MBE Released Questions

Released Questions from the Multistate Bar Examintion

MBE Released Questions

Revised 2011

Copyright 2011 AmeriBar

ISBN 1-44046-980-6

NCBE COPYRIGHT NOTICE

This book contains actual questions that have appeared on the Multistate Bar Examination ("MBE"). Section 1&2 contain the most recently released sets of 100 questions covering all of the testable subjects. Subsequent sections are separated by subject. Subject determinations have been made by the National Conference of Bar Examiners.

Table of Contents

MBE QUESTIONS

AMERIBAR BAR REVIEW

Multistate Bar Examination Released Questions
Section 1

PRACTICE EXAM 1

Question # 1 – Evidence

In a suit based on a will, inheritance of $1 million depended upon whether the wife had survived her husband when both died in the crash of a small airplane. An applicable statute provided that, for purposes of distributing an estate after a common disaster, there was a rebuttable presumption that neither spouse had survived the other. A witness was called to testify that as she approached the plane she heard what she thought was a woman's voice saying, "I'm dying," although by the time the two occupants were removed from the wreckage they were both dead.

Is the witness's testimony admissible?

(A) No, because the matter is governed by the presumption that neither spouse survived the other.
(B) No, because the witness's testimony is too speculative to support a finding.
(C) Yes, because the hearsay rule does not apply to statements by decedents in actions to determine rights under a will.
(D) Yes, because it is relevant and not otherwise prohibited.

Question # 2 - Criminal Law and Procedure

The defendant subsequently moved to suppress the testimony of the teller, claiming the lineup violated his privilege against self-incrimination. At a suppression hearing, the teller testified that she had not gotten a good look at the robber's face, because the robber had been wearing a hat pulled down over most of his face, but that she was certain the defendant was the robber because she had recognized his voice at the lineup.

A defendant was lawfully arrested without a warrant for bank robbery. He was not given *Miranda* warnings, but was immediately taken to a police station where he and five other men were placed in a lineup to be viewed by the bank teller. Each man was required to say the words spoken by the bank robber: "Give me all your money. I've got a gun." After all the men in the lineup spoke those words, the teller identified the defendant as the robber.

Should the defendant's motion be granted?

(A) No, because being required to speak at the lineup, while compelled, was not testimonial or communicative.
(B) No, because testimony of a witness based on firsthand observation is not subject to exclusion as the fruit of the poisonous tree.
(C) Yes, because the defendant was compelled to speak at the lineup, and this compelled speech led to the witness's identification testimony.
(D) Yes, because the defendant was never informed that he could refuse to make a statement and that any statement could be used as evidence against him.

Question # 3 - Constitutional Law

A city owned and operated a municipal bus system. The city sold space on its buses for the posting of placards. Decisions on the type of placards that could be posted on the buses were left wholly to the discretion of the administrator of the bus system. Although most of the placards that appeared on city buses were commercial advertisements, the administrator had often sold space on the buses for placards promoting various political, charitable, and religious causes.

A circus bought space on the city buses for placards advertising its forthcoming performances. An animal rights organization asked the administrator to sell it space for a placard with photographs showing the mistreatment of animals in circus shows.

The administrator denied the organization's request. She said that the display of this placard would be offensive to the circus, which had paid a substantial sum to place its placards on the buses, and that she had been told by a circus employee that none of the photographs on the organization's placard depicted an animal belonging to this particular circus. Under the relevant city ordinance, the administrator's decision was final.

The organization sued the administrator in an appropriate court for a declaration that she could not, consistent with the First Amendment as made applicable to the states by the Fourteenth Amendment, refuse to sell the organization space for its placard for the reasons she gave.

Will the organization prevail?

(A) No, because the administrator's denial of space to the organization was a reasonable time, manner, and place restriction of speech.
(B) No, because a public official may not allow the use of public facilities for the propagation of a message that he or she believes may create a false or misleading impression.
(C) Yes, because a public official may not refuse to permit the dissemination of a message in a public forum wholly on the basis of its content unless that denial is necessary to serve a compelling government interest.
(D) Yes, because a public official may not refuse to allow the use of any public facility to publish a message dealing with an issue of public concern.

Question # 4 – Torts

A landowner who owned a large tract of land in the mountains sought to protect a herd of wild deer that frequented the area. Although the landowner had posted signs that said, "No Hunting—No Trespassing," hunters frequently intruded to kill the deer. Recently, the landowner built an eight-foot chain-link fence, topped by three strands of barbed wire, across a gully on her land that provided the only access to the area frequented by the deer.

A wildlife photographer asked the landowner for permission to enter the property to photograph the deer. Because the landowner feared that any publicity would encourage further intrusions, she denied the photographer's request. Frustrated, the photographer attempted to climb the fence. He became entangled in the barbed wire and suffered extensive lacerations. The wounds became infected and ultimately caused his death. The photographer's personal representative brought an action against the landowner.

Will the plaintiff prevail?

(A) Yes, because the landowner may not use deadly force to protect her land from intrusion.
(B) Yes, because the landowner had no property interest in the deer that entitled her to use force to protect them.
(C) No, because the photographer entered the landowner's land after the landowner had refused him permission to do so.
(D) No, because the potential for harm created by the presence of the barbed wire was apparent.

Question # 5 – Torts

A smoker and a nonsmoker were seated at adjoining tables in a small restaurant. The smoker's table was in the smoking section, and the nonsmoker's table was in the nonsmoking section. When the smoker lit a cigarette, the nonsmoker politely requested that he not smoke, explaining that she had a severe allergy to cigarette smoke. The smoker ignored the nonsmoker's request and continued to smoke. As a result, the nonsmoker was hospitalized with a severe allergic reaction to the smoke.

The nonsmoker brought a battery action against the smoker.

Which of the following questions will NOT be an issue in the battery action?

(A) Did the smoker intend to cause the nonsmoker's contact with the cigarette smoke?
(B) Does smoke have the physical properties necessary for making the kind of contact required for battery?
(C) Is contact with cigarette smoke from a lawful smoking section in a restaurant the kind of contact one must endure as a voluntary restaurant patron?
(D) Was the smoker's conduct unreasonable under the circumstances?

Question # 6 - Criminal Law and Procedure

A federal officer had probable cause to believe a woman had participated in a bank robbery. Two days after the robbery, the woman checked into a local hotel room. When the woman left for the evening, the hotel manager opened the hotel room door so the officer could enter the room and look inside. The officer did not find any of the stolen money but did see, lying open on the bed, the woman's diary. The diary contained an entry describing the woman's involvement in robbing the bank.

The woman was charged in federal court with bank robbery. She moved to suppress the diary.

Should the court suppress the diary?

(A) Yes, because the officer had no warrant.
(B) Yes, because admitting the diary would violate the woman's privilege against self-incrimination.
(C) No, because the hotel manager had actual authority to allow the officer into the hotel room.
(D) No, because the officer reasonably relied on the hotel manager's apparent authority to allow the officer into the hotel room.

Question # 7 - Real Property

Thirty years ago, a landowner conveyed land by warranty deed to a church (a charity) "so long as the land herein conveyed is used as the site for the principal religious edifice maintained by said church."
Twenty years ago, the landowner died intestate, survived by a single heir.

There is no applicable statute. The common law Rule Against Perpetuities is unmodified in the jurisdiction.
One year ago, the church dissolved and its church building situated on the land was demolished.
In an appropriate action, the landowner's heir and the attorney general, who is the appropriate official to assert public interests in charitable trusts, contest the right to the land.

In such action, who will prevail?

(A) The landowner's heir, as successor to the landowner's possibility of reverter.
(B) The landowner's heir, because a charity cannot convey assets donated to it.
(C) The attorney general, because *cy pres* should be applied to devote the land to religious purposes to carry out the charitable intent of the landowner.
(D) The attorney general, because the landowner's attempt to restrict the church's fee simple violated the Rule Against Perpetuities.

Question # 8 - Constitutional Law

With the advice and consent of the Senate, the President entered into a self-executing treaty with a foreign country. The treaty provided that citizens of both nations were required to pay whatever torts damages were awarded against them by a court of either nation.

A man and a woman who were U.S. citizens and residents of the same state were traveling separately in the foreign country when their cars collided. The foreign court awarded the woman a judgment for $500,000 in damages for her injuries from the accident.

In federal district court in their home state, the woman filed suit against the man to enforce the judgment. The man filed a motion to dismiss for lack of jurisdiction.

Should the court grant the motion to dismiss?

(A) Yes, because the citizenship of the parties is not diverse.
(B) Yes, because the traffic accident was a noncommercial transaction outside interstate commerce.
(C) No, because the case falls within the federal question jurisdiction of the court.
(D) No, because the treaty power is plenary and not subject to judicial review.

Question # 9 – Contracts

A fugitive was wanted for murder. The authorities offered the following reward: "$20,000 to anyone who provides information leading to the arrest and conviction of this fugitive." A private detective knew of the reward, located the fugitive, and brought him to the authorities, who arrested him. The authorities then determined that while the fugitive had, in fact, committed the crime, he had been directed to commit the crime by his boss. The authorities and the fugitive then agreed that in exchange for the fugitive's testimony against his boss, all charges against the fugitive would be dropped. The fugitive testified and was released. The authorities refused to pay the reward to the private detective on the ground that the fugitive was never convicted.

Would the private detective be likely to prevail in a breach of contract action against the authorities?

(A) No, because the private detective failed to notify the authorities that he had accepted the reward offer.
(B) No, because the express conditions set out in the reward were not met.
(C) Yes, because the authorities' agreement with the fugitive was against public policy.
(D) Yes, because the authorities themselves prevented the conviction of the fugitive.

Question # 10 – Evidence

A defendant was on trial for burglary. The prosecutor called the arresting officer to testify that shortly after the arrest the defendant had orally admitted her guilt to him. Before the officer testified, the defendant objected that no *Miranda* warning had been given, and she requested a hearing outside the presence of the jury to hear evidence on that issue.

How should the court proceed?

(A) The court should grant the request, because the hearing on the admissibility of the confession must be conducted outside the presence of the jury.
(B) The court may grant or deny the request, because the court has discretion whether to conduct preliminary hearings in the presence of the jury.
(C) The court should deny the request and rule the confession inadmissible, because only signed confessions are permitted in criminal cases.
(D) The court should deny the request and rule the confession admissible, because it is the statement of a party-opponent.

Question # 11 – Torts

Under the Federal Tort Claims Act, with certain exceptions not relevant here, the federal government is liable only for negligence. A federally owned and operated nuclear reactor emitted substantial quantities of radioactive matter that settled on a nearby dairy farm, killing the dairy herd and contaminating the soil. At the trial of an action brought against the federal government by the farm's owner, the trier of fact found that the nuclear plant had a sound design, but that a valve made by the Acme Engineering Company had malfunctioned and allowed the radioactive matter to escape, that Acme Engineering Company is universally regarded as a quality manufacturer of components for nuclear plants, and that there was no way the federal government could have anticipated or prevented the emission of the radioactive matter.

If there is no other applicable statute, for whom should the trial judge enter judgment?

(A) The plaintiff, on the ground that the doctrine of res ipsa loquitur applies.
(B) The plaintiff, on the ground that one who allows dangerous material to escape to the property of another is liable for the damage done.
(C) The defendant, on the ground that a case under the Federal Tort Claims Act has not been proved.
(D) The defendant, on the ground that the Acme Engineering Company is the proximate cause of the owner's damage.

Question # 12 - Criminal Law and Procedure

A state statute provides as follows: "In all criminal cases, whenever the Constitution permits, the burden of proof as to a defense claimed by the defendant shall rest on the defendant, and the magnitude of the burden shall be as great as the Constitution permits."

The same state defines the crime of forcible rape as follows: "Forcible rape consists of sexual penetration inflicted on an unconsenting person by means of force or violence. Consent of the victim is a complete defense to a charge of rape."

At a defendant's trial for forcible rape, he testified that the alleged victim had consented to having sexual intercourse with him.

How should the trial judge instruct the jury regarding the issue of consent?

(A) The burden of proving that the victim consented, by a preponderance of the evidence, rests on the defendant.
(B) The burden of proving that the victim consented, by clear and convincing evidence, rests on the defendant.
(C) The burden of proving that the victim consented, by proof beyond a reasonable doubt, rests on the defendant.
(D) The burden of proving that the victim did not consent, by proof beyond a reasonable doubt, rests on the prosecution.

Question # 13 – Contracts

A buyer and a seller entered into a contract for the sale of 10,000 novelty bracelets. The seller had the bracelets in stock. The contract specified that the seller would ship the bracelets by a third-party carrier. However, the contract did not specify either who was to pay the costs of carriage or the place of tender for the bracelets.

On the above facts, when would the risk of loss of the bracelets pass to the buyer?

(A) When the contract was made.
(B) When the bracelets were identified to the contract by the seller, assuming the goods conformed to the contract.
(C) When the bracelets were delivered to a carrier and a proper contract for their carriage was made.
(D) When the bracelets were unloaded on the buyer's premises by the carrier.

Question # 14 - Constitutional Law

A state legislature received complaints from accident victims who, in the days immediately following their accidents, had received unwelcome and occasionally misleading telephone calls on behalf of medical care providers. The callers warned of the risks of not obtaining prompt medical evaluation to detect injuries resulting from accidents and offered free examinations to determine whether the victims had suffered any injuries.

In response to these complaints, the legislature enacted a law prohibiting medical care providers from soliciting any accident victim by telephone within 30 days of his or her accident.

Which of the following is the most useful argument for the state to use in defending the constitutionality of the law?

(A) Because the commercial speech that is the subject of this law includes some speech that is misleading, the First Amendment does not limit the power of the state to regulate that speech.
(B) Because the law regulates only commercial speech, the state need only demonstrate that the restriction is rationally related to achieving the state's legitimate interests in protecting the privacy of accident victims and in regulating the medical profession.
(C) The state has substantial interests in protecting the privacy of accident victims and in regulating the practice of medical care providers, and the law is narrowly tailored to achieve the state's objectives.
(D) The law is a reasonable time, place, and manner regulation.

Question # 15 – Evidence

A defendant was charged with murder. While walking down the hallway during a recess in the defendant's trial, the judge overheard the defendant say to his attorney, "So what if I did it? There's not enough proof to convict." Upon the judge's reporting the incident to counsel, the prosecutor called the judge as a witness in the trial.

Is the judge's testimony regarding the defendant's statement admissible?

(A) Yes, as the statement of a party-opponent.
(B) Yes, because the defendant's statement, although otherwise privileged, was made without reasonable efforts to preserve confidentiality.
(C) No, because the statement was a privileged attorney-client communication.
(D) No, because a judge may never testify in a trial over which he or she is presiding.

Question # 16 - Real Property

A man borrowed money from a bank and executed a promissory note for the amount secured by a mortgage on his residence. Several years later, the man sold his residence. As provided by the contract of sale, the deed to the buyer provided that the buyer agreed "to assume the existing mortgage debt" on the residence.

Subsequently, the buyer defaulted on the mortgage loan to the bank, and appropriate foreclosure proceedings were initiated. The foreclosure sale resulted in a deficiency.

There is no applicable statute.

Is the buyer liable for the deficiency?

(A) No, because even if the buyer assumed the mortgage, the seller is solely responsible for any deficiency.
(B) No, because the buyer did not sign a promissory note to the bank and therefore has no personal liability.
(C) Yes, because the buyer assumed the mortgage and therefore became personally liable for the mortgage loan and any deficiency.
(D) Yes, because the transfer of the mortgage debt to the buyer resulted in a novation of the original mortgage and loan and rendered the buyer solely responsible for any deficiency.

Question # 17 – Contracts

In a written contract, an architect agreed to draw up the plans for and to supervise construction of a client's new house. In return, the client agreed to pay the architect a fee of $10,000 to be paid upon the house's completion. After completion, the client claimed erroneously but in good faith that the architect's plans were defective. The client orally offered to pay the architect $7,500 in full settlement of the claim for the fee. The architect orally accepted that offer despite the fact that the reasonable value of his services was in fact $10,000. The client paid the architect $7,500 pursuant to their agreement.

The architect subsequently sued the client for the remaining $2,500. In a preliminary finding, the trier of fact found that there were no defects in the architect's plans.

Will the architect be likely to prevail in his action against the client for $2,500?

(A) Yes, because payment of $7,500 cannot furnish consideration for the architect's promise to surrender his claim.
(B) Yes, because the oral agreement to modify the written contract is not enforceable.
(C) No, because the architect's promise to accept $7,500 became binding when the client made the payment.
(D) No, because the architect's acceptance of partial payment constituted a novation.

Question # 18 – Evidence

A defendant's house was destroyed by fire and she was charged with arson. To prove that the defendant had a motive to burn down her house, the government offered evidence that the defendant had fully insured the house and its contents.

Should the court admit this evidence?

(A) No, because the probative value of the evidence of insurance upon the issue of whether the defendant intentionally burned her house down is substantially outweighed by the dangers of unfair prejudice and confusion of the jury.
(B) No, because evidence of insurance is not admissible upon the issue of whether the insured acted wrongfully.
(C) Yes, because evidence of insurance on the house has a tendency to show that the defendant had a motive to burn down the house.
(D) Yes, because any conduct of a party to the case is admissible when offered against the party.

Question # 19 – Torts

The owner of a shopping mall hired a construction company to design and construct the entryway to the mall. The construction company negligently selected an unusually slippery material for the floor covering. A customer at the mall slipped on the floor of the entryway, sustaining injuries. The customer sued the mall owner for the construction company's negligent design of the mall's entryway.

Will the injured customer recover damages?

(A) No, if the construction company was an independent contractor.
(B) No, if no customers had previously slipped on the floor.
(C) Yes, if the customer intended to make a purchase at the mall.
(D) Yes, if the mall's duty to maintain safe conditions was nondelegable.

Question # 20 – Contracts

On June 1, a seller agreed, in a writing signed by both the seller and the buyer, to sell an antique car to a buyer for $20,000. The car was at the time on display in a museum in a different city and was to be delivered to the buyer on August 1. On July 15, before the risk of loss had passed to the buyer, the car was destroyed by fire without fault of either party. Subsequent to the contract but before the fire, the car had increased in value to $30,000. The seller sued the buyer for the contract price of $20,000, and the buyer counterclaimed for $30,000.

Which of the following will the court conclude?

(A) Both claims fail.
(B) Only the seller's claim prevails.
(C) Only the buyer's claim prevails.
(D) Both claims prevail.

Question # 21 - Constitutional Law

A report released by a Senate investigating committee named three U.S. citizens as helping to organize support for terrorist activities. All three were employed by the U.S. government as park rangers.

Congress enacted a statute naming the three individuals identified in the report and providing that they could not hold any position of employment with the federal government.

Which of the following constitutional provisions provides the best means for challenging the constitutionality of the statute?

(A) The bill of attainder clause.
(B) The due process clause.
(C) The *ex post facto* clause.
(D) The takings clause.

Question # 22 - Real Property

A seller owned a single family house. A buyer gave the seller a signed handwritten offer to purchase the house. The offer was unconditional and sufficient to satisfy the statute of frauds, and when the seller signed an acceptance an enforceable contract resulted.

The house on the land had been the seller's home, but he had moved to an apartment, so the house was vacant at all times relevant to the proposed transaction. Two weeks after the parties had entered into their contract, one week after the buyer had obtained a written mortgage lending commitment from a lender, and one week before the agreed-upon closing date, the house was struck by lightning and burned to the ground. The loss was not insured, because three years earlier, the seller had let his homeowner's insurance policy lapse after he had paid his mortgage debt in full.

The handwritten contract was wholly silent as to matters of financing, risk of loss, and insurance. The buyer declared the contract voided by the fire, but the seller asserted a right to enforce the contract despite the loss.
There is no applicable statute.

If a court finds for the seller, what is the likely reason?

(A) The contract was construed against the buyer, who drafted it.
(B) The lender's written commitment to make a mortgage loan to the buyer made the contract of sale fully binding on the buyer.
(C) The risk of loss falls on the party in possession, and constructive possession passed to the buyer on the contract date.

(D) The risk of loss passed to the buyer on the contract date under the doctrine of equitable conversion.

Question # 23 - Criminal Law and Procedure

A federal grand jury was investigating drug trafficking in the jurisdiction. It subpoenaed a witness to testify, and the prosecutor advised the witness that he had a Fifth Amendment privilege not to testify if he so chose. The witness asked that his counsel be allowed to advise him inside the grand jury room, but the prosecutor refused to allow the attorney inside. The witness, after speaking with his attorney outside the grand jury room, decided to testify and ended up making self-incriminating statements.

The witness subsequently was indicted for drug crimes. The indictment was based on the witness's grand jury testimony and on evidence seized in an unconstitutional search of the witness's home.

The witness moved to dismiss the indictment.

Should the court dismiss the indictment?

(A) Yes, because the witness was denied his constitutional right to advice of counsel.
(B) Yes, because the indictment was based upon illegally seized evidence.
(C) No, because the witness waived his constitutional rights by testifying.
(D) No, because the witness had no right to counsel inside the grand jury room and the illegally seized evidence did not affect the validity of the indictment.

Question # 24 – Torts

A hiker sustained a head injury when he was struck by a limb that fell from a tree. At the time of his injury, the hiker was walking through a forest on private property without the property owner's knowledge or permission. It was determined that the limb fell because the tree was infested with termites.

In an action by the hiker against the property owner to recover for his head injury, will the hiker prevail?

(A) No, because the property owner could not foresee that anyone would be injured.
(B) No, because the property owner breached no duty to the hiker, who was a trespasser.
(C) Yes, because the property owner had a duty to prevent the trees on his property from becoming dangerous.
(D) Yes, because the property owner is liable for hidden dangers on his property.

Question # 25 - Criminal Law and Procedure

United States customs officials received an anonymous tip that heroin would be found inside a distinctively marked red package mailed from a foreign country to the United States. Pursuant to this tip, United States customs officers opened the red package and found heroin inside. They then resealed the package and left the heroin inside it. The FBI was notified and, as agents watched, the package was delivered to the address.

The FBI then secured a warrant to search the house for the package. About two hours after the package was delivered, the warrant was executed at the house. The man who opened the door was arrested, and the agents found the package, unopened, in an upstairs bedroom closet. After seizing the package, the agents looked through the rest of the house. In a footlocker in the basement, they found a machine gun.

The man was charged with, among other crimes, unlawful possession of the machine gun. He moved to suppress its use as evidence.

Should the court grant the motion to suppress the machine gun?

(A) Yes, because the search exceeded the authority granted by the warrant.
(B) Yes, because the initial search by the customs officers was without probable cause.
(C) No, because, having found the package, the agents had probable cause to believe more narcotics could be located in the house and the gun was found in a proper search for narcotics.

(D) No, because narcotics dealers are often armed and the search was justified to protect the agents.

Question # 26 – Contracts

A homeowner and a contractor entered into a contract for the construction of a home for the price of $300,000. The contractor was to earn a profit of $10,000 for the job. After the contractor had spent $45,000 on labor and materials, including $5,000 on oak flooring not yet installed, the homeowner informed the contractor that the homeowner had lost his job and could not pay for any services. The homeowner told the contractor to stop working immediately. The reasonable market value of the labor and materials provided by the contractor at that point, including the oak flooring, was $40,000. The contractor used the $5,000 worth of oak flooring on another job.

In an action by the contractor against the homeowner for damages, which of the following would be the largest amount of damages recoverable by the contractor?

(A) $40,000, the reasonable value of the services the contractor had provided.
(B) $40,000, the contractor's construction costs.
(C) $50,000, the contractor's construction costs of $45,000 plus the $10,000 profit minus the $5,000 saved by reusing the oak flooring on another job.
(D) $55,000, the contractor's construction costs of $45,000 plus the $10,000 profit.

Question # 27 - Real Property

A man died testate. The man's estate consisted of a residence as well as significant personal property. By his duly probated will, the man devised the residence to a friend who was specifically identified in the will. The residue of the estate was given to a stated charity.

The man's friend, although alive at the time the man executed the will, predeceased the man. The friend's wife and their child, who has a disability, survived the man.

The value of the residence has increased significantly because of recent zoning changes. There is credible extrinsic evidence that the man wanted his friend to own the residence after the man's death so that the friend and his wife could care for their child there.

There is no applicable statute.

If both the charity and the child claim the residence, to whom should the estate distribute the residence?

(A) The charity, because the devise to the friend adeemed.
(B) The charity, because the devise to the friend lapsed.
(C) The child, because extrinsic evidence exists that the man's intent was to benefit the child.
(D) The child, because no conditions of survivorship were noted in the will.

Question # 28 - Constitutional Law

Several sites on a mountain within federal public lands are regarded as sacred to a group that for years has gathered there to perform religious ceremonies. The United States Forest Service recently issued a permit to a private developer to construct a ski facility in an area that includes the sites that are sacred to the group.

The group filed suit in federal district court against the Forest Service to force cancellation of the permit. The group claimed solely that the permit violated its First Amendment right to the free exercise of religion. The Forest Service conceded that the group's religious beliefs were sincere and that the ski facility would adversely affect the group's religious practices.

In order to prevail in its First Amendment claim, what must the group show?

(A) Construction of the ski facility will have a discriminatory impact on the group's religious practices in relation to the practices of other religious groups.
(B) The burden on the group's religious practices imposed by construction of the ski facility outweighs the government's

interest in allowing the facility.

(C) The Forest Service can achieve its legitimate interest in allowing the ski facility by issuing a permit that is less burdensome on the group's religious practices.

(D) The permit issued by the Forest Service is aimed at suppressing the religious practices of the group.

Question # 29 - Evidence

A defendant was charged with battery for allegedly attacking a man as they left a local bar together. No one else witnessed the fight. At trial, each testified that he had acted only in self-defense. The defendant called his next-door neighbor as a witness to testify as to the defendant's reputation both for truthfulness and for peacefulness. The government objected to the testimony in its entirety.

How should the court proceed?

(A) Admit the evidence in its entirety.

(B) Admit the evidence regarding the defendant's reputation for peacefulness, but exclude the evidence regarding his truthfulness.

(C) Exclude the evidence regarding the defendant's reputation for peacefulness, but admit the evidence regarding his truthfulness.

(D) Exclude the evidence in its entirety.

Question # 30 - Torts

A cigarette maker created and published a magazine advertisement that featured a model dressed as a race-car driver standing in front of a distinctive race car. In fact, the car looked almost exactly like the very unusually marked one driven by a famous and popular driver. The driver in the ad was not identified, and his face was not shown in the advertisement. The cigarette maker published the advertisement without obtaining the famous driver's permission. The race-car driver sued the cigarette maker for economic loss only, based on common law misappropriation of the right of publicity. The cigarette maker moved to dismiss the complaint.

Will the cigarette maker's motion to dismiss the complaint be granted?

(A) No, because there are sufficient indicia of the driver's identity to support a verdict of liability.

(B) Yes, because the driver is a public figure.

(C) Yes, because there was no mention of the driver's name in the ad.

(D) Yes, because the driver did not claim any emotional or dignitary loss.

Question # 31 - Criminal Law and Procedure

In a city, a number of armed bank robberies were committed near closing time by a masked man wearing a white hooded sweatshirt and blue sweatpants. Police saw a man wearing a white hooded sweatshirt and blue sweatpants pacing nervously outside one of the city's banks just before it closed. The police stopped the man and frisked the outer layers of his clothing for weapons, but found none. They asked the man what he was doing outside the bank and pointed out that he was wearing clothing similar to clothing worn by the perpetrator of recent robberies. After pausing for several moments, the man confessed. The police had not provided him with any *Miranda* warnings.

After being charged with the bank robberies, the man moved to suppress his confession. The parties agreed, and the court properly found, that the police had reasonable suspicion but not probable cause at all times before the man confessed.

Should the man's motion to suppress be granted?

(A) Yes, because the confession was the fruit of a Fourth Amendment violation, even though there was no *Miranda* violation.

(B) Yes, because the confession was the fruit of a *Miranda* violation, even though there was no Fourth Amendment violation.

(C) Yes, because the confession was the fruit of both a Fourth Amendment violation and a *Miranda* violation.

(D) No, because there was neither a Fourth Amendment violation nor a *Miranda* violation.

Question # 32 - Real Property

A man owned property that he used as his residence. The man received a loan, secured by a mortgage on the property, from a bank. Later, the man defaulted on the loan. The bank then brought an appropriate action to foreclose the mortgage, was the sole bidder at the judicial sale, and received title to the property as a result of the foreclosure sale.

Shortly after the foreclosure sale, the man received a substantial inheritance. He approached the bank to repurchase the property, but the bank decided to build a branch office on the property and declined to sell.

If the man prevails in an appropriate action to recover title to the property, what is the most likely reason?

(A) He had used the property as his residence.
(B) He timely exercised an equitable right of redemption.
(C) The court applied the doctrine of exoneration.
(D) The jurisdiction provides for a statutory right of redemption.

Question # 33 - Real Property

A farmer borrowed $100,000 from a bank and gave the bank a promissory note secured by a mortgage on the farm that she owned. The bank promptly and properly recorded the mortgage, which contained a due-on-sale provision.

A few years later, the farmer borrowed $5,000 from a second bank and gave it a promissory note secured by a mortgage on her farm. The bank promptly and properly recorded the mortgage.

Subsequently, the farmer defaulted on her obligation to the first bank, which then validly accelerated the debt and instituted nonjudicial foreclosure proceedings as permitted by the jurisdiction. The second bank received notice of the foreclosure sale but did not send a representative to the sale. At the foreclosure sale, a buyer who was not acting in collusion with the farmer outbid all other bidders and received a deed to the farm.

Several months later, the original farmer repurchased her farm from the buyer, who executed a warranty deed transferring the farm to her. After the farmer promptly and properly recorded that deed, the second bank commenced foreclosure proceedings on the farm. The farmer denied the validity of the second bank's mortgage.

Does the second bank continue to have a valid mortgage on the farm?

(A) Yes, because of the doctrine of estoppel by deed.
(B) Yes, because the original owner reacquired title to the farm.
(C) No, because the purchase at the foreclosure sale by the buyer under these facts eliminated the second bank's junior mortgage lien.
(D) No, because of the due-on-sale provision in the farmer's mortgage to the first bank.

Question # 34 - Evidence

At a trial of a contract dispute, the plaintiff offered to testify to what the defendant said in a private conversation between the two of them, which the plaintiff had secretly recorded on an audiotape that she did not offer in evidence.

Is the plaintiff's testimony admissible?

(A) Yes, because the plaintiff has personal knowledge of the statement of a party-opponent.
(B) Yes, because the original document rule does not apply to audiotapes.
(C) No, because the statement must be proved by introduction of the audiotape itself.
(D) No, because of the plaintiff's deception, even if the recording was not illegal.

Question # 35 - Torts

A manufacturing plant located near a busy highway uses and stores highly volatile explosives. The owner of the plant has imposed strict safety measures to prevent an explosion at the plant. During an unusually heavy windstorm, a large tile was blown off the roof of the plant and crashed into the windshield of a passing car, damaging it. The driver of the car brought a strict liability action against the owner of the plant to recover for the damage to the car's windshield.

Is the driver likely to prevail?

(A) No, because the damage to the windshield did not result from the abnormally dangerous aspect of the plant's activity.
(B) No, because the severity of the windstorm was unusual.
(C) Yes, because the plant's activity was abnormally dangerous.
(D) Yes, because the plant's location near a busy highway was abnormally dangerous.

Question # 36 - Contracts

While waiting in line to open an account with a bank, a customer read a poster on the bank's wall that said, "New Customers! $25 FOR 5 MINUTES. If you stand in line for more than five minutes, we will pay you $25! We like happy customers! (This offer may be withdrawn at any time.)" The customer started timing his wait and just as five minutes was about to pass, the bank manager tore the poster down and announced, "The $25 stand-in-line promotion is over." The customer waited in line for 10 more minutes before being served.

In the customer's action against the bank for $25, will the customer prevail?

(A) No, because the bank withdrew its offer before the customer completed the requested performance.
(B) No, because the bank's statement was a nonbinding gift promise.
(C) Yes, because the bank could not revoke its offer once the customer had commenced performance.
(D) Yes, because the customer's presence in line served as notice to the bank that he had accepted.

Question # 37 - Constitutional Law

A federal statute required that any individual or entity owning more than 100 cars had to ensure that at least 10 percent of those cars were electric-powered.

A city filed suit in federal district court against the federal official who enforced this requirement. The city sought an injunction prohibiting enforcement of the statute on the ground that it was unconstitutional.

Should the court grant the injunction?

(A) No, because the statute is valid under the commerce clause and does not violate the Tenth Amendment.
(B) No, because the federal government has sovereign immunity and cannot be sued without its explicit consent.
(C) Yes, because the statute violates the reserved rights of the states under the Tenth Amendment.
(D) Yes, because as applied to state and local governments, the statute exceeds Congress's power under the commerce clause.

Question # 38 - Criminal Law and Procedure

A driver stopped at a red light in his home state. A stranger opened the passenger door, got in, and pointed a gun at the driver. The stranger then directed the driver to keep driving. They drove several miles, crossed into a neighboring state, and drove several more miles. When they reached a remote location, the stranger ordered the driver to pull over. The stranger then robbed the driver of his wallet and cash, and ordered him out of the car. The stranger drove off in the driver's car.

The stranger is charged with kidnapping in the neighboring state, which has adopted the Model Penal Code.

Could the stranger properly be convicted of kidnapping in the neighboring state?

(A) Yes, because the driver was transported under threat of force in the neighboring state.
(B) Yes, because the driver in effect paid ransom for his release.
(C) No, because any kidnapping took place in the driver's home state.
(D) No, because the restraint was incidental to the robbery.

Question # 39 - Contracts

On June 1, a seller received a mail order from a buyer requesting prompt shipment of a specified computer model at the seller's current catalog price. On June 2, the seller mailed to the buyer a letter accepting the order and assuring the buyer that the computer would be shipped on June 3. On June 3, the seller realized that he was out of that computer model and shipped to the buyer a different computer model and a notice of accommodation. On June 5, the buyer received the seller's June 2 letter and the different computer model, but not the notice of accommodation.

At that juncture, which of the following is a correct statement of the parties' legal rights and duties?

(A) The buyer can either accept or reject the different computer model and in either event recover damages, if any, for breach of contract.
(B) The buyer can either accept or reject the different computer model, but if he rejects it, he will thereby waive any remedy for breach of contract.
(C) The seller's prompt shipment of nonconforming goods constituted an acceptance of the buyer's offer, thereby creating a contract for sale of the replacement computer model.
(D) The seller's notice of accommodation was timely mailed and his shipment of the different computer model constituted a counteroffer.

Question # 40 - Evidence

A plaintiff sued a ladder manufacturer for injuries he suffered to his neck and back when a rung of the ladder on which he was standing gave way. When the plaintiff's back and neck continued to be very sore after more than two weeks, his treating physician sent him to an orthopedist for an evaluation. Though the orthopedist did not treat the plaintiff, he diagnosed an acute cervical strain. At trial, the plaintiff called the orthopedist to testify that in response to the orthopedist's inquiry about how the plaintiff had injured his back, the plaintiff told him, "I was standing near the top of a 15-foot ladder when I abruptly fell, landing hard on my back, after which the ladder toppled onto my neck."

Should the statement be admitted?

(A) Yes, because the plaintiff is present and can be cross-examined about it.
(B) Yes, because it was made for the purpose of medical diagnosis or treatment.
(C) No, because it was not made to a treating physician.
(D) No, because it relates to the inception or the cause of the injury rather than the plaintiff's physical condition.

Question # 41 - Constitutional Law

The United States government demonstrated that terrorist attacks involving commercial airliners were perpetrated exclusively by individuals of one particular race. In response, Congress enacted a statute imposing stringent new airport and airline security measures only on individuals of that race seeking to board airplanes in the United States.

Which of the following provides the best ground for challenging the constitutionality of this statute?

(A) The commerce clause of Article I, Section 8.
(B) The due process clause of the Fifth Amendment.
(C) The privileges and immunities clause of Article IV.
(D) The privileges or immunities clause of the Fourteenth Amendment.

Question # 42 - Torts

A consumer bought an electric kitchen blender from the manufacturer. Soon after the purchase, the consumer was using the blender in an appropriate way when the blender jar shattered, throwing a piece of glass into the consumer's eye.

The consumer brought an action against the manufacturer based solely on strict product liability. The consumer's expert testified that the blender was defectively designed. However, because the blender jar was destroyed in the accident, the expert could not determine whether the accident was caused by the design defect or a manufacturing defect. The manufacturer's expert testified that the blender was not defective.

If, at the conclusion of the evidence, both parties move for directed verdicts, how should the trial judge rule?

(A) Direct a verdict for the manufacturer, because the consumer's expert was unable to specify the nature of the defect.
(B) Direct a verdict for the manufacturer, because the consumer's action was brought solely on a strict liability theory.
(C) Direct a verdict for the consumer, because the blender was new when the jar shattered.
(D) Deny both motions and send the case to the jury, because a jury reasonably could conclude that the harm probably was caused by a defect present in the product when it was sold.

Question # 43 - Constitutional Law

Congressional committees heard testimony from present and former holders of licenses issued by state vocational licensing boards. According to the testimony, the boards had unfairly manipulated their disciplinary proceedings in order to revoke the licenses of some license holders as a means of protecting favored licensees from competition.

In response, Congress enacted a statute prescribing detailed procedural requirements for the disciplinary proceedings of all state vocational licensing boards. For example, the statute required the state boards to provide licensees with adequate notice and opportunity for an adjudicatory hearing in all disciplinary proceedings. The statute also prescribed criteria for the membership of all state vocational licensing boards that were designed to ensure that the boards were likely to be neutral.

Which of the following provides the best source of authority for this federal statute?

(A) Section 5 of the Fourteenth Amendment.
(B) The general welfare clause of Article I, Section 8.
(C) The privileges and immunities clause of Article IV, Section 2.
(D) The takings clause of the Fifth Amendment.

Question # 44 - Real Property

A seller who owned land in fee simple entered into a valid written agreement to sell the land to a buyer by installment purchase. The contract stipulated that the seller would deliver to the buyer, upon the payment of the last installment due, "a warranty deed sufficient to convey a fee simple title." The contract contained no other provision that could be construed as referring to title.

The buyer entered into possession of the land. After making 10 of the 300 installment payments obligated under the contract, the buyer discovered that there was outstanding a valid and enforceable mortgage on the land, securing the payment of a debt in the amount of 25 percent of the purchase price that the buyer had agreed to pay. There was no evidence that the seller had ever been late in payments due under the mortgage and there was no evidence of any danger of insolvency of the seller. The value of the land was then four times the amount due on the debt secured by the mortgage.

The buyer quit possession of the land, stopped making payments on the contract, and demanded that the seller repay the amounts that the buyer had paid under the contract. After the seller refused the demand, the buyer sued the seller to recover damages for the seller's alleged breach of the contract.

In such action, should damages be awarded to the buyer?

(A) Yes, because in the absence of a contrary express agreement, an obligation to convey marketable title is implied.
(B) Yes, because an installment purchase contract is treated as a mortgage and the outstanding mortgage impairs the buyer's equity of redemption.
(C) No, because an installment purchase contract is treated as a security device.
(D) No, because the time for the seller to deliver marketable title has not arrived.

Question # 45 - Contracts

On May 1, a seller and a buyer entered into a written contract, signed by both parties, for the sale of a tract of land for $100,000. Delivery of the deed and payment of the purchase price were scheduled for July 1. On June 1, the buyer received a letter from the seller repudiating the contract. On June 5, the buyer bought a second tract of land at a higher price as a substitute for the first tract. On June 10, the seller communicated a retraction of the repudiation to the buyer.

The buyer did not tender the purchase price for the first tract on July 1, but subsequently sued the seller for breach of contract.

Will the buyer likely prevail?

(A) No, because the seller retracted the repudiation prior to the agreed time for performance.
(B) No, because the buyer's tender of the purchase price on July 1 was a constructive condition to the seller's duty to tender a conveyance.
(C) Yes, because the seller's repudiation was nonretractable after it was communicated to the buyer.
(D) Yes, because the buyer bought the second tract as a substitute for the first tract prior to the seller's retraction.

Question # 46 - Torts

A driver negligently ran over a pedestrian. A bystander witnessed the accident from across the street. The bystander ran to the pedestrian, whom he did not know, and administered first aid, but the pedestrian died in the bystander's arms. The bystander suffered serious emotional distress as a result of his failure to save the pedestrian's life, but he experienced no resulting physical manifestations. The bystander brought a negligence action against the driver.

Is the bystander likely to prevail?

(A) No, because the bystander assumed the risk.
(B) No, because the bystander had no familial or other preexisting relationship with the pedestrian.
(C) Yes, because danger invites rescue.
(D) Yes, because the bystander was in the zone of danger.

Question # 47 - Constitutional Law

A state legislature conducted an investigation into a series of fatal accidents in the state involving commercial trucks with trailer exteriors made of polished aluminum. The investigation revealed that the sun's glare off of these trucks blinded the drivers of other vehicles. The state's legislature then enacted a law prohibiting commercial trucks with polished aluminum trailer exteriors from traveling on the state's highways.

Litigation over the state law resulted in a final decision by the United States Supreme Court that the law impermissibly burdened interstate commerce and, therefore, was unconstitutional. Congress later enacted a statute permitting any state to enact a law regulating the degree of light reflectiveness of the exteriors of commercial trucks using the state's highways.

Is this federal statute constitutional?

(A) No, because the U.S. Supreme Court has already determined that state laws of this type impermissibly burden interstate commerce.
(B) No, because Article III vests the judicial power in the federal courts, the essence of judicial power is the ability to render a final judgment, and this statute overrules a final judgment of the federal Supreme Court.
(C) Yes, because Article I, Section 8 grants Congress authority to enact statutes authorizing states to impose burdens on interstate commerce that would otherwise be prohibited.
(D) Yes, because Article I, Section 8 grants Congress authority to enact statutes for the general welfare, and Congress.

Question # 48 - Evidence

A plaintiff sued a defendant for wrongful death arising out of a traffic collision between the plaintiff's decedent and the defendant. At trial, the investigating traffic officer authenticated a tape recording of her shift-end dictation of comments used in preparing the written report of her factual findings. She testified that the tape recording was accurate when made and that she currently had no clear memory of the details of the investigation.

Is the tape recording admissible as evidence?

(A) Yes, under the past recollection recorded exception to the hearsay rule.
(B) Yes, under the public records exception to the hearsay rule.
(C) No, because it is hearsay and is a police report being offered against the defendant in a wrongful death case.
(D) No, because the police report itself is the best evidence.

Question # 49 - Contracts

A debtor's liquidated and undisputed $1,000 debt to a creditor was due on March 1. On March 15, the creditor told the debtor that if the debtor promised to pay the $1,000 on or before December 1, then the creditor wouldn't sue to collect the debt. The debtor orally agreed. On April 1, the creditor sued the debtor to collect the debt that had become due on March 1. The debtor moved to dismiss the creditor's complaint.

Should the court grant the debtor's motion?

(A) No, because there was no consideration to support the creditor's promise not to sue.
(B) No, because there was no consideration to support the debtor's promise to pay $1,000 on December 1.
(C) Yes, because a promise to allow a debtor to delay payment on a past debt is enforceable without consideration.
(D) Yes, because the debtor was bargaining for the creditor's forbearance.

Question # 50 - Criminal Law and Procedure

A man who had become very drunk left a bar and started to walk home. Another patron of the bar, who had observed the man's condition, followed him. The patron saw the man stumble and fall to the ground near an alley. The patron then began to pull out a gun but saw that the man had passed out asleep in the gutter. The patron reached into the man's pocket, grabbed his wallet, and started to walk away. When the patron heard police officers approaching, he dropped the wallet and ran off. The crimes below are listed in descending order of seriousness.

What is the most serious crime for which the patron properly could be convicted?

(A) Robbery
(B) Larceny
(C) Attempted robbery.
(D) Attempted larceny.

Question # 51 - Contracts

On March 1, a homeowner contacted a builder about constructing an addition to the homeowner's house. The builder orally offered to perform the work for $200,000 if his pending bid on another project was rejected. The homeowner accepted the builder's terms and the builder then prepared a written contract that both parties signed. The contract did not refer to the builder's pending bid. One week later, upon learning that his pending bid on the other project had been accepted, the builder refused to perform any work for the homeowner.

Can the homeowner recover for the builder's nonperformance?

(A) No, because efficiency principles justify the builder's services being directed to a higher-valued use.
(B) No, because the builder's duty to perform was subject to a condition.
(C) Yes, because the builder's attempt to condition his duty to perform rendered the contract illusory.
(D) Yes, because the parol evidence rule would bar the builder from presenting evidence of oral understandings not included in the final writing.

Question # 52 - Constitutional Law

A city passed an ordinance requiring individuals to obtain a license in order to care for children under the age of 12 for pay. To receive such a license, the ordinance required the individuals to complete 10 hours of instruction in child care, undergo a background check, and pay a $100 fee. The ordinance affected women disproportionately to men, because female babysitters far outnumbered male babysitters in the city. City officials who promoted the measure said that the certification process would ensure that babysitters were adequately regulated for the health and safety of the city's children.

Is the ordinance constitutional?

(A) No, because it has a disparate impact on women without a showing that the ordinance is necessary to advance a compelling government interest.
(B) No, because it infringes on the freedom of contract without a compelling government interest.
(C) Yes, because any burden it imposes is clearly outweighed by an important government objective.
(D) Yes, because it is rationally related to a legitimate government objective.

Question # 53 - Real Property

By a valid written contract, a seller agreed to sell land to a buyer. The contract stated, "The parties agree that closing will occur on next May 1 at 10 a.m." There was no other reference to closing. The contract was silent as to quality of title.

On April 27, the seller notified the buyer that she had discovered that the land was subject to a longstanding easement in favor of a corporation for a towpath for a canal, should the corporation ever want to build a canal.

The buyer thought it so unlikely that a canal would be built that the closing should occur notwithstanding this outstanding easement. Therefore, the buyer notified the seller on April 28 that he would expect to close on May 1.

When the seller refused to close, the buyer sued for specific performance.

Will the buyer prevail?

(A) No, because the easement renders the seller's title unmarketable.
(B) No, because rights of third parties are unresolved.
(C) Yes, because the decision to terminate the contract for title not being marketable belongs only to the buyer.
(D) Yes, because the seller did not give notice of the easement a reasonable time before the closing date.

Question # 54 - Criminal Law and Procedure

A drug dealer agreed with another individual to purchase heroin from the individual in order to sell it on a city street corner. Unknown to the drug dealer, the other individual was an undercover police officer whose only purpose was to arrest distributors of drugs. The drug dealer made a down payment for the heroin and agreed to pay the remainder after he sold it on the street. As soon as the undercover officer handed over the heroin, other officers moved in and arrested the dealer.

The jurisdiction follows the common law approach to conspiracy.

Could the dealer properly be convicted of conspiring to distribute drugs?

(A) No, because there was no overt act.
(B) No, because there was no plurality of agreement.
(C) Yes, because neither an overt act nor plurality of agreement is required at common law.
(D) Yes, because the dealer believed all the elements of conspiracy were present and cannot take advantage of a mistake of fact or law.

Question # 55 - Constitutional Law

Residents of a city complained that brightly colored signs detracted from the character of the city's historic district and distracted motorists trying to navigate its narrow streets. In response, the city council enacted an ordinance requiring any "sign or visual display" visible on the streets of the historic district to be black and white and to be no more than four feet long or wide.

A political party wanted to hang a six-foot-long red, white, and blue political banner in front of a building in the historic district. The party filed suit to challenge the constitutionality of the sign ordinance as applied to the display of its banner.

Which of the following would be the most useful argument for the political party?

(A) The ordinance is not the least restrictive means of promoting a compelling government interest.
(B) The ordinance is not narrowly tailored to an important government interest, nor does it leave open alternative channels of communication.
(C) The ordinance imposes a prior restraint on political expression.
(D) The ordinance effectively favors some categories of speech over others.

Question # 56 - Contracts

A buyer ordered a new machine from a manufacturer. The machine arrived on time and conformed in all respects to the contract. The buyer, however, rejected the machine because he no longer needed it in his business and returned the machine to the manufacturer. The manufacturer sold many such machines each year and its factory was not operating at full capacity.

In an action by the manufacturer against the buyer for breach of contract, which of the following is NOT a proper measure of the manufacturer's damages?

(A) The contract price of the machine.
(B) The difference between the contract price and the market price of the machine.
(C) The difference between the contract price and the price obtained from a proper resale of the machine.
(D) The profit the manufacturer would have made on the sale of the machine to the buyer.

Question # 57 - Contracts

An insurance company issued an insurance policy to a homeowner. The policy failed to contain certain coverage terms required by a state insurance statute. When the homeowner suffered a loss due to a theft that was within the policy's terms, the insurance company refused to pay, claiming that the contract was unenforceable because it violated the statute.

Will the homeowner succeed in an action against the insurance company to recover for the loss?

(A) No, because the insurance policy is not a divisible contract.
(B) No, because the insurance policy violated the statute.
(C) Yes, because the homeowner belongs to the class of persons intended to be protected by the statute.
(D) Yes, because the insurance policy would be strictly construed against the insurance company as the drafter.

Question # 58 - Criminal Law and Procedure

A foreign diplomat discovered that a small person could enter a jewelry store by crawling through an air vent. The diplomat became friendly with a woman in a bar who he believed was small enough to crawl through the air vent. Without telling her that he was a diplomat, he explained how she could get into the jewelry store. She agreed to help him burglarize the store. Someone overheard their conversation and reported it to the police. Shortly thereafter, the police arrested the diplomat and the woman. Both were charged with conspiracy to commit burglary.

Before trial, the diplomat moved to dismiss the charge against him on the ground that he was entitled to diplomatic immunity. The court granted his motion. The woman then moved to dismiss the conspiracy charge against her.

The jurisdiction has adopted the Model Penal Code version of conspiracy.

Should the woman's motion to dismiss the conspiracy charge against her be granted?

(A) No, because the diplomat's defense does not negate any element of the crime.
(B) No, because the woman was not aware of the diplomat's status.
(C) Yes, because a conspiracy requires two guilty participants.
(D) Yes, because but for the diplomat's conduct, no conspiracy would have occurred.

Question # 59 - Torts

A recently established law school constructed its building in a quiet residential neighborhood. The law school had obtained all of the necessary municipal permits for the construction of the building, which included a large clock tower whose clock chimed every hour. The chimes disturbed only one homeowner in the neighborhood, who had purchased her house prior to the construction of the building. The homeowner was abnormally sensitive to ringing sounds, such as bells and sirens, and found the chimes to be extremely annoying.

In a nuisance action by the homeowner against the law school, will the homeowner prevail?

(A) Yes, because the chimes interfere with the homeowner's use and enjoyment of her property.
(B) Yes, because the homeowner purchased her house prior to the construction of the building.
(C) No, because the chimes do not disturb the other residents of the neighborhood.
(D) No, because the law school had the requisite municipal permits to erect the clock tower.

Question # 60 - Criminal Law and Procedure

A woman told a man to go into her friend's unlocked barn and retrieve an expensive black saddle that she said she had loaned to the friend. The man went to the friend's barn, opened the door, found a black saddle, and took it back to the woman's house. The friend had in fact not borrowed a saddle from the woman, and when the friend discovered her black saddle missing, she suspected that the woman was the thief. The friend used a screwdriver to break into the woman's house to find the saddle. Upon discovering the saddle on the woman's table, the friend took it back and called the police.

The jurisdiction follows the common law, except that burglary covers structures in addition to dwellings and the nighttime element has been eliminated.

Which, if any, of these individuals is guilty of burglary?

(A) All of them.
(B) Only the friend.
(C) Only the man.
(D) Only the woman.

Question # 61 - Evidence

A plaintiff sued his insurance company for the full loss of his banquet hall by fire. The insurance company defended under a provision of the policy limiting liability to 50 percent if "flammable materials not essential to the operation of the business were stored on the premises and caused a fire." The insurance company called the keeper of the city fire inspection records to identify a report prepared and filed by the fire marshal as required by law, indicating that shortly before the fire, the fire marshal had cited the plaintiff for storing gasoline at the banquet hall.

Is the report admissible?

(A) No, because it is hearsay not within any exception.
(B) No, because the proceeding is civil, rather than criminal.
(C) Yes, as a public record describing matters observed as to which there was a duty to report.
(D) Yes, as a record of regularly conducted activity, provided the fire marshal is unavailable.

Question # 62 - Real Property

A rectangular parcel of undeveloped land contained three acres and had 150 feet of frontage on a public street. The applicable zoning ordinance required that a buildable lot contain at least two acres and have frontage of not less than 100 feet on a public street.

A brother and sister owned the land as tenants in common, the brother owning a one-third interest and the sister owning a two-thirds interest. Neither of them owned any other real property.

The sister brought an appropriate action to partition the land and proposed that a two-acre rectangular lot with 100 feet of frontage be set off to her and that a one-acre rectangular lot with 50 feet of frontage be set off to the brother. The brother's defense included a demand that the land be sold and its proceeds be divided one-third to the brother and two-thirds to the sister.

Who will prevail?

(A) The brother, because partition by sale is the preferred remedy, unless a fair price is not the likely result of a sale.
(B) The brother, because the zoning ordinance makes it impossible to divide the land fairly.
(C) The sister, because partition by sale is not appropriate if the subject property can be physically divided.
(D) The sister, because the ratio of the two lots that would result from her proposal conforms exactly to the ownership ratio.

Question # 63 - Criminal Law and Procedure

A woman promised to pay $10,000 to a hit man if he would kill her neighbor in any manner that could not be traced to her. The hit man bought a gun and watched the neighbor's house for an opportunity to shoot him. One evening, unaware of the hit man's presence, the neighbor tripped as he was walking toward his house, falling and hitting his head against the front steps. Believing that the neighbor was unconscious, the hit man ran over to him and shot him twice in the chest.

When the woman learned of the neighbor's death, she paid the hit man $10,000. A medical examiner determined that the neighbor was already dead when the hit man shot him.

The crimes below are listed in descending order of seriousness.

What is the most serious crime for which the woman properly could be convicted?

(A) Murder
(B) Attempted murder.
(C) Conspiracy.
(D) Solicitation.

Question # 64 - Contracts

Under the terms of a written contract, a builder agreed to construct a garage for a homeowner for $10,000. Nothing was stated in the parties' negotiations or in the contract about progress payments during the course of the work.

After completing 25 percent of the garage according to the homeowner's specifications, the builder demanded $2,000 as a reasonable progress payment. The homeowner refused, and the builder abandoned the job.

If each party sues the other for breach of contract, which of the following will the court decide?

(A) Both parties are in breach, and each is entitled to damages, if any, from the other.
(B) Only the builder is in breach and liable for the homeowner's damages, if any.
(C) Only the homeowner is in breach and liable for the builder's damages, if any.
(D) Both parties took reasonable positions, and neither is in breach.

Question # 65 - Torts

A company manufactured metal stamping presses that were usually sold with an installed safety device that made it impossible for a press to close on a worker's hands. The company strongly recommended that its presses be purchased with the safety device installed, but would sell a press without the safety device at a slightly reduced price.

Rejecting the company's advice, a worker's employer purchased a stamping press without the safety device. The press closed on the worker's hand, crushing it.

In an action brought by the worker against the company, will the worker prevail?

(A) Yes, because the company's press was the cause in fact of the worker's injury.
(B) Yes, because the company sold the press to the worker's employer without an installed safety device.

(C) No, because the failure of the worker's employer to purchase the press with a safety device was a superseding intervening cause of the worker's injury.

(D) No, because the company strongly recommended that the worker's employer purchase the press with the safety device.

Question # 66 - Constitutional Law

In one state, certain kinds of advanced diagnostic medical technology were located only in hospitals, where they provided a major source of revenue. In many other states, such technology was also available at "diagnostic centers" that were not affiliated with hospitals.

A group of physicians announced its plan to immediately open in the state a diagnostic center that would not be affiliated with a hospital. The state hospital association argued to the state legislature that only hospitals could reliably handle advanced medical technologies. The legislature then enacted a law prohibiting the operation in the state of diagnostic centers that were not affiliated with hospitals.

The group of physicians filed suit challenging the constitutionality of the state law.

What action should the court take?

(A) Uphold the law, because the provision of medical services is traditionally a matter of legitimate local concern that states have unreviewable authority to regulate.

(B) Uphold the law, because the legislature could rationally believe that diagnostic centers not affiliated with hospitals would be less reliable than hospitals.

(C) Invalidate the law, because it imposes an undue burden on access to medical services in the state.

(D) Dismiss the suit without reaching the merits, because the suit is not ripe.

Question # 67 - Torts

While driving his open-bed truck with a friend in the open bed, the driver swerved, throwing his friend to the pavement. The friend sustained severe injuries. The friend had often ridden in the open bed of the driver's truck, and on some of those occasions the driver had swerved to frighten his friend. The friend sued the driver to recover both compensatory damages for his injuries and punitive damages.

Which cause of action would NOT permit the friend to recover punitive damages?

(A) Assault
(B) Battery
(C) Negligence
(D) Recklessness

Question # 68 - Evidence

A plaintiff sued an individual defendant for injuries suffered in a collision between the plaintiff's car and the defendant's truck while the defendant's employee was driving the truck. The plaintiff sought discovery of any accident report the employee might have made to the defendant, but the defendant responded that no such report existed. Before trial, the defendant moved to preclude the plaintiff from asking the defendant in the presence of the jury whether he destroyed such a report, because the defendant would then invoke his privilege against self-incrimination.

Should the court allow the plaintiff to ask the defendant about the destruction of the report?

(A) No, because a report that was prepared in anticipation of litigation is not subject to discovery.
(B) No, because no inference may properly be drawn from invocation of a legitimate privilege.
(C) Yes, because a party in a civil action may not invoke the privilege against self-incrimination.
(D) Yes, because the defendant's destruction of the report would serve as the basis of an inference adverse to the defendant.

Question # 69 - Contracts

A collector bought from a gallery a painting correctly described in the parties' signed contract as a "one-of-a-kind self-portrait" by a famous artist that had recently died. The contract price was $100,000 in cash, payable one month after a truck carrier delivered the painting to the collector.

The painting was damaged in transit. The collector timely rejected it after inspection and immediately notified the gallery of the rejection. The gallery then sold the painting to a third party. It informed the collector that it would pick up the painting within a couple of weeks. Two weeks later, before the gallery picked up the painting, the collector sold the painting to an art admirer for $120,000 cash, after notifying her about the damage.

If the collector's sale of the painting was NOT an acceptance of the goods, what is the maximum amount that the gallery is entitled to recover from the collector?

(A) $120,000 (damages for conversion).
(B) $100,000 (the collector-gallery contract price).
(C) $20,000 (the excess of the market price over the contract price).
(D) Only the allowance of lost profit to the gallery as a volume dealer.

Question # 70 - Real Property

Six years ago, a landlord and a tenant entered into a 10-year commercial lease of land. The written lease provided that, if a public entity under the power of eminent domain condemned any part of the land, the lease would terminate and the landlord would receive the entire condemnation award. Thereafter, the city condemned approximately two-thirds of the land.

The tenant notified the city and the landlord that an independent appraisal of the value of the tenant's possessory interest established that it substantially exceeded the tenant's obligation under the lease and that the tenant was entitled to share the award. The appraisal was accurate.

In an appropriate action among the landlord, the tenant, and the city as to the right of the tenant to a portion of the condemnation award, for whom will the court likely find?

(A) The landlord, because the condemnation superseded and canceled the lease.
(B) The landlord, because the parties specifically agreed as to the consequences of condemnation.
(C) The tenant, because the landlord breached the landlord's implied warranty of quiet enjoyment.
(D) The tenant, because otherwise the landlord would be unjustly enriched.

Question # 71 - Constitutional Law

In order to reduce the federal deficit, Congress enacted a statute imposing a five percent national retail sales tax. The tax was levied upon all retail sales in the United States and applied equally to the sales of all kinds of goods.

Is this tax constitutional as applied to retail sales of newspapers?

(A) Yes, because it is within Congress's power to tax.
(B) Yes, because the tax is necessary to serve the compelling interest of balancing the federal budget.
(C) No, because retail sales taxes are within the taxing power of the states.
(D) No, because the imposition of a tax on the sale of newspapers violates the freedom of the press.

Question # 72 - Criminal Law and Procedure

The police suspected a woman of growing marijuana in her private residence. Narcotics officers went to her neighborhood in the middle of the night. Nothing unlawful could be seen from the street, so the officers walked into the neighbors' yard and looked through the woman's kitchen window, which had neither drapes nor shades. The officers observed what appeared to be marijuana plants being cultivated under grow lights in the kitchen. Using this information, the officers obtained a search warrant. The execution of that warrant netted numerous marijuana plants.

The woman was charged with possession of marijuana. She moved to suppress the marijuana plants recovered when the warrant was executed, claiming that the evidence supporting the warrant was obtained through a search that violated the

Fourth Amendment.

Should the marijuana plants be suppressed?

(A) No, because regardless of the lawfulness of the police conduct beforehand, they did obtain a warrant to search the woman's home.
(B) No, because the woman could have no reasonable expectation of privacy concerning activities that she exposed to the view of her neighbors.
(C) Yes, because the officers' clandestine observation of the plants violated the woman's reasonable expectation of privacy concerning activities occurring in her home.
(D) Yes, because no unlawful activities could be observed by the officers from any public vantage point.

Question # 73 - Real Property

A niece inherited vacant land from her uncle. She lived in a distant state and decided to sell the land to a colleague who was interested in purchasing the land as an investment. They orally agreed upon a price, and, at the colleague's insistence, the niece agreed to provide him with a warranty deed without any exceptions. The price was paid, the warranty deed was delivered, and the deed was promptly and properly recorded. Neither the niece nor the colleague had, at that point, ever seen the land.

After recording the deed, the colleague visited the land for the first time and discovered that it had no access to any public right-of-way and that none of the surrounding lands had ever been held in common ownership with any previous owner of the tract of land.

The colleague sued the niece for damages.

For whom will the court find?

(A) The colleague, because lack of access makes title unmarketable.
(B) The colleague, because the covenants of warranty and quiet enjoyment in the deed were breached.
(C) The niece, because no title covenants were breached.
(D) The niece, because the agreement to sell was oral.

Question # 74 - Evidence

In a prosecution for aggravated battery, a police officer testified that when he arrested the defendant, he took a knife from the defendant and delivered it to the medical examiner. The medical examiner testified that the knife blade was consistent with the victim's wound but admitted on cross-examination that any number of other knives could also have caused the wound.

Should the judge grant a motion to strike the medical examiner's testimony?

(A) No, because the probative worth of this evidence is for the jury to assess.
(B) Yes, because in light of the medical examiner's admission, his testimony has insufficient probative value.
(C) Yes, because the medical examiner could not state the probability that the wound was caused by the defendant's knife.
(D) Yes, because the probative value is substantially outweighed by the danger of unfair prejudice.

Question # 75 - Torts

In a plaintiff's action for battery, the evidence established that the plaintiff was bad-tempered and, the defendant knew, carried a gun and used it often; that the plaintiff struck the defendant first; that during the altercation, the plaintiff repeatedly tried to get to his gun; and that the blows inflicted upon the plaintiff by the defendant resulted in the plaintiff being hospitalized.

Which finding of fact would be most likely to result in a verdict for the defendant?

(A) The defendant used no more force than he actually believed was necessary to protect himself against death or serious bodily harm.

(B) The defendant used no more force than he reasonably believed was necessary to protect himself against death or serious bodily harm.

(C) The defendant, in fact, feared death or serious bodily harm.

(D) The defendant was justified in retaliating against the plaintiff because the plaintiff struck the first blow.

Question # 76 - Evidence

A defendant was on trial for perjury for having falsely testified in an earlier civil case that he knew nothing about a business fraud. In the perjury trial, the defendant again testified that he knew nothing about the business fraud. In rebuttal, the prosecutor called a witness to testify that after the civil trial was over, the defendant admitted to the witness privately that he had known about the fraud.

Is the witness's testimony in the perjury trial admissible?

(A) Yes, but only to impeach the defendant's testimony.

(B) Yes, both to impeach the defendant's testimony and as substantive evidence of the perjury.

(C) No, because it is hearsay not within any exception.

(D) No, because it relates to the business fraud and not to the commission of perjury.

Question # 77 - Real Property

A landowner mortgaged her land to a nationally chartered bank as security for a loan. The mortgage provided that the bank could, at its option, declare the entire loan due and payable if all or any part of the land, or an interest therein, was sold or transferred without the bank's prior written consent.

Subsequently, the landowner wanted to sell the land to a neighbor by an installment land contract, but the bank refused to consent. The neighbor's credit was good, and all mortgage payments to the bank were fully current.

The landowner and the neighbor consulted an attorney about their proposed transaction, their desire to complete it, and the bank's refusal to consent.

What would the attorney's best advice be?

(A) Even if the landowner transfers to the neighbor by land contract, the bank may accelerate the debt and foreclose if the full amount is not paid.

(B) The due-on-sale clause is void as an illegal restraint on alienation of the fee simple, so they may proceed.

(C) By making the transfer in land contract form, the landowner will prevent enforcement of the due-on-sale clause if the mortgage payments are kept current.

(D) The due-on-sale clause has only the effect that the proposed transfer will automatically make the neighbor personally liable on the debt, whether or not the neighbor specifically agrees to assume it.

Question # 78 - Contracts

On March 1, an excavator entered into a contract with a contractor to perform excavation work on a large project. The contract expressly required that the excavator begin work on June 1 to enable other subcontractors to install utilities. On May 15, the excavator requested a 30-day delay in the start date for the excavation work because he was seriously behind schedule on another project. When the contractor refused to grant the delay, the excavator stated that he would try to begin the work for the contractor on June 1.

Does the contractor have valid legal grounds to cancel the contract with the excavator and hire a replacement?

(A) Yes, because the excavator committed an anticipatory repudiation of the contract by causing the contractor to feel insecure about the performance.

(B) Yes, because the excavator breached the implied covenant of good faith and fair dealing.

(C) No, because the excavator would be entitled to specific performance of the contract if he could begin by June 1.

(D) No, because the excavator did not state unequivocally that he would delay the beginning of his work.

Question # 79 - Constitutional Law

In response to the need for additional toxic waste landfills in a state, the state's legislature enacted a law authorizing a state agency to establish five new state-owned and state-operated toxic waste landfills. The law provided that the agency would decide the locations and sizes of the landfills after an investigation of all potential sites and a determination that the particular sites chosen would not endanger public health and would be consistent with the public welfare.

A community in the state was scheduled for inspection by the agency as a potential toxic waste landfill site. Because the community's residents obtained most of their drinking water from an aquifer that ran under the entire community, a citizens' group, made up of residents of that community, sued the appropriate officials of the agency in federal court. The group sought a declaratory judgment that the selection of the community as the site of a toxic waste landfill would be unconstitutional and an injunction preventing the agency from selecting the community as a site for such a landfill. The agency officials moved to dismiss.

Which of the following is the most appropriate basis for the court to dismiss this suit?

(A) The case presents a nonjusticiable political question.
(B) The interest of the state in obtaining suitable sites for toxic waste landfills is sufficiently compelling to justify the selection of the community as a location for such a facility.
(C) The Eleventh Amendment bars suits of this kind in the federal courts.
(D) The case is not ripe for a decision on the merits.

Question # 80 - Real Property

Fifteen years ago, after a part of the path located on his land and connecting his cabin to the public highway washed out, the man cleared a small part of his neighbor's land and rerouted a section of the path through the neighbor's land.

Twelve years ago, the neighbor leased her land to some hunters. For the next 12 years, the hunters and the man who had rerouted the path used the path for access to the highway.

A month ago, the neighbor discovered that part of the path was on her land. The neighbor told the man that she had not given him permission to cross her land and that she would be closing the rerouted path after 90 days.

The man's land and the neighbor's land have never been in common ownership.

The period of time necessary to acquire rights by prescription in the jurisdiction is 10 years. The period of time necessary to acquire title by adverse possession in the jurisdiction is 10 years.

A man contacted his lawyer regarding his right to use a path that was on his neighbor's vacant land.

What should the lawyer tell the man concerning his right to use the rerouted path on the neighbor's land?

(A) The man has fee title by adverse possession of the land included in the path.
(B) The man has an easement by necessity to use the path.
(C) The man has an easement by prescription to use the path.
(D) The man has no right to use the path.

Question # 81 - Evidence

A plaintiff sued a defendant for injuries allegedly suffered when he slipped and fell on the defendant's business property. Without asking that the defendant's property manager be declared a hostile witness, the plaintiff called him solely to establish that the defendant was the owner of the property where the plaintiff fell. On cross-examination of the manager, the defendant's attorney sought to establish that the defendant had taken reasonable precautions to make the property safe for business invitees.

Should the defendant's cross-examination of the manager be permitted over the plaintiff's objection?

(A) No, because cross-examination should be limited to the subject matter of the direct examination and matters affecting the credibility of the witness.
(B) No, because the court has not declared the manager hostile.
(C) Yes, because the cross-examiner is entitled to explore matters relevant to any issue in the case, including credibility.
(D) Yes, because the manager is the agent of a party, as to whom the scope of cross-examination is unlimited.

Question # 82 - Torts

As a shopper was leaving a supermarket, an automatic door that should have opened outward opened inward, striking and breaking the shopper's nose. The owner of the building had installed the automatic door. The lease, pursuant to which the supermarket leased the building, provided that the supermarket was responsible for all maintenance of the premises.

The shopper sued the supermarket. At trial, neither the shopper nor the supermarket offered any testimony, expert or otherwise, as to why the door had opened inward. At the conclusion of the proofs, both the shopper and the supermarket moved for judgment.

How should the trial judge rule?

(A) Grant judgment for the shopper, because it is undisputed that the door malfunctioned.
(B) Grant judgment for the supermarket, because the shopper failed to join the owner of the building as a defendant.
(C) Grant judgment for the supermarket, because the shopper failed to offer proof of the supermarket's negligence.
(D) Submit the case to the jury, because on these facts negligence may be inferred.

Question # 83 - Torts

A man owned a much-loved cat, worth about $25, that frequently trespassed on a neighbor's property. The neighbor repeatedly asked the man to keep the cat on his own property, but the trespasses did not diminish. Aware of the man's attachment to the cat, the neighbor killed the cat with a shotgun in full view of the man. As a consequence, the man suffered great emotional distress.

In an action by the man against the neighbor, which of the following claims would be likely to result in the greatest monetary recovery?

(A) Battery.
(B) Intentional infliction of mental suffering.
(C) Trespass to a chattel.
(D) Conversion.

Question # 84 - Constitutional Law

National statistics revealed a dramatic increase in the number of elementary and secondary school students bringing controlled substances to school for sale. In response, Congress enacted a statute requiring each state legislature to enact a state law making it a crime for any person to sell, within 1,000 feet of any elementary or secondary school, any controlled substance that had previously been transported in interstate commerce.

Is the federal statute constitutional?

(A) No, because Congress has no authority to require a state legislature to enact any specified legislation.
(B) No, because the sale of a controlled substance in close proximity to a school does not have a sufficiently close nexus to interstate commerce to justify its regulation by Congress.
(C) Yes, because it contains a jurisdictional provision that will ensure, on a case-by-case basis, that any particular controlled substance subject to the terms of this statute will, in fact, affect interstate commerce.
(D) Yes, because Congress possesses broad authority under both the general welfare clause and the commerce clause to regulate any activities affecting education that also have, in inseverable aggregates, a substantial effect on interstate commerce.

Question # 85 - Evidence

When a man entered a bank and presented a check for payment, the bank teller recognized the signature on the check as a forgery because the check was drawn on the account of a customer whose handwriting she knew. The bank teller called the police. Before the police arrived, the man picked up the check from the counter and left.

The man was charged with attempting to cash a forged check. At trial, the prosecutor called the bank teller to testify that the signature on the check was forged.

Is the bank teller's testimony admissible?

(A) Yes, because a bank teller is by occupation an expert on handwriting.
(B) Yes, because it is rationally based on the bank teller's perception and is helpful to the jury.
(C) No, because the bank teller was at fault in allowing loss of the original by failing to secure the check.
(D) No, because it is not possible for either the jury or an expert to compare the signature on the missing check with a signature established as genuine.

Question # 86 - Contracts

An accountant and a bookkeeper, as part of a contract dissolving their accounting business, agreed that each would contribute $100,000 to fund an annuity for a clerk who was a longtime employee of the business. The clerk's position would be terminated due to the dissolution, and he did not have a retirement plan. The accountant and the bookkeeper informed the clerk of their plan to fund an annuity for him. The clerk, confident about his financial future because of the promised annuity, purchased a retirement home. The accountant later contributed his $100,000 to fund the annuity, but the bookkeeper stated that he could afford to contribute only $50,000. The accountant agreed that the bookkeeper should contribute only $50,000.

Does the clerk have a valid basis for an action against the bookkeeper for the unpaid $50,000?

(A) No, because the clerk was bound by the modification of the agreement made by the accountant and the bookkeeper.
(B) No, because the clerk was only a donee beneficiary of the agreement between the accountant and the bookkeeper, and had no vested rights.
(C) Yes, because the clerk's reliance on the promised retirement fund prevented the parties from changing the terms.
(D) Yes, because the promises to establish the fund were made binding by consideration from the clerk's many years of employment.

Question # 87 - Real Property

Twenty-five years ago, a man who owned a 45-acre tract of land conveyed 40 of the 45 acres to a developer by warranty deed. The man retained the rear five-acre portion of the land and continues to live there in a large farmhouse.

The deed to the 40-acre tract was promptly and properly recorded. It contained the following language:

"It is a term and condition of this deed, which shall be a covenant running with the land and binding on all owners, their heirs and assigns, that no use shall be made of the 40-acre tract of land except for residential purposes."

Subsequently, the developer fully developed the 40-acre tract into a residential subdivision consisting of 40 lots with a single-family residence on each lot.

Although there have been multiple transfers of ownership of each of the 40 lots within the subdivision, none of them included a reference to the quoted provision in the deed from the man to the developer, nor did any deed to a subdivision lot create any new covenants restricting use.

Last year, a major new medical center was constructed adjacent to the subdivision. A doctor who owns a house in the subdivision wishes to relocate her medical offices to her house. For the first time, the doctor learned of the restrictive covenant in the deed from the man to the developer. The applicable zoning ordinance permits the doctor's intended use. The man, as owner of the five-acre tract, however, objects to the doctor's proposed use of her property.

There are no governing statutes other than the zoning code. The common law Rule Against Perpetuities is unmodified in the jurisdiction.

Can the doctor convert her house in the subdivision into a medical office?

(A) No, because the owners of lots in the subdivision own property benefitted by the original residential covenant and have the sole right to enforce it.
(B) No, because the man owns property benefitted by the original restrictive covenant and has a right to enforce it.
(C) Yes, because the original restrictive covenant violates the Rule Against Perpetuities.
(D) Yes, because the zoning ordinance allows the doctor's proposed use and preempts the restrictive covenant.

Question # 88 - Contracts

On March 1, a mechanic contracted to repair a textile company's knitting machine by March 6. On March 2, the textile company contracted to manufacture and deliver specified cloth to a customer on March 15. The textile company knew that it would have to use the machine then under repair to perform this contract. Because the customer's order was for a rush job, the two parties included in their contract a liquidated damages clause, providing that the textile company would pay $5,000 for each day's delay in delivery after March 15.

The mechanic was inexcusably five days late in repairing the machine, and, as a result, the textile company was five days late in delivering the cloth to the customer. The textile company paid $25,000 to the customer as liquidated damages and then sued the mechanic for $25,000. Both the mechanic and the textile company knew when making their contract on March 1 that under ordinary circumstances the textile company would sustain few or no damages of any kind as a result of a five-day delay in the machine repair.

Assuming that the $5,000-per-day liquidated damages clause in the contract between the textile company and the customer is valid, which of the following arguments will serve as the mechanic's best defense to the textile company's action?

(A) Time was not of the essence in the contract between the mechanic and the textile company.
(B) The mechanic had no reason to foresee on March 1 that the customer would suffer consequential damages in the amount of $25,000.
(C) By entering into the contract with the customer while knowing that its knitting machine was being repaired, the textile company assumed the risk of any delay loss to the customer.
(D) In all probability, the liquidated damages paid by the textile company to the customer are not the same amount as the actual damages sustained by the customer in consequence of the late delivery of the cloth.

Question # 89 - Real Property

Five years ago, an investor who owned a vacant lot in a residential area borrowed $25,000 from a friend and gave the friend a note for $25,000 due in five years, secured by a mortgage on the lot. The friend neglected to record the mortgage. The fair market value of the lot was then $25,000.

Three years ago, the investor discovered that the friend had not recorded his mortgage and in consideration of $50,000 conveyed the lot to a buyer. The fair market value of the lot was then $50,000. The buyer knew nothing of the friend's mortgage. One month thereafter, the friend discovered the sale to the buyer, recorded his $25,000 mortgage, and notified the buyer that he held a $25,000 mortgage on the lot.

Two years ago, the buyer needed funds. Although she told her bank of the mortgage claimed by the investor's friend, the bank loaned her $15,000, and she gave the bank a note for $15,000 due in two years secured by a mortgage on the lot. The bank promptly and properly recorded the mortgage. At that time, the fair market value of the lot was $75,000.

The recording act of the jurisdiction provides: "No conveyance or mortgage of real property shall be good against subsequent purchasers for value and without notice unless the same be recorded according to law."

Both notes are now due and both the investor and the buyer have refused to pay. The lot is now worth only $50,000.

What are the rights of the investor's friend and the bank in the lot?

(A) Both mortgages are enforceable liens and the friend's has priority because it was first recorded.

(B) Both mortgages are enforceable liens, but the bank's has priority because the buyer was an innocent purchaser for value.

(C) Only the friend's mortgage is an enforceable lien, because the bank had actual and constructive notice of the investor's fraud.

(D) Only the bank's mortgage is an enforceable lien, because the buyer was an innocent purchaser for value.

Question # 90 - Criminal Law and Procedure

A woman offered to pay her friend one-third of the stolen proceeds if the friend would drive the getaway car to be used in a bank robbery. The friend agreed but made the woman promise not to hurt anyone during the robbery.

The woman then drove to a sporting goods store, where she explained to the store owner that she needed a small firearm for use in a bank robbery. The store owner responded that he would charge extra because the woman was so unwise as to confide her unlawful plans for using the weapon, and he sold her a handgun at four times the regular price.

During the robbery, the woman used the gun to threaten a bank teller into handing over the money. The gun discharged by accident and killed a bank customer.

At common law, who in addition to the woman could properly be convicted of murder in the death of the customer?

(A) Both the friend and the store owner.

(B) Neither the friend nor the store owner.

(C) Only the friend.

(D) Only the store owner.

Question # 91 - Evidence

A pedestrian sued a driver for injuries suffered in a hit-and-run accident. At trial, the pedestrian called a witness who testified that he saw the accident and that as the car sped off he accurately dictated the license number into his properly operating pocket dictating machine. The witness stated that he no longer remembered the number.

May the tape recording be played?

(A) Yes, as a present sense impression only.

(B) Yes, as a recorded recollection only.

(C) Yes, as a present sense impression and as a past recollection recorded.

(D) No, because it is hearsay not within any exception.

Question # 92 - Criminal Law and Procedure

A man decided to steal a car he saw parked on a hill. When he got in and started the engine, the car began rolling down the hill. The man quickly discovered that the car's brakes did not work. He crashed through the window of a store at the bottom of the hill.

The man was charged with larceny of the car and with the crime of knowingly damaging the store's property. At trial, the judge instructed the jury that if the jury found both that the man was guilty of larceny of the car and that the damage to the store was the result of that larceny, then it should also find him guilty of malicious damage of property.

The man was convicted on both counts. On appeal, he argued that the conviction for malicious damage of property should be reversed because the instruction was not a correct statement of the law.

Should the man's conviction be affirmed?

(A) Yes, because his intent to steal the car provides the necessary mental element.

(B) Yes, because he was committing a felony.

(C) No, because the instruction wrongly described the necessary mental state.

(D) No, because it would violate double jeopardy to convict the man of two crimes for a single act.

Question # 93 - Contracts

A seller and a buyer entered into a written agreement providing that the seller was to deliver 1,000 cases of candy bars to the buyer during the months of May and June. Under the agreement, the buyer was obligated to make a selection by March 1 of the quantities of the various candy bars to be delivered under the contract. The buyer did not make the selection by March 1, and on March 2 the seller notified the buyer that because of the buyer's failure to select, the seller would not deliver the candy bars. The seller had all of the necessary candy bars on hand on March 1 and made no additional sales or purchases on March 1 or March 2. On March 2, after receiving the seller's notice that it would not perform, the buyer notified the seller of its selection and insisted that the seller perform. The seller refused.

If the buyer sues the seller for breach of contract, is the buyer likely to prevail?

(A) No, because a contract did not exist until selection of the specific candy bars, and the seller withdrew its offer before selection.
(B) No, because selection of the candy bars by March 1 was an express condition to the seller's duty to perform.
(C) Yes, because a delay of one day in making the selection did not have a material effect on the seller.
(D) Yes, because upon the buyer's failure to make a selection by March 1, the seller had a duty to make a reasonable selection.

Question # 94 - Real Property

The grantee's release 10 years ago operates as a waiver regarding any right to purchase that the corporation might have.
A grantor owned two tracts of land, one of 15 acres and another of five acres. The two tracts were a mile apart.

Fifteen years ago, the grantor conveyed the smaller tract to a grantee. The grantor retained the larger tract. The deed to the grantee contained, in addition to proper legal descriptions of both properties and identifications of the parties, the following:

I, the grantor, bind myself and my heirs and assigns that in the event that the larger tract that I now retain is ever offered for sale, I will notify the grantee and his heirs and assigns in writing, and the grantee and his heirs and assigns shall have the right to purchase the larger tract for its fair market value as determined by a board consisting of three qualified expert independent real estate appraisers.

With appropriate references to the other property and the parties, there followed a reciprocal provision that conferred upon the grantor and her heirs and assigns a similar right to purchase the smaller tract, purportedly binding the grantee and his heirs and assigns.

Ten years ago, a corporation acquired the larger tract from the grantor. At that time, the grantee had no interest in acquiring the larger tract and by an appropriate written document released any interest he or his heirs or assigns might have had in the larger tract.

Last year, the grantee died. The smaller tract passed by the grantee's will to his daughter. She has decided to sell the smaller tract. However, because she believes the corporation has been a very poor steward of the larger tract, she refuses to sell the smaller tract to the corporation even though she has offered it for sale in the local real estate market.

The corporation brought an appropriate action for specific performance after taking all of the necessary preliminary steps in its effort to exercise its rights to purchase the smaller tract.

The daughter asserted all possible defenses.

The common law Rule Against Perpetuities is unmodified in the jurisdiction.

If the court rules for the daughter, what is the reason?

(A) The provision setting out the right to purchase violates the Rule Against Perpetuities.
(B) The grantee's release 10 years ago operates as a waiver regarding any right to purchase that the corporation might have.
(C) The two tracts of land were not adjacent parcels of real estate, and thus the right to purchase is in gross and is therefore

unenforceable.

(D) Noncompliance with a right to purchase gives rise to a claim for money damages, but not for specific performance.

Question # 95 - Constitutional Law

In order to combat terrorism, Congress enacted a statute authorizing the President to construct surveillance facilities on privately owned property if the President determined that the construction of such facilities was "necessary to safeguard the security of the United States." The statute provided no compensation for the owner of the land on which such facilities were constructed and provided that the surveillance facilities were to be owned and operated by the United States government.

Pursuant to this statute, the President has determined that the construction of a surveillance facility on a very small, unused portion of an owner's large tract of land is necessary to safeguard the security of the United States. The construction and operation of the facility will not affect any of the uses that the owner is currently making of the entire tract of land.

The owner has filed suit to challenge the constitutionality of the construction of a surveillance facility on the parcel of land at issue without compensation.

How should the court rule?

(A) It would be a taking of the owner's property for which the owner must be compensated.
(B) It would single out the owner for adverse treatment in violation of the equal protection component of the Fifth Amendment.
(C) It would not interfere with any use the owner is currently making of the entire tract of land and, therefore, would not entitle the owner to any compensation.
(D) It would be valid without any compensation, because it has been determined to be necessary to protect a compelling government interest in national security.

Question # 96 - Torts

A child was bitten by a dog while playing in a fenced-in common area of an apartment complex owned by a landlord. The child was the guest of a tenant living in the complex, and the dog was owned by another tenant. The owner of the dog knew that the dog had a propensity to bite, but the landlord did not have any notice of the dog's vicious propensities.

In an action by the child against the landlord, will the child prevail?

(A) Yes, because in these circumstances a landlord is strictly liable.
(B) Yes, because a landlord's duty to protect a tenant's guests from dangerous conditions is nondelegable.
(C) No, because the landlord did not have any notice of the dog's vicious propensities.
(D) No, because a landlord owes no duty to a tenant's gratuitous guests.

Question # 97 - Criminal Law and Procedure

A state grand jury investigating a murder learned that the key suspect might have kept a diary. The grand jury issued a subpoena duces tecum requiring the suspect to produce any diary. The subpoena made clear that the grand jury was seeking only the diary and not any testimony from the suspect. The suspect refused to produce the diary, citing the privilege against self-incrimination.

Under what circumstances, if any, could the grand jury compel production of the diary over the suspect's Fifth Amendment privilege?

(A) It may compel production without granting immunity because the suspect was not compelled to write a diary.
(B) It may compel production only if the suspect is granted use and derivative use immunity from the act of production.
(C) It may compel production only if the suspect is granted transactional immunity.
(D) It may not compel production of a private diary under any circumstances.

Question # 98 - Evidence

A defendant was on trial for tax evasion. The IRS, seeking to establish the defendant's income by showing his expenditures, called on the defendant's attorney to produce records showing only how much the defendant had paid his attorney in fees.

Should the demand for the attorney's fee records be upheld?

(A) Yes, because it calls for relevant information not within the attorney-client privilege.
(B) Yes, because the attorney-client privilege cannot be invoked to conceal evidence of a crime.
(C) No, because the records are protected by the attorney-client privilege.
(D) No, because the records are protected by the attorney work-product doctrine.

Question # 99 - Criminal Law and Procedure

A man was angered after he was unexpectedly laid off from his longtime job as a factory assembly worker. The next day, he returned to the factory floor and indiscriminately fired shotgun rounds in the air. The man later testified, without contradiction, that he had not intended to kill anyone but simply sought to exact revenge on the factory's owners by shutting down operations for the day. Unfortunately, one of the bullets ricocheted off the wall and killed the man's best friend.
The crimes below are listed in descending order of seriousness.

On these facts, what is the most serious offense for which the man properly could be convicted?

(A) Murder
(B) Voluntary manslaughter.
(C) Involuntary manslaughter.
(D) Assault.

Question # 100 - Torts

A food company contracted with a delivery service to supply food to remote areas. The contract between the food company and the delivery service was terminable at will. The delivery service then entered into a contract with an airline company to provide an airplane to deliver the food. The contract between the delivery service and the airline company was also terminable at will.

The food company was displeased with the airline company because of a previous business dispute between them. Upon learning of the delivery service's contract with the airline company, the food company terminated its contract with the delivery service in order to cause the airline company to lose the business. When the food company terminated the delivery service's contract, the delivery service had no choice but to terminate the airline company's contract.

If the airline company sues the delivery service for tortious interference with contract, will the airline company prevail?

(A) No, because the airline company and the delivery service were the parties to the contract.
(B) No, because the airline company was not in privity with the food company.
(C) Yes, because the delivery service did not terminate the contract because of poor performance.
(D) Yes, because the delivery service's termination of the contract made it a party to the food company's acts.

Multistate Bar Examination Released Questions
Section 2

PRACTICE EXAM 2

Question 1 - Contracts

In January, a teacher contracted with a summer camp to serve as its head counselor at a salary of $10,000 for 10 weeks of service from the first of June to the middle of August. In March, the camp notified the teacher that it had hired someone else to act as head counselor and that the teacher's services would not be needed. In April, the teacher spent $200 traveling to interview at the only other nearby summer camp for a position as its head counselor. The teacher was not chosen for that job. The teacher then took a position teaching in a local summer school at a salary of $6,000 for the same 10-week period as the summer camp.

In a breach-of-contract action against the camp, to which of the following amounts, as damages, is the teacher entitled?

(A) $4,000
(B) $4,200
(C) $10,000
(D) $10,200

Question 2 - Constitutional Law

A federal statute imposes an excise tax of $100 on each new computer sold in the United States. It also appropriates the entire proceeds of that tax to a special fund, which is required to be used to purchase licenses for computer software that will be made available for use, free of charge, to any resident of the United States.

Is this statute constitutional?

(A) No, because the federal government may not impose any direct taxes on citizens of the United States.
(B) No, because this statute takes without just compensation the property of persons who hold patents or copyrights on computer software.
(C) Yes, because it is a reasonable exercise of the power of Congress to tax and spend for the general welfare.
(D) Yes, because the patent power authorizes Congress to impose reasonable charges on the sale of technology and to spend   the proceeds of those charges to advance the use of technology in the United States.

Question 3 - Criminal Law and Procedure

Nine gang members were indicted for the murder of a tenth gang member who had become an informant. The gang leader pleaded guilty. At the trial of the other eight, the state's evidence showed the following: The gang leader announced a party to celebrate the recent release of a gang member from jail. But the party was not what it seemed. The gang leader had learned that the recently released gang member had earned his freedom by informing the authorities about the gang's criminal activities. The gang leader decided to use the party to let the other gang members see what happened to a snitch. He told no one about his plan. At the party, after all present had consumed large amounts of liquor, the gang leader announced that the released gang member was an informant and stabbed him with a knife in front of the others. The eight other gang members watched and did nothing while the informant slowly bled to death. The jury found the eight gang members guilty of murder and they appealed.

Should the appellate court uphold the convictions?

(A) No, because mere presence at the scene of a crime is insufficient to make one an accomplice.
(B) No, because murder is a specific intent crime, and there is insufficient evidence to show that they intended to kill.
(C) Yes, because the gang members made no effort to save the informant after he had been stabbed.
(D) Yes, because voluntary intoxication does not negate criminal responsibility.

Question 4 - Real Property

A landlord leased an apartment to a tenant by written lease for two years ending on the last day of a recent month. The lease provided for $700 monthly rental. The tenant occupied the apartment and paid the rent for the first 15 months of the lease term, until he moved to a new job in another city. Without consulting the landlord, the tenant moved a friend into the apartment and signed an informal writing transferring to the friend his "lease rights" for the remaining nine months of the lease. The friend made the next four monthly $700 rental payments to the landlord. For the final five months of the lease term, no rent was paid by anyone, and the friend moved out with three months left of the lease term. The landlord was on an extended trip abroad, and did not learn of the default and the vacancy until last week. The landlord sued the tenant and the friend, jointly and severally, for $3,500 for the last five months' rent.

What is the likely outcome of the lawsuit?

(A) Both the tenant and the friend are liable for the full $3,500, because the tenant is liable on privity of contract and the friend is liable on privity of estate as assignee.
(B) The friend is liable for $1,400 on privity of estate, which lasted only until he vacated, and the tenant is liable for $2,100 on privity of contract and estate for the period after the friend vacated.
(C) The friend is liable for $3,500 on privity of estate and the tenant is not liable, because the landlord's failure to object to the friend's payment of rent relieved the tenant of liability.
(D) The tenant is liable for $3,500 on privity of contract and the friend is not liable, because a sublessee does not have personal liability to the original landlord.

Question 5 - Evidence

In a civil trial for professional malpractice, the plaintiff sought to show that the defendant, an engineer, had designed the plaintiff's flour mill with inadequate power. The plaintiff called an expert witness who based his testimony solely on his own professional experience but also asserted, when asked, that the book *Smith on Milling Systems* was a reliable treatise in the field and consistent with his views. On cross-examination, the defendant asked the witness whether he and Smith were ever wrong. The witness answered, "Nobody's perfect." The defendant asked no further questions. The defendant called a second expert witness and asked, "Do you accept the Smith book as reliable?" The second witness said, "It once was, but it is now badly out of date." The plaintiff requested that the jury be allowed to examine the book and judge for itself the book's reliability.

Should the court allow the jury to examine the book?

(A) No, because the jury may consider only passages read to it by counsel or witness.
(B) No, because the plaintiff's expert in testifying did not rely on the treatise but on his own experience.
(C) Yes, because an expert has testified that the treatise is reliable.
(D) Yes, because the jury is the judge of the weight and credibility to be accorded both written and oral evidence.

Question 6 - Torts

A driver, returning from a long shift at a factory, fell asleep at the wheel and lost control of his car. As a result, his car collided with a police car driven by an officer who was returning to the station after having responded to an emergency. The police officer was injured in the accident. The police officer sued the driver in negligence for her injuries. The driver moved for summary judgment, arguing that the common-law firefighters' rule barred the suit.

Should the court grant the motion?

(A) No, because the firefighters' rule does not apply to police officers.
(B) No, because the police officer's injuries were not related to any special dangers of her job.
(C) Yes, because the accident would not have occurred but for the emergency.
(D) Yes, because the police officer was injured on the job.

Question 7 - Contracts

A lumber supplier agreed to sell and a furniture manufacturer agreed to buy all of the lumber that the manufacturer required over a two-year period. The sales contract provided that payment was due 60 days after delivery, but that a 3% discount would be allowed if the manufacturer paid within 10 days of delivery. During the first year of the contract, the manufacturer regularly paid within the 10-day period and received the 3% discount. Fifteen days after the supplier made its most recent lumber delivery to the manufacturer, the supplier had received no payment from the manufacturer. At this time, the supplier became aware of rumors from a credible source that the manufacturer's financial condition was precarious. The supplier wrote the manufacturer, demanding assurances regarding the manufacturer's financial status. The manufacturer immediately mailed its latest audited financial statements to the supplier, as well as a satisfactory credit report prepared by the manufacturer's banker. The rumors proved to be false. Nevertheless, the supplier refused to resume deliveries. The manufacturer sued the lumber supplier for breach of contract.

Will the manufacturer prevail?

(A) No, because the contract was unenforceable, since the manufacturer had not committed to purchase a definite quantity of lumber.
(B) No, because the supplier had reasonable grounds for insecurity and was therefore entitled to cancel the contract and refuse to make any future deliveries.
(C) Yes, because the credit report and audited financial statements provided adequate assurance of due performance under the contract.
(D) Yes, because the supplier was not entitled to condition resumption of deliveries on the receipt of financial status information.

Question 8 - Constitutional Law

A toy manufacturer that has its headquarters and sole manufacturing plant in the state of Green developed a "Martian" toy that simulates the exploration of Mars by a remote-controlled vehicle. It accurately depicts the Martian landscape and the unmanned exploratory vehicle traversing it. The toy is of high quality, safe, durable, and has sold very well. Other toy manufacturers, all located outside Green, developed similar toys that are lower in price. These manufacturers have contracts to sell their Martian toys to outlets in Green. Although these toys are safe and durable, they depict the Martian landscape less realistically than the toys manufactured in Green. Nevertheless, because of the price difference, sales of these toys have cut severely into the sales of the Martian toys manufactured in Green. The Green legislature subsequently enacted a law "to protect the children of Green from faulty science and to protect Green toy manufacturers from unfair competition." This law forbids the sale in Green of any toy that purports to represent extraterrestrial objects and does not satisfy specified scientific criteria. The Martian toy manufactured in Green satisfies all of these criteria; none of the Martian toys of the competing manufacturers meets the requirements.

Is the Green law constitutional?

(A) No, because it abrogates the obligations of the contracts between the other toy manufacturers and their Green outlets who have agreed to sell their Martian toys.
(B) No, because it imposes an undue burden on interstate commerce.
(C) Yes, because it deals only with a local matter, the sale of toys in Green stores.
(D) Yes, because the state's interest in protecting the state's children from faulty science justifies this burden on interstate commerce.

Question 9 - Real Property

A landowner executed an instrument in the proper form of a deed, purporting to convey his land to a friend. The landowner handed the instrument to the friend, saying, "This is yours, but please do not record it until after I am dead. Otherwise, it will cause me no end of trouble with my relatives." Two days later, the landowner asked the friend to return the deed to him because he had decided that he should devise the land to the friend by will rather than by deed. The friend said that he would destroy the deed and a day or so later falsely told the landowner that the deed had been destroyed. Six months ago, the landowner, who had never executed a will, died intestate, survived by a daughter as his sole heir at law. The day after the landowner's death, the friend recorded the deed from him. As soon as the daughter discovered this recording and the friend's claim to the land, she brought an appropriate action against the friend to quiet title to the land.

For whom should the court hold?

(A) The daughter, because the death of the landowner deprived the subsequent recordation of any effect.
(B) The daughter, because the friend was dishonest in reporting that he had destroyed the deed.
(C) The friend, because the deed was delivered to him.
(D) The friend, because the deed was recorded by him.

Question 10 - Criminal Law and Procedure

An undercover police detective told a local drug dealer that she wanted to buy cocaine, but that she needed time to raise the necessary funds. The drug dealer said that he needed time to get the cocaine. They agreed to meet again in 10 days. An hour later, without a warrant, other officers forcibly entered the drug dealer's apartment and arrested him for attempted possession of a controlled substance.

If the drug dealer is prosecuted in a common-law jurisdiction for attempted possession of cocaine, should he be convicted?

(A) No, because he had not taken sufficient acts toward commission of the crime.
(B) No, because he was illegally arrested.
(C) Yes, because by objective standards an agreement between them had occurred.
(D) Yes, because his intention to obtain the cocaine was unequivocally expressed.

Question 11 - Torts

During a comprehensive evaluation of an adult patient's psychiatric condition, the psychiatrist failed to diagnose the patient's suicidal state. One day after the misdiagnosis, the patient committed suicide. The patient's father, immediately after having been told of his son's suicide, suffered severe emotional distress, which resulted in a stroke. The patient's father was not present at his son's appointment with the psychiatrist and did not witness the suicide. The father brought an action against the psychiatrist to recover for his severe emotional distress and the resulting stroke.

Will the father prevail?

(A) No, because the father did not sustain a physical impact.
(B) No, because the psychiatrist's professional duty did not extend to the harms suffered by the patient's father.
(C) Yes, because the father was a member of the patient's immediate family.
(D) Yes, because the psychiatrist reasonably could have foreseen that a misdiagnosis would result in the patient's suicide and the resulting emotional distress of the patient's father.

Question 12 - Evidence

In a civil trial arising from a car accident at an intersection, the plaintiff testified on direct that he came to a full stop at the intersection. On cross-examination, the defendant's lawyer asked whether the plaintiff claimed that he was exercising due care at the time, and the plaintiff replied that he was driving carefully. At a sidebar conference, the defendant's lawyer sought permission to ask the plaintiff about two prior intersection accidents in the last 12 months where he received traffic citations for failing to stop at stop signs. The plaintiff's lawyer objected.

Should the court allow defense counsel to ask the plaintiff about the two prior incidents?

(A) No, because improperly failing to stop on the recent occasions does not bear on the plaintiff's veracity and does not contradict his testimony in this case.
(B) No, because there is no indication that failing to stop on the recent occasions led to convictions.
(C) Yes, because improperly failing to stop on the recent occasions bears on the plaintiff's credibility, since he claims to have stopped in this case.
(D) Yes, because improperly failing to stop on the recent occasions tends to contradict the plaintiff's claim that he was driving carefully at the time he collided with the defendant.

Question 13 - Constitutional Law

According to a state law, state employees may be fired only "for good cause." A woman who was a resident and an employee of the state was summarily fired on the sole ground that she had notified federal officials that the state was not following federal rules governing the administration of certain federally funded state programs on which she worked. The state denied the woman's request for a hearing to allow her to contest the charge. There is no record of any other state employee having been terminated for this reason.

In a suit to enjoin the state from firing her, which of the following claims provides the LEAST support for the woman's suit?

(A) Firing her unconstitutionally abridges her freedom of speech.
(B) Firing her unconstitutionally denies her a privilege or immunity of state citizenship protected by Article IV.
(C) Firing her violates the supremacy clause of Article VI because it interferes with the enforcement of federal rules.
(D) Firing her without affording an opportunity for a hearing is an unconstitutional denial of procedural due process.

Question 14 - Contracts

A landowner and a contractor entered into a written contract under which the contractor agreed to build a building and pave an adjacent sidewalk for the landowner at a price of $200,000. Later, while construction was proceeding, the landowner and the contractor entered into an oral modification under which the contractor was not obligated to pave the sidewalk, but still would be entitled to $200,000 upon completion. The contractor completed the building. The landowner, after discussions with his landscaper, demanded that the contractor pave the adjacent sidewalk. The contractor refused.

Has the contractor breached the contract?

(A) No, because the oral modification was in good faith and therefore enforceable.
(B) Yes, because a discharge of a contractual obligation must be in writing.
(C) Yes, because the parol evidence rule bars proof of the oral modification.
(D) Yes, because there was no consideration for the discharge of the contractor's duty to pave the sidewalk.

Question 15 - Real Property

A landowner conveyed his land by quitclaim deed to his daughter and son "as joint tenants in fee simple." The language of the deed was sufficient to create a common-law joint tenancy, which is unmodified by statute. The daughter then duly executed a will devising her interest in the land to a friend. Then the son duly executed a will devising his interest in the land to a cousin. The son died, then the daughter died. Neither had ever married. The daughter's friend and the cousin survived.

After both wills have been duly probated, who owns what interest in the land?

(A) The cousin owns the fee simple.
(B) The daughter's friend and the cousin own equal shares as joint tenants.
(C) The daughter's friend and the cousin own equal shares as tenants in common.
(D) The daughter's friend owns the fee simple.

Question 16 - Evidence

A defendant was charged with burglary. At trial, a police officer testified that, after the defendant was arrested and agreed to answer questions, the officer interrogated him with a stenographer present, but that he could not recall what the defendant had said. The prosecutor presented the officer with a photocopy of the stenographic transcript of the interrogation. The officer, after looking at it, was prepared to testify that he recalled that the defendant admitted to being in the area of the burglary. The defendant objected to the officer's testimony on the ground that it violated the "original document" rule (also known as the "best evidence" rule).

Should the officer's testimony concerning the defendant's recorded confession be admitted?

(A) No, because a photocopy cannot be used without a showing that the original is unavailable.
(B) No, because the stenographer has not testified to the accuracy of the transcript.
(C) Yes, because a photocopy is a duplicate of the original.
(D) Yes, because the prosecutor is not attempting to prove the contents of the document.

Question 17 - Criminal Law and Procedure

A state legislature passed a statute providing that juries in criminal trials were to consist of 6 rather than 12 jurors, and providing that jury verdicts did not have to be unanimous but could be based on 5 votes out of 6 jurors. A defendant was tried for murder. Over his objection, he was tried by a jury composed of 6 jurors. The jurors found him guilty by a vote of 5 to 1 and, over the defendant's objection, the court entered a judgment of conviction, which was affirmed on appeal by the state supreme court. The defendant seeks to overturn his conviction in a habeas corpus action in federal court, claiming his constitutional rights were violated by allowing a jury verdict that was not unanimous and by allowing a jury composed of fewer than 12 members.

How is the federal court likely to rule in this action?

(A) It will set aside the conviction, because the jury was composed of fewer than 12 members.
(B) It will set aside the conviction, because the 6-person jury verdict was not unanimous.
(C) It will set aside the conviction for both reasons.
(D) It will uphold the conviction.

Question 18 - Real Property

A grantor executed an instrument in the proper form of a warranty deed purporting to convey a tract of land to his church. The granting clause of the instrument ran to the church "and its successors forever, so long as the premises are used for church purposes." The church took possession of the land and used it as its site of worship for many years. Subsequently, the church wanted to relocate and entered into a valid written contract to sell the land to a buyer for a substantial price. The buyer wanted to use the land as a site for business activities and objected to the church's title. The contract contained no provision relating to the quality of title the church was bound to convey. There is no applicable statute. When the buyer refused to close, the church sued the buyer for specific performance and properly joined the grantor as a party.

Is the church likely to prevail?

(A) No, because the grantor's interest prevents the church's title from being marketable.
(B) No, because the quoted provision is a valid restrictive covenant.
(C) Yes, because a charitable trust to support religion will attach to the proceeds of the sale.
(D) Yes, because the grantor cannot derogate from his warranty to the church.

Question 19 - Evidence

In a civil trial for fraud arising from a real estate transaction, the defendant claimed not to have been involved in the transaction. The plaintiff called a witness to testify concerning the defendant's involvement in the fraudulent scheme, but to the plaintiff's surprise the witness testified that the defendant was not involved, and denied making any statement to the contrary. The plaintiff now calls a second witness to testify that the first witness had stated, while the two were having a dinner conversation, that the defendant was involved in the fraudulent transaction.

Is the testimony of the second witness admissible?

(A) No, because a party cannot impeach the party's own witness.
(B) No, because it is hearsay not within any exception.
(C) Yes, but only to impeach the first witness.
(D) Yes, to impeach the first witness and to prove the defendant's involvement.

Question 20 - Torts

A car owner washed her car while it was parked on a public street, in violation of a statute that prohibits the washing of vehicles on public streets during rush hours. The statute was enacted only to expedite the flow of automobile traffic. Due to a sudden and unexpected cold snap, the car owner's waste water formed a puddle that froze. A pedestrian slipped on the frozen puddle and broke her leg. The pedestrian sued the car owner to recover for her injury. At trial, the only evidence the pedestrian offered as to negligence was the car owner's admission that she had violated the statute. At the conclusion of the proofs, both parties moved for a directed verdict.

How should the trial judge proceed?

(A) Deny both motions and submit the case to the jury, because, on the facts, the jury may infer that the car owner was negligent.
(B) Deny both motions and submit the case to the jury, because the jury may consider the statutory violation as evidence that the car owner was negligent.
(C) Grant the car owner's motion, because the pedestrian has failed to offer adequate evidence that the car owner was negligent.
(D) Grant the pedestrian's motion, because of the car owner's admitted statutory violation.

Question 21 - Constitutional Law

Two tenured professors at a state university drafted a new university regulation prohibiting certain kinds of speech on campus. Students, staff, and faculty convicted by campus tribunals of violating the regulation were made subject to penalties that included fines, suspensions, expulsions, and termination of employment. The regulation was widely unpopular and there was a great deal of public anger directed toward the professors who drafted it. The following year, the state legislature approved a severable provision in the appropriations bill for the university declaring that none of the university's funding could be used to pay the two professors, who were specifically named in the provision. In the past, the professors' salaries had always been paid from funds appropriated to the university by the legislature, and the university had no other funds that could be used to pay them.

If the professors challenge the constitutionality of the appropriations provision, is the court likely to uphold the provision?

(A) No, because it amounts to the imposition of a punishment by the legislature without trial.
(B) No, because it was based on conduct the professors engaged in before it was enacted.
(C) Yes, because the Eleventh Amendment gives the state legislature plenary power to appropriate state funds in the manner that it deems most conducive to the welfare of its people.
Clause 1 of the Constitution.
(D) Yes, because the full faith and credit clause requires the court to enforce the provision strictly according to its terms.

Question 22 - Criminal Law and Procedure

Police officers received a tip that drug dealing was occurring at a certain ground-floor duplex apartment. They decided to stake out the apartment. The stakeout revealed that a significant number of people visited the apartment for short periods of time and then left. A man exited the apartment and started to walk briskly away. The officers grabbed the man and, when he struggled, wrestled him to the ground. They searched him and found a bag of heroin in one of his pockets. After discovering the heroin on the man, the police decided to enter the apartment. They knocked on the door, which was opened by the woman who lived there. The police asked if they could come inside, and the woman gave them permission to do so. Once inside, the officers observed several bags of heroin on the living room table. The woman is charged with possession of the heroin found on the living room table. She moves pretrial to suppress the heroin on the ground that it was obtained by virtue of an illegal search and seizure.

Should the woman's motion be granted?

(A) No, because the tip together with the heroin found in the man's pocket provided probable cause for the search.
(B) No, because the woman consented to the officers' entry.
(C) Yes, because the officers' decision to enter the house was the fruit of an illegal search of the man.
(D) Yes, because the officers did not inform the woman that she could refuse consent.

Question 23 - Real Property

A landowner died, validly devising his land to his wife "for life or until remarriage, then to" their daughter. Shortly after the landowner's death, his daughter executed an instrument in the proper form of a deed, purporting to convey the land to her friend. A year later, the daughter died intestate, with her mother, the original landowner's wife, as her sole heir. The following month, the wife re-married. She then executed an instrument in the proper form of a deed, purporting to convey the land to her new husband as a wedding gift.

Who now owns what interest in the land?

(A) The daughter's friend owns the fee simple.
(B) The wife owns the fee simple.
(C) The wife's new husband has a life estate in the land for the wife's life, with the remainder in the daughter's friend.
(D) The wife's new husband owns the fee simple.

Question 24 - Contracts

During negotiations to purchase a used car, a buyer asked a dealer whether the car had ever been in an accident. The dealer replied: "It is a fine car and has been thoroughly inspected and comes with a certificate of assured quality. Feel free to have the car inspected by your own mechanic." In actuality, the car had been in an accident and the dealer had repaired and repainted the car, successfully concealing evidence of the accident. The buyer declined to have the car inspected by his own mechanic, explaining that he would rely on the dealer's certificate of assured quality. At no time did the dealer disclose that the car had previously been in an accident. The parties then signed a contract of sale. After the car was delivered and paid for, the buyer learned about the car's involvement in a major accident.

If the buyer sues the dealer to rescind the transaction, is the buyer likely to succeed?

(A) No, because the buyer had the opportunity to have the car inspected by his own mechanic and declined to do so.
(B) No, because the dealer did not affirmatively assert that the car had not been in an accident.
(C) Yes, because the contract was unconscionable.
(D) Yes, because the dealer's statement was intentionally misleading and the dealer had concealed evidence of the accident.

Question 25 - Constitutional Law

A state constitution provides that in every criminal trial "the accused shall have the right to confront all witnesses against him face to face." A defendant was convicted in state court of child abuse based on testimony from a six-year-old child. The child testified while she was seated behind one-way glass, which allowed the defendant to see the child but did not allow the child to see the defendant. The defendant appealed to the state supreme court claiming that the inability of the witness to see the defendant while she testified violated both the United States Constitution and the state constitution. Without addressing the federal constitutional issue, the state supreme court reversed the defendant's conviction and ordered a new trial. The state supreme court held that "the constitution of this state is clear, and it requires that while testifying in a criminal trial, a witness must be able to see the defendant." The state petitioned the United States Supreme Court for a writ of certiorari.

On which ground should the United States Supreme Court DENY the state's petition?

(A) A state may not seek appellate review in the United States Supreme Court of the reversal of a criminal conviction by its own supreme court.
(B) The decision of the state supreme court was based on an adequate and independent state ground.
(C) The Sixth Amendment to the United States Constitution does not require that a witness against a criminal defendant be able to see the defendant while the witness testifies.
(D) The state supreme court's decision requires a new trial, and therefore it is not a final judgment.

Question 26 - Criminal Law and Procedure

A husband and wife took their 12-year-old son to a political rally to hear a controversial United States senator speak. The speaker was late, and the wife stepped outside to smoke a cigarette. While there, she saw a man placing what she believed to be a bomb against a wall at the back of the building. She went back inside and told her husband what she had seen. Without alerting anyone, they took their son and left. Some 20 minutes later, the bomb exploded, killing eight persons and injuring 50. In the jurisdiction, murder in the first degree is defined as an intentional homicide committed with premeditation and deliberation; murder in the second degree is defined as all other murder at common law; and manslaughter is defined as either a homicide in the heat of passion arising from adequate provocation or a homicide caused by gross negligence or reckless indifference to consequence.

As to the deaths of the eight persons, what crime, if any, did the wife commit?

(A) Manslaughter.
(B) Murder in the first degree.
(C) Murder in the second degree.
(D) No crime.

Question 27 - Criminal Law and Procedure

A woman decided to steal a necklace that belonged to her neighbor. She knew where the neighbor kept the necklace because she had been in the neighbor's house on many occasions when the neighbor had taken off the necklace and put it away in a jewelry box in the bathroom. One night, the woman went to the neighbor's house. The neighbor was away and the house was dark. The woman opened the bathroom window, saw the jewelry box on the counter, and started to climb inside. As her leg cleared the window sill, the neighbor's cat let out a loud screech. Terrified, the woman bolted back outside and fled.

The crimes below are listed in descending order of seriousness. What is the most serious crime committed by the woman?

(A) Burglary.
(B) Attempted burglary.
(C) Attempted larceny.
(D) No crime.

Question 28 - Torts

A host pointed an unloaded revolver at her guest, threatening to shoot him. The guest knew that the revolver was not loaded, and that the ammunition for the revolver was stored in a locked basement closet, two stories below where the two were then standing.
In an action brought by the guest against the host for assault, will the guest prevail?

(A) No, because the host did not intend to shoot her guest.
(B) No, because the host did not put her guest in apprehension of an imminent contact.
(C) Yes, because the ammunition was accessible to the host.
(D) Yes, because the host threatened her guest with a revolver.

Question 29 - Evidence

A defendant has pleaded not guilty to a federal charge of bank robbery. The principal issue at trial is the identity of the robber. The prosecutor calls the defendant's wife to testify to the clothing that the defendant wore as he left their house on the day the bank was robbed, expecting her description to match that of eyewitnesses to the robbery. Both the defendant and his wife object to her testifying against the defendant.

Should the wife be required to testify?

(A) No, because the defendant has a privilege to prevent his wife from testifying against him in a criminal case.
(B) No, because the wife has a privilege not to testify against her husband in a criminal case.
(C) Yes, because the interspousal privilege does not apply in criminal cases.
(D) Yes, because the wife's viewing of the defendant's clothing was not a confidential communication.

Question 30 - Contracts

On January 5, a creditor lent $1,000 to a debtor under a contract calling for the debtor to repay the loan at the rate of $100 per month payable on the first day of each month. On February 1, at the debtor's request, the creditor agreed to permit payment on February 5. On March 1, the debtor requested a similar time extension and the creditor replied, "Don't bother me each month. Just change the date of payment to the fifth of the month. But you must now make the payments by cashier's check." The debtor said, "Okay," and made payments on March 5 and April 5. On April 6, the creditor sold the loan contract to a bank, but did not tell the bank about the agreement permitting payments on the fifth of the month. On April 6, the bank wrote to the debtor: "Your debt to [the creditor] has been assigned to us. We hereby inform you that all payments must be made on the first day of the month."

Can the debtor justifiably insist that the payment date for the rest of the installments is the fifth of each month?

(A) No, because a contract modification is not binding on an assignee who had no knowledge of the modification.
(B) No, because although the creditor waived the condition of payment on the first of the month, the bank reinstated it.
(C) Yes, because although the creditor waived the condition of payment on the first of the month, the creditor could not assign to the bank his right to reinstate that condition.
(D) Yes, because the creditor could assign to the bank only those rights the creditor had in the contract at the time of the assignment.

Question 31 - Contracts

A buyer entered into a written contract to purchase from a seller 1,000 sets of specially manufactured ball bearings of a nonstandard dimension for a price of $10 per set. The seller correctly calculated that it would cost $8 to manufacture each set. Delivery was scheduled for 60 days later. Fifty-five days later, after the seller had completed production of the 1,000 sets, the buyer abandoned the project requiring use of the specially manufactured ball bearings and repudiated the contract with the seller. After notifying the buyer of his intention to resell, the seller sold the 1,000 sets of ball bearings to a salvage company for $2 per set. The seller sued the buyer for damages.

What damages should the court award to the seller?

(A) $2 per set, representing the difference between the cost of production and the price the buyer agreed to pay.
(B) $6 per set, representing the difference between the cost of manufacture and the salvage price.
(C) $8 per set, representing the lost profits plus the unrecovered cost of production.
(D) Nominal damages, as the seller failed to resell the goods by public auction.

Question 32 - Torts

A construction company was digging a trench for a new sewer line in a street in a high-crime neighborhood. During the course of the construction, there had been many thefts of tools and equipment from the construction area. One night, the construction company's employees neglected to place warning lights around the trench. A delivery truck drove into the trench and broke an axle. While the delivery driver was looking for a telephone to summon a tow truck, thieves broke into the delivery truck and stole $350,000 worth of goods. The delivery company sued the construction company to recover for the $350,000 loss and for $1,500 worth of damage to its truck. The construction company stipulated that it was negligent in failing to place warning lights around the trench, and admits liability for damage to the truck, but denies liability for the loss of the goods.

On cross-motions for summary judgment, how should the court rule?

(A) Deny both motions, because there is evidence to support a finding that the construction company should have realized that its negligence could create an opportunity for a third party to commit a crime.

(B) Grant the construction company's motion, because no one could have foreseen that the failure to place warning lights could result in the loss of a cargo of valuable goods.

(C) Grant the construction company's motion, because the criminal acts of third persons were a superseding cause of the loss.

(D) Grant the delivery company's motion, because but for the construction company's actions, the goods would not have been stolen.

Question 33 - Constitutional Law

Several public high school students asked the superintendent of the public school district whether the minister of a local church could deliver an interdenominational prayer at their graduation ceremony in the school auditorium. None of the students or their guests at graduation would be required to pray while the minister delivered the prayer.

Would the minister's delivery of such a prayer at the public high school graduation be constitutional?

(A) No, because it would be an unconstitutional establishment of religion.

(B) No, because it would deny attendees who are not members of the minister's denomination the right to freely exercise their religion.

(C) Yes, because none of the students or their guests would be required to pray at the graduation ceremony.

(D) Yes, because the idea for the prayer originated with the students and not with school officials.

Question 34 - Evidence

At the defendant's trial for a gang-related murder, the prosecution introduced, as former testimony, a statement by a gang member who testified against the defendant at a preliminary hearing and has now invoked his privilege against self-incrimination.

If the defendant now seeks to impeach the credibility of the gang member, which of the following is the court most likely to admit?

(A) Evidence that the gang member had three misdemeanor convictions for assault.

(B) Testimony by a psychologist that persons with the gang member's background have a tendency to fabricate.

(C) Testimony by a witness that at the time the gang member testified, he was challenging the defendant's leadership role in the gang.

(D) Testimony by a witness that the gang member is a cocaine dealer.

Question 35 - Criminal Law and Procedure

A defendant was charged with manslaughter. At the preliminary hearing, the magistrate dismissed the charge on the grounds that the evidence was insufficient. The prosecutor then brought the case before a grand jury. After hearing the evidence presented by the prosecutor, the grand jury refused to return an indictment. The prosecutor waited a few months until a new grand jury had been impaneled and brought the case before that grand jury, which returned an indictment charging the defendant with manslaughter. The defendant moves to dismiss the indictment on double jeopardy grounds.

Should the motion be granted?

(A) No, because jeopardy had not attached.
(B) No, because there has been no conviction or acquittal.
(C) Yes, because any proceeding after the preliminary hearing would violate double jeopardy.
(D) Yes, because bringing the case before the second grand jury was a violation of double jeopardy.

Question 36 - Constitutional Law

Congress passed a statute directing the United States Forest Service, a federal agency, to issue regulations to control campfires on federal public lands and to establish a schedule of penalties for those who violate the new regulations. The statute provided that the Forest Service regulations should "reduce, to the maximum extent feasible, all potential hazards that arise from campfires on Forest Service lands." The Forest Service issued the regulations and the schedule of penalties directed by Congress. The regulations include a rule that provides for the doubling of the fine for any negligent or prohibited use of fire if the user is intoxicated by alcohol or drugs.

Which of the following is the best argument for sustaining the constitutionality of the Forest Service's rule providing for the fines?

(A) The executive branch of government, of which the Forest Service is part, has inherent rule-making authority over public lands.
(B) The rule is issued pursuant to a valid exercise of Congress's power to delegate rule-making authority to federal agencies.
(C) The rule is justified by a compelling governmental interest in safeguarding forest resources.
(D) The rule relates directly to law enforcement, which is an executive rather than legislative function, and hence it does not need specific congressional authorization.

Question 37 - Evidence

A defendant was charged with aggravated assault. At trial, the victim testified that the defendant beat her savagely, but she was not asked about anything said during the incident. The prosecutor then called a witness to testify that when the beating stopped, the victim screamed: "I'm dying-don't let [the defendant] get away with it!"

Is the testimony of the witness concerning the victim's statement admissible?

(A) No, because it is hearsay not within any exception.
(B) No, because the victim was not asked about the statement.
(C) Yes, as a statement under belief of impending death, even though the victim did not die.
(D) Yes, as an excited utterance.

Question 38 - Contracts

A bakery offered a chef a permanent full-time job as a pastry chef at a salary of $2,000 per month. The chef agreed to take the position and to begin work in two weeks. In her employment application, the chef had indicated that she was seeking a permanent job. One week after the chef was hired by the bakery, a hotel offered the chef a position as a restaurant manager at a salary of $2,500 a month. The chef accepted and promptly notified the bakery that she would not report for work at the bakery.

Is the bakery likely to prevail in a lawsuit against the chef for breach of contract?

(A) No, because a contract for permanent employment would be interpreted to mean the chef could leave at any time.
(B) No, because the position the chef took with the hotel was not substantially comparable to the one she had agreed to take with the bakery.
(C) Yes, because the chef's acceptance of a permanent position meant that she agreed to leave the bakery only after a reasonable time.
(D) Yes, because the chef's failure to give the bakery a chance to match the salary offered by the hotel breached the implied right of first refusal.

Question 39 - Real Property

A creditor received a valid judgment against a debtor and promptly and properly filed the judgment in the county. Two years later, the debtor purchased land in the county and promptly and properly recorded the warranty deed to it. Subsequently, the debtor borrowed $30,000 from his aunt, signing a promissory note for that amount, which note was secured by a mortgage on the land. The mortgage was promptly and properly recorded. The aunt failed to make a title search before making the loan. The debtor made no payment to the creditor and defaulted on the mortgage loan from his aunt. A valid judicial foreclosure proceeding was held, in which the creditor, the aunt, and the debtor were named parties. A dispute arose as to which lien has priority. A statute of the jurisdiction provides: "Any judgment properly filed shall, for 10 years from filing, be a lien on the real property then owned or subsequently acquired by any person against whom the judgment is rendered." A second statute of the jurisdiction provides: "No unrecorded conveyance or mortgage of real property shall be good against subsequent purchasers for value without notice, who shall first record."

Who has the prior lien?

(A) The aunt, because a judgment lien is subordinate to a mortgage lien.
(B) The aunt, because she is a mortgagee under a purchase money mortgage.
(C) The creditor, because its judgment was filed first.
(D) The creditor, because the aunt had a duty to make a title search of the property.

Question 40 - Torts

The personnel director of an investment company told a job applicant during an interview that the company was worth millions of dollars and that the company's portfolio would triple in the next several months. The applicant was very excited about the company's prospects and accepted an offer to work for the company. Two days later, the applicant read in the newspaper that the investment company had filed for bankruptcy reorganization. As a result of reading this news, the applicant suffered severe emotional distress but he immediately found another comparable position.

Is the applicant likely to prevail in his action for negligent misrepresentation?

(A) No, because the applicant did not suffer any physical injury or pecuniary loss.
(B) No, because the personnel director's statement was purely speculative.
(C) Yes, because the applicant relied on the personnel director's misrepresentations about the investment company.
(D) Yes, because the personnel director should have foreseen that his misrepresentations would cause the applicant to be upset.

Question 41 - Constitutional Law

A city zoning ordinance requires anyone who proposes to operate a group home to obtain a special use permit from the city zoning board. The zoning ordinance defines a group home as a residence in which four or more unrelated adults reside. An individual applied for a special use permit to operate a group home for convicts during their transition from serving prison sentences to their release on parole. Although the proposed group home met all of the requirements for the special use permit, the zoning board denied the individual's application because of the nature of the proposed use. The individual sued the zoning board seeking declaratory and injunctive relief on constitutional grounds.

Which of the following best states the appropriate burden of persuasion in this action?

(A) Because housing is a fundamental right, the zoning board must demonstrate that denial of the permit is necessary to serve a compelling state interest.
(B) Because the zoning board's action has the effect of discriminating against a quasi-suspect class in regard to a basic subsistence right, the zoning board must demonstrate that the denial of the permit is substantially related to an important state interest.
(C) Because the zoning board's action invidiously discriminates against a suspect class, the zoning board must demonstrate that denial of the permit is necessary to serve a compelling state interest.
(D) Because the zoning board's action is in the nature of an economic or social welfare regulation, the individual seeking the permit must demonstrate that the denial of the permit is not rationally related to a legitimate state interest.

Question 42 - Criminal Law and Procedure

State troopers lawfully stopped a driver on the turnpike for exceeding the speed limit by four miles per hour. One trooper approached the car to warn the driver to drive within the speed limit. The other trooper remained in the patrol car and ran a computer check of the license number of the driver's car. The computer check indicated that there was an outstanding warrant for the driver's arrest for unpaid traffic tickets. The troopers then arrested the driver. After handcuffing her, the troopers searched her and the car, and discovered 10 glassine bags of heroin in a paper bag on the back seat of the car. Later it was learned that the driver had paid the outstanding traffic tickets 10 days earlier and the warrant had been quashed, but the clerk of the court had failed to update the computer, which continued to list the warrant as outstanding. The driver was charged with unlawful possession of heroin. Her attorney filed a motion to suppress the use as evidence of the heroin found in the car.

Should the motion be granted?

(A) No, because the troopers could reasonably rely on the computer report and the search was incident to arrest.
(B) No, because troopers may lawfully search the passenger compartment of a car incident to a valid traffic stop.
(C) Yes, because there was no arrest for the traffic violation and no lawful arrest could be made on the basis of the warrant.
(D) Yes, because there was no probable cause or reasonable suspicion to believe drugs were in the car.

Question 43 - Contracts

A debtor owed a lender $1,500. The statute of limitations barred recovery on the claim. The debtor wrote to the lender, stating, "I promise to pay you $500 if you will extinguish the debt." The lender agreed.

Is the debtor's promise to pay the lender $500 enforceable?

(A) No, because the debtor made no promise not to plead the statute of limitations as a defense.
(B) No, because there was no consideration for the debtor's promise.
(C) Yes, because the debtor's promise provided a benefit to the lender.
(D) Yes, because the debtor's promise to pay part of the barred antecedent debt is enforceable.

Question 44 - Evidence

A homeowner sued a plumber for damages resulting from the plumber's allegedly faulty installation of water pipes in her basement, causing flooding. At trial, the homeowner was prepared to testify that when she first detected the flooding, she turned off the water and called the plumber at his emergency number for help. The plumber responded, "I'll come by tomorrow and redo the installation for free."

Is the plumber's response admissible?

(A) No, because it is an offer in compromise.
(B) No, because it is hearsay not within any exception.
(C) Yes, as a subsequent remedial measure.
(D) Yes, as evidence of the plumber's fault.

Question 45 - Real Property

An investor purchased a tract of land, financing a large part of the purchase price by a loan from a business partner that was secured by a mortgage. The investor made the installment payments on the mortgage regularly for several years. Then the investor persuaded a neighbor to buy the land, subject to the mortgage to his partner. They expressly agreed that the neighbor would not assume and agree to pay the investor's debt to the partner. The investor's mortgage to the partner contained a due-on-sale clause stating, "If Mortgagor transfers his/her interest without the written consent of Mortgagee first obtained, then at Mortgagee's option the entire principal balance of the debt secured by this Mortgage shall become immediately due and payable." However, without seeking his partner's consent, the investor conveyed the land to the neighbor, the deed stating in pertinent part " . . . , subject to a mortgage to [the partner]," and giving details and recording data related to the mortgage. The neighbor took possession of the land and made several mortgage payments, which the partner accepted. Now, however, neither the neighbor nor the investor has made the last three mortgage payments. The partner has sued the neighbor for the amount of the delinquent payments.

In this action, for whom should the court render judgment?

A)   The neighbor, because she did not assume and agree to pay the investor's mortgage debt.

(B) The neighbor, because she is not in privity of estate with the partner.
(C) The partner, because the investor's deed to the neighbor violated the due-on-sale clause.
(D) The partner, because the neighbor is in privity of estate with the partner.

Question 46 - Constitutional Law

A purchaser bought land in the mountain foothills just outside a resort town and planned to build a housing development there. Soon thereafter, the county in which the land was located unexpectedly adopted a regulation that, for the first time, prohibited all construction in several foothill and mountain areas, including the area of the purchaser's property. The purpose of the county's regulation was "to conserve for future generations the unique natural wildlife and plant habitats" in the mountain areas. Since the adoption of the regulation, the purchaser has been unable to lease or sell the property at any price. Several realtors have advised the purchaser that the property is now worthless. The purchaser sued the county, claiming that the regulation has taken the purchaser's property and that the county therefore owes the purchaser just compensation.

Is the court likely to rule in favor of the purchaser?

(A) No, because the county did not take title to the property from the purchaser.
(B) No, because the regulation has not caused or authorized any uninvited physical invasion or intrusion onto the property.
(C) Yes, because the conservation objective of the county ordinance is not sufficiently compelling to justify the substantial diminution in the property value.
(D) Yes, because the effect of the county's regulation is to deny the purchaser's investment-backed expectation and essentially all economically beneficial use of the property.

Question 47 - Criminal Law and Procedure

A woman who is a computer whiz decided to dedicate herself to exposing persons who traffic in child pornography. She posted a number of sexually oriented photographs on her web site. The file for each photograph contained an embedded Trojan horse program. The defendant downloaded one of those photographs onto his personal computer. Using the embedded program, the woman entered the defendant's computer and found a file containing a pornographic photograph of a child. She copied the file and turned it over to a federal law enforcement agency. A federal agent told her that a successful prosecution would require more than one photograph and offered her a monetary reward for additional photos leading to a conviction of the defendant. The woman entered the defendant's computer again, and this time she found hundreds of child pornography photos, which she turned over to the federal agency. The defendant is charged with multiple counts of violating federal statutes regarding child pornography. He moves to suppress the photographs that the woman discovered on his computer. The motion is based on both the Fourth Amendment and a federal statute forbidding interception of electronic communication without permission. The parties have stipulated that the woman's conduct in downloading photos from the defendant's computer violated the interception statute.

How should the court rule on the defendant's motion to suppress?

(A) Deny it as to all photographs.
(B) Grant it as to all photographs, because the woman acted without probable cause.
(C) Grant it as to all photographs, because the woman violated the federal interception statute.
(D) Grant it only as to the second set of photographs.

Question 48 - Contracts

A car dealer owed a bank $10,000, due on June 1. The car dealer subsequently sold an automobile to a buyer at a price of $10,000, payable at $1,000 per month beginning on June 1. The car dealer then asked the bank whether the bank would accept payments of $1,000 per month for 10 months beginning June 1, without interest, in payment of the debt. The bank agreed to that arrangement and the car dealer then directed the buyer to make the payments to the bank. When the buyer tendered the first payment to the bank, the bank refused the payment, asserting that it would accept payment only from the car dealer. On June 2, the bank demanded that the car dealer pay the debt in full immediately. The car dealer refused to pay and the bank sued the car dealer to recover the $10,000.

In this suit, which of the following arguments best supports the bank's claim for immediate payment?

(A) The agreement to extend the time for payment was not in writing.
(B) The car dealer could not delegate its duty to pay to the buyer.
(C) The car dealer gave no consideration for the agreement to extend the time of payment.
(D) The car dealer's conduct was an attempted novation that the bank could reject.

Question 49 - Evidence

A defendant was charged in federal court with selling a controlled substance (heroin) in interstate commerce. At trial, the prosecutor introduced evidence that the defendant obtained the substance from a supplier in Kansas City and delivered it in Chicago. The defendant denied that the substance in question was heroin, but he introduced no contrary evidence on the issue of transportation.

Which of the following instructions regarding judicial notice may the judge legitimately give the jury?

(A) "If you find that the defendant obtained the drugs in Kansas City and delivered them to Chicago, I instruct you to find that the substance was sold in an interstate transaction."
(B) "If you find that the defendant obtained the drugs in Kansas City and delivered them to Chicago, then the burden of persuasion is on the defendant to establish that the transaction was not interstate."
(C) "If you find that the defendant obtained the drugs in Kansas City and delivered them to Chicago, then you may, but you are not required to, find that the transaction was interstate in nature."
(D) "I instruct you that there is a presumption that the substance was sold in an interstate transaction, but the burden of persuasion on that issue is still on the government."

Question 50 - Torts

An associate professor in the pediatrics department of a local medical school was denied tenure. He asked a national education lobbying organization to represent him in his efforts to have the tenure decision reversed. In response to a letter from the organization on the professor's behalf, the dean of the medical school wrote to the organization explaining truthfully that the professor had been denied tenure because of reports that he had abused two of his former patients. Several months later, after a thorough investigation, the allegations were proven false and the professor was granted tenure. He had remained working at the medical school at full pay during the tenure decision review process and thus suffered no pecuniary harm.

In a suit for libel by the professor against the dean of the medical school, will the professor prevail?

(A) No, because the professor invited the libel.
(B) No, because the professor suffered no pecuniary loss.
(C) Yes, because the dean had a duty to investigate the rumor before repeating it.
(D) Yes, because the dean's defamatory statement was in the form of a writing.

Question 51 - Constitutional Law

A man bought an antique car from a car dealer in State A. Under State A law, a person who buys from such a dealer acquires good title, even if the property was stolen from a previous owner. The man showed the car at an antique car show in State B. A woman recognized the car as having been stolen from her. Under State B law, a person whose property is stolen may reclaim it, even if the current possessor is an innocent purchaser. The woman sued the man in a State B court to reclaim the car. The man defended, claiming that he had good title under the law of State A. Nevertheless, the State B court applied State B law, and the woman prevailed. The man did not appeal. The sheriff gave the woman possession of the car. Several months later, the woman drove the car to State A. The man brought a new suit against the woman, claiming that the State B court in the prior suit should have applied the State A law, which protected innocent purchasers. The woman appeared and moved to dismiss the suit.

What should the State A court do?

(A) Apply the federal law of sale of goods, because the car has moved in interstate commerce.
(B) Apply the State A law, because the car is currently located in State A.
(C) Dismiss the suit, because the State A court must give full faith and credit to the State B judgment.
(D) Remove the case to federal court, because the car has moved in interstate commerce, and therefore the case raises a federal question.

Question 52 - Real Property

A rancher and a farmer own adjacent tracts of rural land. For the past nine years, the rancher has impounded on her land the water that resulted from rain and melting snow, much of which flowed from the farmer's land. The rancher uses the water in her livestock operation. Recently, the farmer increased the size of his farming operation and built a dam on his land near the boundary between the two tracts. Because of the dam, these waters no longer drain from the farmer's land onto the rancher's land. There is no applicable statute. The rancher sued the farmer to restrain him from interfering with the natural flow of the water onto her land.

Who is likely to prevail?

(A) The farmer, because he has the right to use all of the water impounded on his land.
(B) The farmer, because the rancher's past impoundment of water estops her from asserting the illegality of the farmer's dam.
(C) The rancher, because she has acquired riparian rights to use the water.
(D) The rancher, because the farmer is estopped to claim all of the surface water on his land.

Question 53 - Torts

A dentist was anesthetizing a patient's gum before pulling a tooth. Although the dentist used due care, the hypodermic needle broke off in the patient's gum, causing injury. The needle broke because of a manufacturing defect that the dentist could not have detected.

Is the patient likely to recover damages in an action against the dentist based on strict products liability and malpractice?

(A) No, on neither basis.
(B) Yes, based on malpractice, but not on strict products liability.
(C) Yes, based on strict products liability, but not on malpractice.
(D) Yes, on both bases.

Question 54 - Contracts

A bottling company sent a purchase order to a wholesaler that stated, "Ship 100,000 empty plastic bottles at the posted price." Two days after receipt of this purchase order, the wholesaler shipped the bottles and the bottling company accepted delivery of them. A week after the bottles were delivered, the bottling company received the wholesaler's acknowledgement form, which included a provision disclaiming consequential damages. After using the bottles for two months, the bottling company discovered a defect in the bottles that caused its products to leak from them. The bottling company recalled 10,000 of the bottles containing its product, incurring lost profits of $40,000.

Assuming all appropriate defenses are seasonably raised, will the bottling company succeed in recovering $40,000 in consequential damages from the wholesaler?

(A) No, because buyers are generally not entitled to recover consequential damages.
(B) No, because the bottling company's acceptance of the goods also constituted an acceptance of the terms included in the wholesaler's acknowledgement.
(C) Yes, because the disclaimer of consequential damages is unconscionable.
(D) Yes, because the wholesaler's acknowledgement did not alter the terms of an existing contract between the parties.

Question 55 - Criminal Law and Procedure

A state statute defines murder in the first degree as "knowingly causing the death of another person after deliberation upon the matter." Second-degree murder is defined as "knowingly causing the death of another person." Manslaughter is defined as at common law. Deliberation is defined as "cool reflection for any length of time, no matter how brief." The defendant, despondent and angry over losing his job, was contemplating suicide. He took his revolver, went to a bar, and drank until he was very intoxicated. A customer on the next stool was telling the bartender how it was necessary for companies to downsize and become more efficient in order to keep the economy strong. The defendant turned to him and said, "Why don't you shut the hell up." The customer responded, "This is a free country and I can say what I want," all the while shaking his finger at the defendant. The finger-shaking, combined with his already bad disposition and the alcohol, enraged the defendant. Trembling with fury, he snatched his revolver from his pocket and shot and killed the customer.

What crime did the defendant commit?

(A) Manslaughter, because there was a reasonable explanation for his becoming enraged.
(B) Murder in the first degree, because deliberation can take place in an instant.
(C) Murder in the first degree, because he contemplated taking a human life before becoming intoxicated.
(D) Murder in the second degree, because he knowingly caused the customer's death without deliberation.

Question 56 - Constitutional Law

A state statute requires, without exception, that a woman under the age of 18 notify one of her parents at least 48 hours before having an abortion. A proper lawsuit challenges the constitutionality of this state statute.

In that suit, should the court uphold the constitutionality of the statute?

(A) No, because a 48-hour waiting period is excessively long and, therefore, it imposes an undue burden on a woman's right to procure an abortion.
(B) No, because the state law does not provide a bypass procedure that would allow a court to authorize a minor to obtain an abortion without prior parental notification under appropriate circumstances.
(C) Yes, because parents' rights to supervise their minor daughter's health care outweighs any individual right she may have.
(D) Yes, because such parental notification and waiting-period requirements do not impose an undue burden on a minor's right to procure an abortion.

Question 57 - Real Property

A businessman owned a hotel, subject to a mortgage securing a debt he owed to a bank. The businessman later acquired a nearby parking garage, financing a part of the purchase price by a loan from a financing company, secured by a mortgage on the parking garage. Two years thereafter, the businessman defaulted on the loan owed to the bank, which caused the full amount of that loan to become immediately due and payable. The bank decided not to foreclose the mortgage on the hotel at that time, but instead properly sued for the full amount of the defaulted loan. The bank obtained and properly filed a judgment for that amount. A statute of the jurisdiction provides: "Any judgment properly filed shall, for ten years from filing, be a lien on the real property then owned or subsequently acquired by any person against whom the judgment is rendered." There is no other applicable statute, except the statute providing for judicial foreclosure of mortgages, which places no restriction on deficiency judgments. Shortly thereafter, the bank brought an appropriate action for judicial foreclosure of its first mortgage on the hotel and of its judgment lien on the parking garage. The financing company was joined as a party defendant, and appropriately counterclaimed for foreclosure of its mortgage on the parking garage, which was also in default. All procedures were properly followed and the confirmed foreclosure sales resulted in the following: The net proceeds of the sale of the hotel to a third party were $200,000 less than the bank's mortgage balance. The net proceeds of the sale of the parking garage to a fourth party were $200,000 more than the financing company's mortgage balance.

How should the $200,000 surplus arising from the bid on the parking garage be distributed?

A)   It should be paid to the bank.

(B) It should be paid to the businessman.
(C) It should be paid to the financing company.
(D) It should be split equally between the bank and the financing company.

Question 58 - Evidence

In a personal injury case, the plaintiff sued a retail store for injuries she sustained from a fall in the store. The plaintiff alleged that the store negligently allowed its entryway to become slippery due to snow tracked in from the sidewalk. When the plaintiff threatened to sue, the store's manager said, "I know that there was slush on that marble entry, but I think your four-inch-high heels were the real cause of your fall. So let's agree that we'll pay your medical bills, and you release us from any claims you might have." The plaintiff refused the offer. At trial, the plaintiff seeks to testify to the manager's statement that "there was slush on that marble entry."

Is the statement about the slush on the floor admissible?

(A) No, because it is a statement made in the course of compromise negotiations.
(B) No, because the manager denied that the slippery condition was the cause of the plaintiff's fall.
(C) Yes, as an admission by an agent about a matter within the scope of his authority.
(D) Yes, because the rule excluding offers of compromise does not protect statements of fact made during compromise

negotiations.

Question 59 - Torts

In a civil action, the plaintiff sued a decedent's estate to recover damages for the injuries she suffered in a collision between her car and one driven by the decedent. At trial, the plaintiff introduced undisputed evidence that the decedent's car swerved across the median of the highway, where it collided with an oncoming car driven by the plaintiff. The decedent's estate introduced undisputed evidence that, prior to the car's crossing the median, the decedent suffered a fatal heart attack, which she had no reason to foresee, and that, prior to the heart attack, the decedent had been driving at a reasonable speed and in a reasonable manner. A statute makes it a traffic offense to cross the median of a highway.

In this case, for whom should the court render judgment?

(A) The decedent's estate, because its evidence is undisputed.
(B) The decedent's estate, because the plaintiff has not established a prima facie case of liability.
(C) The plaintiff, because the accident was of a type that does not ordinarily happen in the absence of negligence on the actor's part.
(D) The plaintiff, because the decedent crossed the median in violation of the statute.

Question 60 - Constitutional Law

A group of students at a state university's law school wished to debate the future of affirmative action in that state and at that law school. For this debate they requested the use of a meeting room in the law school that is available on a first-come, first-served basis for extracurricular student use. Speakers presenting all sides of the issue were scheduled to participate. The law school administration refused to allow the use of any of its meeting rooms for this purpose solely because it believed that "such a debate, even if balanced, would have a negative effect on the morale of the law school community and might cause friction among the students that would disrupt the institution's educational mission."

Is the refusal of the law school administration to allow the use of its meeting room for this purpose constitutional?

(A) No, because the law school administration cannot demonstrate that its action was necessary to vindicate a compelling state interest.
(B) No, because the law school administration cannot demonstrate that its action was rationally related to a legitimate state interest.
(C) Yes, because the law school administration's only concern was the adverse effect of such a discussion of affirmative action on the immediate audience and the mission of the institution.
(D) Yes, because the law students do not have a right to use a state-owned law school facility for a meeting that is not organized and sponsored by the law school itself.

Question 61 - Real Property

A fee-simple landowner lawfully subdivided his land into 10 large lots. The recorded subdivision plan imposed no restrictions on any of the 10 lots. Within two months after recording the plan, the landowner conveyed Lot 1 to a buyer, by a deed that contained no restriction on the lot's use. There was then a lull in sales. Two years later, the real estate market in the state had generally improved and, during the next six months, the landowner sold and conveyed eight of the remaining nine lots. In each of the eight deeds of conveyance, the landowner included the following language: "It is a term and condition of this conveyance, which shall be a covenant running with the land for the benefit of each of the 10 lots [with an appropriate reference to the recorded subdivision plan], that for 15 years from the date of recording of the plan, no use shall be made of the premises herein conveyed except for single-family residential purposes." The buyer of Lot 1 had actual knowledge of what the landowner had done. The landowner included the quoted language in part because the zoning ordinance of the municipality had been amended a year earlier to permit professional offices in any residential zone. Shortly after the landowner's most recent sale, when he owned only one unsold lot, the buyer of Lot 1 constructed a one-story house on Lot 1 and then conveyed Lot 1 to a doctor. The deed to the doctor contained no reference to any restriction on the use of Lot 1. The doctor applied for an appropriate certificate of occupancy to enable her to use a part of the house on Lot 1 as a medical office. The landowner, on behalf of himself as the owner of the unsold lot, and on behalf of the other lot owners, sued to enjoin the doctor from carrying out her plans and to impose the quoted restriction on Lot 1.

Who is likely to prevail?

(A) The doctor, because Lot 1 was conveyed without the inclusion of the restrictive covenant in the deed to the first buyer and the subsequent deed to the doctor.
(B) The doctor, because zoning ordinances override private restrictive covenants as a matter of public policy.
(C) The landowner, because the doctor, as a successor in interest to the first buyer, is estopped to deny that Lot 1 remains subject to the zoning ordinance as it existed when Lot 1 was first conveyed by the landowner to the first buyer.
(D) The landowner, because with the first buyer's knowledge of the facts, Lot 1 became incorporated into a common scheme.

Question 62 - Contracts

A seller and a buyer have dealt with each other in hundreds of separate grain contracts over the last five years. In performing each contract, the seller delivered the grain to the buyer and, upon delivery, the buyer signed an invoice that showed an agreed upon price for that delivery. Each invoice was silent in regard to any discount from the price for prompt payment. The custom of the grain trade is to allow a 2% discount from the invoice price for payment within 10 days of delivery. In all of their prior transactions and without objection from the seller, the buyer took 15 days to pay and deducted 5% from the invoice price. The same delivery procedure and invoice were used in the present contract as had been used previously. The present contract called for a single delivery of wheat at a price of $300,000. The seller delivered the wheat and the buyer then signed the invoice. On the third day after delivery, the buyer received the following note from the seller: "Payment in full in accordance with signed invoice is due immediately. No discounts permitted." s/Seller.

Which of the following statements concerning these facts is most accurate?

(A) The custom of the trade controls, and the buyer is entitled to take a 2% discount if he pays within 10 days.
(B) The parties' course of dealing controls, and the buyer is entitled to take a 5% discount if he pays within 15 days.
(C) The seller's retraction of his prior waiver controls, and the buyer is entitled to no discount.
(D) The written contract controls, and the buyer is entitled to no discount because of the parol evidence rule.

Question 63 - Torts

A bus passenger was seated next to a woman whom he did not know. The woman stood to exit the bus, leaving a package on the seat. The passenger lightly tapped the woman on the back to get her attention and to inform her that she had forgotten the package. Because the woman had recently had back surgery, the tap was painful and caused her to twist and seriously injure her back.

If the woman sues the passenger to recover for the back injury, will she prevail?

(A) No, because she is presumed to have consented to the ordinary contacts of daily life.
(B) No, because she was not put in apprehension because of the touching.
(C) Yes, because the passenger intentionally touched her.
(D) Yes, because the passenger's intentional touching seriously injured her.

Question 64 - Constitutional Law

The president issued an executive order in an effort to encourage citizens to use the metric (Celsius) system of temperatures. Section 1 of the executive order requires the United States Weather Bureau, a federal executive agency, to state temperatures only in Celsius in all weather reports. Section 2 of the executive order requires all privately owned federally licensed radio and television stations giving weather reports to report temperatures only in Celsius. No federal statute is applicable.

Is the president's executive order constitutional?

(A) Section 1 is constitutional, but Section 2 is not.
(B) Section 2 is constitutional, but Section 1 is not.
(C) Sections 1 and 2 are constitutional.
(D) Sections 1 and 2 are unconstitutional.

Question 65 - Evidence

In a civil action for misrepresentation in the sale of real estate, the parties contested whether the defendant was licensed by the State Board of Realtors, a public agency established by statute to license real estate brokers. The defendant testified she was licensed. On rebuttal, the plaintiff offers a certification, bearing the seal of the secretary of the State Board of Realtors. The certification states that the secretary conducted a thorough search of the agency's records and all relevant databases, and that this search uncovered no record of a license ever having been issued to the defendant. The certification is signed by the secretary.

Is the certification that there was no record of a license issuance admissible?

(A) No, because it is hearsay not within any exception.
(B) No, because the writing was not properly authenticated.
(C) Yes, for the limited purpose of impeaching the defendant.
(D) Yes, to prove the nonexistence of a public record.

Question 66 - Real Property

A seller entered into a written contract to sell a tract of land to an investor. The contract made no mention of the quality of title to be conveyed. Thereafter, the seller and the investor completed the sale, and the seller delivered a warranty deed to the investor. Soon thereafter, the value of the land increased dramatically. The investor entered into a written contract to sell the land to a buyer. The contract between the investor and the buyer expressly provided that the investor would convey a marketable title. The buyer's attorney discovered that the title to the land was not marketable, and had not been marketable when the original seller conveyed to the investor. The buyer refused to complete the sale. The investor sued the original seller on multiple counts. One count was for breach of the contract between the seller and the investor for damages resulting from the seller's failure to convey to the investor marketable title, resulting in the loss of the sale of the land to the subsequent buyer.

Who is likely to prevail on this count?

(A) The investor, because the law implies in the contract a covenant that the title would be marketable.
(B) The investor, because the original seller is liable for all reasonably foreseeable damages.
(C) The original seller, because her contract obligations as to title merged into the deed.
(D) The original seller, because she did not expressly agree to convey marketable title.

Question 67 - Torts

A consumer became physically ill after drinking part of a bottle of soda that contained a large decomposed snail. The consumer sued the store from which she bought the soda to recover damages for her injuries. The parties agreed that the snail was put into the bottle during the bottling process, over which the store had no control. The parties also agreed that the snail would have been visible in the bottle before the consumer opened it.

Will the consumer prevail in her action against the store?

(A) No, because the consumer could have seen the snail in the bottle.
(B) No, because the store was not responsible for the bottling process.
(C) Yes, because the consumer was injured by a defective product sold to her by the store.
(D) Yes, because the store had exclusive control over the bottle before selling it to the consumer.

Question 68 - Evidence

A defendant is on trial for attempted fraud. The state charges that the defendant switched a price tag from a cloth coat to a more expensive fur-trimmed coat and then presented the latter for purchase at the cash register. The defendant testified in her own behalf that the tag must have been switched by someone else. On cross-examination, the prosecutor asks whether the defendant was convicted on two prior occasions of misdemeanor fraud in the defrauding of a retailer by the same means of switching the price tag on a fur-trimmed coat.

Is the question about the convictions for the earlier crimes proper?

(A) It is not proper either to impeach the defendant or to prove that the defendant committed the crime.
(B) It is proper both to prove that the defendant committed the crime and to impeach the defendant.
(C) It is proper to impeach the defendant, but not to prove that the defendant committed the crime.
(D) It is proper to prove the defendant committed the crime, but not to impeach the defendant.

Question 69 - Criminal Law and Procedure

In a criminal trial, the evidence showed that the defendant's neighbor tried to kill the defendant by stabbing him. The defendant ran to his room, picked up a gun, and told his neighbor to back off. The neighbor did not, but continued her attack and stabbed him in the arm. The defendant then shot the neighbor twice. The neighbor fell to the floor and lay quietly moaning. After a few seconds, the defendant fired a third shot into the neighbor. The jury found that the neighbor died instantly from the third shot and that the defendant was no longer in fear of being attacked by her.

The defendant could properly be convicted of which of the following degrees of criminal homicide, if any?

(A) Attempted murder only.
(B) Manslaughter only.
(C) Murder or manslaughter.
(D) No degree of criminal homicide.

Question 70 - Real Property

When a homeowner became ill, he properly executed a deed sufficient to convey his home to his nephew, who was then serving overseas in the military. Two persons signed as witnesses to qualify the deed for recordation under an applicable statute. The homeowner handed the deed to his nephew's friend and said, "I want [the nephew] to have my home. Please take this deed for him." Shortly thereafter, the nephew's friend learned that the homeowner's death was imminent. One day before the homeowner's death, the nephew's friend recorded the deed. The nephew returned home shortly after the homeowner's death. The nephew's friend brought him up to date, and he took possession of the home. The homeowner died intestate, leaving a daughter as his sole heir. She asserted ownership of his home. The nephew brought an appropriate action against her to determine title to the home. The law of the jurisdiction requires only two witnesses for a will to be properly executed.

If the court rules for the nephew and against the daughter, what is the most likely explanation?

(A) The deed was delivered when the homeowner handed it to the nephew's friend.
(B) The delivery of the deed was accomplished by the recording of the deed.
(C) The homeowner's death consummated a valid gift causa mortis to the nephew.
(D) The homeowner's properly executed deed was effective as a testamentary document.

Question 71 - Criminal Law and Procedure

A woman drove her car through the drive-through lane of a fast-food restaurant in the afternoon. When she reached the microphone used to place orders, she said, "There's a man across the street with a rifle. He can see everything you do. If you do not do exactly what I tell you, he will shoot you. Put all the money from the register into a sack and give it to me when I drive up." The clerk did not see anyone across the street and was unsure whether anyone was there. However, unwilling to risk harm to himself, he put $500 in a paper bag and handed it to the woman when she drove up to the delivery window. The woman drove off with the money but was arrested a short time later. She had lied about the man with a rifle and had acted alone.

Of what crime or crimes can the woman be convicted?

(A) Embezzlement.
(B) Obtaining property by false pretenses.
(C) Robbery and larceny.
(D) Robbery or larceny.

Question 72 - Torts

A four-year-old child sustained serious injuries when a playmate pushed him from between two parked cars into the street, where he was struck by a car. The child, by his representative, sued the driver of the car, the playmate's parents, and his own parents. At trial, the child's total injuries were determined to be $100,000. The playmate's parents were determined to be 20% at fault because they had failed to adequately supervise her. The driver was found to be 50% at fault. The child's own parents were determined to be 30% at fault for failure to adequately supervise him. The court has adopted the pure comparative negligence doctrine, with joint and several liability, in place of the common-law rules relating to plaintiff's fault. In addition, the common-law doctrines relating to intra-family liability have been abrogated.

How much, if anything, is the child's representative entitled to recover from the driver?

(A) $30,000
(B) $50,000
(C) $100,000
(D) Nothing

Question 73 - Constitutional Law

The childhood home of a former U.S. president is part of a national park located in a city. The National Park Service entered into a contract with an independent antique collector to acquire items owned by residents of the city during the president's lifetime. According to the contract, the collector purchases items and then sells them to the Park Service at a price equal to the collector's cost plus a 10% commission. Purchases by antique collectors are ordinarily subject to the sales tax of the state in which the city is located. The collector files suit in state court to enjoin collection of the tax on these purchases, claiming that the sales tax is unconstitutional as applied to them.

Should the state court issue the injunction?

(A) No, because as the purchaser of these antiques, the collector rather than the federal government is liable for the tax.
(B) No, because the suit is within the exclusive jurisdiction of the federal courts.
(C) Yes, because the federal government is contractually obligated to pay the amount of the sales tax when it covers the collector's cost of these antiques.
(D) Yes, because under the supremacy clause, the federal program to acquire these antiques preempts the state sales tax on the purchase of these items.

Question 74 - Evidence

The defendant, a young doctor, is charged with falsely claiming deductions on her federal income tax return. At trial, a witness testified for the defendant that she has a reputation in the community for complete honesty. After a sidebar conference at which the prosecutor gave the judge a record showing that the defendant's medical school had disciplined her for altering her transcript, the prosecutor proposes to ask the witness on cross-examination: "Have you ever heard that the defendant falsified her medical school transcript?"

Is the prosecutor's question proper?

(A) No, because it calls for hearsay not within any exception.
(B) No, because its minimal relevance on the issue of income tax fraud is substantially outweighed by the danger of unfair prejudice.
(C) Yes, because an affirmative answer will be probative of the defendant's bad character for honesty and, therefore, her guilt.
(D) Yes, because an affirmative answer will impeach the witness's credibility.

Question 75 - Torts

A homeowner owned a large poisonous snake which had been defanged and was kept in a cage. A storm damaged the homeowner's house and the snake's cage, allowing it to escape. During the cleanup after the storm, a volunteer worker came across the snake. The worker tried to run away from the snake and fell, breaking his arm.

In a suit by the worker against the homeowner based on strict liability in tort to recover for his injury, will the worker prevail?

(A) No, because the snake's escape was caused by a force of nature.
(B) No, because the worker should have anticipated an injury during his volunteer work.
(C) Yes, because the homeowner did not take adequate precautions to secure the snake.
(D) Yes, because the worker's injury was the result of his fear of the escaped snake.

Question 76 - Real Property

A buyer validly contracted in writing to buy land from a seller. The contract had no contingencies and was silent as to risk of loss if there were damage to, or destruction of, property improvements between contract and closing, and as to any duty to carry insurance. As soon as the parties signed the contract, the seller (who had already moved out) canceled her insurance covering the land. The buyer did not know this and did not obtain insurance. A few days later, three weeks before the agreed closing date, the building on the land was struck by lightning and burned to the ground. There is no applicable statute. In an appropriate action, the buyer asserted the right to cancel the contract and to recover his earnest money. The seller said the risk of fire loss passed to the buyer before the fire, so the buyer must perform.

If the seller prevails, what is the most likely explanation?

(A) Once the parties signed the contract, only the buyer had an insurable interest and so could have protected against this loss.
(B) The buyer's constructive possession arising from the contract gave him the affirmative duty of protecting against loss by fire.
(C) The seller's cancellation of her casualty insurance practically construed the contract to transfer the risk of loss to the buyer.
(D) Upon execution of the contract, the buyer became the equitable owner of the land under the doctrine of equitable conversion.

Question 77 - Criminal Law and Procedure

A customer asked to see an expensive watch in a jewelry store. In conversation with the clerk, the customer falsely claimed to be the son of the mayor. When handed the watch, he asked if he could put it on, walk around a bit so he could see how it felt on his wrist, and then briefly step outside to observe it in natural light. The clerk agreed, saying, "I know I can trust someone like you with the merchandise." The customer walked out of the store wearing the watch and never returned. A week later, the clerk was at a gathering when she spotted the customer wearing the watch. She told him that he must either pay for the watch or give it back. He hissed, "I'll knock your block off if you mess with me." Intimidated, the clerk backed off. The following list of crimes is in descending order of seriousness.

What is the most serious crime the customer committed?

(A) Robbery.
(B) Larceny.
(C) False pretenses.
(D) Embezzlement.

Question 78 - Evidence

In a civil action for breach of an oral contract, the defendant admits that there had been discussions, but denies that he ever entered into an agreement with the plaintiff.

Which of the following standards of admissibility should be applied by the court to evidence proffered as relevant to prove whether a contract was formed?

(A) Whether a reasonable juror would find the evidence determinative of whether the contract was or was not formed.
(B) Whether the evidence has any tendency to make the fact of contract formation more or less probable than without the evidence.
(C) Whether the evidence is sufficient to prove, absent contrary evidence, that the contract was or was not formed.
(D) Whether the evidence makes it more likely than not that a contract was or was not formed.

Question 79 - Contracts

A mother, whose adult son was a law school graduate, contracted with a tutor to give the son a bar exam preparation course. "If my son passes the bar exam," the mother explained to the tutor, "he has been promised a job with a law firm that will pay $55,000 a year." The tutor agreed to do the work for $5,000, although the going rate was $6,000. Before the instruction was to begin, the tutor repudiated the contract. Although the mother or the son reasonably could have employed, for $6,000, an equally qualified instructor to replace the tutor, neither did so. The son failed the bar exam and the law firm refused to employ him. It can be shown that had the son received the instruction, he would have passed the bar exam.

If the mother and the son join as parties plaintiff and sue the tutor for breach of contract, how much, if anything, are they entitled to recover?

(A) $1,000, because all other damages could have been avoided by employing another equally qualified instructor.
(B) $55,000, because damages of that amount were within the contemplation of the parties at the time they contracted.
(C) Nominal damages only, because the mother was not injured by the breach and the tutor made no promise to the son.
(D) Nothing, because neither the mother nor the son took steps to avoid the consequences of the tutor's breach.

Question 80 - Constitutional Law

A federal statute required the National Bureau of Standards to establish minimum quality standards for all beer sold in the United States. The statute also provided that public proceedings must precede adoption of the standards, and that once they were adopted, the standards would be subject to judicial review. No standards have yet been adopted. Several officials of the National Bureau of Standards have indicated their personal preference for beer produced by a special brewing process commonly referred to as pasteurization. However, these officials have not indicated whether they intend to include a requirement for pasteurization in the minimum beer quality standards to be adopted by the Bureau. A brewery that produces an unpasteurized beer believes that its brewing process is as safe as pasteurization. The brewery is concerned that, after the appropriate proceedings, the Bureau may adopt quality standards that will prohibit the sale of any unpasteurized beer. As a result, the brewery sued in federal district court to enjoin the Bureau from adopting any standards that would prohibit the sale of unpasteurized beer in this country.

How should the district court dispose of the suit?

(A) Determine whether the Bureau could reasonably believe that pasteurization is the safest process by which to brew beer, and if the Bureau could reasonably believe that, refuse to issue the injunction against the Bureau.
(B) Determine whether the process used by the brewery is as safe as pasteurization and, if it is, issue the injunction against the Bureau.
(C) Refuse to adjudicate the merits of the suit at this time and stay the action until the Bureau has actually issued beer quality standards.
(D) Refuse to adjudicate the merits of the suit, because it does not involve a justiciable case or controversy.

Question 81 - Contracts

A landowner entered into a single contract with a builder to have three different structures built on separate pieces of property owned by the landowner. Each structure was distinct from the other two and the parties agreed on a specific price for each. After completing the first structure in accordance with the terms of the contract, the builder demanded payment of the specified price for that structure. At the same time, the builder told the landowner that the builder was "tired of the construction business" and would not even begin the other two structures. The landowner refused to pay anything to the builder.

Is the builder likely to prevail in a suit for the agreed price of the first structure?

(A) No, because substantial performance is a constructive condition to the landowner's duty to pay at the contract rate.
(B) No, because the builder's cessation of performance without legal excuse is a willful breach of the contract.
(C) Yes, because the contract is divisible, and the landowner will be required to bring a separate claim for the builder's failure to complete the other two structures.
(D) Yes, because the contract is divisible, but the landowner will be able to deduct any recoverable damages caused by the builder's failure to complete the contract.

Question 82 - Real Property

An uncle was the record title holder of a vacant tract of land. He often told friends that he would leave the land to his nephew in his will. The nephew knew of these conversations. Prior to the uncle's death, the nephew conveyed the land by warranty deed to a woman for $10,000. She did not conduct a title search of the land before she accepted the deed from the nephew. She promptly and properly recorded her deed. Last month, the uncle died, leaving the land to the nephew in his duly probated will. Both the nephew and the woman now claim ownership of the land. The nephew has offered to return the $10,000 to the woman.

Who has title to the land?

(A) The nephew, because at the time of the deed to the woman, the uncle was the owner of record.
(B) The nephew, because the woman did not conduct a title search.
(C) The woman, because of the doctrine of estoppel by deed.
(D) The woman, because she recorded her deed prior to the uncle's death.

Question 83 - Torts

A customer fell and injured himself when he slipped on a banana peel while shopping at a grocer's store. The banana peel was fresh and clean except for a mark made by the heel of the customer's shoe. In an action brought by the customer against the grocer, these are the only facts in evidence.

Should the trial judge permit the case to go to the jury?

(A) No, because the customer had an obligation to watch where he stepped.
(B) No, because there is not a reasonable basis for inferring that the grocer knew or should have known of the banana peel.
(C) Yes, because it is more likely than not that the peel came from a banana offered for sale by the grocer.
(D) Yes, because the grocer could foresee that a customer might slip on a banana peel.

Question 84 - Constitutional Law

The United States Congress enacted a federal statute providing that any state may "require labeling to show the state or other geographic origin of citrus fruit that is imported into the receiving state." Pursuant to the federal statute, a state that produced large quantities of citrus fruit enacted a law requiring all citrus fruit imported into the state to be stamped with a two-letter postal abbreviation signifying the state of the fruit's origin. The law did not impose any such requirement for citrus fruit grown within the state. When it adopted the law, the state legislature declared that its purpose was to reduce the risks of infection of local citrus crops by itinerant diseases that have been found to attack citrus fruit. A national association of citrus growers sued to have the state law declared unconstitutional. The association claims that the law is prohibited by the negative implications of the commerce clause of the Constitution.

Which of the following is the best argument in favor of the state's effort to have this lawsuit dismissed?

(A) Any burden on interstate commerce imposed by the state law is outweighed by a legitimate state interest.
(B) Congress has the authority to authorize specified state regulations that would otherwise be prohibited by the negative implications of the commerce clause, and it has done so in this situation.
(C) The state law does not discriminate against out-of-state citrus growers or producers.
(D) The state law furthers a legitimate state interest, the burden it imposes on interstate commerce is only incidental, and the state's interest cannot be satisfied by other means that are less burdensome to interstate commerce.

Question 85 - Contracts

In financial straits and needing $4,000 immediately, a nephew orally asked his uncle for a $4,000 loan. The uncle replied that he would lend the money to the nephew only if the nephew's mother "guaranteed" the loan. At the nephew's suggestion, the uncle then telephoned the nephew's mother, told her about the loan, and asked if she would "guarantee" it. She replied, "Surely. Lend my son the $4,000 and I'll repay it if he doesn't." The uncle then lent $4,000 to the nephew, an amount the nephew orally agreed to repay in six weeks. The next day, the nephew's mother wrote to him and concluded her letter with the words, "Son, I was happy to do you a favor by promising your uncle I would repay your six-week $4,000 loan if you don't. /s/ Mother." Neither the nephew nor his mother repaid the loan when it came due and the uncle sued the mother for breach of contract. In that action, the mother raised the statute of frauds as her only defense.

Will the mother's statute-of-frauds defense be successful?

(A) No, because the amount of the loan was less than $5,000.
(B) No, because the mother's letter satisfies the statute-of-frauds requirement.
(C) Yes, because the mother's promise to the uncle was oral.
(D) Yes, because the nephew's promise to the uncle was oral.

Question 86 - Criminal Law and Procedure

After a liquor store was robbed, the police received an anonymous telephone call naming a store employee as the perpetrator of the robbery. Honestly believing that their actions were permitted by the U.S. Constitution, the police talked one of the employee's neighbors into going to the employee's home with a hidden tape recorder to engage him in a conversation about the crime. During the conversation, the employee admitted committing the robbery. The employee was charged in state court with the robbery. He moved to suppress the recording on the grounds that the method of obtaining it violated his constitutional rights under both the state and federal constitutions. Assume that a clear precedent from the state supreme court holds that the conduct of the police in making the recording violated the employee's rights under the state constitution, and that the exclusionary rule is the proper remedy for this violation.

Should the court grant the employee's motion?

(A) No, because the employee's federal constitutional rights were not violated, and this circumstance overrides any state constitutional provisions.
(B) No, because the police were acting in the good-faith belief that their actions were permitted by the federal Constitution.
(C) Yes, because the making of the recording violated the state constitution.
(D) Yes, because use of the recording would violate the neighbor's federal constitutional rights.

Question 87 - Evidence

At a civil trial for slander, the plaintiff showed that the defendant had called the plaintiff a thief. In defense, the defendant called a witness to testify, "I have been the plaintiff's neighbor for many years, and people in our community generally have said that he is a thief."

Is the testimony concerning the plaintiff's reputation in the community admissible?

(A) No, because character is an essential element of the defense, and proof must be made by specific instances of conduct.
(B) Yes, to prove that the plaintiff is a thief, and to reduce or refute the damages claimed.
(C) Yes, to prove that the plaintiff is a thief, but not on the issue of damages.
(D) Yes, to reduce or refute the damages claimed, but not to prove that the plaintiff is a thief.

Question 88 - Torts

A law student rented a furnished apartment. His landlord began to solicit his advice about her legal affairs, but he refused to provide it. The landlord then demanded that he vacate the apartment immediately. The landlord also engaged in a pattern of harassment, calling the student at home every evening and entering his apartment without his consent during times when he was at school. During these unauthorized visits she removed the handles from the bathroom and kitchen sinks, but did not touch anything belonging to the student. The lease has a year to run, and the student is still living in the apartment. The student has sued the landlord for trespass to land.

Is he likely to prevail?

(A) No, because he has no standing to sue for trespass.
(B) No, because the landlord caused no damage to his property.
(C) Yes, for compensatory damages only.
(D) Yes, for injunctive relief, compensatory damages, and punitive damages.

Question 89 - Contracts

On May 1, an uncle mailed a letter to his adult nephew that stated: "I am thinking of selling my pickup truck, which you have seen and ridden in. I would consider taking $7,000 for it." On May 3, the nephew mailed the following response: "I will buy your pickup for $7,000 cash." The uncle received this letter on May 5 and on May 6 mailed a note that stated: "It's a deal." On May 7, before the nephew had received the letter of May 6, he phoned his uncle to report that he no longer wanted to buy the pickup truck because his driver's license had been suspended.

Which of the following statements concerning this exchange is accurate?

(A) There is a contract as of May 3.
(B) There is a contract as of May 5.
(C) There is a contract as of May 6.
(D) There is no contract.

Question 90 - Real Property

On a parcel of land immediately adjacent to a woman's 50-acre farm, a public school district built a large consolidated high school that included a 5,000-seat lighted athletic stadium. The woman had objected to the district's plans for the stadium and was particularly upset about nighttime athletic events that attracted large crowds and that, at times, resulted in significant noise and light intensity levels. On nights of athletic events, the woman and her family members wore earplugs and could not sleep or enjoy a quiet evening until after 10 p.m. In addition, light from the stadium on those nights was bright enough to allow reading a newspaper in the woman's yard.

Which of the following doctrines would best support the woman's claim for damages?

(A) Constructive eviction.
(B) Private nuisance.
(C) Public nuisance.
(D) Waste.

Question 91 - Criminal Law and Procedure

Four men are charged with conspiracy to commit a series of bank robberies. Nine successful bank robberies took place during the period of the charged conspiracy. Because the robbers wore masks and gloves and stole the bank surveillance tapes, no direct identification of the robbers by the witnesses has been made. Some circumstantial evidence ties each of the men to the overall conspiracy. During cross-examination, a prosecution witness testified that one defendant was in jail on other charges during six of the robberies. That defendant's lawyer has moved for a judgment of acquittal at the close of the government's case.

Should the motion be granted?

(A) No, because a conspirator is not required to agree to all of the objects of the conspiracy.
(B) No, because a conspirator need not be present at the commission of each crime conspired upon.
(C) Yes, provided the defendant has complied with the rule requiring pretrial notice of alibi.
(D) Yes, regardless of compliance with the alibi rule, because the government is bound by exculpatory evidence elicited during its case-in-chief.

Question 92 - Contracts

A seller and a buyer entered into a contract obligating the seller to convey title to a parcel of land to the buyer for $100,000. The agreement provided that the buyer's obligation to purchase the parcel was expressly conditioned upon the buyer's obtaining a loan at an interest rate no higher than 10%. The buyer was unable to do so, but did obtain a loan at an interest rate of 10.5% and timely tendered the purchase price. Because the value of the land had increased since the time of contracting, the seller refused to perform. The buyer sued the seller.

Will the buyer prevail?

(A) No, because an express condition will only be excused to avoid forfeiture.
(B) No, because the contract called for a loan at an interest rate not to exceed 10% and it could not be modified without the consent of the seller.
(C) Yes, because the buyer detrimentally changed position in reliance on the seller's promise to convey.
(D) Yes, because the buyer's obtaining a loan at an interest rate no higher than 10% was not a condition to the seller's duty to perform.

Question 93 - Torts

A bright nine-year-old child attended a day care center after school. The day care center was located near a man-made duck pond on the property of a corporation. During the winter, the pond was used for ice skating when conditions were suitable. At a time when the pond was only partially frozen, the child sneaked away from the center and walked out onto the ice covering the pond. The ice gave way, and the child fell into the cold water. He suffered shock and would have drowned had he not been rescued by a passerby. At the time of the incident, the pond was clearly marked with signs that stated, "THIN ICE - NO SKATING." When the child left the day care center, the center was staffed with a reasonable number of qualified personnel, and the center's employees were exercising reasonable care to ensure that the children in their charge did not leave the premises. The jurisdiction follows a rule of pure comparative negligence.

In a suit brought on the child's behalf against the corporation, who is likely to prevail?

(A) The child, because the corporation owes a duty to keep its premises free of dangerous conditions.
(B) The child, because the pond was an attractive nuisance.
(C) The corporation, because the danger of thin ice may reasonably be expected to be understood by a nine-year-old child.
(D) The corporation, because the day care center had a duty to keep the child off the ice.

Question 94 - Torts

[NOTE: These facts are repeated from question 93.] A bright nine-year-old child attended a day care center after school. The day care center was located near a man-made duck pond on the property of a corporation. During the winter, the pond was used for ice skating when conditions were suitable. At a time when the pond was only partially frozen, the child sneaked away from the center and walked out onto the ice covering the pond. The ice gave way, and the child fell into the cold water. He suffered shock and would have drowned had he not been rescued by a passerby. At the time of the incident, the pond was clearly marked with signs that stated, "THIN ICE - NO SKATING." When the child left the day care center, the center was staffed with a reasonable number of qualified personnel, and the center's employees were exercising reasonable care to ensure that the children in their charge did not leave the premises. The jurisdiction follows a rule of pure comparative negligence.

In a suit brought on the child's behalf against the day care center, who is likely to prevail?

(A) The child, because he left the center while he was under the center's care.
(B) The child, because the day care center is located near a pond.
(C) The day care center, because it was not negligent.
(D) The day care center, because the child was a trespasser.

Question 95 - Constitutional Law

A man intensely disliked his neighbors, who were of a different race. One night, intending to frighten his neighbors, he spray-painted their house with racial epithets and threats that they would be lynched. The man was arrested and prosecuted under a state law providing that "any person who threatens violence against another person with the intent to cause that person to fear for his or her life or safety may be imprisoned for up to five years." In defense, the man claimed that he did not intend to lynch his neighbors, but only to scare them so that they would move away.

Can the man constitutionally be convicted under this law?

(A) No, because he was only communicating his views and had not commenced any overt action against the neighbors.
(B) Yes, because he was engaged in trespass when he painted the words on his neighbors' house.
(C) Yes, because his communication was a threat by which he intended to intimidate his neighbors.
(D) Yes, because his communication was racially motivated and thus violated the protections of the Thirteenth Amendment.

Question 96 - Criminal Law and Procedure

A defendant was charged with assault and battery in a jurisdiction that followed the "retreat" doctrine, and he pleaded self-defense. At his trial, the evidence established the following: A man and his wife were enjoying a drink at a tavern when the defendant entered and stood near the door. The wife whispered to her husband that the defendant was the man who had insulted her on the street the day before. The husband approached the defendant and said, "Get out of here, or I'll break your nose." The defendant said, "Don't come any closer, or I'll hurt you." When the husband raised his fists menacingly, the defendant pulled a can of pepper spray from his pocket, aimed it at the husband's face, and sprayed. The husband fell to the floor, writhing in pain.

Should the defendant be convicted?

A)   No, because he had no obligation to retreat before resorting to non-deadly force.

(B) No, because there is no obligation to retreat when one is in an occupied structure.
(C) Yes, because he failed to retreat even though there was an opportunity available.
(D) Yes, because the husband did not threaten to use deadly force against him.

Question 97 - Contracts

An innkeeper, who had no previous experience in the motel or commercial laundry business and who knew nothing about the trade usages of either business, bought a motel and signed an agreement with a laundry company for the motel's laundry services. The one-year agreement provided for "daily service at $500 a week." From their conversations during negotiation, the laundry company knew that the innkeeper expected laundry services seven days a week. When the laundry company refused to pick up the motel's laundry on two successive Sundays and indicated that it would not ever do so, the innkeeper canceled the agreement. The laundry company sued the innkeeper for breach of contract. At trial, clear evidence was introduced to show that in the commercial laundry business "daily service" did not include service on Sundays.

Will the laundry company succeed in its action?

(A) No, because the laundry company knew the meaning the innkeeper attached to "daily service," and, therefore, the innkeeper's meaning will control.
(B) No, because the parties attached materially different meanings to "daily service," and, therefore, no contract was formed.
(C) Yes, because the parol evidence rule will not permit the innkeeper to prove the meaning she attached to "daily service."
(D) Yes, because the trade usage will control the interpretation of "daily service."

Question 98 - Real Property

A landowner orally gave his neighbor permission to share the use of the private road on the landowner's land so that the neighbor could have more convenient access to the neighbor's land. Only the landowner maintained the road. After the neighbor had used the road on a daily basis for three years, the landowner conveyed his land to a grantee, who immediately notified the neighbor that the neighbor was not to use the road. The neighbor sued the grantee seeking a declaration that the neighbor had a right to continue to use the road.

Who is likely to prevail?

(A) The grantee, because an oral license is invalid.
(B) The grantee, because the neighbor had a license that the grantee could terminate at any time.
(C) The neighbor, because the grantee is estopped to terminate the neighbor's use of the road.
(D) The neighbor, because the neighbor's use of the road was open and notorious when the grantee purchased the land.

Question 99 - Contracts

A carpenter contracted with a homeowner to remodel the homeowner's home for $10,000, to be paid on completion of the work. On May 29, relying on his expectation that he would finish the work and have the homeowner's payment on June 1, the carpenter contracted to buy a car for "$10,000 in cash, if payment is made on June 1; if payment is made thereafter, the price is $12,000." The carpenter completed the work according to specifications on June 1 and demanded payment from the homeowner on that date. The homeowner, without any excuse, refused to pay. Thereupon, the carpenter became very excited, suffered a minor heart attack, and, as a result, incurred medical expenses of $1,000. The reasonable value of the carpenter's services in remodeling the homeowner's home was $13,000.

In an action by the carpenter against the homeowner, which of the following should be the carpenter's measure of recovery?

(A) $10,000, the contract price.
(B) $11,000, the contract price plus $1,000 for the medical expenses incurred because the homeowner refused to pay.
(C) $12,000, the contract price plus $2,000, the bargain that was lost because the carpenter could not pay cash for the car on June 1.
(D) $13,000, the amount the homeowner was enriched by the carpenter's services.

Question 100 - Evidence

A plaintiff sued her employer, alleging that poor working conditions had caused her to develop a stomach ulcer. At trial, the plaintiff's medical expert testified to the cause of the plaintiff's ulcer and stated that his opinion was based in part on information in a letter the plaintiff's personal physician had written to the plaintiff's employer, explaining why the plaintiff had missed work.

When offered to prove the cause of the plaintiff's condition, is the letter from the plaintiff's doctor admissible?

(A) No, because it is hearsay not within any exception.
(B) No, because the plaintiff's physician is not shown to be unavailable.
(C) Yes, because it was relied upon by the plaintiff's medical expert.
(D) Yes, under the business records exception to the hearsay rule.

MBE QUESTIONS

AMERIBAR BAR REVIEW

Multistate Bar Examination Released Questions
Section 3

CONSTITUTIONAL LAW

Question 1

Road Lines is an interstate bus company operating in a five-state area. A federal statute authorizes the Interstate Commerce Commission (ICC) to permit interstate carriers to discontinue entirely any unprofitable route. Road Lines applied to the ICC for permission to drop a very unprofitable route through the sparsely populated Shaley Mountains. The ICC granted that permission even though Road Lines provided the only public transportation into the region.

Foley is the owner of a mountain resort in the Shaley Mountains, whose customers usually arrived on vehicles operated by Road Lines. After exhausting all available federal administrative remedies, Foley filed suit against Road Lines in the trial court of the state in which the Shaley Mountains are located to enjoin the discontinuance by Road Lines of its service to that area. Foley alleged that the discontinuance of service by Road Lines would violate a statute of that state prohibiting common carriers of persons from abandoning service to communities having no alternate form of public transportation.

The state court should

(A) dismiss the action, because Foley lacks standing to sue.
(B) direct the removal of the case to federal court, because this suit involves a substantial federal question.
(C) hear the case on its merits and decide for Foley because, on these facts, a federal agency is interfering with essential state functions.
(D) hear the case on its merits and decide for Road Lines, because a valid federal law preempts the state statute on which Foley relies.

Question 2

Plaintiff challenged the constitutionality of a state tax law, alleging that it violated the equal protection clauses of both the United States Constitution and the state constitution. The state supreme court agreed and held the tax law to be invalid. It said: "We hold that this state tax law violates the equal protection clause of the United States Constitution and also the equal protection clause of the state constitution because we interpret that provision of the state constitution to contain exactly the same prohibition against discriminatory legislation as is contained in the equal protection clause of the

Fourteenth Amendment to the United States Constitution."

The state sought review of this decision in the United States Supreme Court, alleging that the state supreme court's determination of the federal constitutional issue was incorrect.

How should the United States Supreme Court dispose of the case if it believes that this interpretation of the federal Constitution by the state supreme court raises an important federal question and is incorrect on the merits?

(A) Reverse the state supreme court decision, because the equal protection clause of a state constitution must be construed by the state supreme court in a manner that is congruent with the meaning of the equal protection clause of the federal Constitution.
(B) Reverse the state supreme court decision with respect to the equal protection clause of the federal Constitution and remand the case to the state supreme court for further proceedings, because the state and federal constitutional issues are so intertwined that the federal issue must be decided so that this case may be disposed of properly.
(C) Refuse to review the decision of the state supreme court, because it is based on an adequate and independent ground of state law.
(D) Refuse to review the decision of the state supreme court, because a state government may not seek review of decisions of its own courts in the United States Supreme Court.

Question 3

A federal statute prohibits the construction of nuclear energy plants in this country without a license from the Federal Nuclear Plant Siting Commission. The statute provides that the Commission may issue a license authorizing the construction of a proposed nuclear energy plant 30 days after the Commission makes a finding that the plant will comply with specified standards of safety, technological and commercial feasibility, and public convenience. In a severable provision, the Commission's enabling statute also provides that the Congress, by simple majorities in each house, may veto the issuance of a particular license by the Commission if such a veto occurs within 30 days following the required Commission finding.

Early last year, the Commission found that Safenuke, Inc., met all statutory requirements and, therefore, voted to issue Safenuke, Inc., a license authorizing it to construct a nuclear energy plant. Because they believed that the issuance of a license to Safenuke, Inc., was not in accord with the applicable statutory criteria, a majority of each of the two houses of Congress voted, within the specified 30-day period, to veto the license. On the basis of that veto, the Commission refused to issue the license. Subsequently, Safenuke, Inc., sued the Commission in an appropriate federal district court, challenging the constitutionality of the Commission's refusal to issue the license.

In this suit, the court should hold the congressional veto of the license of Safenuke, Inc., to be

(A) invalid, because any determination by Congress that particular agency action does not satisfy statutory criteria violates Article III, Section 1 of the Constitution because it constitutes the performance of a judicial function by the legislative branch.
(B) invalid, because Article I, Section 7 of the Constitution has been interpreted to mean that any action of Congress purporting to alter the legal rights of persons outside of the legislative branch must be presented to the President for his signature or veto.
(C) valid, because Congress has authority under the commerce clause to regulate the construction of nuclear energy plants.
(D) valid, because there is a compelling national interest in the close congressional supervision of nuclear plant siting in light of the grave dangers to the public health and safety that are associated with the operation of such plants.

Question 4

Congressional hearings determined that the use of mechanical power hammers is very dangerous to the persons using them and to persons in the vicinity of the persons using them. As a result, Congress enacted a statute prohibiting the use of mechanical power hammers on all construction projects in the United States. Subsequently, a study conducted by a private research firm concluded that nails driven by mechanical power hammers have longer-lasting joining power than hand-driven nails. After learning about this study, the city council of the city of Green enacted an amendment to its building safety code requiring the use of

mechanical power hammers in the construction of all buildings intended for human habitation.

This amendment to the city of Green's building safety code is

(A) unconstitutional, because it was enacted subsequent to the federal statute.
(B) unconstitutional, because it conflicts with the provisions of the federal statute.
(C) constitutional, because the federal statute does not expressly indicate that it supersedes inconsistent state or local laws.
(D) constitutional, because the long-term safety of human habitations justifies some additional risk to the people engaged in their construction.

Question 5

Modality City has had a severe traffic problem on its streets. As a result, it enacted an ordinance prohibiting all sales to the public of food or other items by persons selling directly from trucks, cars, or other vehicles located on city streets. The ordinance included an inseverable grandfather provision exempting from its prohibition vendors who, for 20 years or more, have continuously sold food or other items from such vehicles located on the streets of Modality City.

Northwind Ice Cream, a retail vendor of ice cream products, qualifies for this exemption and is the only food vendor that does. Yuppee Yogurt is a business similar to Northwind, but Yuppee has been selling to the public directly from trucks located on the streets of Modality City only for the past ten years. Yuppee filed suit in an appropriate federal district court to enjoin enforcement of this ordinance on the ground that it denies Yuppee the equal protection of the laws.

In this case, the court will probably rule that the ordinance is

(A) constitutional, because it is narrowly tailored to implement the city's compelling interest in reducing traffic congestion and, therefore, satisfies the strict scrutiny test applicable to such cases.
(B) constitutional, because its validity is governed by the rational basis test, and the courts consistently defer to economic choices embodied in such legislation if they are even plausibly justifiable.
(C) unconstitutional, because the nexus between the legitimate purpose of the ordinance and

the conduct it prohibits is so tenuous and its provisions are so under-inclusive that the ordinance fails to satisfy the substantial relationship test applicable to such cases.

(D) unconstitutional, because economic benefits or burdens imposed by legislatures on the basis of grandfather provisions have consistently been declared invalid by courts as *per se* violations of the equal protection clause of the Fourteenth Amendment.

Question 6

A federal statute prohibits the sale or resale, in any place in this country, of any product intended for human consumption or ingestion into the human body that contains designated chemicals known to cause cancer, unless the product is clearly labeled as dangerous.

The constitutionality of this federal statute may most easily be justified on the basis of the power of Congress to

(A) regulate commerce among the states.
(B) enforce the Fourteenth Amendment.
(C) provide for the general welfare.
(D) promote science and the useful arts.

Question 7

A federal statute enacted pursuant to the powers of Congress to enforce the Fourteenth Amendment and to regulate commerce among the states prohibits any state from requiring any of its employees to retire from state employment solely because of their age. The statute expressly authorizes employees required by a state to retire from state employment solely because of their age to sue the state government in federal district court for any damages resulting from that state action. On the basis of this federal statute, Retiree sues State X in federal district court. State X moves to dismiss the suit on the ground that Congress lacks authority to authorize such suits against a state.

Which of the following is the strongest argument that Retiree can offer in opposition to the state's motion to dismiss this suit?

(A) When Congress exercises power vested in it by the Fourteenth Amendment and/or the commerce clause, Congress may enact appropriate remedial legislation expressly subjecting the states to private suits for damages in federal court.

(B) When Congress exercises power vested in it by any provision of the Constitution, Congress has

unlimited authority to authorize private actions for damages against a state.

(C) While the Eleventh Amendment restrains the federal judiciary, that amendment does not limit the power of Congress to modify the sovereign immunity of the states.

(D) While the Eleventh Amendment applies to suits in federal court by citizens of one state against another state, it does not apply to such suits by citizens against their own states.

Question 8

A federal law provides that all motor vehicle tires discarded in this country must be disposed of in facilities licensed by the federal Environmental Protection Agency. Pursuant to this federal law and all proper federal procedural requirements, that agency has adopted very strict standards for the licensing of such facilities. As a result, the cost of disposing of tires in licensed facilities is substantial. The state of East Dakota has a very large fleet of motor vehicles, including trucks used to support state-owned commercial activities and police cars. East Dakota disposes of used tires from both kinds of state motor vehicles in a state-owned and - operated facility. This state facility is unlicensed, but its operation in actual practice meets most of the standards imposed by the federal Environmental Protection Agency on facilities it licenses to dispose of tires.

Consistent with United States Supreme Court precedent, may the state of East Dakota continue to dispose of its used tires in this manner?

(A) No, because a state must comply with valid federal laws that regulate matters affecting interstate commerce.

(B) No, because some of the tires come from vehicles that are used by the state solely in its commercial activities.

(C) Yes, because some of the tires come from vehicles that are used by the state in the performance of core state governmental functions such as law enforcement.

(D) Yes, because the legitimate needs of the federal government are satisfied by the fact that the unlicensed state disposal scheme meets, in actual practice, most of the federal standards for the licensing of such facilities.

Question 9

Congress enacted a statute providing grants of federal funds for the restoration and preservation of courthouses that were built before 1900 and are still in use. The statute contains an inseverable condition requiring that any courthouse restored with the aid of such a grant must be equipped with ramps and other facilities necessary to accommodate physically handicapped people.

A law of the state of Blue requires public buildings in Blue to have ramps and other facilities for handicapped people. It exempts from those requirements any building that is more than 70 years old if the State Board of Architects finds that the installation of such facilities would destroy the architectural integrity of the building.

The Red County Courthouse in the state of Blue was built in 1895 and is still in use. It does not contain ramps or other special facilities for handicapped people. The State Board of Architects has determined that the installation of those facilities would destroy the architectural integrity of the building. Nevertheless, the County Board of Red County applies for a federal grant to restore and preserve that county's courthouse.

If the County Board of Red County restores the Red County Courthouse with the aid of a federal restoration and preservation grant, is the board bound to install ramps and other facilities for handicapped people in that building?

(A) Yes, because Congress may impose reasonable conditions related to the public welfare on grants of federal funds to public bodies when the public bodies are free to accept or reject the grants.
(B) Yes, because the rights of handicapped and disabled people are fundamental rights that take precedence, as a constitutional matter, over considerations of architectural integrity.
(C) No, because the Constitution does not authorize the federal government to direct the actions of the states or any of their political subdivisions with respect to matters affecting their own governmental buildings.
(D) No, because any acceptance of this condition by the Red County Board of Supervisors would, as a matter of law, be considered to be under duress.

Question 10

"Look-alike drugs" is the term used to describe nonprescription drugs that look like narcotic drugs and are sold on the streets as narcotic drugs. After extensive hearings, Congress concluded that the sale of look-alike drugs was widespread in this country and was creating severe health and law enforcement problems. To combat these problems, Congress enacted a comprehensive statute that regulates the manufacture, distribution, and sale of all nonprescription drugs in the United States.

Which of the following sources of constitutional authority can most easily be used to justify the authority of Congress to enact this statute?

(A) The spending power.
(B) The commerce clause.
(C) The general welfare clause.
(D) The enforcement powers of the Fourteenth Amendment.

Question 11

After several well-publicized deaths caused by fires in products made from highly flammable fabrics, the state of Orange enacted a statute prohibiting "the manufacture or assembly of any product in this state which contains any fabric that has not been tested and approved for flame retardancy by the Zetest Testing Company." The Zetest Testing Company is a privately owned and operated business located in Orange.

For many years, Fabric Mill, located in the state of Orange, has had its fabric tested for flame retardancy by the Alpha Testing Company, located in the state of Green. Alpha Testing Company is a reliable organization that uses a process for testing and approving fabrics for flame retardancy identical in all respects to that used by the Zetest Testing Company.

Because Fabric Mill wishes to continue to have its fabric tested solely by Alpha Testing Company, Fabric Mill files an action in Orange state court challenging the constitutionality of the Orange statute as applied to its circumstances.

In this suit, the court should hold the statute to be

(A) constitutional, because it is reasonably related to the protection of the reputation of the fabric industry located in the state of Orange.
(B) constitutional, because it is a legitimate means of protecting the safety of the public.
(C) unconstitutional, because it denies to Fabric

Mill the equal protection of the laws.

(D) unconstitutional, because it imposes an unreasonable burden on interstate commerce.

Question 12

Public schools in the state of Green are financed, in large part, by revenue derived from real estate taxes imposed by each school district on the taxable real property located in that district. Public schools also receive other revenue from private gifts, federal grants, student fees, and local sales taxes. For many years, Green has distributed additional funds, which come from the state treasury, to local school districts in order to equalize the funds available on a per-student basis for each public school district. These additional funds are distributed on the basis of a state statutory formula that considers only the number of students in each public school district and the real estate tax revenue raised by that district. The formula does not consider other revenue received by a school district from different sources.

The school boards of two school districts, together with parents and schoolchildren in those districts, bring suit in federal court to enjoin the state from allocating the additional funds from the state treasury to individual districts pursuant to this formula. They allege that the failure of the state, in allocating this additional money, to take into account a school district's sources of revenue other than revenue derived from taxes levied on real estate located there violates the equal protection clause of the Fourteenth Amendment. The complaint does not allege that the allocation of the additional state funds based on the current statutory formula has resulted in a failure to provide minimally adequate education to any child.

Which of the following best describes the appropriate standard by which the court should review the constitutionality of the state statutory funding formula?

(A) Because classifications based on wealth are inherently suspect, the state must demonstrate that the statutory formula is necessary to vindicate a compelling state interest.

(B) Because the statutory funding formula burdens the fundamental right to education, the state must demonstrate that the formula is necessary to vindicate a compelling state interest.

(C) Because no fundamental right or suspect classification is implicated in this case, the

plaintiffs must demonstrate that the funding allocation formula bears no rational relationship to any legitimate state interest.

(D) Because the funding formula inevitably leads to disparities among the school districts in their levels of total funding, the plaintiffs must only demonstrate that the funding formula is not substantially related to the furtherance of an important state interest.

Question 13

The constitution of State X authorizes a five-member state reapportionment board to redraw state legislative districts every ten years. In the last state legislative reapportionment, the board, by a unanimous vote, divided the greater Green metropolitan area, composed of Green City and several contiguous townships, into three equally populated state legislative districts. The result of that districting was that 40% of the area's total black population resided in one of those districts, 45% of the area's total black population resided in the second of those districts, and 15% resided in the third district.

Jones is black, is a registered voter, and is a resident of Green City. Jones brings suit in an appropriate court against the members of the state reapportionment board, seeking declaratory and injunctive relief that would require the boundary lines of the state legislative districts in the greater Green metropolitan area to be redrawn. His only claim is that the current apportionment violates the Fifteenth Amendment and the equal protection clause of the Fourteenth Amendment because it improperly dilutes the voting power of the blacks who reside in that area.

If no federal statute is applicable, which of the following facts, if proven, would most strongly support the validity of the action of the state reapportionment board?

(A) In drawing the current district lines, the reapportionment board precisely complied with state constitutional requirements that state legislative districts be compact and follow political subdivision boundaries to the maximum extent feasible.

(B) The reapportionment board was composed of three white members and two black members and both of the board's black members were satisfied that its plan did not improperly dilute the voting power of the blacks who reside in that area.

(C) Although the rate of voter registration among blacks is below that of voter registration among whites in the greater Green metropolitan area, two black legislators have been elected from that area during the last 15 years.

(D) The total black population of the greater Green metropolitan area amounts to only 15% of the population that is required to comprise a single legislative district.

Question 14

Which of the following acts by the United States Senate would be constitutionally IMPROPER?

(A) The Senate decides, with the House of Representatives, that a disputed state ratification of a proposed constitutional amendment is valid.

(B) The Senate determines the eligibility of a person to serve as a senator.

(C) The Senate appoints a commission to adjudicate finally a boundary dispute between two states.

(D) The Senate passes a resolution calling on the President to pursue a certain foreign policy.

Question 15

The Federal Family Film Enhancement Act assesses an excise tax of 10% on the price of admission to public movie theaters when they show films that contain actual or simulated scenes of human sexual intercourse.

Which of the following is the strongest argument against the constitutionality of this federal act?

(A) The act imposes a prior restraint on the freedom of speech protected by the First Amendment.

(B) The act is not rationally related to any legitimate national interest.

(C) The act violates the equal protection concepts embodied in the due process clause of the Fifth Amendment because it imposes a tax on the price of admission to view certain films and not on the price of admission to view comparable live performances.

(D) The act imposes a tax solely on the basis of the content of speech without adequate justification and, therefore, it is prohibited by the freedom of speech clause of the First Amendment.

Question 16

A city ordinance makes the city building inspector responsible for ensuring that all buildings in that city are kept up to building code standards, and requires the inspector to refer for prosecution all known building code violations. Another ordinance provides that the city building inspector may be discharged for "good cause." The building inspector took a newspaper reporter through a number of run-down buildings in a slum neighborhood. After using various epithets and slurs to describe the occupants of these buildings, the building inspector stated to the reporter: "I do not even try to get these buildings up to code or to have their owners prosecuted for code violations because if these buildings are repaired, the people who live in them will just wreck them again." The reporter published these statements in a story in the local newspaper. The building inspector admitted he made the statements.

On the basis of these statements, the city council discharged the building inspector.

Is the action of the city council constitutional?

(A) Yes, because the statements demonstrate that the building inspector has an attitude toward a certain class of persons that interferes with the proper performance of the obligations of his job.

(B) Yes, because the building inspector is a government employee and a person holding such a position may not make public comments inconsistent with current governmental policy.

(C) No, because the statements were lawful comments on a matter of public concern.

(D) No, because the statements were published in a newspaper that is protected by the First and Fourteenth Amendments.

Question 17

Insurance is provided in the state of Shoshone only by private companies. Although the state insurance commissioner inspects insurance companies for solvency, the state does not regulate their rates or policies. An insurance company charges higher rates for burglary insurance to residents of one part of a county in Shoshone than to residents of another section of the same county because of the different crime rates in those areas.

Foster is a resident of that county who was charged the higher rate by the insurance company because of the location of her residence. Foster sues the insurance company, alleging that the differential in insurance rates unconstitutionally denies her the equal protection of the laws.

Will Foster's suit succeed?

(A)   Yes, because the higher crime rate in Foster's neighborhood demonstrates that the county police are not giving persons who reside there the equal protection of the laws.

(B)   Yes, because the insurance rate differential is inherently discriminatory.

(C)   No, because the constitutional guarantee of equal protection of the laws is not applicable to the actions of these insurance companies.

(D)   No, because there is a rational basis for the differential in insurance rates.

Question 18

The National AIDS Prevention and Control Act is a new, comprehensive federal statute that was enacted to deal with the public health crisis caused by the AIDS virus. Congress and the President were concerned that inconsistent lower court rulings with respect to the constitutionality, interpretation, and application of the statute might adversely affect or delay its enforcement and, thereby, jeopardize the public health. As a result, they included a provision in the statute providing that all legal challenges concerning those matters may be initiated only by filing suit directly in the United States Supreme Court.

The provision authorizing direct review of the constitutionality, interpretation, or application of this statute only in the United States Supreme Court is

(A)   constitutional, because it is authorized by the Article I power of Congress to enact all laws that are "necessary and proper" to implement the general welfare.

(B)   constitutional, because Article III provides that the jurisdiction of the United States Supreme Court is subject to such exceptions and such regulations as Congress shall make.

(C)   unconstitutional, because it denies persons who wish to challenge this statute the equal protection of the laws by requiring

them to file suit in a court different from that in which persons who wish to challenge other statutes may file suit.

(D)   unconstitutional, because it is inconsistent with the specification in Article III of the original jurisdiction of the United States Supreme Court.

Question 19

In order to provide funds for a system of new major airports near the ten largest cities in the United States, Congress levies a tax of $25 on each airline ticket issued in the United States. The tax applies to every airline ticket, even those for travel that does not originate in, terminate at, or pass through any of those ten large cities.

As applied to the issuance in the United States of an airline ticket for travel between two cities that will not be served by any of the new airports, this tax is

(A)   constitutional, because Congress has broad discretion in choosing the subjects of its taxation and may impose taxes on subjects that have no relation to the purpose for which those tax funds will be expended.

(B)   constitutional, because an exemption for the issuance of tickets for travel between cities that will not be served by the new airports would deny the purchasers of all other tickets the equal protection of the laws.

(C)   unconstitutional, because the burden of the tax outweighs its benefits for passengers whose travel does not originate in, terminate at, or pass through any of the ten largest cities.

(D)   unconstitutional, because the tax adversely affects the fundamental right to travel.

Question 20

To encourage the growth of its population, the state of Axbridge established a program that awarded $1,000 to the parents of each child born within the state, provided that at the time of the child's birth the mother and father of the newborn were citizens of the United States.

The Lills are aliens who are permanent residents of the United States and have resided in Axbridge for three years. When their first child was born two months ago, they applied for and were denied the $1,000 award by Axbridge officials on the sole ground that they are not citizens of the United States. The Lills filed suit in federal court contending that their exclusion from the award program was unconstitutional. Assume no federal statute addresses this question.

In this case, the court should hold that the exclusion of aliens from the Axbridge award program is

(A)   constitutional, because the Tenth Amendment reserves to the states plenary authority over the spending of state funds.

(B)   constitutional, because Axbridge has a legitimate interest in encouraging the growth of its population, and a rational legislature could believe that families in which both parents are United States citizens are more likely to stay in Axbridge and contribute to its future prosperity than those in which one or both of the parents are aliens.

(C)   unconstitutional, because strict scrutiny governs judicial review of such state classifications based on alienage, and Axbridge cannot demonstrate that this classification is necessary to advance a compelling state interest.

(D)   unconstitutional, because state classifications based on alienage are impermissible unless explicitly authorized by an act of Congress.

Question 21

Old City police officers shot and killed Jones's friend as he attempted to escape arrest for an armed robbery he had committed. Jones brought suit in federal district court against the Old City Police Department and the city police officers involved, seeking only a judgment declaring unconstitutional the state statute under which the police acted. That newly enacted statute authorized the police to use deadly force when necessary to apprehend a person who has committed a felony. In his suit, Jones alleged that the police would not have killed his friend if the use of deadly force had not been authorized by the statute.

The federal district court should

(A)   decide the case on its merits, because it raises a substantial federal question.

(B)   dismiss the action, because it involves a nonjusticiable political question.

(C)   dismiss the action, because it does not present a case or controversy.

(D)   dismiss the action, because the Eleventh Amendment prohibits federal courts from deciding cases of this type.

Question 22

Lee contracted with Mover, an interstate carrier, to ship household goods from the state of Green to his new home in the state of Pink. A federal statute provides that all liability of an interstate mover to a shipper for loss of or damage to the shipper's goods in transit is governed exclusively by the contract between them. The statute also requires the mover to offer a shipper at least two contracts with different levels of liability. In full compliance with that federal statute, Mover offered Lee a choice between two shipping agreements that provided different levels of liability on the part of Mover. The more expensive contract provided that Mover was fully liable in case of loss or damage. The less expensive contract limited Mover's liability in case of loss or damage to less than full value. Lee voluntarily signed the less expensive contract with Mover, fixing Mover's liability at less than the full value of the shipment.

Mover's truck was involved in an accident in the state of Pink. The accident was entirely a product of the negligence of Mover's driver. Lee's household goods were totally destroyed. In accordance with the contract, Mover reimbursed Lee for less than the full value of the goods. Lee then brought suit against Mover under the tort law of the state of Pink claiming that he was entitled to be reimbursed for the full value of the goods. Mover filed a motion to dismiss.

In this suit, the court should

(A)   dismiss the case, because the federal statute governing liability of interstate carriers is the supreme law of the land and preempts state tort law.

(B)   dismiss the case, because the contractual relationship between Lee and Mover is governed by the obligation of contracts clause of the Constitution.

(C)   deny the motion to dismiss, because the full faith and credit clause of the Constitution requires that state tort law be given effect.

(D)   deny the motion to dismiss, because it is unconstitutional for a federal statute to authorize Mover to contract out of any degree of liability for its own negligence.

Question 23

Metro City operates a cemetery pursuant to a city ordinance. The ordinance requires the operation of the city cemetery to be supported primarily by revenues derived from the sale of cemetery lots to individuals. The ordinance further provides that the purchase of a cemetery lot entitles the owner to perpetual care of the lot, and entitles the owner to erect on the lot, at the owner's expense, a memorial monument or marker of the owner's choice, subject to certain size restrictions.

The Metro City ordinance requires the city to maintain the cemetery, including mowing the grass, watering flowers, and plowing snow, and provides for the expenditure of city tax funds for such maintenance if revenues from the sale of cemetery lots are insufficient. Although cemetery lots are sold at full fair market value, which includes the current value of perpetual care, the revenue from the sale of such lots has been insufficient in recent years to maintain the cemetery. As a result, a small amount of city tax funds has also been used for that purpose.

A group of Metro City taxpayers brings suit against Metro City challenging the constitutionality of the city ordinance insofar as it permits the owner of a cemetery lot to erect a religious memorial monument or marker on his or her lot.

Is this suit likely to be successful?

(A)   No, because only a small amount of city tax funds has been used to maintain the cemetery.

(B)   No, because the purpose of the ordinance is entirely secular, its primary effect neither advances nor inhibits religion, and it does not foster an excessive government entanglement with religion.

(C)   Yes, because city maintenance of any religious object is a violation of the establishment clause of the First Amendment as incorporated into the Fourteenth Amendment.

(D)   Yes, because no compelling governmental interest justifies authorizing private persons to erect religious monuments or markers in a city-operated cemetery.

Question 24

The School Board of the city of Rulb issued a rule authorizing public school principals to punish, after a hearing, students who engage in violations of the board's student behavior code. According to the rule, violators of the behavior code may be punished in a variety of ways including being required to sit in designated school confinement rooms during all

school hours, with their hands clasped in front of them, for a period of up to 15 school days.

Teddy, a fifth grade student in Rulb Elementary School, was charged with placing chewed bubble gum on a classmate's chair, a violation of the student behavior code. He had never violated the code before and was otherwise an attentive and well-behaved student. After a hearing on the charges, Teddy's principal determined that Teddy had violated the behavior code in the manner charged, and ordered Teddy to spend the next 15 school days in the school confinement room with his hands clasped in front of him.

Teddy's parents file suit in federal court challenging, solely on constitutional grounds, the principal's action in ordering Teddy to spend the next 15 school days in the school confinement room with his hands clasped in front of him.

Which of the following arguments would be most helpful to Teddy's parents in this suit?

(A)   Because the school board rule limits the freedom of movement of students and subjects them to bodily restraint, it denies them a privilege and immunity of citizenship guaranteed them by Article IV, Section 2.

(B)   Because the school board rule is substantially overbroad in relation to any legitimate purpose, it constitutes a facial violation of the equal protection clause of the Fourteenth Amendment.

(C)   Because application of the school board rule in this case denies the student freedom of movement and subjects him to bodily restraint in a manner grossly disproportionate to his offense and circumstances, it violates the due process clause of the Fourteenth Amendment.

(D)   Because the school board rule is enforced initially by administrative rather than judicial proceedings, it constitutes a prohibited bill of attainder.

Question 25

A statute of the state of Illitron declares that after five years of continuous service in their positions all state employees, including faculty members at the state university, are entitled to retain their positions during "good behavior." The statute also contains a number of procedural provisions. Any state employee who is dismissed after that five-year period must be given reasons for the dismissal before it takes effect. In addition, such an employee must, upon request, be granted a post-dismissal hearing before an administrative board to seek reinstatement and back pay. The statute precludes any other hearing or opportunity to respond to the charges. That post-dismissal hearing must occur within six months after the dismissal takes effect. The burden of proof at such a hearing is on the state, and the board may uphold the dismissal only if it is supported by a preponderance of the evidence. An employee who is dissatisfied with a decision of the board after a hearing may appeal its decision to the state courts. The provisions of this statute are inseverable.

A teacher who had been employed continuously for seven years as a faculty member at the state university was dismissed. A week before the dismissal took effect, she was informed that she was being dismissed because of a charge that she accepted a bribe from a student in return for raising the student's final grade in her course. At that time she requested an immediate hearing to contest the propriety of her dismissal.

Three months after her dismissal, she was granted a hearing before the state administrative board. The board upheld her dismissal, finding that the charge against her was supported by a preponderance of the evidence presented at the hearing.

The faculty member did not appeal the decision of the state administrative board to the Illitron state courts. Instead, she sought a declaratory judgment in federal district court to the effect that the state statute prescribing the procedures for her dismissal is unconstitutional.

In this case, the federal district court should

(A)   dismiss the suit, because a claim that a state statute is unconstitutional is not ripe for adjudication by a federal court until all judicial remedies in state courts provided for by state law have been exhausted.

(B)   hold the statute unconstitutional, because the due process clause of the Fourteenth Amendment requires a state to demonstrate beyond a reasonable doubt the facts constituting good cause for termination of a state employee.

(C)   hold the statute unconstitutional, because a state may not ordinarily deprive an employee of a property interest in a job

without giving the employee an opportunity for some kind of a pre-dismissal hearing to respond to the charges against that employee.

(D)   hold the statute constitutional, because the due process clause of the Fourteenth Amendment entitles state employees who have a right to their jobs during good behavior only to a statement of reasons for their dismissal and an opportunity for a post-dismissal hearing.

Question 26

Roberts, a professional motorcycle rider, put on a performance in a privately owned stadium during which he leaped his motorcycle over 21 automobiles. Spectators were charged $5 each to view the jump and were prohibited from using cameras. However, the local television station filmed the whole event from within the stadium without the knowledge or consent of Roberts and showed the film in its entirety on the evening newscast that day. Roberts thereafter brought suit to recover damages from the station for the admittedly unauthorized filming and broadcasting of the act. The television station raised only constitutional defenses.
The court should

(A)   hold against Roberts, because the First and Fourteenth Amendments authorize press coverage of newsworthy entertainment events.

(B)   hold against Roberts, because under the First and Fourteenth Amendments news broadcasts are absolutely privileged.

(C)   find the station liable, because its action deprives Roberts of his property without due process.

(D)   find the station liable, because the First and Fourteenth Amendments do not deprive an entertainer of the commercial value of his or her performances.

Question 27

Congress passed a bill prohibiting the President from granting a pardon to any person who had not served at least one-third of the sentence imposed by the court which convicted that person. The President vetoed the bill, claiming that it was unconstitutional. Nevertheless, Congress passed it over his veto by a two-thirds vote of each house.
This act of Congress is

(A)   constitutional, because it was enacted over the

President's veto by a two-thirds vote of each house.

(B)   constitutional, because it is a necessary and proper means of carrying out the powers of Congress.

(C)   unconstitutional, because it interferes with the plenary power of the President to grant pardons.

(D)   unconstitutional, because a Presidential veto based upon constitutional grounds may be overridden only with the concurrence of three-fourths of the state legislatures.

Question 28

Small retailers located in the state of Yellow are concerned about the loss of business to certain large retailers located nearby in bordering states. In an effort to deal with this concern, the legislature of Yellow enacted a statute requiring all manufacturers and wholesalers who sell goods to retailers in Yellow to do so at prices that are no higher than the lowest prices at which they sell them to retailers in any of the states that border Yellow. Several manufacturers and wholesalers who are located in states bordering Yellow and who sell their goods to retailers in those states and in Yellow bring an action in federal court to challenge the constitutionality of this statute.

Which of the following arguments offered by these plaintiffs is likely to be most persuasive in light of applicable precedent?

The state statute

(A)   deprives them of their property or liberty without due process of law.

(B)   imposes an unreasonable burden on interstate commerce.

(C)   deprives them of a privilege or immunity of national citizenship.

(D)   denies them the equal protection of the laws.

Question 29

A federally owned and operated office building in the state of West Dakota is heated with a new, pollution-free heating system. However, in the coldest season of the year, this new system is sometimes insufficient to supply adequate heat to the building. The appropriation statute providing the money for construction of the new heating system permitted use of the old, pollution-generating system when necessary to supply additional heat. When the old heating

system operates (only about two days in any year), the smokestack of the building emits smoke that exceeds the state of West Dakota's pollution-control standards.

May the operators of the federal office building be prosecuted successfully by West Dakota authorities for violating that state's pollution control standards?

(A)   Yes, because the regulation of pollution is a legitimate state police power concern.

(B)   Yes, because the regulation of pollution is a joint concern of the federal government and the state and, therefore, both of them may regulate conduct causing pollution.

(C)   No, because the operations of the federal government are immune from state regulation in the absence of federal consent.

(D)   No, because the violations of the state pollution-control standards involved here are so *de minimis* that they are beyond the legitimate reach of state law.

Question 30

The state of Erehwon has a statute providing that an unsuccessful candidate in a primary election for a party's nomination for elected public office may not become a candidate for the same office at the following general election by nominating petition or by write-in votes.

Sabel sought her party's nomination for governor in the May primary election. After losing in the primary, Sabel filed nominating petitions containing the requisite number of signatures to become a candidate for the office of governor in the following general election. The chief elections officer of Erehwon refused to certify Sabel's petitions solely because of the above statute. Sabel then filed suit in federal district court challenging the constitutionality of this Erehwon statute.

As a matter of constitutional law, which of the following is the proper burden of persuasion in this suit?

(A)   Sabel must demonstrate that the statute is not necessary to achieve a compelling state interest.

(B)   Sabel must demonstrate that the statute is not rationally related to a legitimate state interest.

(C)   The state must demonstrate that the statute is the least restrictive means of achieving a compelling state interest.

(D) The state must demonstrate that the statute is rationally related to a legitimate state interest.

Question 31

A statute of the state of East Dakota requires each insurance company that offers burglary insurance policies in the state to charge a uniform rate for such insurance to all of its customers residing within the same county in that state. So long as it complies with this requirement, a company is free to charge whatever rate the market will bear for its burglary insurance policies.

An insurance company located in the state of East Dakota files suit in federal district court against appropriate East Dakota state officials to challenge this statute on constitutional grounds. The insurance company wishes to charge customers residing within the same county in East Dakota rates for burglary insurance policies that will vary because they would be based on the specific nature of the customer's business, on its precise location, and on its past claims record.

In this suit, the court should

(A) hold the statute unconstitutional, because the statute deprives the insurance company of its liberty or property without due process of law.

(B) hold the statute unconstitutional, because the statute imposes an undue burden on interstate commerce.

(C) hold the statute constitutional, because the statute is a reasonable exercise of the state's police power.

(D) abstain from ruling on the merits of this case until the state courts have had an opportunity to pass on the constitutionality of this state statute.

Question 32

Widgets are manufactured wholly from raw materials mined and processed in the state of Green. The only two manufacturers of widgets in the United States are also located in that state. However, their widgets are purchased by retailers located in every state. The legislature of the state of Green is considering the adoption of a statute that would impose a tax solely on the manufacture of widgets. The tax is to be calculated at 3% of their wholesale value.

Which of the following arguments would be LEAST helpful to the state in defending the constitutionality of this proposed state tax on widgets?

(A) At the time widgets are manufactured and taxed they have not yet entered the channels of interstate commerce.

(B) The economic impact of this tax will be passed on to both in-state and out-of-state purchasers of widgets and, therefore, it is wholly nondiscriminatory in its effect.

(C) Because of the powers reserved to them by the Tenth Amendment, states have plenary authority to construct their tax system in any manner they choose.

(D) A tax on the manufacture of widgets may be imposed only by the state in which the manufacturing occurs and, therefore, it is not likely to create the danger of a multiple tax burden on interstate commerce.

Question 33

Twenty percent of the residents of Green City are members of minority racial groups. These residents are evenly distributed among the many different residential areas of the city. The five city council members of Green City are elected from five single-member electoral districts that are nearly equally populated. No candidate has ever been elected to the city council who was a member of a minority racial group.

A group of citizens who are members of minority racial groups file suit in federal district court seeking a declaratory judgment that the single-member districts in Green City are unconstitutional. They claim that the single-member districting system in that city diminishes the ability of voters who are members of minority racial groups to affect the outcome of city elections. They seek an order from the court forcing the city to adopt an at-large election system in which the five candidates with the greatest vote totals would be elected to the city council. No state or federal statutes are applicable to the resolution of this suit.

Which of the following constitutional provisions provides the most obvious basis for plaintiffs' claim in this suit?

(A) The Thirteenth Amendment.

(B) The due process clause of the Fourteenth Amendment.

(C) The privileges and immunities clause of the Fourteenth Amendment.

(D) The Fifteenth Amendment.

Question 34

The Sports Championship Revenue Enhancement Act is a federal statute that was enacted as part of a comprehensive program to eliminate the federal budget deficit. That act imposed, for a period of five years, a 50% excise tax on the price of tickets to championship sporting events. Such events included the World Series, the Super Bowl, major college bowl games, and similar championship sports events.

This federal tax is probably

(A) constitutional, because the compelling national interest in reducing the federal budget deficit justifies this tax as a temporary emergency measure.
(B) constitutional, because an act of Congress that appears to be a revenue raising measure on its face is not rendered invalid because it may have adverse economic consequences for the activity taxed.
(C) unconstitutional, because a 50% tax is likely to reduce attendance at championship sporting events and, therefore, is not rationally related to the legitimate interest of Congress in eliminating the budget deficit.
(D) unconstitutional, because Congress violates the equal protection component of the Fifth Amendment by singling out championship sporting events for this tax while failing to tax other major sporting, artistic, or entertainment events to which tickets are sold.

Question 35

The Federal Computer Abuse Act establishes the Federal Computer Abuse Commission, authorizes the Commission to issue licenses for the possession of computers on terms that are consistent with the purposes of the act, and makes the unlicensed possession of a computer a crime. The provisions of the Federal Computer Abuse Act are inseverable.

User applied to the Federal Computer Abuse Commission for a license to possess a computer. The Commission held, and User participated in, a trial-type proceeding on User's license application. In that proceeding it was demonstrated that User repeatedly and intentionally used computers to introduce secret destructive computer programs (computer viruses) into electronic data banks without the consent of their owners. As a result, the Commission denied User's application for a license. The license denial was based on a Commission rule authorized by the Computer Abuse Act that prohibited the issuance of computer licenses to persons who had engaged in such conduct. Nevertheless, User retained and continued to use his computer. He was subsequently convicted of the crime of unlicensed possession of a computer. On appeal, he challenges the constitutionality of the licensing provision of the Federal Computer Abuse Act.

In this case, the reviewing court would probably hold that act to be

(A) constitutional, because the Constitution generally authorizes Congress to enact all laws that are necessary and proper to advance the general welfare, and Congress could reasonably believe that possession of computers by people like User constitutes a threat to the general welfare.
(B) constitutional, because Congress may use the authority vested in it by the commerce clause to regulate the possession of computers and the provisions of this act do not violate any prohibitory provision of the Constitution.
(C) unconstitutional, because Congress may not impose a criminal penalty on action that is improper only because it is inconsistent with an agency rule.
(D) unconstitutional, because the mere possession of a computer is a wholly local matter that is beyond the regulatory authority of Congress.

Question 36

The United States Department of Energy regularly transports nuclear materials through Centerville on the way to a nuclear weapons processing plant it operates in a nearby state. The city of Centerville recently adopted an ordinance prohibiting the transportation of any nuclear materials in or through the city. The ordinance declares that its purpose is to protect the health and safety of the residents of that city.

May the Department of Energy continue to transport these nuclear materials through the city of Centerville?

(A) No, because the ordinance is rationally related to the public health and safety of Centerville residents.
(B) No, because the Tenth Amendment reserves to the states certain unenumerated sovereign powers.
(C) Yes, because the Department of Energy is a federal agency engaged in a lawful federal

function and, therefore, its activities may not be regulated by a local government without the consent of Congress.

(D) Yes, because the ordinance enacted by Centerville is invalid because it denies persons transporting such materials the equal protection of the laws.

Question 37

The legislature of the state of Chetopah enacted a statute requiring that all law enforcement officers in that state be citizens of the United States. Alien, lawfully admitted to permanent residency five years before the enactment of this statute, sought employment as a forensic pathologist in the Chetopah coroner's office. He was denied such a job solely because he was not a citizen.

Alien thereupon brought suit in federal district court against appropriate Chetopah officials seeking to invalidate this citizenship requirement on federal constitutional grounds.

The strongest ground upon which to attack this citizenship requirement is that it

(A) constitutes an *ex post facto* law as to previously admitted aliens.
(B) deprives an alien of a fundamental right to employment without the due process of law guaranteed by the Fourteenth Amendment.
(C) denies an alien a right to employment in violation of the privileges and immunities clause of the Fourteenth Amendment.
(D) denies an alien the equal protection of the laws guaranteed by the Fourteenth Amendment.

Question 38

The open-air amphitheater in the city park of Rightville has been utilized for concerts and other entertainment programs. Until this year, each of the groups performing in that city facility was allowed to make its own arrangements for sound equipment and sound technicians.

After recurring complaints from occupants of residential buildings adjacent to the city park about intrusive noise from some performances held in the amphitheater, the Rightville City Council passed an ordinance establishing city control over all sound amplification at all programs held there. The ordinance provided that Rightville's Department of Parks would be the sole provider in the amphitheater of sound amplification equipment and of the

technicians to operate the equipment "to ensure a proper balance between the quality of the sound at such performances and respect for the privacy of nearby residential neighbors."

Which of the following standards should a court use to determine the constitutionality on its face of this content neutral ordinance?

(A) The ordinance is narrowly tailored to serve a substantial government interest, and does not unreasonably limit alternative avenues of expression.
(B) The ordinance is rationally related to a legitimate government interest, and does not unreasonably limit alternative avenues of expression.
(C) The ordinance is rationally related to a legitimate government interest and restricts the expressive rights involved no more than is reasonable under the circumstances.
(D) The ordinance is substantially related to a legitimate governmental interest and restricts the expressive rights involved no more than is reasonable in light of the surrounding circumstances.

Question 39

The state of Orrington wanted to prevent its only major league baseball team, the privately owned and operated Orrington Opossums, from moving to the rival state of Atrium. After a heated political debate in the legislature, Orrington enacted legislation providing for a one-time grant of $10 million in state funds to the Opossums to cover part of the projected income losses the team would suffer during the next five years if it remained in that state. The legislation required that the team remain in the state for at least ten years if it accepted the grant.

After accepting the grant, the owners of the Opossums decided to build a new $150 million stadium in Orrington. As plans for the construction of the new stadium proceeded, it became evident that all of the contractors and subcontractors would be white males, and that they had been chosen by the owners of the Opossums without any public bids because these contractors and subcontractors had successfully built the only other new baseball stadium in the region. Several contractors who were females or members of minority racial groups filed suit against the owners of the Opossums in federal district court to compel public solicitation of bids for the construction of its new stadium on an equal opportunity basis, and to enjoin construction of the stadium until compliance was ensured. Their only claim was that the contracting practices of the owners of the Opossums denied them the equal protection of the laws in violation of the Fourteenth Amendment.

In this suit, the court will probably rule that

(A) the nexus between the actions of the owners of the Opossums and the one-time grant of monies to them by the state is sufficiently substantial to subject their actions to the limitations of the Fourteenth Amendment.

(B) the intense public preoccupation with the activities of major league baseball teams coupled with the fact that baseball is considered to be our national pastime is sufficient to justify application of the Fourteenth Amendment to the activities of major league teams.

(C) in the absence of additional evidence of state involvement in the operations or decisions of the owners of the Opossums, a onetime grant of state monies to them is insufficient to warrant treating their actions as subject to the limitations of the Fourteenth Amendment.

(D) the issues presented by this case are nonjusticiable political questions because there is a lack of judicially manageable standards to resolve them and they are likely to be deeply involved in partisan politics.

Question 40

In response to massive layoffs of employees of automobile assembly plants located in the state of Ames, the legislature of that state enacted a statute which prohibits the parking of automobiles manufactured outside of the United States in any parking lot or parking structure that is owned or operated by the state or any of its instrumentalities. This statute does not apply to parking on public streets.

Which of the following is the strongest argument with which to challenge the constitutionality of this statute?

(A) The statute imposes an undue burden on foreign commerce.

(B) The statute denies the owners of foreign-made automobiles the equal protection of the laws.

(C) The statute deprives the owners of foreign-made automobiles of liberty or property without due process of law.

(D) The statute is inconsistent with the privileges and immunities clause of the Fourteenth Amendment.

Question 41

The National Ecological Balance Act prohibits the destruction or removal of any wild animals located on lands owned by the United States without express permission from the Federal Bureau of Land Management. Violators are subject to fines of up to $1,000 per offense.

After substantial property damage was inflicted on residents of the state of Arkota by hungry coyotes, the state legislature passed the Coyote Bounty Bill, which offers $25 for each coyote killed or captured within the state. The Kota National Forest, owned by the federal government, is located entirely within the state of Arkota. Many coyotes live in the Kota National Forest.

Without seeking permission from the Bureau of Land Management, Hunter shot several coyotes in the Kota National Forest and collected the bounty from the state of Arkota. As a result, he was subsequently tried in federal district court, convicted, and fined $1,000 for violating the National Ecological Balance Act. Hunter appealed his conviction to the United States Court of Appeals.

On appeal, the Court of Appeals should hold the National Ecological Balance Act, as applied to Hunter, to be

(A) constitutional, because the property clause of Article IV, Section 3, of the Constitution authorizes such federal statutory controls and sanctions.

(B) constitutional, because Article I, Section 8, of the Constitution authorizes Congress to enact all laws necessary and proper to advance the general welfare.

(C) unconstitutional, because Congress may not use its delegated powers to override the Tenth Amendment right of the state of Arkota to legislate in areas of traditional state governmental functions, such as the protection of the property of its residents.

(D) unconstitutional, because Congress violates the full faith and credit clause of Article IV when it punishes conduct that has been authorized by state action.

Question 42

A law of the state of Wonatol imposed a generally applicable sales tax payable by the vendor. That law exempted from its provisions the sale of "all magazines, periodicals, newspapers, and books." In order to raise additional revenue, the state legislature eliminated that broad exemption and substituted a narrower exemption. The new, narrower exemption excluded from the state sales tax only the sale of those "magazines, periodicals, newspapers, and books that are published or distributed by a recognized religious faith and that consist wholly of writings sacred to such a religious faith."

Magazine is a monthly publication devoted to history and politics. Magazine paid under protest the sales tax due on its sales according to the amended sales tax law. Magazine then filed suit against the state in an appropriate state court for a refund of the sales taxes paid. It contended that the state's elimination of the earlier, broader exemption and adoption of the new, narrower exemption restricted to sacred writings of recognized religious faiths violates the First and Fourteenth Amendments to the Constitution.

In this case, the court will probably rule that

(A) Magazine lacks standing to sue for a refund of sales taxes imposed by a generally applicable state law because Article III of the Constitution precludes taxpayers from bringing such suits.
(B) the Eleventh Amendment bars the state court from exercising jurisdiction over this suit in the absence of a law of Wonatol expressly waiving the state's immunity.
(C) the new, narrower exemption from the state sales tax law violates the establishment clause of the First and Fourteenth Amendments by granting preferential state support to recognized religious faiths for the communication of their religious beliefs.
(D) the new, narrower exemption from the state sales tax law violates the freedom of the press guaranteed by the First and Fourteenth Amendments because it imposes a prior restraint on nonreligious publications that are required to pay the tax.

Question 43

A statute of the state of Kiowa provided state monetary grants to private dance, theater, and opera groups located in that state. The statute required recipients of such grants to use the granted monies for the acquisition, construction, and maintenance of appropriate facilities for the public performance of their performing arts. The last section of the statute conditioned the award of each such grant on the recipient's agreement to refrain from all kinds of political lobbying calculated to secure additional tax support for the performing arts.

The strongest constitutional basis for an attack upon the validity of the last section of the statute would be based upon the

(A) commerce clause.
(B) obligation of contracts clause.
(C) Fifth Amendment.
(D) First and Fourteenth Amendments.

Question 44

Assume that Congress passed and the President signed the following statute:

"The appellate jurisdiction of the United States Supreme Court shall not extend to any case involving the constitutionality of any state statute limiting the circumstances in which a woman may obtain an abortion, or involving the constitutionality of this statute."

The strongest argument against the constitutionality of this statute is that

(A) Congress may not exercise its authority over the appellate jurisdiction of the Supreme Court in a way that seriously interferes with the establishment of a supreme and uniform body of federal constitutional law.
(B) Congress may only regulate the appellate jurisdiction of the Supreme Court over cases initially arising in federal courts.
(C) the appellate jurisdiction of the Supreme Court may only be altered by constitutional amendment.
(D) the statute violates the equal protection clause of the Fourteenth Amendment.

Question 45

The federal statute admitting the state of Blue to the Union granted Blue certain public lands, and established some very ambiguous conditions on the subsequent disposition of these lands by Blue. This federal statute also required the new state to write those exact same conditions into its state constitution. One hundred years later, a statute of Blue dealing with the sale of these public lands was challenged in a state court lawsuit on the ground that it was inconsistent with the conditions contained in the federal statute, and with the provisions of the Blue Constitution that exactly copy the conditions contained in the federal statute. The trial court decision in this case was appealed to the Blue Supreme Court. In its opinion, the Blue Supreme

Court dealt at length with the ambiguous language of the federal statute and with cases interpreting identical language in federal statutes admitting other states to the union. The Blue Supreme Court opinion did not discuss the similar provisions of the Blue Constitution, but it did hold that the challenged Blue statute is invalid because it is "inconsistent with the language of the federal statute and therefore is inconsistent with the identical provisions of our state constitution."

If the losing party in the Blue Supreme Court seeks review of the decision of that court in the United States Supreme Court, the United States Supreme Court should

(A) accept the case for review and determine the validity and interpretation of the federal statute if it is an important and substantial question.
(B) ask the Blue Supreme Court to indicate more clearly whether it relied on the state constitutional provision in rendering its decision.
(C) decline to review the case on the ground that the decision of the Blue Supreme Court rests on an adequate and independent state ground.
(D) decline to review the case because a decision by a state supreme court concerning the proper disposition of state public lands is not reviewable by the United States Supreme Court.

Question 46

A proposed federal statute would prohibit all types of discrimination against black persons on the basis of their race in every business transaction executed anywhere in the United States by any person or entity, governmental or private.

Is this proposed federal statute likely to be constitutional?

(A) Yes, because it could reasonably be viewed as an exercise of Congress's authority to enact laws for the general welfare.
(B) Yes, because it could reasonably be viewed as a means of enforcing the provisions of the Thirteenth Amendment.
(C) No, because it would regulate purely local transactions that are not in interstate commerce.
(D) No, because it would invade the powers reserved to the states by the Tenth Amendment.

Question 47

Members of a religious group calling itself the Friends of Lucifer believe in Lucifer as their

Supreme Being. The members of this group meet once a year on top of Mt. Snow, located in a U.S. National Park, to hold an overnight encampment and a midnight dance around a large campfire. They believe this overnight encampment and all of its rituals are required by Lucifer to be held on the top of Mt. Snow. U.S. National Park Service rules that have been consistently enforced prohibit all overnight camping and all campfires on Mt. Snow because of the very great dangers overnight camping and campfires would pose in that particular location. As a result, the park Superintendent denied a request by the Friends of Lucifer for a permit to conduct these activities on top of Mt. Snow. The park Superintendent, who was known to be violently opposed to cults and other unconventional groups had, in the past, issued permits to conventional religious groups to conduct sunrise services in other areas of that U.S. National Park.

The Friends of Lucifer brought suit in Federal Court against the U.S. National Park Service and the Superintendent of the park to compel issuance of the requested permit.

As a matter of constitutional law, the most appropriate result in this suit would be a decision that denial of the permit was

(A) invalid, because the free exercise clause of the First Amendment prohibits the Park Service from knowingly interfering with religious conduct.
(B) invalid, because these facts demonstrate that the action of the Park Service purposefully and invidiously discriminated against the Friends of Lucifer.
(C) valid, because the establishment clause of the First Amendment prohibits the holding of religious ceremonies on federal land.
(D) valid, because religiously motivated conduct may be subjected to nondiscriminatory time, place, and manner restrictions that advance important public interests.

Question 48

The Personnel Handbook of Green City contains all of that city's personnel policies. One section of the handbook states that "where feasible and practicable supervisors are encouraged to follow the procedures specified in this Handbook before discharging a city employee." Those specified procedures include a communication to the employee of the reasons for the contemplated discharge and an opportunity for a pre-termination trial-type hearing at which the employee may challenge those reasons. After a year of service, Baker, the secretary to the Green City Council, was discharged without receiving any communication of reasons for her contemplated discharge and without receiving an opportunity for a pre-termination trial-type hearing. Baker files suit in federal district court to challenge her discharge solely on constitutional grounds.

Which of the following best describes the initial burden of persuasion in that suit?

(A) The Green City Council must demonstrate that its personnel handbook created no constitutionally protected interest in city employment or in the procedures by which such employment is terminated.

(B) The Green City Council must demonstrate that Baker's termination was for good cause.

(C) Baker must demonstrate that state law creates a constitutionally protected interest in her employment or in the procedures by which her employment is terminated.

(D) Baker must demonstrate that she reasonably believed that she could work for Green City for as long as she wished.

Question 49

Terrorists in the foreign country of Ruritania kidnapped the United States ambassador to that country. They threatened to kill her unless the President of the United States secured the release of an identified person who was a citizen of Ruritania and was held in a prison of the state of Aurora in the United States pursuant to a valid conviction by that state.

The President responded by entering into an agreement with Ruritania which provided that Ruritania would secure the release of the United States ambassador on a specified date in return for action by the President that would secure the release of the identified person held in the Aurora prison. The President then ordered the governor of Aurora to release the prisoner in question. The governor refused. No federal statutes are applicable.

Which of the following is the strongest constitutional argument for the authority of the President to take action in these circumstances requiring the governor of Aurora to release the Aurora prisoner?

(A) The power of the President to conduct the foreign affairs of the United States includes a plenary authority to take whatever action the

President deems wise to protect the safety of our diplomatic agents.

(B) The power of the President to appoint ambassadors authorizes him to take any action that he may think desirable to protect them from injury because, upon appointment, those officials become agents of the President.

(C) The power of the President to negotiate with foreign nations impliedly authorizes the President to make executive agreements with them which prevail over state law.

(D) The duty of the President to execute faithfully the laws authorizes him to resolve finally any conflicts between state and federal interests, making the determination of such matters wholly nonjusticiable.

Question 50

A newly enacted federal statute appropriates $100 million in federal funds to support basic research by universities located in the United States. The statute provides that "the ten best universities in the United States" will each receive $10 million. It also provides that "the ten best universities" shall be "determined by a poll of the presidents of all the universities in the nation, to be conducted by the United States Department of Education." In responding to that poll, each university president is required to apply the well-recognized and generally accepted standards of academic quality that are specified in the statute. The provisions of the statute are inseverable.

Which of the following statements about this statute is correct?

(A) The statute is unconstitutional, because the reliance by Congress on a poll of individuals who are not federal officials to determine the recipients of its appropriated funds is an unconstitutional delegation of legislative power.

(B) The statute is unconstitutional, because the limitation on recipients to the ten best universities is arbitrary and capricious and denies other high quality universities the equal protection of the laws.

(C) The statute is constitutional, because Congress has plenary authority to determine the objects of its spending and the methods used to achieve them, so long as they may reasonably be deemed to serve the general welfare and do not violate any prohibitory language in the Constitution.

(D) The validity of the statute is nonjusticiable, because the use by Congress of its spending power necessarily involves political considerations that must be resolved finally by those branches of the government that are closest to the political process.

Question 51

The state of Atlantica spends several million dollars a year on an oyster conservation program. As part of that program, the state limits, by statute, oyster fishing in its coastal waters to persons who have state oyster permits. In order to promote conservation, it issues only a limited number of oyster permits each year. The permits are effective for only one year from the date of their issuance and are awarded on the basis of a lottery, in which there is no differentiation between resident and nonresident applicants. However, each nonresident who obtains a permit is charged an annual permit fee that is $5 more than the fee charged residents.

Fisher, Inc., is a large fishing company that operates from a port in another state and is incorporated in that other state. Each of the boats of Fisher, Inc., has a federal shipping license that permits it "to engage in all aspects of the coastal trade, to fish and to carry cargo from place to place along the coast, and to engage in other lawful activities along the coast of the United States." These shipping licenses are authorized by federal statute. Assume no other federal statutes or administrative rules apply.

Although it had previously held an Atlantica oyster permit, Fisher, Inc., did not obtain a permit in that state's lottery this year.

Which of the following is the strongest argument that can be made in support of a continued right of Fisher, Inc., to fish for oysters this year in the coastal waters of Atlantica?

(A) Because the Atlantica law provides higher permit charges for nonresidents, it is an undue burden on interstate commerce.
(B) Because the Atlantica law provides higher permit charges for nonresidents, it denies Fisher, Inc., the privileges and immunities of state citizenship.
(C) Because it holds a federal shipping license, Fisher, Inc., has a right to fish for oysters in Atlantica waters despite the state law.
(D) Because Fisher, Inc., previously held an Atlantica oyster permit and Atlantica knows that company is engaged in a continuing business operation, the refusal to grant Fisher, Inc., a permit this year is a taking of its property without due process of law.

Question 52

The United States Department of the Interior granted Concessionaire the food and drink concession in a federal park located in the state of New Senora. Concessionaire operated his concession out of federally owned facilities in the park. The federal statute authorizing the Interior Department to grant such concessions provided that the grantees would pay only a nominal rental for use of these federal facilities because of the great benefit their concessions would provide to the people of the United States.

The legislature of the state of New Senora enacted a statute imposing an occupancy tax on the occupants of real estate within that state that is not subject to state real estate taxes. The statute was intended to equalize the state tax burden on such occupants with that on people occupying real estate that is subject to state real estate taxes. Pursuant to that statute, the New Senora Department of Revenue attempted to collect the state occupancy tax from Concessionaire because the federal facilities occupied by Concessionaire were not subject to state real estate taxes. Concessionaire sued to invalidate the state occupancy tax as applied to him.

The strongest ground upon which Concessionaire could challenge the occupancy tax is that it violates the

(A) commerce clause by unduly burdening the interstate tourist trade.
(B) privileges and immunities clause of the Fourteenth Amendment by interfering with the fundamental right to do business on federal property.
(C) equal protection of the laws clause of the Fourteenth Amendment because the tax treats him less favorably than federal concessionaires in other states who do not have to pay such occupancy taxes.
(D) supremacy clause of Article VI and the federal statute authorizing such concessions.

Question 53

An ordinance of the city of Green requires that its mayor must have been continuously a resident of the city for at least five years at the time he or she takes office. Candidate, who is thinking about running for mayor in an election that will take place next year, will have been a resident of Green for only four and one-half years at the time the mayor elected then takes office. Before he decides whether to run for the position of mayor, Candidate wants to know whether he could lawfully assume that position if he were elected. As a result, Candidate files suit in the local federal district court for a declaratory judgment that the Green five-year-residence requirement is unconstitutional and that he is entitled to a place on his political party's primary election ballot for mayor. He names the chairman of his political party as the sole defendant but does not join any election official. The chairman responds by joining Candidate in requesting the court to declare the Green residence requirement invalid.

In this case, the court should

(A) refuse to determine the merits of this suit, because there is no case or controversy.
(B) refuse to issue such a declaratory judgment, because an issue of this kind involving only a local election does not present a substantial federal constitutional question.
(C) issue the declaratory judgment, because a residency requirement of this type is a denial of the equal protection of the laws.
(D) issue the declaratory judgment, because Candidate will have substantially complied with the residency requirement.

Question 54

Big City High School has had a very high rate of pregnancy among its students. In order to assist students who keep their babies to complete high school, Big City High School has established an infant day-care center for children of its students, and also offers classes in child-care. Because the child-care classes are always overcrowded, the school limits admission to those classes solely to Big City High School students who are the mothers of babies in the infant day-care center.

Joe, a student at Big City High School, has legal custody of his infant son. The school provides care for his son in its infant day-care center, but will not allow Joe to enroll in the child-care classes. He brings suit against the school challenging, on constitutional grounds, his exclusion from the child-care classes.

Which of the following best states the burden of persuasion in this case?

(A) Joe must demonstrate that the admission requirement is not rationally related to a legitimate governmental interest.
(B) Joe must demonstrate that the admission

requirement is not as narrowly drawn as possible to achieve a substantial governmental interest.
(C) The school must demonstrate that the admission policy is the least restrictive means by which to achieve a compelling governmental interest.
(D) The school must demonstrate that the admission policy is substantially related to an important governmental interest.

Question 55

A statute of the state of Wasminia prohibits the use of state-owned or state-operated facilities for the performance of abortions that are not "necessary to save the life of the mother." That statute also prohibits state employees from performing any such abortions during the hours they are employed by the state.

Citizen was in her second month of pregnancy. She sought an abortion at the Wasminia State Hospital, a state-owned and state-operated facility. Citizen did not claim that the requested abortion was necessary to save her life. The officials in charge of the hospital refused to perform the requested abortion solely on the basis of the state statute. Citizen immediately filed suit against those officials in an appropriate federal district court. She challenged the constitutionality of the Wasminia statute and requested the court to order the hospital to perform the abortion she sought.

In this case, the court will probably hold that the Wasminia statute is

(A) unconstitutional, because a limit on the availability of abortions performed by state employees or in state-owned or state-operated facilities to situations in which it is necessary to save the life of the mother impermissibly interferes with the fundamental right of Citizen to decide whether to have a child.
(B) unconstitutional, because it impermissibly discriminates against poor persons who cannot afford to pay for abortions in privately owned and operated facilities and against persons who live far away from privately owned and operated abortion clinics.
(C) constitutional, because it does not prohibit a woman from having an abortion or penalize her for doing so, it is rationally related to the legitimate governmental goal of encouraging childbirth, and it does not interfere with the voluntary performance of abortions by private physicians in private facilities.
(D) constitutional, because the use of state-owned or

state-operated facilities and access to the services of state employees are privileges and not rights and, therefore, a state may condition them on any basis it chooses.

Question 56

Radon is a harmful gas found in the soil of certain regions of the United States. A statute of the state of Magenta requires occupants of residences with basements susceptible to the intrusion of radon to have their residences tested for the presence of radon and to take specified remedial steps if the test indicates the presence of radon above specified levels. The statute also provides that the testing for radon may be done only by testers licensed by a state agency. According to the statute, a firm may be licensed to test for radon only if it meets specified rigorous standards relating to the accuracy of its testing. These standards may easily be achieved with current technology; but the technology required to meet them is 50% more expensive than the technology required to measure radon accumulations in a slightly less accurate manner.

The United States Environmental Protection Agency (EPA) does not license radon testers. However, a federal statute authorizes the EPA to advise on the accuracy of various methods of radon testing and to provide to the general public a list of testers that use methods it believes to be reasonably accurate.

WeTest, a recently established Magenta firm, uses a testing method that the EPA has stated is reasonably accurate. WeTest is also included by the EPA on the list of testers using methods of testing it believes to be reasonably accurate. WeTest applies for a Magenta radon testing license, but its application is denied because WeTest cannot demonstrate that the method of testing for radon it uses is sufficiently accurate to meet the rigorous Magenta statutory standards. WeTest sues appropriate Magenta officials in federal court claiming that Magenta may not constitutionally exclude WeTest from performing the required radon tests in Magenta.

In this suit, the court will probably rule in favor of

(A) WeTest, because the full faith and credit clause of the Constitution requires Magenta to respect and give effect to the action of the EPA in including WeTest on its list of testers that use reasonably accurate methods.

(B) WeTest, because the supremacy clause of the Constitution requires Magenta to respect and give effect to the action of the EPA in including

WeTest on its list of testers that use reasonably accurate methods.

(C) Magenta, because the federal statute and the action of the EPA in including WeTest on its list of testers that use reasonably accurate methods are not inconsistent with the more rigorous Magenta licensing requirement, and that requirement is reasonably related to a legitimate public interest.

(D) Magenta, because radon exposure is limited to basement areas, which, by their very nature, cannot move in interstate commerce.

Question 57

The legislature of the state of Gray recently enacted a statute forbidding public utilities regulated by the Gray Public Service Commission to increase their rates more than once every two years. Economy Electric Power Company, a public utility regulated by that commission, has just obtained approval of the commission for a general rate increase. Economy Electric has routinely filed for a rate increase every ten to 14 months during the last 20 years. Because of uncertainties about future fuel prices, the power company cannot ascertain with any certainty the date when it will need a further rate increase; but it thinks it may need such an increase sometime within the next 18 months.

Economy Electric files an action in the federal district court in Gray requesting a declaratory judgment that this new statute of Gray forbidding public utility rate increases more often than once every two years is unconstitutional. Assume no federal statute is relevant.

In this case, the court should

(A) hold the statute unconstitutional, because such a moratorium on rate increases deprives utilities of their property without due process of law.

(B) hold the statute constitutional, because the judgment of a legislature on a matter involving economic regulation is entitled to great deference.

(C) dismiss the complaint, because this action is not ripe for decision.

(D) dismiss the complaint, because controversies over state-regulated utility rates are outside of the jurisdiction conferred on federal courts by Article III of the Constitution.

Question 58

Clerk is a clerical worker who has been employed for the past two years in a permanent position in the Wasmania County Public Records Office in the state of Orange. Clerk has been responsible for copying and filing records of real estate transactions in that office. Clerk works in a nonpublic part of the office and has no contact with members of the public. However, state law provides that all real estate records in that office are to be made available for public inspection.

On the day an attempted assassination of the governor of Orange was reported on the radio, Clerk remarked to a coworker, "Our governor is such an evil man, I am sorry they did not get him." Clerk's coworker reported this remark to Clerk's employer, the county recorder. After Clerk admitted making the remark, the county recorder dismissed him stating that "there is no room in this office for a person who hates the governor so much."

Clerk sued for reinstatement and back pay. His only claim is that the dismissal violated his constitutional rights.

In this case, the court should hold that the county recorder's dismissal of Clerk was

(A) unconstitutional, because it constitutes a taking without just compensation of Clerk's property interest in his permanent position with the county.
(B) unconstitutional, because in light of Clerk's particular employment duties his right to express himself on a matter of public concern outweighed any legitimate interest the state might have had in discharging him.
(C) constitutional, because the compelling interest of the state in having loyal and supportive employees outweighs the interest of any state employee in his or her job or in free speech on a matter of public concern.
(D) nonjusticiable, because public employment is a privilege rather than a right and, therefore, Clerk lacked standing to bring this suit.

Question 59

Maple City has an ordinance that prohibits the location of "adult theaters and bookstores" (theaters and bookstores presenting sexually explicit performances or materials) in residential or commercial zones within the city. The ordinance was intended to protect surrounding property from the likely adverse secondary effects of such establishments. "Adult theaters and bookstores" are freely permitted in the areas of the city zoned industrial, where those adverse secondary effects are not as likely. Storekeeper is denied a zoning permit to open an adult theater and bookstore in a building owned by him in an area zoned commercial. As a result, Storekeeper brings suit in an appropriate court challenging the constitutionality of the zoning ordinance.

Which of the following statements regarding the constitutionality of this Maple City ordinance is most accurate?

(A) The ordinance is valid, because a city may enforce zoning restrictions on speech-related businesses to ensure that the messages they disseminate are acceptable to the residents of adjacent property.
(B) The ordinance is valid, because a city may enforce this type of time, place, and manner regulation on speech-related businesses, so long as this type of regulation is designed to serve a substantial governmental interest and does not unreasonably limit alternative avenues of communication.
(C) The ordinance is invalid, because a city may not enforce zoning regulations that deprive potential operators of adult theaters and bookstores of their freedom to choose the location of their businesses.
(D) The ordinance is invalid, because a city may not zone property in a manner calculated to protect property from the likely adverse secondary effects of adult theaters and bookstores.

Question 60

A statute of the state of Orrington provides that assessments of real property for tax purposes must represent the "actual value" of the property. The Blue County Tax Commission, in making its assessments, has uniformly and consistently determined the "actual value" of real property solely by reference to the price at which the particular property was last sold. In recent years, the market values of real property in Blue County have been rising at the rate of 15% per year.

Owner is required to pay real estate taxes on her home in Blue County that are 200% to 300% higher than those paid by many other owners of similar homes in similar neighborhoods in that county, even though the current market values of their respective homes and Owner's home are nearly identical. The reason the taxes on Owner's home are higher than those imposed on the other similar homes in similar neighborhoods is that she bought her home much more recently than the other owners and, therefore, it is assessed at a much higher "actual value" than their homes. Persistent efforts by Owner to have her assessment reduced or the assessments of the others raised by the Blue County Tax Commission have failed.

Owner has now filed suit against the Blue County Tax Commission, charging only that the tax assessment on her property is unconstitutional.

The strongest constitutional argument to support Owner's claim is that the comparative overvaluation of Owner's property by the Blue County Tax Commission in making tax assessments over time

(A) deprives Owner of the equal protection of the laws.
(B) deprives Owner of a privilege or immunity of national citizenship.
(C) constitutes a taking of private property for public use without just compensation.
(D) constitutes an *ex post facto* law.

Questions 61-64 are based on the following fact situation.

The State of Aurora requires licenses of persons "who are engaged in the trade of barbering." It will grant such licenses only to those who are graduates of barber schools located in Aurora, who have resided in the state for two years, and who are citizens of the United States.

Question 61

The requirement that candidates for license must be graduates of barber schools in Aurora is probably

(A) unconstitutional as an undue burden on interstate commerce.
(B) unconstitutional as a violation of the privileges and immunities clause of the Fourteenth Amendment.
(C) constitutional, because the state does not know the quality of out-of-state barber schools.
(D) constitutional, because barbering is a privilege and not a right.

Question 62

The requirement that candidates for licenses must be citizens is

(A) constitutional as an effort to ensure that barbers

speak English adequately.
(B) constitutional as an exercise of the state police power.
(C) unconstitutional as a bill of attainder.
(D) unconstitutional as a denial of equal protection.

Question 63

Assume that a resident of the state of Aurora was denied a license because she had been graduated from an out-of-state barber school. Her suit in federal court to enjoin denial of the license on this ground would be

(A) dismissed, because there is no diversity of citizenship.
(B) dismissed, because of the abstention doctrine.
(C) decided on the merits, because federal jurisdiction extends to controversies between two states.
(D) decided on the merits, because a federal question is involved.

Question 64

Which of the following is the strongest ground on which to challenge the requirement that candidates for barber licenses must have been residents of the state for at least two years?

(A) The privileges and immunities clause of the Fourteenth Amendment
(B) The due process clause of the Fourteenth Amendment
(C) The equal protection clause of the Fourteenth Amendment
(D) The obligation of contracts clause

Question 65

The State of Rio Grande entered into a contract with Roads, Inc., for construction of a four-lane turnpike. Prior to commencement of construction, the legislature, in order to provide funds for parks, repealed the statute authorizing the turnpike and cancelled the agreement with Roads, Inc. Roads, Inc. sued the state to enforce its original agreement. In ruling on this case, a court should hold that the state statute cancelling the agreement is

(A) valid, because constitutionally the sovereign is not liable except with its own consent.
(B) valid, because the legislature is vested with constitutional authority to repeal laws it has enacted.
(C) invalid, because a state is equitably estopped to

disclaim a valid bid once accepted by it.
(D) invalid, because of the constitutional prohibition against impairment of contracts.

Question 66

The strongest constitutional basis for the enactment of a federal statute requiring colleges and universities receiving federal funds to offer student aid solely on the basis of need is the

(A) police power.
(B) war and defense power.
(C) power to tax and spend for the general welfare.
(D) power to enforce the privileges and immunities clause of the Fourteenth Amendment.

Questions 67-68 are based on the following fact situation.

Green is cited for contempt of the House of Representatives after she refused to answer certain questions posed by a House Committee concerning her acts while serving as a United States Ambassador. A federal statute authorizes the Attorney General to prosecute contempts of Congress. Pursuant to this law, the House directs the Attorney General to begin criminal proceedings against Green. A federal grand jury indicts Green, but the Attorney General refuses to sign the indictment.

Question 67

Which of the following best describes the constitutionality of the Attorney General's action?

(A) Illegal, because the Attorney General must prosecute if the House of Representatives directs.
(B) Illegal, because the Attorney General must prosecute those who violate federal law.
(C) Legal, because ambassadors are immune from prosecution for acts committed in the course of their duties.
(D) Legal, because the decision to prosecute is an exclusively executive act.

Question 68

If the Attorney General signs the indictment, the strongest argument Green could urge as a defense is that

(A) Green may refuse to answer the questions if she can demonstrate that they are unrelated to matters upon which Congress may legislate.
(B) the House may question Green on matters

pertaining to the expenditures of funds appropriated by Congress.
(C) only the Senate may question Green on matters that relate to the performance of her duties.
(D) Congress may not ask questions relating to the performance of duties executed by an officer of the executive branch.

Questions 69-70 are based on the following fact situation.

Until 1954, the state of New Atlantic required segregation in all public and private schools, but all public schools are now desegregated. Other state laws, enacted before 1954 and continuing to the present, provide for free distribution of the same textbooks on secular subjects to students in all public and private schools. In addition, the state accredits schools and certifies teachers.

Little White School, a private school that offers elementary and secondary education in the state, denies admission to all non-Caucasians. Stone School is a private school that offers religious instruction.

Question 69

Which of the following is the strongest argument against the constitutionality of free distribution of textbooks to the students at the Little White School?

(A) No legitimate educational function is served by the free distribution of textbooks.
(B) The state may not in any way aid private schools.
(C) The Constitution forbids private bias of any kind.
(D) Segregation is furthered by the distribution of textbooks to these students.

Question 70

Which of the following is the strongest argument in favor of the constitutionality of free distribution of textbooks to the students at Stone School?

(A) Private religious schools, like public nonsectarian schools, fulfill an important educational function.
(B) Religious instruction in private schools is not constitutionally objectionable.
(C) The purpose and effect of the free distribution of these textbooks is secular and does not entangle church and state.
(D) The free exercise clause requires identical treatment by the state of students in public and private schools.

Questions 71-72 are based on the following fact situation.

Barnes was hired as an assistant professor of mathematics at Reardon State College and is now in his third consecutive one-year contract. Under state law, he cannot acquire tenure until after five consecutive annual contracts. In his third year, Barnes was notified that he was not being re-hired for the following year. Applicable state law and college rules did not require either a statement of reasons or a hearing, and in fact neither was offered to Barnes.

Question 71

Which of the following, if established, sets forth the strongest constitutional argument Barnes could make to compel the college to furnish him a statement of reasons for the failure to rehire him and an opportunity for a hearing?

(A) There is no evidence that tenured teachers are any more qualified than he is.
(B) He leased a home in reliance on an oral promise of reemployment by the college president.
(C) He was the only teacher at the college whose contract was not renewed that year.
(D) In the expectation of remaining at the college, he had just moved his elderly parents to the town in which the college is located.

Question 72

Which of the following, if established, most strongly supports the college in refusing to give Barnes a statement of reasons or an opportunity for a hearing?

(A) Barnes' academic performance had been substandard.
(B) A speech he made that was critical of administration policies violated a college regulation concerning teacher behavior.
(C) Barnes worked at the college for less than five years.
(D) Barnes could be replaced with a more competent teacher.

Question 73

National regulation of predatory wild animals on federal lands is most likely

(A) constitutional, because the protection of wild animals is important to the general welfare.
(B) constitutional, because Congress has authority to make regulations respecting federal property.
(C) unconstitutional, because wild animals as defined by state common law are not federal property.
(D) unconstitutional, because regulation and control of wild animals is retained by the states under the Tenth Amendment.

Question 74

In an effort to relieve serious and persistent unemployment in the industrialized state of Onondaga, its legislature enacted a statute requiring every business with annual sales in Onondaga of over one million dollars to purchase goods and/or services in Onondaga equal in value to at least half of the annual sales in Onondaga of the business. Which of the following constitutional provisions is the strongest basis on which to attack this statute?

(A) The due process clause of the Fourteenth Amendment.
(B) The equal protection clause.
(C) The commerce clause.
(D) The privileges and immunities clause of the Fourteenth Amendment.

Questions 75-76 are based on the following fact situation.

The Federal Automobile Safety Act establishes certain safety and performance standards for all automobiles manufactured in the United States. The Act creates a five-member "Automobile Commission" to investigate automobile safety, to make recommendations to Congress for new laws, to make further rules establishing safety and performance standards, and to prosecute violations of the act. The chairman is appointed by the President, two members are selected by the President pro tempore of the Senate, and two by the Speaker of the House of Representatives.

Minicar, Inc., a minor United States car manufacturer, seeks to enjoin enforcement of the Commission's rules.

Question 75

The best argument that Minicar can make is that

(A) legislative power may not be delegated by Congress to an agency in the absence of clear guidelines.
(B) the commerce power does not extend to the manufacture of automobiles not used in interstate

commerce.

(C) Minicar is denied due process of law because it is not represented on the Commission.

(D) the Commission lacks authority to enforce its standards because not all of its members were appointed by the President.

Question 76

The appropriate decision for the court is to

(A) allow the Commission to continue investigating automobile safety and making recommendations to Congress.

(B) allow the Commission to prosecute violations of the act but not allow it to issue rules.

(C) forbid the Commission to take any action under the act.

(D) order that all members of the Commission be appointed by the President by and with the advice and consent of the Senate.

Question 77

In 1963 Hobson was appointed to a tribunal established pursuant to a congressional act. The tribunal's duties were to review claims made by veterans and to make recommendations to the Veterans Administration on their merits. Congress later abolished the tribunal and established a different format for review of such claims. Hobson was offered a federal administrative position in the same bureau at a lesser salary. He thereupon sued the government on the ground that Congress may not remove a federal judge from office during good behavior nor diminish his compensation during continuance in office. Government attorneys filed a motion to dismiss the action. The court should

(A) deny the motion, because of the independence of the federal judiciary constitutionally guaranteed by Article III.

(B) deny the motion, because Hobson has established a property right to his federal employment on the tribunal.

(C) grant the motion, because Hobson lacked standing to raise the question.

(D) grant the motion, because Hobson was not a judge under Article III and is not entitled to life tenure.

Questions 78-79 are based on the following fact situation.

Kane, a member of the legislature of State, is prosecuted in federal court for a violation of the Federal Securities Act arising out of the activities of a state-owned corporation. Kane's defense includes a claim that the alleged wrongful acts were committed in the course of legislative business and are immune from scrutiny.

Question 78

Which of the following is the strongest constitutional argument supporting Kane?

(A) Because of doctrines of federalism, federal law generally cannot be applied to state legislators acting in the course of their official duties.

(B) State legislators enjoy the protection of the speech and debate clause of the United States Constitution.

(C) A federal court must follow state law respecting the scope of legislative immunity.

(D) To apply the Federal Securities Act to state legislators would violate the due process clause.

Question 79

Which of the following is the strongest argument against Kane's constitutional defense?

(A) Congress has plenary power under the commerce clause.

(B) Congress may impose liability on state legislators as a means of guaranteeing a republican form of government.

(C) Congress does not significantly interfere with state government by applying this law to state legislators.

(D) Congress may impose liability on state legislators by virtue of the necessary and proper clause.

Question 80

A newly-enacted state criminal statute provides, in its entirety, "No person shall utter to another person in a public place any annoying, disturbing or unwelcome language." Smith followed an elderly woman for three blocks down a public street, yelling in her ear offensive four-letter words. The woman repeatedly asked Smith to leave her alone, but he refused.

In the subsequent prosecution of Smith, the first under this statute, Smith

(A) can be convicted.

(B) cannot be convicted, because speech of the sort described here may not be punished by the state because of the First and Fourteenth

Amendments.

(C) cannot be convicted, because, though his speech here may be punished by the state, the state may not do so under this statute.

(D) cannot be convicted, because the average user of a public street would think his speech/action here was amusing and ridiculous rather than "annoying," etc.

Question 81

Congressional legislation authorizing marriages and divorces as a matter of federal law on prescribed terms and conditions could most easily be upheld if it

(A) applied only to marriages and divorces in which at least one of the parties is a member of the armed forces.

(B) applied only to marriages performed by federal judges and to divorces granted by federal courts.

(C) implemented an executive agreement seeking to define basic human rights.

(D) applied only to marriages and divorces in the District of Columbia.

Questions 82-84 are based on the following fact situation.

Congress provides by statute that any state that fails to prohibit automobile speeds of over 55 miles per hour on highways within the state shall be denied all federal highway construction funding. The state of Atlantic, one of the richest and most highway-oriented states in the country, refuses to enact such a statute.

Question 82

Which of the following potential plaintiffs is most likely to be able to obtain a judicial determination of the validity of this federal statute?

(A) A taxpayer of the United States and the state of Atlantic who wants his state to get its fair share of federal tax monies for highways, and fears that, if it does not, his state taxes will be increased to pay for the highway construction in the state of Atlantic that federal funds would have financed.

(B) Contractors who have been awarded contracts by the state of Atlantic for specific highway construction projects, which contracts are contingent on payment to the state of the federal highway construction funds to which it would otherwise be entitled.

(C) An automobile owner who lives in the state of

Atlantic and regularly uses its highway system.

(D) An organization dedicated to keeping the federal government within the powers granted it by the Constitution.

Question 83

The strongest argument that can be made in support of the constitutionality of this federal statute is that

(A) the states ceded their authority over highways to the national government when the states accepted federal grants to help finance their highways.

(B) the federal government can regulate the use of state highways without limitation because the federal government paid for some of their construction costs.

(C) Congress could reasonably believe that the 55 mile-an-hour speed limit will assure that the federal money spent on highways results in greater benefit than harm to the public.

(D) a recent public opinion survey demonstrated that 90 percent of the people in this country support a 55 mile-an-hour speed limit.

Question 84

The federal statute relating to disbursement of highway funds conditioned on the 55 mile-an-hour speed limit is probably

(A) unconstitutional.

(B) constitutional only on the basis of the spending power.

(C) constitutional only on the basis of the commerce power.

(D) constitutional on the basis of both the spending power and the commerce power.

Question 85

The city of Newtown adopted an ordinance providing that street demonstrations involving more than 15 persons may not be held in commercial areas during "rush" hours. "Exceptions" may be made to the prohibition "upon 24-hour advance application to an approval by the police department." The ordinance also imposes sanctions on any person "who shall, without provocation, use to or of another, and in his presence, opprobrious words or abusive language tending to cause a breach of the peace." The ordinance has not yet had either judicial or administrative interpretation. Which of the following is the strongest argument for the unconstitutionality of both parts of the ordinance on their face?

(A) No type of prior restraint may be imposed on speech in public places.
(B) Laws regulating, by their terms, expressive conduct or speech may not be overbroad or unduly vague.
(C) The determination as to whether public gatherings may be lawfully held cannot be vested in the police.
(D) The right of association in public places without interference is assured by the First and Fourteenth Amendments.

Questions 86-87 are based on the following fact situation.

While Defendant was in jail on a procuring charge, his landlord called the police because rent had not been paid and because he detected a disagreeable odor coming from Defendant's apartment into the hallways.

The police officer who responded to the call knew that Defendant was in jail. He recognized the stench coming from Defendant's apartment as that of decomposing flesh and, without waiting to obtain a warrant and using the landlord's passkey, entered the apartment with the landlord's consent. The lease to these premises gave the landlord a right of entry, at any reasonable hour, for the purpose of making repairs. The police officer found a large trunk in the bedroom which seemed to be the source of the odor. Upon breaking it open, he found the remains of Rosette, Defendant's former mistress.

Question 86

The landlord's consent to the police officer's search of Defendant's apartment is

(A) a waiver of Defendant's Fourth Amendment rights, because a landlord has implied consent to enter a tenant's apartment.
(B) a waiver of Defendant's Fourth Amendment rights, because the lease gave the landlord express authority to enter the premises.
(C) not a waiver of Defendant's Fourth Amendment rights, because the landlord lacked probable cause to believe a crime was then in the process of commission.
(D) not a waiver of Defendant's Fourth Amendment rights, because the landlord had neither actual nor apparent authority to permit the entry.

Question 87

If Defendant undertakes to challenge the search of his apartment, he has

(A) standing, because the items seized in the search were incriminating in nature.
(B) standing, because he still has a sufficient interest in the apartment even while in jail.
(C) no standing, because his landlord authorized the search.
(D) no standing, because he was out of the apartment when it occurred and had not paid his rent.

Question 88

An appropriations act passed by Congress over the President's veto directs that one billion dollars "shall be spent" by the federal government for the development of a new military weapons system, which is available only from the Arms Corporation. On the order of the President, the Secretary of Defense refuses to authorize a contract for purchase of the weapons system. The Arms Corporation sues the Secretary of Defense alleging an unlawful withholding of these federal funds.

The strongest constitutional argument for the Arms Corporation is that

(A) passage of an appropriation over a veto makes the spending mandatory.
(B) Congress' power to appropriate funds includes the power to require that the funds will be spent as directed.
(C) the President's independent constitutional powers do not specifically refer to spending.
(D) the President's power to withhold such funds is limited to cases where foreign affairs are directly involved.

Questions 89-90 are based on the following fact situation.

The State of Missoula has enacted a new election code designed to increase voter responsibility in the exercise of the franchise and to enlarge citizen participation in the electoral process. None of its provisions conflicts with federal statutes.

Question 89

Which of the following is the strongest reason for finding unconstitutional a requirement in the Missoula election code that each voter must be literate in English?

(A) The requirement violates Article I Section 2 of

the Constitution, which provides that representatives to Congress be chosen "by the People of the several States."

(B) The requirement violates Article I, Section 4 of the Constitution, which gives Congress the power to "make or alter" state regulations providing for the "Times" and "Manner" of holding elections for senators and representatives.

(C) the requirement violates the due process clause of the Fourteenth Amendment.

(D) The requirement violates the equal protection of the laws clause of the Fourteenth Amendment.

Question 90

The Missoula election code provides that in a special-purpose election for directors of a state watershed improvement district, the franchise is limited to landowners within the district, because they are the only ones directly affected by the outcome. Each vote is weighted according to the proportion of the holding of that individual in relation to the total affected property. The best argument in support of the statute and against the application of the "one man, one vote" principle in this situation is that the principle

(A) applies only to elections of individuals to statewide public office.

(B) does not apply where property rights are involved.

(C) does not apply, because the actions of such a district principally affect landowners.

(D) does not apply, because of rights reserved to the states by the Tenth Amendment.

Questions 91-93 are based on the following fact situation.

The State of Yuma provides by statute, "No person may be awarded any state construction contract without agreeing to employ only citizens of the state and of the United States in performance of the contract."

Question 91

In evaluating the constitutionality of this state statute under the supremacy clause, which of the following would be most directly relevant?

(A) The general unemployment rate in the nation.

(B) The treaties and immigration laws of the United States.

(C) The need of the state for this particular statute.

(D) The number of aliens currently residing in Yuma.

Question 92

If the Yuma statute is attacked as violating the commerce clause, which of the following defenses is the *WEAKEST*?

(A) The statute will help protect the workers of the State of Yuma from competition by foreign workers.

(B) The statute will help assure that workers with jobs directly affecting the performance of public contracts are dedicated to their jobs.

(C) The statute will help assure a continuously available and stable work force for the execution of public contracts.

(D) The statute will help assure that only the most qualified individuals work on public contracts.

Question 93

Suppose the state supreme court declares the statute to be unconstitutional on the grounds that it violates the privileges and immunities clause of the Fourteenth Amendment to the federal constitution and the equal protection clause of the state constitution. If the state seeks review in the United States Supreme Court, which of the following statements is most accurate?

(A) The United States Supreme Court may properly review that decision by certiorari only.

(B) The United States Supreme Court may properly review the decision by appeal only.

(C) The United States Supreme Court may properly review that decision by appeal or certiorari.

(D) The United States Supreme Court may not properly review that decision.

Questions 94-96 are based on the following fact situation.

As part of a comprehensive federal aid-to-education program, Congress included the following provisions as conditions for state receipt of federal funds:

(1) Whenever textbooks are provided to students without charge, they must include no religious instruction and must be made available on the same terms to students in all public and private schools accredited by the state educational authority. (2) Salary supplements can be paid to teachers in public and private schools, up to ten percent of existing

salary schedules, where present compensation is less than the average salary for persons of comparable training and experience, provided that no such supplement is paid to any teacher who instructs in religious subjects. (3) Construction grants can be made toward the cost of physical plant at private colleges and universities, provided that no part of the grant is used for buildings in which instruction in religious subject matters is offered.

Question 94

Federal taxpayer Allen challenges the provision that allows the distribution of free textbooks to students in a private school where religious instruction is included in the curriculum. On the question of the adequacy of Allen's standing to raise the constitutional question, the most likely result is that standing will be

(A) sustained, because any congressional spending authorization can be challenged by any taxpayer.
(B) sustained, because the challenge to the exercise of congressional spending power is based on a claimed violation of specific constitutional limitations on the exercise of such power.
(C) denied, because there is insufficient nexus between the taxpayer and the challenged expenditures.
(D) denied, because, in the case of private schools, no state action is involved.

Question 95

Federal taxpayer Bates challenges the salary supplements for teachers in private schools where religious instruction is included in the curriculum. On the substantive constitutional issue, the most likely result is that the salary supplements will be

(A) sustained, because the statute provides that no supplements will be made to teachers who are engaged in any religious instruction.
(B) sustained, because to distinguish between private and public school teachers would violate the religious freedom clause of the First Amendment.
(C) held unconstitutional, because some religions would benefit disproportionately.
(D) held unconstitutional, because the policing of the restriction would amount to an excessive entanglement with religion.

Question 96

Federal taxpayer Bates also challenges the construction grants to church-operated private colleges and universities. The most likely result is that the construction grants will be

(A) sustained, because aid to one aspect of an institution of higher education not shown to be pervasively sectarian does not necessarily free it to spend its other resources for religious purposes.
(B) sustained, because bricks and mortar do not aid religion in a way forbidden by the establishment clause of the First Amendment.
(C) held unconstitutional, because any financial aid to a church-operated school strengthens the religious purposes of the institution.
(D) held unconstitutional, because the grants involve or cause an excessive entanglement with religion.

Question 97

A state accredits both public and private schools, licenses their teachers, and supplies textbooks on secular subjects to all such schools. Country Schoolhouse, a private school that offers elementary and secondary education in the state, denies admission to all non-Caucasians. In a suit to enjoin as unconstitutional the continued racially exclusionary admissions policy of the Country Schoolhouse, which of the following is the strongest argument *AGAINST* the school?

(A) Because education is a public function, the Country Schoolhouse may not discriminate on racial grounds.
(B) The state is so involved in school regulation and support that the equal protection clause of the Fourteenth Amendment is applicable to the school.
(C) The state is constitutionally obligated to eliminate segregation in all public and private educational institutions within the state.
(D) Any school with teachers who are licensed by the state is forbidden to discriminate on racial grounds.

Question 98

A state statute requires that all buses which operate as common carriers on the highways of the state shall be equipped with seat belts for passengers. Transport Lines, an interstate carrier, challenges the validity of the statute and the right of the state to make the requirement. What is the best basis for a constitutional challenge by Transport Lines?

(A) Violation of the due process clause of the Fourteenth Amendment
(B) Violation of the equal protection clause of the Fourteenth Amendment
(C) Unreasonable burden on interstate commerce
(D) Difficulty of enforcement

Question 99

Amy Docent, a state college instructor, was discharged because of her refusal to comply with a state statute requiring public employees to swear or affirm that they will (1) "uphold and defend" the state and federal constitutions and (2) "oppose the overthrow" of the state or federal governments "by force, violence, or by any improper method." The statute had previously been held constitutional by the state supreme court. Docent filed a complaint in federal district court alleging the unconstitutionality of the statute and seeking an injunction and damages.

Which of the following is the state's strongest argument for sustaining the validity of the statute?

(A) Government employment is a privilege, not a right.
(B) The oath as a whole is only a commitment to abide by constitutional processes.
(C) The First and Fourteenth Amendments permit a state to fix the conditions of state employment.
(D) The state has a compelling need to keep disloyal persons out of governmental positions of trust.

Questions 100-101 are based on the following fact situation.

All lawyers practicing in the state of Erewhon must be members of the State Bar Association, by order of the state supreme court. Several state officials serve on the Bar Association's Board of Bar Governors. The Board of Bar Governors authorizes the payment of dues for two staff members to the Cosmopolitan Club, a private dining club licensed to sell alcoholic beverages. The Cosmopolitan Club is frequented by affluent businessmen and professionals and by legislators. It is generally known that the purpose of the membership of the Bar Association staff is to enable them to go where members of the "elite" meet and to lobby for legislation in which the Bar Association is interested. The State Bar Association has numerous committees and subcommittees concerned with family law, real estate law, unauthorized practice, etc., and its recommendations often influence state policy. Some committee meetings are held at the Cosmopolitan Club. The club

is known to have rules which restrict membership by race, religion, and sex.

Plaintiffs, husband and wife, who are members of the Erewhon Bar Association, petition the Board of Bar Governors to adopt a resolution prohibiting the payment of club dues to and the holding of meetings of the Bar Association or its committees at places which discriminate on the basis of race, religion, or sex. After substantial public discussion, the Board of Bar Governors, by a close vote, fails to pass such a resolution. These events receive extensive coverage in the local newspapers. Plaintiffs bring an action in federal court seeking an injunction against such payments and the holding of meetings in such places as the Cosmopolitan Club.

Question 100

The strongest argument for Plaintiffs is

(A) private rights to discriminate and associate freely must defer to a public interest against discrimination on the basis of race, religion, or sex.
(B) the failure of the State Bar Association to pass a resolution forbidding discrimination on the basis of race, religion, or sex constitutes a denial of equal protection.
(C) the State Bar Association is an agency of the state and its payment of dues to such private clubs promotes discrimination on the basis of race, religion, and sex.
(D) the State Bar Association's payment of dues to such private clubs promotes discrimination on the basis of race, religion, and sex.

Question 101

Which of the following actions should a federal district court take with respect to jurisdiction?

(A) Hear the case on the merits, because a federal claim is presented.
(B) Hear the case on the merits, because the expenditure of state funds in support of segregation is forbidden by the Fifth Amendment.
(C) Abstain from jurisdiction, because the constitutional issue should be litigated first in a state court.
(D) Dismiss the case for lack of jurisdiction, because the issue of Bar Association activities is solely within the domain of state law.

Questions 102-103 are based on the following fact situation.

The state of Champlain enacts the Young Adult Marriage Counseling Act, which provides that, before any persons less than 30 years of age may be issued a marriage license, they must receive at least five hours of marriage counseling from a state-licensed social worker. This counseling is designed to assure that applicants for marriage licenses know their legal rights and duties in relation to marriage and parenthood, understand the "true nature" of the marriage relationship, and understand the procedures for obtaining divorces.

Question 102

Pine, aged 25, contemplated marrying Ross, aged 25. Both are residents of the state of Champlain. Pine has not yet proposed to Ross because he is offended by the counseling requirement.

Pine sues in court seeking a declaratory judgment that the Young Adult Marriage Counseling Act is unconstitutional. Which of the following is the clearest ground for dismissal of this action by the court?

(A) Pine and Ross are residents of the same state.
(B) No substantial federal question is presented.
(C) The suit presents a non-justifiable political question.
(D) The suit is unripe.

Question 103

In a case in which the constitutionality of the Young Adult Marriage Counseling Act is in issue, the burden of persuasion will probably be on the

(A) person challenging the law, because there is a strong presumption that elected state legislators acted properly.
(B) person challenging the law, because the Tenth Amendment authorized states to determine the conditions on which they issue marriage licenses.
(C) state, because there is a substantial impact on the right to marry, and that right is fundamental.
(D) state, because there is a substantial impact in the discrete and insular class of young adults.

Question 104

A federal statute requires United States civil service employees to retire at age 75. However, that statute also states that civil service employees of the armed forces must retire at age 65.

Prentis, a 65-year-old service employee of the Department of the Army, seeks a declaratory judgment that would forbid his mandatory retirement until age 75.

The strongest argument that Prentis can make to invalidate the requirement that he retire at age 65 is that the law

(A) denies him a privilege or immunity of national citizenship.
(B) deprives him of a property right without just compensation.
(C) is not within the scope of any of the enumerated powers of Congress in Article I, §8.
(D) invidiously discriminates against him on the basis of age in violation of the Fifth Amendment.

Question 105

Congress passes a law regulating the wholesale retail prices of "every purchase or sale of oil, natural gas, and electric power made in the United States." The strongest argument in support of the constitutionality of this statute is that

(A) the Constitution expressly empowers Congress to enact laws for "the general welfare."
(B) Congress has the authority to regulate such products' interstate transportation and importation from abroad.
(C) Congress may regulate the prices of every purchase and sale of goods and services made in this country, because commerce includes buying and selling.
(D) in inseverable aggregates, the domestic purchases or sales of such products affect interstate or foreign commerce.

Question 106

Congress enacted a statute providing that persons may challenge a state energy law on the ground that it is in conflict with the federal Constitution in either federal or state court. According to this federal statute, any decision by a lower state court upholding a state energy law against a challenge based on the federal Constitution may be appealed directly to the United States Supreme Court.

The provisions of this statute that authorize direct United States Supreme Court review of specified decisions rendered by lower state courts are

(A) constitutional, because congressional control over questions of energy usage is plenary.

(B) constitutional, because Congress may establish the manner in which the appellate jurisdiction of the United States Supreme Court is exercised.

(C) unconstitutional, because they infringe on the sovereign right of states to have their supreme courts review decisions of their lower state courts.

(D) unconstitutional, because under Article III of the Constitution the United States Supreme Court does not have authority to review directly decisions of lower state courts.

Question 107

Congress enacts a criminal statute prohibiting "any person from interfering in any way with any right conferred on another person by the equal protection clause of the Fourteenth Amendment."

Application of this statute to Jones, a private citizen, would be most clearly constitutional if Jones, with threats of violence, coerces

(A) a public school teacher to exclude Black pupils from her class, solely because of their race.

(B) Black pupils, solely because of their race, to refrain from attending a privately owned and operated school licensed by the state.

(C) the bus driver operating a free school bus service under the sponsorship of a local church to refuse to allow Black pupils on the bus, solely because of their race.

(D) the federal official in charge of distributing certain federal benefits directly to students from distributing them to Black pupils, solely because of their race.

Question 108

A federal statute sets up a program of dental education. The statute provides that the Secretary of Health and Human Services "shall, on a current basis, spend all of the money appropriated for this purpose" and "shall distribute the appropriated funds" by a specified formula to state health departments that agree to participate in the program. In the current year Congress has appropriated $100 million for expenditure on this program.

In order to ensure a budget surplus in the current fiscal year, the President issued an executive order directing the various cabinet secretaries to cut expenditures in this year by 10 percent in all categories. He also orders certain programs to be cut more drastically because he believes that "they are not as important to the general welfare as other programs." The President identifies the dental education program as such a program and orders it to be cut by 50 percent. Assume that no other federal statutes are relevant.

To satisfy constitutional requirements, how much money must the Secretary of Health and Human Services distribute for the dental education program this year?

(A) $50 million, because the President could reasonably determine that this program is not as important to the general welfare as other programs.

(B) $50 million, because as chief executive the President has the constitutional authority to control the actions of all of his subordinates by executive order.

(C) $90 million, because any more drastic cut for the program would be a denial of equal protection to beneficiaries of this program as compared to beneficiaries of other programs.

(D) $100 million, because the President may not unilaterally suspend the effect of a valid federal statute imposing a duty to spend appropriated monies.

Question 109

A state statute provides that persons moving into a community to attend a college on a full-time basis may not vote in any elections for local or state officials that are held in that community. Instead, the statute provides that for voting purposes all such persons shall retain their residence in the community from which they came. In that state the age of majority is eighteen.

Which of the following is the strongest argument to demonstrate the unconstitutionality of this state statute?

(A) A state does not have an interest that is sufficiently compelling to justify the exclusion from voting of an entire class of persons.

(B) There are less restrictive means by which the state could assure that only actual residents of a community vote in its elections.

(C) Most persons moving to a community to attend college full-time are likely to have attained the age of majority under the laws of this state.

(D) On its face this statute impermissibly discriminates against interstate commerce.

Question 110

Congress enacts a statute punishing "each and every conspiracy entered into by any two or more persons for the purpose of denying Black persons housing, employment, or education, solely because of their race." Under which of the following constitutional provisions is the authority of Congress to pass such a statute most clearly and easily justifiable?

(A) The obligation of contracts clause
(B) The general welfare clause of Article I, §8
(C) The Thirteenth Amendment
(D) The Fourteenth Amendment

Question 111

A federal criminal law makes it a crime for any citizen of the United States not specifically authorized by the President to negotiate with a foreign government for the purpose of influencing the foreign government in relation to a dispute with the United States. The strongest constitutional ground for the validity of this law is that

(A) under several of its enumerated powers, Congress may legislate to preserve the monopoly of the national government over the conduct of United States foreign affairs.
(B) the President's inherent power to negotiate for the United States with foreign countries authorizes the President, even in the absence of statutory authorization, to punish citizens who engage in such negotiations without permission.
(C) the law deals with foreign relations and therefore is not governed by the First Amendment.
(D) federal criminal laws dealing with international affairs need not be as specific as those dealing with domestic affairs.

Question 112

Pursuant to a state statute, Clovis applied for tuition assistance to attend the Institute of Liberal Arts. He was qualified for such assistance in every way except that he was a resident alien who did not intend to become a United States citizen. The state's restriction of such grants to United States citizens or resident aliens seeking such citizenship is probably

(A) valid, because aliens are not per se "a discrete and insular minority" specially protected by the Fourteenth Amendment.
(B) valid, because the line drawn by the state for extending aid was reasonably related to a legitimate state interest.
(C) invalid, because the justifications for this restriction are insufficient to overcome the burden imposed on a state when it uses such an alienage classification.
(D) invalid, because the privileges and immunities clause of Article IV does not permit such an arbitrary classification.

Question 113

Congress passes an act requiring that all owners of bicycles in the United States register them with a federal bicycle registry. The purpose of the law is to provide reliable evidence of ownership to reduce bicycle theft. No fee is charged for the registration. Although most stolen bicycles are kept or resold by the thieves in the same cities in which the bicycles were stolen, an increasing number of bicycles are being taken to cities in other states for resale.

Is this act of Congress constitutional?

(A) Yes, because Congress has the power to regulate property for the general welfare.
(B) Yes, because Congress could determine that in inseverable aggregates bicycle thefts affect interstate commerce.
(C) No, because most stolen bicycles remain within the state in which they were stolen.
(D) No, because the registration of vehicles is a matter reserved to the states by the Tenth Amendment.

Question 114

A statute of the state of Lanape flatly bans the sale or distribution of contraceptive devices to minors. Drugs, Inc., a national retailer of drugs and related items, is charged with violating the Lanape statute. Which of the following is the strongest constitutional argument Drugs, Inc., could make in defending itself against prosecution for violation of this statute?

(A) The statute constitutes an undue burden on interstate commerce.
(B) The statute denies minors one of their fundamental rights without due process.
(C) The statute denies Drugs, Inc., a privilege or immunity of state citizenship.
(D) The statute violates the First Amendment right to freedom of religion because it regulates morals.

Question 115

Congress enacted a law prohibiting the killing, capture, or removal of any form of wildlife upon or from any federally owned land.

Which of the following is the most easily justifiable source of national authority for this federal law?

(A) The commerce clause of Article I, §8
(B) The privileges and immunities clause of Article IV
(C) The enforcement clause of the Fourteenth Amendment
(D) The property clause of Article IV, §3

Question 116

Congress enacts a law providing that all disagreements between the United States and a state over federal grant-in-aid funds shall be settled by the filing of a suit in the federal district court in the affected state. "The judgment of that federal court shall be transmitted to the head of the federal agency dispensing such funds who, if satisfied that the judgment is fair and lawful, shall execute the judgment according to its terms." This law is

(A) constitutional, because disagreements over federal grant-in-aid funds necessarily involve federal questions within the judicial power of the United States.
(B) constitutional, because the spending of federal monies necessarily includes the authority to provide for the effective settlement of disputes involving them.
(C) unconstitutional, because it vests authority in the federal court to determine a matter prohibited to it by the Eleventh Amendment.
(D) unconstitutional, because it vests authority in a federal court to render an advisory opinion.

Question 117

The President of the United States recognizes the country of Ruritania and undertakes diplomatic relations with its government through the Secretary of State. Ruritania is governed by a repressive totalitarian government.

In an appropriate federal court, Dunn brings a suit against the President and Secretary of State to set aside this action on the ground that it is inconsistent with the principles of our constitutional form of government. Dunn has a lucrative contract with the United States Department of Commerce to provide commercial information about Ruritania.

The contract expressly terminates, however, "when the President recognizes the country of Ruritania and undertakes diplomatic relations with its government."

Which of the following is the most proper disposition of the Dunn suit by the federal court?

(A) Suit dismissed, because Dunn does not have standing to bring this action.
(B) Suit dismissed, because there is no adversity between Dunn and the defendants.
(C) Suit dismissed, because it presents a non-justifiable political question.
(D) Suit decided on the merits.

Question 118

A state statute requires the permanent removal from parental custody of any child who has suffered "child abuse." That term is defined to include "corporal punishment of any sort."

Zeller very gently spanks his six-year-old son on the buttocks whenever he believes that spanking is necessary to enforce discipline on him. Such a spanking occurs not more than once a month and has never physically harmed the child.

The state files suit under the statute to terminate Zeller's parental rights solely because of these spankings. Zeller defends only on the ground that the statute in question is unconstitutional as applied to his admitted conduct. In light of the nature of the rights involved, which of the following is the most probable burden of persuasion on this constitutional issue?

(A) The state has the burden of persuading the court that the application of this statute to Zeller is necessary to vindicate an important state interest.
(B) The state has the burden of persuading the court that the application of this statute to Zeller is rationally related to a legitimate state interest.
(C) Zeller has the burden of persuading the court that the application of this statute to him is not necessary to vindicate an important state interest.
(D) Zeller has the burden of persuading the court that the application of this statute to him is not rationally related to a legitimate state interest.

Question 119

According to a statute of the state of Kiowa, a candidate for state office may have his name placed on the official election ballot only if he files with the appropriate state official a petition containing a specified number of voter signatures. Roderick failed to get his name placed on the state ballot as an independent candidate for governor, because he failed to file a petition with the number of voter signatures required by state statute. In a suit against the appropriate state officials in federal district court, Roderick sought an injunction against the petition signature requirement on the ground that it was unconstitutional.

Which of the following, if established, constitutes the strongest argument for Roderick?

(A) Compliance with the petition signature requirement is burdensome.
(B) The objectives of the statute could be satisfactorily achieved by less burdensome means.
(C) Because of the petition signature requirement, very few independent candidates have ever succeeded in getting on the ballot.
(D) The motivation for the statute was a desire to keep candidates off the ballot if they did not have strong support among voters.

Question 120

Congress passes an Energy Conservation Act. The act requires all users of energy in this country to reduce their consumption by a specified percentage, to be set by a presidential executive order. The act sets forth specific standards the President must use in setting the percentage and detailed procedures to be followed.

The provision that allows the President to set the exact percentage is probably

(A) constitutional, because it creates a limited administrative power to implement the statute.
(B) constitutional, because inherent executive powers permit such action even without statutory authorization.
(C) unconstitutional as an undue delegation of legislative power to the executive.
(D) unconstitutional, because it violates the due process clause of the Fifth Amendment.

Question 121

The federal government has complete jurisdiction over certain park land located within the state of Plains. To conserve the wildlife that inhabits that land the federal government enacts a statute forbidding all hunting of animals in the federal park. That statute also forbids the hunting of animals that have left the federal park and have entered the state of Plains.

Hanson has a hunting license from the state of Plains authorizing him to hunt deer anywhere in the state. On land within the state of Plains located adjacent to the federal park, Hanson shoots a deer he knows has recently left the federal land.

Hanson is prosecuted for violating the federal hunting law. The strongest ground supporting the constitutionality of the federal law forbidding the hunting of wild animals that wander off federal property is that

(A) this law is a necessary and proper means of protecting United States property.
(B) the animals are moving in the stream of interstate commerce.
(C) the police powers of the federal government encompass protection of wild animals.
(D) shooting wild animals is a privilege, not a right.

Questions 122-123 are based on the following fact situation.

Three states, East Winnetka, Midland, and West Hampton, are located next to one another in that order. The states of East Winnetka and West Hampton permit the hunting and trapping of snipe, but the state of Midland strictly forbids it in order to protect snipe, a rare species of animal, from extinction. The state of Midland has a state statute that provides "Possession of snipe traps is prohibited. Any game warden finding a snipe trap within the state shall seize and destroy it." Snipe traps cost about $15 each.

Prentis is a resident of West Hampton and an ardent snipe trapper. She drove her car to East Winnetka to purchase a new improved snipe trap from a manufacturer there. In the course of her trip back across Midland with the trap in her car, Prentis stopped in a Midland state park to camp for a few nights. While she was in that park, a Midland game warden saw the trap, which was visible on the front seat of her car. The warden seized the trap and destroyed it in accordance with the Midland statute after Prentis admitted that the seized item was a prohibited snipe trap. No federal statutes or federal administrative regulations apply.

Question 122

For this question only, assume that Prentis demonstrates that common carriers are permitted to transport snipe traps as cargo across Midland for delivery to another state and that in practice the Midland statute is enforced only against private individuals transporting those traps in private vehicles. If Prentis challenges the application of the Midland statute to her on the basis only of a denial of equal protection, the application of the statute will probably be found

(A) constitutional, because the traps constitute contraband in which Prentis could have no protected property interest.
(B) constitutional, because there is a rational basis for differentiating between the possession of snipe traps as interstate cargo by common carriers and the possession of snipe traps by private individuals.
(C) unconstitutional, because the state cannot demonstrate a compelling public purpose for making this differentiation between common carriers and such private individuals.
(D) unconstitutional, because interstate travel is a fundamental right that may not be burdened by state law.

Question 123

For this question only, assume that a valid federal administrative rule, adopted under a federal consumer product safety act, regulates the design of snipe traps. The rule was issued to prevent traps from causing injury to human beings, e.g., by pinching fingers while persons were setting the traps. No other federal law applies. Which of the following best states the effect of the federal rule on the Midland state statute?

(A)   The federal rule preempts the Midland state statute, because the federal rule regulates the same subject matter, snipe traps.
(B)   The federal rule preempts the Midland state statute, because the federal rule does not contain affirmative authorization for continued state regulation.
(C)   The federal rule does not preempt the Midland state statute, because the Midland state statute regulates wild animals, a field of exclusive state power.
(D)   The federal rule does not preempt the Midland state statute, because the purposes of the federal rule and the Midland state statute are different.

Question 124

There is high and persistent unemployment in the industrialized state of Green. Its legislature therefore enacted a statute requiring every business with annual

sales in Green of over $1 million to purchase each year goods and/or services in Green equal in value to at least half of its sales in Green.

Which of the following parties most clearly has standing to contest the constitutionality of this statute of Green in federal court?

(A) A business in another state that supplies from that other state 95 percent of the goods and services bought by a corporation that has annual sales in Green of $20 million
(B) A corporation selling $300,000 worth of goods in Green but presently purchasing only $10,000 in goods and services in Green
(C) The governor of an adjacent state on behalf of the state and its residents
(D) The owner of high-grade, secured bonds issued by a corporation with sales in Green of $10 million that currently purchases only $1 million in goods and services in Green

Question 125

A state statute makes fraud for personal financial gain a crime. Jones was convicted of violating this statute on three separate occasions. Following his most recent conviction, he professed to have undergone a religious conversion and proclaimed himself to be the divine minister of "St. Rockport," an alleged messiah who would shortly be making his appearance on earth. Jones solicited cash donations from the public to support his efforts to spread the word of St. Rockport and his coming appearance on earth.

Following complaints by several contributors who claimed he defrauded them, Jones was again charged with fraud under this state statute. The charge was that Jones "should have known that his representations about St. Rockport were false and, therefore, that he made them solely to collect cash donations for his personal gain." A witness for the prosecution in Jones' trial stated that Jones had admitted that, at times, he had doubts about the existence of St. Rockport. Jones was the only religious minister prosecuted for fraud under this state statute.

The strongest constitutional defense that Jones could assert would be that this prosecution

(A) deprived him of the equal protection of the laws because other religious ministers have not been charged under this statute.
(B) denied him procedural due process because it

placed upon Jones the burden of rebutting evidence, submitted by the state, of his bad faith in raising this money.

(C) denied him rights conferred by the obligation of contracts clause by preventing him from taking money from persons who wished to contract with him to spread the word of St. Rockport.

(D) denied him the free exercise of religion in violation of the First and Fourteenth Amendments because it required the state to determine the truth or falsity of the content of his religious beliefs.

Question 126

Argus Corporation is privately owned and incorporated in the state of Kiowa. It contracted with the United States to construct a dam across the Big Sandy River in the state of Arapaho. The state of Arapaho imposed a gross receipts tax on all business conducted within the state. Arapaho sued Argus Corporation to collect that tax on the receipts Argus received under this federal contract. No federal statutes or administrative rules are applicable, and the contract between the United States and the Argus Corporation does not mention state taxation.

The court should hold the state tax, as applied here, to be

(A) constitutional, because a state has exclusive jurisdiction over all commercial transactions executed wholly within its borders.

(B) constitutional, because private contractors performing work under a federal contract are not immune in these circumstances from nondiscriminatory state taxation.

(C) unconstitutional, because it violates the supremacy clause.

(D) unconstitutional, because it imposes an undue burden on interstate commerce.

Question 127

On a wholly random basis, a state agency has given a few probationary employees who were not rehired at the end of their probationary period a statement of reasons and an opportunity for a hearing; but the agency has very rarely done so. No statute or rule of the agency required such a statement of reasons or a hearing.

The employment of Masters, a probationary employee, was terminated without a statement of reasons or an opportunity for a hearing. The agency

did not even consider whether it should give him either.

A suit by Masters requesting a statement of reasons and a hearing will probably be

(A) successful on the grounds that failure to give Masters reasons and an opportunity for a hearing constituted a bill of attainder.

(B) successful on the grounds that an agency's inconsistent practices, even if unintentional, deny adversely affected persons the equal protection of the laws.

(C) unsuccessful, because Masters does not have a right to be rehired that is protected by procedural due process.

(D) unsuccessful, because the conditions of state employment are matters reserved to the states by the Tenth Amendment.

Question 128

A state statute provides that only citizens of the United States may be employed by that state. In an action brought in a federal court, a resident alien who was prevented from obtaining state employment as a garbage collector solely because of his alien status challenged the statute's constitutionality as applied to his circumstances.

Which of the following statements concerning the burden of persuasion applicable to this suit is correct?

(A) The alien must demonstrate that there is no rational relationship between the citizenship requirement and any legitimate state interest.

(B) The alien must demonstrate that the citizenship requirement is not necessary to advance an important state interest.

(C) The state must demonstrate that there is a rational relationship between the citizenship requirement and a legitimate state interest.

(D) The state must demonstrate that the citizenship requirement is necessary to advance an important state interest.

Question 129

The High National Grasslands is owned by the United States and is located in the center of a large western state. Acting pursuant to a federal statute authorizing such action, the United States Bureau of Land Management leased the grazing rights in the High National Grasslands to ranchers located nearby. Grazingland Company owns a vast amount of rangeland adjacent to the High National Grasslands and leases its land for livestock grazing purposes to the same ranchers, but at prices higher than those charged by the Bureau. Grazingland Company sued the Bureau in an appropriate federal district court to restrain the Bureau from competing with that company by leasing the High National Grasslands.

Which of the following constitutional provisions may most easily and directly be used to justify the federal statute authorizing this leasing program of the Bureau of Land Management?

(A) The general welfare clause of Article I, §8
(B) The federal property clause of Article IV, §3
(C) The commerce clause of Article I, §8
(D) The supremacy clause of Article VI

Question 130

Zall, a resident of the state of Paxico, brought suit in federal district court against Motors, Inc., a Paxico corporation. Zall seeks recovery of $12,000 actual and $12,000 punitive damages arising from Motors' sale to him of a defective automobile. Zall's suit is based only on a common-law contract theory.

From a constitutional standpoint, should the federal district court hear this suit on its merits?

(A) Yes, because Article III vests federal courts with jurisdiction over cases involving the obligation of contracts.
(B) Yes, because it is an action affecting interstate commerce.
(C) No, because this suit is not within the jurisdiction of an Article III court.
(D) No, because there is no case or controversy within the meaning of Article III.

Question 131

A generally applicable state statute requires an autopsy by the county coroner in all cases of death that are not obviously of natural causes. The purpose of this law is to ensure the discovery and prosecution of all illegal activity resulting in death. In the 50 years since its enactment, the statute has been consistently enforced.

Mr. and Mrs. Long are sincere practicing members of a religion that maintains it is essential for a deceased person's body to be buried promptly and without any invasive procedures, including an autopsy. When the Longs' son died of mysterious causes and an autopsy was scheduled, the Longs filed an action in state court challenging the constitutionality of the state

statute, and seeking an injunction prohibiting the county coroner from performing an autopsy on their son's body. In this action, the Longs claimed only that the application of this statute in the circumstances of their son's death would violate their right to the free exercise of religion as guaranteed by the First and Fourteenth Amendments. Assume that no federal statutes are applicable.

As applied to the Longs' case, the court should rule that the state's autopsy statute is

(A)   constitutional, because a dead individual is not a person protected by the due process clause of the Fourteenth Amendment.
(B)   constitutional, because it is a generally applicable statute and is rationally related to a legitimate state purpose.
(C)   unconstitutional, because it is not necessary to vindicate a compelling state interest.
(D)   unconstitutional, because it is not substantially related to an important state interest.

Question 132

The mineral alpha is added to bodies of fresh water to prevent the spread of certain freshwater parasites. The presence of those parasites threatens the health of the organisms living in rivers and streams throughout the country and imperils the freshwater commercial fishing industry. Alpha is currently mined only in the state of Blue.

In order to raise needed revenue, Congress recently enacted a statute providing for the imposition of a $100 tax on each ton of alpha mined in the United States. Because it will raise the cost of alpha, this tax is likely to reduce the amount of alpha added to freshwater rivers and streams and, therefore, is likely to have an adverse effect on the interstate freshwater commercial fishing industry. The alpha producers in Blue have filed a lawsuit in federal court challenging this tax solely on constitutional grounds.

Is this tax constitutional?

(A) No, because only producers in Blue will pay the tax and, therefore, it is not uniform among the states and denies alpha producers the equal protection of the laws.
(B) No, because it is likely to have an adverse effect on the freshwater commercial fishing industry and Congress has a responsibility under the commerce clause to protect, foster, and advance such interstate industries.

(C) Yes, because the tax is a necessary and proper means of exercising federal authority over the navigable waters of the United States.

(D) Yes, because the power of Congress to impose taxes is plenary, this tax does not contain any provisions extraneous to tax needs or purposes, and it is not barred by any prohibitory language in the Constitution.

Question 133

Water District is an independent municipal water-supply district incorporated under the applicable laws of the state of Green. The district was created solely to supply water to an entirely new community in a recently developed area of Green. That new community is racially, ethnically, and socioeconomically diverse, and the community has never engaged in any discrimination against members of minority groups.

The five-member, elected governing board of the newly created Water District contains two persons who are members of racial minority groups. At its first meeting, the governing board of Water District adopted a rule unqualifiedly setting aside 25% of all positions on the staff of the District and 25% of all contracts to be awarded by the District to members of racial minority groups. The purpose of the rule was "to help redress the historical discrimination against these groups in this country and to help them achieve economic parity with other groups in our society." Assume that no federal statute applies.

A suit by appropriate parties challenges the constitutionality of these set-asides.

In this suit, the most appropriate ruling on the basis of applicable United States Supreme Court precedent would be that the set-asides are

(A) unconstitutional, because they would deny other potential employees or potential contractors the equal protection of the laws.

(B) unconstitutional, because they would impermissibly impair the right to contract of other potential employees or potential contractors.

(C) constitutional, because they would assure members of racial minority groups the equal protection of the laws.

(D) constitutional, because the function and activities of Water District are of a proprietary nature rather than a governmental nature and, therefore, are not subject to the usual requirements of the Fourteenth Amendment.

Question 134

Current national statistics show a dramatic increase in the number of elementary and secondary school students bringing controlled substances (drugs) to school for personal use or distribution to others. In response, Congress enacted a statute requiring each state legislature to enact a state law that makes it a state crime for any person to possess, use, or distribute, within 1,000 feet of any elementary or secondary school, any controlled substance that has previously been transported in interstate commerce and that is not possessed, used, or distributed pursuant to a proper physician's prescription.

This federal statute is

(A) unconstitutional, because Congress has no authority to require a state legislature to enact any specified legislation.

(B) unconstitutional, because the possession, use, or distribution, in close proximity to a school, of a controlled substance that has previously been transported in interstate commerce does not have a sufficiently close nexus to such commerce to justify its regulation by Congress.

(C) constitutional, because it contains a jurisdictional provision that will ensure, on a case-by-case basis, that any particular controlled substance subject to the terms of this statute will, in fact, affect interstate commerce.

(D) constitutional, because Congress possesses broad authority under both the general welfare clause and the commerce clause to regulate any activities affecting education that also have, in inseverable aggregates, a substantial effect on interstate commerce.

Question 135

Congress recently enacted a statute imposing severe criminal penalties on anyone engaged in trading in the stock market who, in the course of that trading, takes "unfair advantage" of other investors who are also trading in the stock market. The statute does not define the term "unfair advantage." There have been no prosecutions under this new statute. The members of an association of law school professors that is dedicated to increasing the clarity of the language used in criminal statutes believe that this statute is unconstitutionally vague. Neither the association nor any of its members is currently engaged in, or intends in the future to engage in, trading in the stock market. The association and its members bring suit against the Attorney General of the United States in a federal district court, seeking an injunction against the enforcement of this statute on the ground that it is unconstitutional.

May the federal court determine the merits of this suit?

(A) Yes, because the suit involves a dispute over the constitutionality of a federal statute.
(B) Yes, because the plaintiffs seek real relief of a conclusive nature--an injunction against enforcement of this statute.
(C) No, because the plaintiffs do not have an interest in the invalidation of this statute that is adequate to ensure that the suit presents an Article III controversy.
(D) No, because a suit for an injunction against enforcement of a criminal statute may not be brought in federal court at any time prior to a bona fide effort to enforce that statute.

Question 136

City enacted an ordinance banning from its public sidewalks all machines dispensing publications consisting wholly of commercial advertisements. The ordinance was enacted because of a concern about the adverse aesthetic effects of litter from publications distributed on the public sidewalks and streets. However, City continued to allow machines dispensing other types of publications on the public sidewalks. As a result of the City ordinance, 30 of the 300 sidewalk machines that were dispensing publications in City were removed.

Is this City ordinance constitutional?

(A) Yes, because regulations of commercial speech are subject only to the requirement that they be rationally related to a legitimate state goal, and that requirement is satisfied here.
(B) Yes, because City has a compelling interest in protecting the aesthetics of its sidewalks and streets, and such a ban is necessary to vindicate this interest.
(C) No, because it does not constitute the least restrictive means with which to protect the aesthetics of City's sidewalks and streets.
(D) No, because there is not a reasonable fit between the legitimate interest of City in preserving the aesthetics of its sidewalks and streets and the means it chose to advance that interest.

Question 137

The state of Brunswick enacted a statute providing for the closure of the official state records of arrest and prosecution of all persons acquitted of a crime by a court or against whom criminal charges were filed and subsequently dropped or dismissed. The purpose of this statute is to protect these persons from further publicity or embarrassment relating to those state proceedings. However, this statute does not prohibit the publication of such information that is in the possession of private persons.

A prominent businessman in Neosho City in Brunswick was arrested and charged with rape. Prior to trial, the prosecutor announced that new information indicated that the charges should be dropped. He then dropped the charges without further explanation, and the records relating thereto were closed to the public pursuant to the Brunswick statute.

The Neosho City Times conducted an investigation to determine why the businessman was not prosecuted, but was refused access to the closed official state records. In an effort to determine whether the law enforcement agencies involved were properly doing their duty, the Times filed suit against appropriate state officials to force opening of the records and to invalidate the statute on constitutional grounds.

Which of the following would be most helpful to the state in defending the constitutionality of this statute?

(A) The fact that the statute treats in an identical manner the arrest and prosecution records of all persons who have been acquitted of a crime by a court or against whom criminal charges were filed and subsequently dropped or dismissed.
(B) The argument that the rights of the press are no greater than those of citizens generally.
(C) The fact that the statute only prohibits public access to these official state records and does not prohibit the publication of information they contain that is in the possession of private persons.
(D) The argument that the state may seal official records owned by the state on any basis its legislature chooses.

Question 138

A federal statute appropriated $7 million for a nationwide essay contest on "How the United States Can Best Stop Drug Abuse." The statute indicates that its purpose is to generate new, practical ideas for eliminating drug abuse in the United States.

Contest rules set forth in the statute provide that winning essays are to be selected on the basis of the "originality, aptness, and feasibility of their ideas." The statute expressly authorizes a first prize of $1 million, 50 second prizes of $100,000 each, and 100 third prizes of $10,000 each. It also states that judges for the contest are to be appointed by the President of the United States with the advice and consent of the Senate, and that all residents of the United States who are not employees of the federal government are eligible to enter and win the contest. A provision of the statute authorizes any taxpayer of the United States to challenge its constitutionality.

In a suit by a federal taxpayer to challenge the constitutionality of the statute, the court should

(A) refuse to decide its merits, because the suit involves policy questions that are inherently political and, therefore, nonjusticiable.
(B) hold the statute unconstitutional, because it does not provide sufficient guidelines for awarding the prize money appropriated by Congress and, therefore, unconstitutionally delegates legislative power to the contest judges.
(C) hold the statute unconstitutional, because its relationship to legitimate purposes of the spending power of Congress is too tenuous and conjectural to satisfy the necessary and proper clause of Article I.
(D) hold the statute constitutional, because it is reasonably related to the general welfare, it states concrete objectives, and it provides adequate criteria for conducting the essay contest and awarding the prize money.

Question 139

Kelly County, in the state of Green, is located adjacent to the border of the state of Red. The communities located in Kelly County are principally suburbs of Scarletville, a large city located in Red, and therefore there is a large volume of traffic between that city and Kelly County. While most of that traffic is by private passenger automobiles, some of it is by taxicabs and other kinds of commercial vehicles.

An ordinance of Kelly County, the stated purpose of which is to reduce traffic congestion, provides that only taxicabs registered in Kelly County may pick up or discharge passengers in the county. The ordinance also provides that only residents of Kelly County may register taxicabs in that county.

Which of the following is the proper result in a suit brought by Scarletville taxicab owners challenging the constitutionality of this Kelly County ordinance?

(A) Judgment for Scarletville taxicab owners, because the fact that private passenger automobiles contribute more to the traffic congestion problem in Kelly County than do taxicabs indicates that the ordinance is not a reasonable means by which to solve that problem.
(B) Judgment for Scarletville taxicab owners, because the ordinance unduly burdens interstate commerce by insulating Kelly County taxicab owners from out-of-state competition without adequate justification.
(C) Judgment for Kelly County, because the ordinance forbids taxicabs registered in other counties of Green as well as in states other than Green to operate in Kelly County and, therefore, it does not discriminate against interstate commerce.
(D) Judgment for Kelly County, because Scarletville taxicab owners do not constitute a suspect class and the ordinance is reasonably related to the legitimate governmental purpose of reducing traffic congestion.

Question 140

A city ordinance requires a taxicab operator's license to operate a taxicab in King City. The ordinance states that the sole criteria for the issuance of such a license are driving ability and knowledge of the geography of King City. An applicant is tested by the city for these qualifications with a detailed questionnaire, written and oral examinations, and a practical behind-the-wheel demonstration.

The ordinance does not limit the number of licenses that may be issued. It does, however, allow any citizen to file an objection to the issuance of a particular license, but only on the ground that an applicant does not possess the required qualifications. City licensing officials are also authorized by the ordinance to determine, in their discretion, whether to hold an evidentiary hearing on an objection before issuing a license.

Sandy applies for a taxicab operator's license and is found to be fully qualified after completing the usual licensing process. Her name is then posted as a prospective licensee, subject only to the objection process. John, a licensed taxicab driver, files an objection to the issuance of such a license to Sandy solely on the ground that the grant of a license to

Sandy would impair the value of John's existing license. John demands a hearing before a license is issued to Sandy so that he may have an opportunity to prove his claim. City licensing officials refuse to hold such a hearing, and they issue a license to Sandy.

John petitions for review of this action by city officials in an appropriate court, alleging that the Constitution requires city licensing officials to grant his request for a hearing before issuing a license to Sandy.

In this case, the court should rule for

(A) John, because the due process clause of the Fourteenth Amendment requires all persons whose property may be adversely affected by governmental action to be given an opportunity for a hearing before such action occurs.
(B) John, because the determination of whether to hold a hearing may not constitutionally be left to the discretion of the same officials whose action is being challenged.
(C) city officials, because John had the benefit of the licensing ordinance and, therefore, may not now question actions taken under it.
(D) city officials, because the licensing ordinance does not give John any property interest in being free of competition from additional licensees.

Question 141

A statute of State X permits a person's name to appear on the general election ballot as a candidate for statewide public office if the person pays a $100 filing fee and provides proof from the State Elections Board that he or she was nominated in the immediately preceding primary election by one of the state's two major political parties. It also permits the name of an independent candidate or a candidate of a smaller party to appear on the general election ballot if that person pays a filing fee of $1,000, and submits petitions signed by at least 3% of the voters who actually cast ballots for the office of governor in the last State X election. State X maintains that these filing requirements are necessary to limit the size of the election ballot, to eliminate frivolous candidacies, and to help finance the high cost of elections.

Historically, very few of State X's voters who are members of racial minority groups have been members of either of the two major political parties. Recently, a new political party has been formed by some of these voters.

Which of the following constitutional provisions would be most helpful to the new political party as a basis for attacking the constitutionality of this statute of State X?

(A) The First Amendment.
(B) The Thirteenth Amendment.
(C) The Fourteenth Amendment.
(D) The Fifteenth Amendment.

Question 142

A federal statute provides that the cities in which certain specified airports are located may regulate the rates and services of all limousines that serve those airports, without regard to the origin or destination of the passengers who use the limousines.

The cities of Redville and Greenville are located adjacent to each other in different states. The airport serving both of them is located in Redville and is one of those airports specified in the federal statute. The Redville City Council has adopted a rule that requires any limousines serving the airport to charge only the rates authorized by the Redville City Council.

Airline Limousine Service has a lucrative business transporting passengers between Greenville and the airport in Redville, at much lower rates than those required by the Redville City Council. It transports passengers in interstate traffic only; it does not provide local service within Redville. The new rule adopted by the Redville City Council will require Airline Limousine Service to charge the same rates as limousines operating only in Redville.

Must Airline Limousine Service comply with the new rule of the Redville City Council?

(A) Yes, because the airport is located in Redville and, therefore, its city council has exclusive regulatory authority over all transportation to and from the airport.
(B) Yes, because Congress has authorized this form of regulation by Redville and, therefore, removed any constitutional impediments to it that may have otherwise existed.
(C) No, because the rule would arbitrarily destroy a lucrative existing business and, therefore, would amount to a taking without just compensation.
(D) No, because Airline Limousine Service is engaged in interstate commerce and this rule is an undue burden on that commerce.

Question 143

A federal statute with inseverable provisions established a new five-member National Prosperity Board with broad regulatory powers over the operation of the securities, banking, and commodities industries, including the power to issue rules with the force of law. The statute provides for three of the board members to be appointed by the President with the advice and consent of the Senate. They serve seven-year terms and are removable only for good cause. The other two members of the board were designated in the statute to be the respective general counsel of the Senate and House of Representatives Committees on Government Operations. The statute stipulated that they were to serve on the board for as long as they continued in those positions.

Following all required administrative procedures, the board issued an elaborate set of rules regulating the operations of all banks, securities dealers, and commodities brokers. The Green Light Securities Company, which was subject to the board's rules, sought a declaratory judgment that the rules were invalid because the statute establishing the board was unconstitutional.

In this case, the court should rule that the statute establishing the National Prosperity Board is

(A) unconstitutional, because all members of federal boards having broad powers that are quasi-legislative in nature, such as rulemaking, must be appointed by Congress.
(B) unconstitutional, because all members of federal boards exercising executive powers must be appointed by the President or in a manner otherwise consistent with the appointments clause of Article II.
(C) constitutional, because the necessary and proper clause authorizes Congress to determine the means by which members are appointed to boards created by Congress under its power to regulate commerce among the states.
(D) constitutional, because there is a substantial nexus between the power of Congress to legislate for the general welfare and the means specified by Congress in this statute for the appointment of board members.

Question 144

A federal statute provides that the United States Supreme Court has authority to review any case filed in a United States Court of Appeals, even though that case has not yet been decided by the court of appeals.

The Environmental Protection Agency (EPA), an agency in the executive branch of the federal government, issued an important environmental rule. Although the rule had not been enforced against them, companies that would be adversely affected by the rule filed a petition for review of the rule in a court of appeals, seeking a declaration that the rule was invalid solely because it was beyond the statutory authority of the EPA. The companies made no constitutional claim. A statute specifically provides for direct review of EPA rules by a court of appeals without any initial action in a district court.

The companies have filed a petition for a writ of certiorari in the Supreme Court requesting immediate review of this case by the Supreme Court before the court of appeals has actually decided the case. The EPA acknowledges that the case is important enough to warrant Supreme Court review and that it should be decided promptly, but it asks the Supreme Court to dismiss the petition on jurisdictional grounds.

The best constitutional argument in support of the EPA's request is that

(A) the case is not within the original jurisdiction of the Supreme Court as defined by Article III, and it is not a proper subject of that court's appellate jurisdiction because it has not yet been decided by any lower court.
(B) the case is appellate in nature, but it is beyond the appellate jurisdiction of the Supreme Court, because Article III states that its jurisdiction extends only to cases arising under the Constitution.
(C) Article III precludes federal courts from reviewing the validity of any federal agency rule in any proceeding other than an action to enforce the rule.
(D) Article III provides that all federal cases, except those within the original jurisdiction of the Supreme Court, must be initiated by an action in a federal district court.

Question 145

In recent years, several large corporations incorporated and headquartered in State A have suddenly been acquired by out-of-state corporations that have moved all of their operations out of State A. Other corporations incorporated and headquartered in State A have successfully resisted such attempts at acquisition by out-of-state corporations, but they have suffered severe economic injury during those acquisition attempts.

In an effort to preserve jobs in State A and to protect its domestic corporations against their sudden acquisition by out-of-state purchasers, the legislature of State A enacts a statute governing acquisitions of shares in all corporations incorporated in State A. This statute requires that any acquisition of more than 25% of the voting shares of a corporation incorporated in State A that occurs over a period of less than one year must be approved by the holders of record of a majority of the shares of the corporation as of the day before the commencement of the acquisition of those shares. The statute expressly applies to acquisitions of State A corporations by both in-state and out-of-state entities.

Assume that no federal statute applies.

Is this statute of State A constitutional?

(A) No, because one of the purposes of the statute is to prevent out-of-state entities from acquiring corporations incorporated and headquartered in State A.
(B) No, because the effect of the statute will necessarily be to hinder the acquisition of State A corporations by other corporations, many of whose shareholders are not residents of State A and, therefore, it will adversely affect the interstate sale of securities.
(C) Yes, because the statute imposes the same burden on both in-state and out-of-state entities wishing to acquire a State A corporation, it regulates only the acquisition of State A corporations, and it does not create an impermissible risk of inconsistent regulation on this subject by different states.
(D) Yes, because corporations exist only by virtue of state law and, therefore, the negative implications of the commerce clause do not apply to state regulations governing their creation and acquisition.

Question 146

The legislature of State X enacts a statute that it believes reconciles the state's interest in the preservation of human life with a woman's right to reproductive choice. That statute permits a woman to have an abortion on demand during the first trimester of pregnancy but prohibits a woman from having an abortion after that time unless her physician determines that the abortion is necessary to protect the woman's life or health.

If challenged on constitutional grounds in an appropriate court, this statute will probably be held

(A) constitutional, because the state has made a rational policy choice that creates an equitable balance between the compelling state interest in protecting fetal life and the fundamental right of a woman to reproductive choice.
(B) constitutional, because recent rulings by the United States Supreme Court indicate that after the first trimester a fetus may be characterized as a person whose right to life is protected by the due process clause of the Fourteenth Amendment.
(C) unconstitutional, because the state has, without adequate justification, placed an undue burden on the fundamental right of a woman to reproductive choice prior to fetal viability.
(D) unconstitutional, because a statute unqualifiedly permitting abortion at one stage of pregnancy, and denying it at another with only minor exceptions, establishes an arbitrary classification in violation of the equal protection clause of the Fourteenth Amendment.

Question 147

The vaccination of children against childhood contagious diseases (such as measles, diphtheria and whooping cough) has traditionally been a function of private doctors and local and state health departments. Because vaccination rates have declined in recent years, especially in urban areas, the President proposes to appoint a Presidential Advisory Commission on Vaccination which would be charged with conducting a national publicity campaign to encourage vaccination as a public health measure. No federal statute authorizes or prohibits this action by the President. The activities of the Presidential Advisory Commission on Vaccination would be financed entirely from funds appropriated by Congress to the Office of the President for "such other purposes as the President may think appropriate."

May the President constitutionally create such a commission for this purpose?

(A) Yes, because the President has plenary authority to provide for the health, safety, and welfare of the people of the United States.
(B) Yes, because this action is within the scope of executive authority vested in the President by the Constitution, and no federal statute prohibits it.
(C) No, because the protection of children against common diseases by vaccination is a traditional state function and, therefore, is reserved to the states by the Tenth Amendment.

(D) No, because Congress has not specifically authorized the creation and support of such a new federal agency.

Question 148

Central City in the state of Green is a center for businesses that assemble personal computers. Components for these computers are manufactured elsewhere in Green and in other states, then shipped to Central City, where the computers are assembled. An ordinance of Central City imposes a special license tax on all of the many companies engaged in the business of assembling computers in that city. The tax payable by each such company is a percentage of the company's gross receipts.

The Green statute that authorizes municipalities to impose this license tax has a "Green content" provision. To comply with this provision of state law, the Central City license tax ordinance provides that the tax paid by any assembler of computers subject to this tax ordinance will be reduced by a percentage equal to the proportion of computer components manufactured in Green.

Assembler is a company that assembles computers in Central City and sells them from its offices in Central City to buyers throughout the United States. All of the components of its computers come from outside the state of Green. Therefore, Assembler must pay the Central City license tax in full without receiving any refund. Other Central City computer assemblers use components manufactured in Green in varying proportions and, therefore, are entitled to partial reductions of their Central City license tax payments.

Following prescribed procedure, Assembler brings an action in a proper court asking to have Central City's special license tax declared unconstitutional on the ground that it is inconsistent with the negative implications of the commerce clause.

In this case, the court should rule

(A) against Assembler, because the tax falls only on companies resident in Central City and, therefore, does not discriminate against or otherwise adversely affect interstate commerce.

(B) against Assembler, because the commerce clause does not interfere with the right of a state to foster and support businesses located within its borders by encouraging its residents to purchase the products of those businesses.

(C) for Assembler, because any tax on a company engaged in interstate commerce, measured in

whole or in part by its gross receipts, is a per se violation of the negative implications of the commerce clause.

(D) for Assembler, because the tax improperly discriminates against interstate commerce by treating in-state products more favorably than out-of-state products.

Question 149

An ordinance of Central City requires every operator of a taxicab in the city to have a license and permits revocation of that license only for "good cause." The Central City taxicab operator's licensing ordinance conditions the issuance of such a license on an agreement by the licensee that the licensee "not display in or on his or her vehicle any bumper sticker or other placard or sign favoring a particular candidate for any elected municipal office." The ordinance also states that it imposes this condition in order to prevent the possible imputation to the city council of the views of its taxicab licensees and that any licensee who violates this condition shall have his or her license revoked.

Driver, the holder of a Central City taxicab operator's license, decorates his cab with bumper stickers and other signs favoring specified candidates in a forthcoming election for municipal offices. A proceeding is initiated against him to revoke his taxicab operator's license on the sole basis of that admitted conduct.

In this proceeding, does Driver have a meritorious defense based on the United States Constitution?

(A) No, because he accepted the license with knowledge of the condition and, therefore, has no standing to contest it.

(B) No, because a taxicab operator's license is a privilege and not a right and, therefore, is not protected by the due process clause of the Fourteenth Amendment.

(C) Yes, because such a proceeding threatens Driver with a taking of property, his license, without just compensation.

(D) Yes, because the condition imposed on taxicab operators' licenses restricts political speech based wholly on its content, without any adequate governmental justification.

Question 150

Agitator, a baseball fan, has a fierce temper and an extremely loud voice. Attending a baseball game in which a number of calls went against the home team,

Agitator repeatedly stood up, brandished his fist, and angrily shouted, "Kill the umpires." The fourth time he engaged in this conduct, many other spectators followed Agitator in rising from their seats, brandishing fists, and shouting, "Kill the umpires."

The home team lost the game. Although no violence ensued, spectators crowded menacingly around the umpires after the game. As a result, the umpires were able to leave the field and stadium only with the help of a massive police escort.

For his conduct, Agitator was charged with inciting to riot and was convicted in a jury trial in state court. He appealed. The state supreme court reversed his conviction. In its opinion, the court discussed in detail decisions of the United States Supreme Court dealing with the First Amendment free speech clause as incorporated into the Fourteenth Amendment. At the end of that discussion, however, the court stated that it "need not resolve how, on the basis of these cases," the United States Supreme Court would decide Agitator's case. "Instead," the court stated, "this court has always given the free-speech guarantee of the state's constitution the broadest possible interpretation. As a result, we hold that in this case, where no riot or other violence actually occurred, the state constitution does not permit this conviction for incitement to riot to stand."

The United States Supreme Court grants a writ of certiorari to review this decision of the state supreme court.

In this case, the United States Supreme Court should

(A) affirm the state supreme court's decision, because Agitator's ballpark shout is commonplace hyperbole that cannot, consistently with the First and Fourteenth Amendments, be punished.
(B) remand the case to the state supreme court with directions that it resolve the First and Fourteenth Amendment free-speech issue that it discussed in such detail.
(C) dismiss the writ as improvidently granted, because the state supreme court's decision rests on an independent and adequate state law ground.
(D) reverse the decision of the state supreme court, because incitement to violent action is not speech protected by the First and Fourteenth Amendments.

Question 151

The state of Green imposes a tax on the "income" of each of its residents. As defined in the taxing statute, "income" includes the fair rental value of the use of any automobile provided by the taxpayer's employer for the taxpayer's personal use. The federal government supplies automobiles to some of its employees who are resident in Green so that they may perform their jobs properly. A federal government employee supplied with an automobile for this purpose may also use it for the employee's own personal business.

Assume there is no federal legislation on this subject.

May the state of Green collect this tax on the fair rental value of the personal use of the automobiles furnished by the federal government to these employees?

(A) No, because such a tax would be a tax on the United States.
(B) No, because such a tax would be a tax upon activities performed on behalf of the United States, since the automobiles are primarily used by these federal employees in the discharge of their official duties.
(C) Yes, because the tax is imposed on the employees rather than on the United States, and the tax does not discriminate against persons who are employed by the United States.
(D) Yes, because an exemption from such state taxes for federal employees would be a denial to others of the equal protection of the laws.

Question 152

The King City zoning ordinance contains provisions restricting places of "adult entertainment" to two specified city blocks within the commercial center of the city. These provisions of the ordinance define "adult entertainment" as "live or filmed nudity or sexual activity, real or simulated, of an indecent nature."

Sam proposes to operate an adult entertainment establishment outside the two-block area zoned for such establishments but within the commercial center of King City. When his application for permission to do so is rejected solely because it is inconsistent with provisions of the zoning ordinance, he sues the appropriate officials of King City, seeking to enjoin them from enforcing the adult entertainment provisions of the ordinance against him. He asserts that these provisions of the ordinance violate the First Amendment as made applicable to King City by the Fourteenth Amendment.

In this case, the court hearing Sam's request for an injunction would probably hold that the adult entertainment provisions of the King City zoning ordinance are

(A) constitutional, because they do not prohibit adult entertainment everywhere in King City, and the city has a substantial interest in keeping the major part of its commercial center free of uses it considers harmful to that area.

(B) constitutional, because adult entertainment of the kind described in these provisions of the King City ordinance is not protected by the free speech guarantee of the First and Fourteenth Amendments.

(C) unconstitutional, because they prohibit in the commercial area of the city adult entertainment that is not "obscene" within the meaning of the First and Fourteenth Amendments.

(D) unconstitutional, because zoning ordinances that restrict freedom of speech may be justified only by a substantial interest in preserving the quality of a community's residential neighborhoods.

Question 153

John is a licensed barber in State A. The State A barber licensing statute provides that the Barber Licensing Board may revoke a barber license if it finds that a licensee has used his or her business premises for an illegal purpose.

John was arrested by federal narcotics enforcement agents on a charge of selling cocaine in his barbershop in violation of federal laws. However, the local United States Attorney declined to prosecute and the charges were dropped.

Nevertheless, the Barber Licensing Board commenced a proceeding against John to revoke his license on the ground that John used his business premises for illegal sales of cocaine. At a subsequent hearing before the board, the only evidence against John was affidavits by unnamed informants, who were not present or available for cross-examination. Their affidavits stated that they purchased cocaine from John in his barbershop. Based solely on this evidence, the board found that John used his business premises for an illegal purpose and ordered his license revoked.

In a suit by John to have this revocation set aside, his best constitutional argument is that

(A) John's inability to cross-examine his accusers

denied him a fair hearing and caused him to be deprived of his barber license without due process of law.

(B) the administrative license revocation proceeding was invalid, because it denied full faith and credit to the dismissal of the criminal charges by the United States Attorney.

(C) Article III requires a penalty of the kind imposed on John to be imposed by a court rather than an administrative agency.

(D) the existence of federal laws penalizing the illegal sale of cocaine preempts state action relating to drug trafficking of the kind involved in John's case.

Question 154

The state of Red sent three of its employees to a city located in the state of Blue to consult with a chemical laboratory there about matters of state business. While in the course of their employment, the three employees of Red negligently released into local Blue waterways some of the chemical samples they had received from the laboratory in Blue.

Persons in Blue injured by the release of the chemicals sued the three Red state employees and the state of Red in Blue state courts for the damages they suffered. After a trial in which all of the defendants admitted jurisdiction of the Blue state court and fully participated, plaintiffs received a judgment against all of the defendants for $5 million, which became final.

Subsequently, plaintiffs sought to enforce their Blue state court judgment by commencing a proper proceeding in an appropriate court of Red. In that enforcement proceeding, the state of Red argued, as it had done unsuccessfully in the earlier action in Blue state court, that its liability is limited by a law of Red to $100,000 in any tort case. Because the three individual employees of Red are able to pay only $50,000 of the judgment, the only way the injured persons can fully satisfy their Blue state court judgment is from the funds of the state of Red.

Can the injured persons recover the full balance of their Blue state court judgment from the state of Red in the enforcement proceeding they filed in a court of Red?

(A) Yes, because the final judgment of the Blue court is entitled to full faith and credit in the courts of Red.

(B) Yes, because a limitation on damage awards against Red for tortious actions of its agents would violate the equal protection clause of the

Fourteenth Amendment.

(C) No, because the Tenth Amendment preserves the right of a state to have its courts enforce the state's public policy limiting its tort liability.

(D) No, because the employees of Red were negligent and, therefore, their actions were not authorized by the state of Red.

Question 155

Alex contracted for expensive cable television service for a period of six months solely to view the televised trial of Clark, who was on trial for murder in a court of the state of Green.

In the midst of the trial, the judge prohibited any further televising of Clark's trial because he concluded that the presence of television cameras was disruptive.

Alex brought an action in a federal district court against the judge in Clark's case asking only for an injunction that would require the judge to resume the televising of Clark's trial. Alex alleged that the judge's order to stop the televising of Clark's trial deprived him of property his investment in cable television service without due process of law.

Before Alex's case came to trial, Clark's criminal trial concluded in a conviction and sentencing. There do not appear to be any obvious errors in the proceeding that led to the result in Clark's case. After Clark's conviction and sentencing, the defendant in Alex's case moved to dismiss that suit.

The most proper disposition of this motion by the federal court would be to

(A) defer action on the motion until after any appellate proceedings in Clark's case have concluded, because Clark might appeal, his conviction might be set aside, he might be tried again, and television cameras might be barred from the new trial.

(B) defer action on the motion until after the Green Supreme Court expresses a view on its proper disposition, because the state law of mootness governs suits in federal court when the federal case is inexorably intertwined with a state proceeding.

(C) grant the motion, because the subject matter of the controversy between Alex and the defendant has ceased to exist and there is no strong likelihood that it will be revived.

(D) deny the motion, because Alex has raised an important constitutional question whether his

investment in cable service solely to view Clark's trial is property protected by the due process clause of the Fourteenth Amendment.

Question 156

Company wanted to expand the size of the building it owned that housed Company's supermarket by adding space for a coffeehouse. Company's building was located in the center of five acres of land owned by Company and devoted wholly to parking for its supermarket customers.

City officials refused to grant a required building permit for the coffeehouse addition unless Company established in its store a child care center that would take up space at least equal to the size of the proposed coffeehouse addition, which was to be 20% of the existing building. This action of City officials was authorized by provisions of the applicable zoning ordinance.

In a suit filed in state court against appropriate officials of City, Company challenged this child care center requirement solely on constitutional grounds. The lower court upheld the requirement even though City officials presented no evidence and made no findings to justify it other than a general assertion that there was a shortage of child care facilities in City. Company appealed.

The court hearing the appeal should hold that the requirement imposed by City on the issuance of this building permit is

(A) constitutional, because the burden was on Company to demonstrate that there was no rational relationship between this requirement and a legitimate governmental interest, and Company could not do so because the requirement is reasonably related to improving the lives of families and children residing in City.

(B) constitutional, because the burden was on Company to demonstrate that this requirement was not necessary to vindicate a compelling governmental interest, and Company could not do so on these facts.

(C) unconstitutional, because the burden was on City to demonstrate that this requirement was necessary to vindicate a compelling governmental interest, and City failed to meet its burden under that standard.

(D) unconstitutional, because the burden was on City to demonstrate a rough proportionality between this requirement and the impact of Company's proposed action on the community, and City failed to do so.

Question 157

The governor of the state of Green proposes to place a Christmas nativity scene, the components of which would be permanently donated to the state by private citizens, in the Green Capitol Building rotunda where the Green Legislature meets annually. The governor further proposes to display this state-owned nativity scene annually from December 1 to December 31, next to permanent displays that depict the various products manufactured in Green. The governor's proposal is supported by all members of both houses of the legislature.

If challenged in a lawsuit on establishment clause grounds, the proposed nativity scene display would be held

(A) unconstitutional, because the components of the nativity scene would be owned by the state rather than by private persons.

(B) unconstitutional, because the nativity scene would not be displayed in a context that appeared to depict and commemorate the Christmas season as a primarily secular holiday.

(C) constitutional, because the components of the nativity scene would be donated to the state by private citizens rather than purchased with state funds.

(D) constitutional, because the nativity scene would be displayed alongside an exhibit of various products manufactured in Green.

Question 158

Congress wishes to enact legislation prohibiting discrimination in the sale or rental of housing on the basis of the affectional preference or sexual orientation of the potential purchaser or renter. Congress wishes this statute to apply to all public and private vendors and lessors of residential property in this country, with a few narrowly drawn exceptions.

The most credible argument for congressional authority to enact such a statute would be based upon the

(A) general welfare clause of Article I, Section 8, because the conduct the statute prohibits could reasonably be deemed to be harmful to the national interest.

(B) commerce clause of Article I, Section 8, because, in inseverable aggregates, the sale or rental of

almost all housing in this country could reasonably be deemed to have a substantial effect on interstate commerce.

(C) enforcement clause of the Thirteenth Amendment, because that amendment clearly prohibits discrimination against the class of persons protected by this statute.

(D) enforcement clause of the Fourteenth Amendment, because that amendment prohibits all public and private actors from engaging in irrational discrimination.

Question 159

A city owns and operates a large public auditorium. It leases the auditorium to any group that wishes to use it for a meeting, lecture, concert, or contest. Each user must post a damage deposit and pay rent, which is calculated only for the actual time the building is used by the lessee. Reservations are made on a first-come, first-served basis.

A private organization that permits only males to serve in its highest offices rented the auditorium for its national convention. The organization planned to install its new officers at that convention. It broadly publicized the event, inviting members of the general public to attend the installation ceremony at the city auditorium. No statute or administrative rule prohibits the organization from restricting its highest offices to men.

An appropriate plaintiff sues the private organization seeking to enjoin it from using the city auditorium for the installation of its new officers. The sole claim of the plaintiff is that the use of this auditorium by the organization for the installation ceremony is unconstitutional because the organization disqualifies women from serving in its highest offices.

Will the plaintiff prevail?

(A) Yes, because the Fourteenth Amendment prohibits such an organization from discriminating against women in any of its activities to which it has invited members of the general public.

(B) Yes, because the organization's use of the city auditorium for this purpose subjects its conduct to the provisions of the Fourteenth Amendment.

(C) No, because the freedom of association protected by the Fourteenth Amendment prohibits the city from interfering in any way with the organization's use of city facilities.

(D) No, because this organization is not a state actor and, therefore, its activities are not subject to the provisions of the Fourteenth Amendment.

Question 160

State Y has a state employee grievance system that requires any state employee who wishes to file a grievance against the state to submit that grievance for final resolution to a panel of three arbitrators chosen by the parties from a statewide board of 13 arbitrators. In any given case, the grievant and the state alternate in exercising the right of each party to eliminate five members of the board, leaving a panel of three members to decide their case. At the present time, the full board is composed of seven male arbitrators and six female arbitrators.

Ellen, a female state employee, filed a sexual harassment grievance against her male supervisor and the state. Anne, the state's attorney, exercised all of her five strikes to eliminate five of the female arbitrators. At the time she did so, Anne stated that she struck the five female arbitrators solely because she believed women, as a group, would necessarily be biased in favor of another woman who was claiming sexual harassment. Counsel for Ellen eliminated four males and one female arbitrator, all solely on grounds of specific bias or conflicts of interest. As a result, the panel was all male.

When the panel ruled against Ellen on the merits of her case, she filed an action in an appropriate state court, challenging the panel selection process as a gender-based denial of equal protection of the laws.

In this case, the court should hold that the panel selection process is

(A) unconstitutional, because the gender classification used by the state's attorney in this case does not satisfy the requirements of intermediate scrutiny.
(B) unconstitutional, because the gender classification used by the state's attorney in this case denies the grievant the right to a jury made up of her peers.
(C) constitutional, because the gender classification used by the state's attorney in this case satisfies the requirements of the strict scrutiny test.
(D) constitutional, because the gender classification used by the state's attorney in this case satisfies the requirements of the rational basis test.

Question 161

Senator makes a speech on the floor of the United States Senate in which she asserts that William, a federal civil servant with minor responsibilities, was twice convicted of fraud by the courts of State X. In making this assertion, Senator relied wholly on research done by Frank, her chief legislative assistant. In fact, it was a different man named William and not William the civil servant, who was convicted of these crimes in the state court proceedings. This mistake was the result of carelessness on Frank's part.

No legislation affecting the appointment or discipline of civil servants or the program of the federal agency for which William works was under consideration at the time Senator made her speech about William on the floor of the Senate.

William sues Senator and Frank for defamation. Both defendants move to dismiss the complaint.

As a matter of constitutional law, the court hearing this motion should

(A) grant it as to Frank, because he is protected by the freedom of speech guarantee against defamation actions by government officials based on his mere carelessness; but deny it as to Senator, because, as an officer of the United States, she is a constituent part of the government and, therefore, has no freedom of speech rights in that capacity.
(B) grant it as to both defendants, because Senator is immune to suit for any speech she makes in the Senate under the speech or debate clause of Article I, Section 6, and Frank may assert Senator's immunity for his assistance to her in preparing the speech.
(C) deny it as to both defendants, because any immunity of Senator under the speech or debate clause does not attach to a speech that is not germane to pending legislative business, and Frank is entitled to no greater immunity than the legislator he was assisting.
(D) deny it as to Frank, because he is not a legislator protected by the speech or debate clause; but grant it as to Senator, because she is immune from suit for her speech by virtue of that clause.

Question 162

Doctor, a resident of the city of Greenville in the state of Green, is a physician licensed to practice in both Green and the neighboring state of Red. Doctor finds that the most convenient place to treat her patients who need hospital care is in the publicly owned and operated Redville Municipal Hospital of the city of Redville in the state of Red, which is located just across the state line from Greenville. For many years Doctor had successfully treated her patients in that hospital. Early this year she was notified that she could no longer treat patients in the Redville hospital because she was not a resident of Red, and a newly adopted rule of Redville Municipal Hospital, which was adopted in conformance with all required procedures, stated that every physician who practices in that hospital must be a resident of Red.

Which of the following constitutional provisions would be most helpful to Doctor in an action to challenge her exclusion from the Redville hospital solely on the basis of this hospital rule?

(A) The bill of attainder clause.
(B) The privileges and immunities clause of Article IV.
(C) The due process clause of the Fourteenth Amendment.
(D) The ex post facto clause.

Question 163

A statute of the state of Texona prohibits any retailer of books, magazines, pictures, or posters from "publicly displaying or selling to any person any material that may be harmful to minors because of the violent or sexually explicit nature of its pictorial content." Violation of this statute is a misdemeanor.

Corner Store displays publicly and sells magazines containing violent and sexually explicit pictures. The owner of this store is prosecuted under the above statute for these actions.

In defending against this prosecution in a Texona trial court, the argument that would be the best defense for Corner Store is that the statute violates the

(A) First Amendment as it is incorporated into the Fourteenth Amendment, because the statute is excessively vague and overbroad.
(B) First Amendment as it is incorporated into the Fourteenth Amendment, because a state may not prohibit the sale of violent or sexually explicit material in the absence of proof that the material is utterly without any redeeming value in the marketplace of ideas.
(C) equal protection of the laws clause, because the statute irrationally treats violent and sexually explicit material that is pictorial differently from such material that is composed wholly of printed words.
(D) equal protection of the laws clause, because the

statute irrationally distinguishes between violent and sexually explicit pictorial material that may harm minors and such material that may harm only adults.

Question 164

A statute authorizes a specified federal administrative agency to issue rules governing the distribution of federal grant funds for scientific research. The statute provides that, in issuing those rules, the agency must follow procedures and substantive standards contained in the statute. In a severable provision, the statute also provides that otherwise valid rules issued by the agency under authority delegated to it by this statute may be set aside by a majority vote of a designated standing joint committee of Congress.

The provision of this statute relating to the power of the designated standing joint committee of Congress is

(A) constitutional, because it is a necessary and proper means of ensuring that the rules issued by this agency are actually consistent with the will of Congress.
(B) constitutional, because discretionary money grants authorized by statute are privileges, not rights, and, therefore, Congress has greater freedom to intervene in their administration than it has to intervene in the administration of regulatory laws.
(C) unconstitutional, because it denies equal protection of the laws to members of Congress who are not appointed to the joint legislative committee authorized to set aside rules of this agency.
(D) unconstitutional, because it authorizes a congressional change of legal rights and obligations by means other than those specified in the Constitution for the enactment of laws.

Question 165

A statute of the state of Tuscarora made it a misdemeanor to construct any building of more than five stories without an automatic fire sprinkler system.

A local construction company built in Tuscarora a ten-story federal office building. It constructed the building according to the precise specifications of a federal contract authorized by federal statutes. Because the building was built without the automatic fire sprinkler system required by state law, Tuscarora prosecutes the private contractor.

Which of the following is the company's strongest defense to that prosecution?

(A) The state sprinkler requirement denies the company property or liberty without due process.
(B) The state sprinkler requirement denies the company equal protection of the laws.
(C) As applied, the state sprinkler requirement violates the supremacy clause.
(D) As applied, the state sprinkler requirement violates the obligation of contracts clause.

MBE QUESTIONS

AMERIBAR BAR REVIEW

Multistate Bar Examination Released Questions – Section 4

CONTRACTS

Question 1

On August 1, Geriatrics, Inc., operating a "lifetime care" home for the elderly, admitted Ohlster, who was 84 years old, for a trial period of two months. On September 25, Ohlster and Geriatrics entered into a written lifetime care contract with an effective commencement date of October 1. The full contract price was $20,000, which, as required by the terms of the contract, Ohlster prepaid to Geriatrics on September 25. Ohlster died of a heart attack on October 2.

In a restitutionary action, can the administratrix of Ohlster's estate, a surviving sister, recover on behalf of the estate either all or part of the $20,000 paid to Geriatrics on September 25?

(A) Yes, because Geriatrics would otherwise be unjustly enriched at Ohlster's expense.
(B) Yes, under the doctrine of frustration of purpose.
(C) No, because Ohlster's life span and the duration of Geriatrics' commitment to him was a risk assumed by both parties.
(D) No, but only if Geriatrics can show that between September 25 and Ohlster's death it rejected, because of its commitment to Ohlster, an application for lifetime care from another elderly person.

Question 2

Swatter, a baseball star, contracted with the Municipal Symphony Orchestra, Inc., to perform for $5,000 at a children's concert as narrator of "Peter and the Wolf." Shortly before the concert, Swatter became embroiled in a highly publicized controversy over whether he had cursed and assaulted a baseball fan. The orchestra canceled the contract out of concern that attendance might be adversely affected by Swatter's appearance.

Swatter sued the orchestra for breach of contract. His business agent testified without contradiction that the cancellation had resulted in Swatter's not getting other contracts for performances and endorsements.

The trial court instructed the jury, in part, as follows: "If you find for the plaintiff, you may award damages for losses which at the time of contracting could reasonably have been foreseen by the defendant as a probable result of its breach. However, the law does not permit recovery for the loss of prospective profits of a

new business caused by breach of contract."

On Swatter's appeal from a jury verdict for Swatter, and judgment thereon, awarding damages only for the $5,000 fee promised by the orchestra, the judgment will probably be

(A) affirmed, because the trial court stated the law correctly.
(B) affirmed, because the issue of damages for breach of contract was solely a jury question.
(C) reversed, because the test for limiting damages is what the breaching party could reasonably have foreseen at the time of the breach.
(D) reversed, because under the prevailing modern view, lost profits of a new business are recoverable if they are established with reasonable certainty.

Questions 3-4 are based on the following fact situation.

Under a written agreement Superpastries, Inc., promised to sell its entire output of baked buns at a specified unit price to Bonnie's Buns, Inc., a retailer, for one year. Bonnie's Buns promised not to sell any other supplier's baked buns.

Question 3

For this question only, assume the following facts. Shortly after making the contract, and before Superpastries had tendered any buns, Bonnie's Buns decided that the contract had become undesirable because of a sudden, sharp decline in its customers' demand for baked buns. It renounced the agreement, and Superpastries sues for breach of contract.

Which of the following will the court probably decide?

(A) Bonnie's Buns wins, because mutuality of obligation was lacking in that Bonnie's Buns made no express promise to buy any of Superpastries' baked buns.
(B) Bonnie's Buns wins, because the agreement was void for indefiniteness of quantity and total price for the year involved.
(C) Superpastries wins, because Bonnie's Buns' promise to sell at retail Superpastries' baked buns exclusively, if it sold any such buns at all, implied a promise to use its best efforts to sell Superpastries' one-year output of baked buns.
(D) Superpastries wins, because under the applicable law both parties to a sale-of-goods

contract impliedly assume the risk of price and demand fluctuations.

Question 4

For this question only, assume the following facts. The parties' contract included a provision for termination by either party at any time upon reasonable notice. After six months of performance on both sides, Superpastries, claiming that its old bun-baker had become uneconomical and that it could not afford a new one, dismantled the bun-baker and began using the space for making dog biscuits. Superpastries' output of baked buns having ceased, Bonnie's Buns sued for breach of contract. Bonnie's Buns moves for summary judgment on liability, and Superpastries moves for summary judgment of dismissal.

Which of the following should the court rule?

(A) Summary judgment for Bonnie's Buns, because as a matter of law Superpastries could not discontinue production of baked buns merely because it was losing money on that product.
(B) Summary judgment for Superpastries, because its cessation of baked-bun production and Bonnie's Buns' awareness thereof amounted as a matter of law to valid notice of termination as permitted by the contract.
(C) Both motions denied, because there are triable issues of fact as to whether Superpastries gave reasonable notice of termination or whether its losses from continued production of baked buns were sufficiently substantial to justify cessation of production.
(D) Both motions denied: Superpastries may legally cease production of baked buns, but under the circumstances it must share with Bonnie's Buns its profits from the manufacture of dog biscuits until the end of the first year.

Questions 5-6 are based on the following fact situation.

On July 18, Snowco, a shovel manufacturer, received an order for the purchase of 500 snow shovels from Acme, Inc., a wholesaler. Acme had mailed the purchase order on July 15. The order required shipment of the shovels no earlier than September 15 and no later than October 15. Typed conspicuously across the front of the order form was the following: "Acme, Inc., reserves the right to cancel this order at any time before September 1." Snowco's mailed response, saying "We accept your order," was received by Acme on July 21.

Question 5

As of July 22, which of the following is an accurate statement as to whether a contract was formed?

(A) No contract was formed, because of Acme's reservation of the right to cancel.
(B) No contract was formed, because Acme's order was only a revocable offer.
(C) A contract was formed, but prior to September 1 it was terminable at the will of either party.
(D) A contract was formed, but prior to September 1 it was an option contract terminable only at the will of Acme.

Question 6

For this question only, assume the following facts. Acme did not cancel the order, and Snowco shipped the shovels to Acme on September 15. When the shovels, conforming to the order in all respects, arrived on October 10, Acme refused to accept them.

Which of the following is an accurate statement as of October 10 after Acme rejected the shovels?

(A) Acme's order for the shovels, even if initially illusory, became a binding promise to accept and pay for them.
(B) Acme's order was an offer that became an option after shipment by Snowco.
(C) Acme's right to cancel was a condition subsequent, the failure of which resulted in an enforceable contract.
(D) In view of Acme's right to cancel its order prior to September 1, the shipment of the shovels on September 15 was only an offer by Snowco.

Question 7

Hydro-King, Inc., a high-volume, pleasure-boat retailer, entered into a written contract with Zuma, signed by both parties, to sell Zuma a power boat for $12,000. The manufacturer's price of the boat delivered to Hydro-King was $9,500. As the contract provided, Zuma paid Hydro-King $4,000 in advance and promised to pay the full balance upon delivery of the boat. The contract contained no provision for liquidated damages. Prior to the agreed delivery date, Zuma notified Hydro-King that he would be financially unable to conclude the purchase; and Hydro-King thereupon resold the same boat that Zuma had ordered to a third person for $12,000 cash.

If Zuma sues Hydro-King for restitution of the $4,000 advance payment, which of the following should the court decide?

(A) Zuma's claim should be denied, because, as the party in default, he is deemed to have lost any right to restitution of a benefit conferred on Hydro-King.

(B) Zuma's claim should be denied, because, but for his repudiation, Hydro-King would have made a profit on two boat-sales instead of one.

(C) Zuma's claim should be upheld in the amount of $4,000 minus the amount of Hydro-King's lost profit under its contract with Zuma.

(D) Zuma's claims should be upheld in the amount of $3,500 ($4,000 minus $500 as statutory damages under the UCC).

Question 8

Dewar, a developer, needing a water well on one of his projects, met several times about the matter with Waterman, a well driller. Subsequently, Waterman sent Dewar an unsigned typewritten form captioned "WELL DRILLING PROPOSAL" and stating various terms the two had discussed but not agreed upon, including a "proposed price of $5,000." The form concluded, "This proposal will not become a contract until signed by you [Dewar] and then returned to and signed by me [Waterman]."

Dewar signed the form and returned it to Waterman, who neglected to sign it but promptly began drilling the well at the proposed site on Dewar's project. After drilling for two days, Waterman told Dewar during one of Dewar's daily visits that he would not finish unless Dewar would agree to pay twice the price recited in the written proposal. Dewar refused, Waterman quit, and Dewar hired Subbo to drill the well to completion for a price of $7,500.

In an action by Dewar against Waterman for damages, which of the following is the probable decision?

(A) Dewar wins, because his signing of Waterman's form constituted an acceptance of an offer by

Waterman.

(B) Dewar wins, because Waterman's commencement of performance constituted an acceptance by Waterman of an offer by Dewar and an implied promise by Waterman to complete the well.

(C) Waterman wins, because he never signed the proposal as required by its terms.

(D) Waterman wins, because his commencement of performance merely prevented Dewar from revoking his offer, made on a form supplied by Waterman, and did not obligate Waterman to complete the well.

Questions 9-10 are based on the following fact situation.

Ohner and Planner signed a detailed writing in which Planner, a landscape architect, agreed to landscape and replant Ohner's residential property in accordance with a design prepared by Planner and incorporated in the writing. Ohner agreed to pay $10,000 for the work upon its completion. Ohner's spouse was not a party to the agreement, and had no ownership interest in the premises.

Question 9

For this question only, assume the following facts. Shortly before the agreement was signed, Ohner and Planner orally agreed that the writing would not become binding on either party unless Ohner's spouse should approve the landscaping design.

If Ohner's spouse disapproves the design and Ohner refuses to allow Planner to proceed with the work, is evidence of the oral agreement admissible in Planner's action against Ohner for breach of contract?

(A) Yes, because the oral agreement required approval by a third party.

(B) Yes, because the evidence shows that the writing was intended to take effect only if the approval occurred.

(C) No, because the parol evidence rule bars evidence of a prior oral agreement even if the latter is consistent with the terms of a partial integration.

(D) No, because the prior oral agreement contradicted the writing by making the parties' duties conditional.

Question 10

For this question only, assume the following facts. At Ohner's insistence, the written Ohner-Planner agreement contained a provision that neither party would be bound unless Ohner's law partner, an avid student of landscaping, should approve Planner's design. Before Planner commenced the work, Ohner's law partner, in the presence of both Ohner and Planner, expressly disapproved the landscaping design. Nevertheless, Ohner ordered Planner to proceed with the work, and Planner reluctantly did so. When Planner's performance was 40% complete, Ohner repudiated his duty, if any, to pay the contract price or any part thereof.

If Planner now sues Ohner for damages for breach of contract, which of the following concepts best supports Planner's claim?

(A) Substantial performance.
(B) Promissory estoppel.
(C) Irrevocable waiver of condition.
(D) Unjust enrichment.

Questions 11-12 are based on the following fact situation.

Gyro, an expert in lifting and emplacing equipment atop tall buildings, contracted in a signed writing to lift and emplace certain air-conditioning equipment atop Tower's building. An exculpatory clause in the contract provided that Gyro would not be liable for any physical damage to Tower's building occurring during installation of the air-conditioning equipment.

There was also a clause providing for per diem damages if Gyro did not complete performance by a specified date and a clause providing that "time is of the essence." Another clause provided that any subsequent agreement for extra work under the contract must be in writing and signed by both parties.

With ample time remaining under the contract for commencement and completion of his performance, Gyro notified Tower that he was selling his business to Copter, who was equally expert in lifting and emplacing equipment atop tall buildings, and that Copter had agreed to "take over the Gyro-Tower contract."

Question 11

If Tower refuses to accept Copter's services,

which of the following clauses in the Gyro-Tower contract will best support Tower's contention that Gyro's duties under the contract were not delegable without Tower's consent?

(A) The exculpatory clause.
(B) The liquidated-damage clause.
(C) The "time is of the essence" clause.
(D) The extra-work clause.

Question 12

For this question only, assume that Tower orally agreed with Gyro to accept Copter's services and that Copter performed on time but negligently installed the wrong air-conditioning equipment.

Will Tower succeed in an action against Gyro for damages for breach of contract?

(A) Yes, because Tower did not agree to release Gyro from liability under the Gyro-Tower contract.
(B) Yes, because Tower received no consideration for the substitution of Copter for Gyro.
(C) No, because by accepting the substitution of Copter for Gyro, Tower effected a novation, and Gyro was thereby discharged of his duties under the Gyro-Tower contract.
(D) No, because the liquidated-damage clause in the Gyro-Tower contract provided only for damages caused by delay in performance.

Questions 13-14 are based on the following fact situation.

Elda, the aged mother of Alice and Barry, both adults, wished to employ a live-in companion so that she might continue to live in her own home. Elda, however, had only enough income to pay one-half of the companion's $2,000 monthly salary. Learning of their mother's plight, Alice and Barry agreed with each other in a signed writing that on the last day of January and each succeeding month during their mother's lifetime, each would give Elda $500. Elda then hired the companion.

Alice and Barry made the agreed payments in January, February, and March. In April, however, Barry refused to make any payment and notified Alice and Elda that he would make no further payments.

Question 13

Will Elda succeed in an action for $500 brought

against Barry after April 30?

(A) Yes, because by making his first three payments, Barry confirmed his intent to contract.
(B) Yes, because Elda is an intended beneficiary of a contract between Alice and Barry.
(C) No, because a parent cannot sue her child for breach of a promise for support.
(D) No, because Alice and Barry intended their payments to Elda to be gifts.

Question 14

For this question only, assume that there is a valid contract between Alice and Barry and that Elda has declined to sue Barry.

Will Alice succeed in an action against Barry in which she asks the court to order Barry to continue to make his payments to Elda under the terms of the Alice-Barry contract?

(A) Yes, because Alice's remedy at law is inadequate.
(B) Yes, because Alice's burden of supporting her mother will be increased if Barry does not contribute his share.
(C) No, because a court will not grant specific performance of a promise to pay money.
(D) No, because Barry's breach of contract has caused no economic harm to Alice.

Question 15

Barrel, a retailer of guns in State X, U.S.A., received on June 1 the following signed letter from Slidebolt, a gun-wholesaler in another state: "We have just obtained 100 of the assault rifles you inquired about and can supply them for $250 each. We can guarantee shipment no later than August 1."

On June 10, Slidebolt sold and delivered the same rifles to another merchant for $300 each. Unaware of that transaction, Barrel on the morning of June 11 mailed Slidebolt a letter rejecting the latter's offer, but, changing his mind an hour later, retrieved from his local post office the letter of rejection and immediately dispatched to Slidebolt a letter of acceptance, which Slidebolt received on June 14.

On June 9, a valid federal statute making the interstate sale of assault rifles punishable as a crime had become effective, but neither Barrel nor Slidebolt was aware until June 15 that the statute was already in effect.

As between Barrel and Slidebolt, which of the following is an accurate statement?

(A) No contract was formed, because Slidebolt's June 10 sale of the rifles to another merchant revoked the offer to Barrel.
(B) If a contract was formed, it is voidable because of mutual mistake.
(C) If a contract was formed, it is unenforceable because of supervening impracticability.
(D) No contract was formed, because Barrel's June 11 rejection was effective on dispatch.

Questions 16-17 are based on the following fact situation.

Spender owed Midas $1,000, plus interest at 8% until paid, on a long-overdue promissory note, collection of which would become barred by the statute of limitations on June 30. On the preceding April 1, Spender and Midas both signed a writing in which Spender promised to pay the note in full on the following December 31, plus interest at 8% until that date, and Midas promised not to sue on the note in the meantime. Midas, having received some advice from his non-lawyer brother-in-law, became concerned about the legal effect of the April 1 agreement. On May 1, acting pro se as permitted by the rules of the local small claims court, he filed suit to collect the note.

Question 16

Assuming that there is no controlling statute, is the April 1 agreement an effective defense for Spender?

(A) Yes, because Spender's promise to pay interest until December 31 was consideration for Midas's promise not to sue.
(B) Yes, because the law creates a presumption that Spender relied on Midas's promise not to sue.
(C) No, because there was no consideration for Midas's promise not to sue, in that Spender was already obligated to pay $1,000 plus interest at 8% until the payment date.
(D) No, because Spender's April 1 promise is enforceable with or without consideration.

Question 17

For this question only, assume that on January 2

of the following year Midas's suit has not come to trial, Spender has not paid the note, Midas has retained a lawyer, and the lawyer, with leave of court, amends the complaint to add a second count to enforce the promise Spender made in the April 1 agreement.

Does the new count state a claim upon which relief can be granted?

(A) Yes, because Spender's failure to pay the note, plus interest, on December 31 makes Midas's breach of promise not to sue before that date no longer material.

(B) Yes, because Spender's April 1 promise is enforceable by reason of his moral obligation to pay the debt.

(C) No, because such relief would undermine the policy of the statute of limitations against enforcement of stale claims.

(D) No, because Spender's April 1 promise was lawfully conditioned upon Midas's forbearing to sue prior to December 31.

Question 18

Pater and his adult daughter, Carmen, encountered Tertius, an old family friend, on the street. Carmen said to Tertius, "How about lending me $1,000 to buy a used car? I'll pay you back with interest one year from today." Pater added, "And if she doesn't pay it back as promised, I will." Tertius thereupon wrote out and handed to Carmen his personal check, payable to her, for $1,000, and Carmen subsequently used the funds to buy a used car. When the debt became due, both Carmen and Pater refused to repay it, or any part of it.

In an action by Tertius against Pater to recover $1,000 plus interest, which of the following statements would summarize Pater's best defense?

(A) He received no consideration for his conditional promise to Tertius.

(B) His conditional promise to Tertius was not to be performed in less than a year from the time it was made.

(C) His conditional promise to Tertius was not made for the primary purpose of benefiting himself (Pater).

(D) The loan by Tertius was made without any agreement concerning the applicable interest rate.

Questions 19-20 are based on the following fact situation.

Betty Bower, an adult, asked Jeff Geetus to lend her $1,000. Geetus replied that he would do so only if Bower's father, Cash, would guarantee the loan. At Bower's request, Cash mailed a signed letter to Geetus: "If you lend $1,000 to my daughter, I will repay it if she doesn't." On September 15, Geetus, having read Cash's letter, lent $1,000 to Bower, which Bower agreed to repay in installments of $100 plus accrued interest on the last day of each month beginning October 31. Cash died on September 16. Later that same day, unaware of Cash's death, Geetus mailed a letter to Cash advising that he had made the $1,000 loan to Bower on September 15.

Bower did not pay the installments due on October 31, November 30, or December 31, and has informed Geetus that she will be unable to make repayments in the foreseeable future.

Question 19

On January 15, Geetus is entitled to a judgment against Bower for which of the following amounts?

(A) Nothing, because if he sues before the entire amount is due, he will be splitting his cause of action.

(B) $300 plus the accrued interest, because Bower's breach is only a partial breach.

(C) $1,000 plus the accrued interest, because Bower's unexcused failure to pay three installments is a material breach.

(D) $1,000 plus the accrued interest, because the failure to pay her debts as they come due indicates that Bower is insolvent and Geetus is thereby entitled to accelerate payment of the debt.

Question 20

For this question only, assume that Bower's entire $1,000 debt is due and that she has failed to repay any part of it. In an action by Geetus against Cash's estate for $1,000 plus accrued interest, which of the following, if any, will serve as (an) effective defense(s) for Cash's estate?

I. There was no consideration to support Cash's promise, because he did not receive any benefit.

II. Cash died before Geetus accepted his offer.

III. Cash died before Geetus notified him that his offer had been accepted.

(A) I only.
(B) II only.
(C) I and III only.
(D) Neither I nor II nor III.

Questions 21-22 are based on the following fact situation.

Tune Corporation, a radio manufacturer, and Bill's Comex, Inc., a retailer, after extensive negotiations entered into a final, written agreement in which Tune agreed to sell and Bill's agreed to buy all of its requirements of radios, estimated at 20 units per month, during the period January 1, 1988, and December 31, 1990, at a price of $50 per unit. A dispute arose in late December, 1990, when Bill's returned 25 undefective radios to Tune for full credit after Tune had refused to extend the contract for a second three-year period.

In an action by Tune against Bill's for damages due to return of the 25 radios, Tune introduces the written agreement, which expressly permitted the buyer to return defective radios for credit but was silent as to return of undefective radios for credit. Bill's seeks to introduce evidence that during the three years of the agreement it had returned, for various reasons, 125 undefective radios, for which Tune had granted full credit. Tune objects to the admissibility of this evidence.

Question 21

The trial court will probably rule that the evidence proffered by Bill's is

(A) inadmissible, because the evidence is barred by the parol evidence rule.
(B) inadmissible because the express terms of the agreement control when those terms are inconsistent with the course of performance.
(C) admissible, because the evidence supports an agreement that is not within the relevant statute of frauds.
(D) admissible, because course-of-performance evidence, when available, is considered the best indication of what the parties intended the writing to mean.

Question 22

For this question only, assume the following facts. When Bill's returned the 25 radios in question, it included with the shipment a check payable to Tune for the balance admittedly due on all <u>other</u> merchandise sold and delivered to Bill's. The check was conspicuously marked, "Payment in full for all goods sold to Bill's to date." Tune's credit manager, reading this check notation and knowing that Bill's had also returned the 25 radios for full credit, deposited the check without protest in Tune's local bank account. The canceled check was returned to Bill's a week later.

Which of the following defenses would best serve Bill's?

(A) Tune's deposit of the check and its return to Bill's after payment estopped Tune thereafter to assert that Bill's owed any additional amount.
(B) By depositing the check without protest and with knowledge of its wording, Tune discharged any remaining duty to pay on the part of Bill's.
(C) By depositing the check without protest and with knowledge of its wording, Tune entered into a novation discharging any remaining duty to pay on the part of Bill's.
(D) The parties' good-faith dispute over return of the radios suspended the duty of Bill's, if any, to pay any balance due.

Questions 23-24 are based on the following fact situation.

Alice entered into a contract with Paul by the terms of which Paul was to paint Alice's office for $1,000 and was required to do all of the work over the following weekend so as to avoid disruption of Alice's business.

Question 23

For this question only, assume the following facts. If Paul had started to paint on the following Saturday morning, he could have finished before Sunday evening. However, he stayed home that Saturday morning to watch the final game of the World Series on TV, and did not start to paint until Saturday afternoon. By late Saturday afternoon, Paul realized that he had underestimated the time it would take to finish the job if he continued to work alone. Paul phoned Alice at her home and accurately informed her that it was impossible to finish the work over the weekend unless he hired a helper. He also stated that to do so would require an additional charge of $200 for the work. Alice told Paul that she apparently had no choice but to pay "whatever it takes" to get the work done as scheduled.

Paul hired Ted to help finish the painting and paid Ted $200. Alice has offered to pay Paul $1,000. Paul is demanding $1,200.

How much is Paul likely to recover?

(A) $1,000 only, because Alice received no consideration for her promise to pay the additional sum.
(B) $1,000 only, because Alice's promise to pay "whatever it takes" is too uncertain to be enforceable.
(C) $1,200, in order to prevent Alice's unjust enrichment.
(D) $1,200, because the impossibility of Paul's completing the work alone discharged the original contract and a new contract was formed.

Question 24

For this question only, assume the following facts. Paul commenced work on Saturday morning, and had finished half the painting by the time he quit work for the day. That night, without the fault of either party, the office building was destroyed by fire.

Which of the following is an accurate statement?

(A) Both parties' contractual duties are discharged, and Paul can recover nothing from Alice.
(B) Both parties' contractual duties are discharged, but Paul can recover in quasi-contract from Alice.
(C) Only Paul's contractual duty is discharged, because Alice's performance (payment of the agreed price) is not impossible.
(D) Only Paul's contractual duty is discharged, and Paul can recover his reliance damages from Alice.

Question 25

Seisin and Vendee, standing on Greenacre, orally agreed to its sale and purchase for $5,000, and orally marked its bounds as "that line of trees down there, the ditch that intersects them, the fence on the other side, and that street on the fourth side."

In which of the following is the remedy of reformation most appropriate?

(A) As later reduced to writing, the agreement by clerical mistake included two acres that are actually beyond the fence.
(B) Vendee reasonably thought that two acres beyond the fence were included in the oral agreement but Seisin did not. As later reduced to writing, the agreement included the two acres.
(C) Vendee reasonably thought that the price orally agreed upon was $4,500, but Seisin did not. As later reduced to writing, the agreement said $5,000.
(D) Vendee reasonably thought that a dilapidated shed backed up against the fence was to be torn down and removed as part of the agreement, but Seisin did not. As later reduced to writing, the agreement said nothing about the shed.

Question 26

Fruitko, Inc., ordered from Orchard, Inc., 500 bushels of No. 1 Royal Fuzz peaches, at a specified price, "for prompt shipment." Orchard promptly shipped 500 bushels, but by mistake shipped No. 2 Royal Fuzz peaches instead of No. 1. The error in shipment was caused by the negligence of Orchard's shipping clerk.

Which of the following best states Fruitko's rights and duties upon delivery of the peaches?

(A) Orchard's shipment of the peaches was a counteroffer and Fruitko can refuse to accept them.
(B) Orchard's shipment of the peaches was a counteroffer but, since peaches are perishable, Fruitko, if it does not want to accept them, must reship the peaches to Orchard in order to mitigate Orchard's losses.
(C) Fruitko must accept the peaches because a contract was formed when Orchard shipped them.
(D) Although a contract was formed when Orchard shipped the peaches, Fruitko does not have to accept them.

Question 27

Debtor's $1,000 contractual obligation to Aunt was due on July 1. On the preceding June 15, Aunt called Niece and said, "As my birthday gift to you, you may collect on July 1 the $1,000 Debtor owes me." Aunt also called Debtor and told him to pay the $1,000 to Niece on July 1. On July 1, Debtor, saying that he did not like Niece and wouldn't pay anything to her, paid the $1,000 to Aunt, who accepted it without objection.

Will Niece succeed in an action for $1,000 against Debtor?

(A) Yes, because Aunt had effectively assigned the $1,000 debt to her.
(B) Yes, because Aunt's calls to Niece and Debtor effected a novation.
(C) No, because Aunt's acceptance of the $1,000, without objection, was in effect the revocation of a gratuitous assignment.
(D) No, because Debtor cannot be compelled to render performance to an assignee whom he finds personally objectionable.

Question 28

On March 1, Hotz Apartments, Inc., received from Koolair, Inc., a letter offering to sell Hotz 1,200 window air conditioners suitable for the apartments in Hotz's buildings. The Koolair offer stated that it would remain open until March 20, but that Hotz's acceptance must be received on or before that date. On March 16, Hotz posted a letter of acceptance. On March 17, Koolair telegraphed Hotz to advise that it was revoking the offer. The telegram reached Hotz on March 17, but Hotz's letter did not arrive at Koolair's address until March 21.

As of March 22, which of the following is a correct statement?

(A) The telegram revoking the offer was effective upon receipt.
(B) The offer was revocable at any time for lack of consideration.
(C) The mail was the only authorized means of revocation.
(D) Under the terms of Koolair's offer, Hotz's attempted acceptance was ineffective.

Question 29

Stirrup, a rancher, and Equinox, a fancier of horses, signed the following writing: "For $5,000, Stirrup will sell to Equinox a gray horse that Equinox may choose from among the grays on Stirrup's ranch."

Equinox refused to accept delivery of a gray horse

timely tendered by Stirrup or to choose among those remaining, on the ground that during their negotiations Stirrup had orally agreed to include a saddle, worth $100, and also to give Equinox the option to choose a gray or a brown horse. Equinox insisted on one of Stirrup's brown horses, but Stirrup refused to part with any of his browns or with the saddle as demanded by Equinox.

If Equinox sues Stirrup for damages and seeks to introduce evidence of the alleged oral agreement, the court probably will

(A) admit the evidence as to both the saddle and the option to choose a brown horse.
(B) admit the evidence as to the saddle but not the option to choose a brown horse.
(C) admit the evidence as to the option to choose a brown horse but not the promise to include the saddle.
(D) not admit any of the evidence.

Question 30

Testator, whose nephew Bypast was his only heir, died leaving a will that gave his entire estate to charity. Bypast, knowing full well that Testator was of sound mind all of his life, and having no evidence to the contrary, nevertheless filed a suit contesting Testator's will on the ground that Testator was incompetent when the will was signed. Craven, Testator's executor, offered Bypast $5,000 to settle the suit, and Bypast agreed.

If Craven then repudiates the agreement and the foregoing facts are proved or admitted in Bypast's suit against Craven for breach of contract, is Bypast entitled to recover under the prevailing view?

(A) Yes, because the Bypast-Craven agreement was a bargained-for exchange.
(B) Yes, because the law encourages the settlement of disputed claims.
(C) No, because Bypast did not bring the will contest in good faith.
(D) No, because an agreement to oust the court of its jurisdiction to decide a will contest is contrary to public policy.

Questions 31-32 are based on the following fact situation.

Green contracted in a signed writing to sell Greenacre, a 500-acre tract of farmland, to Farmer, The contract provided for exchange of the deed and purchase price of $500,000 in cash on January 15. Possession was to be given to Farmer on the same date. On January 15, Green notified Farmer that because the tenant on Greenacre wrongfully refused to quit the premises until January 30, Green would be unable to deliver possession of Greenacre until then, but he assured Farmer that he would tender the deed and possession on that date. When Green tendered the deed and possession on January 30, Farmer refused to accept either, and refused to pay the $500,000. Throughout the month of January, the market value of Greenacre was $510,000, and its fair monthly rental value was $5,000.

Question 31

Will Green probably succeed in an action against Farmer for specific performance?

(A) Yes, because the court will excuse the delay in tender on the ground that there was a temporary impossibility caused by the tenant's holding over.
(B) Yes, because time is ordinarily not of the essence in a land-sale contract.
(C) No, because Green breached by failing to tender the deed and possession on January 15.
(D) No, because Green's remedy at law for monetary relief is adequate.

Question 32

For this question only, make the following assumptions. On January 30, Farmer accepted a conveyance and possession of Greenacre and paid the $500,000 purchase price, but notified Green that he was reserving any rights he might have to damages caused by Green's breach. Farmer intended to use the land for raising cattle and had entered into a contract for the purchase of 500 head of cattle to be delivered to Greenacre on January 15. Because he did not have possession of Greenacre on that date, he had to rent another pasture at a cost of $2,000 to graze the cattle for 15 days. Green had no reason to know that Farmer intended to use Greenacre for raising cattle or that he was purchasing cattle to be grazed on Greenacre.

In an action by Farmer against Green for damages, Farmer is entitled to recover

(A) nothing, because by paying the purchase price on January 30, he waived whatever cause of action he may have had.

(B) nominal damages only, because the market value of the land exceeded the contract price.
(C) $2,500 only (the fair rental value of Greenacre for 15 days).
(D) $2,500 (the fair rental value of Greenacre for 15 days), plus $2,000 (the cost of grazing the cattle elsewhere for 15 days).

Question 33

On December 1, Broker contracted with Collecta to sell her one of a certain type of rare coin for $12,000, delivery and payment to occur on the next March 1. To fulfill that contract, and without Collecta's knowledge, Broker contracted on January 1 to purchase for $10,000 a specimen of that type coin from Hoarder, delivery and payment to occur on February 1. The market price of such coins had unexpectedly fallen to $8,000 by February 1, when Hoarder tendered the coin and Broker repudiated.

On February 25, the market in such coins suddenly reversed and had stabilized at $12,000 on March 1. Broker, however, had failed to obtain a specimen of the coin and repudiated his agreement with Collecta when she tendered the $12,000 agreed price on March 1.

Later that day, after learning by chance of Broker's dealing with Collecta, Hoarder telephoned Collecta and said: "Listen, Broker probably owes me at least $2,000 in damages for refusing wrongfully to buy my coin for $10,000 on February 1 when the market was down to $8,000. But I'm in good shape in view of the market's recovery since then, and I think you ought to get after the so-and-so."

If Collecta immediately sues Broker for his breach of the Broker-Hoarder contract, which of the following will the court probably decide?

(A) Broker wins, because Collecta, if a beneficiary at all of the Broker-Hoarder contract, was only an incidental beneficiary.
(B) Broker wins, because as of March 1 neither Hoarder nor Collecta had sustained any damage from Broker's repudiation of both contracts.
(C) Collecta wins, because she was an intended beneficiary of the Broker-Hoarder contract, under which damages for Broker's repudiation became fixed on February 1.
(D) Collecta wins, because she took an effective assignment of Hoarder's claim for damages against Broker when Hoarder suggested that

Collecta "get after the so-and-so."

Question 34

For an agreed price of $20 million, Bildko, Inc., contracted with Venture to design and build on Venture's commercial plot a 15-story office building. In excavating for the foundation and underground utilities, Bildko encountered a massive layer of granite at a depth of 15 feet. By reasonable safety criteria, the building's foundation required a minimum excavation of 25 feet. When the contract was made, neither Venture nor Bildko was aware of the subsurface granite, for the presence of which neither party had hired a qualified expert to test.

Claiming accurately that removal of enough granite to permit the construction as planned would cost him an additional $3 million and a probable net loss on the contract of $2 million, Bildko refused to proceed with the work unless Venture would promise to pay an additional $2.5 million for the completed building.

If Venture refuses and sues Bildko for breach of contract, which of the following will the court probably decide?

(A) Bildko is excused under the modern doctrine of supervening impossibility, which includes severe impracticability.
(B) Bildko is excused, because the contract is voidable on account of the parties' mutual mistake concerning an essential underlying fact.
(C) Venture prevails, because Bildko assumed the risk of encountering subsurface granite that was unknown to Venture.
(D) Venture prevails, unless subsurface granite was previously unknown anywhere in the vicinity of Venture's construction site.

Question 35

Wastrel, a notorious spendthrift who was usually broke for that reason, received the following letter from his Uncle Bullion, a wealthy and prudent man; "I understand you're in financial difficulties again. I promise to give you $5,000 on your birthday next month, but you'd better use it wisely or you'll never get another dime from me." Wastrel thereupon signed a contract with a car dealer to purchase a $40,000 automobile and to make a $5,000 down payment on the day after his birthday.

If Wastrel sues Bullion for $5,000 after the latter learned of the car-purchase contract and then repudiated his promise, which of the following is Bullion's best defense?

(A) A promise to make a gift in the future is not enforceable.
(B) Reliance by the promisee on a promise to make a future gift does not make the promise enforceable unless the value of the promised gift is substantially equivalent to the promisee's loss by reliance.
(C) Reliance by the promisee on a promise to make a future gift does not make the promise enforceable unless that reliance also results in an economic benefit to the promisor.
(D) Reliance by the promisee on a promise to make a future gift does not make the promise enforceable unless injustice can be avoided only by such enforcement.

Questions 36-37 are based on the following fact situation.

Mural a wallpaper hanger, sent Gennybelle, a general contractor, this telegram:

> Will do all paperhanging on new Doctors' Building, per owner's specs, for $14,000 if you accept within reasonable time after main contract awarded.
>
> /s/   Mural

Three other competing hangers sent Gennybelle similar bids in the respective amounts of $18,000, $19,000, and $20,000. Gennybelle used Mural's $14,000 figure in preparing and submitting her own sealed bid on Doctors' Building. Before the bids were opened, Mural truthfully advised Gennybelle that the former's telegraphic sub-bid had been based on a $4,000 computational error and was therefore revoked. Shortly thereafter, Gennybelle was awarded the Doctors' Building construction contract and subsequently contracted with another paperhanger for a price of $18,000. Gennybelle now sues Mural to recover $4,000.

Question 36

Which of the following, if proved, would most strengthen Gennybelle's prospect of recovery?

(A) After Mural's notice of revocation, Gennybelle made a reasonable effort to subcontract with another paperhanger at the lowest possible price.

(B) Gennybelle had been required by the owner to submit a bid bond and could not have withdrawn or amended her bid on the main contract without forfeiting that bond,

(C) Mural was negligent in erroneously calculating the amount of his sub-bid.

(D) Gennybelle dealt with all of her subcontractors in good faith and without seeking to renegotiate (lower) the prices they had bid.

Question 37

Which of the following, if proved, would best support Mural's defense?

(A) Gennybelle gave Mural no consideration for an irrevocable sub-bid.

(B) Mural's sub-bid expressly requested Gennybelle's acceptance after awarding of the main contract.

(C) Even after paying $18,000 for the paperhanging, Gennybelle would make a net profit of $100,000 on the Doctors' Building contract.

(D) Before submitting her own bid, Gennybelle had reason to suspect that Mural had made a computational mistake in figuring his sub-bid.

Questions 38-39 are based on the following fact situation.

For several weeks Mater, a wealthy, unemployed widow, and Nirvana Motors, Inc., negotiated unsuccessfully over the purchase price of a new Mark XX Rolls-Royce sedan, which, as Nirvana knew, Mater wanted her son Dilbert to have as a wedding gift. On April 27, Nirvana sent Mater a signed, dated memo saying, "If we can arrive at the same price within the next week, do we have a deal?" Mater wrote "Yes" and her signature at the bottom of this memo and delivered it back to Nirvana on April 29.

On May 1, Mater wrote Nirvana a signed letter offering to buy "one new Mark XX Rolls-Royce sedan, with all available equipment, for $180,000 cash on delivery not later than June 1." By coincidence, Nirvana wrote Mater a signed letter on May 1 offering to sell her "one new Mark XX Rolls-Royce sedan, with all available equipment, for $180,000 cash on delivery not later than June

1." These letters crossed in the mails and were respectively received and read by Mater and Nirvana on May 2.

Question 38

If Mater subsequently asserts and Nirvana denies that the parties had a binding contract on May 3, which of the following most persuasively supports Mater's position?

(A) A sale-of-goods contract may be made in any manner sufficient to show agreement, even though the moment of its making is undetermined.

(B) A sale-of-goods contract does not require that an acceptance be a mirror image of the offer.

(C) With respect both to the making of an agreement and the requirement of consideration, identical cross-offers are functionally the same as an offer followed by a responsive acceptance.

(D) Since Nirvana was a merchant in the transaction and Mater was not, Nirvana is estopped to deny that the parties' correspondence created a binding contract.

Question 39

For this question only, assume the following facts. On May 4, Mater and Nirvana Motors both signed a single document evidencing a contract for the sale by Nirvana to Mater, "as a wedding gift for Mater's son Dilbert," a new Mark XX Rolls-Royce sedan, under the same terms as previously stated in their correspondence. On May 5, Mater handed Dilbert a carbon copy of this document. In reliance on the prospective gift, Dilbert on May 20 sold his nearly new Cheetah (an expensive sports car) to a dealer at a "bargain" price of $50,000 and immediately informed Mater and Nirvana that he had done so.

On May 25, however, Mater and Nirvana Motors by mutual agreement rescinded in a signed writing "any and all agreements heretofore made between the undersigned parties for the sale-and-purchase of a new Mark XX Rolls-Royce sedan." Later that day, Nirvana sold for $190,000 cash to another buyer the only new Mark XX Rolls-Royce that it had in stock or could readily obtain elsewhere. On June 1, Dilbert tendered $180,000 in cash to Nirvana Motors and demanded delivery to him "within a reasonable time" of a new Mark XX Rolls-Royce sedan with all available equipment.

Nirvana rejected the tender and denied any obligation.

If Dilbert sues Nirvana for breach of contract, which of the following will the court probably decide?

(A) Dilbert wins, because his rights as an assignee for value of the May 4 Mater-Nirvana contract cannot be cut off by agreement between the original parties.
(B) Dilbert wins, because his rights as a third-party intended beneficiary became vested by his prejudicial reliance in selling his Cheetah on May 20.
(C) Nirvana wins, because Dilbert, if an intended beneficiary at all of the Mater-Nirvana contract, was only a donee beneficiary.
(D) Nirvana wins, because it reasonably and prejudicially relied on its contract of mutual rescission with Mater by selling the only readily available new Mark XX Rolls-Royce sedan to another buyer.

Question 40

On June 1, Buyem, Inc., a widget manufacturer, entered into a written agreement with Mako, Inc., a tool maker, in which Mako agreed to produce and sell to Buyem 12 sets of newly designed dies to be delivered August 1 for the price of $50,000, payable ten days after delivery. Encountering unexpected expenses in the purchase of special alloy steel required for the dies, Mako advised Buyem that production costs would exceed the contract price; and on July 1 Buyem and Mako signed a modification to the June 1 agreement increasing the contract price to $60,000. After timely receipt of 12 sets of dies conforming to the contract specifications, Buyem paid Mako $50,000 but refused to pay more.

Which of the following concepts of the Uniform Commercial Code, dealing expressly with the sale of goods, best supports an action by Mako to recover $10,000 for breach of Buyem's July 1 promise?

(A) Bargained-for exchange.
(B) Promissory estoppel.
(C) Modification of contracts without consideration.
(D) Unconscionability in the formation of contracts.

Questions 41-42 are based on the following fact situation.

Structo contracted with Bailey to construct for $500,000 a warehouse and an access driveway at highway level. Shortly after commencing work on the driveway, which required for the specified level some excavation and removal of surface material, Structo unexpectedly encountered a large mass of solid rock.

Question 41

For this question only, assume the following facts. Structo informed Bailey (accurately) that because of the rock the driveway as specified would cost at least $20,000 more than figured, and demanded for that reason a total contract price of $520,000. Since Bailey was expecting warehousing customers immediately after the agreed completion date, he signed a writing promising to pay the additional $20,000. Following timely completion of the warehouse and driveway, which conformed to the contract in all respects, Bailey refused to pay Structo more than $500,000.

What is the maximum amount to which Structo is entitled?

(A) $500,000, because there was no consideration for Bailey's promise to pay the additional $20,000.
(B) $500,000, because Bailey's promise to pay the additional $20,000 was exacted under duress.
(C) $520,000, because the modification was fair and was made in the light of circumstances not anticipated by the parties when the original contract was made.
(D) $520,000, provided that the reasonable value of Structo's total performance was that much or more.

Question 42

For this question only, assume the following facts. Upon encountering the rock formation, Structo, instead of incurring additional costs to remove it, built the access driveway over the rock with a steep grade down to the highway. Bailey, who was out of town for several days, was unaware of this nonconformity until the driveway had been finished. As built, it is too steep to be used safely by trucks or cars, particularly in the wet or icy weather frequently occurring in the area. It would cost $30,000 to tear out and rebuild the driveway at highway level. As built, the warehouse, including the driveway, has a fair market value of $550,000. Bailey has paid $470,000 to Structo, but refuses to pay more because of the nonconforming driveway, which Structo has refused to tear out and rebuild.

If Structo sues Bailey for monetary relief, what is the maximum amount Structo is entitled to recover?

(A) $30,000, because the fair market value of the warehouse and driveway "as is" exceeds the contract price by $50,000 (more than the cost of correcting the driveway).
(B) $30,000, because Structo substantially performed and the cost of correcting the driveway would involve economic waste.
(C) $30,000, minus whatever amount Structo saved by not building the driveway at the specified level.
(D) Nothing, because Bailey is entitled to damages for the cost of correcting the driveway.

Questions 43-44 are based on the following fact situation.

Responding to County's written advertisement for bids, Tyres was the successful bidder for the sale of tires to County for County's vehicles. Tyres and County entered into a signed, written agreement that specified, "It is agreed that Tyres will deliver all tires required by this agreement to County, in accordance with the attached bid form and specifications, for a one-year period beginning September 1, 1990." Attached to the agreement was a copy of the bid form and specifications. In the written advertisement to which Tyres had responded, but not in the bid form, County had stated, "Multiple awards may be issued if they are in the best interests of County." No definite quantity of tires to be bought by County from Tyres was specified in any of these documents.

In January 1991, Tyres learned that County was buying some of its tires from one of Tyres's competitors. Contending that the Tyres-County agreement was a requirements contract, Tyres sued County for the damages caused by County's buying some of its tires from the competitor.

Question 43

If County defends by offering proof of the advertisement concerning the possibility of

multiple awards, should the court admit the evidence?

(A) Yes, because the provision in the written agreement, "all tires required by this agreement," is ambiguous.
(B) Yes, because the advertisement was in writing.
(C) No, because of the parol evidence rule.
(D) No, because it would make the contract illusory.

Question 44

If the court concludes that the Tyres-County contract is an agreement by County to buy its tire requirements from Tyres, Tyres probably will

(A) recover under the contracts clause of the United States Constitution.
(B) recover under the provisions of the Uniform Commercial Code.
(C) not recover, because the agreement lacks mutuality of obligation.
(D) not recover, because the agreement is indefinite as to quantity.

Question 45

Rollem, an automobile retailer, had an adult daughter, Betsy, who needed a car in her employment but had only $3,000 with which to buy one. Rollem wrote to her, "Give me your $3,000 and I'll give you the car on our lot that we have been using as a demonstrator." Betsy thanked her father and paid him the $3,000. As both Rollem and Betsy knew, the demonstrator was reasonably worth $10,000. After Betsy had paid the $3,000, but before the car had been delivered to her, one of Rollem's sales staff sold and delivered the same car to a customer for $10,000. Neither the salesperson nor the customer was aware of the transaction between Rollem and Betsy.

Does Betsy, after rejecting a tendered return of the $3,000 by Rollem, have an action against him for breach of contract?

(A) Yes, because Rollem's promise was supported by bargained-for consideration.
(B) Yes, because Rollem's promise was supported by the moral obligation a father owes his child as to the necessities of modern life.
(C) No, because the payment of $3,000 was inadequate consideration to support Rollem's promise.

(D) No, because the salesperson's delivery of the car to the customer made it impossible for Rollem to perform.

Question 46

Loomis, the owner and operator of a small business, encourages "wellness" on the part of his employees and supports various physical-fitness programs to that end. Learning that one of his employees, Graceful, was a dedicated jogger, Loomis promised to pay her a special award of $100 if she could and would run one mile in less than six minutes on the following Saturday. Graceful thanked him, and did in fact run a mile in less than six minutes on the day specified. Shortly thereafter, however, Loomis discovered that for more than a year Graceful had been running at least one mile in less than six minutes every day as a part of her personal fitness program. He refused to pay the $100.

In an action by Graceful against Loomis for breach of contract, which of the following best summarizes the probable decision of the court?

(A) Loomis wins, because it is a compelling inference that Loomis's promise did not induce Graceful to run the specified mile.
(B) Loomis wins, because Graceful's running of the specified mile was beneficial, not detrimental, to her in any event.
(C) Graceful wins, because running a mile in less than six minutes is a significantly demanding enterprise.
(D) Graceful wins, because she ran the specified mile as requested, and her motives for doing so are irrelevant.

Questions 47-48 are based on the following fact situation.

Under the terms of a written contract, Karp agreed to construct for Manor a garage for $10,000. Nothing was said in the parties' negotiations or in the contract about progress payments during the course of the work.

Question 47

For this question only, assume the following facts. After completing 25% of the garage strictly according to Manor's specifications, Karp demanded payment of $2,000 as a "reasonable progress payment." Manor refused, and Karp

abandoned the job.

If each party sues the other for breach of contract, which of the following will the court decide?

(A) Both parties are in breach, and each is entitled to damages, if any, from the other.
(B) Only Karp is in breach and liable for Manor's damages, if any.
(C) Only Manor is in breach and liable for Karp's damages, if any.
(D) Both parties took reasonable positions, and neither is in breach.

Question 48

For this question only, assume the following facts. After completing 25% of the garage strictly according to Manor's specifications, Karp assigned his rights under the contract to Banquo as security for an $8,000 loan. Banquo immediately notified Manor of the assignment. Karp thereafter, without legal excuse, abandoned the job before it was half-complete. Karp subsequently defaulted on the loan from Banquo. Karp has no assets. It will cost Manor at least $8,000 to get the garage finished by another builder.

If Banquo sues Manor for $8,000, which of the following will the court decide?

(A) Banquo wins, because the Karp-Manor contract was in existence and Karp was not in breach when Banquo gave Manor notice of the assignment.
(B) Banquo wins, because Banquo as a secured creditor over Karp is entitled to priority over Manor's unsecured claim against Karp.
(C) Manor wins, because his right to recoupment on account of Karp's breach is available against Banquo as Karp's assignee.
(D) Manor wins, because his claim against Karp arose prior to Karp's default on his loan from Banquo.

Question 49

On June 1, Topline Wholesale, Inc., received a purchase-order form from Wonder-Good, Inc., a retailer and new customer, in which the latter ordered 1,000 anti-recoil widgets for delivery no later than August 30 at a delivered total price of $10,000, as quoted in Topline's current catalog.

Both parties are merchants with respect to widgets of all types. On June 2, Topline mailed to Wonder-Good its own form, across the top of which Topline's president had written, "We are pleased to accept your order." This form contained the same terms as Wonder-Good's form except for an additional printed clause in Topline's form that provided for a maximum liability of $100 for any breach of contract by Topline.

As of June 5, when Wonder-Good received Topline's acceptance form, which of the following is an accurate statement concerning the legal relationship between Topline and Wonder-Good?

(A) There is no contract, because the liability-limitation clause in Topline's form is a material alteration of Wonder-Good's offer.
(B) There is no contract, because Wonder-Good did not consent to the liability-limitation clause in Topline's form.
(C) There is an enforceable contract whose terms include the liability-limitation clause in Topline's form, because liquidation of damages is expressly authorized by the Uniform Commercial Code.
(D) There is an enforceable contract whose terms do not include the liability-limitation clause in Topline's form.

Questions 50-51 are based on the following fact situation.

Dominique obtained a bid of $10,000 to tear down her old building and another bid of $90,000 to replace it with a new structure in which she planned to operate a sporting goods store. Having only limited cash available, Dominique asked Hardcash for a $100,000 loan. After reviewing the plans for the project, Hardcash in a signed writing promised to lend Dominique $100,000 secured by a mortgage on the property and repayable over ten years in equal monthly installments at 10% annual interest. Dominique promptly accepted the demolition bid and the old building was removed, but Hardcash thereafter refused to make the loan. Despite diligent efforts, Dominique was unable to obtain a loan from any other source.

Question 50

Does Dominique have a cause of action against Hardcash?

(A) Yes, because by having the building demolished, she accepted Hardcash's offer to make the loan.
(B) Yes, because her reliance on Hardcash's promise was substantial, reasonable, and foreseeable.
(C) No, because there was no bargained-for exchange of consideration for Hardcash's promise to make the loan.
(D) No, because Dominique's inability to obtain a loan from any other source demonstrated that the project lacked the financial soundness that was a constructive condition to Hardcash's performance.

Question 51

For this question only, assume that Dominique has a cause of action against Hardcash.

If she sues him for monetary relief, what is the probable measure of her recovery?

(A) Expectancy damages, measured by the difference between the value of the new building and the old building, less the amount of the proposed loan ($100,000).
(B) Expectancy damages, measured by the estimated profits from operating the proposed sporting goods store for ten years, less the cost of repaying a $100,000 loan at 10% interest over ten years.
(C) Reliance damages, measured by the $10,000 expense of removing the old building, adjusted by the decrease or increase in the market value of Dominique's land immediately thereafter.
(D) Nominal damages only, because both expectancy and reliance damages are speculative, and there is no legal or equitable basis for awarding restitution.

Questions 52-53 are based on the following fact situation.

In a writing signed by both parties on December 1, Kranc agreed to buy from Schaff a gasoline engine for $1,000, delivery to be made on the following February 1. Through a secretarial error, the writing called for delivery on March 1, but neither party noticed the error until February 1. Before signing the agreement, Kranc and Schaff orally agreed that the contract of sale would be effective only if Kranc should notify

Schaff in writing not later than January 2 that Kranc had arranged to resell the engine to a third person. Otherwise, they agreed orally, "There is no deal." On December 15, Kranc entered into a contract with Trimota to resell the engine to Trimota at a profit.

Question 52

For this question only, assume the following facts. Kranc did not give Schaff notice of the resale until January 25, and Schaff received it by mail on January 26. Meantime, the value of the engine had unexpectedly increased about 75% since December 1, and Schaff renounced the agreement.

If Kranc sues Schaff on February 2 for breach of contract, which of the following is Schaff's best defense?

(A) The secretarial error in the written delivery-term was a mutual mistake concerning a basic fact, and the agreement is voidable by either party.
(B) Kranc's not giving written notice by January 2 of his resale was a failure of a condition precedent to the existence of a contract.
(C) In view of the unexpected 75% increase in value of the engine after December 1, Schaff's performance is excused by the doctrine of commercial frustration.
(D) The agreement, if any, is unenforceable because a material term was not included in the writing.

Question 53

For this question only, assume the following facts. On December 16, Kranc notified Schaff by telephone of Kranc's resale agreement with Trimota, and explained that a written notice was unfeasible because Kranc's secretary was ill. Schaff replied, "That's okay. I'll get the engine to you on February 1, as we agreed." Having learned, however, that the engine had increased in value about 75% since December 1, Schaff renounced the agreement on February 1.

If Kranc sues Schaff on February 2 for breach of contract, which of the following concepts best supports Kranc's claim?

(A) Substantial performance.
(B) Nonoccurrence of a condition subsequent.
(C) Waiver of condition.
(D) Novation of buyers.

Questions 54-55 are based on the following fact situation.

Walker, who knew nothing about horses, inherited Aberlone, a thoroughbred colt whose disagreeable behavior made him a pest around the barn. Walker sold the colt for $1,500 to Sherwood, an experienced racehorse-trainer who knew of Walker's ignorance about horses. At the time of sale, Walker said to Sherwood, "I hate to say it, but this horse is bad-tempered and nothing special."

Question 54

For this question only, assume that soon after the sale, Aberlone won three races and earned $400,000 for Sherwood.

Which of the following additional facts, if established by Walker, would best support his chance of obtaining rescission of the sale to Sherwood?

(A) Walker did not know until after the sale that Sherwood was an experienced racehorse-trainer.
(B) At a pre-sale exercise session of which Sherwood knew that Walker was not aware, Sherwood clocked Aberlone in record-setting time, far surpassing any previous performance.
(C) Aberlone was the only thoroughbred that Walker owned, and Walker did not know how to evaluate young and untested racehorses.
(D) At the time of the sale, Walker was angry and upset over an incident in which Aberlone had reared and thrown a rider.

Question 55

Which one of the following scenarios would best support an action by Sherwood, rather than Walker, to rescind the sale?

(A) In his first race after the sale, Aberlone galloped to a huge lead but dropped dead 100 yards from the finish line because of a rare congenital heart defect that was undiscoverable except by autopsy.
(B) Aberlone won $5 million for Sherwood over a three-year racing career but upon being retired was found to be incurably sterile and useless as a breeder.
(C) After Aberlone had won three races for Sherwood, it was discovered that by clerical

error, unknown to either party, Aberlone's official birth registration listed an undistinguished racehorse as the sire rather than the famous racehorse that in fact was the sire.

(D) A week after the sale, Aberlone went berserk and inflicted injuries upon Sherwood that required his hospitalization for six months and a full year for his recovery.

Questions 56-57 are based on the following fact situation.

Kabb, the owner of a fleet of taxis, contracted with Petrol, a dealer in petroleum products, for the purchase and sale of Kabb's total requirements of gasoline and oil for one year. As part of that agreement, Petrol also agreed with Kabb that for one year Petrol would place all his advertising with Ada Artiste, Kabb's wife, who owned her own small advertising agency. When Artiste was informed of the Kabb-Petrol contract, she declined to accept an advertising account from the Deturgid Soap Company because she could not handle both the Petrol and Deturgid accounts during the same year.

Question 56

For this question only, assume the following facts. During the first month of the contract, Kabb purchased substantial amounts of his gasoline from a supplier other than Petrol, and Petrol thereupon notified Artiste that he would no longer place his advertising with her agency.

In an action against Petrol for breach of contract, Artiste probably will

(A) succeed, because she is a third-party beneficiary of the Kabb-Petrol contract.
(B) succeed, because Kabb was acting as Artiste's agent when he contracted with Petrol.
(C) not succeed, because the failure of a constructive condition precedent excused Petrol's duty to place his advertising with Artiste.
(D) not succeed, because Artiste did not provide any consideration to support Petrol's promise to place his advertising with her.

Question 57

For this question only, make the following assumptions. Artiste was an intended beneficiary under the Kabb-Petrol contract. Kabb performed his contract with Petrol for six months, and

during that time Petrol placed his advertising with Artiste. At the end of the six months, Kabb and Artiste were divorced, and Kabb then told Petrol that he had no further obligation to place his advertising with Artiste. Petrol thereupon notified Artiste that he would no longer place his advertising with her.

In an action against Petrol for breach of contract, Artiste probably will

(A) succeed, because, on the facts of this case, Petrol and Kabb could not, without Artiste's consent, modify their contract so as to discharge Petrol's duties to Artiste.
(B) succeed, because Kabb acted in bad faith in releasing Petrol from his duty with respect to Artiste.
(C) not succeed, because, absent a provision in the contract to the contrary, the promisor and promisee of a third-party beneficiary contract retain by law the right to modify or terminate the contract.
(D) not succeed, because the agency relationship, if any, between Kabb and Artiste terminated upon their divorce.

Questions 58-59 are based on the following fact situation.

Mermaid owns an exceptionally seaworthy boat that she charters for sport fishing at a $500 daily rate. The fee includes the use of the boat with Mermaid as the captain, and one other crew member, as well as fishing tackle and bait. On May 1, Phinney agreed with Mermaid that Phinney would have the full-day use of the boat on May 15 for himself and his family for $500. Phinney paid an advance deposit of $200 and signed an agreement that the deposit could be retained by Mermaid as liquidated damages in the event Phinney canceled or failed to appear.

Question 58

For this question only, assume the following facts. At the time of contracting, Mermaid told Phinney to be at the dock at 5 a.m. on May 15. Phinney and his family, however, did not show up on May 15 until noon. Meantime, Mermaid agreed at 10 a.m. to take Tess and her family out fishing for the rest of the day. Tess had happened to come by and inquire about the possibility of such an outing. In view of the late hour, Mermaid charged Tess $400 and stayed out two hours beyond the customary return time. Phinney's failure to appear until noon was due to the fact that he had been trying to charter another boat across the bay at a lower rate and had gotten lost after he was unsuccessful in getting such a charter.

Which of the following is an accurate statement concerning the rights of the parties?

(A) Mermaid can retain the $200 paid by Phinney, because it would be difficult for Mermaid to establish her actual damages and the sum appears to have been a reasonable forecast in light of anticipated loss of profit from the charter.
(B) Mermaid is entitled to retain only $50 (10% of the contract price) and must return $150 to Phinney.
(C) Mermaid must return $100 to Phinney in order to avoid her own unjust enrichment at Phinney's expense.
(D) Mermaid must return $100 to Phinney, because the liquidated-damage clause under the circumstances would operate as a penalty.

Question 59

For this question only, assume the following facts. On May 15 at 1 a.m., the Coast Guard had issued offshore "heavy weather" warnings and prohibited all small vessels the size of Mermaid's from leaving the harbor. This prohibition remained in effect throughout the day. Phinney did not appear at all on May 15, because he had heard the weather warnings on his radio.

Which of the following is an accurate statement?

(A) The contract is discharged because of impossibility, and Phinney is entitled to return of his deposit.
(B) The contract is discharged because of mutual mistake concerning an essential fact, and Phinney is entitled to return of his deposit.
(C) The contract is not discharged, because its performance was possible in view of the exceptional seaworthiness of Mermaid's boat, and Phinney is not entitled to return of his deposit.
(D) The contract is not discharged, and Phinney is not entitled to return of his deposit, because the liquidated-damage clause in effect allocated the risk of bad weather to Phinney.

Question 60

Trawf, the manager of a state fair, contracted with Schweinebauch, a renowned hog breeder, to exhibit Schweinebauch's world champion animal, Megahawg, for the three weeks of the annual fair, at the conclusion of which Schweinebauch would receive an honorarium of $300. Two days before the opening of the fair, Megahawg took sick with boarsitis, a communicable disease among swine, and, under the applicable state quarantine law, very probably could not be exhibited for at least a month.

Upon learning this, Trawf can legally pursue which of the following courses of action with respect to his contract with Schweinebauch?

(A) Suspend his own performance, demand assurances from Schweinebauch, and treat a failure by Schweinebauch to give them as an actionable repudiation.
(B) Suspend his own performance and recover damages from Schweinebauch for breach of contract unless Schweinebauch at once supplies an undiseased hog of exhibition quality as a substitute for Megahawg.
(C) Terminate his own performance and treat Megahawg's illness as discharging all remaining duties under the contract.
(D) Terminate the contract, but only if he (Trawf) seeks promptly to obtain for the exhibit a suitable substitute for Megahawg from another hog owner.

Question 61

In a signed writing, Nimrod contracted to purchase a 25-foot travel trailer from Trailco for $15,000, cash on delivery no later than June 1. Nimrod arrived at the Trailco sales lot on Sunday, May 31, to pay for and take delivery of the trailer, but refused to do so when he discovered that the spare tire was missing.

Trailco offered to install a spare tire on Monday when its service department would open, but Nimrod replied that he did not want the trailer and would purchase another one elsewhere.

Which of the following is accurate?

(A) Nimrod had a right to reject the trailer, but Trailco was entitled to a reasonable opportunity to cure the defect.

(B) Nimrod had a right to reject the trailer and terminate the contract under the perfect tender rule.

(C) Nimrod was required to accept the trailer, because the defect could be readily cured.

(D) Nimrod was required to accept the trailer, because the defect did not substantially impair its value.

Question 62

Buyem faxed the following signed message to Zeller, his long-time widget supplier: "Urgently need blue widgets. Ship immediately three gross at your current list price of $600." Upon receipt of the fax, Zeller shipped three gross of red widgets to Buyem, and faxed to Buyem the following message: "Temporarily out of blue. In case red will help, am shipping three gross at the same price. Hope you can use them."

Upon Buyem's timely receipt of both the shipment and Zeller's fax, which of the following best describes the rights and duties of Buyem and Zeller?

(A) Buyem may accept the shipment, in which case he must pay Zeller the list price, or he must reject the shipment and recover from Zeller for total breach of contract.

(B) Buyem may accept the shipment, in which case he must pay Zeller the list price, or he may reject the shipment, in which case he has no further rights against Zeller.

(C) Buyem may accept the shipment, in which case he must pay Zeller the list price, less any damages sustained because of the nonconforming shipment, or he may reject the shipment and recover from Zeller for total breach of contract, subject to Zeller's right to cure.

(D) Buyem may accept the shipment, in which case he must pay Zeller the list price, less any damages sustained because of the nonconforming shipment, or he may reject the shipment provided that he promptly covers by obtaining conforming widgets from another supplier.

Questions 63-64 are based on the following fact situation.

Staff, Inc., a flour wholesaler, contracted to deliver to Eclaire, a producer of fine baked goods, her flour requirements for a one-year period. Before delivery of the first scheduled installment, Staff sold its business and "assigned" all of its sale contracts to Miller, Inc., another reputable and long-time flour wholesaler. Staff informed Eclaire of this transaction.

Question 63

For this question only, assume that when Miller tendered the first installment to Eclaire in compliance with the Staff-Eclaire contract, Eclaire refused to accept the goods.

Which of the following arguments, if any, legally support(s) Eclaire's rejection of the goods?

I.   Executory requirements contracts are nonassignable.

II.   Duties under an executory bilateral contract are assumable only by an express promise to perform on the part of the delegatee.

III. Language of "assignment" in the transfer for value of a bilateral sale-of-goods contract affects only a transfer of rights, not a delegation of duties.

(A) I only.
(B) II and III only.
(C) I and II and III.
(D) Neither I nor II nor III.

Question 64

For this question only, assume that Eclaire accepted Miller's delivery of the first installment under the Staff-Eclaire contract, but that Eclaire paid the contract price for that installment to Staff and refused to pay anything to Miller.

In an action by Miller against Eclaire for the contractual amount of the first installment, which of the following, if any, will be an effective defense for Eclaire?

I.   Eclaire had not expressly agreed to accept Miller as her flour supplier.

II.   Eclaire's payment of the contractual installment to Staff discharged her obligation.

III. Staff remained obligated to Eclaire even though Staff had assigned the contract to Miller.

(A) I only.
(B) II only.
(C) I and III only.
(D) Neither I nor II nor III.

Question 65

Client consulted Lawyer about handling the sale of Client's building, and asked Lawyer what her legal fee would be. Lawyer replied that her usual charge was $100 per hour, and estimated that the legal work on behalf of Client would cost about $5,000 at that rate. Client said, "Okay; let's proceed with it," and Lawyer timely and successfully completed the work. Because of unexpected title problems, Lawyer reasonably spent 75 hours on the matter and shortly thereafter mailed Client a bill for $7,500, with a letter itemizing the work performed and time spent. Client responded by a letter expressing his good-faith belief that Lawyer had agreed to a total fee of no more than $5,000. Client enclosed a check in the amount of $5,000 payable to Lawyer and conspicuously marked, "Payment in full for legal services in connection with the sale of Client's building." Despite reading the "Payment in full..." language, Lawyer, without any notation of protest or reservation of rights, endorsed and deposited the check to her bank account. The check was duly paid by Client's bank. A few days later, Lawyer unsuccessfully demanded payment from Client of the $2,500 difference between the amount of her bill and the check, and now sues Client for that difference.

What, if anything, can Lawyer recover from Client?

(A) Nothing, because the risk of unexpected title problems in a real-property transaction is properly allocable to the seller's attorney and thus to Lawyer in this case.
(B) Nothing, because the amount of Lawyer's fee was disputed in good faith by Client, and Lawyer impliedly agreed to an accord and satisfaction.
(C) $2,500, because Client agreed to an hourly rate for as many hours as the work reasonably required, and the sum of $5,000 was merely an estimate.
(D) The reasonable value of Lawyer's services in excess of $5,000, if any, because there was no specific agreement on the total amount of Lawyer's fee.

Questions 66-67 are based on the following fact situation.

On November 1, Debbit, an accountant, and Barrister, a lawyer, contracted for the sale by Debbit to Barrister of the law books Debbit had inherited from his father. Barrister agreed to pay the purchase price of $10,000 when Debbit delivered the books on December 1.

On November 10, Barrister received a signed letter from Debbit that stated: "I have decided to dispose of the book stacks containing the law books you have already purchased. If you want the stacks, I will deliver them to you along with the books on December 1 at no additional cost to you. Let me know before November 15 whether you want them. I will not sell them to anyone else before then." On November 14, Barrister faxed and Debbit received the following message: "I accept your offer of the stacks." Debbit was not a merchant with respect to either law books or book stacks.

Question 66

Debbit is contractually obligated to deliver the stacks because

(A) Barrister provided a new bargained-for exchange by agreeing to take the stacks.
(B) Debbit's letter (received by Barrister on November 10) and Barrister's fax-message of November 14 constituted an effective modification of the original sale-of-books contract.
(C) Barrister's fax-message of November 14 operated to rescind unilaterally the original sale-of-books contract.
(D) Debbit's letter (received by Barrister on November 10) waived the bargained-for consideration that would otherwise be required.

Question 67

For this question only, assume that on November 12 Debbit told Barrister that he had decided not to part with the stacks.

Will this communication operate as a legally effective revocation of his offer to deliver the stacks?

(A) Yes, because Barrister had a pre-existing obligation to pay $10,000 for the law books.
(B) Yes, because Debbit was not a merchant with respect to book stacks.
(C) No, because Debbit had given a signed assurance that the offer would be held open until November 15.
(D) No, because by delaying his acceptance until

November 14, Barrister detrimentally relied on Debbit's promise not to sell the stacks to anyone else in the meantime.

Questions 68-69 are based on the following fact situation.

On November 15, Joiner in a signed writing contracted with Galley for an agreed price to personally remodel Galley's kitchen according to specifications provided by Galley, and to start work on December 1. Joiner agreed to provide all materials for the job in addition to all of the labor required.

Question 68

For this question only, assume that on November 26 Joiner without legal excuse repudiated the contract and that Galley, after a reasonable and prolonged effort, could not find anyone to remodel his kitchen for a price approximating the price agreed to by Joiner.

If one year later Galley brings an action for specific performance against Joiner, which of the following will provide Joiner with the best defense?

(A) An action for equitable relief not brought within a reasonable time is barred by laches.
(B) Specific performance is generally not available as a remedy to enforce a contractual duty to perform personal services.
(C) Specific performance is generally not available as a remedy in the case of an anticipatory repudiation.
(D) Specific performance is not available as a remedy where even nominal damages could have been recovered as a remedy at law.

Question 69

For this question only, assume the following facts. On November 26, Galley without legal excuse repudiated the contract. Notwithstanding Galley's repudiation, however, Joiner subsequently purchased for $5,000 materials that could only be used in remodeling Galley's kitchen, and promptly notified Galley, "I will hold you to our contract." If allowed to perform, Joiner would have made a profit of $3,000 on the job.

If Galley refuses to retract his repudiation, and Joiner sues him for damages, what is the maximum that Joiner is entitled to recover?

(A) Nothing, because he failed to mitigate his damages.
(B) $3,000, his expectancy damages.
(C) $5,000, on a restitutionary theory.
(D) $5,000, his reliance damages, plus $3,000, his expectancy damages.

Question 70

Which of the following fact patterns most clearly suggests an implied-in-fact contract?

(A) A county tax assessor mistakenly bills Algernon for taxes on Bathsheba's property, which Algernon, in good faith, pays.
(B) Meddick, a physician, treated Ryder without Ryder's knowledge or consent, while Ryder was unconscious as the result of a fall from his horse.
(C) Asphalt, thinking that he was paving Customer's driveway, for which Asphalt had an express contract, mistakenly paved Nabor's driveway while Nabor looked on without saying anything or raising any objection.
(D) At her mother's request, Iris, an accountant, filled out and filed her mother's "E-Z" income-tax form (a simple, short form).

Question 71

Happy-Time Beverages agreed in writing with Fizzy Cola Company to serve for three years as a distributor in a six-county area of Fizzy Cola, which contains a small amount of caffeine. Happy-Time promised in the contract to "promote in good faith the sale of Fizzy Cola" in that area; but the contract said nothing about restrictions on the products that Happy-Time could distribute.

Six months later, Happy-Time agreed with the Cool Cola Company to distribute its caffeine-free cola beverages in the same six-county area.

If Fizzy Cola Company sues Happy-Time for breach of their distribution contract, which of the following facts, if established, would most strengthen Fizzy's case?

(A) Cool Cola's national advertising campaign disparages the Fizzy Cola product by saying, "You don't need caffeine and neither does your cola."

(B) Since Happy-Time began to distribute Cool Cola, the sales of Fizzy Cola have dropped 3% in the six-county area.

(C) Prior to signing the contract with Fizzy Cola Company, a representative of Happy-Time said that the deal with Fizzy would be "an exclusive."

(D) For many years in the soft-drink industry, it has been uniform practice for distributors to handle only one brand of cola.

Question 72

Bitz, an amateur computer whiz, agreed in writing to design for the Presskey Corporation, a distributor of TV game systems, three new games a year for a five-year period. The writing provided, in a clause separately signed by Bitz, that "No modification shall be binding on Presskey unless made in writing and signed by Presskey's authorized representative."

Because of family problems, Bitz delivered and Presskey accepted only two game-designs a year for the first three years; but the games were a commercial success and Presskey made no objection. Accordingly, Bitz spent substantial sums on new computer equipment that would aid in speeding up future design work. In the first quarter of the fourth year, however, Presskey terminated the contract on the ground that Bitz had breached the annual-quantity term.

In Bitz's suit against Presskey for damages, the jury found that the contract had been modified by conduct and the trial court awarded Bitz substantial compensatory damages.

Is this result likely to be reversed on appeal?

(A) Yes, because the contract's no-oral- modification clause was not expressly waived by Presskey.

(B) Yes, because the contract's no-oral- modification clause was a material part of the agreed exchange and could not be avoided without new consideration.

(C) No, because the contract's no-oral- modification clause was unconscionable as against an amateur designer.

(D) No, because Presskey by its conduct waived the annual-quantity term and Bitz materially changed his position in reasonable reliance on that waiver.

Question 73

Freund, a U.S. west-coast manufacturer, gave Wrench, a hardware retailer who was relocating to the east coast, the following "letter of introduction" to Tuff, an east-coast hardware wholesaler.

> This will introduce you to my good friend and former customer, Wrench, who will be seeking to arrange the purchase of hardware inventory from you on credit. If you will let him have the goods, I will make good any loss up to $25,000 in the event of his default.

> /Signed/ Freund

Wrench presented the letter to Tuff, who then sold and delivered $20,000 worth of hardware to Wrench on credit. Tuff promptly notified Freund of this sale.

Which of the following is NOT an accurate statement concerning the arrangement between Freund and Tuff?

(A) It was important to enforceability of Freund's promise to Tuff that it be embodied in a signed writing.

(B) By extending the credit to Wrench, Tuff effectively accepted Freund's offer for a unilateral contract.

(C) Although Freund received no consideration from Wrench, Freund's promise is enforceable by Tuff.

(D) Freund's promise is enforceable by Tuff whether or not Tuff gave Freund seasonable notice of the extension of credit to Wrench.

Questions 74-75 are based on the following fact situation.

Broker needed a certain rare coin to complete a set that he had contracted to assemble and sell to Collecta. On February 1, Broker obtained such a coin from Hoarda in exchange for $1,000 and Broker's signed, written promise to re-deliver to Hoarda "not later than December 31 this year" a comparable specimen of the same kind of coin without charge to Hoarda. On February 2, Broker consummated sale of the complete set to Collecta.

On October 1, the market price of rare coins suddenly began a rapid, sustained rise; and on

October 15 Hoarda wrote Broker for assurance that the latter would timely meet his coin-replacement commitment. Broker replied, "In view of the surprising market, it seems unfair that I should have to replace your coin within the next few weeks."

Question 74

For this question only, assume the following facts. Having received Broker's message on October 17, Hoarda sued Broker on November 15 for the market value of a comparable replacement-coin as promised by Broker in February. The trial began on December 1.

If Broker moves to dismiss Hoarda's complaint, which of the following is Broker's best argument in support of the motion?

(A) Broker did not repudiate the contract on October 17, and may still perform no later than the contract deadline of December 31.
(B) Even if Broker repudiated on October 17, Hoarda's only action would be for specific performance because the coin is a unique chattel.
(C) Under the doctrine of impossibility, which includes unusually burdensome and unforeseen impracticability, Broker is temporarily excused by the market conditions from timely performance of his coin-replacement obligation.
(D) Even if Broker repudiated on October 17, Hoarda has no remedy without first demanding in writing that Broker retract his repudiation.

Question 75

For this question only, assume the following facts. After receiving Broker's message on October 17, Hoarda telephoned Broker, who said, "I absolutely will not replace your coin until the market drops far below its present level." Hoarda then sued Broker on November 15 for the market value of a comparable replacement-coin as promised by Broker in February. The trial began on December 1.

If Broker moves to dismiss Hoarda's complaint, which of the following is Hoarda's best argument in opposing the motion?

(A) Hoarda's implied duty of good faith and fair dealing in enforcement of the contract required her to mitigate her losses on the rising market by suing promptly, as she did, after becoming

reasonably apprehensive of a prospective breach by Broker.
(B) Although the doctrine of anticipatory breach is not applicable under the prevailing view if, at the time of repudiation, the repudiatee owes the repudiator no remaining duty of performance, the doctrine applies in this case because Hoarda, the repudiatee, remains potentially liable under an implied warranty that the coin advanced to Broker was genuine.
(C) When either party to a sale-of-goods contract repudiates with respect to a performance not yet due, the loss of which will substantially impair the value of the contract to the other, the aggrieved party may in good faith resort to any appropriate remedy for breach.
(D) Anticipatory repudiation, as a deliberate disruption without legal excuse of an ongoing contractual relationship between the parties, may be treated by the repudiatee at her election as a present tort, actionable at once.

Question 76

Slalome, a ski-shop operator, in a telephone conversation with Mitt, a glove manufacturer, ordered 12 pairs of vortex-lined ski gloves at Mitt's list price of $600 per dozen "for delivery in 30 days." Mitt orally accepted the offer, and immediately faxed to Slalome this signed memo: "Confirming our agreement today for your purchase of a dozen pairs of vortex-lined ski gloves for $600, the shipment will be delivered in 30 days." Although Slalome received and read Mitt's message within minutes after its dispatch, she changed her mind three weeks later about the purchase and rejected the conforming shipment when it timely arrived.

On learning of the rejection, does Mitt have a cause of action against Slalome for breach of contract?

(A) Yes, because the gloves were identified to the contract and tendered to Slalome.
(B) Yes, because Mitt's faxed memo to Slalome was sufficient to make the agreement enforceable.
(C) No, because the agreed price was $600 and Slalome never signed a writing evidencing a contract with Mitt.
(D) No, because Slalome neither paid for nor accepted any of the goods tendered.

Question 77

A burglar stole Collecta's impressionist painting valued at $400,000. Collecta, who had insured the painting for $300,000 with Artistic Insurance Co., promised to pay $25,000 to Snoop, a full-time investigator for Artistic, if he effected the return of the painting to her in good condition. By company rules, Artistic permits its investigators to accept and retain rewards from policyholders for the recovery of insured property. Snoop, by long and skillful detective work, recovered the picture and returned it undamaged to Collecta.

If Collecta refuses to pay Snoop anything, and he sues her for $25,000, what is the probable result under the prevailing modern rule?

(A) Collecta wins, because Snoop owed Artistic a preexisting duty to recover the picture if possible.
(B) Collecta wins, because Artistic, Snoop's employer, had a preexisting duty to return the recovered painting to Collecta.
(C) Snoop wins, because Collecta will benefit more from return of the $400,000 painting than from receiving the $300,000 policy proceeds.
(D) Snoop wins, because the preexisting duty rule does not apply if the promisee's (Snoop's) duty was owed to a third person.

Questions 78-79 are based on the following fact situation.

Sue Starr, a minor both in fact and appearance, bought on credit and took delivery of a telescope from 30-year-old Paul Prism for an agreed price of $100. Upon reaching her majority soon thereafter, Starr encountered Prism and said, "I am sorry for not having paid you that $100 for the telescope when the money was due, but I found out it was only worth $75. So I now promise to pay you $75." Starr subsequently repudiated this promise and refused to pay Prism anything.

Question 78

In an action for breach of contract by Prism against Starr, Prism's probable recovery is

(A) nothing, because Starr was a minor at the time of the original transaction.
(B) nothing, because there was no consideration for the promise made by Starr after reaching majority.

(C) $75.
(D) $100.

Question 79

For this question only, assume that Starr bought the telescope from Prism after reaching her majority and promised to pay $100 "as soon as I am able."

What effect does this quoted language have on enforceability of the promise?

(A) None.
(B) It makes the promise illusory.
(C) It requires Starr to prove her inability to pay.
(D) It requires Prism to prove Starr's ability to pay.

Question 80

Tess Traviata owed Dr. Paula Pulmonary, a physician, $25,000 for professional services. Dr. Pulmonary orally assigned this claim to her adult daughter, Bridey, as a wedding gift. Shortly thereafter, on suffering sudden, severe losses in the stock market, Dr. Pulmonary assigned by a signed writing the same claim to her stockbroker, Margin, in partial satisfaction of advances legally made by Margin in Dr. Pulmonary's previous stock-market transactions. Subsequently, Traviata, without knowledge of either assignment, paid Dr. Pulmonary the $25,000 then due, which Dr. Pulmonary promptly lost at a horse track, although she remains solvent.

Assuming that Article 9 of the Uniform Commercial Code does NOT apply to either of the assignments in this situation, which of the following is a correct statement of the parties' rights and liabilities?

(A) As the assignee prior in time, Bridey can recover $25,000 from Traviata, who acted at her peril in paying Dr. Pulmonary.
(B) As the sole assignee for value, Margin can recover $25,000 from Traviata, who acted at her peril in paying Dr. Pulmonary.
(C) Neither Bridey nor Margin can recover from Traviata, but Bridey, though not Margin, can recover $25,000 from Dr. Pulmonary.
(D) Neither Bridey nor Margin can recover from Traviata, but Margin, though not Bridey, can recover $25,000 from Dr. Pulmonary.

Questions 81-82 are based on the following fact situation.

Ames had painted Bell's house under a contract which called for payment of $2,000. Bell, contending in good faith that the porch had not been painted properly, refused to pay anything.

On June 15, Ames mailed a letter to Bell stating, "I am in serious need of money. Please send the $2,000 to me before July 1." On June 18, Bell replied, "I will settle for $1,800 provided you agree to repaint the porch." Ames did not reply to this letter.

Thereafter Bell mailed a check for $1,800 marked "Payment in full on the Ames-Bell painting contract as per letter dated June 18." Ames received the check on June 30. Because he was badly in need of money, Ames cashed the check without objection and spent the proceeds but has refused to repaint the porch.

Question 81

Bell's refusal to pay anything to Ames when he finished painting was a

(A) partial breach of contract only if Ames had properly or substantially painted the porch.
(B) partial breach of contract whether or not Ames had properly or substantially painted the porch.
(C) total breach of contract only if Ames had properly or substantially painted the porch.
(D) total breach of contract whether or not Ames had properly or substantially painted the porch.

Question 82

After cashing the check Ames sued Bell for $200.00. Ames probably will

(A) succeed if he can prove that he had painted the porch according to specifications.
(B) succeed, because he cashed the check under economic duress.
(C) not succeed, because he cashed the check without objection.
(D) not succeed, because he is entitled to recover only the reasonable value of his services.

Question 83

In an action by Bell against Ames for any provable damages Bell sustained because the porch was not repainted, Bell probably will

(A) succeed, because by cashing the check Ames impliedly promised to repaint the porch.
(B) succeed, because Ames accepted Bell's offer by not replying to the letter of June 18.
(C) not succeed, because Bell's letter of June 18 was a counter-offer which Ames never accepted.
(D) not succeed, because there is no consideration to support Ames' promise, if any.

Question 84

Albert engaged Bertha, an inexperienced actress, to do a small role in a new Broadway play for a period of six months at a salary of $200 a week. Bertha turned down another role in order to accept this engagement. On the third day of the run, Bertha was hospitalized with influenza and Helen was hired to do the part. A week later, Bertha recovered, but Albert refused to accept her services for the remainder of the contract period. Bertha then brought an action against Albert for breach of contract.

Which of the following is Bertha's best legal theory?

(A) Her acting contract with Albert was legally severable into weekly units.
(B) Her performance of the literal terms of the contract was physically impossible.
(C) Her reliance on the engagement with Albert by declining another acting role created an estoppel against Albert.
(D) Her failure to perform for one week was not a material failure so as to discharge Albert's duty to perform.

Question 85

Testator, whose nephew Bypast was his only heir, died leaving a will that gave his entire estate to charity. Bypast, knowing full well that Testator was of sound mind all of his life, and having no evidence to the contrary, nevertheless filed a suit contesting Testator's will on the ground that Testator was incompetent when the will was signed. Craven, Testator's executor, offered Bypast $5,000 to settle the suit, and Bypast agreed.

If Craven then repudiates the agreement and the foregoing facts are proved or admitted in Bypast's suit against Craven for breach of contract, is Bypast entitled to recover under the prevailing view?

(A) Yes, because the Bypast-Craven agreement was a bargained-for exchange.
(B) Yes, because the law encourages the settlement of disputed claims.
(C) No, because Bypast did not bring the will contest in good faith.
(D) No, because an agreement to oust the court of its jurisdiction to decide a will contest is contrary to public policy.

Questions 86-89 are based on the following fact situation.

On March 1, Zeller orally agreed to sell his land, Homestead, to Byer for $46,000 to be paid on March 31. Byer orally agreed to pay $25,000 of the purchase price to Quincy in satisfaction of a debt which Zeller said he had promised to pay Quincy.

On March 10, Byer dictated the agreement to his secretary but omitted all reference to the payment of the $25,000 to Quincy. In typing the agreement, the secretary mistakenly typed in $45,000 rather than $46,000 as the purchase price. Neither Byer nor Zeller carefully read the writing before signing it on March 15. Neither noticed the error in price and neither raised any question concerning omission of the payment to Quincy.

Question 86

In an action by Quincy against Byer for $25,000, which of the following is (are) correct?

I.   Byer could successfully raise the Statute of Frauds as a defense because the Byer-Zeller agreement was to answer for the debt of another.
II. Byer could successfully raise the Statute of Frauds as a defense because the Byer-Zeller agreement was for the sale of an interest in land.

(A) I only
(B) II only
(C) Both I and II
(D) Neither I nor II

Question 87

Which of the following would be most important in deciding an action by Quincy against Byer for $25,000?

(A) Whether the Byer-Zeller agreement was completely integrated.
(B) Whether Byer was negligent in not having carefully read the written agreement.
(C) Whether Zeller was negligent in not having carefully read the written agreement.
(D) Whether Quincy was a party to the contract.

Question 88

In an action by Quincy against Byer for $25,000, which of the following, if proved, would best serve Byer as a defense?

(A) There was no consideration to support Zeller's antecedent promise to pay Quincy the $25,000.
(B) On March 5, before Quincy was aware of the oral agreement between Zeller and Byer, Zeller agreed with Byer not to pay any part of the purchase price to Quincy.
(C) Whatever action Quincy may have had against Byer was barred by the statute of limitations prior to March 1.
(D) Before he instituted his action against Byer, Quincy had not notified either Byer or Zeller that he had accepted the Byer-Zeller arrangement for paying Quincy.

Question 89

If Byer refused to pay more than $45,000 for Homestead, in an action by Zeller against Byer for an additional $1,000, it would be to Zeller's advantage to try to prove that

(A) the writing was intended only as a sham.
(B) the writing was only a partial integration.
(C) there was a mistake in integration.
(D) there was a misunderstanding between Zeller and Byer concerning the purchase price.

Questions 90-94 are based on the following fact situation.

While negligently driving his father's uninsured automobile, 25-year-old Arthur crashed into an automobile driven by Betty. Both Arthur and Betty were injured. Charles, Arthur's father, erroneously believing that he was liable because he owned the automobile, said to Betty: "I will see to it that you are reimbursed for any losses you incur as a result of the accident." Charles also called Physician and told him to take care of Betty, and that he, Charles, would pay the bill.

Arthur, having no assets, died as a result of his injuries. Dodge, one of Arthur's creditors, wrote to Charles stating that Arthur owed him a clothing bill of $200 and that he was going to file a claim against Arthur's estate. Charles replied: "If you don't file a claim against Arthur's estate, I will pay what he owed you."

Question 90

In an action by Betty against Charles for wages lost while she was incapacitated as a result of the accident, which of the following would be Charles' best defense?

(A) Lack of consideration
(B) Mistake of fact as to basic assumption
(C) Statute of Frauds
(D) Indefiniteness of Charles' promise

Question 91

Which of the following, if true, would be significant in determining whether or not there was bargained-for consideration to support Charles' promise to Physician?

  I.   Physician had not begun treating Betty before Charles called him.
  II. Charles had a contract with Betty.

(A) I only
(B) II only
(C) Both I and II
(D) Neither I nor II

Question 92

If Physician discontinued treating Betty before she had fully recovered and Betty brought an action against Physician for breach of contract, which of the following arguments, if any, by Physician would probably be effective in defense?

  I.   Betty furnished no consideration, either express or implied.

  II. Physician's contract was with Charles and not with Betty.
  III. Whatever contract Physician may have had with Betty was discharged by novation on account of the agreement with Charles.

(A) I only
(B) I and II only
(C) II and III only
(D) Neither I nor II nor III

Question 93

If Dodge did not file action against Arthur's estate, would Dodge succeed in an action against Charles for $200?

(A) Yes, because Dodge had detrimentally relied on Charles' promise.
(B) Yes, because Charles' promise was supported by a bargained-for exchange.
(C) No, because Dodge's claim against Arthur's estate was worthless.
(D) No, because Charles at most had only a moral obligation to pay Arthur's debts.

Question 94

Assume that Charles, honestly believing that he owed Dodge nothing, refused to pay anything to Dodge, who honestly believed that Charles owed him $200. If Dodge then accepts $150 from Charles in settlement of the claim, will Dodge succeed in an action against Charles for the remaining $50?

(A) Yes, because Arthur's debt of $200 was liquidated and undisputed.
(B) Yes, because Dodge honestly believed that he had a legal right against Charles for the full $200.
(C) No, because Charles honestly believed that Dodge did not have a legal right against him for the $200.
(D) No, because Charles was not contractually obligated to pay Dodge $200 in the first place.

Questions 95-100 are based on the following fact situation.

On March 1, Computer Programs, Inc. (CP) orally agreed with Holiday Department Store (HDS) to write a set of programs for HDS's computer and to coordinate the programs with

HDS's billing methods. A subsequent memo, signed by both parties, provided in its entirety:

> HDS will pay CP $20,000 in two equal installments within one month of completion if CP is successful in shortening by one-half the processing time for the financial transactions now handled on HDS's Zenon 747 computer; CP to complete by July 1. This agreement may be amended only by a signed writing.

On June 6, CP demanded $10,000, saying the job was one-half done. After HDS denied liability, the parties orally agreed that HDS should deposit $20,000 in escrow, pending completion to the satisfaction of HDS's computer systems manager. The escrow deposit was thereupon made. On July 5, CP completed the programs, having used an amount of time in which it could have earned $18,000 had it devoted that time to other jobs. Tests by CP and HDS's computer systems manager then showed that the computer programs, not being perfectly coordinated with HDS's billing methods, cut processing time by only 47 percent. They would, however, save HDS $12,000 a year. Further, if HDS would spend $5,000 to change its invoice preparation methods, as recommended by CP, the programs would cut processing time by a total of 58 percent, saving HDS another $8,000 a year. HDS's computer systems manager refused in good faith to certify satisfactory completion. HDS requested the escrow agent to return the $20,000 and asserted that nothing was owed to CP even though HDS continued to use the programs.

Question 95

If HDS denies liability on the ground that CP had orally agreed to coordinate with HDS's methods of accounting, and CP seeks in litigation to bar introduction of that agreement because of the parol evidence rule, HDS's most effective argument is that

(A) the parol evidence rule does not bar the introduction of evidence for the purpose of interpreting a written agreement.
(B) the memorandum was not a completely integrated agreement.
(C) HDS detrimentally relied on the oral promise of coordination in signing the memorandum.
(D) the memorandum was not a partially integrated agreement.

Question 96

If CP in fact had half-completed the job on June 6, would it then have been entitled to $10,000?

(A) Yes, because June 6 was within one month of completion.
(B) Yes, because CP had done one-half the job.
(C) No, because of a constructive condition precedent requiring at least substantial completion of the work before HDS would have a duty to pay.
(D) No, because "within one month of completion" would, in these circumstances, be interpreted to mean "within one month after completion."

Question 97

Was the escrow agreement a valid modification?

(A) Yes, because it was the compromise of an honest dispute.
(B) Yes, because the Statute of Frauds does not apply to subsequent oral modifications.
(C) No, because it was oral.
(D) No, because it was not supported by consideration.

Question 98

Assume for this question only that the programs completed on July 5 had cut processing time by one-half for all of HDS's financial transactions. Is HDS entitled to renounce the contract because of CP's delay in completion?

(A) Yes, because "CP to complete by July 1" is an express condition.
(B) Yes, because the doctrine of substantial performance does not apply to commercial contracts.
(C) No, because both parties manifested an understanding that time was not of the essence.
(D) No, because the contract did not contain a liquidated damages clause dealing with delay in completion.

Question 99

Assume for this question only that CP's delay in completion did not give HDS the right to renounce the contract and that the parties' escrow agreement was enforceable. Is CP entitled to recover damages for breach of the contract?

(A) Yes, because CP had substantially performed.
(B) Yes, because the program would save HDS $12,000 a year.
(C) No, because shortening the processing time by one-half was an express condition subsequent.
(D) No, because HDS's computer systems manager did not certify satisfactory completion of the programs.

Question 100

Assume for this question only that CP was in breach of contract because of its four-day delay in completion and that an express condition precedent to HDS's duty to pay the contract price has failed. Can CP nevertheless recover the reasonable value of its service?

(A) Yes, because continued use of the programs by HDS would save at least $12,000 a year.
(B) Yes, because HDS was continuing to use programs created by CP for which, as HDS knew, CP expected to be paid.
(C) No, because failure of an express condition precedent excused HDS from any duty to compensate CP.
(D) No, because such a recovery by CP would be inconsistent with a claim by HDS against CP for breach of contract.

Questions 101-105 are based on the following fact situation.

During 1976 a series of arsons, one of which damaged the Humongous Store, occurred in the City of Swelter. In early 1977 Swelter's City Council adopted this resolution:

> The City will pay $10,000 for the arrest and conviction of anyone guilty of any of the 1976 arsons committed here.

The foregoing was telecast by the city's sole television station once daily for one week. Subsequently, Humongous, by a written memorandum to Gimlet, a private detective, proposed to pay Gimlet $200 "for each day's work you actually perform in investigating our fire." Thereafter, in August, 1977, the City Council by resolution repealed its reward offer and caused this resolution to be broadcast once daily for a week over two local radio stations, the local television station having meanwhile ceased operations. In September, 1977, a Humongous

employee voluntarily confessed to Gimlet to having committed all of the 1976 arsons. Humongous' president thereupon paid Gimlet at the proposed daily rate for his investigation and suggested that Gimlet also claim the city's reward, of which Gimlet had been previously unaware. Gimlet immediately made the claim. In December, 1977, as a result of Gimlet's investigation, the Humongous employee was convicted of burning the store. The city, which has no immunity to suit, has since refused to pay Gimlet anything, although he swears that he never heard of the city's repealer before claiming its reward.

Question 101

In which of the following ways could the city reward offer be effectively accepted?

(A) Only by an offeree's return promise to make a reasonable effort to bring about the arrest and conviction of an arsonist within the scope of the offer.
(B) Only by an offeree's making the arrest and assisting in the successful conviction of an arsonist within the scope of the offer.
(C) By an offeree's supplying information leading to arrest and conviction of an arsonist within the scope of the offer.
(D) By an offeree's communication of assent through the same medium (television) used by the city in making its offer.

Question 102

With respect to duration, the city's reward offer was terminable

(A) by lapse of time, on December 31 of the year in which it was made.
(B) not by lapse of time, but only by effective revocation.
(C) not by revocation, but only by lapse of a reasonable time.
(D) either by lapse of a reasonable time or earlier by effective revocation.

Question 103

If the city's reward offer was revocable, revocation could be effectively accomplished only

(A) by publication in the legal notices of a local newspaper.

(B) in the same manner as made, i.e., by local telecast at least once daily for one week.

(C) in the same manner as made or by a comparable medium and frequency of publicity.

(D) by notice mailed to all residents of the city and all other reasonably identifiable, potential offerees.

Question 104

Which of the following best characterizes the relationship between Humongous and Gimlet?

(A) A unilateral offer of employment by Humongous which became irrevocable for a reasonable number of days after Gimlet commenced his investigation of the store's arson.

(B) An employment for compensation subject to a condition precedent that Gimlet succeed in his investigation.

(C) A series of daily bilateral contracts, Humongous exchanging an express promise to pay the daily rate for Gimlet's implied promise to pursue his investigation with reasonable diligence.

(D) A series of daily unilateral contracts, Humongous exchanging an express promise to pay the daily rate for Gimlet's daily activity of investigating the store's arson.

Question 105

In a suit by Gimlet against the city to recover the $10,000 reward, which of the following, in light of the facts given, most usefully supports Gimlet's claim?

(A) The city was benefited as a result of Gimlet's services.

(B) The city's offer was in the nature of a bounty, so that the elements of contract are not essential to the city's liability.

(C) The fact that the city attempted to revoke its offer only a few months after making it demonstrated that the attempted revocation was in bad faith.

(D) Although there was no bargained-for exchange between Gimlet and the city, Gimlet's claim for the reward is supported by a moral obligation on the part of the city.

Question 106

Landover, the owner in fee simple of Highacre, an apartment house property, entered into an enforceable written agreement with VanMeer to sell Highacre to VanMeer. The agreement provided that a good and marketable title was to be conveyed free and clear of all encumbrances. However, the agreement was silent as to the risk of fire prior to closing, and there is no applicable statute in the state where the land is located. The premises were not insured. The day before the scheduled closing date, Highacre was wholly destroyed by fire. When VanMeer refused to close, Landover brought an action for specific performance. If Landover prevails, the most likely reason will be that

(A) the failure of VanMeer to insure his interest as the purchaser of Highacre precludes any relief for him.

(B) the remedy at law is inadequate in actions concerning real estate contracts and either party is entitled to specific performance.

(C) equity does not permit consideration of surrounding circumstances in actions concerning real estate contracts.

(D) the doctrine of equitable conversion applies.

Question 107

On March 1, Mechanic agreed to repair Ohner's machine for $5,000, to be paid on completion of the work. On March 15, before the work was completed, Mechanic sent a letter to Ohner with a copy to Jones, telling Ohner to pay the $5,000 to Jones, who was one of Mechanic's creditors. Mechanic then completed the work.

Which of the following, if true, would best serve Ohner as a defense in an action brought against him by Jones for $5,000?

(A) Jones was incapable of performing Mechanic's work.

(B) Mechanic had not performed his work in a workmanlike manner.

(C) On March 1, Mechanic had promised Ohner that he would not assign the contract.

(D) Jones was not the intended beneficiary of the Ohner-Mechanic contract.

Questions 108-110 are based on the following fact situation.

BCD, a manufacturer of computers, pays its salespeople a salary of $1,000 per month and a commission of 5 percent on billings actually rendered for machines that they sell. BCD salespeople are employed at will under written agreements which provide that in order to receive a commission the salesperson must be in the employment of the company when the bill is sent to the customer.

In 1976, John, a salesperson for BCD, worked for eight months to get an order from Bobb Corporation for a large $750,000 computer. He consulted extensively with Bobb's top executives and worked with its operating personnel to develop detailed specifications for the new equipment. He also promised Bobb, with BCD's knowledge and approval, to assist Bobb for six months after installation in making the equipment work.

On January 1, 1977, Bobb signed an order, and on March 1, the computer was installed. On March 15, BCD fired John on the stated ground that he had failed to meet his 1975 and 1976 sales quotas. John thought that BCD was correct in this statement. Another salesperson, Franklin, was thereupon assigned to service the Bobb account. On March 31, BCD billed Bobb for the computer.

Question 108

Assume for this question only that BCD's termination of John's employment was not wrongful. If John, after demand and refusal, sues BCD for the Bobb sale commission, which of the following is the most likely to result?

(A) John will win, because he had procured the sale of the computer.
(B) John will win, because he had promised Bobb to assist in making the equipment work.
(C) BCD will win, because Franklin is entitled to the commission on a *quantum meruit* basis.
(D) BCD will win, because John was not employed as a BCD salesperson when Bobb was billed for the computer.

Question 109

Assume for this question only that BCD's termination of John's employment was not wrongful. If John sues BCD for the reasonable value of his services, which of the following is the most likely result.

(A) John will win, because BCD benefited as a result of John's services.
(B) John will win, because BCD made an implied-in-fact promise to pay a reasonable commission for services that result in sales.
(C) John will lose, because there is an express

contractual provision pre-empting the subject of compensation for his services.
(D) John will lose, because he cannot perform his agreement to assist the customer for six months.

Question 110

Which of the following additional facts, if shown by the evidence, would support a claim by John against BCD?

I.   BCD terminated John because Franklin is the son of the company's president, who wanted his son to have the commission instead of John.
II.   BCD and John were mistaken; John had in fact exceeded his sales quotas for 1975 and 1976.
III. John had worked for BCD as a salesperson for 20 years.

(A) I only
(B) II only
(C) I and II only
(D) I, II, and III

Questions 111-114 are based on the following fact situation.

Sartorial, Inc., a new business enterprise about to commence the manufacture of clothing, entered into written agreement to purchase all of its monthly requirements of a certain elasticized fabric for a period of three years from the Stretch Company at a specified unit price and agreed delivery and payment terms. The agreement also provided:

1.   The parties covenant not to assign this contract.
2.   Payments coming due hereunder for the first two months shall be made directly by Sartorial to Virginia Wear and Son, Inc., a creditor of Stretch.

Stretch promptly made an "assignment of the contract" to Finance Company as security for a $100,000 loan. Sartorial subsequently ordered, took delivery of and paid Stretch the agreed price ($5,000) for Sartorial's requirement of the fabric for the first month of its operation.

Question 111

Which of the following accurately states the

legal effect of the covenant not to assign the contract?

(A) The covenant made the assignment to Finance Company ineffective.
(B) The covenant had no legal effect.
(C) Stretch's assignment was a breach of its contract with Sartorial but was nevertheless effective to transfer to Finance Company Stretch's rights against Sartorial.
(D) By normal interpretation, a covenant against assignment in a sale-of-goods agreement applies only to the buyer, not the seller.

Question 112

Assume for this question only that the assignment from Stretch to Finance Company was effective, and that Sartorial was unaware of the assignment when it paid Stretch the $5,000. Which of the following is correct?

(A) Sartorial is liable to Finance Company for $5,000.
(B) Stretch is liable to Finance Company for $5,000.
(C) Sartorial and Stretch are each liable to Finance Company for $2,500.
(D) Neither Sartorial nor Stretch is liable to Finance Company for any amount.

Question 113

Assume for this question only that the assignment from Stretch to Finance Company was effective, and that Virginia Wear and Son, Inc., did not become aware of the original agreement between Sartorial and Stretch until after Stretch's acceptance of the $5,000 payment from Sartorial. Which of the following, if any, is (are) correct?

    I.   Virginia Wear and Son, Inc., was an incidental beneficiary of the Sartorial-Stretch agreement.

    II.   Virginia Wear and Son, Inc., has a prior right to Sartorial's $5,000 payment as against either Stretch or Finance Company.

(A) I only
(B) II only
(C) Both I and II
(D) Neither I nor II

Question 114

Assume for this question only that, two weeks after making the $5,000 payment to Stretch, Sartorial by written notice to Stretch terminated the agreement for purchase of the elasticized fabric because market conditions had in fact forced Sartorial out of the clothing manufacture business. In an immediate suit by Finance Company against Sartorial for total breach, which of the following would be useful in Sartorial's defense?

(A) Stretch's rights under its agreement with Sartorial were personal and therefore nonassignable.
(B) Stretch's "assignment of the contract" to Finance Company to secure a loan would normally be interpreted as a delegation of Stretch's duties under the contract as well as an assignment of its rights; and its duties, owed to Sartorial, were personal and therefore non-delegable.
(C) The original contract between Sartorial and Stretch was unenforceable by either party for want of a legally sufficient consideration for Stretch's promise to supply Sartorial's requirements of the elasticized fabric.
(D) Sartorial ceased in good faith to have any further requirements for elasticized fabric.

Question 115

Seth owned a vacant lot known as Richacre. Seth entered into a written contract with Bob to build a house of stated specifications on Richacre and to sell the house and lot to Bob. The contract provided for an "inside date" of April 1,1977, and an "outside date" of May 1, 1977, for completion of the house and delivery of a deed. Neither party tendered performance on the dates stated. On May 3, 1977, Bob notified Seth in writing of Bob's election to cancel the contract because of Seth's failure to deliver title by May 1. On May 12, Seth notified Bob that some unanticipated construction difficulties had been encountered but that Seth was entitled to a reasonable time to complete in any event. The notification also included a promise that Seth would be ready to perform by May 29 and that he was setting that date as an adjourned closing date. Seth obtained a certificate of occupancy and appropriate documents of title, and he tendered performance on May 29. Bob refused. Seth brought an action to recover damages for breach of contract.

The decision in the case will most likely be

determined by whether

(A) Seth acted with due diligence in completing the house.
(B) Bob can prove actual "undue hardship" caused by the delay.
(C) the expressions "inside date" and "outside date" are construed to make time of the essence.
(D) there is a showing of good faith in Bob's efforts to terminate the contract.

Questions 116-117 are based on the following fact situation.

Addle, who has been in the painting and contracting business for ten years and has a fine reputation, contracts to paint Boone's barn. Boone's barn is a standard red barn with loft. The contract has no provision regarding assignment.

Question 116

If Addle assigns the contract to Coot, who has comparable experience and reputation, which of the following statements is correct?

(A) Addle is in breach of contract.
(B) Boone may refuse to accept performance by Coot.
(C) Boone is required to accept performance by Coot.
(D) There is a novation.

Question 117

If Addle assigns the contract to Coot and thereafter Coot does not meet the contract specifications in painting Boone's barn, Boone

(A) has a cause of action against Addle for damages.
(B) has a cause of action only against Coot for damages.
(C) has a cause of action against Addle for damages only after he has first exhausted his remedies against Coot.
(D) does not have a cause of action against Addle for damages, because he waived his rights against Addle by permitting Coot to perform the work.

Questions 118-120 are based on the following fact situation.

Johnston bought 100 bolts of standard blue wool,

No. 1 quality, from McHugh. The sales contract provided that Johnston would make payment prior to inspection. The 100 bolts were shipped, and Johnston paid McHugh. Upon inspection, however, Johnston discovered that the wool was No. 2 quality. Johnston thereupon tendered back the wool to McHugh and demanded return of his payment. McHugh refused on the ground that there is no difference between No. 1 quality wool and No. 2 quality wool.

Question 118

Which of the following statements regarding the contract provision for pre-inspection payment is correct?

(A) It constitutes an acceptance of the goods.
(B) It constitutes a waiver of the buyer's remedy of private sale in the case of nonconforming goods.
(C) It does not impair a buyer's right of inspection or his remedies.
(D) It is invalid.

Question 119

What is Johnston's remedy because the wool was nonconforming?

(A) Specific performance.
(B) Damages measured by the difference between the value of the goods delivered and the value of conforming goods.
(C) Damages measured by the price paid plus the difference between the contract price and the cost of buying substitute goods.
(D) None, since he waived his remedies by agreeing to pay before inspection.

Question 120

Can Johnston resell the wool?

(A) Yes, in a private sale.
(B) Yes, in a private sale but only after giving McHugh reasonable notice of his intention to resell.
(C) Yes, but only at a public sale.
(D) No.

Questions 121-123 are based on the following fact situation.

Duffer and Slicker, who lived in different suburbs twenty miles apart, were golfing acquaintances at the Interurban Country Club. Both were traveling salesmen—Duffer for a pharmaceutical house and Slicker for a widget manufacturer. Duffer wrote Slicker by United States mail on Friday, October 8:

> I need a motorcycle for transportation to the country club, and will buy your Sujocki for $1,200 upon your bringing it to my home address above [stated in the letterhead] on or before noon, November 12 next. This offer is not subject to countermand.
>
>   Sincerely,
>
>   [signed] Duffer

Slicker replied by mail the following day:

> I accept your offer, and promise to deliver the bike as you specified.
>
>   Sincerely,
>
>   [signed] Slicker

This letter, although properly addressed, was misdirected by the postal service and not received by Duffer until November 10. Duffer had bought another Sujocki bike from Koolcat for $1,050 a few hours before.

Koolcat saw Slicker at the Interurban Country Club on November 11 and said: "I sold my Sujocki to Duffer yesterday for $1,050. Would you consider selling me yours for $950?" Slicker replied: "I'll let you know in a few days."

On November 12, Slicker took his Sujocki to Duffer's residence; he arrived at 11:15 a.m. Duffer was asleep and did not answer Slicker's doorbell rings until 12:15 p.m. Duffer then rejected Slicker's bike on the ground that he had already bought Koolcat's.

Question 121

In Duffer's letter of October 8, what was the legal effect of the language: "This offer is not subject to countermand"?

(A) Under the Uniform Commercial Code the offer was irrevocable until noon, November 12.
(B) Such language prevented an effective acceptance by Slicker prior to noon, November 12.

(C) At common law, such language created a binding option in Slicker's favor.
(D) Such language did not affect the offerer's power of revocation of the offer.

Question 122

In a lawsuit by Slicker against Duffer for breach of contract, what would the court probably decide regarding Slicker's letter of October 9?

(A) The letter bound both parties to a unilateral contract as soon as Slicker mailed it.
(B) Mailing of the letter by Slicker did not, of itself, prevent a subsequent, effective revocation by Duffer of his offer.
(C) The letter bound both parties to a bilateral contract, but only when received by Duffer on November 10.
(D) Regardless of whether Duffer's offer had proposed a unilateral or a bilateral contract, the letter was an effective acceptance upon receipt, if not upon dispatch.

Question 123

What is the probable legal effect of Koolcat's conversation with Slicker and report that he (Koolcat) had sold his Sujocki to Duffer on November 10?

(A) This report had no legal effect because Duffer's offer was irrevocable until November 12.
(B) Unless a contract had already been formed between Slicker and Duffer, Koolcat's report to Slicker operated to terminate Slicker's power of accepting Duffer's offer.
(C) This report has no legal effect because the offer had been made by a prospective buyer (Duffer) rather than a prospective seller.
(D) Koolcat's conversation with Slicker on November 11 terminated Duffer's original offer and operated as an offer by Koolcat to buy Slicker's Sujocki for $950.

Questions 124-125 are based on the following fact situation.

On May 1 Ohner telegraphed Byer, "Will sell you any or all of the lots in Grover subdivision at $5,000 each. Details will follow in letter." The letter contained all the necessary details concerning terms of payment, insurance, mortgages, etc., and provided, "This offer remains open until June 1."

On May 2, after he had received the telegram but before he had received the letter, Byer telegraphed Ohner, "Accept your offer with respect to lot 101." Both parties knew that there were fifty lots in the Grove subdivision and that they were numbered 101 through 150.

Question 124

For this question only, assume that on May 5 Ohner telephoned Byer that he had sold lots 102 through 150 to someone else on May 4 and that Byer thereafter telegraphed Ohner, "Will take the rest of the lots." Assume further that there is no controlling statute. In an action by Byer against Ohner for breach of contract, Byer probably will

(A) succeed, because Ohner had promised him that the offer would remain open until June 1.
(B) succeed, because Ohner's attempted revocation was by telephone.
(C) not succeed, because Byer's power of acceptance was terminated by Ohner's sale of the lots to another party.
(D) not succeed, because Byer's power of acceptance was terminated by an effective revocation.

Question 125

For this question only, assume that on May 6 Byer telegraphed Ohner, "Will take the rest of the lots," and that on May 8 Ohner discovered that he did not have good title to the remaining lots. Which of the following would provide the best legal support to Ohner's contention that he was not liable for breach of contract as to the remaining forty-nine lots?

(A) Impossibility of performance.
(B) Unilateral mistake as to basic assumption.
(C) Termination of the offer by Byer's having first contracted to buy lot 101.
(D) Excuse by failure of an implied condition precedent.

Questions 126-129 are based on the following fact situation.

Victim, injured by Driver in an auto accident, employed attorney First to represent him in the matter. Victim was chronically insolvent and expressed doubt whether he could promptly get necessary medical treatment. Accordingly, First wrote into their contract his promise to Victim "to pay from any settlement with Driver

compensation to any physician who provides professional services for Victim's injuries." The contract also provided that First's duties were "non-assignable." First immediately filed suit against Driver. Victim then sought and received medical treatment, reasonably valued at $1,000, from Doctor, but failed to inform Doctor of First's promise.

After receiving a bill from Doctor for $1,000, Victim immediately wrote Doctor explaining that he was unable to pay and enclosing a copy of his contract with First.

Victim then asked First about payment of this bill, but First requested a release from their employment contract, stating that he would like to refer Victim's claim to attorney Second and that Second was willing to represent Victim in the pending lawsuit. Victim wrote a letter to First releasing him from their contract and agreeing to Second's representation. A copy of this letter was sent to Doctor. Second subsequently promised First to represent Victim and soon negotiated a settlement of Victim's claim against Driver which netted $1,000, all of which was paid by Victim to creditors other than Doctor. Victim remains insolvent.

Question 126

In an action by Doctor against Victim to recover $1,000, Doctor's best theory of recovery is that Doctor

(A) is a creditor beneficiary of the employment contract between Victim and First.
(B) is a donee beneficiary of the employment contract between Victim and First.
(C) provided services essential to the preservation of Victim's health.
(D) has a claim based upon an implied-in-fact contract with Victim.

Question 127

In an action by Doctor against First upon First's employment contract with Victim, First is likely to argue in defense that

(A) the anti-assignment clause in First's contract with Victim is void as against public policy.
(B) First has relied to his detriment on Victim's letter of release.
(C) third parties cannot acquire valid claims under an attorney-client contract.

(D) Doctor has not materially changed his position in reliance upon First's employment contract.

Question 128

In an action by Doctor against First upon First's employment contract with Victim, if First attempted to use Victim's release as a defense, Doctor is likely to argue that

(A) the release was ineffective, because Doctor had impliedly assented to the Victim-First contract.
(B) the release was ineffective, because Victim would thereby be unjustly enriched.
(C) there was no consideration for Victim's release of First.
(D) First's contract duties were too personal to be effectively delegated to Second.

Question 129

In an action by Doctor against Second, Second is most likely to argue on these facts that

(A) Second made only a gratuitous promise to First.
(B) at the time Second promised to represent Victim, Doctor was only a member of an unidentified class of beneficiaries.
(C) there is insufficient evidence to support a finding that Doctor was either a creditor or donee beneficiary of Second's promise to First.
(D) there is insufficient evidence to support a finding that Doctor substantially changed his position in reliance on Second's promise.

Questions 130-132 are based on the following fact situation.

On March 1, Green and Brown orally agreed that Brown would erect a boathouse on Green's lot and dig a channel from the boathouse, across Clark's lot, to a lake. Clark had already orally agreed with Green to permit the digging of the channel across Clark's lot. Brown agreed to begin work on the boathouse on March 15, and to complete all the work before June 1. The total price of $10,000 was to be paid by Green in three installments: $2,500 on March 15; $2,500 when the boathouse was completed; $5,000 when Brown finished the digging of the channel.

Question 130

Assume that Green tendered the $2,500 on March 15, and that Brown refused to accept it or to perform. In an action by Green against Brown for breach of contract, which of the following can Brown successfully use as a defense?

    I.   The Clark-Green agreement permitting the digging of the channel across Clark's lot was not in writing.

    II.   The Green-Brown agreement was not in writing.

(A) I only
(B) II only
(C) Both I and II
(D) Neither I nor II

Question 131

Assume that Green paid the $2,500 on March 15 and that Brown completed the boathouse according to specifications, but that Green then refused to pay the second installment and repudiated the contract. Assume further that the absence of a writing is not raised as a defense. Which of the following is (are) correct?

    I.   Brown has a cause of action against Green and his damages will be $2,500.

    II.   Brown can refuse to dig the channel and not be liable for breach of contract.

(A) I only
(B) II only
(C) Both I and II
(D) Neither I nor II

Question 132

Assume that Green paid the $2,500 on March 15, that Brown completed the boat-house, that Green paid the second installment of $2,500, and that Brown completed the digging of the channel but not until July 1. Assume further that the absence of a writing is not raised as a defense. Which of the following is (are) correct?

    I.   Green has a cause of action against Brown for breach of contract.

    II.   Green is excused from paying the $5,000.

(A) I only
(B) II only
(C) Both I and II
(D) Neither I nor II

Questions 133-134 are based on the following fact situation.

Seller and Buyer execute an agreement for the sale of real property on September 1, 1971. The jurisdiction in which the property is located recognized the principle of equitable conversion and has no statute pertinent to this problem.

Question 133

Assume for this question only that Seller dies before closing and his will leaves his personal property to Perry and his real property to Rose. There being no breach of the agreement by either party, which of the following is correct?

(A) Death, an eventuality for which the parties could have provided, terminates the agreement if they did not so provide.
(B) Rose is entitled to the proceeds of the sale when it closes, because the doctrine of equitable conversion does not apply to these circumstances.
(C) Perry is entitled to the proceeds of the sale when it closes.
(D) Title was rendered unmarketable by Seller's death.

Question 134

Assume for this question only that Buyer dies before closing, there being no breach of the agreement by either party. Which of the following is appropriate in most jurisdictions?

(A)   Buyer's heir may specifically enforce the agreement.
(B)   Seller has the right to return the down payment and cancel the contract.
(C)   Death terminates the agreement.
(D)   Any title acquired would be unmarketable by reason of Buyer's death.

Questions 135-137 are based on the following fact situation.

Farquart had made a legally binding promise to furnish his son Junior and the latter's fiancée a house on their wedding day, planned for June 10, 1972. Pursuant to that promise, Farquart telephoned his old contractor-friend Sawtooth on May 1, 1971, and made the following oral agreement—each making full and accurate written notes thereof:

Sawtooth was to cut 30 trees into fireplace logs from a specified portion of a certain one-acre plot owned by Farquart, and Farquart was to pay therefore $20 per tree. Sawtooth agreed further to build a house on the plot conforming to the specifications of Plan OP5 published by Builders, Inc. for a construction price of $18,000. Farquart agreed to make payments of $2,000 on the first of every month for nine months beginning August 1, 1971, upon monthly presentation of certificate by Builders, Inc. that the specifications of Plan OP5 were being met.

Sawtooth delivered the cut logs to Farquart in July 1971, when he also began building the house. Farquart made three $2,000 payments for the work done in July, August, and September 1971, without requiring a certificate. Sawtooth worked through October, but no work was done from November 1, 1971, to the end of February 1972, because of bad weather, and Farquart made no payments during that period. Sawtooth did not object. On March 1, 1972, Sawtooth demanded payment of $2,000; but Farquart refused on the grounds that no construction work had been done for four months and Builders had issued no certificate. Sawtooth thereupon abandoned work and repudiated the agreement.

Question 135

Assuming that Sawtooth committed a total breach on March 1, 1972, what would be the probable measure of Farquart's damages in an action against Sawtooth for breach of contract?

(A) Restitution of the three monthly installments paid in August, September, and October.
(B) What it would cost to get the house completed by another contractor, minus installments not yet paid to Sawtooth.
(C) The difference between the market value of the partly built house, as of the time of Sawtooth's breach, and the market value of the house if completed according to specifications.
(D) In addition to other legally allowable damages, an allowance for Farquart's mental distress if the house cannot be completed in time for Junior's wedding on June 10, 1972.

Question 136

Assuming that Sawtooth committed a total

breach on March 1, 1972, and assuming further that he was aware when the agreement was made of the purpose for which Farquart wanted the completed house, which of the following, if true, would best support Farquart's claim for consequential damages on account of delay beyond June 10, 1972, in getting the house finished?

(A) Junior and his bride, married on June 10, 1972, would have to pay storage charges on their wedding gifts and new furniture until the house could be completed.
(B) Junior's fiancée jilted Junior on June 10, 1972, and ran off with another man who had a new house.
(C) Farquart was put to additional expense in providing Junior and his bride, married on June 10, 1972, with temporary housing.
(D) On June 10, 1972, Farquart paid a $5,000 judgment obtained against him in a suit filed March 15, 1972, by an adjoining landowner on account of Farquart's negligent excavation, including blasting, in an attempt to finish the house himself after Sawtooth's repudiation.

Question 137

Fruitko, Inc., ordered from Orchard, Inc., 500 bushels of No. 1 Royal Fuzz peaches, at a specified price, "for prompt shipment." Orchard promptly shipped 500 bushels, but by mistake shipped No. 2 Royal Fuzz peaches instead of No. 1. The error in shipment was caused by the negligence of Orchard's shipping clerk.

Which of the following best states Fruitko's rights and duties upon delivery of the peaches?

(A) Orchard's shipment of the peaches was a counteroffer and Fruitko can refuse to accept them.
(B) Orchard's shipment of the peaches was a counteroffer but, since peaches are perishable, Fruitko, if it does not want to accept them, must reship the peaches to Orchard in order to mitigate Orchard's losses.
(C) Fruitko must accept the peaches because a contract was formed when Orchard shipped them.
(D) Although a contract was formed when Orchard shipped the peaches, Fruitko does not have to accept them.

Questions 138-139 are based on the following fact situation.

Alpha and Beta made a written contract pursuant to which Alpha promised to convey a specified apartment house to Beta in return for Beta's promise (1) to convey a 100-acre farm to Alpha and (2) to pay Alpha $1,000 in cash six months after the exchange of the apartment house and the farm. The contract contained the following provision: "It is understood and agreed that Beta's obligation to pay the $1,000 six months after the exchange of the apartment house and the farm shall be voided if Alpha has not, within three months after the aforesaid exchange, removed the existing shed in the parking area in the rear of the said apartment house."

Question 138

Which of the following statements concerning the order of performances is *LEAST* accurate?

(A) Alpha's tendering of good title to the apartment house is a condition precedent to Beta's duty to convey good title to the farm.
(B) Beta's tendering of good title to the farm is a condition precedent to Alpha's duty to convey good title to the apartment house.
(C) Beta's tendering of good title to the farm is a condition subsequent to Alpha's duty to convey good title to the apartment house.
(D) Alpha's tendering of good title to the apartment house and Beta's tendering of good title to the farm are concurrent conditions.

Question 139

Alpha's removal of the shed from the parking area of the apartment house is

(A) a condition subsequent in form but precedent in substance to Beta's duty to pay the $1,000.
(B) a condition precedent in form but subsequent in substance to Beta's duty to pay the $1,000.
(C) a condition subsequent to Beta's duty to pay the $1,000.
(D) not a condition, either precedent or subsequent, to Beta's duty to pay the $1,000.

Question 140

Professor James said to Mary Digit, president of the X-L Secretarial Service, "Since you folks have done good typing work for me in the past, I promise to bring you the manuscript for my new book."

"When?" asked Mary Digit.

"First chapter next Monday," replied the Professor.

"Wouldn't that be nice," said Mary Digit.

The following Monday James, foregoing the services of another secretarial service, brought chapter one to the X-L office but Mary Digit refused to take it, saying that they were all booked up for three weeks.

Which of the following facts or inferences would be most helpful in an action by James against X-L?

(A) "When" and "Wouldn't that be nice" implied a promise to type the manuscript.
(B) James relied on Mary Digit's statement by bringing the manuscript to X-L.
(C) X-L had done good work for James in the past.
(D) James had foregone the services of another secretarial service.

Questions 141-144 are based on the following fact situation.

On November 1, the following notice was posted in a privately-operated law school:

> The faculty, seeking to encourage legal research, offers to any student at this school who wins the current National Obscenity Law Competition the additional prize of $500. All competing papers must be submitted to the Dean's office before May 1.

(The National Competition is conducted by an outside agency, unconnected with any law school.) Student read this notice on November 2, and thereupon intensified his effort to make his paper on obscenity law, which he started in October, a winner. Student also left on a counter in the Dean's office a signed note saying, "I accept the faculty's $500 Obscenity Competition offer." This note was inadvertently placed in Student's file and never reached the Dean or any faculty member personally. On the following April 1, the above notice was removed and the following substituted therefore:

> The faculty regrets that our offer regarding the National Obscenity Law Competition must be withdrawn.

Student's paper was submitted through the Dean's office on April 15. On May 1, it was announced that Student had won the National Obscenity Law Competition and the prize of $1,000. The law faculty refused to pay anything.

Question 141

Assuming that the faculty's notice of November 1 was posted on a bulletin board or other conspicuous place commonly viewed by all persons in the law school, such notice constituted a

(A) preliminary invitation to deal, analogous to newspaper advertisements for the sale of goods by merchants.
(B) contractual offer, creating a power of acceptance.
(C) preliminary invitation, because no offeree was named therein.
(D) promise to make a conditional, future gift of money.

Question 142

As to Student, was the offer effectively revoked?

(A) Yes, by the faculty's second notice.
(B) No, because it became irrevocable after a reasonable time had elapsed.
(C) No, because of Student's reliance, prior to April 1, on the offer.
(D) No, unless Student became aware of the April 1 posting and removal before submitting the paper.

Question 143

The offer proposed a

(A) unilateral contract only.
(B) bilateral contract only.
(C) unilateral contract or bilateral contract at the offeree's option.
(D) unilateral contract which ripened into a bilateral contract, binding on both parties, as soon as Student intensified his effort in response to the offer.

Question 144

The promise of the faculty on November 1 was

(A) enforceable on principles of promissory estoppel.
(B) enforceable by Student's personal representative even if Student had been killed in an accident on

April 16.

(C) not enforceable on policy grounds because it produced a noncommercial agreement between a student and his teachers, analogous to intramural family agreement and informal social commitments.

(D) not enforceable, because Student, after entering the National Competition in October, was already under a duty to perform to the best of his ability.

Questions 145-147 are based on the following fact situation.

Paul and Daniel entered a contract in writing on November 1, the essential part of which read as follows:

"Paul to supply Daniel with 200 personalized Christmas cards on or before December 15, 1970, bearing a photograph of Daniel and his family, and Daniel to pay $100 thirty days thereafter. Photograph to be taken by Paul at Daniel's house. Cards guaranteed to be fully satisfactory and on time." Because Daniel suddenly became ill, Paul was unable to take the necessary photograph of Daniel and his family until the first week of December.

The final week's delay was caused by Paul's not being notified promptly by Daniel of his recovery. Before taking the photograph of Daniel and his family, Paul advised Daniel that he was likely to be delayed a day or two beyond December 15 in making delivery because of the time required to process the photograph and cards. Daniel told Paul to take the photograph anyway. The cards were finally delivered by Paul to Daniel on December 17, Paul having diligently worked on them in the interim. Although the cards pleased the rest of the family, Daniel refused to accept them because, as he said squinting at one of the cards at arm's length without bothering to put on his reading glasses, "The photograph makes me look too old. Besides, the cards weren't delivered on time."

Question 145

In an action by Paul against Daniel, which of the following would be Daniel's best defense?

(A) The cards, objectively viewed, were not satisfactory.
(B) The cards, subjectively viewed, were not satisfactory.
(C) The cards were not delivered on time.

(D) Daniel's illness excused him from further obligation under the contract.

Question 146

Which of the following statements is most accurate?

(A) Payment by Daniel of the $100 was a condition precedent to Paul's duty of performance.
(B) The performances of Paul and Daniel under the contract were concurrently conditional.
(C) Payment by Daniel of the $100 was a condition subsequent to Paul's duty of performance.
(D) Performance by Paul under the contract was a condition precedent to Daniel's duty of payment of the $100.

Question 147

Which of the following statements regarding the legal effect of Daniel's illness is *LEAST* accurate?

(A) Daniel's illness and the related development excused Paul from his obligations to deliver the cards on or before December 15.
(B) Prompt notice by Daniel to Paul of Daniel's recovery from illness was an implied condition of Paul's duty under the circumstances.
(C) Paul was under a duty of immediate performance of his promise to deliver the cards, as of December 15, by reason of the express language of the contract and despite the illness of Daniel and the related developments.
(D) Daniel's conduct after his illness constituted a waiver of the necessity of Paul's performing on or before December 15.

Question 148

Chase, as seller, and Scott, as buyer, enter into a written contract for the sale and purchase of land which is complete in all respects except that no reference is made to the quality of title to be conveyed. Which of the following will result?

(A) The contract will be unenforceable.
(B) Chase will be required to convey a marketable title.
(C) Chase will be required to convey only what he owned on the date of the contract.
(D) Chase will be required to convey only what he owned on the date of the contract plus whatever additional title rights he may acquire prior to the closing date.

Questions 149-151 are based on the following fact situation.

Brill saved the life of Ace's wife, Mary, who thereafter changed her will to leave Brill $1,000. However, upon Mary's death she had no property except an undivided interest in real estate held in tenancy by the entirety of Ace. The property had been purchased by Ace from an inheritance.

After Mary died, Ace signed and delivered to Brill the following instrument: "In consideration of Brill's saving my wife's life and his agreement to bring no claims against my estate based on her will, I hereby promise to pay Brill $1,000."

Upon Ace's death, Brill filed a claim for $1,000. Ace's executor contested the claim on the ground that the instrument was not supported by sufficient consideration.

Question 149

In most states, would Brill's saving of Mary's life be regarded as sufficient consideration for Ace's promise?

(A) Yes, because Ace was thereby morally obligated to Brill.
(B) Yes, because Ace was thereby materially benefited.
(C) No, because Ace had not asked Brill to save her.
(D) No, because the value of Brill's act was too uncertain.

Question 150

With respect to the recital that Brill had agreed not to file a claim against Ace's estate, what additional fact would most strengthen Brill's claim?

(A) Brill's agreement was made in a writing he signed.
(B) Brill reasonably believed he had a valid claim when the instrument was signed.
(C) Mary had contributed to accumulation of the real property.
(D) Brill paid Ace $1 when he received the instrument.

Question 151

On which of the following theories would it be most likely that Brill could recover?

(A) Ace and Brill have made a compromise.
(B) Ace must give restitution for benefits it would be unjust to retain.
(C) Ace is bound by promissory estoppel.
(D) Ace executed a binding unilateral contract.

Question 152

On January 15, Carpenter agreed to repair Householder's house according to certain specifications and to have the work completed by April 1. On March 1, Householder's property was inundated by flood waters which did not abate until March 15. Householder could not get the house in a condition which would permit Carpenter to begin the repairs until March 31. On that date Carpenter notified Householder that he would not repair the house.

Which one of the following facts, if it was the only one true and known to both parties on January 15, would best serve Carpenter as the basis for a defense in an action brought against him by Householder for breach of contract?

(A) Carpenter's busy schedule permitted him to work on Householder's house only during the month of March.
(B) Any delay in making the repairs would not seriously affect Householder's use of the property.
(C) The cost of making repairs was increasing at the rate of 3 percent a month.
(D) The area around Householder's property was frequently flooded during the month of March.

Question 153

In a telephone call on March 1, Adams, an unemployed, retired person, said to Dawes, "I will sell my automobile for $3,000 cash. I will hold this offer open through March 14." On March 12, Adams called Dawes and told her that he had sold the automobile to Clark. Adams in fact had not sold the automobile to anyone. On March 14, Dawes learned that Adams still owned the automobile, and on that date called Adams and said, "I'm coming over to your place with $3,000." Adams replied, "Don't bother, I won't deliver the automobile to you under any circumstances." Dawes protested, but made no further attempt to pay for or take delivery of the automobile.

In an action by Dawes against Adams for breach of contract, Dawes probably will

(A) succeed, because Adams had assured her that the offer would remain open through March 14.
(B) succeed, because Adams had not in fact sold the automobile to Clark.
(C) not succeed, because Dawes had not tendered the $3,000 to Adams on or before March 14.
(D) not succeed, because on March 12 Adams had told Dawes that he had sold the automobile to Clark.

Question 154

Carver is a chemical engineer. She has no interest in or connection with Chemco. Carver noticed that Chemco's most recent publicly issued financial statement listed, as part of Chemco's assets, a large inventory of a certain special chemical compound. This asset was listed at a cost of $100,000, but Carver knew that the ingredients of the compound were in short supply and that the current market value of the inventory was in excess of $1,000,000. There was no current public quotation of the price of Chemco stock. The book value of Chemco stock, according to the statement, was $5 a share; its actual value was $30 a share.

Knowing these facts, Carver offered to purchase from Page at $6 a share the 1,000 shares of Chemco stock owned by Page. Page and Carver had not previously met. Page sold the stock to Carver for $6 a share.

If Page asserts a claim based on misrepresentation against Carver, will Page prevail?

(A) Yes, because Carver knew that the value of the stock was greater than the price she offered.
(B) Yes, if Carver did not inform Page of the true value of the inventory.
(C) No, unless Carver told Page that the stock was not worth more than $6 a share.
(D) No, if Chemco's financial statement was available to Page.

Questions 155-156 are based on the following fact situation.

In a written contract Singer agreed to deliver to Byer 500 described chairs at $20 each F.O.B. Singer's place of business. The contract provided that "neither party will assign this contract

without the written consent of the other." Singer placed the chairs on board a carrier on January 30. On February 1 Singer said in a signed writing, "I hereby assign to Wheeler all my rights under the Singer-Byer contract." Singer did not request and did not get Byer's consent to this transaction. On February 2 the chairs while in transit were destroyed in a derailment of the carrier's railroad car.

Question 155

In an action by Wheeler against Byer, Wheeler probably will recover

(A) $10,000, the contract price.
(B) the difference between the contract price and the market value of the chairs.
(C) nothing, because the chairs had not been delivered.
(D) nothing, because the Singer-Byer contract forbade an assignment.

Question 156

In an action by Byer against Singer for breach of contract, Byer probably will

(A) succeed, because the carrier will be deemed to be Singer's agent.
(B) succeed, because the risk of loss was on Singer.
(C) not succeed, because of impossibility of performance.
(D) not succeed, because the risk of loss was on Byer.

Question 157

After several days of negotiations, Ohner wrote to Plummer: "Will pay you $3,000 if you will install new plumbing in my office building according to the specifications I have sent you.

I must have your reply by March 30." Plummer replied by a letter that Ohner received on March 15: "Will not do it for less than $3,500." On March 20, Plummer wrote to Ohner: "Have changed my mind. I will do the work for $3,000. Unless I hear from you to the contrary, I will begin work on April 5." Ohner received this letter on March 22 but did not reply to it. Plummer, without Ohner's knowledge, began the work on April 5.

Which of the following best characterizes the legal relationship between Ohner and Plummer as of April 5?

(A) A contract was formed on March 20 when Plummer posted his letter.
(B) A contract was formed on March 22 when Ohner received Plummer's letter.
(C) A contract was formed on April 5 when Plummer began work.
(D) There was no contract between the parties as of April 5.

Questions 158-159 are based on the following fact situation.

On January 15, in a signed writing, Artisan agreed to remodel Ohner's building according to certain specifications, Ohner to pay the agreed price of $5,000 to Artisan's niece, Roberta Neese, as a birthday present. Neese did not learn of the agreement until her birthday on May 5.

Before they signed the writing, Artisan and Ohner had orally agreed that their "written agreement will be null and void unless Ohner is able to obtain a $5,000 loan from the First National Bank before January 31."

Question 158

For this question only, assume that Ohner was unable to obtain the loan, and, on January 31, phoned Artisan and told him, "Don't begin the work. The deal is off." In an action for breach of contract brought against Ohner by the proper party, will Ohner be successful in asserting as a defense his inability to obtain a loan?

(A) Yes, because obtaining a loan was a condition precedent to the existence of an enforceable contract.
(B) Yes, because the agreement about obtaining a loan is a modification of a construction contract and is not required to be in writing.
(C) No, because the agreement about obtaining a loan contradicts the express and implied terms of the writing.
(D) No, because Ohner is estopped to deny the validity of the written agreement.

Question 159

For this question only, assume that Ohner obtained the loan, that Artisan completed the remodeling on May 1, and that on May 3, at Artisan's request, Ohner paid the $5,000 to

Artisan. If Neese learns of Ohner's payment to Artisan on May 5, at the same time she learns of the written Artisan-Ohner Contract, will she succeed in action against Ohner for $5,000?

(A) Yes, because she is an intended beneficiary of the written Artisan-Ohner contract.
(B) Yes, because the written Artisan-Ohner contract operated as an assignment to Neese, and Artisan thereby lost whatever rights he may have had to the $5,000.
(C) No, because Neese had not furnished any consideration to support Ohner's promise to pay $5,000 to her.
(D) No, because on May 3, Artisan and Ohner effectively modified their written contract, thereby depriving Neese of whatever right she may have had under that contract.

Questions 160-161 are based on the following fact situation.

When Esther, Gray's 21-year-old daughter, finished college, Gray handed her a signed memorandum stating that if she would go to law school for three academic years, he would pay her tuition, room, and board and would "give her a $1,000 bonus" for each "A" she got in law school. Esther's uncle, Miller, who was present on this occasion, read the memorandum and thereupon said to Esther, "and if he doesn't pay your expenses, I will." Gray paid her tuition, room, and board for her first year but died just before the end of that year. Subsequently, Esther learned that she had received two "A's" in the second semester. The executor of Gray's estate has refused to pay her anything for the two "A's" and has told her that the estate will no longer pay her tuition, room, and board in law school.

Question 160

In an action by Esther against Miller on account of the executor's repudiation of Gray's promise to pay future tuition, room, and board, which of the following would be Miller's strongest defense?

(A) The parties did not manifestly intend a contract.
(B) Gray's death terminated the agreement.
(C) The agreement was oral.
(D) The agreement was divisible.

Question 161

In an action against Gray's estate for $2,000 on

account of the two "A's" if the only defense raised is lack of consideration, Esther probably will

(A) succeed under the doctrine of promissory estoppel.
(B) succeed on a theory of bargained-for exchange for her father's promise.
(C) not succeed, because the $1,000 for each "A" was promised only as a bonus.
(D) not succeed, because Esther was already legally obligated to use her best efforts in law school.

Question 162

Zeller contracted in writing to deliver to Baker 100 bushels of wheat on August 1 at $3.50 a bushel. Because his suppliers had not delivered enough wheat to him by that time, Zeller on August 1 had only 95 bushels of wheat with which to fulfill his contract with Baker.

If Zeller tenders 95 bushels of wheat to Baker on August 1, and Baker refused to accept or pay for any of the wheat, which of the following best states the legal relationship between Zeller and Baker?

(A) Zeller has a cause of action against Baker, because Zeller has substantially performed his contract.
(B) Zeller is excused from performing his contract because of impossibility of performance.
(C) Baker has a cause of action against Zeller for Zeller's failure to deliver 100 bushels of wheat.
(D) Baker is obligated to give Zeller a reasonable time to attempt to obtain the other five bushels of wheat.

Questions 163-164 are based on the following fact situation.

On March 31, Selco and Byco entered into a written agreement in which Selco agreed to fabricate and sell to Byco 10,000 specially designed brake linings for a new type of power brake manufactured by Byco. The contract provided that Byco would pay half of the purchase price on May 15 in order to give Selco funds to "tool up" for the work; that Selco would deliver 5,000 brake linings on May 31; that Byco would pay the balance of the purchase price on June 15; and that Selco would deliver the balance of the brake linings on June 30.

On May 10, Selco notified Byco that it was

doubtful whether Selco could perform because of problems encountered in modifying its production machines to produce the brake linings. On May 15, however, Selco assured Byco that the production difficulties had been overcome, and Byco paid Selco the first 50 percent installment of the purchase price. Selco did not deliver the first 5,000 brake linings on May 31, or at any time thereafter; and on June 10, Selco notified Byco that it would not perform the contract.

Question 163

Which of the following correctly states Byco's rights and obligations immediately after receipt of Selco's notice on May 10?

(A) Byco can treat the notice as an anticipatory repudiation, and has a cause of action on May 10 for breach of the entire contract.
(B) Byco can treat the notice as an anticipatory repudiation, and can sue to enjoin an actual breach by Selco on May 31.
(C) Byco has no cause of action for breach of contract, but can suspend its performance and demand assurances that Selco will perform.
(D) Byco has no cause of action for breach of contract, and must pay the installment of the purchase price due on May 15 to preserve its rights under the contract.

Question 164

Which of the following is *NOT* a correct statement of the parties' legal status immediately after Selco's notice on June 10?

(A) Byco has a cause of action for total breach of contract because of Selco's repudiation, but that cause of action will be lost if Selco retracts its repudiation before Byco changes it position or manifests to Selco that Byco considers the repudiation final.
(B) Byco can bring suit to rescind the contract even if it elects to await Selco's performance for a commercially reasonable time.
(C) Byco can await performance by Selco for a commercially reasonable time, but if Byco awaits performance beyond that period, it cannot recover any resulting damages that it reasonably could have avoided.
(D) Byco has a cause of action for breach of contract that it can successfully assert only after it has given Selco a commercially reasonable time to perform.

Questions 165-166 are based on the following fact situation.

The Kernel Corporation, through its president, Demeter Gritz, requested from Vault Finance, Inc., a short-term loan of $100,000. On April 1, Gritz and Vault's loan officer agreed orally that Vault would make the loan on the following terms: (1) The loan would be repaid in full on or before the following July 1 and would carry interest at an annual rate of 15 percent (a lawful rate under the applicable usury law); and (2) Gritz would personally guarantee repayment. The loan was approved and made on April 5. The only document evidencing the loan was a memorandum, written and supplied by Vault and signed by Gritz for Kernel, that read in its entirety:

> "April 5
>
> In consideration of a loan advanced on this date, Kernel Corporation hereby promises to pay Vault Finance, Inc., $100,000 on September 1.
>
> Kernel Corporation
>
> By /s/ Demeter Gritz
> Demeter Gritz, President"

Kernel Corporation did not repay the loan on or before July 1, although it had sufficient funds to do so. On July 10, Vault sued Kernel as principal debtor and Gritz individually as guarantor for $100,000, plus 15 percent interest from April 5.

Question 165

At the trial, can Vault prove Kernel's oral commitment to repay the loan on or before July 1?

(A) Yes, because the oral agreement was supported by an independent consideration.
(B) Yes, because the evidence of the parties' negotiations is relevant to their contractual intent concerning maturity of the debt.
(C) No, because such evidence is barred by the preexisting duty rule.
(D) No, because such evidence contradicts the writing and is barred by the parol evidence rule.

Question 166

At the trial, can Vault prove Gritz's oral promise to guarantee the loan?

(A) Yes, because Gritz signed the memorandum.
(B) Yes, because, as president of the debtor-company, Gritz is a third-party beneficiary of the loan.
(C) No, because there was no separate consideration for Gritz's promise.
(D) No, because such proof is barred by the statute of frauds.

Question 167

O'Neal entered into a written contract to sell her house and six acres known as Meadowacre to Perez for $75,000. Delivery of the deed and payment of the purchase price were to be made six months after the contract. The contract provided that Meadowacre was to be conveyed "subject to easements, covenants, and restrictions of record." The contract was not recorded.

After the contract was signed but before the deed was delivered, Electric Company decided to run a high-voltage power line in the area and required an easement through a portion of Meadowacre. O'Neal, by deed, granted an easement to Electric Company in consideration of $5,000; the deed was duly recorded.

The power line would be a series of towers with several high-voltage lines that would be clearly visible from the house on Meadowacre but would in no way interfere with the house.

When Perez caused the title to Meadowacre to be searched, the deed of easement to Electric Company was found. O'Neal appeared at the time and place scheduled for the closing and proffered an appropriate deed to Perez and demanded the purchase price. Perez refused to accept the deed. In an appropriate action for specific performance against Perez, O'Neal demanded $75,000.

In this action, O'Neal should

(A) obtain an order for specific performance at a price of $75,000.
(B) obtain an order for specific performance at a price of $70,000.
(C) lose, because Perez did not contract to take subject to the easement to Electric Company.
(D) lose, because a high-voltage power line is a

nuisance per se.

Question 168

Osif owned Broadacres in fee simple. For a consideration of $5,000, Osif gave Bard a written option to purchase Broadacres for $300,000. The option was assignable. For a consideration of $10,000, Bard subsequently gave an option to Cutter to purchase Broadacres for $325,000. Cutter exercised his option.

Bard thereupon exercised his option. Bard paid the agreed price of $300,000 and took title to Broadacres by deed from Osif. Thereafter, Cutter refused to consummate his purchase.

Bard brought an appropriate action against Cutter for specific performance, or, if that should be denied, then for damages. Cutter counterclaimed for return of the $10,000. In this action the court will

(A) grant money damages only to Bard.
(B) grant specific performance to Bard.
(C) grant Bard only the right to retain the $10,000.
(D) require Bard to refund the $10,000 to Cutter.

Questions 169-171 are based on the following fact situation.

A written contract was entered into between Bouquet, a financier-investor, and Vintage Corporation, a winery and grape-grower. The contract provided that Bouquet would invest $1,000,000 in Vintage for its capital expansion and, in return, that Vintage, from grapes grown in its famous vineyards, would produce and market at least 500,000 bottles of wine each year for five years under the label "Premium Vintage-Bouquet."

The contract included provisions that the parties would share equally the profits and losses from the venture and that, if feasible, the wine would be distributed by Vintage only through Claret, a wholesale distributor of fine wines. Neither Bouquet nor Vintage had previously dealt with Claret. Claret learned of the contract two days later from reading a trade newspaper. In reliance thereon, he immediately hired an additional sales executive and contracted for enlargement of his wine storage and display facility.

Question 169

If Vintage refuses to distribute the wine through Claret and Claret then sues Vintage for breach of contract, is it likely that Claret will prevail?

(A) Yes, because Vintage's performance was to run to Claret rather than to Bouquet.
(B) Yes, because Bouquet and Vintage could reasonably foresee that Claret would change his position in reliance on the contract.
(C) No, because Bouquet and Vintage did not expressly agree that Claret would have enforceable rights under their contract.
(D) No, because Bouquet and Vintage, having no apparent motive to benefit Claret, appeared in making the contract to have been protecting or serving only their own interests.

Question 170

For this question only, assume the following facts. Amicusbank lent Bouquet $200,000 and Bouquet executed a written instrument providing that Amicusbank "is entitled to collect the debt from my share of the profits, if any, under the Vintage-Bouquet contract." Amicusbank gave prompt notice of this transaction to Vintage.

If Vintage thereafter refuses to account for any profits to Amicusbank and Amicusbank sues Vintage for Bouquet's share of profits then realized, Vintage's strongest argument in defense is that

(A) the Bouquet-Vintage contract did not expressly authorize an assignment of rights.
(B) Bouquet and Vintage are partners, not simply debtor and creditor.
(C) Amicusbank is not an assignee of Bouquet's rights under the Bouquet-Vintage contract.
(D) Amicusbank is not an intended third-party beneficiary of the Bouquet-Vintage contract.

Question 171

For this question only, assume the following facts. Soon after making its contract with Bouquet, Vintage, without Bouquet's knowledge or assent, sold its vineyards but not its winery to Agribiz, a large agricultural corporation. Under the terms of this sale, Agribiz agreed to sell to Vintage all grapes grown on the land for five years. Agribiz's employees have no experience in winegrape production, and Agribiz has no reputation in the wine industry as a grape producer or otherwise. The Bouquet-Vintage contract was silent on the matter of Vintage's selling any or all of its business assets.

If Bouquet seeks an appropriate judicial remedy against Vintage for entering into the Vintage-Agribiz transaction, is Bouquet likely to prevail?

(A) Yes, because the Vintage-Agribiz transaction created a significant risk of diminishing the profits in which Bouquet would share under his contract with Vintage.
(B) Yes, because the Bouquet-Vintage contract did not contain a provision authorizing a delegation of Vintage's duties.
(C) No, because Vintage remains in a position to perform under the Bouquet-Vintage contract.
(D) No, because Vintage, as a corporation, must necessarily perform its contracts by delegating duties to individuals.

Questions 172-173 are based on the following fact situation.

On June 1, Kravat, a manufacturer of men's neckties, received the following order from Clothier: "Ship 500 two-inch ties, assorted stripes, your catalogue No. V34. Delivery by July 1."

On June 1, Kravat shipped 500 three-inch ties that arrived at Clothier's place of business on June 3. Clothier immediately telegraphed Kravat: "Reject your shipment. Order was for two-inch ties." Clothier, however, did not ship the ties back to Kravat. Kravat replied by telegram: "Will deliver proper ties before July 1." Clothier received this telegram on June 4, but did not reply to it.

On June 30, Kravat tendered 500 two-inch ties in assorted stripes, designated in his catalogue as item No. V34; but Clothier refused to accept them.

Question 172

Did Clothier properly reject the ties delivered on June 3?

(A) Yes, because the ties were nonconforming goods.
(B) Yes, because Kravat did not notify Clothier that the ties were shipped as an accommodation to Clothier.
(C) No, because Kravat could accept Clothier's offer by prompt shipment of either conforming or nonconforming goods.

(D) No, because Clothier waived his right to reject the ties by not returning them promptly to Kravat.

Question 173

Did Clothier properly reject the ties tendered on June 30?

(A) Yes, because Kravat's shipping the three-inch ties on June 1 was a present breach of contract.
(B) Yes, because Kravat's shipping the three-inch ties on June 1 was an anticipatory repudiation.
(C) No, because Kravat cured the June 1 defective delivery by his tender of conforming goods on June 30.
(D) No, because a contract for the sale of goods can be modified without consideration.

Question 174

Santos agreed to sell and Perrine agreed to buy a described lot on which a single-family residence had been built. Under the contract, Santos agreed to convey marketable title subject only to conditions, covenants, and restrictions of record and all applicable zoning laws and ordinances. The lot was subject to a 10-foot side line setback originally set forth in the developer's duly recorded subdivision plot. The applicable zoning ordinance zones the property for single-family units and requires an 8.5-foot side line setback.

Prior to closing, a survey of the property was made. It revealed that a portion of Santos' house was 8.4 feet from the side line.

Perrine refused to consummate the transaction on the ground that Santos' title is not marketable. In an appropriate action, Santos seeks specific performance. Who will prevail in such an action?

(A) Santos, because any suit against Perrine concerning the setback would be frivolous.
(B) Santos, because the setback violation falls within the doctrine *de minimis non curat lex.*
(C) Perrine, because any variation, however small, amounts to a breach of contract.
(D) Perrine, because the fact that Perrine may be exposed to litigation is sufficient to make the title unmarketable.

Questions 175-176 are based on the following fact situation.

Mater, a wealthy widow, wishing to make a

substantial and potentially enduring gift to her beloved adult stepson Prodigal, established with the Vault Savings and Loan Association a passbook savings account by an initial deposit of $10,000.

Question 175

For this question only, assume the following facts. The passbook was issued solely in Prodigal's name; but Mater retained possession of it, and Prodigal was not then informed of the savings account. Subsequently, Mater became disgusted with Prodigal's behavior and decided to give the same savings account solely to her beloved adult daughter Distaff. As permitted by the rules of Vault Savings and Loan, Mater effected this change by agreement with Vault. This time she left possession of the passbook with Vault. Shortly thereafter, Prodigal learned of the original savings account in his name and the subsequent switch to Distaff's name.

If Prodigal now sues Vault Savings and Loan for $10,000 plus accrued interest, will the action succeed?

(A) Yes, because Prodigal was a third-party intended beneficiary of the original Mater-Vault deposit agreement.
(B) Yes, because Prodigal was a constructive assignee of Mater's claim, as depositor, to the savings account.
(C) No, because Prodigal never obtained possession of the passbook.
(D) No, because Prodigal's right, if any, to the funds on deposit was effectively abrogated by the second Mater-Vault deposit agreement.

Question 176

For this question only, assume the following facts. The passbook was issued by Vault to Mater solely in her own name. That same day, disinterested witnesses being present, she handed the passbook to Prodigal and said, "As a token of my love and affection for you, I give you this $10,000 savings account." Shortly thereafter, she changed her mind and wrote Prodigal, "I hereby revoke my gift to you of the $10,000 savings account with Vault Savings and Loan Association. Please return my passbook immediately. Signed: Mater." Prodigal received the letter but ignored it, and Mater died unexpectedly a few days later.

In litigation between Prodigal and Mater's estate, which of the following is a correct statement of the parties' rights with respect to the money on deposit with Vault?

(A) The estate prevails, because Mater's gift to Prodigal was revocable and was terminated by her death.
(B) The estate prevails, because Mater's gift to Prodigal was revocable and was terminated by her express revocation.
(C) Prodigal prevails, because he took Mater's claim to the savings account by a gratuitous but effective and irrevocable assignment from Mater.
(D) Prodigal prevails, because his failure to reject the gift, even if the assignment was revocable, created an estoppel against Mater and her estate.

Questions 177-178 are based on the following fact situation.

On October 1, Toy Store, Inc., entered into a written contract with Fido Factory, Inc., for the purchase at $20 per unit of 1,000 mechanical dogs, to be specially manufactured by Fido according to Toy Store's specifications. Fido promised to deliver all of the dogs "not later than November 15, for the Yule shopping season," and Toy Store promised to pay the full $20,000 price upon delivery. In order to obtain operating funds, Fido as borrower entered into a written loan agreement on October 5 with the High Finance Company. In relevant part, this agreement recited, "Fido Factory hereby transfers and assigns to High Finance its (Fido Factory's) October 1 mechanical dog contract with Toy Store, as security for a 50-day loan of $15,000, the advance and receipt of which are hereby acknowledged by Fido Factory . . . . " No copy of this agreement, or statement relating to it, was filed in an office of public record.

On October 15, Fido notified Toy Store, "We regret to advise that our master shaft burned out last night because our night supervisor let the lubricant level get too low. We have just fired the supervisor, but the shaft cannot be repaired or replaced until about January 1. We can guarantee delivery of your order, however, not later than January 20." Toy Store rejected this proposal as unacceptable and immediately contracted with the only other available manufacturer to obtain the 1,000 dogs at $30 per unit by November 15.

Question 177

For this question only, assume that on November 1, Toy Store sues Fido for damages and alleges the above facts, except those relating to the Fido-High Finance loan agreement. Upon Fido's motion to dismiss the complaint, the court should

(A) sustain the motion, because Fido on October 15 stated its willingness, and gave assurance of its ability, to perform the contract in January.
(B) sustain the motion, because Toy Store's lawsuit is premature in any case until after November 15.
(C) deny the motion, because Toy Store's complaint alleges an actionable tort by Fido.
(D) deny the motion, because Toy Store's complaint alleges an actionable breach of contract by Fido.

Question 178

For this question only, assume that by November 16, Fido, without legal excuse, has delivered no dogs, and that Toy Store has brought an action against Fido. In an action brought on November 16 by Toy Store against High Finance Company on account of Fido's default, Toy Store can recover

(A) nothing, because the October 5 assignment by Fido to High Finance of Fido's contract with Toy Store was only an assignment for security.
(B) nothing, because no record of the October 5 transaction between Fido and High Finance was publicly filed.
(C) $10,000 damages, because Toy Store was a third-party intended beneficiary of the October 5 transaction between Fido and High Finance.
(D) $10,000 in damages, because the October 5 transaction between Fido and High Finance effected, with respect to Toy Store as creditor, a novation of debtors.

Question 179

In March, when Ohm was 17, Stereo delivered to Ohm a television set. At that time

Ohm agreed in writing to pay $400 for the set on July 1 when he would reach his eighteenth birthday. Eighteen is the applicable statutory age of majority, and on that date Ohm was to receive the proceeds of a trust. On July 1, when the reasonable value of the television set was $250, Ohm sent Stereo a signed letter stating, "I'll only pay you $300; that is all the set is worth."

In an action against Ohm for money damages on July 2, what is the maximum amount that Stereo

will be entitled to recover?

(A) Nothing
(B) $250, the reasonable value of the set
(C) $300, the amount Ohm promised to pay in his letter of July 1
(D) $400, the original sale price

Questions 180-181 are based on the following fact situation.

Eureka, Inc., inventor of the LBVC, a laser-beam vegetable chopper, ran a television ad that described the chopper and said, "The LBVC is yours for only $49.99 if you send your check or money order to Box 007, Greenville. Not available in stores." Gourmet, who owned a retail specialty shop, wrote Eureka, "What's your best, firm price for two dozen LBVC's?" Eureka sent a written reply that said in its entirety, "We quote you for prompt acceptance $39.99 per unit for 24 LBVC's." Gourmet subsequently mailed a check to Eureka in the appropriate amount, with a memo enclosed saying, "I accept your offer for 24 LBVC's."

Question 180

A contract would arise from these communications only if

(A) both parties were merchants.
(B) Eureka had at least 24 LBVC's in stock when Gourmet's check and memo were received.
(C) Gourmet's check and memo were mailed within three months after his receipt of Eureka's letter.
(D) Gourmet's check and memo were mailed within a reasonable time after his receipt of Eureka's letter.

Question 181

For this question only, assume the following facts: Eureka shipped 24 LBVC's to Gourmet after receiving his check and memo, and with the shipment sent Gourmet an invoice that conspicuously stated, among other things, the following lawful provision: "These items shall not be offered for resale at retail." Gourmet received and read but disregarded the invoice restriction and displayed the 24 LBVC's for resale. Eureka has a cause of action against Gourmet for breach of contract only if

(A) Eureka, as inventor of the LBVC, was not a merchant.

(B) the invoice restriction was a material alteration of pre-existing terms.
(C) Eureka's written reply that quoted $39.99 per LBVC, but did not contain a restriction on retail sales, was not an offer that Gourmet accepted by ordering 24 LBVC's.
(D) Gourmet was consciously aware when taking delivery of the goods that the television ad had said, "Not available in stores."

Questions 182-183 are based on the following fact situation.

In a writing signed by both parties, Paul Plannah, a renowned architect, agreed for a fee of $25,000 to design and supervise construction of a new house for Phoebe Threedee, a famous sculptor, the fee to be paid upon completion of the house. Plannah and Threedee got along poorly, and, when the design plans were about two-thirds complete, they had a heated argument over the proper location of a marble staircase. Hoping to avoid such encounters, Plannah, without Threedee's knowledge, assigned to Donna Drafty, a newly-licensed architect practicing solo, "all of my rights and duties under my design and construction supervision contract with Threedee." Drafty expressly promised Plannah to carry out the work to the best of Drafty's ability.

Question 182

For this question only, assume that Threedee on learning of the assignment refused to allow Drafty to proceed as architect and brought an action against Plannah to compel him to resume and complete performance of the contract.

Is Threedee entitled to such relief?

(A) Yes, because Plannah's services under the contract are unique.
(B) Yes, because Plannah has personally completed two-thirds of the design work.
(C) No, because the Plannah-Threedee contract is one for personal services by Plannah.
(D) No, because Plannah effectively delegated his remaining duties under the Plannah-Threedee contract to Drafty.

Question 183

For this question only, assume that Threedee allowed Drafty to proceed with the design work but that Drafty without legal excuse abandoned the project shortly after construction began.

Which of the following legal conclusions are correct?

I.   Plannah is liable to Threedee for legal damages, if any, caused by Drafty's default.
II. Drafty is liable to Threedee for legal damages, if any, caused by Drafty's default.
III. Threedee is indebted to Drafty, on a divisible contract theory, for a prorated portion of the agreed $25,000 architect's fee promised to Plannah.

(A) I and II only
(B) I and III only
(C) II and III only
(D) I, II, and III

Question 184

The German-made Doppelpferd, featuring sleek styling and remarkable fuel efficiency, is the most popular automobile in the United States. Its U.S. sales are booming, and the average retail markup in such sales is 30 percent. Hardsell Motors, Inc., a franchised Doppelpferd dealer in the United States, contracted with Shift to sell him a new Doppelpferd for $9,000 cash, the sale to be consummated after delivery to Hardsell of the car, which Hardsell ordered from the manufacturer specifically for Shift. The signed retail contractual document was a contract drafted by Hardsell's lawyer, and Shift did not question or object to any of its terms, including the price inserted by Hardsell. When the car arrived from Germany, Shift repudiated the contract. Hardsell at once sold the car for $9,000 cash to Karbuff, for whom Hardsell had also ordered from the manufacturer a Doppelpferd identical to Shift's.

In an action against Shift for breach of contract, Hardsell will probably recover

(A) $9,000 minus what it cost Hardsell to purchase the car from the manufacturer.
(B) $9,000 minus the wholesale price of an identical Doppelpferd in the local wholesale market among dealers.
(C) nominal damages only, because Hardsell resold the car to Karbuff without lowering the retail price.
(D) nothing, because the parties' agreement was an

adhesion contract and therefore unconscionable.

Questions 185-186 are based on the following fact situation.

On January 1, Awl and Howser agreed in writing that Awl would build a house on Howser's lot according to Howser's plans and specifications for $60,000, the work to commence on April 1. Howser agreed to make an initial payment of $10,000 on April 1, and to pay the balance upon completion of the work.

On February 1, Awl notified Howser that he (Awl) would lose money on the job at that price, and would not proceed with the work unless Howser would agree to increase the price to $90,000. Howser thereupon, without notifying Awl, agreed in writing with Gutter for Gutter, commencing April 1, to build the house for $75,000, which was the fair market cost of the work to be done.

On April 1, both Awl and Gutter showed up at the building site to begin work, Awl telling Howser that he had decided to "take the loss" and would build the house for $60,000 as originally agreed. Howser dismissed Awl and allowed Gutter to begin work on the house.

Question 185

In a contract action by Awl against Howser, which of the following would the court decide under the prevailing American view?

(A) Howser will win, because Awl in legal effect committed a total breach of contract.
(B) Howser will win, because Gutter's contract price was $15,000 lower than the $90,000 demanded by Awl on February 1.
(C) Awl will win, because Howser did not tell him before April 1 about the contract with Gutter.
(D) Awl will win, because he attempted to perform the contract as originally agreed.

Question 186

For this question only, assume that Awl is liable to Howser for breach of contract and also assume the following additional facts: Gutter finished the house on schedule and then showed Howser that he (Gutter) had spent $85,000 on the job. Howser thereupon paid Gutter the full balance of their contract price plus an additional $10,000, so that

Gutter would not lose money.

In a contract action by Howser against Awl, Howser will recover

(A) the difference between the fair market value of the completed house and Awl's original contract price.
(B) $30,000, the difference between Awl's original contract price and the amount Awl demanded on February 1.
(C) $25,000, the difference between Awl's original contract price and the total amount Howser paid Gutter for building the house.
(D) $15,000, the difference between Awl's original contract price and Gutter's contract price.

Question 187

Ann leased commercial property to Brenda for a period of ten years. The lease contained the following provision: "No subleasing or assignment will be permitted unless with the written consent of the lessor." One year later, Brenda assigned all interest in the lease to Carolyn, who assumed and agreed to perform the lessee's obligations under the terms of the lease. Ann learned of the assignment and wrote to Brenda that she had no objection to the assignment to Carolyn and agreed to accept rent from Carolyn instead of Brenda.

Thereafter, Carolyn paid rent to Ann for a period of five years. Carolyn then defaulted and went into bankruptcy. In an appropriate action, Ann sued Brenda for rent due.

If Ann loses, it will be because there was

(A) laches.
(B) an accord and satisfaction.
(C) a novation.
(D) an attornment.

Questions 188-189 are based on the following fact situation.

On January 2, Hugh Homey and Sue Structo entered into a written contract in which Structo agreed to build on Homey's lot a new house for Homey, according to plans and specifications furnished by Homey's architect, Barbara Bilevel, at a contract price of $200,000. The contract provided for specified progress payments and a final payment of $40,000 upon Homey's acceptance of the house and issuance of a certificate of final approval by the architect. Further, under a "liquidated damages" clause in the agreement, Structo promised to pay Homey $500 for each day's delay in completing the house after the following October 1. Homey, however, told Structo on January 2, before the contract was signed, that he would be on an around-the-world vacation trip most of the summer and fall and would not return to occupy the house until November 1.

Question 188

For this question only, assume the following facts. Because she was overextended on other construction jobs, Structo did not complete the house until October 15. Homey returned on November 1 as planned and occupied the house. Ten days later, after making the $40,000 final payment to Structo, Homey learned for the first time that the house had not been completed until October 15.

If Homey sues Structo for breach of contract on account of the fifteen-day delay in completion, which of the following will the court probably decide?

(A) Homey will recover damages as specified in the contract, i.e., $500 multiplied by fifteen.
(B) Homey will recover his actual damages, if any, caused by the delay in completion.
(C) Having waived the delay by occupying the house and making the final payment, Homey will recover nothing.
(D) Homey will recover nothing because the contractual completion date was impliedly modified to November 1 when Homey on January 2 advised Structo about Homey's prospective trip and return date.

Question 189

For this question only, assume the following facts. Structo completed the house on October 14 and, when Homey returned on November 1, requested the final payment of $40,000 and issuance of a certificate of final approval by the architect, Bilevel. Homey, however, refused to pay any part of the final installment after Bilevel told him, "Structo did a great job and I find no defects worth mentioning; but Structo's contract price was at least $40,000 too high, especially in view of the big drop in housing values within the past ten months. I will withhold the final

certificate, and you just hold on to your money."

If Structo sues Homey for the $40,000 final payment after Bilevel's refusal to issue a final certificate, which of the following will the court probably decide?

(A) Structo wins, because nonoccurrence of the condition requiring Bilevel's certificate of final approval was excused by Bilevel's bad-faith refusal to issue the certificate.
(B) Structo wins, but, because all contractual conditions have not occurred, her recovery is limited to restitution of the benefit conferred on Homey, minus progress payments already received.
(C) Homey wins, provided he can prove by clear and convincing evidence that the fair-market value of the completed house is $160,000 or less.
(D) Homey wins, provided he can prove by clear and convincing evidence that total payments to Structo of $160,000 will yield a fair net profit.

Question 190

On August 1, Geriatrics, Inc., operating a "lifetime care" home for the elderly, admitted Ohlster, who was 84 years old, for a trial period of two months. On September 25, Ohlster and Geriatrics entered into a written lifetime care contract with an effective commencement date of October 1. The full contract price was $20,000, which, as required by the terms of the contract, Ohlster prepaid to Geriatrics on September 25. Ohlster died of a heart attack on October 2.

In a restitutionary action, can the administratrix of Ohlster's estate, a surviving sister, recover on behalf of the estate either all or part of the $20,000 paid to Geriatrics on September 25?

(A) Yes, because Geriatrics would otherwise be unjustly enriched at Ohlster's expense.
(B) Yes, under the doctrine of frustration of purpose.
(C) No, because Ohlster's life span and the duration of Geriatrics' commitment to him was a risk assumed by both parties.
(D) No, but only if Geriatrics can show that between September 25 and Ohlster's death it rejected, because of its commitment to Ohlster, an application for lifetime care from another elderly person.

Question 191

Five years ago, Sally acquired Blackacre,

improved with a 15-year-old dwelling. This year Sally listed Blackacre for sale with Bill, a licensed real estate broker. Sally informed Bill of several defects in the house that were not readily discoverable by a reasonable inspection, including a leaky basement, an inadequate water supply, and a roof that leaked. Paul responded to Bill's advertisement, was taken by Bill to view Blackacre, and decided to buy it. Bill saw to it that the contract specified the property to be "as is" but neither Bill nor Sally pointed out the defects to Paul, who did not ask about the condition of the dwelling. After closing and taking possession, Paul discovered the defects, had them repaired, and demanded that Sally reimburse him for the cost of the repairs. Sally refused and Paul brought an appropriate action against Sally for damages.

If Sally wins, it will be because

(A) Sally fulfilled the duty to disclose defects by disclosure to Bill.
(B) the contract's "as is" provision controls the rights of the parties.
(C) Bill became the agent of both Paul and Sally and thus knowledge of the defects was imputed to Paul.
(D) the seller of a used dwelling that has been viewed by the buyer has no responsibility toward the buyer.

Question 192

Hydro-King, Inc., a high-volume, pleasure-boat retailer, entered into a written contract with Zuma, signed by both parties, to sell Zuma a power boat for $12,000. The manufacturer's price of the boat delivered to Hydro-King was $9,500. As the contract provided, Zuma paid Hydro-King $4,000 in advance and promised to pay the full balance upon delivery of the boat. The contract contained no provision for liquidated damages. Prior to the agreed delivery date, Zuma notified Hydro-King that he would be financially unable to conclude the purchase; and Hydro-King thereupon resold the same boat that Zuma had ordered to a third person for $12,000 cash.

If Zuma sues Hydro-King for restitution of the $4,000 advance payment, which of the following should the court decide?

(A) Zuma's claim should be denied, because, as the party in default, he is deemed to have lost any

right to restitution of a benefit conferred on Hydro-King.
(B) Zuma's claim should be denied, because, but for his repudiation, Hydro-King would have made a profit on two boat-sales instead of one.
(C) Zuma's claim should be upheld in the amount of $4,000 minus the amount of Hydro-King's lost profit under its contract with Zuma.
(D) Zuma's claims should be upheld in the amount of $3,500 ($4,000 minus $500 as statutory damages under the UCC).

Questions 193-194 are based on the following fact situation.

Ohner and Planner signed a detailed writing in which Planner, a landscape architect, agreed to landscape and replant Ohner's residential property in accordance with a design prepared by Planner and incorporated in the writing. Ohner agreed to pay $10,000 for the work upon its completion. Ohner's spouse was not a party to the agreement, and had no ownership interest in the premises.

Question 193

For this question only, assume the following facts. Shortly before the agreement was signed, Ohner and Planner orally agreed that the writing would not become binding on either party unless Ohner's spouse should approve the landscaping design.

If Ohner's spouse disapproves the design and Ohner refuses to allow Planner to proceed with the work, is evidence of the oral agreement admissible in Planner's action against Ohner for breach of contract?

(A) Yes, because the oral agreement required approval by a third party.
(B) Yes, because the evidence shows that the writing was intended to take effect only if the approval occurred.
(C) No, because the parol evidence rule bars evidence of a prior oral agreement even if the latter is consistent with the terms of a partial integration.
(D) No, because the prior oral agreement contradicted the writing by making the parties' duties conditional.

Question 194

For this question only, assume the following

facts. At Ohner's insistence, the written Ohner-Planner agreement contained a provision that neither party would be bound unless Ohner's law partner, an avid student of landscaping, should approve Planner's design. Before Planner commenced the work, Ohner's law partner, in the presence of both Ohner and Planner, expressly disapproved the landscaping design. Nevertheless, Ohner ordered Planner to proceed with the work, and Planner reluctantly did so. When Planner's performance was 40 percent complete, Ohner repudiated his duty, if any, to pay the contract price or any part thereof.

If Planner now sues Ohner for damages for breach of contract, which of the following concepts best supports Planner's claim?

(A) Substantial performance
(B) Promissory estoppel
(C) Irrevocable waiver of condition
(D) Unjust enrichment

Question 195

Fruitko, Inc., ordered from Orchard, Inc., 500 bushels of No. 1 Royal Fuzz peaches, at a specified price, "for prompt shipment." Orchard promptly shipped 500 bushels, but by mistake shipped No. 2 Royal Fuzz peaches instead of No. 1. The error in shipment was caused by the negligence of Orchard's shipping clerk.

Which of the following best states Fruitko's rights and duties upon delivery of the peaches?

(A) Orchard's shipment of the peaches was a counteroffer and Fruitko can refuse to accept them.
(B) Orchard's shipment of the peaches was a counteroffer but, since peaches are perishable, Fruitko, if it does not want to accept them, must reship the peaches to Orchard in order to mitigate Orchard's losses.
(C) Fruitko must accept the peaches because a contract was formed when Orchard shipped them.
(D) Although a contract was formed when Orchard shipped the peaches, Fruitko does not have to accept them.

Question 196

Pater and his adult daughter, Carmen, encountered Tertius, an old family friend, on the street. Carmen said to Tertius, "How about lending me $1,000 to buy a used car? I'll pay you back with interest one year from today." Pater added, "And if she doesn't pay it back as promised, I will." Tertius thereupon wrote out and handed to Carmen his personal check, payable to her, for $1,000, and Carmen subsequently used the funds to buy a used car. When the debt became due, both Carmen and Pater refused to repay it, or any part of it.

In an action by Tertius against Pater to recover $1,000 plus interest, which of the following statements would summarize Pater's best defense?

(A) He received no consideration for his conditional promise to Tertius.
(B) His conditional promise to Tertius was not to be performed in less than a year from the time it was made.
(C) His conditional promise to Tertius was not made for the primary purpose of benefiting himself (Pater).
(D) The loan by Tertius was made without any agreement concerning the applicable interest rate.

Questions 197-198 are based on the following fact situation.

Pam and Dora own adjoining lots in the central portion of a city. Each of their lots had an office building. Dora decided to raze the existing building on her lot and to erect a building of greater height. Dora has received all governmental approvals required to pursue her project.

There is no applicable statute or ordinance (other than those dealing with various approvals for zoning, building, etc.).

Question 197

After Dora had torn down the existing building, she proceeded to excavate deeper. Dora used shoring that met all local, state, and federal safety regulations, and the shoring was placed in accordance with those standards.

Pam notified Dora that cracks were developing in the building situated on Pam's lot. Dora took the view that any subsidence suffered by Pam was due to the weight of Pam's building, and correctly asserted that none would have occurred had Pam's soil been in its natural state. Dora continued to excavate.

The building on Pam's lot did suffer extensive damage, requiring the expenditure of $750,000 to remedy the defects.

Which of the following is the best comment concerning Pam's action to recover damages from Dora?

(A) Dora is liable, because she removed necessary support for Pam's lot.
(B) Dora cannot be held liable simply upon proof that support was removed, but may be held liable if negligence is proved.
(C) Once land is improved with a building, the owner cannot invoke the common-law right of lateral support.
(D) Dora's only obligation was to satisfy all local, state, and federal safety regulations.

Question 198

Assume that no problems with subsidence or other misadventures occurred during construction of Dora's new building. However, when it was completed, Pam discovered that the shadow created by the new higher building placed her building in such deep shade that her ability to lease space was diminished and that the rent she could charge and the occupancy rate were substantially lower. Assume that these facts are proved in an appropriate action Pam instituted against Dora for all and any relief available.

Which of the following is the most appropriate comment concerning this lawsuit?

(A) Pam is entitled to a mandatory injunction requiring Dora to restore conditions to those existing with the prior building insofar as the shadow is concerned.
(B) The court should award permanent damages, in lieu of an injunction, equal to the present value of all rents lost and loss on rents for the reasonable life of the building.
(C) The court should award damages for losses suffered to the date of trial and leave open recovery of future damages.
(D) Judgment should be for Dora, because Pam has no cause of action.

Questions 199-200 are based on the following fact situation.

Tune Corporation, a radio manufacturer, and

Bill's Comex, Inc., a retailer, after extensive negotiations entered into a final, written agreement in which Tune agreed to sell and Bill's agreed to buy all of its requirements of radios, estimated at 20 units per month, during the period January 1, 1988, and December 31, 1990, at a price of $50 per unit. A dispute arose in late December, 1990, when Bill's returned 25 undefective radios to Tune for full credit after Tune had refused to extend the contract for a second three-year period.

In an action by Tune against Bill's for damages due to return of the 25 radios, Tune introduces the written agreement, which expressly permitted the buyer to return defective radios for credit but was silent as to return of undefective radios for credit. Bill's seeks to introduce evidence that during the three years of the agreement it had returned, for various reasons, 125 undefective radios, for which Tune had granted full credit. Tune objects to the admissibility of this evidence.

Question 199

The trial court will probably rule that the evidence proffered by Bill's is

(A) inadmissible, because the evidence is barred by the parol evidence rule.
(B) inadmissible, because the express terms of the agreement control when those terms are inconsistent with the course of performance.
(C) admissible, because the evidence supports an agreement that is not within the relevant statute of frauds.
(D) admissible, because course-of-performance evidence, when available, is considered the best indication of what the parties intended the writing to mean.

Question 200

For this question only, assume the following facts. When Bill's returned the 25 radios in question, it included with the shipment a check payable to Tune for the balance admittedly due on all *other* merchandise sold and delivered to Bill's. The check was conspicuously marked, "Payment in full for all goods sold to Bill's to date." Tune's credit manager, reading this check notation and knowing that Bill's had also returned the 25 radios for full credit, deposited the check without protest in Tune's local bank account. The canceled check was returned to

Bill's a week later.

Which of the following defenses would best serve Bill's?

(A) Tune's deposit of the check and its return to Bill's after payment estopped Tune thereafter to assert that Bill's owed any additional amount.
(B) By depositing the check without protest and with knowledge of its wording, Tune discharged any remaining duty to pay on the part of Bill's.
(C) By depositing the check without protest and with knowledge of its wording, Tune entered into a novation discharging any remaining duty to pay on the part of Bill's.
(D) The parties' good-faith dispute over return of the radios suspended the duty of Bill's, if any, to pay any balance due.

Question 201

Testator, whose nephew Bypast was his only heir, died leaving a will that gave his entire estate to charity. Bypast, knowing full well that Testator was of sound mind all of his life, and having no evidence to the contrary, nevertheless filed a suit contesting Testator's will on the ground that Testator was incompetent when the will was signed. Craven, Testator's executor, offered Bypast $5,000 to settle the suit, and Bypast agreed.

If Craven then repudiates the agreement and the foregoing facts are proved or admitted in Bypast's suit against Craven for breach of contract, is Bypast entitled to recover under the prevailing view?

(A) Yes, because the Bypast-Craven agreement was a bargained-for exchange.
(B) Yes, because the law encourages the settlement of disputed claims.
(C) No, because Bypast did not bring the will contest in good faith.
(D) No, because an agreement to oust the court of its jurisdiction to decide a will contest is contrary to public policy.

Question 202

On July 15, in a writing signed by both parties, Fixtures, Inc., agreed to deliver to Druggist on August 15 five storage cabinets from inventory for a total price of $5,000 to be paid on delivery. On August 1, the two parties orally agreed to postpone the delivery date to August 20. On August 20, Fixtures tendered the cabinets to Druggist, who refused to accept or pay for them on the ground that they were not tendered on Augustÿ15, even though they otherwise met the contract specifications.

Assuming that all appropriate defenses are seasonably raised, will Fixtures succeed in an action against Druggist for breach of contract?

(A) Yes, because neither the July 15 agreement nor the August 1 agreement was required to be in writing.
(B) Yes, because the August 1 agreement operated as a waiver of the August 15 delivery term.
(C) No, because there was no consideration to support the August 1 agreement.
(D) No, because the parol evidence rule will prevent proof of the August 1 agreement.

Question 203

By the terms of a written contract signed by both parties on January 15, M.B. Ram, Inc., agreed to sell a specific ICB personal computer to Marilyn Materboard for $3,000, and Materboard agreed to pick up and pay for the computer at Ram's store on February 1. Materboard unjustifiably repudiated on February 1. Without notifying Materboard, Ram subsequently sold at private sale the same specific computer to Byte, who paid the same price ($3,000) in cash. The ICB is a popular product. Ram can buy from the manufacturer more units than it can sell at retail.

If Ram sues Materboard for breach of contract, Ram will probably recover

(A) nothing, because it received a price on resale equal to the contract price that Materboard had agreed to pay.
(B) nothing, because Ram failed to give Materboard proper notice of Ram's intention to resell.
(C) Ram's anticipated profit on the sale to Materboard plus incidental damages, if any, because Ram lost that sale.
(D) $3,000 (the contract price), because Materboard intentionally breached the contract by repudiation.

Questions 204-205 are based on the following fact pattern.

In a single writing, Painter contracted with Farmer to paint three identical barns on her rural estate for

$2,000 each. The contract provided for Farmer's payment of $6,000 upon Painter's completion of the work on all three barns. Painter did not ask for any payment when the first barn was completely painted, but she demanded $4,000 after painting the second barn.

Question 204

Is Farmer obligated to make the $4,000 payment?

(A) No, because Farmer has no duty under the contract to pay anything to Painter until all three barns have been painted.
(B) No, because Painter waived her right, if any, to payment on a per-barn basis by failing to demand $2,000 upon completion of the first barn.
(C) Yes, because the contract is divisible.
(D) Yes, because Painter has substantially performed the entire contract.

Question 205

For this question only, assume that Farmer rightfully refused Painter's demand for payment.

If Painter immediately terminates the contract without painting the third barn, what is Painter entitled to recover from Farmer?

(A) Nothing, because payment was expressly conditioned on completion of all three barns.
(B) Painter's expenditures plus anticipated "profit" in painting the first two barns, up to a maximum recovery of $4,000.
(C) The reasonable value of Painter's services in painting the two barns, less Farmer's damages, if any, for Painter's failure to paint the third barn.
(D) The amount that the combined value of the two painted barns has been increased by Painter's work.

Questions 206-207 are based on the following fact situation.

On December 15, Lawyer received from Stationer, Inc., a retailer of office supplies, an offer consisting of its catalog and a signed letter stating, "We will supply you with as many of the items in the enclosed catalog as you order during the next calendar year. We assure you that this offer and the prices in the catalog will remain firm throughout the coming year."

Question 206

For this question only, assume that no other correspondence passed between Stationer and Lawyer until the following April 15 (four months later), when Stationer received from Lawyer a faxed order for "100 reams of your paper, catalog item #101."

Did Lawyer's April 15 fax constitute an effective acceptance of Stationer's offer at the prices specified in the catalog?

(A) Yes, because Stationer had not revoked its offer before April 15.
(B) Yes, because a one-year option contract had been created by Stationer's offer.
(C) No, because under applicable law the irrevocability of Stationer's offer was limited to a period of three months.
(D) No, because Lawyer did not accept Stationer's offer within a reasonable time.

Question 207

For this question only, assume that on January 15, having at that time received no reply from Lawyer, Stationer notified Lawyer that effective February 1, it was increasing the prices of certain specified items in its catalog.

Is the price increase effective with respect to catalog orders Stationer receives from Lawyer during the month of February?

(A) No, because Stationer's original offer, including the price term, became irrevocable under the doctrine of promissory estoppel.
(B) No, because Stationer is a merchant with respect to office supplies; and its original offer, including the price term, was irrevocable throughout the month of February.
(C) Yes, because Stationer received no consideration to support its assurance that it would not increase prices.
(D) Yes, because the period for which Stationer gave assurance that it would not raise prices was longer than three months.

Questions 208-210 are based on the following fact situation.

Buyer, Inc., contracted in writing with Shareholder, who owned all of XYZ Corporation's outstanding stock, to purchase all of her stock at a specified price per share. At the time this contract was executed, Buyer's contracting officer said to Shareholder, "Of course, our commitment to buy is conditioned on our obtaining approval of the contract from Conglomerate, Ltd., our parent company." Shareholder replied, "Fine. No problem."

Question 208

For this question only, assume that Conglomerate orally approved the contract, but that Shareholder changed her mind and refused to consummate the sale on two grounds:

(1) when the agreement was made there was no consideration for her promise to sell; and

(2) Conglomerate's approval of the contract was invalid.

If Buyer sues Shareholder for breach of contract, is Buyer likely to prevail?

(A) Yes, because Buyer's promise to buy, bargained for and made in exchange for Shareholder's promise to sell, was good consideration even though it was expressly conditioned on an event that was not certain to occur.
(B) Yes, because any possible lack of consideration for Shareholder's promise to sell was expressly waived by Shareholder when the agreement was made.
(C) No, because mutuality of obligation between the parties was lacking when the agreement was made.
(D) No, because the condition of Conglomerate's approval of the contract was an essential part of the agreed exchange and was not in a signed writing.

Question 209

For this question only, assume the following facts. Shareholder subsequently refused to consummate the sale on the ground that Buyer had neglected to request Conglomerate's approval of the contract, which was true. Conglomerate's chief executive officer, however, is prepared to testify that Conglomerate would have routinely approved the contract if requested to do so. Buyer can also prove that it has made a substantial sale of other assets to finance the stock purchase, although it admittedly had not anticipated any such necessity when it entered into the stock purchase agreement.

If Buyer sues Shareholder for breach of contract,

is Buyer likely to prevail?

(A) Yes, because the condition of Conglomerate's approval of the contract, being designed to protect only Buyer and Conglomerate, can be and has been waived by those entities.
(B) Yes, because Buyer detrimentally relied on Shareholder's commitment by selling off other assets to finance the stock purchase.
(C) No, because the express condition of Conglomerate's approval had not occurred prior to the lawsuit.
(D) No, because obtaining Conglomerate's approval of the contract was an event within Buyer's control and Buyer's failure to obtain it was itself a material breach of contract.

Question 210

For this question only, assume the following facts. Shareholder is willing and ready to consummate the sale of her stock to Buyer, but the latter refuses to perform on the ground (which is true) that Conglomerate has firmly refused to approve the contract.

If Shareholder sues Buyer for breach of contract and seeks to exclude any evidence of the oral condition requiring Conglomerate's approval, the court will probably

(A) admit the evidence as proof of a collateral agreement.
(B) admit the evidence as proof of a condition to the existence of an enforceable obligation, and therefore not within the scope of the parol evidence rule.
(C) exclude the evidence on the basis of a finding that the parties' written agreement was a complete integration of their contract.
(D) exclude the evidence as contradicting the terms of the parties' written agreement, whether or not the writing was a complete integration of the contract.

Questions 211-212 are based on the following fact situation.

Tenant rented a commercial building from Landlord, and operated a business in it. The building's large front window was smashed by vandals six months before expiration of the Tenant-Landlord lease. Tenant, who was obligated thereunder to effect and pay for repairs in such cases, promptly contracted with Glazier to replace the window for $2,000, due 30 days after satisfactory completion of the work. Landlord was then unaware of the Tenant-Glazier contract. Glazier was aware that the building was under lease, but dealt entirely with Tenant.

Sixty days after Glazier's satisfactory completion of the window replacement, and prior to the expiration of Tenant's lease, Tenant, then insolvent, ceased doing business and vacated the building. In so doing, Tenant forfeited under the lease provisions its right to the return of a $2,000 security deposit with Landlord. The deposit had been required, however, for the express purpose (as stated in the lease) of covering any damage to the leased property except ordinary wear and tear. The only such damage occurring during Tenant's occupancy was the smashed window. Glazier's $2,000 bill for the window replacement is wholly unpaid.

Question 211

Assuming that Glazier has no remedy quasi in rem under the relevant state mechanic's lien statute, which of the following would provide Glazier's best chance of an effective remedy in personam against Landlord?

(A) An action in quasi contract for the reasonable value of a benefit unofficiously and non-gratuitously conferred on Landlord.
(B) An action based on promissory estoppel.
(C) An action based on an implied-in-fact contract.
(D) An action as third-party intended beneficiary of the Tenant-Landlord lease.

Question 212

For this question only, assume the following facts. Upon vacating the building, Tenant mailed a $1,000 check to Glazier bearing on its face the following conspicuous notation: "This check is in full and final satisfaction of your $2,000 window replacement bill." Without noticing this notation, Glazier cashed the check and now sues Tenant for the $1,000 difference.

If Tenant's only defense is accord and satisfaction, is Tenant likely to prevail?

(A) No, because Glazier failed to notice Tenant's notation on the check.
(B) No, because the amount owed by Tenant to Glazier was liquidated and undisputed.
(C) Yes, because by cashing the check Glazier

impliedly agreed to accept the $1,000 as full payment of its claim.
(D) Yes, because Glazier failed to write a reservation-of-rights notation on the check before cashing it.

Question 213

Bye Bye telegraphed Vendor on June 1, "At what price will you sell 100 of your QT-Model garbage-disposal units for delivery around June 10?" Thereafter, the following communications were exchanged:

1.   Telegram from Vendor received by Bye Bye on June 2: "You're in luck. We have only 100 QT's, all on clearance at 50% off usual wholesale of $120 per unit, for delivery at our shipping platform on June 12."

2.   Letter from Bye Bye received in U.S. mail by Vendor on June 5: "I accept. Would prefer to pay in full 30 days after invoice."

3.   Telegram from Vendor received by Bye Bye on June 6: "You must pick up at our platform and pay C.O.D."

4.   Letter from Bye Bye received in U.S. mail by Vendor on June 9: "I don't deal with people who can't accommodate our simple requests."

5.   Telegram from Bye Bye received by Vendor on June 10, after Vendor had sold and delivered all 100 of the QT's to another buyer earlier that day: "Okay. I'm over a barrel and will pick up the goods on your terms June 12."

Bye Bye now sues Vendor for breach of contract.

Which of the following arguments will best serve Vendor's defense?

(A) Vendor's telegram received on June 2 was merely a price quotation, not an offer.
(B) Bye Bye's letter received on June 5 was not an acceptance because it varied the terms of Vendor's initial telegram.
(C) Bye Bye's use of the mails in response to Vendor's initial telegram was an ineffective method of acceptance.
(D) Bye Bye's letter received on June 9 was an unequivocal refusal to perform that excused Vendor even if the parties had previously formed a contract.

Questions 214-215 are based on the following fact situation.

Gourmet, a famous chef, entered into a written agreement with his friend Deligor, a well-known interior decorator respected for his unique designs, in which Deligor agreed, for a fixed fee, to design the interior of Gourmet's new restaurant, and, upon Gourmet's approval of the design plan, to decorate and furnish the restaurant accordingly. The agreement was silent as to assignment or delegation by either party. Before beginning the work, Deligor sold his decorating business to Newman under an agreement in which Deligor assigned to Newman, and Newman agreed to complete, the Gourmet-Deligor contract. Newman, also an experienced decorator of excellent repute, advised Gourmet of the assignment, and supplied him with information confirming both Newman's financial responsibility and past commercial success.

Question 214

Is Gourmet obligated to permit Newman to perform the Gourmet-Deligor agreement?

(A) Yes, because the agreement contained no prohibition against assignment or delegation.
(B) Yes, because Gourmet received adequate assurances of Newman's ability to complete the job.
(C) No, because Deligor's duties were of a personal nature, involving his reputation, taste, and skill.
(D) No, because Deligor's purported delegation to Newman of his obligations to Gourmet effected a novation.

Question 215

If Gourmet allows Newman to perform and approves his design plan, but Newman fails without legal excuse to complete the decorating as agreed, against whom does Gourmet have an enforceable claim for breach of contract?

(A) Deligor only, because Deligor's agreement with Newman did not discharge his duty to Gourmet, and Newman made no express promise to Gourmet.
(B) Newman only, because Deligor's duty to Gourmet was discharged when Deligor obtained a skilled decorator (Newman) to perform the Gourmet-Deligor contract.
(C) Newman only, because Gourmet was an intended beneficiary of the Deligor-Newman agreement, and Deligor's duty to Gourmet was discharged

when Gourmet permitted Newman to do the work and approved Newman's design.
(D) Either Deligor, because his agreement with Newman did not discharge his duty to Gourmet; or Newman, because Gourmet was an intended beneficiary of the Deligor-Newman agreement.

Questions 216-217 are based on the following fact situation.

Landholder was land-rich by inheritance but money-poor, having suffered severe losses on bad investments, but still owned several thousand acres of unencumbered timberland.

He had a large family, and his normal, fixed personal expenses were high. Pressed for cash, he advertised a proposed sale of standing timber on a choice 2,000-acre tract. The only response was an offer by Logger, the owner of a large, integrated construction enterprise, after inspection of the advertised tract.

Question 216

For this question only, assume the following facts. Logger offered to buy, sever, and remove the standing timber from the advertised tract at a cash price 70% lower than the regionally prevailing price for comparable timber rights. Landholder, by then in desperate financial straits and knowing little about timber values, signed and delivered to Logger a letter accepting the offer.

If, before Logger commences performance, Landholder's investment fortunes suddenly improve and he wishes to get out of the timber deal with Logger, which of the following legal concepts affords his best prospect of effective cancellation?

(A) Bad faith.
(B) Equitable estoppel.
(C) Unconscionability.
(D) Duress.

Question 217

For this question only, assume the following facts. Logger offered a fair price for the timber rights in question, and Landholder accepted the offer. The 2,000-acre tract was an abundant wild-game habitat and had been used for many years, with Landholder's permission, by area hunters. Logger's performance of the timber contract would destroy this habitat. Without legal excuse and over Landholder's strong objection, Logger repudiated the contract before commencing performance. Landholder could not afford to hire a lawyer and take legal action, and made no attempt to assign any cause of action he might have had against Logger.

If Logger is sued for breach of the contract by Landholder's next-door neighbor, whose view of a nearby lake is obscured by the standing timber, the neighbor will probably

(A) lose, as only an incidental beneficiary, if any, of the Logger-Landholder contract.
(B) lose, as a maintainer of nuisance litigation.
(C) prevail, as a third-party intended beneficiary of the Logger-Landholder contract.
(D) prevail, as a surrogate for Landholder in view of his inability to enforce the contract.

Question 218

Agreement, between Land, Inc. (hereafter called `Owner'), and Builder, Inc., and Boss, its President (hereafter called `Contractor'), witnesseth:" The signatures to the contract appeared in the following format:

LAND, INC.

By /s/ Oscar Land

President

BUILDER, INC.

By /s/ George Mason

Vice President

/s/ Mary Boss, President

Mary Boss

Builder, Inc., became insolvent and defaulted. Land, Inc., sued Boss individually for the breach, and at the trial Boss proffered evidence from the pre-contract negotiations that only Builder, Inc., was to be legally responsible for performing the contract.

If the court finds the contract to be completely

integrated, is Boss's proffered evidence admissible?

(A) Yes, because the writing is ambiguous as to whether or not Boss was intended individually to be a contracting party.
(B) Yes, because the evidence would contradict neither the recital nor the form of Boss's signature.
(C) No, because the legal effect of Boss's signature cannot be altered by evidence of prior understandings.
(D) No, because of the application of the "four corners" rule, under which the meaning of a completely integrated contract must be ascertained solely from its own terms.

Questions 219-220 are based on the following fact situation.

Fixtures, Inc., in a signed writing, contracted with Apartments for the sale to Apartments of 50 identical sets of specified bathroom fixtures, 25 sets to be delivered on March 1, and the remaining 25 sets on April 1. The agreement did not specify the place of delivery, or the time or place of payment.

Question 219

Which of the following statements is correct?

(A) Fixtures must tender 25 sets to Apartments at Apartments' place of business on March 1, but does not have to turn them over to Apartments until Apartments pays the contract price for the 25 sets.
(B) Fixtures has no duty to deliver the 25 sets on March 1 at Fixtures' place of business unless Apartments tenders the contract price for the 25 sets on that date.
(C) Fixtures must deliver 25 sets on March 1, and Apartments must pay the contract price for the 25 sets within a reasonable time after their delivery.
(D) Fixtures must deliver 25 sets on March 1, but Apartments' payment is due only upon the delivery of all 50 sets.

Question 220

For this question only, make the following assumptions. On March 1, Fixtures tendered 24 sets to Apartments and explained, "One of the 25 sets was damaged in transit from the manufacturer to us, but we will deliver a replacement within 5 days."

Which of the following statements is correct?

(A) Apartments is entitled to accept any number of the 24 sets, reject the rest, and cancel the contract both as to any rejected sets and the lot due on April.
(B) Apartments is entitled to accept any number of the 24 sets and to reject the rest, but is not entitled to cancel the contract as to any rejected sets or the lot due on April 1.
(C) Apartments must accept the 24 sets but is entitled to cancel the rest of the contract.
(D) Apartments must accept the 24 sets and is not entitled to cancel the rest of the contract.

Question 221

On March 1, Mechanic contracted to repair Textiles' knitting machine and to complete the job by March 6. On March 2, Textiles contracted to manufacture and deliver specified cloth to Knitwear on March 15. Textiles knew that it would have to use the machine then under repair to perform this contract. Because the Knitwear order was for a rush job, Knitwear and Textiles included in their contract a liquidated damages clause, providing that Textiles would pay $5,000 for each day's delay in delivery after March 15.

Mechanic was inexcusably five days late in repairing the machine, and, as a result, Textiles was five days late in delivering the cloth to Knitwear. Textiles paid $25,000 to Knitwear as liquidated damages and now sues Mechanic for $25,000. Both Mechanic and Textiles knew when making their contract on March 1 that under ordinary circumstances Textiles would sustain little or no damages of any kind as a result of a five-day delay in the machine repair.

Assuming that the $5,000 liquidated damages clause in the Knitwear-Textiles contract is valid, which of the following arguments will serve as Mechanic's best defense to Textiles' action?

(A) Time was not of the essence in the Mechanic-Textiles contract.
(B) Mechanic had no reason to foresee on March 1 that Knitwear would suffer consequential damages in the amount of $25,000.
(C) By entering into the Knitwear contract while knowing that its knitting machine was being repaired, Textiles assumed the risk of any delay loss to Knitwear.

(D) In all probability, the liquidated damages paid by Textiles to Knitwear are not the same amount as the actual damages sustained by Knitwear in consequence of Textiles' late delivery of the cloth.

Question 222

A written construction contract, under which Contractor agreed to build a new house for Owner at a fixed price of $200,000, contained the following provision:

Prior to construction or during the course thereof, this contract may be modified by mutual agreement of the parties as to "extras" or other departures from the plans and specifications provided by Owner and attached hereto. Such modifications, however, may be authorized only in writing, signed by both parties.

During construction, Contractor incorporated into the structure overhanging gargoyles and other "extras" orally requested by Owner for orally agreed prices in addition to the contract price. Owner subsequently refused to pay anything for such extras, aggregating $30,000 at the agreed prices, solely on the ground that no written, signed authorization for them was ever effected.

If Contractor sues Owner on account of the "extras," which, if any, of the following will effectively support Owner's defense?

    I.   The parol evidence rule.
    II.   The preexisting duty rule.
    III.   Failure of an express condition.
    IV.   The statute of frauds.

(A) I and III only.
(B) I and IV only.
(C) II and IV only.
(D) Neither I, II, III, nor IV.

Questions 223-224 are based on the following fact situation.

On April 1, Owner and Buyer signed a writing in which Owner, "in consideration of $100 to be paid to Owner by Buyer," offered Buyer the right to purchase Greenacre for $100,000 within 30 days. The writing further provided, "This offer will become effective as an option only if and when the $100 consideration is in fact paid." On April 20, Owner, having received no payment or other communication from Buyer, sold and conveyed Greenacre to Citizen for $120,000. On April 21, Owner received a letter from Buyer enclosing a cashier's check for $100 payable to Owner and stating, "I am hereby exercising my option to purchase Greenacre and am prepared to close whenever you're ready."

Question 223

Which of the following, if proved, best supports Buyer's suit against Owner for breach of contract?

(A) Buyer was unaware of the sale to Citizen when Owner received the letter and check from Buyer on April 21.
(B) On April 15, Buyer decided to purchase Greenacre, and applied for and obtained a commitment from Bank for a $75,000 loan to help finance the purchase.
(C) When the April 1 writing was signed, Owner said to Buyer, "Don't worry about the $100; the recital of `$100 to be paid' makes this deal binding."
(D) Owner and Buyer are both professional dealers in real estate.

Question 224

For this question only, assume that, for whatever reason, Buyer prevails in the suit against Owner.

Which of the following is Buyer entitled to recover?

(A) Nominal damages only, because the remedy of specific performance was not available to Buyer.
(B) The fair market value, if any, of an assignable option to purchase Greenacre for $100,000.
(C) $20,000, plus the amount, if any, by which the fair market value of Greenacre on the date of Owner's breach exceeded $120,000.
(D) The amount, if any, by which the fair market value of Greenacre on the date of Owner's breach exceeded $100,000.

Questions 225-226 are based on the following fact situation.

On June 1, Seller and Buyer contracted in writing for the sale and purchase of Seller's cattle ranch (a large single tract), and to close the transaction on December 1.

Question 225

For this question only, assume the following facts. On October 1, Buyer told Seller, "I'm increasingly unhappy about our June 1 contract because of the current cattle market, and do not intend to buy your ranch unless I'm legally obligated to do so."

If Seller sues Buyer on October 15 for breach of contract, Seller will probably

(A) win, because Buyer committed a total breach by anticipatory repudiation on October 1.
(B) win, because Buyer's October 1 statement created reasonable grounds for Seller's insecurity with respect to Buyer's performance.
(C) lose, because the parties contracted for the sale and conveyance of a single tract, and Seller cannot bring suit for breach of such a contract prior to the agreed closing date.
(D) lose, because Buyer's October 1 statement to Seller was neither a repudiation nor a present breach of the June 1 contract.

Question 226

For this question only, assume the following facts. Buyer unequivocally repudiated the contract on August 1. On August 15, Seller urged Buyer to change her mind and proceed with the scheduled closing on December 1. On October 1, having heard nothing further from Buyer, Seller sold and conveyed his ranch to Rancher without notice to Buyer. On December 1, Buyer attempted to close under the June 1 contract by tendering the full purchase price to Seller. Seller rejected the tender.

If Buyer sues Seller for breach of contract, Buyer will probably

(A) win, because Seller failed seasonably to notify Buyer of any pending sale to Rancher.
(B) win, because Seller waived Buyer's August 1 repudiation by urging her to retract it on August 15.
(C) lose, because Buyer did not retract her repudiation before Seller materially changed his position in reliance thereon by selling the ranch to Rancher.
(D) lose, because acceptance of the purchase price by Seller was a concurrent condition to Seller's obligation to convey the ranch to Buyer on December 1.

Question 227

Kontractor agreed to build a power plant for a public utility. Subbo agreed with Kontractor to lay the foundation for $200,000. Subbo supplied goods and services worth $150,000, for which Kontractor made progress payments aggregating $100,000 as required by the subcontract. Subbo then breached by refusing unjustifiably to perform further. Kontractor reasonably spent $120,000 to have the work completed by another subcontractor.

Subbo sues Kontractor for the reasonable value of benefits conferred, and Kontractor counterclaims for breach of contract.

Which of the following should be the court's decision?

(A) Subbo recovers $50,000, the benefit conferred on Kontractor for which Subbo has not been paid.
(B) Subbo recovers $30,000, the benefit Subbo conferred on Kontractor minus the $20,000 in damages incurred by Kontractor.
(C) Kontractor recovers $20,000, the excess over the contract price that was paid by Kontractor for the performance it had bargained to receive from Subbo.
(D) Neither party recovers anything, because Subbo committed a material, unexcused breach and Kontractor received a $50,000 benefit from Subbo for which Subbo has not been paid.

Questions 228-229 are based on the following fact situation.

Computers, Inc., contracted in writing with Bank to sell and deliver to Bank a mainframe computer using a new type of magnetic memory, then under development but not perfected by Computers, at a price substantially lower than that of a similar computer using current technology. The contract's delivery term was "F.O.B. Bank, on or before July 31."

Question 228

For this question only, assume that Computers tendered the computer to Bank on August 15, and that Bank rejected it because of the delay.

If Computers sues Bank for breach of contract, which of the following facts, if proved, will best support a recovery by Computers?

(A) The delay did not materially harm Bank.

(B) Computers believed, on the assumption that Bank was getting a "super deal" for its money, that Bank would not reject because of the late tender of delivery.
(C) Computers' delay in tender was caused by a truckers' strike.
(D) A usage in the relevant trade allows computer sellers a 30-day leeway in a specified time of delivery, unless the usage is expressly negated by the contract.

Question 229

For this question only, assume the following facts. After making the contract with Bank, Computers discovered that the new technology it intended to use was unreliable and that no computer manufacturer could yet build a reliable computer using that technology. Computers thereupon notified Bank that it was impossible for Computers or anyone else to build the contracted-for computer "in the present state of the art."

If Bank sues Computers for failure to perform its computer contract, the court will probably decide the case in favor of

(A) Computers, because its performance of the contract was objectively impossible.
(B) Computers, because a contract to build a machine using technology under development imposes only a duty on the builder to use its best efforts to achieve the result contracted for.
(C) Bank, because the law of impossibility does not apply to merchants under the applicable law.
(D) Bank, because Computers assumed the risk, in the given circumstances, that the projected new technology would not work reliably.

Question 230

Loyal, aged 60, who had no plans for early retirement, had worked for Mutate, Inc., for 20 years as a managerial employee-at-will when he had a conversation with the company's president, George Mutant, about Loyal's post-retirement goal of extensive travel around the United States. A month later, Mutant handed Loyal a written, signed resolution of the company's Board of Directors stating that when and if Loyal should decide to retire, at his option, the company, in recognition of his past service, would pay him a $2,000-per-month lifetime pension. (The company had no regularized retirement plan for at-will employees.) Shortly thereafter, Loyal retired and immediately bought a $30,000 recreational vehicle for his planned travels. After receiving the promised $2,000 monthly pension from Mutate, Inc., for six months, Loyal, now unemployable elsewhere, received a letter from Mutate, Inc., advising him that the pension would cease immediately because of recessionary budget constraints affecting in varying degrees all managerial salaries and retirement pensions.

In a suit against Mutate, Inc., for breach of contract, Loyal will probably

(A) win, because he retired from the company as bargained-for consideration for the Board's promise to him of a lifetime pension.
(B) win, because he timed his decision to retire and to buy the recreational vehicle in reasonable reliance on the Board's promise to him of a lifetime pension.
(C) lose, because the Board's promise to him of a lifetime pension was an unenforceable gift promise.
(D) lose, because he had been an employee-at-will throughout his active service with the company.

Question 231

In exchange for a valid and sufficient consideration, Goodbar orally promised Walker, who had no car and wanted a minivan, "to pay to anyone from whom you buy a minivan within the next six months the full purchase-price thereof." Two months later, Walker bought a used minivan on credit from Minivanity Fair, Inc., for $8,000. At the time, Minivanity Fair was unaware of Goodbar's earlier promise to Walker, but learned of it shortly after the sale.

Can Minivanity Fair enforce Goodbar's promise to Walker?

(A) Yes, under the doctrine of promissory estoppel.
(B) Yes, because Minivanity Fair is an intended beneficiary of the Goodbar-Walker contract.
(C) No, because Goodbar's promise to Walker is unenforceable under the suretyship clause of the statute of frauds.
(D) No, because Minivanity Fair was neither identified when Goodbar's promise was made nor aware of it when the minivan-sale was made.

Question 232

Breeder bought a two-month-old registered boar at auction from Pigstyle for $800. No express

warranty was made. Fifteen months later, tests by experts proved conclusively that the boar had been born incurably sterile. If this had been known at the time of the sale, the boar would have been worth no more than $100.

In an action by Breeder against Pigstyle to avoid the contract and recover the price paid, the parties stipulate that, as both were and had been aware, the minimum age at which the fertility of a boar can be determined is about 12 months.

Which of the following will the court probably decide?

(A) Breeder wins, because the parties were mutually mistaken as to the boar's fertility when they made the agreement.
(B) Breeder wins, because Pigstyle impliedly warranted that the boar was fit for breeding.
(C) Pigstyle wins, because Breeder assumed the risk of the boar's sterility.
(D) Pigstyle wins, because any mistake involved was unilateral, not mutual.

Question 233

Gourmet purchased the front portion of the land needed for a restaurant he desired to build and operate, but the back portion was the subject of a will dispute between Hope and Faith (two sisters). Hope's attorney advised her that her claim was doubtful. Gourmet, knowing only that the unresolved dispute existed, agreed in a signed writing to pay Hope $6,000, payable $1,000 annually, in exchange for a quitclaim deed (a deed containing no warranties) from Hope, who promptly executed such a deed to Gourmet and received Gourmet's first annual payment. Shortly thereafter, the probate court handed down a decision in Faith's favor, ruling that Hope had no interest in the land. This decision has become final. Gourmet subsequently defaulted when his second annual installment came due.

In an action against Gourmet for breach of contract, Hope will probably

(A) lose, because she was aware at the time of the agreement with Gourmet that her claim to the property quitclaimed was doubtful.
(B) lose, because Hope suffered no legal detriment in executing the quitclaim deed.
(C) win, because Gourmet bargained for and received in exchange a quitclaim deed from Hope.

(D) win, because Gourmet, by paying the first $1,000 installment, is estopped to deny that his agreement with Hope is an enforceable contract.

Question 234

Retailer, a dry goods retailer, telephoned Manufacturer, a towel manufacturer, and offered to buy for $5 each a minimum of 500 and a maximum of 1,000 large bath towels, to be delivered in 30 days. Manufacturer orally accepted this offer and promptly sent the following letter to Retailer, which Retailer received two days later: "This confirms our agreement today by telephone to sell you 500 large bath towels for 30-day delivery. /s/ Manufacturer." Twenty-eight days later, Manufacturer tendered to Retailer 1,000 (not 500) conforming bath towels, all of which Retailer rejected because it had found a better price term from another supplier. Because of a glut in the towel market, Manufacturer cannot resell the towels except at a loss.

In a suit by Manufacturer against Retailer, which of the following will be the probable decision?

(A) Manufacturer can enforce a contract for 1,000 towels, because Retailer ordered and Manufacturer tendered that quantity.
(B) Manufacturer can enforce a contract for 500 towels, because Manufacturer's letter of confirmation stated that quantity term.
(C) There is no enforceable agreement, because Retailer never signed a writing.

(D) There is no enforceable agreement, because Manufacturer's letter of confirmation did not state a price term.

Question 235

Buyer mailed a signed order to Seller that read: "Please ship us 10,000 widgets at your current price." Seller received the order on January 7 and that same day mailed to Buyer a properly stamped, addressed, and signed letter stating that the order was accepted at Seller's current price of $10 per widget. On January 8, before receipt of Seller's letter, Buyer telephoned Seller and said, "I hereby revoke my order." Seller protested to no avail. Buyer received Seller's letter on January 9. Because of Buyer's January 8 telephone message, Seller never shipped the goods.

Under the relevant and prevailing rules, is there a contract between Buyer and Seller as of January 10?

(A) No, because the order was an offer that could be accepted only by shipping the goods; and the offer was effectively revoked before shipment.
(B) No, because Buyer never effectively agreed to the $10 price term.
(C) Yes, because the order was, for a reasonable time, an irrevocable offer.
(D) Yes, because the order was an offer that Seller effectively accepted before Buyer attempted to revoke it.

AMERIBAR BAR REVIEW

Multistate Bar Examination Released Questions-Section 5

CRIMINAL LAW & PROCEDURE

Question 1

While walking home one evening, Harold, an off-duty police officer, was accosted by Jones, a stranger. Jones had been drinking and mistakenly thought Harold was a man who was having an affair with his wife. Intending to frighten Harold but not to harm him, Jones pulled out a knife, screamed obscenities, and told Harold he was going to kill him. Frightened and reasonably believing Jones was going to kill him and that using deadly force was his only salvation, Harold took out his service revolver and shot and killed Jones. Harold is charged with murder.

Harold's claim of self-defense should be

(A) sustained, because Harold reasonably believed Jones was planning to kill him and that deadly force was required.
(B) sustained, because the killing was in hot blood upon sufficient provocation.
(C) denied, because Jones did not in fact intend to harm Harold and Harold was incorrect in believing that he did.
(D) denied, because Harold was not defending his home and had an obligation to retreat or to repel with less than deadly force.

Question 2

Shore decided to destroy his dilapidated building in order to collect the insurance money. He hired Parsons to burn down the building. Parsons broke into the building and carefully searched it to make sure no one was inside. He failed, however, to see a vagrant asleep in an office closet. He started a fire. The building was destroyed, and the vagrant died from burns a week later. Two days after the fire, Shore filed an insurance claim in which he stated that he had no information about the cause of the fire.

If Shore is guilty of felony-murder, it is because the vagrant's death occurred in connection with the felony of

(A) arson.
(B) fraud.
(C) conspiracy.
(D) burglary.

Questions 3-5 are based on the following fact situation.

A jurisdiction has the following decisional law on questions of principal and accomplice liability:

CASE A: Defendant, a hardware store owner, sold several customers an item known as a "SuperTrucker," which detects police radar and enables speeders to avoid detection. When one of the devices broke down and the speeder was arrested, he confessed that he often sped, secure in the knowledge that his "SuperTrucker" would warn him of police radar in the vicinity. Held: Defendant guilty as an accomplice to speeding.

CASE B: Defendant told Arnold that Defendant had stored some stereo equipment in a self-storage locker. He gave Arnold a key and asked Arnold to pick up the equipment and deliver it to Defendant's house. Arnold complied, and removed the equipment from the locker, using the key. In fact, the equipment belonged to Defendant's neighbor, whose locker key Defendant had found in the driveway. Held: Defendant guilty as an accomplice to burglary.

CASE C: Tooley, a city council member, accepted a bribe from Defendant in exchange for his vote on Defendant's application for a zoning variance. A statute prohibits the taking of bribes by public officials.

<u>Held:</u> Defendant not guilty as an accomplice to Tooley's violation of the bribery statute.

CASE D: Defendant, an innkeeper, sometimes let his rooms to prostitutes, whom he knew to be using the rooms to ply their trade. He charged the prostitutes the same price as other guests at his inn. <u>Held:</u> Defendant not guilty as an accomplice to prostitution.

Question 3

Lipsky, a college student, purchased narcotics from Speed, whom he believed to be a "street person" but who was in fact an undercover police agent. Lipsky has been charged as an accomplice to the sale of narcotics.

(A) He should be convicted on the authority of Case A.
(B) convicted on the authority of Case B.
(C) acquitted on the authority of Case C.
(D) acquitted on the authority of Case D.

Question 4

In this jurisdiction, conviction for statutory rape requires proof of the defendant's knowledge that the victim is underage. Howard, who knew that Sarah was underage, encouraged George, who was unaware of Sarah's age, to have sex with Sarah. Howard has been charged as an accomplice to statutory rape.

He should be

(A) convicted on the authority of Case A.
(B) convicted on the authority of Case B.
(C) acquitted on the authority of Case C.
(D) acquitted on the authority of Case D.

Question 5

Larson, a plastic surgeon, agreed to remove the fingerprints from the hands of "Fingers" Malloy, whom Larson knew to be a safecracker. Larson charged his usual hourly rate for the operation. Afterward, Malloy burglarized a bank safe and was convicted of burglary.

Charged with burglary, Larson should be

(A) convicted on the authority of Case A.
(B) convicted on the authority of Case B.
(C) acquitted on the authority of Case C.
(D) acquitted on the authority of Case D.

Question 6

After waiting until all the customers had left, Max entered a small grocery store just before closing time. He went up to the lone clerk in the store and said, "Hand over all the money in the cash register or you will get hurt." The clerk fainted and struck his head on the edge of the counter. As Max went behind the counter to open the cash register, two customers entered the store. Max ran out before he was able to open the register drawer.

On this evidence Max could be convicted of

(A) robbery.
(B) assault and robbery.
(C) attempted robbery.
(D) assault and attempted robbery.

Questions 7-8 are based on the following fact situation.

Police received information from an undercover police officer that she had just seen two men (whom she described) in a red pickup truck selling marijuana to schoolchildren near the city's largest high school. A few minutes later, two police officers saw a pickup truck fitting the description a half block from the high school. The driver of the truck matched the description of one of the men described by the undercover officer.

The only passenger was a young woman who was in the back of the truck. The police saw her get out and stand at a nearby bus stop. They stopped the truck and searched the driver. In the pocket of the driver's jacket, the police found a small bottle of pills that they recognized as narcotics. They then broke open a locked toolbox attached to the flatbed of the truck and found a small sealed envelope inside. They opened it and found marijuana. They also found a quantity of cocaine in the glove compartment.

After completing their search of the driver and the truck, the police went over to the young woman and searched her purse. In her purse, they found a small quantity of heroin. Both the driver and the young woman were arrested and charged with unlawful possession of narcotics.

Question 7

If the driver moves to suppress the use as evidence of the marijuana and cocaine found in the search of the truck, the court should

(A) grant the motion as to both the marijuana and the cocaine.
(B) grant the motion as to the marijuana but deny it as to the cocaine.
(C) deny the motion as to the marijuana but grant it as to the cocaine.
(D) deny the motion as to both the marijuana and the cocaine.

Question 8

If the young woman moves to suppress the use as evidence of the heroin, the court should

(A) grant the motion, because she did not fit the description given by the informant and her mere presence does not justify the search.
(B) grant the motion, because the police should have seized her purse and then obtained a warrant to search it.
(C) deny the motion, because she had been a passenger in the truck and the police had probable cause to search the truck.
(D) deny the motion, because she was planning to leave the scene by bus and so exigent circumstances existed.

Question 9

Smith joined a neighborhood gang. At a gang meeting, as part of the initiation process, the leader ordered Smith to kill Hardy, a member of a rival gang. Smith refused, saying he no longer wanted to be part of the group. The leader, with the approval of the other members, told Smith that he had become too involved with the gang to quit and that they would kill him if he did not accomplish the murder of Hardy. The next day Smith shot Hardy to death while Hardy was sitting on his motorcycle outside a restaurant.

Smith is charged with first-degree murder. First-degree murder is defined in the jurisdiction as the intentional premeditated killing of another. Second-degree murder is all other murder at common law.

If Smith killed Hardy because of the threat to his own life, Smith should be found

(A) not guilty, because of the defense of duress.
(B) not guilty, because of the defense of necessity.

(C) guilty of first-degree murder.
(D) guilty of second-degree murder.

Question 10

Arnold decided to destroy an old warehouse that he owned because the taxes on the structure exceeded the income that he could receive from it. He crept into the building in the middle of the night with a can of gasoline and a fuse and set the fuse timer for 30 minutes. He then left the building. The fuse failed to ignite, and the building was not harmed.

Arson is defined in this jurisdiction as "The intentional burning of any building or structure of another, without the consent of the owner." Arnold believed, however, that burning one's own building was arson, having been so advised by his lawyer.

Has Arnold committed attempted arson?

(A) Yes, because factual impossibility is no defense.
(B) Yes, because a mistake of law even on the advice of an attorney is no defense.
(C) No, because his mistake negated a necessary mental state.
(D) No, because even if his actions had every consequence he intended, they would not have constituted arson.

Question 11

Suspecting that Scott had slain his wife, police detectives persuaded one of Scott's employees to remove a drinking glass from Scott's office so that it could be used for fingerprint comparisons with a knife found near the body. The fingerprints matched. The prosecutor announced that he would present comparisons and evidence to the grand jury. Scott's lawyer immediately filed a motion to suppress the evidence of the fingerprint comparisons to bar its consideration by the grand jury, contending that the evidence was illegally acquired.

The motion should be

(A) granted, because, if there was no probable cause, the grand jury should not consider the evidence.
(B) granted, because the employee was acting as a police agent and his seizure of the glass without a warrant was unconstitutional.
(C) denied, because motions based on the exclusionary rule are premature in grand jury proceedings.
(D) denied, because the glass was removed from Scott's possession by a private citizen and not a police officer.

Question 12

In which of the following cases is Morrow most likely to be convicted if she is charged with receiving stolen property?

(A) Morrow bought a car from Aster, who operates a used car lot. Before the purchase, Aster told Morrow that the car had been stolen, which was true. Unknown to Morrow, Aster is an undercover police agent who is operating the lot in cooperation with the police in exchange for leniency in connection with criminal charges pending against him.
(B) Morrow bought a car from Ball. Before the purchase, Ball told Morrow that the car was stolen. Ball had stolen the car with the help of Eames, who, unknown to Morrow or Ball, was an undercover police agent who feigned cooperation with Ball in the theft of the car.
(C) Morrow bought a car from Cooper. Before the purchase, Cooper told Morrow that the car was stolen. Unknown to Morrow, Cooper had stolen the car from a parking lot and had been caught by the police as he was driving it away. He agreed to cooperate with the police and carry through with his prearranged sale of the car to Morrow.

(D) Morrow bought a car from Dixon. Before the purchase, Dixon told Morrow that the car was stolen. Unknown to Morrow, Dixon was in fact the owner of the car but had reported it to the police as stolen and had collected on a fraudulent claim of its theft from his insurance company.

Question 13

Dan entered the police station and announced that he wanted to confess to a murder. The police advised Dan of the Miranda warnings, and Dan signed a written waiver. Dan described the murder in detail and pinpointed the location where a murder victim had been found a few weeks before. Later, a court-appointed psychiatrist determined that Dan was suffering from a serious mental illness that interfered with his ability to make rational choices and to understand his rights and that the psychosis had induced his confession.

Dan's confession is

(A) admissible, because there was no coercive police conduct in obtaining Dan's statement.
(B) admissible, because Dan was not in custody.
(C) inadmissible, because Dan's confession was a product of his mental illness and was therefore involuntary.
(D) inadmissible, because under these circumstances, there was no valid waiver of Miranda warnings.

Question 14

In which of the following situations would a court applying common-law doctrine be most likely to convict Defendant of the crime charged, despite Defendant's mistake?

(A) Defendant was charged with bigamy. He married his neighbor four years after her husband was reported missing at sea. The rescued husband returns alive. A state statute provides that a person is presumed dead after five years of unexplained absence. Defendant believed the statutory period was three years.
(B) Defendant was charged with murder after he shot and killed a man who had extorted money from him. Defendant mistakenly thought the victim had raised his hand to shoot, when, in fact, the victim was shaking his fist at Defendant to frighten him.
(C)   Defendant was charged with assault with intent to rape a woman who he mistakenly believed had agreed to have sexual intercourse with him.
(D)   Defendant was charged with burglary. He had broken into an office where he once worked and had taken a typewriter that he erroneously believed had been given to him before he was fired.

Question 15

Kathy, a two-year-old, became ill with meningitis. Jim and Joan, her parents, were members of a group that believed fervently that if they prayed enough, God would not permit their child to die. Accordingly, they did not seek medical aid for Kathy and refused all offers of such aid. They prayed continuously. Kathy died of the illness within a week.

Jim and Joan are charged with murder in a common-law jurisdiction.

Their best defense to the charge is that

(A) they did not intend to kill or to harm Kathy.
(B) they were pursuing a constitutionally protected religious belief.
(C) Kathy's death was not proximately caused by their conduct.
(D) they neither premeditated nor deliberated.

Question 16

At a party for coworkers at Defendant's home, Victim accused Defendant of making advances toward his wife. Victim and his wife left the party. The next day at work, Defendant saw Victim and struck him on the head with a soft-drink bottle. Victim fell into a coma and died two weeks after the incident.

This jurisdiction defines aggravated assault as an assault with any weapon or dangerous implement and punishes it as a felony. It defines murder as the unlawful killing of a person with malice aforethought or in the course of an independent felony.

Defendant may be found guilty of murder

(A) only if the jury finds that Defendant intended to kill Victim.
(B) only if the jury finds that Defendant did not act in a rage provoked by Victim's accusations.
(C) if the jury finds that Defendant intended either to kill or to inflict serious bodily harm.
(D) if the jury finds that the killing occurred in the course of an aggravated assault.

Question 17

David entered the county museum at a time when it was open to the public, intending to steal a Picasso etching. Once inside, he took what he thought was the etching from an unlocked display case and concealed it under his coat. However, the etching was a photocopy of an original that had been loaned to another museum. A sign over the display case containing the photocopy said that similar photocopies were available free at the entrance. David did not see the sign.

Burglary in the jurisdiction is defined as "entering a building unlawfully with the intent to commit a crime."

David is guilty of:

(A) burglary and larceny.
(B) burglary and attempted larceny.
(C) larceny.
(D) attempted larceny.

Questions 18-19 are based on the following fact situation.

Jack, a bank teller, was fired by Morgan, the president of the bank. Jack decided to take revenge against Morgan, but decided against attempting it personally, because he knew Morgan was protected around the clock by bank security guards. Jack knew that Chip had a violent temper and was very jealous. Jack falsely told Chip that Chip's wife, Elsie, was having an affair with Morgan. Enraged, Chip said, "What am I going to do?" Jack said, "If it were my wife, I'd just march into his office and blow his brains out." Chip grabbed a revolver and rushed to the bank. He walked into the bank, carrying the gun in his hand. One of the security guards, believing a holdup was about to occur, shot and killed Chip.

Question 18

If charged with murder of Chip, Jack should be found

(A) guilty, based upon extreme recklessness.
(B) guilty, based upon transferred intent.
(C) not guilty, because he did not intend for Chip to be shot by the security guard.
(D) not guilty, because he did not shoot Chip and he was not acting in concert with the security guard.

Question 19

If charged with attempted murder of Morgan, Jack should be found

(A) guilty, because he intended to kill Morgan and used Chip to carry out his plan.

(B) guilty, because he was extremely reckless as to Morgan.

(C) not guilty, because Morgan was never in imminent danger of being killed.

(D) not guilty, because Chip, if successful, would be guilty of no more than manslaughter and an accessory cannot be guilty of a higher crime than the principal.

Question 20

Miller was indicted in a state court in January 1985 for a robbery and murder that occurred in December 1982. He retained counsel, who filed a motion to dismiss on the ground that Miller had been prejudiced by a 25-month delay in obtaining the indictment. Thereafter, Miller, with his counsel, appeared in court for arraignment and stated that he wished to plead guilty.

The presiding judge asked Miller whether he understood the nature of the charges, possible defenses, and maximum allowable sentences. Miller replied that he did, and the judge reviewed all of those matters with him. He then asked Miller whether he understood that he did not have to plead guilty. When Miller responded that he knew that, the judge accepted the plea and sentenced Miller to 25 years.

Six months later, Miller filed a motion to set aside his guilty plea on each of the following grounds.

Which of these grounds provides a constitutional basis for relief?

(A) The judge did not rule on his motion to dismiss before accepting the guilty plea.

(B) The judge did not determine that Miller had robbed and killed the victim.

(C) The judge did not determine whether Miller understood that he had a right to jury trial.

(D) The judge did not determine whether the prosecutor's file contained any undisclosed exculpatory material.

Question 21

Sally told Michael she would like to have sexual intercourse with him and that he should come to her apartment that night at 7 p.m. After Michael arrived, he and Sally went into the bedroom. As Michael started to remove Sally's blouse, Sally said she had changed her mind. Michael tried to convince her to have intercourse with him, but after ten minutes of her sustained refusals, Michael left the apartment. Unknown to Michael, Sally was 15 years old. Because she appeared to be older, Michael believed her to be about 18 years old.

A statute in the jurisdiction provides: "A person commits rape in the second degree if he has sexual intercourse with a girl, not his wife, who is under the age of 16 years."

If Michael is charged with attempting to violate this statute, he is

(A) guilty, because no mental state is required as to the element of age.

(B) guilty, because he persisted after she told him she had changed her mind.

(C) not guilty, because he reasonably believed she had consented and voluntarily withdrew after she told him she had changed her mind.

(D) not guilty, because he did not intend to have intercourse with a girl under the age of 16.

Question 22

One evening, Parnell had several drinks and then started to drive home. As he was proceeding down Main Boulevard, an automobile pulled out of a side street to his right. Parnell's car struck this automobile broadside. The driver of the other car was killed as a result of the collision. A breath analysis test administered after the accident showed that Parnell satisfied the legal definition of intoxication.

If Parnell is prosecuted for manslaughter, his best chance for acquittal would be based on an argument that

(A) the other driver was contributorily negligent.
(B) the collision would have occurred even if Parnell had not been intoxicated.
(C) because of his intoxication he lacked the mens rea needed for manslaughter.
(D) driving while intoxicated requires no mens rea and so cannot be the basis for misdemeanor manslaughter.

Question 23

John asked Doris to spend a weekend with him at his apartment and promised her they would get married on the following Monday. Doris agreed and also promised John that she would not tell anyone of their plans. Unknown to Doris, John had no intention of marrying her. After Doris came to his apartment, John told Doris he was going for cigarettes. He called Doris's father and told him that he had his daughter and would kill her if he did not receive $100.000. John was arrested on Sunday afternoon when he went to pick up the $100,000. Doris was still at the apartment and knew nothing of John's attempt to get the money.

John is guilty of

(A) kidnapping.
(B) attempted kidnapping.
(C) kidnapping or attempted kidnapping but not both.
(D) neither kidnapping nor attempted kidnapping.

Question 24

A grand jury indicted Alice on a charge of arson, and a valid warrant was issued for her arrest. Paul, a police officer, arrested Alice and informed her of what the warrant stated. However, hoping that Alice might say something incriminating, he did not give her Miranda warnings. He placed her in the back seat of his patrol car and was driving her to the police station when she said, "Look, I didn't mean to burn the building; it was an accident. I was just burning some papers in a wastebasket."

At the station, after being given Miranda warnings, Alice stated she wished to remain silent and made no other statements.

Alice moved to suppress the use of her statement to Paul as evidence on two grounds: first, that the statement was acquired without giving Miranda warnings, and second, that the police officer had deliberately elicited her incriminating statement after she was in custody.

As to Alice's motion to suppress, the court should

(A) deny the motion.
(B) grant the motion only on the basis of the first ground stated.
(C) grant the motion only on the basis of the second ground stated.
(D) grant the motion on either ground.

Question 25

Miller's, a department store, had experienced a growing incidence of shoplifting. At the store's request, the police concealed Best, a woman who was a detective, at a vantage point above the women's apparel fitting rooms where she could see into these rooms, where customers tried on clothes. Detective Best saw Davis enter a fitting room, stuff a dress into her pocketbook, leave the fitting room, and start for the street door. By prearranged signal, Best notified another police officer near the door, who detained Davis as Davis started to go out into the street. Davis was placed under arrest, and the dress was retrieved from her purse.

Davis is charged with shoplifting.

Her motion to prevent the introduction of the dress into evidence will be

(A) granted, because the police should have secured a search warrant to search her bag.
(B) granted, because a customer has a reasonable expectation of privacy while using a department store fitting room,
(C) denied, because the search and seizure were made incident to a valid arrest based on probable cause.
(D) denied, because Detective Best could see into the room and thus Davis's activities were legitimately in plain view.

Question 26

A statute provides: A person commits the crime of rape if he has sexual intercourse with a female, not his wife, without her consent.

Dunbar is charged with the rape of Sally. At trial, Sally testifies to facts sufficient for a jury to find that Dunbar had sexual intercourse with her, that she did not consent, and that the two were not married. Dunbar testifies in his own defense that he believed that Sally had consented to sexual intercourse and that she was his common-law wife.

At the conclusion of the case, the court instructed the jury that in order to find Dunbar guilty of rape, it must find beyond a reasonable doubt that he had sexual intercourse with Sally without her consent.

The court also instructed the jury that it should find the defendant not guilty if it found either that Sally was Dunbar's wife or that Dunbar reasonably believed that Sally had consented to the sexual intercourse, but that the burden of persuasion as to these issues was on the defendant.

The jury found Dunbar guilty, and Dunbar appealed, contending that the court's instructions on the issues of whether Sally was his wife and whether he reasonably believed she had consented violated his constitutional rights.

Dunbar's constitutional rights were

(A) violated by the instructions as to both issues.
(B) violated by the instruction as to whether Sally was his wife, but not violated by the instruction on belief as to consent.
(C) violated by the instruction on belief as to consent, but not violated by the instruction as to whether Sally was his wife.
(D) not violated by either part of the instructions.

Questions 27-28 are based on the following fact situation.

Morten was the general manager and chief executive officer of the Woolen Company, a knitting mill.

Morten delegated all operational decision making to Crouse, the supervising manager of the mill. The child labor laws in the jurisdiction provide, "It is a violation of the law for one to employ a person under the age of 17 years for full-time labor." Without Morten's knowledge, Crouse hired a number of 15- and 16-year-olds to work at the mill full time. He did not ask their ages and they did not disclose them. Crouse could have discovered their ages easily by asking for identification, but he did not do so because he was not aware of the law and believed that company policy was to hire young people.

Question 27

If the statute is interpreted to create strict liability and Crouse is charged with violating it, Crouse is

(A) guilty, because he should have inquired as to the ages of the children.
(B) guilty, because he hired the children.
(C) not guilty, because in law the Woolen Company, not Crouse, is the employer of the children.
(D) not guilty, because he believed he was following company policy and was not aware of the violation.

Question 28

If the statute is interpreted to create strict liability and Morten is convicted of violating it, his contention that his conviction would violate the federal Constitution is

(A) correct, because it is a violation of due process to punish without a voluntary act.
(B) correct, because criminal liability is personal and the Woolen Company is the employer of the children, not Morten.
(C) incorrect, because regulatory offenses are not subject to due process limitations.
(D) incorrect, because he was in a position to exercise control over the hiring of employees for Woolen Company.

Question 29

A statute in the jurisdiction defines murder in the first degree as knowingly killing another person after deliberation. Deliberation is defined as "cool reflection for any length of time no matter how brief." Murder in the second degree is defined as "all other murder at common law except felony-murder." Felony-murder is murder in the third degree. Manslaughter is defined by the common law.

At 2 a.m., Duncan held up an all-night liquor store using an assault rifle. During the holdup, two police cars with flashing lights drove up in front of the store. In order to create a situation where the police would hesitate to come into the store (and thus give Duncan a chance to escape out the back) Duncan fired several rounds through the front window of the store. Duncan then ran out the back but upon discovering another police car there, surrendered quietly. One of the shots he fired while in the store struck and killed a burglar who was stealing items from a closed store across the street.

The most serious degree of criminal homicide Duncan is guilty of is

(A) murder in the first degree.
(B) murder in the second degree.
(C) murder in the third degree.
(D) manslaughter.

Question 30

Smith is a new lawyer who has three clients, all of whom are indigent. To improve the appearance of his office, he decided to purchase some new furniture and to pay for it out of future earnings. Wearing an expensive suit borrowed from a friend, Smith went to a furniture store and asked to purchase on credit a desk and various other items of furniture. Smith told the store owner that he was a very able lawyer with a growing practice and that he expected to do very well in the future. The store owner agreed to sell him the items on credit, and Smith promised to make monthly payments of $800. Smith has never had an income from his practice of more than $150 a month. Smith's business did not improve, and he did not make any payments to the furniture store. After three months, the store owner repossessed the items.

If Smith is charged with obtaining property by false pretenses, his best argument for being NOT guilty would be that

(A) even if he misled the store owner, he intended to pay for the items.
(B) he did not misrepresent any material fact.

(C) the store owner got his property back and so suffered no harm.
(D) the store owner could have asked for payment in full at the time of the purchase.

Question 31

Larson was charged with the murder of a man who had been strangled and whose body was found in some woods near his home. Larson suffers from a neurological problem that makes it impossible for him to remember an occurrence for longer than 48 hours.

After Larson was charged, the police visited him and asked if they might search his home. Larson consented. The police found a diary written by Larson. An entry dated the same day as the victim's disappearance read, "Indescribable excitement. Why did no one ever tell me that killing gave such pleasure to the master?"

Larson was charged with murder. His attorney has moved to exclude the diary from evidence on the ground that its admission would violate Larson's privilege against self-incrimination. Counsel has also argued that Larson could not give informed consent to the search because more than 48 hours had passed since the making of the entry and hence he could not remember the existence of the incriminating entry at the time he gave his consent. There is no evidence that the police officers who secured Larson's consent to the search were aware of his memory impairment.

With regard to the diary, the court should

(A) admit it, because Larson's consent was not obtained by intentional police misconduct and Larson was not compelled to make the diary entry.
(B) admit it, pursuant to the good-faith exception to the exclusionary rule.
(C) exclude it, because Larson was not competent to consent to a search.
(D) exclude it, because use of the diary as evidence would violate Larson's privilege against self-incrimination.

Question 32

Dawson was charged with felony murder because of his involvement in a bank robbery. The evidence at trial disclosed that Smith invited Dawson to go for a ride in his new car, and after a while asked Dawson to drive. As Smith and Dawson drove around town, Smith explained to Dawson that he planned to rob the bank and that he needed Dawson to drive the getaway car. Dawson agreed to drive to the bank and to wait outside while Smith went in to rob it. As they approached the bank, Dawson began to regret his agreement to help with the robbery. Once there, Smith got out of the car. As Smith went out of sight inside the bank, Dawson drove away and went home. Inside the bank, Smith killed a bank guard who tried to prevent him from leaving with the money. Smith ran outside and, finding that his car and Dawson were gone, ran down an alley. He was apprehended a few blocks away. Dawson later turned himself in after hearing on the radio that Smith had killed the guard.

The jurisdiction has a death penalty that applies to felony murder.

Consistent with the law and the Constitution, the jury may convict Dawson of

(A) felony murder and impose the death penalty.
(B) felony murder but not impose the death penalty.
(C) bank robbery only.
(D) no crime.

Question 33

Jones wanted to kill Adams because he believed Adams was having an affair with Jones's wife. Early one morning, armed with a pistol, he crouched behind some bushes on a park hillside overlooking a path upon which Adams frequently jogged. On this morning, however, Jones saw Adams jogging on another path about a half mile away. Nonetheless, Jones fired five shots at Adams. None of the five shots came anywhere close to Adams as he was well out of the range of the pistol Jones was using.

Jones is

(A) guilty of attempted murder, if he was not aware of the limited range of his pistol.
(B) guilty of attempted murder, if a reasonable person would not have been aware of the limited range of his pistol.
(C) not guilty of attempted murder, or any lesser included offense, because, under the circumstances, it was impossible for him to have killed Adams.
(D) not guilty of attempted murder, but guilty of assault.

Question 34

Ralph and Sam were engaged in a heated discussion over the relative merits of their favorite professional football teams when Ralph said, "You have to be one of the dumbest persons around." Sam slapped Ralph. Ralph drew a knife and stabbed Sam in the stomach. Other persons then stepped in and stopped any further fighting. Despite the pleas of the other persons, Sam refused to go to a hospital or to seek medical treatment. About two hours later, he died as the result of a loss of blood. Ralph was charged with the murder of Sam. At trial, medical evidence established that if Sam had been taken to a hospital, he would have survived.

At the end of the case, Ralph moves for a judgment of acquittal or, in the alternative, for an instruction on the elements of voluntary manslaughter.

The court should

(A) grant the motion for acquittal.
(B) deny the motion for acquittal, but instruct on manslaughter because there is evidence of adequate provocation.
(C) deny both motions, because Ralph failed to retreat.
(D) deny both motions, because malice may be proved by the intentional use of a deadly weapon on a vital part of the body.

Question 35

Plagued by neighborhood youths who had been stealing lawn furniture from his back yard, Armando remained awake nightly watching for them. One evening Armando heard noises in his backyard. He yelled out, warning intruders to leave. Receiving no answer, he fired a shotgun filled with nonlethal buckshot into bushes along his back fence where he believed the intruders might be hiding. A six-year-old child was hiding in the bushes and was struck in the eye by some of the pellets, causing loss of sight.

If Armando is charged with second-degree assault, which is defined in the jurisdiction as "maliciously causing serious physical injury to another," he is

(A) not guilty, because the child was trespassing and he was using what he believed was nondeadly force.
(B) not guilty, because he did not intend to kill or to cause serious physical injury.
(C) guilty, because he recklessly caused serious physical injury.
(D) guilty, because there is no privilege to use force against a person who is too young to be criminally responsible.

Question 36

Phillips bought a new rifle and wanted to try it out by doing some target shooting. He went out into the country to an area where he had previously hunted. Much to his surprise, he noticed that the area beyond a clearing contained several newly constructed houses that had not been there before. Between the houses there was a small playground where several children were playing. Nevertheless, Phillips nailed a paper target to a tree and went to a point where the tree was between himself and the playground. He then fired several shots at the target. One of the shots missed the target and the tree and hit and killed one of the children in the playground.

Phillips was convicted of murder. He appealed, contending that the evidence was not sufficient to support a conviction of murder.

The appellate court should

(A) affirm the conviction, as the evidence is sufficient to support a conviction of murder.
(B) reverse the conviction and remand for a new trial, because the evidence is not sufficient for murder but will support a conviction of voluntary manslaughter.
(C) reverse the conviction and remand for a new trial, because the evidence is not sufficient for murder but will support a conviction of involuntary manslaughter.
(D) reverse the conviction and order the case dismissed, because the evidence is sufficient only for a finding of negligence and negligence alone cannot support a criminal conviction.

Question 37

Suffering from painful and terminal cancer, Willa persuaded Harold, her husband, to kill her to end her misery. As they reminisced about their life together and reaffirmed their love for each other, Harold tried to discourage Willa from giving up. Willa insisted, however, and finally Harold held a gun to her head and killed her.

The most serious degree of criminal homicide of which Harold can be legally convicted is

(A) no degree of criminal homicide.
(B) involuntary manslaughter.
(C) voluntary manslaughter.
(D) murder.

Question 38

Dart is charged with the statutory offense of "knowingly violating a regulation of the State Alcoholic Beverage Control Board" and specifically that he knowingly violated regulation number 345-90 issued by the State Alcoholic Beverage Control Board. That regulation prohibits the sale of alcoholic beverages to any person under the age of 18 and also prohibits the sale of any alcoholic beverage to a person over the age of 17 and under the age of 22 without the presentation of such person's driver's license or other identification showing the age of the purchaser to be 18 or older.

The evidence showed that Dart was a bartender in a tavern and sold a bottle of beer to a person who was 17 years old and that Dart did not ask for or see the purchaser's driver's license or any other identification.

Which of the following, if found by the jury, would be of the most help to Dart?

(A) The purchaser had a driver's license that falsely showed his age to be 21.
(B) Dart had never been told he was supposed to check identification of persons over 17 and under 22 before selling them alcohol.
(C) Dart did not know that the regulations classified beer as an alcoholic beverage.
(D) Dart mistakenly believed the purchaser to be 24 years old.

Question 39

Smith and Penn were charged with murder. Each gave a confession to the police that implicated both of them. Smith later retracted her confession, claiming that it was coerced.

Smith and Penn were tried together. The prosecutor offered both confessions into evidence. Smith and Penn objected. After a hearing, the trial judge found that both confessions were voluntary and admitted both into evidence. Smith testified at trial. She denied any involvement in the crime and claimed that her confession was false and the result of coercion. Both defendants were convicted.

On appeal, Smith contends her conviction should be reversed because of the admission into evidence of Penn's confession.

Smith's contention is

(A) correct, unless Penn testified at trial.
(B) correct, whether or not Penn testified at trial.
(C) incorrect, because Smith testified in her own behalf.
(D) incorrect, because Smith's own confession was properly admitted into evidence.

Question 40

Lester was engaged to marry Sylvia. One evening, Lester became enraged at the comments of Sylvia's eight-year-old daughter, Cynthia, who was complaining, in her usual fashion, that she did not want her mother to marry Lester. Lester, who had had too much to drink, began beating her. Cynthia suffered some bruises and a broken arm. Sylvia took Cynthia to the hospital. The police were notified by the hospital staff. Lester was indicted for felony child abuse.

Lester pleaded with Sylvia to forgive him and to run away with him. She agreed. They moved out of state and took Cynthia with them. Without the testimony of the child, the prosecution was forced to dismiss the case.

Some time later, Sylvia returned for a visit with her family and was arrested and indicted as an accessory-after-the-fact to child abuse.

At her trial, the court should

(A) dismiss the charge, because Lester had not been convicted.
(B) dismiss the charge, because the evidence shows that any aid she rendered occurred after the crime was completed.
(C) submit the case to the jury, on an instruction to convict only if Sylvia knew Lester had been indicted.
(D) submit the case to the jury, on an instruction to convict only if her purpose in moving was to prevent Lester's conviction.

Question 41

Robert walked into a store that had a check-cashing service and tried to cash a $550 check which was payable to him. The attendant on duty refused to cash the check because Robert did not have two forms of identification, which the store's policies required. Robert, who had no money except for the check and who needed cash to pay for food and a place to sleep, became agitated. He put his hand into his pocket and growled, "Give me the money or I'll start shooting." The attendant, who knew Robert as a neighborhood character, did not believe that he was violent or had a gun. However, because the attendant felt sorry for Robert, he handed over the cash. Robert left the check on the counter and departed. The attendant picked up the check and found that Robert had failed to endorse it.

If Robert is guilty of any crime, he is most likely guilty of

(A) robbery.
(B) attempted robbery.
(C) theft by false pretenses.
(D) larceny by trick.

Question 42

A kidnapping statute in State A makes it a crime for a person, including a parent, to "take a child from the custody of his custodial parent, knowing he has no privilege to do so."

After a bitter court battle Ann and Dave were divorced and Ann was given custody of their daughter, Maria. Dave later moved to State B where he brought an action to obtain custody of Maria. A local judge awarded him custody. His attorney incorrectly advised him that, under this award, he was entitled to take Maria away from Ann. Dave drove to State A, picked Maria up at her preschool, and took her back to State B with him.

He was indicted for kidnapping in State A, extradited from State B, and tried. At trial, he testified that he had relied on his attorney's advice in taking Maria, and that at the time he believed his conduct was not illegal.

If the jury believes his testimony, Dave should be

(A) acquitted, because he acted on the advice of an attorney.
(B) acquitted, because he lacked a necessary mental element of the crime.
(C) convicted, because reliance on an attorney's advice is not a defense.
(D) convicted, provided a reasonable person would have known that the attorney's advice was erroneous.

Question 43

Donald was arrested in Marilyn's apartment after her neighbors had reported sounds of a struggle and the police had arrived to find Donald bent over Marilyn's prostrate body. Marilyn was rushed to the hospital where she lapsed into a coma. Despite the explanation that he was trying to revive Marilyn after she suddenly collapsed, Donald was charged with attempted rape and assault after a neighbor informed the police that she had heard Marilyn sobbing, "No, please no, let me alone."

At trial, the forensic evidence was inconclusive. The jury acquitted Donald of attempted rape but convicted him of assault. While he was serving his sentence for assault, Marilyn, who had never recovered from the coma, died. Donald was then indicted and tried on a charge of felony murder. In this common-law jurisdiction, there is no statute that prevents a prosecutor from proceeding in this manner, but Donald argued that a second trial for felony murder after his original trial for attempted rape and assault would violate the double jeopardy clause.

His claim is

(A) correct, because he was acquitted of the attempted rape charge.
(B) correct, because he was convicted of the assault charge.
(C) incorrect, because Marilyn had not died at the time of the first trial and he was not placed in jeopardy for murder.
(D) incorrect, because he was convicted of the assault charge.

Question 44

Devlin was charged with murder. Several witnesses testified that the crime was committed by a person of Devlin's general description who walked with a severe limp. Devlin in fact walks with a severe limp. He objected to a prosecution request that the court order him to walk across the courtroom in order to display his limp to the jury to assist it in determining whether Devlin was the person that the witnesses had seen.

Devlin's objection will most likely be

(A) sustained, because the order sought by the prosecution would violate Devlin's privilege against self-incrimination.
(B) sustained, because the order sought by the prosecution would constitute an illegal search and seizure.
(C) denied, because the order sought by the prosecution is a legitimate part of a proper courtroom identification process.
(D) denied, because a criminal defendant has no legitimate expectation of privacy.

Question 45

Smith asked Jones if he would loan him $500, promising to repay the amount within two weeks. Jones loaned him the $500. The next day Smith took the money to the race track and lost all of it betting on horse races. He then left town for six months. He has not repaid Jones.

Smith has committed

(A) both larceny by trick and obtaining money by false pretenses (although he can only be convicted of one offense).
(B) larceny by trick only.
(C) obtaining money by false pretenses only.
(D) neither larceny by trick nor obtaining money by false pretenses.

Question 46

Sam told Horace, his neighbor, that he was going away for two weeks and asked Horace to keep an eye on his house. Horace agreed. Sam gave Horace a key to use to check on the house.

Horace decided to have a party in Sam's house. He invited a number of friends. One friend, Lewis, went into Sam's bedroom, took some of Sam's rings, and put them in his pocket.

Which of the following is true?

(A) Horace and Lewis are guilty of burglary.
(B) Horace is guilty of burglary and Lewis is guilty of larceny.
(C) Horace is guilty of trespass and Lewis is guilty of larceny.
(D) Lewis is guilty of larceny and Horace is not guilty of any crime.

Question 47

Police received an anonymous tip that Tusitala was growing marijuana in her backyard, which was surrounded by a 15-foot high, solid wooden fence. Officer Boa was unable to view the yard from the street, so he used a police helicopter to fly over Tusitala's house. Boa identified a large patch of marijuana plants growing right next to the house and used this observation to obtain a search warrant.

Tusitala is prosecuted for possession of marijuana and moves to suppress use of the marijuana in evidence.

The court should

(A) grant the motion, because the only purpose of Boa's flight was to observe the yard.

(B) grant the motion, because Tusitala had a reasonable expectation of privacy in the curtilage around her house and the police did not have a warrant.

(C) deny the motion, because a warrant is not required for a search of a residential yard.

(D) deny the motion, because Tusitala had no reasonable expectation of privacy from aerial observation.

Question 48

On October 22, Officer Jones submitted an application for a warrant to search 217 Elm Street for cocaine. In the application, Officer Jones stated under oath that he believed there was cocaine at that location because of information supplied to him on the morning of October 22 by Susie Schultz. He described Schultz as a cocaine user who had previously supplied accurate information concerning the use of cocaine in the community and summarized what Schultz had told him as follows: the previous night, October 21, Schultz was in Robert Redd's house at 217 Elm Street. Redd gave her cocaine. She also saw three cellophane bags containing cocaine in his bedroom.

The warrant was issued and a search of 217 Elm Street was conducted on October 22. The search turned up a quantity of marijuana but no cocaine. Robert Redd was arrested and charged with possession of marijuana. Redd moved to suppress the use of the marijuana as evidence contending that Susie Schultz was not in 217 Elm Street on October 21 or at any other time.

If, after hearing evidence, the judge concludes that the statement in the application attributed to Susie Schultz is incorrect, the judge should grant the motion to suppress

(A) because the application contains a material statement that is false.

(B) because of the false statement and because no cocaine was found in the house.

(C) only if he also finds that Susie Schultz's statement was a deliberate lie.

(D) only if he also finds that Officer Jones knew the statement was false.

Question 49

Steve, in desperate need of money, decided to hold up a local convenience store. Determined not to harm anyone, he carried a toy gun that resembled a real gun. In the store, he pointed the toy gun at the clerk and demanded money. A customer who entered the store and saw the robbery in progress pulled his own gun and fired at Steve. The bullet missed Steve but struck and killed the clerk.

Steve was charged with felony murder.

His best argument for being found NOT guilty is that he

(A) did not intend to kill.

(B) did not commit the robbery because he never acquired any money from the clerk.

(C) did not intend to create any risk of harm.

(D) is not responsible for the acts of the customer.

Question 50

State Y employs the Model Penal Code or American Law Institute test for insanity, and requires the state to prove sanity, when it is in issue, beyond a reasonable doubt. At Askew's trial for murder, he pleaded insanity. The state put on an expert psychiatrist who had examined Askew. He testified that, in his opinion, Askew was sane at the time of the murder. Askew's attorney did not introduce expert testimony on the question of sanity. Rather, he presented lay witnesses who testified that, in their opinion, Askew was insane at the time of the murder. At the end of the trial, each side moves for a directed verdict on the question of sanity.

Which of the following correctly describes the judge's situation?

(A) She may grant a directed verdict for the defense if she believes that the jury could not find the prosecution to have proved sanity beyond a reasonable doubt.
(B) She may grant a directed verdict for the prosecution if she believes that Askew's witnesses on the insanity question are not believable.
(C) She may not grant a directed verdict for the defense, because the state had expert testimony and the defense only lay witnesses.
(D) She may grant a directed verdict for the prosecution if she is convinced by their experts that Askew was sane beyond a reasonable doubt.

Question 51

Trelawney worked at a day-care center run by the Happy Faces Day Care Corporation. At the center, one of the young charges, Smith, often arrived with bruises and welts on his back and legs. A statute in the jurisdiction requires all day-care workers to report to the police cases where there is probable cause to suspect child abuse and provides for immediate removal from the home of any suspected child abuse victims. Trelawney was not aware of this statute. Nevertheless, he did report Smith's condition to his supervisor, who advised him to keep quiet about it so the day-care center would not get into trouble for defaming a parent. About two weeks after Trelawney first noticed Smith's condition, Smith was beaten to death by his father. Trelawney has been charged with murder in the death of Smith. The evidence at trial disclosed, in addition to the above, that the child had been the victim of beatings by the father for some time, and that these earlier beatings had been responsible for the marks that Trelawney had seen. Smith's mother had been aware of the beatings but had not stopped them because she was herself afraid of Smith's father.

Trelawney's best argument that he is NOT guilty of murder is

(A) he was not aware of the duty-to-report statute.
(B) he lacked the mental state necessary to the commission of the crime.
(C) his omission was not the proximate cause of death.
(D) the day-care corporation, rather than Trelawney, was guilty of the omission, which was sanctioned by its supervisory-level agent.

Question 52

Despondent over losing his job, Wilmont drank all night at a bar. While driving home, he noticed a car following him and, in his intoxicated state, concluded he was being followed by robbers. In fact, a police car was following him on suspicion of drunk driving. In his effort to get away, Wilmont sped through a stop sign and struck and killed a pedestrian. He was arrested by the police.

Wilmont is prosecuted for manslaughter.

He should be

(A) acquitted, because he honestly believed he faced an imminent threat of death or severe bodily injury.
(B) acquitted, because his intoxication prevented him from appreciating the risk he created.
(C) convicted, because he acted recklessly and in fact was in no danger.
(D) convicted, because he acted recklessly and his apprehension of danger was not reasonable.

Questions 53-54 are based on the following fact situation.

The police suspected that Yancey, a 16-year-old high school student, had committed a series of burglaries. Two officers went to Yancey's high school and asked the principal to call Yancey out of class and to search his backpack. While the officers waited, the principal took Yancey into the hall where she asked to look in his backpack. When Yancey refused, the principal grabbed it from him, injuring Yancey's shoulder in the process. In the backpack, she found jewelry that she turned over to the officers.

The officers believed that the jewelry had been taken in one of the burglaries. They arrested Yancey, took him to the station, and gave him Miranda warnings. Yancey asked to see a lawyer. The police called Yancey's parents to the station. When Yancey's parents arrived, the police asked them to speak with Yancey. They put them in a room and secretly recorded their conversation with a concealed electronic device. Yancey broke down and confessed to his parents that he had committed the burglaries.

Yancey was charged with the burglaries.

Question 53

Yancey moves to suppress the use of the jewelry.

The court should

(A) deny the motion on the ground that the search was incident to a lawful arrest.
(B) deny the motion on the ground that school searches are reasonable if conducted by school personnel on school grounds on the basis of reasonable suspicion.
(C) grant the motion on the ground that the search was conducted with excessive force.
(D) grant the motion on the ground that the search was conducted without probable cause or a warrant.

Question 54

Assume for this question only that the court denied the motion to suppress the jewelry. Yancey moves to suppress the use of the statement Yancey made to his parents.

The best argument for excluding it would be that

(A) Yancey was in custody at the time the statement was recorded.
(B) the police did not comply with Yancey's request for a lawyer.
(C) once Yancey had invoked his right to counsel, it was improper for the police to listen to any of his private conversations.
(D) the meeting between Yancey and his parents was arranged by the police to obtain an incriminating statement.

Question 55

Defendant was upset because he was going to have to close his liquor store due to competition from a discount store in a new shopping mall nearby. In desperation, he decided to set fire to his store to collect the insurance. While looking through the basement for flammable material, he lit a match to read the label on a can. The match burned his finger and, in a reflex action, he dropped the match. It fell into a barrel and ignited some paper. Defendant made no effort to put out the fire but instead left the building. The fire spread and the store was destroyed by fire. Defendant was eventually arrested and indicted for arson.

Defendant is

(A) guilty, if he could have put out the fire before it spread and did not do so because he wanted the building destroyed.
(B) guilty, if he was negligent in starting the fire.
(C) not guilty, because even if he wanted to burn the building there was no concurrence between his mens rea and the act of starting the fire.
(D) not guilty, because his starting the fire was the result of a reflex action and not a voluntary act.

Question 56

Unprepared for a final examination, Slick asked his girlfriend, Hope, to set off the fire alarms in the university building 15 minutes after the test commenced. Hope did so. Several students were injured in the panic that followed as people were trying to get out of the building. Slick and Hope are prosecuted for battery and for conspiracy to commit battery.

They are

(A) guilty of both crimes.
(B) guilty of battery but not guilty of conspiracy.
(C) not guilty of battery but guilty of conspiracy.
(D) not guilty of either crime.

Question 57

In which of the following situations is the defendant most likely to be convicted, even though he did not intend to bring about the harm that the statute defining the offense is designed to prevent?

(A) Defendant was the president of an aspirin manufacturing company. A federal inspector discovered that a large number of aspirin tablets randomly scattered through several bottles in a carton ready for shipment were laced with arsenic. Defendant is charged with attempted introduction of adulterated drugs into interstate commerce.
(B) Defendant struck Victim in the face with a baseball bat, intending to inflict a serious injury. Victim died after being hospitalized for three days. Defendant is charged with murder.
(C) Defendant burglarized a jewelry store, intending to steal some diamonds. As he entered the store, he short-circuited the store's burglar alarm system, thereby preventing a warning of his entry to police. The smoldering wires eventually caused a fire that destroyed the store. Defendant is charged with arson.
(D) Defendant wanted to frighten Victim's friend by placing a plastic rattlesnake in his lunch box. When Victim mistakenly took the lunch box and opened it, believing it to be his own, the plastic rattlesnake popped out. As a result of the fright, Victim suffered a heart attack and died. Defendant is charged with manslaughter.

Question 58

Eddie worked as the cashier in a restaurant. One night after the restaurant had closed, Eddie discovered that the amount of cash in the cash register did not match the cash register receipt tapes. He took the cash and the tapes, put them in a bag, gave them to Rita, the manager of the restaurant, and reported the discrepancy. Rita immediately accused him of taking money from the register and threatened to fire him if he did not make up the difference. Rita placed the bag in the office safe. Angered by what he considered to be an unjust accusation, Eddie waited until Rita left the room and then reached into the still open safe, took the bag containing the cash, and left.

Eddie is guilty of

(A) larceny.
(B) embezzlement.
(C) either larceny or embezzlement but not both.
(D) neither larceny nor embezzlement.

Question 59

A grand jury returned an indictment charging Daniels with bank robbery, and when he could not make bond he was jailed pending trial. He had received Miranda warnings when arrested and had made no statement at that time. The prosecutor arranged to have Innis, an informant, placed as Daniels's cellmate and instructed Innis to find out about the bank robbery without asking any direct questions about it. Innis, once in the cell, constantly boasted about the crimes that he had committed. Not to be outdone, Daniels finally declared that he had committed the bank robbery with which he was charged.

At Daniels's trial, his attorney moved to exclude any testimony from Innis concerning Daniels's boast.

The motion should be

(A) granted, because Daniels's privilege against self-incrimination was violated.
(B) granted, because Daniels's right to counsel was violated.
(C) denied, because Daniels had received Miranda warnings.
(D) denied, because Daniels was not interrogated by Innis.

Question 60

Kingsley was prosecuted for selling cocaine to an undercover police agent. At his trial, he testified that he only sold the drugs to the agent, whom Kingsley knew as "Speedy," because Speedy had told him that he (Speedy) would be killed by fellow gang members unless he supplied them with cocaine. The prosecution did not cross-examine Kingsley. As rebuttal evidence, however, the prosecutor introduced records, over Kingsley's objection, showing that Kingsley had two prior convictions for narcotics-related offenses. The court instructed the jury concerning the defense of entrapment and added, also over Kingsley's objection but in accord with state law, that it should acquit on the ground of entrapment only if it found that the defendant had established the elements of the defense by a preponderance of the evidence. Kingsley was convicted.

On appeal, Kingsley's conviction should be

(A) reversed, because it was an error for the court to admit the evidence of his prior convictions as substantive evidence.
(B) reversed, because it was a violation of due process to impose on the defense a burden of persuasion concerning entrapment.
(C) reversed, for both of the above reasons.
(D) affirmed, because neither of the above reasons constitutes a ground for reversal.

Question 61

Davis decided to kill Adams. He set out for Adams' house. Before he got there he saw Brooks, who resembled Adams. Thinking Brooks was Adams, Davis shot at Brooks. The shot missed Brooks but wounded Case, who was some distance away. Davis had not seen Case.

In a prosecution under a statute that proscribes attempt to commit murder, the district attorney should indicate that the intended victim(s) was (were)

(A) Adams only.
(B) Brooks only.
(C) Case only.
(D) Adams and Brooks.

Question 62

A state statute requires any person licensed to sell prescription drugs to file with the State Board of Health a report listing the types and amounts of such drugs sold if his sales of such drugs exceed $50,000 during a calendar year. The statute makes it a misdemeanor to "knowingly fail to file" such a report.

Nelson, who is licensed to sell prescription drugs, sold $63,000 worth of prescription drugs during 1976 but did not file the report. Charged with committing the misdemeanor, Nelson testifies that he did a very poor job of keeping records and did not realize that his sales of prescription drugs had exceeded $50,000. If the jury believes Nelson he should be found

(A) guilty, because this is a public welfare offense.
(B) guilty, because he cannot be excused on the basis of his own failure to keep proper records.
(C) not guilty, because the statute punishes omissions and he was not given fair warning of his duty to act.
(D) not guilty, because he was not aware of the value of the drugs he had sold.

Question 63

John was fired from his job. Too proud to apply for unemployment benefits, he used his savings to feed his family. When one of his children became ill, he did not seek medical attention for the child at a state clinic because he did not want to accept what he regarded as charity. Eventually, weakened by malnutrition, the child died as a result of the illness. John has committed

(A) murder.
(B) involuntary manslaughter.
(C) voluntary manslaughter.
(D) no form of criminal homicide.

Question 64

A state statute divides murder into degrees. First degree murder is defined as murder with premeditation and deliberation or a homicide in the commission of arson, rape, robbery, burglary or kidnapping. Second degree murder is all other murder at common law.

In which of the following situations is Defendant most likely to be guilty of first degree murder?

(A) Immediately after being insulted by Robert, Defendant takes a knife and stabs and kills Robert.
(B) Angered over having been struck by Sam, Defendant buys rat poison and puts it in Sam's coffee. Sam drinks the coffee and dies as a result.
(C) Intending to injure Fred, Defendant lies in wait and, as Fred comes by, Defendant strikes him with a broom handle. As a result of the blow, Fred dies.
(D) Defendant, highly intoxicated, discovers a revolver on a table. He picks it up, points it at Alice, and pulls the trigger. The gun discharges, and Alice is killed.

Question 65

On a camping trip in a state park, Rose discovered metal signs near a rubbish heap stating, "Natural Wildlife Area—No Hunting." She took two of the signs and used them to decorate her room at home. She is charged with violation of a state statute which provides, "Any person who appropriates to his own use property owned by the state shall be guilty of a crime and shall be punished by a fine of not more than $1,000, or by imprisonment for not more than five years, or by both such fine and imprisonment."

At trial, Rose admits taking the signs but says she believed they had been thrown away. In fact, the signs had not been abandoned.

Rose should be found

(A) guilty, because this is a public welfare offense.
(B) guilty, because she should have inquired whether the signs were abandoned.
(C) not guilty if the jury finds she honestly believed the signs had been abandoned.
(D) not guilty unless the jury finds that the state had taken adequate steps to inform the public that the signs had not been abandoned.

Question 66

Ted frequently visited Janet, his next-door neighbor. Janet was separated from her husband, Howard. Howard resided with his mother but jointly owned the house in which Janet resided. Late one night, Ted and Janet were sitting on the bed in Janet's bedroom drinking when Howard burst through the door and told Ted, "Get out." When Ted refused, Howard challenged him to go outside and "fight it out." Ted again refused. Howard then pulled a knife from his pocket and lunged at Ted. Ted grabbed a lamp, struck Howard on the head, and killed him. Ted is charged with murder. On a charge of murder, Ted should be found

(A) not guilty, because Ted had as much right as Howard to be in the house.
(B) not guilty, because Howard attacked Ted with a deadly weapon.
(C) guilty, because Ted's presence in Janet's bedroom prompted Howard's attack.
(D) guilty, because Ted's failure to obey Howard's order to leave the house made him a trespasser.

Question 67

In which of the following cases is a conviction of the named defendant for robbery LEAST likely to be upheld?

(A) Johnson forced his way into a woman's home, bound her, and compelled her to tell him that her jewelry was in an adjoining room. Johnson went to the room, took the jewelry and fled.
(B) A confederate of Brown pushed a man in order to cause him to lose his balance and drop his briefcase. Brown picked up the briefcase and ran off with it.
(C) Having induced a woman to enter his hotel room, Ritter forced her to telephone her maid to tell the maid to bring certain jewelry to the hotel. Ritter locked the woman in the bathroom while he accepted the jewelry from the maid when she arrived.
(D) Hayes unbuttoned the vest of a man too drunk to notice and removed his wallet. A minute later, the victim missed his wallet and accused Hayes of taking it. Hayes pretended to be insulted, slapped the victim, and went off with the wallet.

Questions 68-70 are based on the following fact situation.

Harry met Bill, who was known to him to be a burglar, in a bar. Harry told Bill that he needed money. He promised to pay Bill $500 if Bill would go to Harry's house the following night and take some silverware. Harry explained to Bill that, although the silverware was legally his, his wife would object to his selling it.

Harry pointed out his home, one of a group of similar tract houses. He drew a floor plan of the house that showed the location of the silverware. Harry said that his wife usually took several sleeping pills before retiring, and that he would make sure that she took them the next night. He promised to leave a window unlocked.

Everything went according to the plan except that Bill, deceived by the similarity of the tract houses, went to the wrong house. He found a window unlocked, climbed in and found silver where Harry had indicated. He took the silver to the cocktail lounge where the payoff was to take place. At that point police arrested the two men.

Question 68

If Harry were charged with burglary, his best argument for acquittal would be that

(A) there was no breaking.
(B) he consented to the entry.
(C) no overt act was committed by him.
(D) there was no intent to commit a felony.

Question 69

Bill's best argument for acquittal of burglary is that he

(A) acted under a mistake of law.
(B) had the consent of the owner.
(C) reasonably thought he was in Harry's house.
(D) found the window unlocked.

Question 70

If Harry and Bill are charged with a conspiracy to commit burglary, their best argument for acquittal is that

(A) Bill was the alter ego of Harry.
(B) they did not intend to commit burglary.
(C) there was no overt act.
(D) there was no agreement.

Question 71

Defendant is charged with assault and battery. The state's evidence shows that Victim was struck in the face by Defendant's fist. In which of the following situations is Defendant most likely to be not guilty of assault and battery?

(A) Defendant had been hypnotized at a party and ordered by the hypnotist to strike the person he disliked the most.
(B) Defendant was suffering from an epileptic seizure and had no control over his motions.
(C) Defendant was heavily intoxicated and was shadow boxing without realizing that Victim was near him.
(D) Defendant, who had just awakened from a deep sleep, was not fully aware of what was happening and mistakenly thought Victim was attacking him.

Question 72

Police Officer stopped Dexter for speeding late one night. Noting that Dexter was nervous, he ordered him from the car and placed him under arrest for speeding. By state law, Police Officer was empowered to arrest Dexter and take him to the nearest police station for booking. He searched Dexter's person and discovered a package of heroin in his jacket pocket.

Dexter is charged with possession of heroin. At trial, Dexter's motion to prevent introduction of the heroin into evidence, on the ground that the search violated his federal constitutional rights, will most probably be

(A) denied, because the search was incident to a valid custodial arrest.
(B) denied, because Police Officer acted under a reasonable suspicion and legitimate concern for his own personal safety.
(C) granted, because there was no reasonable or proper basis upon which to justify conducting the search.
(D) granted if Police Officer was not in fear and had no suspicion that Dexter was transporting narcotics.

Question 73

Donna was arrested and taken to police headquarters, where she was given her Miranda warnings. Donna indicated that she wished to telephone her lawyer and was told that she could do so after her fingerprints had been taken. While being fingerprinted, however, Donna blurted out, "Paying a lawyer is a waste of money because I know you have me."

At trial, Donna's motion to prevent the introduction of the statement she made while being fingerprinted will most probably be

(A) granted, because Donna's request to contact her attorney by telephone was reasonable and should have been granted immediately.
(B) granted, because of the "fruit of the poisonous tree" doctrine.
(C) denied, because the statements were volunteered and not the result of interrogation.
(D) denied, because fingerprinting is not a critical stage of the proceeding requiring the assistance of counsel.

Question 74

Driving down a dark road, Defendant accidentally ran over a man. Defendant stopped and found that the victim was dead. Defendant, fearing that he might be held responsible, took the victim's wallet, which contained a substantial amount of money. He removed the identification papers and put the wallet and money back into the victim's pocket. Defendant is not guilty of

(A) larceny, because he took the papers only to prevent identification and not for his own use.
(B) larceny, because he did not take anything from a living victim.
(C) robbery, because he did not take the papers by means of force or putting in fear.
(D) robbery, because he did not take anything of monetary value.

Question 75

Al and Bill are identical twins. Al, angry at David, said, "You'd better stay out of my way. The next time I find you around here, I'll beat you up." Two days later, while in the neighborhood, David saw Bill coming toward him. As Bill came up to David, Bill raised his hand. Thinking Bill was Al and fearing bodily harm, David struck Bill.

If Bill asserts a claim against David and David relies on the privilege of self-defense, David will
(A) not prevail, because Bill was not an aggressor.
(B) not prevail unless Bill intended his gesture as a threat.
(C) prevail if David honestly believed that Bill would attack him.
(D) prevail only if a reasonable person under the circumstances would have believed that Bill would attack him.

Question 76

Suspecting that students were using narcotics, the president of a private college arranged for local police to place concealed microphones in several suites of the dormitory. Using these microphones, the college security officers recorded a conversation in which Green, a student, offered to sell marijuana to another student. The tape was turned over to the local police, who played it for a local judge. The judge issued a warrant to search Green's room. The room was searched by police, and marijuana was discovered.

Green is charged with unlawful possession of narcotics. At trial, Green's motion to prevent the introduction of the marijuana into evidence will most probably be

(A) denied, because the college president, in loco parentis, had the responsibility of preventing unlawful activity by students under the president's supervision.
(B) denied, because there was probable cause to make the search and police obtained a warrant before commencing the search.
(C) granted, because Green's privacy was unreasonably invaded.
(D) granted, because the electronic surveillance was "fundamentally unfair."

Question 77

Tom had a heart ailment so serious that his doctors had concluded that only a heart transplant could save his life. They therefore arranged to have him flown to Big City to have the operation performed.

Dan, Tom's nephew, who stood to inherit from him, poisoned him. The poison produced a reaction which required postponing the journey. The plane on which Tom was to have flown crashed, and all aboard were killed. By the following day, Tom's heart was so weakened by the effects of the poison that he suffered a heart attack and died. If charged with criminal homicide, Dan should be found

(A) guilty.
(B) not guilty, because his act did not hasten the deceased's death, but instead prolonged it by one day.
(C) not guilty, because the deceased was already suffering from a fatal illness.
(D) not guilty, because the poison was not the sole cause of death.

Question 78

In which of the following situations is Defendant most likely to be not guilty of the charge made?

(A) Police arrested Thief and recovered goods he had stolen. At the direction of the police, Thief took the goods to Defendant. Defendant, believing the goods to be stolen, purchased them. Defendant is charged with attempting to receive stolen property.
(B) Defendant misrepresented his identity to secure a loan from a bank. The banker was not deceived and refused to grant the loan. Defendant is charged with attempting to obtain property by false pretenses.
(C) Believing that state law made it a crime to purchase codeine without a prescription, Defendant purchased, without a prescription, cough syrup containing codeine. Unknown to Defendant, the statute had been repealed and codeine could be legally purchased without a prescription. Defendant is charged with attempting to purchase codeine without a prescription.
(D) Defendant, intending to kill Selma, shot at Selma. Unknown to Defendant, Selma had died of a heart attack minutes before Defendant shot at her. Defendant is charged with attempted murder.

Question 79

In an action to recover for personal injuries arising out of an automobile accident, Plaintiff called Bystander to testify. Claiming the privilege against self-incrimination, Bystander refuses to answer a question as to whether she was at the scene of the accident. Plaintiff moves that Bystander be ordered to answer the question. The judge should allow Bystander to remain silent only if

(A) the judge is convinced that she will incriminate herself.
(B) there is clear and convincing evidence that she will incriminate herself.
(C) there is a preponderance of evidence that she will incriminate herself.
(D) the judge believes that there is some reasonable possibility that she will incriminate herself.

Question 80

In which of the following situations is Defendant most likely to be guilty of common-law murder?

(A) Angered because his neighbor is having a noisy party, Defendant fires a rifle into the neighbor's house. The bullet strikes and kills a guest at the party.
(B) During an argument, Harry slaps Defendant. Angered, Defendant responds by shooting and killing Harry.
(C) Defendant drives his car through a red light and strikes and kills a pedestrian who is crossing the street.
(D) Using his fist, Defendant punches Walter in the face. As a result of the blow, Walter falls and hits his head on a concrete curb, suffers a concussion, and dies.

Questions 81-83 are based on the following fact situation.

Defendant became intoxicated at a bar. He got into his car and drove away. Within a few blocks, craving another drink, he stopped his car in the middle of the street, picked up a brick, and broke the display window of a liquor store. As he was reaching for a bottle, the night watchman arrived. Startled, Defendant turned and struck the watchman on the head with the bottle, killing him. Only vaguely aware of what was happening, Defendant returned to his car, consumed more liquor, and then drove off at a high speed. He ran a red light and struck and killed a pedestrian who was crossing the street.

Relevant statutes define burglary to include "breaking and entering a building not used as a dwelling with the intent to commit a crime therein." Manslaughter is defined as the "killing of a human being in a criminally reckless manner." Criminal recklessness is "consciously disregarding a substantial and unjustifiable risk resulting from the actor's conduct." Murder is defined as "the premeditated and intentional killing of another or the killing of another in the commission of committing rape, robbery, burglary, or arson." Another statute provides that intoxication is not a defense to crime unless it negates an element of the offense.

Defendant was charged with the murder of the watchman and manslaughter in the death of the pedestrian. Assume that he is tried separately on each charge.

Question 81

At Defendant's trial for the murder of the watchman, the court should in substance charge the jury on the issue of the defense of intoxication that

(A) intoxication is a defense to the underlying crime of burglary if Defendant, due to drunkenness, did not form an intent to commit a crime within the building, in which case there can be no conviction for murder unless Defendant intentionally and with premeditation killed the watchman.
(B) voluntary intoxication is not a defense to the crime of murder.
(C) Defendant is guilty of murder despite his intoxication only if the state proves beyond a reasonable doubt that the killing of the watchman was premeditated and intentional.
(D) voluntary intoxication is a defense to the crime of murder if Defendant would not have killed the watchman but for his intoxication.

Question 82

At Defendant's trial on the charge of manslaughter in the death of the pedestrian, his best argument would be that

(A) he was too intoxicated to realize he was creating a substantial and unjustifiable risk in the manner in which he was operating his car.
(B) when he got in the car his acts were not voluntary because he was too intoxicated to know where he was or what he was doing.
(C) the pedestrian was contributorily negligent in failing to see Defendant's car approaching.
(D) he was too intoxicated to form any intent to voluntarily operate the automobile.

Question 83

The state's best argument to counter Defendant's argument in Question 82 on the intoxication issue in the manslaughter death of the pedestrian is that

(A) intoxication is no defense to the crime charged, because manslaughter is historically a general intent crime.
(B) intoxication is a defense only to a specific intent crime, and no specific intent is involved in the definition of the crime of manslaughter.
(C) conscious risk-taking refers to Defendant's entire course of conduct, including drinking with the knowledge that he might become intoxicated and seriously injure or kill someone while driving.
(D) whether Defendant was intoxicated or not is not the crucial issue here; the real issue is whether the manner in which Defendant was operating his car can be characterized under the facts as criminally reckless.

Questions 84-85 are based on the following fact situation.

Statutes in the jurisdiction define criminal assault as "an attempt to commit a criminal battery" and criminal battery as "causing an offensive touching."

As Edward was walking down the street, a gust of wind blew his hat off. Edward reached out, trying to grab his hat, and narrowly missed striking Margaret in the face with his hand. Margaret, fearful of being struck by Edward, pushed Edward away.

Question 84

If charged with criminal assault, Edward should be found

(A) guilty, because he caused Margaret to be in apprehension of an offensive touching.
(B) guilty, because he should have realized he might strike someone by reaching out.
(C) not guilty, because he did not intend to hit Margaret.
(D) not guilty, because he did not hit Margaret.

Question 85

If charged with criminal battery, Margaret should be found

(A) guilty, because she intentionally pushed Edward.
(B) guilty, because she caused the touching of Edward whether she meant to do so or not.
(C) not guilty, because a push is not an offensive touching.
(D) not guilty, because she was justified in pushing Edward.

Question 86

Police were concerned about an increase in marijuana traffic in Defendant's neighborhood. One night, Police Officers, accompanied by dogs trained to sniff out marijuana, went into the back yard of Defendant's house and onto his porch. Defendant and his friend were inside having dinner. The dogs acted as if they smelled marijuana. Police Officers knocked on the back door. Defendant answered the door and let them in. Defendant was immediately placed under arrest. After a brief search, Police Officers confiscated a large quantity of marijuana which they found in Defendant's linen closet.

Defendant's motion to prevent introduction of the marijuana into evidence will most probably be

(A) denied, because the search was incident to a valid arrest.
(B) denied, because Defendant permitted Police Officers to enter his house.
(C) granted, because under the circumstances the police activity violated Defendant's reasonable expectations of privacy.
(D) granted, because this kind of detection by trained dogs has not been scientifically verified and cannot be the basis for probable cause.

Question 87

Alan, who was already married, went through a marriage ceremony with Betty and committed bigamy. Carl, his friend, who did not know of Alan's previous marriage, had encouraged Alan to marry Betty and was best man at the ceremony. If Carl is charged with being an accessory to bigamy, he should be found

(A) not guilty, because his encouragement and assistance was not the legal cause of the crime.
(B) not guilty, because he did not have the mental state required for aiding and abetting.

(C) guilty, because he encouraged Alan, and his mistake as to the existence of a prior marriage is not a defense to a charge of bigamy.
(D) guilty, because he was present when the crime occurred and is thus a principal in the second degree.

Question 88

Darlene was arrested on a murder charge. She was given Miranda warnings and refused to talk further with the police. At trial, she testified in her own defense. She recounted in some detail her whereabouts on the day of the crime and explained why she could not have committed the crime. On cross-examination and over defense objection, the prosecution emphasized the fact that she did not tell the police this story following her arrest. The prosecution thereby suggested that her testimony was false.

Defendant was convicted. On appeal, she claims error in the prosecutor's cross-examination. Her conviction will most probably be

(A) affirmed, because defendant's silence at time of arrest is tantamount to a prior inconsistent statement, giving rise to an inference that the story was fabricated.
(B) affirmed, because defendant's silence was not used as direct evidence but only for impeachment, a purpose consistent with legitimate cross-examination.
(C) reversed, because post-arrest silence constituted defendant's exercise of her Miranda rights and use of that silence against her at trial violated due process.
(D) reversed, because to require the defense to acquaint the prosecution with defendant's testimony prior to trial would constitute unconstitutional pre-trial discovery.

Question 89

In which of the following situations is Defendant most likely to be guilty of larceny?

(A) Defendant took Sue's television set, with the intention of returning it the next day. However, he dropped it and damaged it beyond repair.
(B) Defendant went into Tom's house and took $100 in the belief that Tom had damaged Defendant's car to that amount.
(C) Mistakenly believing that larceny does not include the taking of a dog, Defendant took his neighbor's dog and sold it.
(D) Unreasonably mistaking George's car for his own, Defendant got into George's car in a parking lot and drove it home.

Question 90

Jim watched a liquor store furtively for some time, planning to hold it up. He bought a realistic-looking toy gun for the job. One night, just before the store's closing time, he drove to the store, opened the front door and entered. He reached in his pocket for the toy gun, but he became frightened and began to move back toward the front door. However, the shopkeeper had seen the butt of the gun. Fearing a hold up, the shopkeeper produced a gun from under the counter, pointed it at Jim, and yelled, "Stop!" Jim ran to the door and the toy gun fell from his pocket. The shopkeeper fired. The shot missed Jim, but struck and killed a passerby outside the store.

A statute in the jurisdiction defines burglary as "breaking and entering any building or structure with the intent to commit a felony or to steal therein." On a charge of burglary, Jim's best defense would be that

(A) the intent required was not present.
(B) the liquor store was open to the public.
(C) he had a change of heart and withdrew before committing any crime inside the store.
(D) he was unsuccessful, and so at most could be guilty of attempted burglary.

Question 91

Jackson and Brannick planned to break into a federal government office to steal food stamps. Jackson telephoned Crowley one night and asked whether Crowley wanted to buy some "hot" food stamps. Crowley, who understood that "hot" meant stolen, said, "Sure, bring them right over." Jackson and Brannick then successfully executed their scheme. That same night they delivered the food stamps to Crowley, who bought them for $500. Crowley did not ask when or by whom the stamps were stolen. All three were arrested. Jackson and Brannick entered guilty pleas in federal court to a charge of larceny in connection with the theft. Crowley was brought to trial in the state court on a charge of conspiracy to steal food stamps.

On the evidence stated, Crowley should be found

(A) guilty, because, when a new confederate enters a conspiracy already in progress, he becomes a party to it.
(B) guilty, because he knowingly and willingly aided and abetted the conspiracy and is chargeable as a principal.
(C) not guilty, because, although Crowley knew the stamps were stolen, he neither helped to plan nor participated or assisted in the theft.
(D) not guilty, because Jackson and Brannick had not been convicted of or charged with conspiracy, and Crowley cannot be guilty of conspiracy by himself.

Questions 92-93 are based on the following fact situation.

Jack and Paul planned to hold up a bank. They drove to the bank in Jack's car. Jack entered while Paul remained as lookout in the car. After a few moments, Paul panicked and drove off.

Jack looked over the various tellers, approached one and whispered nervously, "Just hand over the cash. Don't look around, don't make a false move—or it's your life." The teller looked at the fidgeting Jack, laughed, flipped him a dollar bill and said, "Go on, beat it." Flustered, Jack grabbed the dollar and left.

Soon after leaving the scene, Paul was stopped by the police for speeding. Noting his nervous condition, the police asked Paul if they might search the car. Paul agreed. The search turned up heroin concealed in the lid of the trunk.

Question 92

Paul's best defense to a charge of robbery would be that

(A) Jack alone entered the bank.
(B) Paul withdrew before commission of the crime when he fled the scene.
(C) Paul had no knowledge of what Jack whispered to the teller.
(D) the teller was not placed in fear by Jack.

Question 93

The prosecution's best argument to sustain the validity of the search of Jack's car would be that

(A) the search was reasonable under the circumstances, including Paul's nervous condition.
(B) the search was incident to a valid arrest.
(C) Paul had, under the circumstances, sufficient standing and authority to consent to the search.
(D) exigent circumstances, including the inherent mobility of a car, justified the search.

Question 94

Adam and Bailey, brothers, operated an illicit still. They customarily sold to anyone unless they suspected the person of being a revenue agent or an informant. One day when Adam was at the still alone, he was approached by Mitchell who asked to buy a gallon of liquor. Mitchell was in fact a revenue officer. After Adam had sold him the liquor, Mitchell revealed his identity. Adam grabbed one of the rifles that the brothers kept handy in case of trouble with the law, and shot and wounded Mitchell. Other officers, hiding nearby, overpowered and arrested Adam.

Shortly thereafter, Bailey came on the scene. The officers in hiding had been waiting for him. One of them approached him and asked to buy liquor. Bailey was suspicious and refused to sell. The officers nevertheless arrested him.

Adam and Bailey were charged with conspiracy to violate revenue laws, illegal selling of liquor, and battery of the officer.

On the charge of battery, which statement concerning Adam and Bailey is true?

(A) Neither is guilty.
(B) Both are guilty.
(C) Adam is guilty but Bailey is not, because the conspiracy had terminated with the arrest of Adam.
(D) Adam is guilty but Bailey is not, because Adam's act was outside the scope of the conspiracy.

Question 95

Defendant was driving his automobile at a legal speed in a residential zone. A child darted out in front of him and was run over and killed before Defendant could prevent it. Defendant's driver's license had expired three months previously; Defendant had neglected to check when it was due to expire. Driving without a valid license is a misdemeanor in the jurisdiction. On a charge of manslaughter, Defendant should be found

(A) guilty under the misdemeanor-manslaughter rule.
(B) guilty, because the licensing requirements are to protect life, and failure to obey is negligence.
(C) not guilty, because the offense was not the proximate cause of the death.
(D) not guilty, because there was no criminal intent.

Question 96

In which of the following situations is Defendant's claim of intoxication most likely to result in his being found not guilty?

(A) Defendant is charged with manslaughter for a death resulting from an automobile accident. Defendant, the driver, claims he was so drunk he was unable to see the other car involved in the accident.
(B) Defendant is charged with assault with intent to kill Watts as a result of his wounding Watts by shooting him. Defendant claims he was so drunk he did not realize anyone else was around when he fired the gun.
(C) Defendant is charged with armed robbery. He claims he was so drunk he did not know if the gun was loaded.
(D) Defendant is charged with statutory rape after he has sexual intercourse with a girl aged 15 in a jurisdiction where the age of consent is 16. Defendant claims he was so drunk he did not realize the girl was a minor.

Question 97

Defendant was tried for robbery. Victim and Worth were the only witnesses called to testify. Victim testified that Defendant threatened her with a knife, grabbed her purse, and ran off with it. Worth testified that he saw Defendant grab Victim's purse and run away with it but that he neither saw a knife nor heard any threats. On this evidence the jury could properly return a verdict of guilty of

(A) robbery only.
(B) larceny only.

(C) either robbery or larceny.
(D) both robbery and larceny.

Question 98

Defendant visited a fellow college student, James, in James' dormitory room. They drank some beer. James produced a box containing marijuana cigarettes and asked if Defendant wanted one. Defendant, afraid of being caught, declined and urged James to get rid of the marijuana. James refused.

Shortly thereafter, both went out to get more beer, leaving the door to James' room standing open. Making an excuse about having dropped his pen, Defendant went back into James' room. Still apprehensive about their being caught with the marijuana cigarettes, he took the cigarettes and flushed them down the toilet. He was sure James was too drunk to notice that the cigarettes were missing.

Defendant is charged with larceny and burglary (defined in the jurisdiction as breaking and entering the dwelling of another with intent to commit any felony or theft). He should be found guilty of

(A)   burglary only.
(B)   larceny only.
(C)   both burglary and larceny.
(D)   neither burglary nor larceny.

Questions 99-100 are based on the following fact situation.

Bill and Chuck hated Vic and agreed to start a fight with Vic and, if the opportunity arose, to kill him.

Bill and Chuck met Vic in the street outside a bar and began to push him around. Ray, Sam, and Tom, who also hated Vic, stopped to watch. Ray threw Bill a knife. Sam told Bill, "Kill him." Tom, who made no move and said nothing, hoped that Bill would kill Vic with the knife. Chuck held Vic while Bill stabbed and killed him.

Question 99

On a charge of murdering Vic, Sam is

(A) not guilty, because his words did not create a "clear and present danger" not already existing.
(B) not guilty, because mere presence and oral encouragement, whether or not he has the requisite intent, will not make him guilty as an accomplice.
(C) guilty, because, with the intent to have Bill kill Vic, he shouted encouragement to Bill.
(D) guilty, because he aided and abetted the murder through his mere presence plus his intent to see Vic killed.

Question 100

On a charge of murdering Vic, Tom is

(A) not guilty, because mere presence, coupled with silent approval and intent, is not sufficient.
(B) not guilty, because he did not tell Bill ahead of time that he hoped Bill would murder Vic.
(C) guilty, because he had a duty to stop the killing and made no attempt to do so.
(D) guilty, because he was present and approved of what occurred.

Questions 101-102 each describe an offense. Select from the choices (A-D) the most serious offense of which the defendant could be properly convicted.

(A) Involuntary manslaughter

(B) Voluntary manslaughter
(C) Murder
(D) None of the above

Question 101

Defendant, an avid fan of his home town football team, shot at the leg of a star player for a rival team, intending to injure his leg enough to hospitalize him for a few weeks, but not to kill him. The victim died of loss of blood.

Question 102

Defendant, a worker in a metal working shop, had long been teasing Vincent, a young colleague, by calling him insulting names and ridiculing him. One day Vincent responded to the teasing by picking up a metal bar and attacking Defendant. Defendant could have escaped from the shop. He parried the blow with his left arm, and with his right hand struck Vincent a blow on his jaw from which the young man died.

Questions 103-104 are based on the following fact situation.

Johnson took a diamond ring to a pawnshop and borrowed $20 on it. It was agreed that the loan was to be repaid within 60 days and if it was not, the pawnshop owner, Defendant, could sell the ring. A week before expiration of the 60 days, Defendant had an opportunity to sell the ring to a customer for $125. He did so, thinking it unlikely that Johnson would repay the loan and if he did, Defendant would be able to handle him somehow, even by paying him for the ring if necessary. Two days later, Johnson came in with the money to reclaim his ring. Defendant told him that it had been stolen when his shop was burglarized one night and that therefore he was not responsible for its loss.

Larceny, embezzlement, and false pretenses are separate crimes in the jurisdiction.

Question 103

It is most likely that Defendant has committed which of the following crimes?

(A) Larceny
(B) Embezzlement
(C) Larceny by trick
(D) Obtaining by false pretenses

Question 104

Suppose in the case above, instead of denying liability, Defendant told Johnson the truth—that he sold the ring because he thought Johnson would not reclaim it—and offered to give Johnson $125. Johnson demanded his ring. Defendant said, "Look buddy, that's what I got for it and it's more than it's worth." Johnson reluctantly took the money. Defendant could most appropriately be found guilty of

(A) Larceny
(B) Embezzlement
(C) False pretenses
(D) None of the above

Question 105

Brown suffered from the delusion that he was a special agent of God. He frequently experienced hallucinations in the form of hearing divine commands. Brown believed God told him several times that the local Roman Catholic bishop was corrupting the diocese into heresy, and that the bishop should be "done away with." Brown, a devout Catholic, conceived of himself as a religious martyr. He knew that shooting bishops for heresy is against the criminal law. He nevertheless carefully planned how he might kill the bishop. One evening Brown shot the bishop, who was taken to the hospital where he died two weeks later.

Brown told the police he assumed the institutions of society would support the ecclesiastical hierarchy, and he expected to be persecuted for his God-inspired actions. Psychiatrist Stevens examined Brown and found that Brown suffered from schizophrenic psychosis, that in the absence of this psychosis he would not have shot the bishop, and that because of the psychosis Brown found it extremely difficult to determine whether he should obey the specific command that he do away with the bishop or the general commandment "Thou shalt not kill." Brown was charged with murder.

If Brown interposes an insanity defense and the jurisdiction in which he is tried has adopted only the M'Naghten test of insanity, then the strongest argument for the defense under that test is that

(A) Brown did not know the nature of the act he was performing.
(B) Brown did not know that his act was morally wrong.
(C) Brown did not know the quality of the act he was performing.
(D) Brown's acts were the product of a mental disease.

Question 106

At the trial of Davis for a murder that occurred in Newtown, the prosecution called Waite, who testified that she saw Davis kill the victim. Davis believed that Waite was 600 miles away in Old Town, engaged in the illegal sale of narcotics, on the day in question. On cross-examination by Davis, Waite was asked whether she had in fact sold narcotics in Old Town on that date. Waite refused to answer on the ground of self-incrimination.

The judge, over the prosecutor's objection, ordered that if Waite did not testify, her direct testimony should be stricken. The order to testify or have the testimony stricken can best be supported on the basis that

(A) Waite had not been charged with any crime and, thus, could claim no privilege against self-incrimination.
(B) Waite's proper invocation of the privilege prevented adequate cross-examination.
(C) the public interest in allowing an accused to defend himself or herself outweighs the interest of a non-party witness in the privilege.
(D) the trial record, independent of testimony, does not establish that Waite's answer could incriminate her.

Question 107

A state statute makes it a felony for any teacher at a state institution of higher education to accept anything of value from a student at the same institution. Monroe, a student at the state university, offered Professor Smith, his English teacher, $50 in exchange for a good grade in his English course. Smith agreed and took the money. Professor Smith and Monroe are tried jointly for violation of the state statute. Professor Smith is charged with violating the statute and Monroe with aiding and abetting him.

Monroe's best argument for a dismissal of the charge against him is that

(A) a principal and an accessory cannot be tried together, since the principal must be convicted first.
(B) he cannot be an accessory, since he is the victim of the crime.
(C) the legislature did not intend to punish the person giving the thing of value.
(D) he did not assist Professor Smith in violating the statute.

Question 108

In which of the following situations is Defendant most likely to be guilty of the crime charged?

(A) Without the permission of Owner, Defendant takes Owner's car with the intention of driving it three miles to a grocery store and back. Defendant is charged with larceny.

(B) Defendant gets permission to borrow Owner's car for the evening by falsely promising to return it, although he does not intend to do so. Two days later, he changes his mind and returns the car. Defendant is charged with larceny by trick.

(C) Defendant gets permission to borrow Owner's car for the evening by misrepresenting his identity and falsely claiming he has a valid driver's license. He returns the car the next day. Defendant is charged with obtaining property by false pretenses.

(D) With permission, Defendant, promising to return it by 9:00 p.m., borrows Owner's car. Later in the evening, Defendant decides to keep the car until the next morning and does so. Defendant is charged with embezzlement.

Question 109

While testifying as a witness in a civil trial, Walters was asked on cross-examination if he had been convicted in the circuit court of Jasper County of stealing $200 from his employer on August 16, 1977. Walters said, "No, I have never been convicted of any crime." In fact, Walters had pleaded guilty to such a charge and had been placed on probation.

Walters was then charged with perjury on the ground that his statement denying the conviction was false. A statute in the jurisdiction defines perjury as knowingly making a false statement while under oath.

At trial, the state proved Walters' statement and the prior conviction. Walters testified that the attorney who represented him in the theft case had told him that, because he had been placed on probation, he had not been convicted of a crime. Walters had served his probationary period satisfactorily and been discharged from probation. The alleged advice of the attorney was incorrect.

If the jury believes Walters, it should find him

(A) guilty, because his mistake was one of law.

(B) guilty, because reliance on the advice of an attorney is not a defense.

(C) not guilty if the jury also finds that his reliance on the attorney's advice was reasonable.

(D) not guilty, because he lacked the necessary mental state.

Question 110

Davison was driving through an apartment building area plagued with an unusually high incidence of burglaries and assaults. Acting pursuant to a police department plan to combat crime by the random stopping of automobiles in the area between midnight and 6:00 a.m., a police officer stopped Davison and asked him for identification. As Davison handed the officer his license, the officer directed a flashlight into the automobile and saw what appeared to be the barrel of a shotgun protruding from under the front seat on the passenger side of the car. The officer ordered Davison from the car, searched him, and discovered marijuana cigarettes and a shotgun.

At Davison's trial for unlawful possession of narcotics, his motion to suppress the use of the marijuana as evidence should be

(A) sustained, because the marijuana was discovered as a result of the unlawful stopping of Davison's automobile.

(B) sustained, because the use of the flashlight constituted a search of the interior of Davison's automobile without probable cause.

(C) denied, because the officer's conduct was consistent with the established police plan.

(D) denied, because the discovery of the gun in plain view created the reasonable suspicion necessary to justify the arrest and search of Davison.

Question 111

In which of the following situations is defendant most likely to be guilty of common-law murder?

(A) During an argument in a bar, Norris punches Defendant. Defendant, mistakenly believing that Norris is about to stab him, shoots and kills Norris.
(B) While committing a robbery of a liquor store, Defendant accidentally drops his revolver, which goes off. The bullet strikes and kills Johnson, a customer in the store.
(C) While hunting deer, Defendant notices something moving in the bushes. Believing it to be a deer, Defendant fires into the bushes. The bullet strikes and kills Griggs, another hunter.
(D) In celebration of the Fourth of July, Defendant discharges a pistol within the city limits in violation of a city ordinance. The bullet ricochets off the street and strikes and kills Abbott.

Question 112

Dutton, disappointed by his 8-year-old son's failure to do well in school, began systematically depriving the child of food during summer vacation. Although his son became seriously ill from malnutrition, Dutton failed to call a doctor. He believed that as a parent he had the sole right to determine whether the child was fed or received medical treatment. Eventually the child died. An autopsy disclosed that the child had suffered agonizingly as a result of the starvation, that a physician's aid would have alleviated the suffering, and that although the child would have died in a few months from malnutrition, the actual cause of death was an untreatable form of cancer.

The father was prosecuted for murder, defined in the jurisdiction as "unlawful killing of a human being with malice aforethought." The father should be

(A) acquitted, because of the defendant's good faith belief concerning parental rights in supervising children.
(B) acquitted, because summoning the physician or feeding the child would not have prevented the child's death from cancer.
(C) convicted, because the father's treatment of his son showed reckless indifference to the value of life.
(D) convicted, because the child would have died from malnutrition had he not been afflicted with cancer.

Question 113

Vance had cheated Dodd in a card game. Angered, Dodd set out for Vance's house with the intention of shooting him. Just as he was about to set foot on Vance's property, Dodd was arrested by a police officer who noticed that Dodd was carrying a revolver. A statute in the jurisdiction makes it a crime to "enter the property of another with the intent to commit any crime of violence thereon."

If charged with attempting to violate the statute, Dodd should be found

(A) not guilty, because the statute defines an attempted crime and there cannot be an attempt to attempt.
(B) not guilty, because to convict him would be to punish him simply for having a guilty mind.
(C) guilty, because he was close enough to entering the property and he had the necessary state of mind.
(D) guilty, because this is a statute designed to protect the public from violence and Dodd was dangerous.

Question 114

Dillon held up a gasoline station. During the robbery he shot and killed a customer who attempted to apprehend him. Dillon was prosecuted for premeditated murder and convicted. Thereafter, he was indicted for armed robbery of the station.

Before the trial, his attorney moved to dismiss the indictment on the ground that further proceedings were unconstitutional because of Dillon's prior conviction.

The motion to dismiss should be

(A) granted, because once Dillon was convicted on any of the charges arising out of the robbery, the prosecution was constitutionally estopped from proceeding against Dillon on any charge stemming from the same transaction.
(B) granted, because the double jeopardy clause prohibits a subsequent trial on what is essentially a lesser included offense.
(C) denied, because there is no constitutional requirement that all known charges against Dillon be brought in the same prosecution.
(D) denied, because estoppel does not apply when the defendant is charged with violating two different statutes.

Questions 115-117 are based on the following fact situation.

Adams, Bennett, and Curtis are charged in a common law jurisdiction with conspiracy to commit larceny. The state introduced evidence that they agreed to go to Nelson's house to take stock certificates from a safe in Nelson's bedroom, that they went to the house, and that they were arrested as they entered Nelson's bedroom.

Adams testified that he thought the stock certificates belonged to Curtis, that Nelson was improperly keeping them from Curtis, and that he went along to aid in retrieving Curtis' property.

Bennett testified that he suspected Adams and Curtis of being thieves and joined up with them in order to catch them. He also testified that he made an anonymous telephone call to the police alerting them to the crime and that the call caused the police to be waiting for them when they walked into Nelson's bedroom.

Curtis did not testify.

Question 115

If the jury believes Adams, it should find him

(A) guilty, because there was an agreement and the entry into the bedroom is sufficient for the overt act.
(B) guilty, because good motives are not a defense to criminal liability.
(C) not guilty, because he did not have a corrupt motive.
(D) not guilty, because he did not intend to steal.

Question 116

If the jury believes Bennett, it should find him

(A) guilty, because there was an agreement and the entry into the bedroom is sufficient for the overt act.
(B) guilty, because he is not a police officer and thus cannot claim any privilege of apprehending criminals.
(C) not guilty, because he did not intend to steal.
(D) not guilty, because he prevented the theft from occurring.

Question 117

If the jury believes both Adams and Bennett, it should find Curtis

(A) guilty, because there was an agreement and the entry into the bedroom is sufficient for the overt act.
(B) guilty, because he intended to steal.

(C) not guilty, because a conviction would penalize him for exercising his right not to be a witness.
(D) not guilty, because Adams and Bennett did not intend to steal.

Question 118

Dobbs, while intoxicated, drove his car through a playground crowded with children just to watch the children run to get out of his way. His car struck one of the children, killing her instantly.

Which of the following is the best theory for finding Dobbs guilty of murder?

(A) Transferred intent
(B) Felony murder, with assault with a deadly weapon as the underlying felony
(C) Intentional killing, since he knew that the children were there and he deliberately drove his car at them
(D) Commission of an act highly dangerous to life, without an intent to kill but with disregard of the consequences

Question 119

Which of the following is most likely to be found to be a strict liability offense?

(A) A city ordinance providing for a fine of not more than $200 for shoplifting
(B) A federal statute making it a felony to possess heroin
(C) A state statute making it a felony to fail to register a firearm
(D) A state statute making the sale of adulterated milk a misdemeanor

Question 120

Donaldson broke into Professor Ruiz' office in order to look at examination questions. The questions were locked in a drawer, and Donaldson could not find them. Donaldson believed that looking at examination questions was a crime, but in this belief he was mistaken.

Charged with burglary, Donaldson should be

(A) acquitted, because he did not complete the crime and he has not been charged with attempt.
(B) acquitted, because what he intended to do when he broke in was not a crime.
(C) convicted, because he had the necessary mental state and committed the act of breaking and entering.
(D) convicted, because factual impossibility is not a defense.

Question 121

Dent, while eating in a restaurant, noticed that a departing customer at the next table had left a five-dollar bill as a tip for the waitress. Dent reached over, picked up the five-dollar bill, and put it in his pocket. As he stood up to leave, another customer who had seen him take the money ran over to him and hit him in the face with her umbrella. Enraged, Dent choked the customer to death.

Dent is charged with murder. He requests the court to charge the jury that they can find him guilty of voluntary manslaughter rather than murder. Dent's request should be

(A) granted, because the jury could find that Dent acted recklessly and not with the intent to cause death or serious bodily harm.
(B) granted, because the jury could find that being hit in the face with an umbrella constitutes adequate provocation.
(C) denied, because the evidence shows that Dent intended to kill or to cause serious bodily harm.
(D) denied, because the evidence shows that Dent provoked the assault on himself by his criminal misconduct.

Question 122

Young, believing that Brown suffered from arthritis, told her that for $100 he could cure her with a device he had invented. The device was a large box with a series of electric light bulbs along the sides. Brown, after examining the device, agreed to take the treatment, which consisted of placing her hands inside the box for several ten-minute periods. Brown gave Young $100 and went through the treatment.

Young is charged with obtaining money by false pretenses. Each of the following, if true, will absolve Young of guilt for obtaining money by false pretenses EXCEPT:

(A) Young honestly believed that the device would cure arthritis, but his belief was unreasonable.
(B) Brown honestly believed that the device would cure arthritis, but her belief was unreasonable.
(C) Young was playing a practical joke on Brown and intended to return the money.
(D) Brown was an undercover police officer and did not believe that the device would cure arthritis.

Question 123

Dann was an alcoholic who frequently experienced auditory hallucinations that commanded him to engage in bizarre and sometimes violent behavior. He generally obeyed their commands. The hallucinations appeared more frequently when he was intoxicated, but he sometimes experienced them when he had not been drinking.

After Dann had been drinking continuously for a three-day period, an elderly woman began to reproach him about his drunken condition, slapping him on the face and shoulders as she did so. Dann believed that he was being unmercifully attacked and heard the hallucinatory voice telling him to strangle his assailant. He did so, and she died.

If Dann is charged with second degree murder, Dann's best chance of acquittal would be to rely on a defense of

(A) intoxication.
(B) lack of malice aforethought.
(C) self-defense.
(D) insanity.

Question 124

James and Mary Green were walking to their car one evening after having seen a movie. As they were passing a dark alleyway, Daves leaped out brandishing a gun. He pushed Mary against the wall of a nearby building, held the gun to her head, and demanded money from James. James handed over his cash. Daves grabbed the cash and ran away.

Which of the following, listed in descending order of seriousness, is the most serious crime for which Daves may be convicted?

(A) Robbery from James Green
(B) Larceny from James Green
(C) Assault on James and Mary Green
(D) Assault on Mary Green

Questions 125-126 are based on the following fact situation.

Dunbar and Balcom went into a drugstore, where Dunbar reached into the cash register and took out $200. Stone, the owner of the store, came out of a back room, saw what had happened, and told Dunbar to put the money back. Balcom then took a revolver from under his coat and shot and killed Stone.

Dunbar claims that Stone owed her $200 and that she went to the drugstore to try to collect the debt. She said that she asked Balcom to come along just in case Stone made trouble but that she did not plan on using any force and did not know that Balcom was armed.

Question 125

If Dunbar is prosecuted for murder on the basis of felony murder and the jury believes her claim, she should be found

(A) guilty, because her companion, Balcom, committed a homicide in the course of a felony.
(B) guilty, because her taking Balcom with her to the store created the risk of death that occurred during the commission of a felony.
(C) not guilty, because she did not know that Balcom was armed and thus did not have the required mental state for felony murder.
(D) not guilty, because she believed she was entitled to the money and thus did not intend to steal.

Question 126

If Dunbar is prosecuted for murder on the basis of being an accessory to Balcom in committing a murder and the jury believes her claim, she should be found

(A) guilty, because in firing the shot Balcom was trying to help her.
(B) guilty, because she and Balcom were acting in concert in a dangerous under-taking.
(C) not guilty, because she had no idea that Balcom was armed and she did not plan to use force.
(D) not guilty, because she was exercising self-help and did not intend to steal.

Question 127

Damson was short of money. He decided to go into Waters' house to take Waters' silverware and then to sell it. That night, while Waters was away, Damson entered by picking the lock on the front door. He picked up a chest of silverware from the dining room and went out the front door of the house to his car. As he was putting the chest of silverware into the trunk, he had second thoughts and decided that he did not wish to become a thief. He reentered the house and replaced the chest of silverware where he had found it. As he came out of the house the second time, he was arrested by the police, who had been called by a neighbor.

Damson is

(A) guilty of burglary and larceny.
(B) guilty of burglary and attempted larceny.
(C) guilty of burglary but not guilty of any larceny offense.
(D) not guilty of burglary or any larceny offense.

Question 128

Which of the following is LEAST likely to be the underlying felony in a prosecution for felony murder?

(A) Arson
(B) Manslaughter
(C) Attempted rape
(D) Burglary

Question 129

Alford was a suspect in a homicide committed during a robbery of a liquor store. Barber was a friend of

Alford. Police telephoned Barber and asked if he would help locate Alford. Barber agreed and met the police officers at headquarters later that night.

After a discussion during which police asked questions about Alford and the homicide, Barber said that he wanted to get something "off his chest" and advised the officers that he was in on the robbery but that Alford had shot the owner of the store without his permission or prior knowledge. The officers then for the first time gave Barber his Miranda warnings.

Barber was indicted for felony murder. He moved to prevent the introduction of his statement into evidence. His motion should be

(A) granted, because Barber was effectively in custody and entitled to receive Miranda warnings at the beginning of the discussion.
(B) granted, because Barber's rights to counsel and to due process were violated by the interrogation at police headquarters.
(C) denied, because his statement was freely and voluntarily given and he was not entitled to Miranda warnings.
(D) denied, because by visiting headquarters voluntarily, Barber waived his right to have Miranda warnings at the beginning of the discussion.

Question 130

Downs was indicted in state court for bribing a public official. During the course of the investigation, police had demanded and received from Downs' bank the records of Downs' checking account for the preceding two years. The records contained incriminating evidence.

On the basis of a claim of violation of his constitutional rights, Downs moves to prevent the introduction of the records in evidence. His motion should be

(A) granted, because a search warrant should have been secured for seizure of the records.
(B) granted, because the records covered such an extensive period of time that their seizure unreasonably invaded Downs' right of privacy.
(C) denied, because the potential destructibility of the records, coupled with the public interest in proper enforcement of the criminal laws, created an exigent situation justifying the seizure.
(D) denied, because the records were business records of the bank in which Downs had no legitimate expectation of privacy.

Question 131

A statute in a jurisdiction makes it a crime to sell ammunition to a minor (defined as a person under the age of eighteen). The courts have interpreted this statute as creating a strict liability offense that does not require knowledge of the age of the purchaser and as creating vicarious liability. Duncan, who was sixteen years old, but looked four or five years older, entered a store owned by Matthews and asked a clerk for a box of .22 caliber shells. Matthews had instructed her employees not to sell ammunition to minors. The clerk asked Duncan his age. Duncan said he was twenty. The clerk then placed a box of shells on the counter and asked, "Anything else?" Duncan said that was all he wanted but then discovered he did not have enough money to pay for the shells, so the clerk put the box back onto the shelf.

If Matthews, the owner of the store, is charged with attempting to violate the statute, her best argument would be that

(A) it was impossible for the sale to have occurred.
(B) she had strictly instructed her employees not to sell ammunition to minors.
(C) Duncan lied about his age.
(D) the clerk did not have the mental state needed for attempt.

Questions 132-133 are based on the following fact situation.

Hammond decided to kill his wife by poisoning her. He asked his friend, Jordan, a pharmacist, to obtain some curare, a deadly poison, and to give it to him without recording the transaction. Because Jordan suspected Hammond's motive, she supplied Hammond with a small quantity of Marvane, an antibiotic, instead of curare. Marvane is harmless if administered in small quantities, except for the less than 1 percent of the population who are allergic to the drug. Hammond injected his wife with the Marvane while she slept. She was allergic to the drug and died from the injection. Jordan was distraught and confessed the entire affair to the police, explaining that she had failed to report Hammond's conduct to the authorities because she feared that it would end their friendship if she did.

Question 132

Jordan is an accomplice to

(A) murder.
(B) manslaughter.
(C) criminally negligent homicide.
(D) no degree of criminal homicide.

Question 133

In a common-law jurisdiction, Hammond is guilty of

(A) murder only.
(B) murder and conspiracy.
(C) attempted murder only.
(D) attempted murder and conspiracy.

Question 134

During the night, Murphy broke into a house with the intention of stealing a typewriter. On not finding a typewriter, she became angry, poured lighter fluid onto a couch, and set it on fire. The flames destroyed the couch and also burned a portion of the ceiling in the room.

In a common-law jurisdiction, Murphy is guilty of

(A) burglary only.
(B) arson only.
(C) burglary and attempted arson.
(D) burglary and arson.

Question 135

Dirk broke into Vera's house one night. As he started to stuff silverware into a sack, he was surprised by Vera, who had arrived home earlier than usual. Dirk struck Vera on the head with a candlestick and tied her up. He finished filling his sack and left.

The police discovered Vera several hours later and rushed her to the hospital. Dirk was apprehended by the police early the following morning with the loot still in his possession. He was taken to police headquarters, given Miranda warnings, and asked if he wished to make a statement about the prior evening's events. The police did not mention that Vera had been seriously injured and was in the hospital. Dirk said he understood his rights and was willing to talk. He then admitted that he committed the burglary of Vera's house. The following day, Vera died from injuries caused by the blow to her head.

If, at Dirk's trial for murder, Dirk moves to prevent introduction of the confession into evidence, his motion should most probably be

(A) denied, because failure of the police to advise Dirk of Vera's condition was harmless error since felony murder does not require intent to kill or injure.
(B) denied, because Dirk's waiver of his rights did not depend upon the nature of the charges that were later filed against him.
(C) granted, because Dirk could not make a knowing and intelligent waiver unless he had information concerning Vera's condition.
(D) granted, because the use of a confession to burglary in a prosecution for murder violates due process where the police withheld information about the potential seriousness of the offense.

Question 136

Smythe was charged with the murder of his wife. In his defense, he testified that at the time he killed her, he believed that his wife was planning to destroy the world by detonating a massive explosive device that she had developed and built in the basement of their home. He further testified that he had tried many times to dissuade his wife from her plan and had tried to destroy devices that she stored in the basement. She had, he testified, foiled his efforts by on two occasions signing papers for his hospitalization, which lasted for a brief period each time. He said that he had concluded that the only way to prevent her scheme was to kill her and that he had become so obsessed with the importance of doing so that he could think of nothing else. One day when he saw her open the door to the basement he lunged at her and pushed her down the steps to her death.

The best defense raised by Smythe's testimony is

(A) lack of the requisite mental element.
(B) lack of the requisite act element.
(C) insanity.
(D) belief that the situation justified his actions.

Question 137

Rimm and Hill were fooling around with a pistol in Hill's den. Rimm aimed the pistol in Hill's direction and fired three shots slightly to Hill's right. One shot ricocheted off the wall and struck Hill in the back, killing him instantly.

The most serious crime of which Rimm can be convicted is

(A) murder.
(B) voluntary manslaughter.
(C) involuntary manslaughter.
(D) assault with a dangerous weapon.

Question 138

Beth wanted to make some money, so she decided to sell cocaine. She asked Albert, who was reputed to have access to illegal drugs, to supply her with cocaine so she could resell it. Albert agreed and sold Beth a bag of white powder. Beth then repackaged the white powder into smaller containers and sold one to Carol, an undercover police officer, who promptly arrested Beth. Beth immediately confessed and said that Albert was her supplier. Upon examination, the white powder was found not to be cocaine or any type of illegal substance.

If Albert knew the white powder was not cocaine but Beth believed it was, which of the following is correct?

(A) Both Albert and Beth are guilty of attempting to sell cocaine.
(B) Neither Albert nor Beth is guilty of attempting to sell cocaine.
(C) Albert is guilty of attempting to sell cocaine, but Beth is not.
(D) Albert is not guilty of attempting to sell cocaine, but Beth is.

Question 139

After being fired from his job, Mel drank almost a quart of vodka and decided to ride the bus home. While on the bus, he saw a briefcase he mistakenly thought was his own, and began struggling with the passenger carrying the briefcase. Mel knocked the passenger to the floor, took the briefcase, and fled. Mel was arrested and charged with robbery.

Mel should be:

(A) acquitted, because he used no threats and was intoxicated.
(B) acquitted, because his mistake negated the required specific intent.
(C) convicted, because his intoxication was voluntary.
(D) convicted, because mistake is no defense to robbery.

Question 140

Joe and Marty were coworkers. Joe admired Marty's wristwatch and frequently said how much he wished he had one like it. Marty decided to give Joe the watch for his birthday the following week.

On the weekend before Joe's birthday, Joe and Marty attended a company picnic. Marty took his watch off and left it on a blanket when he went off to join in a touch football game. Joe strolled by, saw the watch on the blanket, and decided to steal it. He bent over and picked up the watch. Before he could pocket it, however, Marty returned. When he saw Joe holding the watch, he said, "Joe, I know how much you like that watch. I was planning to give it to you for your birthday. Go ahead and take it now." Joe kept the watch.

Joe has committed

(A) larceny.
(B) attempted larceny.
(C) embezzlement.
(D) no crime.

Questions 141-142 are based on the following fact situation.

Jones, a marijuana farmer, had been missing for several months. The sheriff's department received an anonymous tip that Miller, a rival marijuana farmer, had buried Jones in a hillside about 200 yards from Miller's farmhouse. Sheriff's deputies went to Miller's farm. They cut the barbed wire that surrounded the hillside and entered, looking for the grave. They also searched the adjacent fields on Miller's farm that were within the area enclosed by the barbed wire and discovered clothing that belonged to Jones hanging on a scarecrow. Miller observed their discovery and began shooting. The deputies returned the fire. Miller dashed to his pickup truck to escape. Unable to start the truck, he fled across a field toward the barn. A deputy tackled him just as he entered the barn.

As Miller attempted to get up, the deputy pinned his arms behind his back. Another deputy threatened, "Tell us what you did with Jones or we will shut you down and see your family on relief." Miller responded that he had killed Jones in a fight but did not report the incident because he did not want authorities to enter his land and discover his marijuana crop. Instead, he buried him behind the barn. Miller was thereafter charged with murder.

Question 141

If Miller moves to suppress his admission about killing his neighbor, the court should

(A) grant the motion, because Miller did not voluntarily waive his right to silence.
(B) grant the motion, because the statement was the product of the warrantless entry and search of Miller's farm.
(C) deny the motion, because the deputy was in hot pursuit when he questioned Miller.
(D) deny the motion, because Miller was questioned during a police emergency search.

Question 142

If Miller moves to exclude the introduction of Jones's clothing into evidence, the court should

(A) grant the motion, because the deputies had not obtained a warrant.
(B) grant the motion, because the deputies' conduct in its entirety violated Miller's right to due process of law.
(C) deny the motion, because Miller had no expectation of privacy in the fields around his farmhouse.
(D) deny the motion, because the clothing was not Miller's property.

Question 143

Martha's high school teacher told her that she was going to receive a failing grade in history, which would prevent her from graduating. Furious, she reported to the principal that the teacher had fondled her, and the teacher was fired. A year later, still unable to get work because of the scandal, the teacher committed suicide. Martha, remorseful, confessed that her accusation had been false.

If Martha is charged with manslaughter, her best defense would be that she

(A) committed no act that proximately caused the teacher's death.
(B) did not intend to cause the teacher's death.
(C) did not act with malice.
(D) acted under extreme emotional distress.

Question 144

Two police officers in uniform were on foot patrol in a neighborhood frequented by drug sellers. They saw Sandra, who, when she saw them, turned around and started to walk quickly away. The police ran after her and shouted, "Stop and don't take another step, lady!" Sandra turned, looked at the police, and stopped. She put her arms up in the air. As the police approached, she threw a small object into nearby bushes. The police retrieved the object, which turned out to be a small bag of cocaine, and then arrested Sandra.

Sandra is charged with possession of the cocaine. She moves pretrial to suppress its use as evidence on the ground that it was obtained as the result of an illegal search and seizure.

Her motion should be

(A) granted, because the police did not know the item was cocaine until after they had seized it.
(B) granted, because the police acquired the cocaine as the result of an unlawful seizure.
(C) denied, because the police had probable cause to seize the package.
(D) denied, because Sandra voluntarily discarded the contraband.

Question 145

On May 1, 1987, a car driven by Debra struck Peggy, a pedestrian. On July 1, 1987, with regard to this incident, Debra pleaded guilty to reckless driving (a misdemeanor) and was sentenced to 30 days in jail and a fine of $1,000. She served the sentence and paid the fine. On April 1, 1988, Peggy died as a result of the injuries she suffered in the accident. On March 1, 1991, a grand jury indicted Debra on a charge of manslaughter of Peggy. On May 15, 1991, trial had not begun and Debra filed a motion to dismiss the indictment on the ground of double jeopardy in that her conviction of reckless driving arose out of the same incident, and on the ground that the three-year statute of limitations for manslaughter had run.

Debra's motion should be

(A) granted only on double jeopardy grounds.
(B) granted only on statute of limitations grounds.
(C) granted on either double jeopardy grounds or statute of limitations grounds.
(D) denied on both grounds.

Question 146

FBI agents, without a warrant and without permission of Mexican law enforcement or judicial officers, entered Mexico, kidnapped Steven, an American citizen wanted in the United States for drug smuggling violations, and forcibly drove him back to Texas. Thereafter, the agents, again without a warrant, broke into the Texas home of Joan, wanted as a confederate of Steven, and arrested her.

Steven and Joan were both indicted for narcotics violations. Both moved to dismiss the indictment on the ground that their arrests violated the Fourth Amendment.

The court should

(A) grant the motions of both Steven and Joan.
(B) grant the motion of Steven and deny the motion of Joan.
(C) grant the motion of Joan and deny the motion of Steven.
(D) deny the motions of both Steven and Joan.

Question 147

Smart approached Johnson and inquired about hiring someone to kill his girlfriend's parents. Unknown to Smart, Johnson was an undercover police officer who pretended to agree to handle the job and secretly taped subsequent conversations with Smart concerning plans and payment. A few days before the payment was due, Smart changed his mind and called the plan off. Nevertheless, Smart was charged with solicitation to commit murder.

Smart should be

(A) acquitted, because he withdrew before payment and commission of the act.
(B) acquitted, because no substantial acts were performed.
(C) convicted, because the offense was completed before his attempt to withdraw.
(D) convicted, because Johnson agreed to commit the offense.

Question 148

Defendant is charged with murder. The evidence shows that she pointed a gun at Victim and pulled the trigger. The gun discharged, killing Victim. The gun belonged to Victim.

Defendant testifies that Victim told her, and she believed, that the "gun" was a stage prop that could fire only blanks, and that she fired the gun as part of rehearsing a play with Victim at his house.

If the jury believes Defendant's testimony and finds that her mistaken belief that the gun was a prop was reasonable, they should find her

(A) guilty of murder.
(B) guilty of manslaughter.
(C) guilty of either murder or manslaughter.
(D) not guilty of murder or manslaughter.

Question 149

In which of the following situations would Defendant's mistake most likely constitute a defense to the crime charged?

(A) A local ordinance forbids the sale of alcoholic beverages to persons under 18 years of age. Relying on false identification, Defendant sells champagne to a 16-year-old high school student. Defendant is charged with illegal sale of alcoholic beverages.
(B) Mistaking Defendant for a narcotics suspect, an undercover police officer attempts to arrest him. Defendant, unaware that the person who has grabbed him is an officer, hits him and knocks him unconscious. Defendant is charged with assault.
(C) Defendant, aged 23, has sexual intercourse with a 15-year-old prostitute who tells Defendant that she is 18. Defendant is charged with the felony of statutory rape under a statute that makes sexual relations with a child under 16 a felony.
(D) Relying on erroneous advice from his attorney that, if his wife has abandoned him for more than a year, he is free to marry, Defendant remarries and is subsequently charged with bigamy.

Question 150

State X enacted a statute "to regulate administratively the conduct of motor vehicle junkyard businesses in order to deter motor vehicle theft and trafficking in stolen motor vehicles or parts thereof." The statute requires a junkyard owner or operator "to permit representatives of the Department of Motor Vehicles or of any law enforcement agency upon request during normal business hours to take physical inventory of motor vehicles and parts thereof on the premises." The statute also states that a failure to comply with any of its requirements constitutes a felony.

Police officers assigned to Magnolia City's Automobile Crimes Unit periodically visited all motor vehicle junkyards in town to make the inspections permitted by the statute. Janet owned such a business in Magnolia City. One summer day, the officers asked to inspect the vehicles on her lot. Janet said, "Do I have a choice?" The officers told her she did not. The officers conducted their inspection and discovered three stolen automobiles.

Janet is charged with receiving stolen property. Janet moves pretrial to suppress the evidence relating to the three automobiles on the ground that the inspection was unconstitutional.

Her motion should be

(A) sustained, because the statute grants unbridled discretion to law enforcement officers to make warrantless searches.
(B) sustained, because the stated regulatory purpose of the statute is a pretext to circumvent the warrant requirement in conducting criminal investigations.
(C) denied, because the statute deals reasonably with a highly regulated industry.
(D) denied, because administrative searches of commercial establishments do not require warrants.

Question 151

Rachel, an antique dealer and a skilled calligrapher, crafted a letter on very old paper. She included details that would lead knowledgeable readers to believe the letter had been written by Thomas Jefferson to a friend. Rachel, who had a facsimile of Jefferson's autograph, made the signature and other writing on the letter resemble Jefferson's. She knew that the letter would attract the attention of local collectors. When it did and she was contacted about selling it, she said that it had come into her hands from a foreign collector who wished anonymity, and that she could make no promises about its authenticity. As she had hoped, a collector paid her $5,000 for the letter. Later the collector discovered the letter was not authentic, and handwriting analysis established that Rachel had written the letter.

In a jurisdiction that follows the common-law definition of forgery, Rachel has

(A) committed both forgery and false pretenses.
(B) committed forgery, because she created a false document with the intent to defraud, but has not committed false pretenses, since she made no representation as to the authenticity of the document.
(C) not committed forgery, because the document had no apparent legal significance, but has committed false pretenses, since she misrepresented the source of the document.
(D) not committed forgery, because the document had no apparent legal significance, and has not committed false pretenses, since she made no representation as to authenticity of the document.

Question 152

Nora, executive director of an equal housing opportunity organization, was the leader of a sit-in at the offices of a real estate management company. The protest was designed to call attention to the company's racially discriminatory rental practices. When police demanded that Nora desist from trespassing on the company's property, she refused and was arrested. In Nora's trial for trespass, the prosecution peremptorily excused all nonwhites from the jury, arguing to the court that even though Nora was white, minority groups would automatically support Nora because of her fight against racism in housing accommodations.

If Nora is convicted of trespass by an all-white jury and appeals, claiming a violation of her constitutional rights, the court should

(A) affirm the conviction, because Nora was not a member of the class discriminated against.
(B) affirm the conviction, because peremptory challenge of the nonwhites did not deny Nora the right to an impartial jury.
(C) reverse the conviction, because racially based peremptory challenges violate equal protection of the law.
(D) reverse the conviction, because Nora was denied the right to have her case heard by a fair cross section of the community.

Question 153

The legislature of State X is debating reforms in the law governing insanity. Two reforms have been proposed. Proposal A would eliminate the insanity defense altogether. Proposal B would retain the defense but place on the defendant the burden of proving insanity by a preponderance of the evidence. Opponents of the reforms argue that the proposals would be unconstitutional under the due process clause of the United States Constitution.

Which of the proposed reforms would be unconstitutional?

(A) Both proposals.
(B) Neither proposal.
(C) Proposal A only.
(D) Proposal B only.

Question 154

Homer lived on the second floor of a small convenience store/gas station that he owned. One night he refused to sell Augie a six-pack of beer after hours, saying he could not violate the state laws. Augie became enraged and deliberately drove his car into one of the gasoline pumps, severing it from its base. There was an ensuing explosion causing a ball of fire to go from the underground gasoline tank into the building. As a result, the building burned to the ground and Homer was killed.

In a common-law jurisdiction, if Augie is charged with murder and arson, he should be

(A) convicted of both offenses.
(B) convicted of involuntary manslaughter and acquitted of arson.
(C) convicted of arson and involuntary manslaughter.
(D) acquitted of both offenses.

Question 155

At a party, Diane and Victor agreed to play a game they called "spin the barrel." Victor took an unloaded revolver, placed one bullet in the barrel, and spun the barrel. Victor then pointed the gun at Diane's head and pulled the trigger once. The gun did not fire. Diane then took the gun, pointed it at Victor, spun the barrel, and pulled the trigger once. The gun fired, and Victor fell over dead.

A statute in the jurisdiction defines murder in the first degree as an intentional and premeditated killing or one occurring during the commission of a common-law felony, and murder in the second degree as all other murder at common law. Manslaughter is defined as a killing in the heat of passion upon an adequate legal provocation or a killing caused by gross negligence.

The most serious crime for which Diane can properly be convicted is

(A) murder in the first degree, because the killing was intentional and premeditated and, in any event, occurred during commission of the felony of assault with a deadly weapon.
(B) murder in the second degree, because Diane's act posed a great threat of serious bodily harm.
(C) manslaughter, because Diane's act was grossly negligent and reckless.
(D) no crime, because Victor and Diane voluntarily agreed to play a game and each assumed the risk of death.

Questions 156-158 are based on the following fact situation.

The police had, over time, accumulated reliable information that Jason operated a large cocaine-distribution network, that he and his accomplices often resorted to violence, and that they kept a small arsenal of weapons in his home.

One day, the police received reliable information that a large brown suitcase with leather straps containing a supply of cocaine had been delivered to Jason's home and that it would be moved to a distribution point the next morning. The police obtained a valid search warrant to search for and seize the brown suitcase and the cocaine and went to Jason's house.

The police knocked on Jason's door and called out, "Police. Open up. We have a search warrant." After a few seconds with no response, the police forced the door open and entered. Hearing noises in the basement, the police ran down there and found Jason with a large brown suitcase with leather straps. They seized the suitcase and put handcuffs on Jason. A search of his person revealed a switchblade knife and a .45-caliber pistol. Jason cursed the police and said, "You never would have caught me with the stuff if it hadn't been for that lousy snitch Harvey!"

The police then fanned out through the house, looking in every room and closet. They found no one else, but one officer found an Uzi automatic weapon in a box on a closet shelf in Jason's bedroom.

In addition to charges relating to the cocaine in the suitcase, Jason is charged with unlawful possession of weapons.

Jason moves pretrial to suppress the use as evidence of the weapons seized by the police and of the statement he made.

Question 156

As to the switchblade knife and the .45-caliber pistol, Jason's motion to suppress should be

(A) granted, because the search and seizure were the result of illegal police conduct in executing the search warrant.
(B) granted, because the police did not inform Jason that he was under arrest and did not read him his Miranda rights.
(C) denied, because the search and seizure were incident to a lawful arrest.
(D) denied, because the police had reasonable grounds to believe that there were weapons in the house.

Question 157

As to Jason's statement, his motion to suppress should be

(A) granted, because the entry by forcing open the door was not reasonable.
(B) granted, because the police failed to read Jason his Miranda rights.
(C) denied, because the statement was volunteered.
(D) denied, because the statement was the product of a lawful public safety search.

Question 158

As to the Uzi automatic weapon, Jason's motion to suppress should be

(A) granted, because the search exceeded the scope needed to find out if other persons were present.
(B) granted, because once the object of the warrant the brown suitcase had been found and seized, no further search of the house is permitted.
(C) denied, because the police were lawfully in the bedroom and the weapon was immediately identifiable as being subject to seizure.
(D) denied, because the police were lawfully in the house and had probable cause to believe that weapons were in the house.

Question 159

Sam and two of his friends were members of a teenage street gang. While they were returning from a dance late one evening, their car collided with a car driven by an elderly woman. After an argument, Sam attacked the elderly woman with his fists and beat her to death. Sam's two friends watched, and when they saw the woman fall to the ground they urged Sam to flee. Sam was eventually apprehended and tried for manslaughter, but the jury could not decide on a verdict.

If Sam's companions are subsequently tried as accomplices to manslaughter, they should be

(A) acquitted, because Sam was not convicted of the offense.
(B) acquitted, because they did not assist or encourage Sam to commit the crime.
(C) convicted, because they urged him to flee.
(D) convicted, because they made no effort to intervene.

Question 160

During an altercation between Oscar and Martin at a company picnic, Oscar suffered a knife wound in his abdomen and Martin was charged with assault and attempted murder. At his trial, Martin seeks to offer evidence that he had been drinking at the picnic and was highly intoxicated at the time of the altercation.

In a jurisdiction that follows the common-law rules concerning admissibility of evidence of intoxication, the evidence of Martin's intoxication should be

(A) admitted without limitation.
(B) admitted subject to an instruction that it pertains only to the attempted murder charge.
(C) admitted subject to an instruction that it pertains only to the assault charge.
(D) excluded altogether.

Question 161

In a jurisdiction that has abolished the felony-murder rule, but otherwise follows the common law of murder, Sally and Ralph, both armed with automatic weapons, went into a bank to rob it. Ralph ordered all the persons in the bank to lie on the floor. When some were slow to obey, Sally, not intending to hit anyone, fired about 15 rounds into the air. One of these ricocheted off a stone column and struck and killed a customer in the bank.

Sally and Ralph were charged with murder of the customer.

Which of the following is correct?

(A) Sally can be convicted of murder, because she did the act of killing, but Ralph cannot be convicted of either murder or manslaughter.
(B) Neither can be guilty of murder, but both can be convicted of manslaughter based upon an unintentional homicide.
(C) Sally can be convicted only of manslaughter, but Ralph cannot be convicted of murder or manslaughter.
(D) Both can be convicted of murder.

Question 162

While browsing in a clothing store, Alice decided to take a purse without paying for it. She placed the purse under her coat and took a couple of steps toward the exit. She then realized that a sensor tag on the purse would set off an alarm. She placed the purse near the counter from which she had removed it.

Alice has committed:

(A) no crime, because the purse was never removed from the store.
(B) no crime, because she withdrew from her criminal enterprise.
(C) only attempted larceny, because she intended to take the purse out of the store.
(D) larceny, because she took the purse from its original location and concealed it with the intent to steal.

Question 163

At 11:00 p.m., John and Marsha were accosted in the entrance to their apartment building by Dirk, who was armed as well as masked. Dirk ordered the couple to take him into their apartment. After they entered the apartment, Dirk forced Marsha to bind and gag her husband John and then to open a safe which contained a diamond necklace. Dirk then tied her up and fled with the necklace. He was apprehended by apartment building security guards. Before the guards could return to the apartment, but after Dirk was arrested, John, straining to free himself, suffered a massive heart attack and died.

Dirk is guilty of:

(A) burglary, robbery, and murder.
(B) robbery and murder only.
(C) burglary and robbery only.
(D) robbery only.

Question 164

Grace, while baby-sitting one night, noticed that Sam, who lived next door, had left his house but that the door did not close completely behind him. Grace said to Roy, the 11-year-old boy she was baby-sitting with, "Let's play a game. You go next door and see if you can find my portable television set, which I lent to Sam, and bring it over here." Grace knew that Sam had a portable television set and Grace planned to keep the set for herself. Roy thought the set belonged to Grace, went next door, found the television set, and carried it out the front door. At that moment, Sam returned home and discovered Roy in his front yard with the television set. Roy explained the "game" he and Grace were playing. Sam took back his television set and called the police.

Grace is:

(A) not guilty of larceny or attempted larceny, because Roy did not commit any crime.
(B) not guilty of larceny but guilty of attempted larceny, because she never acquired possession of the television set.
(C) guilty of larceny as an accessory to Roy.
(D) guilty of larceny by the use of an innocent agent.

Question 165

Matt and his friend Fred were watching a football game at Matt's home when they began to argue. Fred became abusive, and Matt asked him to leave. Fred refused, walked into the kitchen, picked up a knife, and said he would cut Matt's heart out. Matt pulled a gun from under the sofa, walked to his front door, opened it, and again told Fred to leave. Fred again refused. Instead, he walked slowly toward Matt, brandishing the knife in a threatening manner. Matt, rather than running out the door himself, shot in Fred's direction, intending only to scare him. However, the bullet struck Fred, killing him instantly.

Charged with murder, Matt should be:

(A) convicted, because the use of deadly force was unreasonable under the circumstances.
(B) convicted, because he had a clear opportunity and duty to retreat.
(C) acquitted, because he did not intend to kill Fred.
(D) acquitted, because he was acting in self-defense and had no duty to retreat.

Question 166

Hannah, who was homeless, broke into the basement of a hotel and fell asleep. She was awakened by a security guard, who demanded that she leave. As Hannah was leaving, she cursed the security guard. Angered, the guard began to beat Hannah on her head with his flashlight. After the second blow, Hannah grabbed a fire extinguisher and sprayed the guard in his face, causing him to lose his sight in one eye.

The jurisdiction defines aggravated assault as assault with intent to cause serious bodily injury.

The most serious crime for which Hannah could properly be convicted is

(A) aggravated assault.
(B) burglary.

(C) assault.
(D) trespass.

Question 167

Scott held up a drugstore at 10:30 at night, and drove away. His car broke down in an isolated area just outside the small city in which the crime occurred. Scott walked to the nearest house and asked Henry, the homeowner, if he could stay until the next morning, explaining that he had been searching for his sister's home and had run out of gas. Henry agreed to let him sleep on a couch in the basement. During the course of the night, Henry began to doubt the story Scott had told him. Early the next morning, Henry called the police and said he was suspicious and frightened of a stranger whom he had allowed to stay the night. The police went immediately to the house to assist Henry and walked through the open front door. They found Scott and Henry drinking coffee in the kitchen. When they saw Scott, they realized he matched the description of the drugstore robber. They arrested Scott and in his jacket they found drugs taken during the robbery.

Scott moves to suppress the evidence of the drugs.

If the court finds that the police did not have probable cause to believe Scott was the robber until they saw him inside Henry's house and realized he matched the description, the court should

(A) grant the motion, because, as a guest, Scott has sufficient standing to contest the entry of the house without a warrant.
(B) grant the motion, because, as a guest, Scott has sufficient standing to contest the lack of probable cause at the time of the entry.
(C) deny the motion, because Scott had no ownership or other possessory interest in the premises.
(D) deny the motion, because the police had the permission of the owner to enter the house.

Question 168

Eighteen-year-old Kenneth and his 14-year-old girlfriend, Emma, made plans to meet in Kenneth's apartment to have sexual intercourse, and they did so. Emma later told her mother about the incident. Kenneth was charged with statutory rape and conspiracy to commit statutory rape.

In the jurisdiction, the age of consent is 15, and the law of conspiracy is the same as at common law.

Kenneth was convicted of both charges and given consecutive sentences. On appeal, he contends that his conspiracy conviction should be reversed.

That conviction should be

(A) affirmed, because he agreed with Emma to commit the crime.
(B) reversed, because Emma could not be a conspirator to this crime.
(C) reversed, because the crime is one that can only be committed by agreement and thus Wharton's Rule bars conspiracy liability.
(D) reversed, because one cannot conspire with a person too young to consent.

Question 169

Sam decided to kill his boss, Anna, after she told him that he would be fired if his work did not improve. Sam knew Anna was scheduled to go on a business trip on Monday morning. On Sunday morning, Sam went to the company parking garage and put a bomb in the company car that Anna usually drove. The bomb was wired to go off when the car engine started. Sam then left town. At 5 a.m. Monday, Sam, after driving all night, was overcome with remorse and had a change of heart. He called the security officer on duty at the company and told him about the bomb. The security officer said he would take care of the matter. An hour later, the officer put a note on Anna's desk telling her of the message. He then looked at the car but could not see any signs of a bomb. He printed a sign saying "DO NOT USE THIS CAR," put it on the windshield, and went to call the police. Before the police arrived, Lois, a company vice president, got into the car and started the engine. The bomb went off, killing her.

The jurisdiction defines murder in the first degree as any homicide committed with premeditation and deliberation or any murder in the commission of a common-law felony. Second-degree murder is defined as all other murder at common law. Manslaughter is defined by the common law.

Sam is guilty of

(A) murder in the first degree, because, with premeditation and deliberation, he killed whoever would start the car.
(B) murder in the second degree, because he had no intention of killing Lois.
(C) manslaughter, because at the time of the explosion, he had no intent to kill, and the death of Lois was in part the fault of the security officer.
(D) only attempted murder of Anna, because the death of Lois was the result of the security officer's negligence.

MBE QUESTIONS

AMERIBAR BAR REVIEW

Multistate Bar Examination Released Questions – Section 6

EVIDENCE

Question 1

In a prosecution of Doris for murder, the government seeks to introduce a properly authenticated note written by the victim that reads: "Doris did it." In laying the foundation for admitting the note as a dying declaration, the prosecution offered an affidavit from the attending physician that the victim knew she was about to die when she wrote the note.

The admissibility of the note as a dying declaration is

(A) a preliminary fact question for the judge, and the judge must not consider the affidavit.
(B) a preliminary fact question for the judge, and the judge may properly consider the affidavit.
(C) a question of weight and credibility for the jury, and the jury must not consider the affidavit,
(D) a question of weight and credibility for the jury, and the jury may properly consider the affidavit.

Question 2

Dirk is on trial for the brutal murder of Villas. Dirk's first witness, Wesley, testified that in her opinion Dirk is a peaceful and nonviolent person. The prosecution does not cross-examine Wesley, who is then excused from further attendance.

Which one of the following is INADMISSIBLE during the prosecution's rebuttal?

(A) Testimony by Wesley's former employer that Wesley submitted a series of false expense vouchers two years ago.
(B) Testimony by a police officer that Dirk has a long-standing reputation in the community as having a violent temper.
(C) Testimony by a neighbor that Wesley has a long-standing reputation in the community as an untruthful person.
(D) Testimony by Dirk's former cell mate that he overheard Wesley offer to provide favorable testimony if Dirk would pay her $5,000.

Question 3

Deeb was charged with stealing furs from a van. At trial, Wallace testified she saw Deeb take the furs.
The jurisdiction in which Deeb is being tried does not allow in evidence lie detector results. On cross-examination by Deeb's attorney, Wallace was asked, "The light was too dim to identify Deeb, wasn't it?"

She responded, "I'm sure enough that it was Deeb that I passed a lie detector test administered by the police."

Deeb's attorney immediately objects and moves to strike.
The trial court should

(A) grant the motion, because the question was leading.
(B) grant the motion, because the probative value of the unresponsive testimony is substantially outweighed by the danger of unfair prejudice.
(C) deny the motion, because it is proper rehabilitation of an impeached witness.
(D) deny the motion, because Deeb's attorney "opened the door" by asking the question.

Question 4

Park sued Officer Dinet for false arrest. Dinet's defense was that, based on a description he heard over the police radio, he reasonably believed Park was an armed robber. Police radio dispatcher Brigg, reading from a note, had broadcast the description of an armed robber on which Dinet claims to have relied.
The defendant offers the following items of evidence:

    I. Dinet's testimony relating the description he heard.
    II. Brigg's testimony relating the description he read over the radio.
    III. The note containing the description Brigg testifies he read over the radio.

Which of the following are admissible on the issue of what description Dinet heard?

(A) I and II only.
(B) I and III only.
(C) II and III only.
(D) I, II, and III.

Question 5

Dalton is on trial for burglary. During cross-examination of Dalton, the prosecutor wants to inquire about Dalton's earlier conviction for falsifying a credit application.

Which of the following facts concerning the conviction would be the best reason for the trial court's refusing to allow such examination?

(A) Dalton was released from prison 12 years ago.
(B) Dalton was put on probation rather than imprisoned.
(C) It was for a misdemeanor rather than a felony.
(D) It is on appeal.

Question 6

Perez sued Dawson for damages arising out of an automobile collision. At trial, Perez called Minter, an eyewitness to the collision. Perez expected Minter to testify that she had observed Dawson's automobile for five seconds prior to the collision and estimated Dawson's speed at the time of the collision to have been 50 miles per hour. Instead, Minter testified that she estimated Dawson's speed to have been 25 miles per hour.

Without finally excusing Minter as a witness, Perez then called Wallingford, a police officer, to testify that Minter had told him during his investigation at the accident scene that Dawson "was doing at least 50."
Wallingford's testimony is

(A) admissible as a present sense impression.
(B) admissible to impeach Minter.
(C) inadmissible, because Perez may not impeach his own witness.
(D) inadmissible, because it is hearsay not within any exception.

Question 7

Deetz was prosecuted for homicide. He testified that he shot in self-defense. In rebuttal, Officer Watts testified that he came to the scene in response to a telephone call from Deetz. Watts offers to testify that he asked, "What is the problem here, sir?" and Deetz replied, "I was cleaning my gun and it went off accidentally."

The offered testimony is

(A) admissible, as an excited utterance.
(B) admissible, to impeach Deetz and as evidence that he did not act in self-defense.
(C) inadmissible, because of Deetz's privilege against self-incrimination.
(D) inadmissible, because it tends to exculpate without corroboration.

Question 8

Park sued Dunlevy for copyright infringement for using in Dunlevy's book some slightly disguised house plans on which Park held the copyright. Park is prepared to testify that he heard Dunlevy's executive assistant for copyright matters say that Dunlevy had obtained an advance copy of the plans from Park's office manager.

Park's testimony is

(A) admissible as reporting a statement of an employee of a party opponent.
(B) admissible as a statement of a co-conspirator.
(C) inadmissible, because it is hearsay not within any exception.
(D) inadmissible, because there is no showing that the assistant was authorized to speak for Dunlevy.

Question 9

Decker, charged with armed robbery of a store, denied that he was the person who had robbed the store.
In presenting the state's case, the prosecutor seeks to introduce evidence that Decker had robbed two other stores in the past year.

This evidence is

(A) admissible, to prove a pertinent trait of Decker's character and Decker's action in conformity therewith.
(B) admissible, to prove Decker's intent and identity.
(C) inadmissible, because character must be proved by reputation or opinion and may not be proved by specific acts.
(D) inadmissible, because its probative value is substantially outweighed by the danger of unfair prejudice.

Question 10

Paulsen Corporation sued Dorr for ten fuel oil deliveries not paid for. Dorr denied that the deliveries were made. At trial, Paulsen calls its office manager, Wicks, to testify that Paulsen employees always record each delivery in duplicate, give one copy to the customer, and place the other copy in Paulsen's files; that he (Wicks) is the custodian of those files; and that his examination of the files before coming to court revealed that the ten deliveries were made.

Wicks's testimony that the invoices show ten deliveries is

(A) admissible, because it is based on regularly kept business records.
(B) admissible, because Wicks has first- hand knowledge of the contents of the records.
(C) inadmissible, because the records must be produced in order to prove their contents.
(D) inadmissible, because the records are self-serving.

Question 11

In litigation on a federal claim, Plaintiff had the burden of proving that Defendant received a notice. Plaintiff relied on the presumption of receipt by offering evidence that the notice was addressed to Defendant, properly stamped, and mailed. Defendant, on the other hand, testified that she never received the notice.

Which of the following is correct?

(A) The jury must find that the notice was received.
(B) The jury may find that the notice was received.
(C) The burden shifts to Defendant to persuade the jury of nonreceipt.
(D) The jury must find that the notice was not received, because the presumption has been rebutted and there is uncontradicted evidence of nonreceipt.

Question 12

In a medical malpractice suit by Payne against Dr. Dock, Payne seeks to introduce a properly authenticated photocopy of Payne's hospital chart. The chart contained a notation made by a medical resident that an aortic clamp had broken during Payne's surgery. The resident made the notation in the regular course of practice, but had no personal knowledge of the operation, and cannot remember which of the operating physicians gave him the information.

The document is

(A) admissible as a record of regularly conducted activity.
(B) admissible as recorded recollection.
(C) inadmissible as a violation of the best evidence rule.
(D) inadmissible, because it is hearsay within hearsay.

Question 13

Parr sued Davis for damages for physical injuries allegedly caused by Davis's violation of the federal civil rights law. The incident occurred wholly within the state of Chippewa but the case was tried in federal court. The Chippewa state code says, "The common-law privileges are preserved intact in this state."

At trial, Davis called Dr. Webb, Parr's physician, to testify to confidential statements made to him by Parr in furtherance of medical treatment for the injuries allegedly caused by Davis. Parr objects, claiming a physician-patient privilege.

The court should apply

(A) state law and recognize the claim of privilege.
(B) federal law and recognize the claim of privilege.
(C) state law and reject the claim of privilege.
(D) federal law and reject the claim of privilege.

Question 14

In a prosecution of Dahle for assault, Wharton is called to testify that the victim, Valerian, had complained to Wharton that Dahle was the assailant.

Wharton's testimony is most likely to be admitted if Wharton is

(A) a doctor, whom Valerian consulted for treatment.
(B) a minister, whom Valerian consulted for counseling.
(C) Valerian's husband, whom she telephoned immediately after the event.
(D) a police officer, whom Valerian called on instructions from her husband.

Question 15

At Darrow's trial for stealing an automobile, Darrow called a character witness, Goode, who testified that Darrow had an excellent reputation for honesty. In rebuttal, the prosecutor calls Wick to testify that he recently saw Darrow cheat on a college examination.

This evidence should be

(A) admitted, because Darrow has "opened the door" to the prosecutor's proof of bad character evidence.
(B) admitted, because the cheating involves "dishonesty or false statement."
(C) excluded, because it has no probative value on any issue in the case.
(D) excluded, because Darrow's cheating can be inquired into only on cross examination of Goode.

Question 16

Pitt sued Dill for damages for back injuries received in a car wreck. Dill disputed the damages and sought to prove that Pitt's disability, if any, resulted from a childhood horseback riding accident. Pitt admitted the childhood accident, but contended it had no lasting effect.

Pitt calls Dr. Webb, an orthopedist who had never examined Pitt, and poses to Webb a hypothetical question as to the cause of the disability that omits any reference to the horseback riding accident. The question was not provided to opposing counsel before trial.

The best ground for objecting to this question would be that

(A) Webb lacked firsthand knowledge concerning Pitt's condition.
(B) the hypothetical question omitted a clearly significant fact.
(C) hypothetical questions are no longer permitted.
(D) sufficient notice of the hypothetical question was not given to opposing counsel before trial.

Question 17

Daggett was prosecuted for murder of Vales, whose body was found one morning in the street near Daggett's house. The state calls Witt, a neighbor, to testify that during the night before the body was found he heard Daggett's wife scream, "You killed him! You killed him!"

Witt's testimony is

(A)   admissible as a report of a statement of belief.
(B)   admissible as a report of an excited utterance.
(C)   inadmissible, because it reports a privileged spousal communication.
(D)   inadmissible on spousal immunity grounds, but only if the wife objects.

Question 18

Darby was prosecuted for sexually abusing his 13-year-old stepdaughter, Wendy. Wendy testified to Darby's conduct. On cross-examination, defense counsel asks Wendy, "Isn't it true that shortly before you complained that Darby abused you, he punished you for maliciously ruining some of his phonograph records?"

The question is

(A) proper, because it relates to a possible motive for Wendy to accuse Darby falsely.
(B) proper, because Wendy's misconduct is relevant to her character for veracity.
(C) improper, because the incident had nothing to do with Wendy's truthfulness.

(D) improper, because it falls outside the scope of direct examination.

Question 19

Paul sued Dyer for personal injuries sustained when Dyer's car hit Paul, a pedestrian. Immediately after the accident, Dyer got out of his car, raced over to Paul, and said, "Don't worry, I'll pay your hospital bill."

Paul's testimony concerning Dyer's statement is

(A) admissible, because it is an admission of liability by a party opponent.
(B) admissible, because it is within the excited utterance exception to the hearsay rule.
(C) inadmissible to prove liability, because it is an offer to pay medical expenses.
(D) inadmissible, provided that Dyer kept his promise to pay Paul's medical expenses.

Question 20

Dooley and Melville were charged with conspiracy to dispose of a stolen diamond necklace. Melville jumped bail and cannot be found. Proceeding to trial against Dooley alone, the prosecutor calls Wixon, Melville's girlfriend, to testify that Melville confided to her that "Dooley said I still owe him some of the money from selling that necklace."
Wixon's testimony is

(A) admissible as evidence of a statement by party-opponent Dooley.
(B) admissible as evidence of a statement against interest by Melville.
(C) inadmissible, because Melville's statement was not in furtherance of the conspiracy.
(D) inadmissible, because Melville is not shown to have firsthand knowledge that the necklace was stolen.

Question 21

In a civil action for personal injury, Payne alleges that he was beaten up by Dabney during an altercation in a crowded bar. Dabney's defense is that he was not the person who hit Payne. To corroborate his testimony about the cause of his injuries, Payne seeks to introduce, through the hospital records custodian, a notation in a regular medical record made by an emergency room doctor at the hospital where Payne was treated for his injuries. The notation is: "Patient says he was attacked by Dabney."

The notation is

(A) inadmissible, unless the doctor who made the record is present at trial and available for cross-examination.
(B) inadmissible as hearsay not within any exception.
(C) admissible as hearsay within the exception for records of regularly conducted activity.
(D) admissible as a statement made for the purpose of medical diagnosis or treatment.

Question 22

Dexter was tried for the homicide of a girl whose strangled body was found beside a remote logging road with her hands taped together. After Dexter offered evidence of alibi, the state calls Wilma to testify that Dexter had taped her hands and tried to strangle her in the same location two days before the homicide but that she escaped.

The evidence is

(A) admissible, as tending to show Dexter is the killer.
(B) admissible, as tending to show Dexter's violent nature.
(C) inadmissible, because it is improper character evidence.
(D) inadmissible, because it is unfairly prejudicial.

Question 23

Davidson and Smythe were charged with burglary of a warehouse. They were tried separately. At Davidson's trial, Smythe testified that he saw Davidson commit the burglary. While Smythe is still subject to recall as a witness, Davidson calls Smythe's cellmate, Walton, to testify that Smythe said, "I broke into the warehouse alone because Davidson was too drunk to help."
This evidence of Smythe's statement is

(A) admissible as a declaration against penal interest.
(B) admissible as a prior inconsistent statement.
(C) inadmissible, because it is hearsay not within any exception.
(D) inadmissible, because the statement is not clearly corroborated.

Question 24

Parker sues Dix for breach of a promise made in a letter allegedly written by Dix to Parker. Dix denies writing the letter.

Which of the following would NOT be a sufficient basis for admitting the letter into evidence?

(A) Testimony by Parker that she is familiar with Dix's signature and recognizes it on the letter.
(B) Comparison by the trier of fact of the letter with an admitted signature of Dix.
(C) Opinion testimony of a nonexpert witness based upon familiarity acquired in order to authenticate the signature.
(D) Evidence that the letter was written in response to one written by Parker to Dix.

Question 25

In a prosecution of Dale for murdering Vera, Dale testified that the killing had occurred in self defense when Vera tried to shoot him. In rebuttal, the prosecution seeks to call Walter, Vera's father, to testify that the day before the killing Vera told Walter that she loved Dale so much she could never hurt him. Walter's testimony is

(A) admissible within the hearsay exception for statements of the declarant's then existing state of mind.
(B) admissible, because Vera is unavailable as a witness.
(C) inadmissible as hearsay not within any exception.
(D) inadmissible, because Vera's character is not an issue

Question 26

Defendant is on trial for the crime of obstructing justice by concealing records subpoenaed May 1, in a government investigation. The government calls Attorney to testify that on May 3, Defendant asked him how to comply with the regulations regarding the transfer of records to a safe-deposit box in Mexico.
The testimony of Attorney is

(A) privileged, because it relates to conduct outside the jurisdiction of the United States.
(B) privileged, because an attorney is required to keep the confidences of his clients.
(C) not privileged, provided Attorney knew of the concededly illegal purpose for which the advice was sought.
(D) not privileged, whether or not Attorney knew of the concededly illegal purpose for which the advice was sought.

Question 27

Denn is on trial for arson. In its case in chief, the prosecution offers evidence that Denn had secretly obtained duplicate insurance from two companies on the property that burned and that Denn had threatened to kill his ex-wife if she testified for the prosecution.

The court should admit evidence of

(A) Denn's obtaining duplicate insurance only.
(B) Denn's threatening to kill his ex-wife only.
(C) both Denn's obtaining duplicate insurance and threatening to kill his ex-wife.
(D) neither Denn's obtaining duplicate insurance nor threatening to kill his ex-wife.

Question 28

Roberta Monk, a famous author, had a life insurance policy with Drummond Life Insurance Company. Her son, Peter, was beneficiary. Roberta disappeared from her residence in the city of Metropolis two years ago and has not been seen since. On the day that Roberta disappeared, Sky Airlines Flight 22 left Metropolis for Rio de Janeiro and vanished; the plane's passenger list included a Roberta Rector.

Peter is now suing Drummond Life Insurance Company for the proceeds of his mother's policy. At trial, Peter offers to testify that his mother told him that she planned to write her next novel under the pen name of Roberta Rector.

Peter's testimony is

(A) admissible as circumstantial evidence that Roberta Monk was on the plane.
(B) admissible as a party admission, because Roberta and Peter Monk are in privity with each other.
(C) inadmissible, because Roberta Monk has not been missing more than seven years.
(D) inadmissible, because it is hearsay not within any exception.

Question 29

Which of the following items of evidence is LEAST likely to be admitted without a supporting witness?

(A) In a libel action, a copy of a newspaper purporting to be published by Defendant Newspaper Publishing Company.
(B) In a case involving contaminated food, a can label purporting to identify the canner as Defendant Company.
(C) In a defamation case, a document purporting to be a memorandum from the Defendant Company

president to "All Personnel," printed on Defendant's letterhead.
(D) In a case involving injury to a pedestrian, a pamphlet on stopping distances issued by the State Highway Department.

Question 30

Under the rule allowing exclusion of relevant evidence because its probative value is substantially outweighed by other considerations, which of the following is NOT to be considered?

(A) The jury may be confused about the appropriate application of the evidence to the issues of the case.
(B) The evidence is likely to arouse unfair prejudice on the part of the jury,
(C) The opponent is surprised by the evidence and not fairly prepared to meet it.
(D) The trial will be extended and made cumbersome by hearing evidence of relatively trivial consequence.

Question 31

In contract litigation between Pixley and Dill, a fact of consequence to the determination of the action is whether Pixley provided Dill with a required notice at Dill's branch office "in the state capital." Pixley introduced evidence that he gave notice at Dill's office in the city of Capitan. Although Capitan is the state's capital, Pixley failed to offer proof of that fact.

Which of the following statements is most clearly correct with respect to possible judicial notice of the fact that Capitan is the state's capital?

(A) The court may take judicial notice even though Pixley does not request it.
(B) The court may take judicial notice only if Pixley provides the court with an authenticated copy of the statute that designates Capitan as the capital.
(C) If the court takes judicial notice, the burden of persuasion on the issue of whether Capitan is the capital shifts to Dill.
(D) If the court takes judicial notice, it should instruct the jury that it may, but is not required to, accept as conclusive the fact that Capitan is the capital.

Question 32

In an automobile negligence action by Popkin against Dwyer, Juilliard testified for Popkin. Dwyer later called Watts, who testified that Juilliard's reputation for truthfulness was bad.

On cross-examination of Watts, Popkin's counsel asks, "Isn't it a fact that when you bought your new car last year, you made a false affidavit to escape paying the sales tax?"

This question is

(A) proper, because it will indicate Watts's standard of judgment as to reputation for truthfulness.
(B) proper, because it bears on Watts's credibility.
(C) improper, because character cannot be proved by specific instances of conduct.
(D) improper, because one cannot impeach an impeaching witness.

Question 33

Poole sued Darrel for unlawfully using Poole's idea for an animal robot as a character in Darrel's science fiction movie. Darrel admitted that he had received a model of an animal robot from Poole, but he denied that it had any substantial similarity to the movie character. After the model had been returned to Poole, Poole destroyed it.

In order for Poole to testify to the appearance of the model, Poole

(A) must show that he did not destroy the model in bad faith.
(B) must give advance notice of his intent to introduce the oral testimony.
(C) must introduce a photograph of the model if one exists.
(D) need do none of the above, because the "best evidence rule" applies only to writings, recordings, and photographs.

Question 34

In a prosecution of Drew for forgery, the defense objects to the testimony of West, a government expert, on the ground of inadequate qualifications. The government seeks to introduce a letter from the expert's former criminology professor, stating that West is generally acknowledged in his field as well qualified.

On the issue of the expert's qualifications, the letter may be considered by

(A) the jury, without regard to the hearsay rule.
(B) the judge, without regard to the hearsay rule.

(C) neither the judge nor the jury, because it is hearsay not within any exception.
(D) both the judge and the jury, because the letter is not offered for a hearsay purpose.

Question 35

In a federal court diversity action by Plant against Decord on an insurance claim, a question arose whether the court should apply a presumption that, where both husband and wife were killed in a common accident, the husband died last.

Whether this presumption should be applied is to be determined according to

(A) traditional common law.
(B) federal statutory law.
(C) the law of the state whose substantive law is applied.
(D) the federal common law.

Question 36

Dahle is charged with possession of heroin. Prosecution witness Walker, an experienced dog trainer, testified that he was in the airport with a dog trained to detect heroin. As Dahle approached, the dog immediately became alert and pawed and barked frantically at Dahle's briefcase. Dahle managed to run outside and throw his briefcase into the river, from which it could not be recovered. After Walker's experience is established, he is asked to testify as an expert that the dog's reaction told him that Dahle's briefcase contained heroin.

Walker's testimony is

(A) admissible, as evidence of Dahle's guilt.
(B) admissible, because an expert may rely on hearsay.
(C) inadmissible, because it is based on hearsay not within any exception.
(D) inadmissible, because of the unreliability of the reactions of an animal.

Question 37

Peterson sued Dylan for libel. After Peterson testified that Dylan wrote to Peterson's employer that Peterson was a thief, Dylan offers evidence that Peterson once stole money from a former employer.

The evidence of Peterson's prior theft is

(A) admissible, as substantive evidence to prove that Peterson is a thief.
(B) admissible, but only to impeach Peterson's credibility.
(C) inadmissible, because character may not be shown by specific instances of conduct.
(D) inadmissible, because such evidence is more unfairly prejudicial than probative.

Question 38

Dickinson was charged with possession of cocaine. At Dickinson's trial, the prosecution established that, when approached by police on a suburban residential street corner, Dickinson dropped a plastic bag and ran, and that when the police returned to the corner a few minutes later after catching Dickinson, they found a plastic bag containing white powder. Dickinson objects to introduction of this bag (the contents of which would later be established to be cocaine), citing lack of adequate identification.

The objection should be

(A) overruled, because there is sufficient evidence to find that the bag was the one Dickinson dropped.
(B) overruled, because the objection should have been made on the basis of incomplete chain of custody.
(C) sustained, because Dickinson did not have possession of the bag at the time he was arrested.
(D) sustained, unless the judge makes a finding by a preponderance of the evidence that the bag was the one dropped by Dickinson.

Question 39

A threatening telephone call that purports to be from Defendant to Witness is most likely to be admitted against Defendant if

(A) the caller identified himself as Defendant.
(B) Witness had previously given damaging testimony against Defendant in another lawsuit.
(C) Witness had given his unlisted number only to Defendant and a few other persons.
(D) Witness believes that Defendant is capable of making such threats.

Question 40

In an automobile collision case brought by Poe against Davies, Poe introduced evidence that Ellis made an excited utterance that Davies ran the red light.

Davies called Witt to testify that later Ellis, a bystander, now deceased, told Witt that Davies went through a yellow light.

Witt's testimony should be

(A) excluded, because it is hearsay not within any exception.
(B) excluded, because Ellis is not available to explain or deny the inconsistency.
(C) admitted only for the purpose of impeaching Ellis.
(D) admitted as impeachment and as substantive evidence of the color of the light.

Question 41

Pate sued Dr. Doke for psychiatric malpractice and called Dr. Will as an expert witness. During Will's direct testimony, Will identified a text as a reliable authority in the field. He seeks to read to the jury passages from this book on which he had relied in forming his opinion on the proper standard of care.

The passage is

(A) admissible, as a basis for his opinion and as substantive evidence of the proper standard of care.
(B) admissible, as a basis for his opinion but not as substantive evidence of the proper standard of care.
(C) inadmissible, because a witness's credibility cannot be supported unless attacked.
(D) inadmissible, because the passage should be received as an exhibit and not read to the jury by the witness.

Question 42

In a suit by Palmer against Denby, Palmer sought to subpoena an audiotape on which Denby had narrated his version of the dispute for his attorney. Counsel for Denby moves to quash the subpoena on the ground of privilege.

The audiotape is most likely to be subject to subpoena if

(A) Denby played the audiotape for his father to get his reactions.
(B) the lawsuit involved alleged criminal behavior by Denby.
(C) Denby has been deposed and there is good reason to believe that the audiotape may contain inconsistent statements.

(D) Denby is deceased and thus unavailable to give testimony in person.

Question 43

Pawn sued Dalton for injuries received when she fell down a stairway in Dalton's apartment building. Pawn, a guest in the building, alleged that she caught the heel of her shoe in a tear in the stair carpet. Pawn calls Witt, a tenant, to testify that Young, another tenant, had said to him a week before Pawn's fall: "When I paid my rent this morning, I told the manager he had better fix that torn carpet."

Young's statement, reported by Witt, is

(A) admissible, to prove that the carpet was defective.
(B) admissible, to prove that Dalton had notice of the defect.
(C) admissible, to prove both that the carpet was defective and that Dalton had notice of the defect.
(D) inadmissible, because it is hearsay not within any exception.

Question 44

Defendant was prosecuted for bankruptcy fraud. Defendant's wife, now deceased, had testified adversely to Defendant during earlier bankruptcy proceedings that involved similar issues. Although the wife had been cross-examined, no serious effort was made to challenge her credibility despite the availability of significant impeachment information. At the fraud trial, the prosecutor offers into evidence the testimony given by Defendant's wife at the bankruptcy proceeding.

This evidence should be

(A) admitted, under the hearsay exception for former testimony.
(B) admitted, because it is a statement by a person identified with a party.
(C) excluded, because it is hearsay not within any exception.
(D) excluded, because Defendant has the right to prevent use of his spouse's testimony against him in a criminal case.

Question 45

Defendant was charged with possession of cocaine with intent to distribute. He had been stopped while driving a car and several pounds of cocaine were found in the trunk. In his opening statement, defendant's counsel asserted that his client had no key to the trunk and no knowledge of its contents. The prosecutor offers the state motor vehicle registration, shown to have been found in the glove compartment of the car, listing Defendant as the owner.

The registration should be

(A) admitted, as a statement against interest.
(B) admitted, as evidence of Defendant's close connection with the car and, therefore, knowledge of its contents.
(C) excluded, unless authenticated by testimony of or certification by a state official charged with custody of vehicle registration records.
(D) excluded, as hearsay not within any exception.

Question 46

Post sued Dint for dissolution of their year-long partnership. One issue concerned the amount of money Post had received in cash. It was customary for Dint to give Post money from the cash register as Post needed it for personal expenses. Post testified that, as he received money, he jotted down the amounts in the partnership ledger. Although Dint had access to the ledger, he made no changes in it. The ledger was admitted into evidence. Dint seeks to testify to his memory of much larger amounts he had given Post.

Dint's testimony is

(A) admissible, because it is based on Dint's firsthand knowledge.
(B) admissible, because the ledger entries offered by a party opponent opened the door.
(C) inadmissible, because the ledger is the best evidence of the amounts Post received.
(D) inadmissible, because Dint's failure to challenge the accuracy of the ledger constituted an adoptive admission.

Question 47

Dix is on trial for killing Vetter. The prosecutor calls Winn to testify that after being shot, Vetter said, "Dix did it." Before the testimony is given, Dix's lawyer asks for a hearing on whether Vetter believed his death was imminent when he made the statement.

Before permitting evidence of the dying declaration, the judge should hear evidence on the issue from

(A) both sides, with the jury not present, and decide whether Winn may testify to Vetter's statement.
(B) both sides, with the jury present, and decide whether Winn may testify to Vetter's statement.
(C) both sides, with the jury present, and allow the jury to determine whether Winn may testify to Vetter's statement.
(D) the prosecutor only, with the jury not present, and if the judge believes a jury could reasonably find that Vetter knew he was dying, permit Winn to testify to the statement, with Dix allowed to offer evidence on the issue as a part of the defendant's case.

Question 48

Park sued Davis Co. for injuries suffered in the crash of Park's dune buggy, allegedly caused by a defective auto part manufactured by Davis Co. Davis Co. claims that the part was a fraudulent imitation, not produced by Davis Co.

Which of the following is NOT admissible on the issue of whether the part was manufactured by Davis Co.?

(A) The fact that the defective part bears Davis Co.'s insignia or trademark.
(B) Testimony that the part was purchased from a parts house to which Davis Co. regularly sold parts.
(C) The part itself and a concededly genuine part manufactured by Davis Co. (for the jury's comparison).
(D) A judgment for another plaintiff against Davis Co. in another case involving substantially similar facts.

Question 49

Dean was prosecuted in federal court for making threats against the President of the United States. Dean was a voluntary patient in a private psychiatric hospital and told a nurse, shortly before the President came to town, that Dean planned to shoot the President. The nurse reported the threat to FBI agents.

Dean's motion to prevent the nurse from testifying is likely to be

(A) successful, because the statement was made in a medical setting.
(B) successful, because the nurse violated a confidence in reporting the statement.

(C) unsuccessful, because the statement was not within any privilege.
(D) unsuccessful, because Dean had not been committed involuntarily by court order.

Question 50

Damson was charged with murder, and Wagner testified for the prosecution. On cross-examination of Wagner, Damson seeks to elicit an admission that Wagner was also charged with the same murder and that the prosecutor told her, "If you testify against Damson, we will drop the charges against you after the conclusion of Damson's trial."

The evidence about the prosecutor's promise is

(A) admissible, as proper impeachment of Wagner.
(B) admissible, as an admission by an agent of a party-opponent.
(C) inadmissible, because the law encourages plea-bargaining.
(D) inadmissible, because the evidence is hearsay not within any exception.

Question 51

Prescott sued Doxie for fraud. After verdict for Prescott, Doxie talked with juror Wall about the trial.

Doxie's motion for a new trial would be most likely granted if Wall is willing to testify that he voted for Prescott because he

(A) misunderstood the judge's instructions concerning the standard of proof in a fraud case.
(B) was feeling ill and needed to get home quickly.
(C) relied on testimony that the judge had stricken and ordered the jury to disregard.
(D) learned from a court clerk that Doxie had been accused of fraud in several recent lawsuits.

Question 52

Deben was charged with using a forged prescription from a Dr. Kohl to obtain Percodan® from Smith's Drugstore on May 1. At trial, Smith identified Deben as the customer, but Deben testified that he had not been in the store.

In rebuttal, the prosecutor calls Wallman and Witler to testify that on May 1 a man they identified as Deben had presented prescriptions for Percodan® from a Dr. Kohl at, respectively, Wallman's Drugs and Witler's Drugstore.

Wallman's and Witler's testimony is

(A) admissible, to prove a pertinent trait of Deben's character and Deben's action in conformity therewith.
(B) admissible, to identify the man who presented the prescription at Smith's Drugstore.
(C) inadmissible, because it proves specific acts rather than reputation or opinion.
(D) inadmissible, because other crimes may not be used to show propensity.

Question 53

Dove is on trial for theft. At trial, the prosecutor called John and May Wong. They testified that, as they looked out their apartment window, they saw thieves across the street break the window of a jewelry store, take jewelry, and leave in a car. Mrs. Wong telephoned the police and relayed to them the license number of the thieves' car as Mr. Wong looked out the window with binoculars and read it to her. Neither of them has any present memory of the number. The prosecutor offers as evidence a properly authenticated police tape recording of May Wong's telephone call with her voice giving the license number, which is independently shown to belong to Dove's car.

The tape recording of May Wong's stating the license number is

(A) admissible, under the hearsay exception for present sense impressions.
(B) admissible, as nonhearsay circumstantial evidence.
(C) inadmissible, because it is hearsay not within any exception.
(D) inadmissible, because May Wong never had firsthand knowledge of the license number.

Question 54

Pike sued Day City Community Church for damages he suffered when Pike crashed his motorcycle in an attempt to avoid a cow that had escaped from its corral. The cow and corral belonged to a farm that had recently been left by will to the church. At trial, Pike seeks to ask Defendant's witness, Winters, whether she is a member of that church.

The question is

(A) improper, because evidence of a witness's religious beliefs is not admissible to impeach credibility.

(B) improper, because it violates First Amendment and privacy rights.
(C) proper, for the purpose of ascertaining partiality or bias.
(D) proper, for the purpose of showing capacity to appreciate the nature and obligation of an oath.

Question 55

Mr. Denby was charged with the sale of narcotics. The federal prosecutor arranged with Mrs. Denby for her to testify against her husband in exchange for leniency in her case. At trial, the prosecution calls Mrs. Denby, who had been granted immunity from prosecution, to testify, among other things, that she saw her husband sell an ounce of heroin.

Which of the following statements is most clearly correct in the federal courts?

(A) Mrs. Denby cannot be called as a witness over her husband's objection.
(B) Mrs. Denby can be called as a witness but cannot testify, over Mr. Denby's objection, that she saw him sell heroin.
(C) Mrs. Denby can refuse to be a witness against her husband.
(D) Mrs. Denby can be required to be a witness and to testify that she saw her husband sell heroin.

Question 56

Daniel is on trial for evading $100,000 in taxes. The prosecution offers in evidence an anonymous letter to the IRS, identified as being in Daniel's handwriting, saying, "I promised my mother on her deathbed I would try to pay my back taxes. Here is $10,000. I'll make other payments if you promise not to prosecute. Answer yes by personal ad saying, 'OK on tax deal.'"

The letter is

(A) admissible, as a statement of present intention or plan.
(B) admissible, as an admission of a party opponent.
(C) inadmissible, because it is an effort to settle a claim.
(D) inadmissible, because the probative value is substantially outweighed by the risk of unfair prejudice.

Question 57

Doppler is charged with aggravated assault on Vezy, a game warden. Doppler testified that, when he was confronted by Vezy, who was armed and out of uniform, Doppler believed Vezy was a robber and shot in self-defense. The state calls Willy to testify that a year earlier, he had seen Doppler shoot a man without provocation and thereafter falsely claim self-defense.

Willy's testimony is

(A) admissible, as evidence of Doppler's untruthfulness.
(B) admissible, as evidence that Doppler did not act in self-defense on this occasion.
(C) inadmissible, because it is improper character evidence.
(D) inadmissible, because it is irrelevant to the defense Doppler raised.

Question 58

Pamela sued Driver for damages for the death of Pamela's husband Ronald, resulting from an automobile collision. At trial, Driver calls Ronald's doctor to testify that the day before his death, Ronald, in great pain, said, "It was my own fault; there's nobody to blame but me."

The doctor's testimony should be admitted as

(A) a statement against interest.
(B) a dying declaration.
(C) a statement of Ronald's then existing state of mind.
(D) an excited utterance.

Question 59

Prine sued Dover for an assault that occurred March 5 in California. To support his defense that he was in Utah on that date, Dover identifies and seeks to introduce a letter he wrote to his sister a week before the assault in which he stated that he would see her in Utah on March 5.

The letter is

(A) admissible, within the state of mind exception to the hearsay rule.
(B) admissible, as a prior consistent statement to support Dover's credibility as a witness.
(C) inadmissible, because it lacks sufficient probative value.
(D) inadmissible, because it is a statement of belief to prove the fact believed.

Question 60

Plaza Hotel sued Plaza House Hotel for infringement of its trade name. To establish a likelihood of name confusion, Plaintiff Plaza Hotel offers a series of memoranda which it had asked its employees to prepare at the end of each day listing instances during the day in which telephone callers, cab drivers, customers, and others had confused the two names.

The memoranda should be

(A) excluded, because they are more unfairly prejudicial and confusing than probative.
(B) excluded, because they are hearsay not within any exception.
(C) admitted, because they are records of regularly conducted business activity.
(D) admitted, because they are past recollection recorded.

Question 61

Peter sued Don for breach of contract. The court admitted testimony by Peter that Don and his wife quarreled frequently, a fact of no consequence to the lawsuit. Don seeks to testify in response that he and his wife never quarreled. The court

(A) must permit Don to answer if he had objected to Peter's testimony.
(B) may permit Don to answer, whether or not he had objected to Peter's testimony.
(C) may permit Don to answer only if he had objected to Peter's testimony.
(D) cannot permit Don to answer, whether or not he had objected to Peter's testimony.

Question 62

Mary Webb, a physician, called as a witness by the defendant in the case of Parr v. Doan, was asked to testify to statements made by Michael Zadok, her patient, for the purpose of obtaining treatment from Dr. Webb. Which of the following is the best basis for excluding evidence of Zadok's statements in a jurisdiction with a doctor-patient privilege?

(A) An objection by Dr. Webb asserting her privilege against disclosure of confidential communications made by a patient.
(B) An objection by Parr's attorney on the grounds of the doctor-patient privilege.
(C) A finding by the trial judge that Zadok had left the office without actually receiving treatment.
(D) The assertion of a privilege by Zadok's attorney, present at the trial as a spectator at Zadok's request, and allowed by the trial judge to speak.

Question 63

A leading question is LEAST likely to be permitted over objection when

(A) asked on cross-examination of an expert witness.
(B) asked on direct examination of a young child.
(C) asked on direct examination of a disinterested eyewitness.
(D) related to preliminary matters such as the name or occupation of the witness.

Question 64

Lawyers Abel and Baker are the members of the law partnership of Abel and Baker in a small town that has only one other lawyer in it. Abel and Baker do a substantial amount of personal injury work. Client was severely and permanently injured in an automobile collision when struck by an automobile driven by Motorist. Client employed the Abel and Baker firm to represent her in obtaining damages for her injuries. At the time Client employed Abel and Baker, the statute of limitations had six weeks to run on her claim. The complaint was prepared but not filed. Abel and Baker each thought that the other would file the complaint. The statute of limitations ran on Client's claim against Motorist.

Client has filed suit against Abel and Baker for negligence. That case is on trial with a jury in a court of general jurisdiction.

In order to establish a breach of standard of care owed to her by Abel and Baker, Client

(A) must have a legal expert from the same locality testify that defendants' conduct was a breach.
(B) must have a legal expert from the same state testify that defendants' conduct was a breach.
(C) can rely on the application of the jurors' common knowledge as to whether there was a breach.
(D) can rely on the judge, as an expert in the law, to advise the jury whether there was a breach.

Questions 65-68 are based on the following fact situation.

Penn sues Duke's Bar for injuries suffered in an automobile accident caused by Chase, who had been a patron of Duke's Bar. Penn claims that Chase was permitted to drink too much liquor at Duke's Bar before the accident.

Question 65

Wood, a patron of Duke's Bar, testified that on the night of the accident Chase was drunk. Wood then proposed to testify that he remarked to his companion, "Chase is so drunk he can't even stand up." Wood's remark to his companion is

(A) admissible as an excited utterance.
(B) admissible as a prior consistent statement.
(C) admissible as a statement by Wood regarding a condition he observed, made while he was observing it.
(D) inadmissible if there was no evidence that Wood had expertise in determining drunkenness.

Question 66

Duke's Bar called Chase to testify and expected him to say that he was sober when he left Duke's Bar; however, on direct examination Chase testified that he may have had a little too much to drink at Duke's Bar. Duke's Bar now seeks to confront Chase with his statement made on deposition that he was sober when he left Duke's Bar. Which of the following is true concerning this statement?

(A) It may be used only to refresh Chase's recollection.
(B) It is admissible for impeachment and as substantive evidence that Chase was sober.
(C) It is inadmissible, because Duke's Bar cannot impeach its own witness.
(D) It is inadmissible, because it is hearsay, not within any exception.

Question 67

Penn offers evidence that, after the accident the manager of Duke's Bar established house rules limiting all customers to two drinks per hour, with a maximum limit of four drinks per night. This evidence is

(A) admissible to show that the prior conduct of Duke's Bar was negligent.
(B) admissible to show that Duke's Bar was aware of the need for taking precautionary measure.
(C) inadmissible, because subsequent measures by an employee are not binding on Duke's Bar.
(D) inadmissible, because its admission would discourage the taking of such remedial measures.

Question 68

Penn offers evidence that, after the accident, the owner of Duke's Bar visited him at the hospital and, offering to pay all of Penn's medical expenses, said, "That's the least I can do after letting Chase leave the bar so drunk last night." The statement that Chase was drunk when he left the bar on the night of the accident is

(A) admissible as an admission by the owner of Duke's Bar that Chase was drunk when he left the bar.
(B) admissible as a factual admission made in connection with an offer of compromise.
(C) inadmissible as hearsay, not within any exception.
(D) inadmissible as a statement made in connection with an offer to pay medical expenses.

Question 69

In a narcotics conspiracy prosecution against Daly, the prosecutor offers in evidence a tape recording of a telephone call allegedly made by Daly. A lay witness is called to testify that the voice on the recording is Daly's. Her testimony to which of the following would be the LEAST sufficient basis for admitting the recording?

(A) She had heard the same voice on a similar tape recording identified to her by Daly's brother.
(B) She had heard Daly speak many times, but never over the telephone.
(C) She had, specifically for the purpose of preparing to testify, talked with Daly over the telephone at a time after the recording was made.
(D) She had been present with Daly when he engaged in the conversation in question but had heard only Daly's side of the conversation.

Question 70

Potts sued Dobbs on a product liability claim. Louis testified for Potts. On cross-examination, which of the following questions is the trial judge most likely to rule improper?

(A) "Isn't it a fact that you are Potts' close friend?"
(B) "Isn't it true that you are known in the community as 'Louie the Lush' because of your addiction to alcohol?"
(C) "Didn't you fail to report some income on your tax return last year?"
(D) "Weren't you convicted, seven years ago in this court, of obtaining money under false pretenses?"

Question 71

In an action to recover for personal injuries arising out of an automobile accident, Plaintiff called Bystander to testify. Claiming the privilege against self-incrimination, Bystander refuses to answer a question as to whether she was at the scene of the accident. Plaintiff moves that Bystander be ordered to answer the question. The judge should allow Bystander to remain silent only if

(A) the judge is convinced that she will incriminate herself.
(B) there is clear and convincing evidence that she will incriminate herself.
(C) there is a preponderance of evidence that she will incriminate herself.
(D) the judge believes that there is some reasonable possibility that she will incriminate herself.

Questions 72-76 are based on the following fact situation.

Miller is tried for armed robbery of the First Bank of City.

Question 72

The prosecution, in its case in chief, offers evidence that when Miller was arrested one day after the crime, he had a quantity of heroin and a hypodermic needle in his possession. This evidence should be

(A) admitted to prove Miller's motive to commit the crime.
(B) admitted to prove Miller's propensity to commit crimes.
(C) excluded, because its probative value is substantially outweighed by the danger of unfair prejudice.
(D) excluded, because such evidence may be offered only to rebut evidence of good character offered by defendant.

Question 73

The prosecutor offers the testimony of a bartender that when he saw the money in Miller's wallet, he said, "You must have robbed a bank," to which Miller made no reply. This evidence is

(A) admissible to prove that Miller's conduct caused the bartender to believe that Miller robbed the bank.
(B) admissible as a statement made in the presence of the defendant.

(C) inadmissible, because it would violate Miller's privilege against self-incrimination.
(D) inadmissible, because Miller had no reason to respond to the bartender's statement.

Question 74

At the request of police, the teller who was robbed prepared a sketch bearing a strong likeness to Miller, but the teller died in an automobile accident before Miller was arrested. At trial the prosecution offers the sketch. The sketch is

(A) admissible as an identification of a person after perceiving him.
(B) admissible as past recollection recorded.
(C) inadmissible as hearsay, not within any exception.
(D) inadmissible as an opinion of the teller.

Question 75

Miller testified on direct examination that he had never been in the First Bank of City. His counsel asks, "What, if anything, did you tell the police when you were arrested?" If his answer would be, "I told them I had never been in the bank," this answer would be

(A) admissible to prove Miller had never been in the bank.
(B) admissible as a prior consistent statement.
(C) inadmissible as hearsay, not within any exception.
(D) inadmissible, because it was a self-serving statement by a person with a substantial motive to fabricate.

Question 76

On cross-examination of Miller, the prosecutor asks Miller whether he was convicted the previous year of tax fraud. This question is

(A) proper to show that Miller is inclined to lie.
(B) proper to show that Miller is inclined to steal money.
(C) improper, because the conviction has insufficient similarity to the crime charged.
(D) improper, because the probative value of the evidence is outweighed by the danger of unfair prejudice.

Questions 77-78 are based on the following fact situation.

Peri sued Denucci for a libelous letter received by Investigator. The authenticity and contents of the letter are disputed.

Question 77

Peri's attorney asks Investigator to testify that, a week before receiving the libelous letter, he had written to Denucci inquiring about Peri. The testimony is

(A) admissible provided this inquiry was made in the regular course of Investigator's business.
(B) admissible without production of the inquiry letter or the showing of its unavailability.
(C) inadmissible unless Peri's attorney has given Denucci notice of Investigator's intended testimony.
(D) inadmissible unless the inquiry letter itself is shown to be unavailable.

Question 78

Investigator, if permitted, will testify that, "I received a letter that I cannot now find, which read:

'Dear Investigator,

You inquired about Peri. We fired him last month when we discovered that he had been stealing from the stockroom.

              Denucci'."

The testimony should be admitted in evidence only if the

(A) jury finds that Investigator has quoted the letter precisely.
(B) jury is satisfied that the original letter is unavailable.
(C) judge is satisfied that Investigator has quoted the letter precisely.
(D) judge finds that the original letter is unavailable.

Questions 79-82 are based on the following fact situation.

Drew was tried for the July 21 murder of Victor.

Question 79

In his case in chief, Drew called as his first witness, Wilma to testify to Drew's reputation in his community as a "peaceable man." The testimony is

(A) admissible as tending to prove Drew is believable.

(B) admissible as trying to prove Drew is innocent.

(C) inadmissible, because Drew has not testified.

(D) inadmissible, because reputation is not a proper way to prove character.

Question 80

Drew called William to testify that on July 20 Drew said that he was about to leave that day to visit relatives in a distant state. The testimony is

(A) admissible, because it is a declaration of present mental state.

(B) admissible, because it is not hearsay.

(C) inadmissible, because it is irrelevant.

(D) inadmissible, because it is hearsay, not within any exception.

Question 81

Drew called Wilson to testify to alibi. On cross-examination of Wilson, the prosecution asked, "Isn't it a fact that you are Drew's first cousin?" The question is

(A) proper, because it goes to bias.

(B) proper, because a relative is not competent to give reputation testimony.

(C) improper, because the question goes beyond the scope of direct examination.

(D) improper, because the evidence being sought is irrelevant.

Question 82

Drew called Warren to testify to alibi. On cross-examination of Warren, the prosecutor asked, "Weren't you on the jury that acquitted Drew of another criminal charge?" The best reason for sustaining an objection to this question is that

(A) the question goes beyond the scope of direct examination.

(B) the probative value of the answer would be outweighed by its tendency to mislead.

(C) the question is leading.

(D) prior jury service in a case involving a party renders the witness incompetent.

Question 83

Re-direct examination of a witness must be permitted in which of the following circumstances?

(A) To reply to any matter raised in cross-examination.

(B) Only to reply to significant new matter raised in cross-examination.

(C) Only to reiterate the essential elements of the case.

(D) Only to supply significant information inadvertently omitted on direct examination.

Question 84

Alice was held up at the point of a gun, an unusual revolver with a red painted barrel, while she was clerking in a neighborhood grocery store. Dennis is charged with armed robbery of Alice.

The prosecutor calls Winthrop to testify that, a week after the robbery of Alice, he was robbed by Dennis with a pistol that had red paint on the barrel. Winthrop's testimony is

(A) admissible as establishing an identifying circumstance.

(B) admissible as showing that Dennis was willing to commit robbery.

(C) inadmissible, because it is improper character evidence.

(D) inadmissible, because its probative value is substantially outweighed by the danger of unfair prejudice.

Questions 85-86 are based on the following fact situation.

Rider, a bus passenger, sued Transit Company for injuries to his back from an accident caused by Transit's negligence. Transit denies that Rider received any injury in the accident.

Question 85

Rider's counsel seeks to introduce an affidavit he obtained in preparation for trial from Dr. Bond who has since died. The affidavit avers that Dr. Bond examined Rider two days after the Transit Company accident and found him suffering from a recently incurred back injury. The judge should rule the affidavit

(A) admissible, as a statement of present bodily condition made to a physician.

(B) admissible, as prior recorded testimony.

(C) inadmissible, because it is irrelevant.

(D) inadmissible, because it is hearsay, not within any exception.

Question 86

Transit Company calls Observer to testify that right after the accident, Rider told him that he had recently suffered a recurrence of an old back injury. The judge should rule Observer's testimony

(A) admissible, as an admission of a party opponent.
(B) admissible, as a spontaneous declaration.
(C) inadmissible, because it is irrelevant.
(D) inadmissible, because it is hearsay, not within any exception.

Question 87

Pace sues Def Company for injuries suffered when Pace's car collided with Def Company's truck. Def's general manager prepared a report of the accident at the request of the company's attorney in preparation for the trial, and delivered the report to the attorney. Pace demands that the report be produced. Will production of the report be required?

(A) Yes, because business reports are not generally privileged.
(B) No, because it is a privileged communication from client to the attorney.
(C) No, because such reports contain hearsay.
(D) No, because such reports are self-serving.

Question 88

Park brought an action against Dan for injuries received in an automobile accident, alleging negligence in that Dan was speeding and inattentive. Park calls White to testify that Dan had a reputation in the community of being a reckless driver and was known as "dare-devil Dan." White's testimony is

(A) admissible as habit evidence.
(B) admissible, because it tends to prove that Dan was negligent at the time of this collision.
(C) inadmissible, because Dan has not offered testimony of his own good character.
(D) inadmissible to show negligence.

Question 89

Alex and Sam were arrested for holding up a gas station. They were taken to police headquarters and placed in a room for interrogation. As a police officer addressing both started to give them the Miranda warnings prior to the questioning, Alex said, "Look, Sam planned the damned thing and I was dumb enough to go along with it. We robbed the place—what else is there to say?" Sam said nothing. Sam

was escorted into another room and a full written confession was then obtained from Alex.

If Sam is brought to trial on an indictment charging him with robbery, the fact that Sam failed to object to Alex's statement and remained silent after Alex had implicated him in the crime should be ruled

(A) admissible, because his silence was an implied admission by Sam that he had participated in the crime.
(B) admissible, because a statement of a participant in a crime is admissible against another participant.
(C) inadmissible, because, under the circumstances, there was no duty or responsibility on Sam's part to respond.
(D) inadmissible, because whatever Alex may have said has no probative value in a trial against Sam.

Question 90

In a suit attacking the validity of a deed executed fifteen years ago, Plaintiff alleges mental incompetency of Joe, the grantor, and offers in evidence a properly authenticated affidavit of Harry, Joe's brother. The affidavit, which was executed shortly after the deed, stated that Harry had observed Joe closely over a period of weeks, that Joe had engaged in instances of unusual behavior (which were described), and that Joe's appearance had changed from one of neatness and alertness to one of disorder and absentmindedness. The judge should rule Harry's affidavit

(A) inadmissible as opinion.
(B) inadmissible as hearsay, not within any exception.
(C) admissible as an official document.
(D) admissible as an ancient document.

Question 91

The police, answering a complaint about noise, arrived at Sam's apartment and found Sam's wife dead on the living room floor. One of the officers turned to Sam and said "What happened?" Sam replied, "She was a bitch and I took care of her." At Sam's trial his statement should be ruled

(A) admissible, because the statement was part of the res gestae.
(B) admissible, because the statement was made at the scene, was essentially volunteered, and was not a product of a custodial interrogation.

(C) inadmissible, because the statement is ambiguous and not necessarily incriminatory.

(D) inadmissible, because Sam was effectively in police custody and should have been given the Miranda warnings.

Question 92

John Smith has denied his purported signature on a letter which has become critical in a breach of contract suit between Smith and Miller. At trial, Miller's counsel calls Alice, a teacher, who testifies that she taught John Smith mathematics in school ten years earlier, knows his signature, and proposes to testify that the signature to the letter is that of John Smith.

Smith's counsel objects. The trial judge should

(A) sustain the objection on the ground that identification of handwriting requires expert testimony and the teacher does not, per se, qualify as an expert.

(B) sustain the objection on the ground that the best evidence of Smith's handwriting would be testimony by a person who had examined his writing more recently than ten years ago.

(C) overrule the objection on the ground that a schoolteacher qualifies as an expert witness for the purpose of identifying handwriting.

(D) overrule the objection on the ground that a layman may identify handwriting if he has seen the person in question write, and has an opinion concerning the writing in question.

Questions 93-94 are based on the following fact situation.

Paula sued for injuries she sustained in a fall in a hotel hallway connecting the lobby of the hotel with a restaurant located in the hotel building. The hallway floor was covered with vinyl tile. The defendants were Horne, owner of the hotel building, and Lee, lessee of the restaurant. The evidence was that the hallway floor had been waxed approximately an hour before Paula slipped on it, and although the wax had dried, there appeared to be excessive dried wax caked on several of the tiles. Home's defense was that the hallway was a part of the premises leased to Lee over which he retained no control, and Lee denied negligence and alleged contributory negligence.

Question 93

Lee offered to prove by Marks, the restaurant manager, that in the week immediately preceding

Paula's fall at least 1,000 people had used the hallway in going to and from the restaurant, and Marks had neither seen anyone fall nor received reports that anyone had fallen. The trial judge should rule this evidence

(A) admissible, because it tends to prove that Paula did not use the care exercised by reasonably prudent people.

(B) admissible, because it tends to prove that Lee was generally careful in maintaining the floor.

(C) inadmissible, because Marks' testimony is self-serving.

(D) inadmissible, because it does not bear on the issue of Lee's exercise of due care on this specific occasion.

Question 94

If Paula offered to prove that the day after she fell Horne had the vinyl tile taken up and replaced with a new floor covering, the trial judge should rule the evidence

(A) admissible, because it is relevant to the issue of whether Horne retained control of the hallway.

(B) admissible, because it is relevant to the issue of awareness of the unsafe condition of the hallway at the time of Paula's fall.

(C) inadmissible, because there was no showing that the new floor covering would be any safer than the old.

(D) inadmissible, because to admit such would discourage a policy of making repairs to prevent further injury, regardless of fault.

Questions 95-96 are based on the following fact situation.

Price sued Derrick for injuries Price received in an automobile accident. Price claims Derrick was negligent in (a) exceeding the posted speed limit of 35 m.p.h., (b) failing to keep a lookout, and (c) crossing the center line.

Question 95

Bystander, Price's eyewitness, testified on cross-examination that Derrick was wearing a green sweater at the time of the accident. Derrick's counsel calls Wilson to testify that Derrick's sweater was blue. Wilson's testimony is

(A) admissible as substantive evidence of a material fact.

(B) admissible as bearing on Bystander's truthfulness and veracity.

(C) inadmissible, because it has no bearing on the capacity of Bystander to observe.

(D) inadmissible, because it is extrinsic evidence of a collateral matter.

Question 96

Derrick testified in his own behalf that he was going 30 m.p.h. On cross-examination, Price's counsel did not question Derrick with regard to his speed. Subsequently, Price's counsel calls Officer to testify that, in his investigation following the accident, Derrick told him he was driving 40 m.p.h. Officer's testimony is

(A) admissible as a prior inconsistent statement.

(B) admissible as an admission.

(C) inadmissible, because it lacks a foundation.

(D) inadmissible, because it is hearsay, not within any exception.

Questions 97-98 are based on the following fact situation.

Peters sued Davis for $100,000 for injuries received in a traffic accident. Davis charges Peters with contributory negligence and alleges that Peters failed to have his lights on at a time when it was dark enough to require them.

Question 97

Davis calls Bystander to testify that Passenger, who was riding in Peters' automobile and who also was injured, confided to him at the scene of the accident that "we should have had our lights on." Bystander's testimony is

(A) admissible as an admission of a party opponent.

(B) admissible as a declaration against interest.

(C) inadmissible, because it is hearsay, not within any exception.

(D) inadmissible, because it is opinion.

Question 98

Davis offers to have Bystander testify that he was talking to Witness when he heard the crash and heard Witness, now deceased, exclaim, "That car doesn't have any lights on." Bystander's testimony is

(A) admissible as a statement of present sense impression.

(B) admissible, because Witness is not available to testify.

(C) inadmissible as hearsay, not within any exception.

(D) inadmissible, because of the Dead Man's Statute.

Questions 99-100 are based on the following fact situation.

Owner and his employee, Driver, consult Attorney about a motor vehicle collision resulting in a suit by Litigant against Owner and Driver as joint defendants. Attorney calls Irving, his investigator, into the conference to make notes of what is said, and those present discuss the facts of the collision and Owner's insurance. Owner thereafter files a cross-claim against Driver for indemnity for any damages obtained by Litigant.

Question 99

Litigant calls Driver to testify in Litigant's case in chief to admissions made by Owner in the conference. On objection by Owner, the court should rule that Driver's testimony is

(A) admissible, because of the presence of persons in the conference other than Attorney and Owner.

(B) admissible, because Driver is an adverse party in the lawsuit.

(C) inadmissible, because of the attorney-client privilege.

(D) inadmissible, because the best evidence is Irving's notes of the conference.

Question 100

Driver calls Irving in his defense against the cross-claim. He seeks to have Irving testify to an admission made by Owner in the conference. On objection by Owner, the court should rule Irving's testimony

(A) admissible, because the attorney-client privilege does not apply, in suits between those conferring with him, to joint consultations with an attorney.

(B) admissible, because the attorney-client privilege does not apply to testimony by one who does not stand in a confidential relationship with the person against whom the evidence is offered.

(C) admissible, because the conference was not intended to be confidential, since it concerned anticipated testimony in open court.

(D) inadmissible, because Owner has not waived the attorney-client privilege.

Questions 101-103 are based on the following fact situation.

Pemberton and three passengers, Able, Baker, and Charley, were injured when their car was struck by a truck owned by Mammoth Corporation and driven by Edwards. Helper, also a Mammoth employee, was riding in the truck. The issues in Pemberton v. Mammoth include the negligence of Edwards in driving too fast and failing to wear glasses, and of Pemberton in failing to yield the right of way.

Question 101

Pemberton's counsel proffers evidence showing that shortly after the accident Mammoth put a speed governor on the truck involved in the accident. The judge should rule the proffered evidence

(A) admissible as an admission of a party.
(B) admissible as res gestae.
(C) inadmissible for public policy reasons.
(D) inadmissible, because it would lead to the drawing of an inference on an inference.

Question 102

Pemberton's counsel seeks to introduce Helper's written statement that Edwards, Mammoth's driver, had left his glasses (required by his operator's license) at the truck stop when they had left five minutes before the accident. The judge should rule the statement admissible only if

(A) Pemberton first proves that Helper is an agent of Mammoth and that the statement concerned a matter within the scope of his agency.
(B) Pemberton produces independent evidence that Edwards was not wearing corrective lenses at the time of the accident.
(C) Helper is shown to be beyond the process of the court and unavailable to testify.
(D) the statement was under oath in affidavit form.

Question 103

Mammoth's counsel seeks to have Sheriff testify that while he was investigating the accident he was told by Pemberton, "This was probably our fault." The judge should rule the proffered evidence

(A) admissible as an admission of a party.
(B) admissible, because it is a statement made to a police officer in the course of an official investigation.

(C) inadmissible, because it is a mixed conclusion of law and fact.
(D) inadmissible, because it is hearsay, not within any exception.

Question 104

In a contract suit between Terrell and Ward, Ward testifies that he recalls having his first conversation with Terrell on January 3. When asked how he remembers the date, he answers, "In the conversation, Terrell referred to a story in that day's newspaper announcing my daughter's engagement." Terrell's counsel moves to strike the reference to the newspaper story. The judge should

(A) grant the motion on the ground that the best evidence rule requires production of the newspaper itself.
(B) grant the motion, because the reference to the newspaper story does not fit within any established exception to the hearsay rule.
(C) deny the motion on the ground that the court may take judicial notice of local newspapers and their contents.
(D) deny the motion on the ground that a witness may refer to collateral documents without providing the documents themselves.

Question 105

Drew is charged with the murder of Pitt. The prosecutor introduced testimony of a police officer that Pitt told a priest, administering the last rites, "I was stabbed by Drew. Since I am dying, tell him I forgive him." Thereafter, Drew's attorney offers the testimony of Wall that the day before, when Pitt believed he would live, he stated that he had been stabbed by Jack, an old enemy. The testimony of Wall is

(A) admissible under an exception to the hearsay rule.
(B) admissible to impeach the dead declarant.
(C) inadmissible, because it goes to the ultimate issue in the case.
(D) inadmissible, because it is irrelevant to any substantive issue in the case.

Question 106

Dexter was tried for the homicide of a girl whose strangled body was found beside a remote logging road with her hands taped together. After Dexter offered evidence of alibi, the state calls Wilma to testify that Dexter had taped her hands and tried to strangle her in the same location two days before the homicide but that she escaped.

The evidence is

(A) admissible as tending to show Dexter is the killer.
(B) admissible as tending to show Dexter's violent nature.
(C) inadmissible, because it is improper character evidence.
(D) inadmissible, because it is unfairly prejudicial.

Questions 107-108 are based on the following fact situation.

In a trial between Jones and Smith, an issue arose about Smith's ownership of a horse, which had caused damage to Jones' crops.

Question 107

Jones offered to testify that he looked up Smith's telephone number in the directory, called that number, and that a voice answered "This is Smith speaking." At this Jones asked, "Was that your horse that tramped across my cornfield this afternoon?" The voice replied "Yes." The judge should rule the testimony

(A) admissible, because the answering speaker's identification of himself, together with the usual accuracy of the telephone directory and transmission system, furnishes sufficient authentication.
(B) admissible, because judicial notice may be taken of the accuracy of telephone directories.
(C) inadmissible unless Jones can further testify that he was familiar with Smith's voice and that it was in fact Smith to whom he spoke.
(D) inadmissible unless Smith has first been asked whether or not the conversation took place and has been given the opportunity to admit, deny, or explain.

Question 108

Jones seeks to introduce in evidence a photograph of his cornfield in order to depict the nature and extent of the damage done. The judge should rule the photograph

(A) admissible if Jones testifies that it fairly and accurately portrays the condition of the cornfield after the damage was done.
(B) admissible if Jones testifies that the photograph was taken within a week after the alleged occurrence.
(C) inadmissible if Jones fails to call the photographer to testify concerning the circumstances under which the photograph was taken.
(D) inadmissible if it is possible to describe the damage to the cornfield through direct oral testimony.

Question 109

Patty sues Mart Department Store for personal injuries, alleging that while shopping she was knocked to the floor by a merchandise cart being pushed by Handy, a stock clerk, and that as a consequence her back was injured.

Handy testified that Patty fell near the cart but was not struck by it. Thirty minutes after Patty's fall, Handy, in accordance with regular practice at Mart, had filled out a printed form, "Employee's Report of Accident—Mart Department Store," in which he stated that Patty had been leaning over to spank her young child and in so doing had fallen near his cart. Counsel for Mart offers in evidence the report, which had been given him by Handy's supervisor.

The judge should rule the report offered by Mart

(A) admissible as res gestae.
(B) admissible as a business record.
(C) inadmissible, because it is hearsay, not within any exception.
(D) inadmissible, because Handy is available as a witness.

Questions 110-112 are based on the following fact situation.

Dann, who was charged with the crime of assaulting Smith, admitted striking Smith but claimed to have acted in self-defense when he was attacked by Smith, who was drunk and belligerent after a football game.

Question 110

Dann offered testimony of Employer, that he had known and employed Dann for twelve years and knew Dann's reputation among the people with whom he lived and worked to be that of a peaceful, law-abiding, nonviolent person. The trial judge should rule this testimony

(A) admissible, because it is relevant to show the improbability of Dann's having committed an unprovoked assault.
(B) admissible, because it is relevant to a determination of the extent of punishment if Dann is convicted.
(C) not admissible, because whether Dann is normally a person of good character is irrelevant to the specific charge.
(D) not admissible, because it is irrelevant without a showing that Employer was one of the persons among whom Dann lived and worked.

Question 111

On cross-examination of Employer (Dann's), the state's attorney asked Employer if he had heard that Dann often engaged in fights and brawls. The trial judge should rule the question

(A) not objectionable, because evidence of Dann's previous fights and brawls may be used to prove his guilt.
(B) not objectionable, because it tests Employer's knowledge of Dann's reputation.
(C) objectionable, because it seeks to put into evidence separate, unrelated offenses.
(D) objectionable, because no specific time or incidents are specified and inquired about.

Question 112

Dann's friend Frank was called to testify that Smith had a reputation among the people with whom he lived and worked for law-breaking and frequently engaging in brawls. The trial judge should rule the testimony

(A) admissible to support Dann's theory of self-defense, touching on whether Dann or Smith was the aggressor.
(B) admissible if Frank testifies further as to specific acts of misconduct on Smith's part of which Frank has personal knowledge.
(C) inadmissible on the question of Dann's guilt because Dann, not Smith, is on trial.
(D) inadmissible, because Frank failed to lay a proper foundation.

Questions 113-115 are based on the following fact situation.

Carr ran into and injured Pedersen, a pedestrian. With Carr in his car were Wanda and Walter Passenger. Passerby saw the accident and called the police department, which sent Sheriff to investigate.

All of these people were available as potential witnesses in the case of Pedersen v. Carr. Pedersen alleges that Carr, while drunk, struck Pedersen who was in a duly marked crosswalk.

Question 113

Pedersen's counsel wishes to prove that after the accident Carr went to Pedersen and offered $1,000 to settle Pedersen's claim. The trial judge should rule this evidence

(A) admissible as an admission of a party.
(B) admissible as an admission to show Carr's liability, provided the court gives a cautionary instruction that the statement should not be considered as bearing on the issue of damages.
(C) inadmissible since it is not relevant either to the question of liability or the question of damages.
(D) inadmissible, because even though relevant and an admission, the policy of the law is to encourage settlement negotiations.

Question 114

Pedersen's counsel wants to have Sheriff testify to the following statement made to him by Walter Passenger, out of the presence of Carr: "We were returning from a party at which we had all been drinking." The trial judge should rule this testimony

(A) admissible as an admission of a party.
(B) admissible as a declaration against interest.
(C) inadmissible, because it is hearsay, not within any exception.
(D) inadmissible, because it would lead the court into nonessential side issues.

Question 115

On the evening of the day of the accident, Walter Passenger wrote a letter to his sister in which he described the accident. When Walter says he cannot remember some details of the accident, Pedersen's counsel seeks to show him the letter to assist him in his testimony on direct examination. The trial judge should rule this

(A) permissible under the doctrine of present recollection refreshed.

(B) permissible under the doctrine of past recollection recorded.

(C) objectionable, because the letter was not a spontaneous utterance.

(D) objectionable, because the letter is a self-serving declaration in so far as the witness, Walter, is concerned.

Question 116

Dever was indicted for the murder of Vickers by poison. At trial, the prosecutor calls the county coroner, Dr. Wolfe, who is a board-certified pathologist, to testify that, in accord with good practice in her specialty, she has studied microphotographic slides, made under her supervision by medical assistants, of tissue taken from Vickers' corpse and that it is Wolfe's opinion, based on that study, that Vickers died of poisoning. The slides have not been offered in evidence.

Dr. Wolfe's opinion should be

(A) excluded, because the cause of death is a critical issue to be decided by the trier of fact.

(B) excluded, because her opinion is based on facts not in evidence.

(C) admitted, because Wolfe followed accepted medical practice in arriving at her opinion.

(D) admitted, because her opinion is based on matters observed pursuant to a duty imposed by law.

Question 117

At the trial of Davis for a murder that occurred in Newtown, the prosecution called Waite, who testified that she saw Davis kill the victim. Davis believed that Waite was 600 miles away in Old Town, engaged in the illegal sale of narcotics, on the day in question. On cross-examination by Davis, Waite was asked whether she had in fact sold narcotics in Old Town on that date. Waite refused to answer on the ground of self-incrimination.

The judge, over the prosecutor's objection, ordered that if Waite did not testify, her direct testimony should be stricken. The order to testify or have the testimony stricken can best be supported on the basis that

(A) Waite had not been charged with any crime and, thus, could claim no privilege against self-incrimination.

(B) Waite's proper invocation of the privilege prevented adequate cross-examination.

(C) the public interest in allowing an accused to defend himself or herself outweighs the interest of a non-party witness in the privilege.

(D) the trial record, independent of testimony, does not establish that Waite's answer could incriminate her.

Question 118

Cars driven by Pugh and Davidson collided, and Davidson was charged with driving while intoxicated in connection with the accident. She pleaded guilty and was merely fined, although under the statute the court could have sentenced her to two years in prison.

Thereafter, Pugh, alleging that Davidson's intoxication had caused the collision, sued Davidson for damages. At trial, Pugh offers the properly authenticated record of Davidson's conviction. The record should be

(A) admitted as proof of Davidson's character.

(B) admitted as proof of Davidson's intoxication.

(C) excluded, because the conviction was not the result of a trial.

(D) excluded, because it is hearsay, not within any exception.

Question 119

Pitt sued Dow for damages for injuries that Pitt incurred when a badly rotted limb fell from a curbside tree in front of Dow's home and hit Pitt. Dow claimed that the tree was on city property and thus was the responsibility of the city. At trial, Pitt offered testimony that a week after the accident, Dow had cut the tree down with a chainsaw. The offered evidence is

(A) inadmissible, because there is a policy to encourage safety precautions.

(B) inadmissible, because it is irrelevant to the condition of the tree at the time of the accident.

(C) admissible to show the tree was on Dow's property.

(D) admissible to show the tree was in a rotted condition.

Question 120

Dean, charged with murder, was present with her attorney at a preliminary examination when White, who was the defendant in a separate prosecution for concealing the body of the murder victim, testified for the prosecution against Dean. When called to testify at Dean's trial, White refused to testify, though ordered to do so.

The prosecution offers evidence of White's testimony at the preliminary examination. The evidence is

(A) admissible as former testimony.
(B) admissible as past recollection recorded.
(C) inadmissible, because it would violate White's privilege against self-incrimination.
(D) inadmissible, because it is hearsay, not within any exception.

Question 121

Potts, a building contractor, sued Dennis for failure to pay on a small cost-plus construction contract. At trial, Potts, who personally supervised all of the work, seeks to testify to what he remembers about the amount of pipe used, the number of workers used on the job, and the number of hours spent grading.

Dennis objects on the ground that Potts had routinely recorded these facts in notebooks which are in Potts' possession.

Potts' testimony is

(A) admissible as a report of regularly conducted business activity.
(B) admissible as based on first-hand knowledge.
(C) inadmissible, because it violates the best evidence rule.
(D) inadmissible, because a summary of writings cannot be made unless the originals are available for examination.

Question 122

A grand jury was investigating a bank robbery. The only information known to the prosecutor was a rumor that Taylor might have been involved. The grand jury subpoenaed Taylor. He refused to answer questions about the robbery and was granted use immunity. He then testified that he and Simmons had robbed the bank. The grand jury indicted both Taylor and Simmons for the bank robbery. The prosecutor permitted Simmons to enter a plea to a lesser offense in exchange for Simmons' agreement to testify against Taylor. The prosecutor had no evidence as to the identity of the robbers except the testimony of Simmons and Taylor.

At Taylor's trial, his objection to Simmons' being permitted to testify should be

(A) sustained, because the prosecutor may not bargain away the rights of one codefendant in a deal with another.
(B) sustained, because Simmons' testimony was acquired as a result of Taylor's grand jury testimony.
(C) overruled, because the police suspected Taylor even before he testified in the grand jury hearing.
(D) overruled, because a witness cannot be precluded from testifying if his testimony is given voluntarily.

Question 123

Dryden is tried on a charge of driving while intoxicated. When Dryden was booked at the police station, a videotape was made that showed him unsteady, abusive, and speaking in a slurred manner. If the prosecutor lays a foundation properly identifying the tape, should the court admit it in evidence and permit it to be shown to the jury?

(A) Yes, because it is an admission.
(B) Yes, because its value is not substantially outweighed by unfair prejudice.
(C) No, because the privilege against self-incrimination is applicable.
(D) No, because specific instances of conduct cannot be proved by extrinsic evidence.

Question 124

Powers sued Debbs for battery. At trial, Powers' witness Wilson testified that Debbs had made an unprovoked attack on Powers.

On cross-examination, Debbs asks Wilson about a false claim that Wilson had once filed on an insurance policy. The question is

(A) proper, because the conduct involved untruthfulness.
(B) proper provided that the conduct resulted in conviction of Wilson.
(C) improper, because the impeachment involved a specific instance of misconduct.
(D) improper, because the claim form would be the best evidence.

Question 125

While crossing Spruce Street, Pesko was hit by a car that she did not see. Pesko sued Dorry for her injuries.

At trial, Pesko calls Williams, a police officer, to testify that, ten minutes after the accident, a driver stopped him and said, "Officer, a few minutes ago I saw a hit-and-run accident on Spruce Street involving a blue convertible, which I followed to the drive-in restaurant at Oak and Third," and that a few seconds later Williams saw Dorry sitting alone in a blue convertible in the drive-in restaurant's parking lot.

Williams' testimony about the driver's statement should be

(A) admitted as a statement of recent perception.
(B) admitted as a present sense impression.
(C) excluded, because it is hearsay, not within any exception.
(D) excluded, because it is more prejudicial than probative.

Question 126

Pratt sued Danvers for injuries suffered by Pratt when their automobiles collided. At trial Pratt offers into evidence a properly authenticated letter from Danvers that says, "your claim seems too high, but, because I might have been a little negligent, I'm prepared to offer you half of what you ask."

The letter is

(A) admissible as an admission by a party-opponent.
(B) admissible as a statement against pecuniary interest.
(C) inadmissible, because Danver's statement is lay opinion on a legal issue.
(D) inadmissible, because Danver's statement was made in an effort to settle the claim.

Question 127

Darden was prosecuted for armed robbery. At trial, Darden testified in his own behalf, denying that he had committed the robbery. On cross-examination, the prosecutor intends to ask Darden whether he had been convicted of burglary six years earlier.

The question concerning the burglary conviction is

(A) proper if the court finds that the probative value for impeachment outweighs the prejudice to Darden.
(B) proper, because the prosecutor is entitled to make this inquiry as a matter of right.
(C) improper, because burglary does not involve dishonesty or false statement.
(D) improper, because the conviction must be proved by court record, not by question on cross-examination.

Question 128

In Peel's personal injury action, Wilson, a physician who had no previous knowledge of the matter, sat in court and heard all the evidence about Peel's symptoms and conditions.

Wilson is called to give her opinion whether Peel's injuries are permanent. May Wilson so testify?

(A) Yes, provided she first identifies the data on which her opinion is based.
(B) Yes, because an expert may base her opinion on facts made known to her at the trial.
(C) No, because she has no personal knowledge of Peel's condition.
(D) No, because permanence of injury is an issue to be decided by the jury.

Question 129

In a tort action, Fisher testified against Dawes. Dawes then called Jones, who testified that Fisher had a bad reputation for veracity. Dawes then also called Weld to testify that Fisher once perpetrated a hoax on the police.

Weld's testimony is

(A) admissible, provided that the hoax involves untruthfulness.
(B) admissible, provided that the hoax resulted in conviction of Fisher.
(C) inadmissible, because it is merely cumulative impeachment.
(D) inadmissible, because it is extrinsic evidence of a specific instance of misconduct.

Question 130

David is being tried in federal court for criminal conspiracy with John to violate federal narcotics law. At trial, the prosecutor calls David's new wife, Wanda, and asks her to testify about a meeting between David and John that she observed before she married David.

Which of the following is the most accurate statement of the applicable rule concerning whether Wanda may testify?

(A) The choice is Wanda's.
(B) The choice is David's.
(C) Wanda is permitted to testify only if both Wanda and David agree.
(D) Wanda is compelled to testify even if both Wanda and David object.

Question 131

In a civil suit by Pine against Decker, Decker called Wall, a chemist, as an expert witness and asked him a number of questions about his education and experience in chemistry. Over Pine's objection that Wall was not shown to be qualified in chemistry, the trial court permitted Wall to testify as to his opinion in response to a hypothetical question.

On cross-examination, Pine asked Wall if he had failed two chemistry courses while doing his graduate work. The answer should be

(A) admitted, because it is relevant to the weight to be given to Wall's testimony.
(B) admitted, because specific acts bearing on truthfulness may be inquired about on cross-examination.
(C) excluded, because the court has determined that Wall is qualified to testify as an expert.
(D) excluded, because Wall's character has not been put in issue.

Question 132

In a contract suit by Perez against Drake, each of the following is an accepted method of authenticating Drake's signature on a document offered by Perez EXCEPT:

(A) A non-expert who, in preparation for trial, has familiarized himself with Drake's usual signature testifies that, in his opinion, the questioned signature is genuine.

(B) The jury, without the assistance of an expert, compares the questioned signature with an admittedly authentic sample of Drake's handwriting.
(C) A witness offers proof that the signature is on a document that has been in existence for at least 20 years, that was in a place where it would be if it was authentic, and that has no suspicious circumstances surrounding it.
(D) A witness testifies that Drake admitted that the signature is his.

Question 133

Paulsen sued Daly for nonpayment of a personal loan to Daly, as evidenced by Daly's promissory note to Paulsen. Paulsen called Walters to testify that he knows Daly's handwriting and that the signature on the note is Daly's. On direct examination, to identify himself, Walters gave his name and address and testified that he had been employed by a roofing company for seven years.

During presentation of Daly's case, Daly called Wilson to testify that she is the roofing company's personnel manager and that she had determined, by examining the company's employment records, that Walters had worked there only three years. The trial judge should rule that Wilson's testimony is

(A) inadmissible, because it is not the best evidence.
(B) inadmissible, because it is impeachment on a collateral question.
(C) admissible as evidence of a regularly conducted activity.
(D) admissible as tending to impeach Walters' credibility.

Question 134

Dray was prosecuted for bank robbery. At trial, the bank teller, Wall, was unable to identify Dray, now bearded, as the bank robber. The prosecutor then showed Wall a group of photographs, and Wall testified that she had previously told the prosecutor that the middle picture (concededly a picture of Dray before he grew a beard) was a picture of the bank robber.

Wall's testimony is

(A) inadmissible, because it is hearsay, not within any exception.
(B) inadmissible, because it is a violation of Dray's right of confrontation.
(C) admissible as prior identification by the witness.

(D) admissible as past recollection recorded.

Question 135

Duncan was charged with aggravated assault. At trial Duncan did not testify; however, he sought to offer opinion evidence of his good character for truth and veracity.

This testimony should be

(A) admitted, because a criminal defendant is entitled to offer evidence of his good character.
(B) admitted, because a party's credibility is necessarily in issue.
(C) excluded, because character is not admissible to prove conduct in conformity therewith.
(D) excluded, because it is evidence of a trait not pertinent to the case.

Question 136

An issue in Parker's action against Daves for causing Parker's back injury was whether Parker's condition had resulted principally from a similar occurrence five years before, with which Daves had no connection.

Parker called Watts, his treating physician, who offered to testify that when she saw Parker after the latest occurrence, Parker told her that before the accident he had been working full time, without pain or limitation of motion, in a job that involved lifting heavy boxes.

Watts' testimony should be

(A) admitted, because it is a statement of Parker's then existing physical condition.
(B) admitted, because it is a statement made for purposes of medical diagnosis or treatment.
(C) excluded, because it is hearsay, not within any exception.
(D) excluded, because Parker is available as a witness.

Question 137

West, a witness in a contract case, testified on direct examination that four people attended a meeting. When asked to identify them, she gave the names of three but despite trying was unable to remember the name of the fourth person.

The attorney who called her as a witness seeks to show her his handwritten notes of the part of his pretrial interview with her in which she provided all four names.

The trial court is likely to consider the showing of the notes taken as

(A) a proper attempt to introduce recorded recollection.
(B) a proper attempt to refresh West's recollection.
(C) an improper attempt to lead the witness.
(D) an improper attempt to support West's credibility.

Question 138

In Peck's antitrust suit against manufacturers of insulation, Peck's interrogatories asked for information concerning total sales of insulation by each of the defendant manufacturers in a particular year. The defendants replied to the interrogatories by referring Peck to the Insulation Manufacturer's Annual Journal for the information.

If, at trial, Peck offers the annual as evidence of the sales volume, this evidence is

(A) admissible as an adoptive admission of the defendants.
(B) admissible as a business record.
(C) inadmissible, because it is hearsay, not within any exception.
(D) inadmissible as lacking sufficient authentication.

Question 139

Parmott sued Dexter in an automobile collision case. At trial, Parmott wishes to show by extrinsic evidence that Wade, Dexter's primary witness, is Dexter's partner in a gambling operation.

This evidence is

(A) admissible as evidence of Wade's character.
(B) admissible as evidence of Wade's possible bias in favor of Dexter.
(C) inadmissible, because criminal conduct can be shown only by admission or record of conviction.
(D) inadmissible, because bias must be shown on cross-examination and not by extrinsic evidence.

Question 140

Able, an attorney, sued Clinton, a client, for his fee, based on an agreed hourly rate. Clinton subpoenaed the attorney's time records for the days on which he purported to have worked for Clinton, in order to show that Able had billed an impossible number of hours to Clinton and others on those days. Clinton's subpoena provided that any information concerning the matters handled for other clients be deleted or masked. Able moved to quash the subpoena on the ground of attorney-client privilege.

The subpoena should be

(A) upheld, because the information about hours billed is not within the privilege.
(B) upheld, because an attorney has no right to invoke his clients' privilege without instructions from the clients.
(C) quashed, because an attorney is entitled to a right of privacy for the work product in his files.
(D) quashed, because no permission was obtained from the other clients to divulge information from their files.

Question 141

In litigation over the estate of Baggs, who died intestate, Payton, who is eighteen years old, claimed to be Baggs' niece and entitled, therefore, to a share of his large estate. In support of her claim, Payton offered in evidence a Bible, properly identified as having belonged to Baggs' family, in the front of which was a list of family births, marriages, and deaths. The list recorded Payton's birth to Baggs' oldest sister.

To prove that Payton is Baggs' niece, the Bible listing is

(A) admissible as an ancient document.
(B) admissible as a family record.
(C) inadmissible, because it is hearsay, not within any exception.
(D) inadmissible, because there was no showing of firsthand knowledge by the one who wrote it.

Question 142

Pullen used aluminum brackets in her business. On the telephone listed as hers in the telephone book, Pullen received a call in which the caller said, "This is John Denison of Denison Hardware Company. We have a special on aluminum brackets this week at 30 percent off." Pullen ordered brackets from the caller. When the brackets were never delivered, Pullen sued Denison for breach of contract.

At trial, Denison, who denies having made the telephone call, objects to Pullen's testimony concerning it. When asked, Pullen testifies that, aside from the telephone call, she had never heard Denison speak until she met him in the judge's chambers before the trial and that, in her opinion, the voice on the telephone was Denison's.

The strongest argument for admission of Pullen's testimony concerning the telephone call is that

(A) the call related to business reasonably transacted over the telephone.
(B) the call was received at a number assigned to Pullen by the telephone company.
(C) after hearing Denison speak in chambers, Pullen recognized Denison's voice as that of the person on the telephone.
(D) self-identification is sufficient authentication of a telephone call.

Question 143

Pack sued Donlon for slander, alleging that Donlon had publicly accused Pack of being a thief. In his answer, Donlon admitted making the accusation, but alleged that it was a true statement.

At trial, Donlon offers evidence that Pack stole a ring worth $10,000 from a jewelry store.

Evidence concerning this theft should be

(A) admitted, because specific instances of conduct may be proved when character is directly in issue.
(B) admitted, because Pack's action constituted a felony.
(C) excluded, because character must be shown by reputation or opinion.
(D) excluded, because its relevance is substantially outweighed by the danger of unfair prejudice.

Question 144

Perez sued Dawson for damages arising out of an automobile collision. At trial, Perez called Minter, an eyewitness to the collision. Perez expected Minter to testify that she had observed Dawson's automobile for five seconds prior to the collision and estimated Dawson's speed at the time of the collision to have been 50 miles per hour. Instead, Minter testified that she estimated Dawson's speed to have been 25 miles per hour.

Without finally excusing Minter as a witness, Perez then called Wallingford, a police officer, to testify that Minter had told him during his investigation at the accident scene that Dawson "was doing at least 50."

Wallingford's testimony is

(A) admissible as a present sense impression.
(B) admissible to impeach Minter.
(C) inadmissible, because Perez may not impeach his own witness.
(D) inadmissible, because it is hearsay, not within any exception.

Question 145

Dalton is on trial for burglary. During cross-examination of Dalton, the prosecutor wants to inquire about Dalton's earlier conviction for falsifying a credit application.

Which of the following facts concerning the conviction would be the best reason for the trial court's refusing to allow such examination?

(A) Dalton was released from prison 12 years ago.
(B) Dalton was put on probation rather than imprisoned.
(C) It was for a misdemeanor rather than a felony.
(D) It is on appeal.

Question 146

Deetz was prosecuted for homicide. He testified that he shot in self-defense. In rebuttal, Officer Watts testified that he came to the scene in response to a telephone call from Deetz. Watts offers to testify that he asked, "What is the problem here, sir?" and Deetz replied, "I was cleaning my gun and it went off accidentally."

The offered testimony is

(A) admissible as an excited utterance.
(B) admissible to impeach Deetz and as evidence that he did not act in self-defense.
(C) inadmissible, because of Deetz's privilege against self-incrimination.
(D) inadmissible, because it tends to exculpate without corroboration.

Question 147

Decker, charged with armed robbery of a store, denied that he was the person who had robbed the store.

In presenting the state's case, the prosecutor seeks to introduce evidence that Decker had robbed two other stores in the past year.

This evidence is

(A) admissible to prove a pertinent trait of Decker's character and Decker's action in conformity therewith.
(B) admissible to prove Decker's intent and identity.
(C) inadmissible, because character must be proved by reputation or opinion and may not be proved by specific acts.
(D) inadmissible, because its probative value is substantially outweighed by the danger of unfair prejudice.

Question 148

Paul sued Dyer for personal injuries sustained when Dyer's car hit Paul, a pedestrian. Immediately after the accident, Dyer got out of his car, raced over to Paul, and said, "Don't worry, I'll pay your hospital bill."

Paul's testimony concerning Dyer's statement is

(A) admissible, because it is an admission of liability by a party opponent.
(B) admissible, because it is within the excited utterance exception to the hearsay rule.
(C) inadmissible to prove liability, because it is an offer to pay medical expenses.
(D) inadmissible, provided that Dyer kept his promise to pay Paul's medical expenses.

Question 149

In a civil action for personal injury, Payne alleges that he was beaten up by Dabney during an altercation in a crowded bar. Dabney's defense is that he was not the person who hit Payne. To corroborate his testimony about the cause of his injuries, Payne seeks to introduce, through the hospital records custodian, a notation in a regular medical record made by an emergency room doctor at the hospital where Payne was treated for his injuries. The notation is: "Patient says he was attacked by Dabney."

The notation is

(A) inadmissible, unless the doctor who made the record is present at trial and available for cross-examination.

(B) inadmissible as hearsay, not within any exception.

(C) admissible as hearsay, within the exception for records of regularly conducted activity.

(D) admissible as a statement made for the purpose of medical diagnosis or treatment.

Question 150

In a federal investigation of Defendant for tax fraud, the grand jury seeks to obtain a letter written January 15 by Defendant to her attorney in which she stated: "Please prepare a deed giving my ranch to University but, in order to get around the tax law, I want it back-dated to December 15." The attorney refuses to produce the letter on the ground of privilege.

Production of the letter should be

(A) prohibited, because the statement is protected by the attorney-client privilege.

(B) prohibited, because the statement is protected by the client's privilege against self-incrimination.

(C) required, because the statement was in furtherance of crime or fraud.

(D) required, because the attorney-client privilege belongs to the client and can be claimed only by her.

Question 151

Plaintiff sued Defendant for breach of a commercial contract in which Defendant had agreed to sell Plaintiff all of Plaintiff's requirements for widgets. Plaintiff called Expert Witness to testify as to damages. Defendant seeks to show that Expert Witness had provided false testimony as a witness in his own divorce proceedings.

This evidence should be

(A) admitted only if elicited from Expert Witness on cross-examination.

(B) admitted only if the false testimony is established by clear and convincing extrinsic evidence.

(C) excluded, because it is impeachment on a collateral issue.

(D) excluded, because it is improper character evidence.

Question 152

Plaintiff sued Defendant for illegal discrimination, claiming that Defendant fired him because of his race. At trial, Plaintiff called Witness, expecting him to testify that Defendant had admitted the racial motivation. Instead, Witness testified that Defendant said that he had fired Plaintiff because of his frequent absenteeism. While Witness is still on the stand, Plaintiff offers a properly authenticated secret tape recording he had made at a meeting with Witness in which Witness related Defendant's admissions of racial motivation.

The tape recording is

(A) admissible as evidence of Defendant's racial motivation and to impeach Witness's testimony.

(B) admissible only to impeach Witness's testimony.

(C) inadmissible, because it is hearsay not within any exception.

(D) inadmissible, because a secret recording is an invasion of Witness's right of privacy under the U.S. Constitution.

Question 153

At Dove's trial for theft, Mr. Wong, called by the prosecutor, testified to the following: 1) that from his apartment window, he saw thieves across the street break the window of a jewelry store, take jewelry, and leave in a car; 2) that Mrs. Wong telephoned the police and relayed to them the license number of the thieves' car as Mr. Wong looked out the window with binoculars and read it to her; 3) that he has no present memory of the number, but that immediately afterward he listened to a playback of the police tape recording giving the license number (which belongs to Dove's car) and verified that she had relayed the number accurately.

Playing the tape recording for the jury would be

(A) proper, because it is recorded recollection.

(B) proper, because it is a public record or report.

(C) improper, because it is hearsay not within any exception.

(D) improper, because Mrs. Wong lacked firsthand knowledge of the license number.

Question 154

Plaintiff's estate sued Defendant Stores claiming that Guard, one of Defendant's security personnel, wrongfully shot and killed Plaintiff when Plaintiff fled after being accused of shoplifting. Guard was convicted of manslaughter for killing Plaintiff. At his criminal trial Guard, who was no longer working for Defendant, testified that Defendant's security director had instructed him to stop shoplifters "at all costs." Because Guard's criminal conviction is on appeal, he refuses to testify at the civil trial. Plaintiff's estate then offers an authenticated transcript of Guard's criminal trial testimony concerning the instructions of Defendant's security director.

This evidence is

(A)   admissible as a statement of an agent of a party-opponent.
(B)   admissible, because the instruction from the security director is not hearsay.
(C)   admissible, although hearsay, as former testimony.
(D)   inadmissible, because it is hearsay not within any exception.

Question 155

Mrs. Pence sued Duarte for shooting her husband from ambush. Mrs. Pence offers to testify that, the day before her husband was killed, he described to her a chance meeting with Duarte on the street in which Duarte said, "I'm going to blow your head off one of these days."

The witness's testimony concerning her husband's statement is

(A)   admissible, to show Duarte's state of mind.
(B)   admissible, because Duarte's statement is that of a party-opponent.
(C)   inadmissible, because it is improper evidence of a prior bad act.
(D)   inadmissible, because it is hearsay not within any exception.

Question 156

Defendant is on trial for robbing a bank in State A. She testified that she was in State B at the time of the robbery. Defendant calls her friend, Witness, to testify that two days before the robbery Defendant told him that she was going to spend the next three days in State B.

Witness's testimony is

(A) admissible, because the statement falls within the present sense impression exception to the hearsay rule.

(B) admissible, because a statement of plans falls within the hearsay exception for then-existing state of mind.
(C) inadmissible, because it is offered to establish an alibi by Defendant's own statement.
(D) inadmissible, because it is hearsay not within any exception.

Question 157

Paul sued Donna for breach of contract. Paul's position was that Joan, whom he understood to be Donna's agent, said: "On behalf of Donna, I accept your offer." Donna asserted that Joan had no actual or apparent authority to accept the offer on Donna's behalf.

Paul's testimony concerning Joan's statement is

(A) admissible, provided the court first finds by a preponderance of the evidence that Joan had actual or apparent authority to act for Donna.
(B) admissible, upon or subject to introduction of evidence sufficient to support a finding by the jury that Joan had actual or apparent authority to act for Donna.
(C) inadmissible, if Joan does not testify and her absence is not excused.
(D) inadmissible, because it is hearsay not within any exception.

Question 158

Defendant is on trial for the murder of his father. Defendant's defense is that he shot his father accidentally. The prosecutor calls Witness, a police officer, to testify that on two occasions in the year prior to this incident, he had been called to Defendant's home because of complaints of loud arguments between Defendant and his father, and had found it necessary to stop Defendant from beating his father.

The evidence is

(A) inadmissible, because it is improper character evidence.
(B) inadmissible, because Witness lacks firsthand knowledge of who started the quarrels.
(C) admissible to show that Defendant killed his father intentionally.
(D) admissible to show that Defendant is a violent person.

Question 159

Plaintiff is suing Doctor for medical malpractice occasioned by allegedly prescribing an incorrect medication, causing Plaintiff to undergo substantial hospitalization. When Doctor learned of the medication problem, she immediately offered to pay Plaintiff's hospital expenses. At trial, Plaintiff offers evidence of Doctor's offer to pay the costs of his hospitalization.

The evidence of Doctor's offer is

(A) admissible as a nonhearsay statement of a party.
(B) admissible, although hearsay, as a statement against interest.
(C) inadmissible, because it is an offer to pay medical expenses.
(D) inadmissible, because it is an offer to compromise.

Question 160

Plaintiff sued Defendant Auto Manufacturing for his wife's death, claiming that a defective steering mechanism on the family car caused it to veer off the road and hit a tree when his wife was driving. Defendant claims that the steering mechanism was damaged in the collision and offers testimony that the deceased wife was intoxicated at the time of the accident.

Testimony concerning the wife's intoxication is

(A) admissible to provide an alternate explanation of the accident's cause.
(B) admissible as proper evidence of the wife's character.
(C) inadmissible, because it is improper to prove character evidence by specific conduct.
(D) inadmissible, because it is substantially more prejudicial than probative.

Question 161

Plaintiff Construction Co. sued Defendant Development Co. for money owed on a cost-plus contract that required notice of proposed expenditures beyond original estimates. Defendant asserted that it never received the required notice. At trial Plaintiff calls its general manager, Witness, to testify that it is Plaintiff's routine practice to send cost overrun notices as required by the contract. Witness also offers a photocopy of the cost overrun notice letter to Defendant on which Plaintiff is relying, and which he has taken from Plaintiff's regular business files.

On the issue of giving notice, the letter copy is

(A) admissible, though hearsay, under the business record exception.
(B) admissible, because of the routine practices of the company.
(C) inadmissible, because it is hearsay not within any exception.
(D) inadmissible, because it is not the best evidence of the notice.

Question 162

Plaintiff sued Defendant under an age discrimination statute, alleging that Defendant refused to hire Plaintiff because she was over age 65. Defendant's defense was that he refused to employ Plaintiff because he reasonably believed that she would be unable to perform the job. Defendant seeks to testify that Employer, Plaintiff's former employer, advised him not to hire Plaintiff because she was unable to perform productively for more than four hours a day.

The testimony of Defendant is

(A) inadmissible, because Defendant's opinion of Plaintiff's abilities is not based on personal knowledge.
(B) inadmissible, because Employer's statement is hearsay not within any exception.
(C) admissible as evidence that Plaintiff would be unable to work longer than four hours per day.
(D) admissible as evidence of Defendant's reason for refusing to hire Plaintiff.

Question 163

In a jurisdiction without a Dead Man's Statute, Parker's estate sued Davidson claiming that Davidson had borrowed from Parker $10,000, which had not been repaid as of Parker's death. Parker was run over by a truck. At the accident scene, while dying from massive injuries, Parker told Officer Smith to "make sure my estate collects the $10,000 I loaned to Davidson."

Smith's testimony about Parker's statement is

(A) inadmissible, because it is more unfairly prejudicial than probative.
(B) inadmissible, because it is hearsay not within any exception.
(C) admissible as an excited utterance.
(D) admissible as a statement under belief of impending death.

Question 164

Defendant is charged with murder in connection with a carjacking incident during which Defendant allegedly shot Victim while attempting to steal Victim's car. The prosecutor calls Victim's four-year-old son, whose face was horribly disfigured by the same bullet, to testify that Defendant shot his father and him.

The son's testimony should be

(A) admitted, provided the prosecutor first provides evidence that persuades the judge that the son is competent to testify despite his tender age.
(B) admitted, provided there is sufficient basis for believing that the son has personal knowledge and understands his obligation to testify truthfully.
(C) excluded, because it is insufficiently probative in view of the son's tender age.
(D) excluded, because it is more unfairly prejudicial than probative.

Question 165

On trial for murdering her husband, Defendant testified she acted in self-defense. Defendant calls Expert, a psychologist, to testify that under hypnosis Defendant had described the killing, and that in Expert's opinion Defendant had been in fear for her life at the time of the killing.

Is Expert's testimony admissible?

(A) Yes, because Expert was able to ascertain that Defendant was speaking truthfully.
(B) Yes, because it reports a prior consistent statement by a witness (Defendant) subject to examination concerning it.
(C) No, because reliance on information tainted by hypnosis is unconstitutional.
(D) No, because it expresses an opinion concerning Defendant's mental state at the time of the killing.

Question 166

Plaintiff sued Defendant for injuries suffered in a car accident allegedly caused by brakes that had been negligently repaired by Defendant. At a settlement conference, Plaintiff exhibited the brake shoe that caused the accident and pointed out the alleged defect to an expert, whom Defendant had brought to the conference. No settlement was reached. At trial, the brake shoe having disappeared, Plaintiff seeks to testify concerning the condition of the shoe.

Plaintiff's testimony is

(A) admissible, because Defendant's expert had been able to examine the shoe carefully.
(B) admissible, because Plaintiff had personal knowledge of the shoe's condition.
(C) inadmissible, because the brake shoe was produced and examined as a part of settlement negotiations.
(D) inadmissible, unless Plaintiff establishes that the disappearance was not his fault.

Question 167

Defendant is on trial for nighttime breaking and entering of a warehouse. The warehouse owner had set up a camera to take infrared pictures of any intruders. After an expert establishes the reliability of infrared photography, the prosecutor offers the authenticated infrared picture of the intruder to show the similarities to Defendant.

The photograph is

(A) admissible, provided an expert witness points out to the jury the similarities between the person in the photograph and Defendant.
(B) admissible, allowing the jury to compare the person in the photograph and Defendant.
(C) inadmissible, because there was no eyewitness to the scene available to authenticate the photograph.
(D) inadmissible, because infrared photography deprives a defendant of the right to confront witnesses.

Question 168

Defendant is on trial for extorting $10,000 from Victim. An issue is the identification of the person who made a telephone call to Victim. Victim is prepared to testify that the caller had a distinctive accent like Defendant's, but that he cannot positively identify the voice as Defendant's. Victim recorded the call but has not brought the tape to court, although its existence is known to Defendant.

Victim's testimony is

(A) inadmissible, because Victim cannot sufficiently identify the caller.
(B) inadmissible, because the tape recording of the conversation is the best evidence.

(C) admissible, because Defendant waived the "best evidence" rule by failing to subpoena the tape.

(D) admissible, because Victim's lack of certainty goes to the weight to be given Victim's testimony, not to its admissibility.

Question 169

Plaintiff sued Defendant for personal injuries suffered in a train-automobile collision. Plaintiff called an eyewitness, who testified that the train was going 20 miles per hour. Defendant then offers the testimony of an experienced police accident investigator that, based on his training and experience and on his examination of the physical evidence, it is his opinion that the train was going between 5 and 10 miles per hour.

Testimony by the investigator is

(A) improper, because there cannot be both lay and expert opinion on the same issue.

(B) improper, because the investigator is unable to establish the speed with a sufficient degree of scientific certainty.

(C) proper, because a police accident investigator has sufficient expertise to express an opinion on speed.

(D) proper, because Plaintiff first introduced opinion evidence as to speed.

Question 170

At Devlin's trial for burglary, Jaron supported Devlin's alibi that they were fishing together at the time of the crime. On cross-examination, Jaron was asked whether his statement on a credit card application that he had worked for his present employer for the last five years was false. Jaron denied that the statement was false.

The prosecutor then calls Wilcox, the manager of the company for which Jaron works, to testify that although Jaron had been first employed five years earlier and is now employed by the company, there had been a three-year period during which he had not been so employed.

The testimony of Wilcox is

(A) admissible, in the judge's discretion, because Jaron's credibility is a fact of major consequence to the case.

(B) admissible, as a matter of right, because Jaron "opened the door" by his denial on cross-examination.

(C) inadmissible, because whether Jaron lied in his application is a matter that cannot be proved by extrinsic evidence.

(D) inadmissible, because the misstatement by Jaron could have been caused by misunderstanding of the application form.

Question 171

Passenger is suing Defendant for injuries suffered in the crash of a small airplane, alleging that Defendant had owned the plane and negligently failed to have it properly maintained. Defendant has asserted in defense that he never owned the plane or had any responsibility to maintain it. At trial, Passenger calls Witness to testify that Witness had sold to Defendant a liability insurance policy on the plane.

The testimony of Witness is

(A) inadmissible, because the policy itself is required under the original document rule.

(B) inadmissible, because of the rule against proof of insurance where insurance is not itself at issue.

(C) admissible to show that Defendant had little motivation to invest money in maintenance of the airplane.

(D) admissible as some evidence of Defendant's ownership of or responsibility for the airplane.

Question 172

Pedestrian died from injuries caused when Driver's car struck him. Executor, Pedestrian's executor, sued Driver for wrongful death. At trial, Executor calls Nurse to testify that two days after the accident, Pedestrian said to Nurse, "The car that hit me ran the red light." Fifteen minutes thereafter, Pedestrian died.

As a foundation for introducing evidence of Pedestrian's statement, Executor offers to the court Doctor's affidavit that Doctor was the intern on duty the day of Pedestrian's death and that several times that day Pedestrian had said that he knew he was about to die.

Is the affidavit properly considered by the court in ruling on the admissibility of Pedestrian's statement?

(A) No, because it is hearsay not within any exception.

(B) No, because it is irrelevant since dying declarations cannot be used except in prosecutions for homicide.

(C) Yes, because, though hearsay, it is a statement of then-existing mental condition.

(D) Yes, because the judge may consider hearsay in ruling on preliminary questions.

Question 173

Plaintiff sued Defendant for personal injuries arising out of an automobile accident.

Which of the following would be ERROR?

(A) The judge allows Defendant's attorney to ask Defendant questions on cross-examination that go well beyond the scope of direct examination by Plaintiff, who has been called as an adverse witness.

(B) The judge refuses to allow Defendant's attorney to cross-examine Defendant by leading questions.

(C) The judge allows cross-examination about the credibility of a witness even though no question relating to credibility has been asked on direct examination.

(D) The judge, despite Defendant's request for exclusion of witnesses, allows Plaintiff's eyewitness to remain in the courtroom after testifying, even though the eyewitness is expected to be recalled for further cross-examination.

Question 174

Phil is suing Dennis for injuries suffered in an automobile collision. At trial Phil's first witness, Wanda, testified that, although she did not see the accident, she heard her friend Frank say just before the crash, "Look at the crazy way old Dennis is driving!" Dennis offers evidence to impeach Frank by asking Wanda, "Isn't it true that Frank beat up Dennis just the day before the collision?"

The question is

(A) proper, because it tends to show the possible bias of Frank against Dennis.

(B) proper, because it tends to show Frank's character.

(C) improper, because Frank has no opportunity to explain or deny.

(D) improper, because impeachment cannot properly be by specific instances.

Question 175

Defendant was charged with attempted murder of Victor in a sniping incident in which Defendant allegedly shot at Victor from ambush as Victor drove his car along an expressway. The prosecutor offers evidence that seven years earlier Defendant had fired a shotgun into a woman's home and that Defendant had once pointed a handgun at another driver while driving on the street.

This evidence should be

(A) excluded, because such evidence can be elicited only during cross-examination.

(B) excluded, because it is improper character evidence.

(C) admitted as evidence of Defendant's propensity toward violence.

(D) admitted as relevant evidence of Defendant's identity, plan, or motive.

Question 176

At Defendant's murder trial, Defendant calls Witness as his first witness to testify that Defendant has a reputation in their community as a peaceable and truthful person. The prosecutor objects on the ground that Witness's testimony would constitute improper character evidence.

The court should

(A) admit the testimony as to peaceableness, but exclude the testimony as to truthfulness.

(B) admit the testimony as to truthfulness, but exclude the testimony as to peaceableness.

(C) admit the testimony as to both character traits.

(D) exclude the testimony as to both character traits.

Question 177

In a federal civil trial, Plaintiff wishes to establish that, in a state court, Defendant had been convicted of fraud, a fact that Defendant denies.

Which mode of proof of the conviction is LEAST likely to be permitted?

(A) A certified copy of the judgment of conviction, offered as a self-authenticating document.

(B) Testimony of Plaintiff, who was present at the time of the sentence.

(C) Testimony by a witness to whom Defendant made an oral admission that he had been convicted.

(D) Judicial notice of the conviction, based on the court's telephone call to the clerk of the state court, whom the judge knows personally.

Question 178

Plaintiff sued Defendant for injuries sustained in an automobile collision. During Plaintiff's hospital stay, Doctor, a staff physician, examined Plaintiff's X rays and said to Plaintiff, "You have a fracture of two vertebrae, C4 and C5." Intern, who was accompanying Doctor on her rounds, immediately wrote the diagnosis on Plaintiff's hospital record. At trial, the hospital records custodian testifies that Plaintiff's hospital record was made and kept in the ordinary course of the hospital's business.

The entry reporting Doctor's diagnosis is

(A) inadmissible, because no foundation has been laid for Doctor's competence as an expert.
(B) inadmissible, because Doctor's opinion is based upon data that are not in evidence.
(C) admissible as a statement of then-existing physical condition.
(D) admissible as a record of regularly conducted business activity.

Question 179

Defendant is on trial for participating in a drug sale. The prosecution calls Witness, an undercover officer, to testify that, when Seller sold the drugs to Witness, Seller introduced Defendant to Witness as "my partner in this" and Defendant shook hands with Witness but said nothing.

Witness's testimony is

(A) inadmissible, because there is no evidence that Seller was authorized to speak for Defendant.
(B) inadmissible, because the statement of Seller is hearsay not within any exception.
(C) admissible as a statement against Defendant's penal interest.
(D) admissible as Defendant's adoption of Seller's statement.

Question 180

At Defendant's trial for sale of drugs, the government called Witness to testify, but Witness refused to answer any questions about Defendant and was held in contempt of court. The government then calls Officer to testify that, when Witness was arrested for possession of drugs and offered leniency if he would identify his source, Witness had named Defendant as his source.

The testimony offered concerning Witness's identification of Defendant is

(A) admissible as a prior inconsistent statement by Witness.
(B) admissible as an identification of Defendant by Witness after having perceived him.
(C) inadmissible, because it is hearsay not within any exception.
(D) inadmissible, because Witness was not confronted with the statement while on the stand.

Question 181

In an arson prosecution the government seeks to rebut Defendant's alibi that he was in a jail in another state at the time of the fire. The government calls Witness to testify that he diligently searched through all the records of the jail and found no record of Defendant's having been incarcerated there during the time Defendant specified.

The testimony of Witness is

(A) admissible as evidence of absence of an entry from a public record.
(B) admissible as a summary of voluminous documents.
(C) inadmissible, because it is hearsay not within any exception.
(D) inadmissible, because the records themselves must be produced.

Question 182

PullCo sued Davidson, its former vice president, for return of $230,000 that had been embezzled during the previous two years. Called by PullCo as an adverse witness, Davidson testified that his annual salary had been $75,000, and he denied the embezzlement. PullCo calls banker Witt to show that, during the two-year period, Davidson had deposited $250,000 in his bank account.

Witt's testimony is

(A) admissible as circumstantial evidence of Davidson's guilt.
(B) admissible to impeach Davidson.
(C) inadmissible, because its prejudicial effect substantially outweighs its probative value.

(D) inadmissible, because the deposits could have come from legitimate sources.

Question 183

Susan entered a guilty plea to a charge of embezzlement. Her attorney hired a retired probation officer as a consultant to gather information for the preparation of a sentencing plan for Susan that would avoid jail. For that purpose, the consultant interviewed Susan for three hours.

Thereafter, the prosecution undertook an investigation of Susan's possible involvement in other acts of embezzlement. The consultant was subpoenaed to testify before a grand jury. The consultant refused to answer any questions concerning her conversation with Susan. The prosecution has moved for an order requiring her to answer those questions.

The motion should be

(A) denied, on the basis of the attorney-client privilege.
(B) denied, in the absence of probable cause to believe the interview developed evidence relevant to the grand jury's inquiry.
(C) granted, because the consultant is not an attorney.
(D) granted, because exclusionary evidentiary rules do not apply in grand jury proceedings.

AMERIBAR BAR REVIEW

Multistate Bar Examination Released Questions – Section 7

REAL PROPERTY

Question 1

Anna entered a hospital to undergo surgery and feared that she might not survive. She instructed her lawyer by telephone to prepare a deed conveying Blackacre, a large tract of undeveloped land, as a gift to her nephew, Bernard, who lived in a distant state. Her instructions were followed, and, prior to her surgery, she executed a document in a form sufficient to constitute a deed of conveyance. The deed was recorded by the lawyer promptly and properly as she instructed him to do. The recorded deed was returned to the lawyer by the land record office, Anna, in fact, recovered from her surgery and the lawyer returned the recorded deed to her.

Before Anna or the lawyer thought to inform Bernard of the conveyance, Bernard was killed in an auto accident. Bernard's will left all of his estate to a satanic religious cult. Anna was very upset at the prospect of the cult's acquiring Blackacre.

The local taxing authority assessed the next real property tax bill on Blackacre to Bernard's estate.

Anna brought an appropriate action against Bernard's estate and the cult to set aside the conveyance to Bernard.

If Anna loses, it will be because

(A) the gift of Blackacre was inter vivos rather than causa mortis.
(B) the showing of Bernard's estate as the owner of Blackacre on the tax rolls supplied what otherwise would be a missing essential element for a valid conveyance.
(C) disappointing Bernard's devisee would violate the religious freedom provisions of the First Amendment to the Constitution.
(D) delivery of the deed is presumed from the recording of the deed.

Question 2

Amos owned Greenfield, a tract of land. His friend Bert wanted to buy Greenfield and offered $20,000 for it. Amos knew that Bert was insolvent, but replied, "As a favor to you as an old friend, I will sell Greenfield to you for $20,000, even though it is worth much more, if you can raise the money within one month." Bert wrote the following words, and no more, on a piece of paper: "I agree to sell Greenfield for $20,000." Amos then signed the piece of paper and gave it to Bert.

Three days later, Amos received an offer of $40,000 for Greenfield. He asked Bert if he had raised the $20,000. When Bert answered, "Not yet," Amos told him that their deal was off and that he was going to accept the $40,000 offer.

The next week, Bert secured a bank commitment to enable him to purchase Greenfield. Bert immediately brought an appropriate action against Amos to compel Amos to convey Greenfield to him. The following points will be raised during the course of the trial.

I. The parol evidence rule.
II. Construction of the contract as to time of performance.
III. Bert's ability to perform.

Which will be relevant to a decision in favor of Bert?
(A) I only.
(B) I and II only.
(C) II and III only.
(D) I, II, and III.

Question 3

Two adjacent, two-story, commercial buildings were owned by Simon. The first floors of both buildings were occupied by various retail establishments. The second floors were rented to various other tenants. Access to the second floor of each building was reached by a common stairway located entirely in Building 1. While the buildings were being used in this manner, Simon sold Building 1 to Edward by warranty deed which made no mention of any rights concerning the stairway. About two years later Simon sold Building 2 to Dennis. The stairway continued to be used by the occupants of both buildings. The stairway became unsafe as a consequence of regular wear and tear. Dennis entered upon Edward's building and began the work of repairing the stairway. Edward demanded that Dennis discontinue the repair work and vacate Edward's building. When Dennis refused, Edward brought an action to enjoin Dennis from continuing the work.

Judgment should be for

(A) Edward, because Dennis has no rights in the stairway.

(B) Edward, because Dennis's rights in the stairway do not extend beyond the normal life of the existing structure.
(C) Dennis, because Dennis has an easement in the stairway and an implied right to keep the stairway in repair.
(D) Dennis, because Dennis has a right to take whatever action is necessary to protect himself from possible tort liability to persons using the stairway.

Question 4

Aris was the owner in fee simple of adjoining lots known as Lot 1 and Lot 2. He built a house in which he took up residence on Lot 1. Thereafter, he built a house on Lot 2, which he sold, house and lot, to Baker. Consistent with the contract of sale and purchase, the deed conveying Lot 2 from Aris to Baker contained the following clause:

In the event Baker, his heirs or assigns, decide to sell the property hereby conveyed and obtain a purchaser ready, willing, and able to purchase Lot 2 and the improvements thereon on terms and conditions acceptable to Baker, said Lot 2 and improvements shall be offered to Aris, his heirs or assigns, on the same terms and conditions. Aris, his heirs or assigns, as the case may be, shall have ten days from said offer to accept said offer and thereby to exercise said option.

Three years after delivery and recording of the deed and payment of the purchase price, Baker became ill and moved to a climate more compatible with his health. Baker's daughter orally offered to purchase the premises from Baker at its then fair market value. Baker declined his daughter's offer but instead deeded Lot 2 to his daughter as a gift.

Immediately thereafter, Baker's daughter sold Lot 2 to Charles at the then fair market value of Lot 2. The sale was completed by the delivery of deed and payment of the purchase price. At no time did Baker or his daughter offer to sell Lot 2 to Aris.

Aris learned of the conveyance to Baker's daughter and the sale by Baker's daughter to Charles one week after the conveyance of Lot 2 from Baker's daughter to Charles. Aris promptly brought an appropriate action against Charles to enforce rights created in him by the deed of Aris to Baker. Aris tendered the amount paid by Charles into the court for whatever disposition the court deemed proper. The common-law Rule Against Perpetuities is unmodified by statute.

Which of the following will determine whether Aris will prevail?

I.   The parol evidence rule.
II.   The Statute of Frauds.
III. The type of recording statute of the jurisdiction in question.
IV.   The Rule Against Perpetuities.

(A) I only.
(B) IV only.
(C) I and IV only.
(D) II and III only.

Question 5

Len owned two adjoining parcels known as Lot 1 and Lot 2. Both parcels fronted on Main Street and abutted a public alley in the rear. Lot 1 was improved with a commercial building that covered all of the Main Street frontage of Lot 1; there was a large parking lot on the rear of Lot 1 with access from the alley only.

Fifteen years ago, Len leased Lot 1 to Tenny for 15 years. Tenny has continuously occupied Lot 1 since that time. Thirteen years ago, without Len's permission, Tenny began to use a driveway on Lot 2 as a better access between Main Street and the parking lot than the alley.

Eight years ago, Len conveyed Lot 2 to Owen and, five years ago, Len conveyed Lot 1 to Tenny by a deed that recited "together with all the appurtenances,"

Until last week, Tenny continuously used the driveway over Lot 2 to Tenny's parking lot in the rear of Lot 1.

Last week Owen commenced construction of a building on Lot 2 and blocked the driveway used by Tenny. Tenny has commenced an action against Owen to restrain him from blocking the driveway from Main Street to the parking lot at the rear of Lot 1.

The period of time to acquire rights by prescription in the jurisdiction is ten years.

If Tenny loses, it will be because

(A)   Len owned both Lot 1 and Lot 2 until eight years ago.
(B)   Tenny has access to the parking lot from the alley.

(C)   mere use of an easement is not adverse possession.

(D)   no easement was mentioned in the deed from Len to Owen.

Question 6

Arnold and Beverly owned a large tract of land, Blackacre, in fee simple as joint tenants with rights of survivorship. While Beverly was on an extended safari in Kenya, Arnold learned that there were very valuable coal deposits within Blackacre, but he made no attempt to inform Beverly. Thereupon, Arnold conveyed his interest in Blackacre to his wife, Alice, who immediately reconveyed that interest to Arnold. The common-law joint tenancy is unmodified by statute.

Shortly thereafter, Arnold was killed in an automobile accident. His will, which was duly probated, specifically devised his one-half interest in Blackacre to Alice.

Beverly then returned from Kenya and learned what had happened. Beverly brought an appropriate action against Alice, who claimed a one-half interest in Blackacre, seeking a declaratory judgment that she, Beverly, was the sole owner of Blackacre.

In this action, who should prevail?

(A)   Alice, because Arnold and Beverly were tenants in common at the time of Arnold's death.

(B)   Alice, because Arnold's will severed the joint tenancy.

(C)   Beverly, because the joint tenancy was reestablished by Alice's reconveyance to Arnold.

(D)   Beverly, because Arnold breached his fiduciary duty as her joint tenant.

Question 7

At the time of his death last week, Test owned Blackacre, a small farm. By his duly probated will, drawn five years ago, Test did the following:

> (1)   devised Blackacre "to Arthur for the life of Baker, then to Casper";
>
> (2)   gave "all the rest, residue and remainder of my Estate, both real and personal, to my friend Fanny."

At his death, Test was survived by Arthur, Casper, Sonny (Test's son and sole heir), and Fanny. Baker had died a week before Test.

Title to Blackacre is now in

(A)   Arthur for life, remainder to Casper.
(B)   Casper, in fee simple.
(C)   Sonny, in fee simple.
(D)   Fanny, in fee simple.

Question 8

Allen owned Greenacre in fee simple of record on January 10. On that day, Maria loaned Allen $50,000 and Allen mortgaged Greenacre to Maria as security for the loan. The mortgage was recorded on January 18.

Allen conveyed Greenacre to Barnes for a valuable consideration on January 11. Maria did not know of this, nor did Barnes know of the mortgage to Maria, until both discovered the facts on January 23, the day on which Barnes recorded Allen's deed.

The recording act of the jurisdiction provides: "No unrecorded conveyance or mortgage of real property shall be good against subsequent purchasers for value without notice, who shall first record." There is no provision for a period of grace and there is no other relevant statutory provision.

Maria sued Barnes to establish that her mortgage was good against Greenacre.

The court should decide for

(A) Barnes, because he paid valuable consideration without notice before Maria recorded her mortgage.

(B) Barnes, because Maria's delay in recording means that she is estopped from asserting her priority in time.

(C) Maria, because Barnes did not record his deed before her mortgage was recorded.

(D) Maria, because after the mortgage to her, Allen's deed to Barnes was necessarily subject to her mortgage.

Question 9

Frank owned two adjacent parcels, Blackacre and Whiteacre. Blackacre fronts on a poor unpaved public road, while Whiteacre fronts on Route 20, a paved major highway. Fifteen years ago, Frank conveyed to his son, Sam, Blackacre "together with a right-of-way 25 feet wide over the east side of Whiteacre to Route

20." At that time, Blackacre was improved with a ten-unit motel.

Ten years ago, Frank died. His will devised Whiteacre "to my son, Sam, for life, remainder to my daughter, Doris." Five years ago, Sam executed an instrument in the proper form of a deed, purporting to convey Blackacre and Whiteacre to Joe in fee simple. Joe then enlarged the motel to 12 units. Six months ago, Sam died and Doris took possession of Whiteacre. She brought an appropriate action to enjoin Joe from using the right-of-way.

In this action, who should prevail?

(A)   Doris, because merger extinguished the easement.
(B)   Doris, because Joe has overburdened the easement.
(C)   Joe, because he has an easement by necessity.
(D)   Joe, because he has the easement granted by Frank to Sam.

Question 10

Twenty-five years ago, Seller conveyed Blackacre to Buyer by a warranty deed. Seller at that time also executed and delivered an instrument in the proper form of a deed, purporting to convey Whiteacre to Buyer. Seller thought she had title to Whiteacre but did not; therefore, no title passed by virtue of the Whiteacre deed. Whiteacre consisted of three acres of brushland adjoining the west boundary of Blackacre. Buyer has occasionally hunted rabbits on Whiteacre, but less often than annually. No one else came on Whiteacre except occasional rabbit hunters.

Twenty years ago, Buyer planted a row of evergreens in the vicinity of the opposite (east) boundary of Blackacre and erected a fence just beyond the evergreens to the east. In fact both the trees and the fence were placed on Greenacre, owned by Neighbor, which bordered the east boundary of Blackacre. Buyer was unsure of the exact boundary, and placed the trees and the fence in order to establish his rights up to the fence. The fence is located ten feet within Greenacre.

Now, Buyer has had his property surveyed and the title checked and has learned the facts.

The period of time to acquire title by adverse possession in the jurisdiction is 15 years.

Buyer consulted his lawyer, who properly advised that, in an appropriate action, Buyer would probably obtain title to

(A)   Whiteacre but not to the ten-foot strip of Greenacre.
(B)   the ten-foot strip of Greenacre but not to Whiteacre.
(C)   both Whiteacre and the ten-foot strip of Greenacre.
(D)   neither Whiteacre nor the ten-foot strip of Greenacre.

Question 11

Mom owned Blackacre, a two-family apartment house on a small city lot not suitable for partition-in-kind. Upon Mom's death, her will devised Blackacre to "my sons, Joe and John."

A week ago, Ken obtained a money judgment against Joe, and properly filed the judgment in the county where Blackacre is located. A statute in the jurisdiction provides: any judgment properly filed shall, for ten years from filing, be a lien on the real property then owned or subsequently acquired by any person against whom the judgment is rendered.

Joe needed cash, but John did not wish to sell Blackacre. Joe commenced a partition action against John and Ken.

Assume that the court properly ordered a partition by judicial sale.

After the sale, Ken's judgment will be a lien on

(A)   all of Blackacre.
(B)   only a one-half interest in Blackacre.
(C)   all of the proceeds of sale of Blackacre.
(D)   only the portion of the proceeds of sale due Joe.

Question 12

Adam entered into a valid written contract to sell Blackacre, a large tract of land, to Betsy. At that time, Blackacre was owned by Adam's father, Fred; Adam had no title to Blackacre and was not the agent of Fred.

After the contract was executed and before the scheduled closing date, Fred died intestate, leaving Adam as his sole heir. Shortly thereafter, Adam received an offer for Blackacre that was substantially higher than the purchase price in the contract with Betsy. Adam refused to close with Betsy although she was ready, willing, and able to close pursuant to the contract.

Betsy brought an appropriate action for specific performance against Adam.

In that action, Betsy should be awarded

(A)   nothing, because Adam had no authority to enter into the contract with Betsy.
(B)   nothing, because the doctrine of after-acquired title does not apply to executory contracts.
(C)   judgment for specific performance, because Adam acquired title prior to the scheduled closing.
(D)   judgment for specific performance, to prevent unjust enrichment of Adam.

Question 13

Leaseco owned Blackacre, a tract of 100 acres. Six years ago, Leaseco leased a one-acre parcel, Oneacre, located in the northeasterly corner of Blackacre, for a term of 30 years, to Eatco. Eatco intended to and did construct a fast-food restaurant on Oneacre.

The lease provided that:

   1.   Eatco was to maintain Oneacre and improvements thereon, to maintain full insurance coverage on Oneacre, and to pay all taxes assessed against Oneacre.

   2.   Leaseco was to maintain the access roads and the parking lot areas platted on those portions of Blackacre that adjoined Oneacre and to permit the customers of Eatco to use them in common with the customers of the other commercial users of the remainder of Blackacre.

   3.   Eatco was to pay its share of the expenses for the off-site improvements according to a stated formula.

Five years ago, Leaseco sold Oneacre to Jones, an investor; the conveyance was made subject to the lease to Eatco. However, Jones did not assume the obligations of the lease and Leaseco retained the remainder of Blackacre. Since that conveyance five years ago, Eatco has paid rent to Jones.

Eatco refused to pay its formula share of the off-site improvement costs as provided in the lease. Leaseco brought an appropriate action against Eatco to recover such costs.

The most likely outcome would be in favor of

(A) Leaseco, because the use of the improvements by the customers of Eatco imposes an implied obligation on Eatco.
(B) Leaseco, because the conveyance of Oneacre to Jones did not terminate Eatco's covenant to contribute.
(C) Eatco, because the conveyance of Oneacre to Jones terminated the privity of estate between Leaseco and Eatco.
(D) Eatco, because Jones, as Eatco's landlord, has the obligation to pay the maintenance costs by necessary implication.

Question 14

Five years ago, Sally acquired Blackacre, improved with a 15-year-old dwelling. This year Sally listed Blackacre for sale with Bill, a licensed real estate broker. Sally informed Bill of several defects in the house that were not readily discoverable by a reasonable inspection, including a leaky basement, an inadequate water supply, and a roof that leaked. Paul responded to Bill's advertisement, was taken by Bill to view Blackacre, and decided to buy it. Bill saw to it that the contract specified the property to be "as is" but neither Bill nor Sally pointed out the defects to Paul, who did not ask about the condition of the dwelling. After closing and taking possession, Paul discovered the defects, had them repaired, and demanded that Sally reimburse him for the cost of the repairs. Sally refused and Paul brought an appropriate action against Sally for damages.

If Sally wins, it will be because

(A)   Sally fulfilled the duty to disclose defects by disclosure to Bill.
(B)   the contract's "as is" provision controls the rights of the parties.
(C)   Bill became the agent of both Paul and Sally and thus knowledge of the defects was imputed to Paul.
(D)   the seller of a used dwelling that has been viewed by the buyer has no responsibility toward the buyer.

Question 15

Hal and Wan owned Blackacre as joint tenants, upon which was situated a two-family house. Hal lived in one of the two apartments and rented the other apartment to Tent. Hal got in a fight with Tent and injured him. Tent obtained and properly filed a judgment for $10,000 against Hal.

The statute in the jurisdiction reads: Any judgment properly filed shall, for ten years from filing, be a lien on the real property then owned or subsequently acquired by any person against whom the judgment is rendered.

Wan, who lived in a distant city, knew nothing of Tent's judgment. Before Tent took any further action, Hal died. The common-law joint tenancy is unmodified by statute.

Wan then learned the facts and brought an appropriate action against Tent to quiet title to Blackacre.

The court should hold that Tent has
(A) a lien against the whole of Blackacre, because he was a tenant of both Hal and Wan at the time of the judgment.
(B) a lien against Hal's undivided one-half interest in Blackacre, because his judgment was filed prior to Hal's death.
(C) no lien, because Wan had no actual notice of Tent's judgment until after Hal's death.
(D) no lien, because Hal's death terminated the interest to which Tent's lien attached.

Question 16

Orin owned in fee simple Blueacre, a farm of 300 acres. He died and by will duly admitted to probate devised Blueacre to his surviving widow, Wilma, for life with remainder in fee simple to his three children, Cindy, Clara, and Carter. All three children survived Orin.

At the time of Orin's death, there existed a mortgage on Blueacre that Orin had given ten years before to secure a loan for the purchase of the farm. At his death, there remained unpaid $40,000 in principal, payable in installments of $4,000 per year for the next ten years. In addition, there was due interest at the rate of 10% per annum, payable annually with the installment of principal. Wilma took possession and out of a gross income of $50,000 per year realized $25,000 net after paying all expenses and charges

except the installment of principal and interest due on the mortgage.

Carter and Cindy wanted the three children, including Clara, to each contribute one-third of the amounts needed to pay the mortgage installments. Clara objected, contending that Wilma should pay all of these amounts out of the profits she had made in operation of the farm. When foreclosure of the mortgage seemed imminent, Clara sought legal advice.

If Clara obtained sound advice relating to her rights, she was told that

(A) her only protection would lie in instituting an action for partition to compel the sale of the life estate of Wilma and to obtain the value of Clara's one-third interest in remainder.
(B) she could obtain appropriate relief to compel Wilma personally to pay the sums due because the income is more than adequate to cover these amounts.
(C) she could be compelled personally to pay her share of the amounts due because discharge of the mortgage enhances the principal.
(D) she could not be held personally liable for any amount but that her share in remainder could be lost if the mortgage installments are not paid.

Question 17

Adam had promised Bob that, if at any time Adam decided to sell his summer cottage property known as Blackacre, he would give Bob the opportunity to purchase Blackacre.

At a time when Bob was serving overseas with the United States Navy, Adam decided to sell Blackacre and spoke to Barbara, Bob's mother. Before Bob sailed, he had arranged for Barbara to become a joint owner of his various bank accounts so that Barbara would be able to pay his bills when he was gone. When she heard from Adam, Barbara took the necessary funds from Bob's account and paid Adam $20,000, the fair market value of Blackacre. Adam executed and delivered to Barbara a deed in the proper form purporting to convey Blackacre to Bob. Barbara promptly and properly recorded the deed.

Shortly thereafter, Barbara learned that Bob had been killed in an accident at sea one week before the delivery of the deed. Bob's Last Will, which has now been duly probated, leaves his entire estate to First Church. Barbara is the sole heir-at-law of Bob.

There is no statute dealing with conveyances to dead persons.

Title to Blackacre is now in

(A) First Church.
(B) Barbara.
(C) Adam free and clear.
(D) Adam, subject to a lien to secure $20,000 to Bob's estate.

Question 18

Rohan executed and delivered a promissory note and a mortgage securing the note to Acme Mortgage Company, which was named as payee in the note and as mortgagee in the mortgage. The note included a statement that the indebtedness evidenced by the note was "subject to the terms of a contract between the maker and the payee of the note executed on the same day" and that the note was "secured by a mortgage of even date." The mortgage was promptly and properly recorded. Subsequently, Acme sold the Rohan note and mortgage to XYZ Bank and delivered to XYZ Bank a written assignment of the Rohan note and mortgage. The assignment was promptly and properly recorded. Acme retained possession of both the note and the mortgage in order to act as collecting agent. Later, being short of funds, Acme sold the note and mortgage to Peterson at a substantial discount. Acme executed a written assignment of the note and mortgage to Peterson and delivered to him the note, the mortgage, and the assignment. Peterson paid value for the assignment without actual knowledge of the prior assignment to XYZ Bank and promptly and properly recorded his assignment. The principal of the note was not then due, and there had been no default in payment of either interest or principal.

If the issue of ownership of the Rohan note and mortgage is subsequently raised in an appropriate action by XYZ Bank to foreclose, the court should hold that

(A)   Peterson owns both the note and the mortgage.
(B)   XYZ Bank owns both the note and the mortgage.
(C)   Peterson owns the note and XYZ Bank owns the mortgage.
(D)   XYZ Bank owns the note and Peterson owns the mortgage.

Question 19

Stoven, who owned Craigmont in fee simple, mortgaged Craigmont to Ulrich to secure a loan of $100,000. The mortgage was promptly and properly recorded. Stoven later mortgaged Craigmont to Martin to secure a loan of $50,000, The mortgage was promptly and properly recorded. Subsequently, Stoven conveyed Craigmont to Fritsch. About a year later, Fritsch borrowed $100,000 from Zorn, an elderly widow, and gave her a mortgage on Craigmont to secure repayment of the loan. Zorn did not know about the mortgage held by Martin. The understanding between Fritsch and Zorn was that Fritsch would use the $100,000 to pay off the mortgage held by Ulrich and that Zorn would, therefore, have a first mortgage on Craigmont. Zorn's mortgage was promptly and properly recorded. Fritsch paid the $100,000 received from Zorn to Ulrich and obtained and recorded a release of the Ulrich mortgage.

The $50,000 debt secured by the Martin mortgage was not paid when it was due, and Martin brought an appropriate action to foreclose, joining Stoven, Fritsch, and Zorn as defendants and alleging that Martin's mortgage was senior to Zorn's mortgage on Craigmont.

If the court rules that Zorn's mortgage is entitled to priority over Martin's mortgage, which of the following determinations are necessary to support that ruling?

I. Ulrich's mortgage was originally senior to Martin's mortgage.
II. Zorn is entitled to have Ulrich's mortgage revived for her benefit, and Zorn is entitled to be subrogated to Ulrich's original position as senior mortgagee.
III. There are no countervailing equities in favor of Martin.

(A)   I and II only.
(B)   I and III only.
(C)   II and III only.
(D)   I, II, and III.

Question 20

Olin owned Blueacre, a valuable tract of land located in York County, Olin executed a document in the form of a warranty deed of Blueacre, which was regular in all respects except that the only language designating the grantees in each of the granting and habendum clauses was: "The leaders of all the Protestant Churches in York County." The instrument was acknowledged as required by statute and promptly and properly recorded. Olin told his lawyer, but no one else, that he had made the conveyance as he did because he abhorred sectarianism in the Protestant movement and because he thought that the leaders would devote the asset to lessening sectarianism.

Olin died suddenly and unexpectedly a week later, leaving a will that bequeathed and devised his entire estate to Plum. After probate of the will became final and the administration on Olin's estate was closed, Plum instituted an appropriate action to quiet title to Blueacre and properly served as defendant each Protestant church situated in the county.

The only evidence introduced consisted of the chain of title under which Olin held, the probated will, the recorded deed, the fact that no person knew about the deed except Olin and his lawyer, and the conversation Olin had with his lawyer described above.

In such action, judgment should be for

(A)   Plum,   because   there   is   inadequate identification of grantees in the deed.
(B)   Plum, because the state of the evidence would not support a finding of delivery of the
        deed.
(C)   the defendants, because a deed is prima facie valid until rebutted.
(D)   the   defendants,   because   recording established delivery prima facie until rebutted.

Question 21

Blackacre was a tract of 100 acres retained by Byron, the owner, after he had developed the adjoining 400 acres as a residential subdivision. Byron had effectively imposed restrictive covenants on each lot in the 400 acres. Chaney offered Byron a good price for a five-acre tract located in a corner of Blackacre far away from the existing 400-acre residential subdivision. Byron conveyed the five-acre tract to Chaney and imposed the same restrictive covenants on the five-acre tract as he had imposed on the lots in the adjoining 400 acres. Byron further covenanted that when he sold the remaining 95 acres of Blackacre he would impose the same restrictive covenants in the deed or deeds for the 95 acres. Byron's conveyance to Chaney was promptly and properly recorded.

However, shortly thereafter, Byron conveyed the remaining 95 acres to Dart for $100,000 by a deed that

made no mention of any restrictive covenants. Dart had no actual knowledge of the restrictive covenants in Chaney's deed.   Dart now proposes to build an industrial park which would violate such restrictive covenants if they are applicable.

The recording act of the jurisdiction provides: "No conveyance or mortgage of real property shall be good against subsequent purchasers for value and without notice unless the same be recorded according to law."

In an appropriate action by Chaney to enforce the restrictive covenants against Dart's 95-acre tract, if Dart wins it will be because

(A)   the deed imposing the restrictions was not in the chain of title for the 95 acres when Dart bought.
(B)   the disparity in acreage means that the covenant can only be personal to Byron.
(C)   negative reciprocal covenants are not generally recognized.
(D)   a covenant to impose restrictions is an illegal restraint on alienation.

Question 22

Owen owned Greenacre, a tract of land, in fee simple. By warranty deed he conveyed Greenacre to Lafe for life "and from and after the death of Lafe to Rem, her heirs and assigns."

Subsequently Rem died, devising all of her estate to Dan. Rem was survived by Hannah, her sole heir-at-law.

Shortly thereafter Lafe died, survived by Owen, Dan, and Hannah.

Title to Greenacre now is in

(A) Owen, because the contingent remainder never vested and Owen's reversion was entitled to possession immediately upon Lafe's death.
(B) Dan, because the vested remainder in Rem was transmitted by her will.
(C) Hannah, because she is Rem's heir.
(D) either Owen or Hannah, depending upon whether the destructibility of contingent remainders is recognized in the applicable jurisdiction.

Questions 23-24 are based on the following fact situation.

Pam and Dora own adjoining lots in the central portion of a city. Each of their lots had an office building. Dora decided to raze the existing building on her lot and to erect a building of greater height. Dora has received all governmental approvals required to pursue her project.

There is no applicable statute or ordinance (other than those dealing with various approvals for zoning, building, etc.).

Question 23

After Dora had torn down the existing building, she proceeded to excavate deeper. Dora used shoring that met all local, state, and federal safety regulations, and the shoring was placed in accordance with those standards.

Pam notified Dora that cracks were developing in the building situated on Pam's lot. Dora took the view that any subsidence suffered by Pam was due to the weight of Pam's building, and correctly asserted that none would have occurred had Pam's soil been in its natural state. Dora continued to excavate.

The building on Pam's lot did suffer extensive damage, requiring the expenditure of $750,000 to remedy the defects.

Which of the following is the best comment concerning Pam's action to recover damages from Dora?

(A) Dora is liable, because she removed necessary support for Pam's lot.
(B) Dora cannot be held liable simply upon proof that support was removed, but may be held liable if negligence is proved.
(C) Once land is improved with a building, the owner cannot invoke the common-law right of lateral support.
(D) Dora's only obligation was to satisfy all local, state, and federal safety regulations.

Question 24

Assume that no problems with subsidence or other misadventures occurred during construction of Dora's new building. However, when it was completed, Pam discovered that the shadow created by the new higher building placed her building in such deep shade that her ability to lease space was diminished and that the rent she could charge and the occupancy rate were substantially lower. Assume that these facts are proved in an appropriate action Pam instituted against Dora for all and any relief available.

Which of the following is the most appropriate comment concerning this lawsuit?

(A) Pam is entitled to a mandatory injunction requiring Dora to restore conditions to those existing with the prior building insofar as the shadow is concerned.
(B) The court should award permanent damages, in lieu of an injunction, equal to the present value of all rents lost and loss on rents for the reasonable life of the building.
(C) The court should award damages for losses suffered to the date of trial and leave open recovery of future damages.
(D) Judgment should be for Dora, because Pam has no cause of action.

Question 25

Able, owner of Blackacre and Whiteacre, two adjoining parcels, conveyed Whiteacre to Baker and covenanted in the deed to Baker that when he, Able, sold Blackacre he would impose restrictive covenants to prohibit uses that would compete with the filling station that Baker intended to construct and operate on Whiteacre. The deed was not recorded.

Baker constructed and operated a filling station on Whiteacre and then conveyed Whiteacre to Dodd, who continued the filling station use. The deed did not refer to the restrictive covenant and was promptly and properly recorded.

Able then conveyed Blackacre to Egan, who knew about Abie's covenant with Baker to impose a covenant prohibiting the filling station use but nonetheless completed the transaction when he noted that no such covenant was contained in Able's deed to him. Egan began to construct a filling station on Blackacre.

Dodd brought an appropriate action to enjoin Egan from using Blackacre for filling station purposes.

If Dodd prevails, it will be because

(A)   Egan had actual knowledge of the covenant to impose restrictions.
(B)   Egan is bound by the covenant because of the doctrine of negative reciprocal covenants.

(C)   business-related restrictive covenants are favored in the law.
(D)   Egan has constructive notice of the possibility of the covenant resulting from the circumstances.

Question 26

Owen contracted to sell Vacantacre to Perry. The written contract required Owen to provide evidence of marketable title of record, specified a closing date, stated that "time is of the essence," and provided that at closing, Owen would convey by warranty deed. Perry paid Owen $2,000 earnest money toward the $40,000 purchase price.

The title evidence showed that an undivided one-eighth interest in Vacantacre was owned by Alice. Perry immediately objected to title and said he would not close on Owen's title. Owen responded, accurately, that Alice was his daughter who would be trekking in Nepal until two weeks after the specified closing date. He said that she would gladly deed her interest upon her return, and that meanwhile his deed warranting title to all of Vacantacre would fully protect Perry. Owen duly tendered his deed but Perry refused to close.

Perry brought an appropriate action to recover the $2,000 earnest money promptly after the specified closing date. Owen counterclaimed for specific performance, tendering a deed from himself and Alice, who had by then returned.

The court will hold for

(A)   Owen, because Alice's deed completing the transfer was given within a reasonable time.
(B)   Owen, because his warranty deed would have given Perry adequate interim protection.
(C)   Perry, because Owen's title was not marketable and time was of the essence.
(D)   Perry, because under the circumstances the earnest money amount was excessive.

Question 27

Owen owned Greenacre in fee simple. The small house on Greenacre was occupied, with Owen's oral permission, rent-free, by Able, Owen's son, and Baker, a college classmate of Able. Able was then 21 years old.

Owen, by properly executed instrument, conveyed Greenacre to "my beloved son, Able, his heirs and assigns, upon the condition precedent that he earn a college degree by the time he reaches the age of 30. If, for any reason, he does not meet this condition, then Greenacre shall become the sole property of my beloved daughter, Anna, her heirs and assigns." At the time of the conveyance, Able and Baker attended a college located several blocks from Greenacre. Neither had earned a college degree.

One week after the delivery of the deed to Able, Able recorded the deed and immediately told Baker that he, Able, was going to begin charging Baker rent since "I am now your landlord." There is no applicable statute.

Able and Baker did not reach agreement, and Able served the appropriate notice to terminate whatever tenancy Baker had. Able then sought, in an appropriate action, to oust Baker.

Who should prevail?

(A)   Able, because the conveyance created a fee simple subject to divestment in Able.
(B)   Able, because Owen's conveyance terminated Baker's tenancy.
(C)   Baker, because Owen's permission to occupy preceded Owen's conveyance to Able.
(D)   Baker, because Baker is a tenant of Owen, not of Able.

Question 28

Owens owned Whiteacre, a dwelling house situated on a two-acre lot in an area zoned for single-family residential uses only. Although it was not discernible from the outside, Whiteacre had been converted by Owens from a single-family house to a structure that contained three separate apartments, in violation of the zoning ordinance. Further, the conversion was in violation of the building code.

Owens and Peters entered into a valid written contract for the purchase and sale of Whiteacre. The contract provided that Owens was to convey to Peters a marketable title. The contract was silent as to zoning. Peters had fully inspected Whiteacre.

Prior to the closing, Peters learned that Whiteacre did not conform to the zoning ordinance and refused to close although Owens was ready, willing, and able to perform his contract obligations. Owens brought an appropriate action for specific performance against Peters.

In that action, Owens should

(A)   win, because Owens was able to convey a marketable title.
(B)   win, because Peters was charged with knowledge of the zoning ordinance prior to entering the contract.
(C)   lose, because the illegal conversion of Whiteacre creates the risk of litigation.
(D)   lose, because the illegal conversion of Whiteacre was done by Owens rather than by a predecessor.

Question 29

Ozzie owned and occupied Blackacre, which was a tract of land improved with a one-family house. His friend Victor orally offered Ozzie $50,000 for Blackacre, the fair market value, and Ozzie accepted. Because they were friends, they saw no need for attorneys or written contracts and shook hands on the deal. Victor paid Ozzie $5,000 down in cash and agreed to pay the balance of $45,000 at an agreed closing time and place.

Before the closing, Victor inherited another home and asked Ozzie to return his $5,000. Ozzie refused, and, at the time set for the closing, Ozzie tendered a good deed to Victor and declared his intention to vacate Blackacre the next day. Ozzie demanded that Victor complete the purchase. Victor refused. The fair market value of Blackacre has remained $50,000.

In an appropriate action brought by Ozzie against Victor for specific performance, if Ozzie loses, the most likely reason will be that

(A)   the agreement was oral.
(B)   keeping the $5,000 is Ozzie's exclusive remedy.
(C)   Victor had a valid reason for not closing.
(D)   Ozzie remained in possession on the day set for the closing.

Question 30

Twenty years ago, Test, who owned Blackacre, a one-acre tract of land, duly delivered a deed of Blackacre "to School District so long as it is used for school purposes." The deed was promptly and properly recorded. Five years ago, Test died leaving Sonny as his only heir but, by his duly probated will, he left "all my Estate to my friend Fanny."

Last month, School District closed its school on Blackacre and for valid consideration duly executed and delivered a quitclaim deed of Blackacre to Owner, who planned to use the land for commercial development. Owner has now brought an appropriate action to quiet title against Sonny, Fanny, and School District.

The only applicable statute is a provision in the jurisdiction's probate code which provides that any property interest which is descendible is devisable.

In such action, the court should find that title is now in

(A)   Owner.
(B)   Sonny.
(C)   Fanny.
(D)   School District.

Question 31

By warranty deed, Marta conveyed Blackacre to Beth and Christine "as joint tenants with right of survivorship." Beth and Christine are not related. Beth conveyed all her interest to Eugenio by warranty deed and subsequently died intestate. Thereafter, Christine conveyed to Darin by warranty deed.

There is no applicable statute, and the jurisdiction recognizes the common-law joint tenancy.

Title to Blackacre is in

(A) Darin.
(B) Marta.
(C) Darin and Eugenio.
(D) Darin and the heirs of Beth.

Question 32

Lanny, the owner of Whiteacre in fee simple, leased Whiteacre to Teri for a term of ten years by properly executed written instrument. The lease was promptly and properly recorded. It contained an option for Teri to purchase Whiteacre by tendering $250,000 as purchase price any time "during the term of this lease." One year later, Teri, by a properly executed written instrument, purported to assign the option to Oscar, expressly retaining all of the remaining term of the lease. The instrument of assignment was promptly and properly recorded.

Two years later, Lanny contracted to sell Whiteacre to Jones and to convey a marketable title "subject to the rights of Teri under her lease." Jones refused to close because of the outstanding option assigned to Oscar.

Lanny brought an appropriate action against Jones for specific performance.

If judgment is rendered in favor of Lanny, it will be because the relevant jurisdiction has adopted a rule on a key issue as to which various state courts have split.

Which of the following identifies the determinative rule or doctrine upon which the split occurs, and states the position favorable to Lanny?

(A) In a contract to buy, any form of "subject to a lease" clause that fails to mention expressly an existing option means that the seller is agreeing to sell free and clear of any option originally included in the lease.
(B) Marketable title can be conveyed so long as any outstanding option not mentioned in the purchase contract has not yet been exercised.
(C) Options to purchase by lessees are subject to the Rule Against Perpetuities.
(D) Options to purchase contained in a lease cannot be assigned separately from the lease.

Question 33

Blackacre is a large tract of land owned by a religious order known as The Seekers. On Blackacre, The Seekers erected a large residential building where its members reside. Blackacre is surrounded by rural residential properties and its only access to a public way is afforded by an easement over a strip of land 30 feet wide. The easement was granted to The Seekers by deed from Sally, the owner of one of the adjacent residential properties. The Seekers built a driveway on the strip, and the easement was used for 20 years without incident or objection.

Last year, as permitted by the applicable zoning ordinance, The Seekers constructed a 200-bed nursing home and a parking lot on Blackacre, using all of Blackacre that was available for such development. The nursing home was very successful, and on Sundays visitors to the nursing home overflowed the parking facilities on Blackacre and parked all along the driveway from early in the

morning through the evening hours. After two Sundays of the resulting congestion and inconvenience, Sally erected a barrier across the driveway on Sundays preventing any use of the driveway by anyone seeking access to Blackacre. The Seekers objected.

Sally brought an appropriate action to terminate the easement.

The most likely result in this action is that the court will hold for

(A) Sally, because The Seekers excessively expanded the use of the dominant tenement.
(B) Sally, because the parking on the driveway exceeded the scope of the easement.
(C) The Seekers, because expanded use of the easement does not terminate the easement.
(D) The Seekers, because Sally's use of self-help denies her the right to equitable relief.

Question 34

Three months ago, Bert agreed in writing to buy Sam's single-family residence, Liveacre, for $110,000. Bert paid Sam a $5,000 deposit to be applied to the purchase price. The contract stated that Sam had the right at his option to retain the deposit as liquidated damages in the event of Bert's default. The closing was to have taken place last week. Six weeks ago, Bert was notified by his employer that he was to be transferred to another job 1,000 miles away. Bert immediately notified Sam that he could not close, and therefore he demanded the return of his $5,000. Sam refused, waited until after the contract closing date, listed with a broker, and then conveyed Liveacre for $108,000 to Conner, a purchaser found by the real estate broker. Conner paid the full purchase price and immediately recorded his deed. Conner knew of the prior contract with Bert. In an appropriate action, Bert seeks to recover the $5,000 deposit from Sam.

The most probable result will be that Sam

(A) must return the $5,000 to Bert, because Sam can no longer carry out his contract with Bert.
(B) must return the $5,000 to Bert, because Bert was legally justified in not completing the contract.
(C) must return $3,000 to Bert, because Sam's damages were only $2,000.
(D) may keep the $5,000 deposit, because Bert breached the contract.

Question 35

Able was the owner of Blackacre, an undeveloped city lot. Able and Baker executed a written document in which Able agreed to sell Blackacre to Baker and Baker agreed to buy Blackacre from Able for $100,000; the document did not provide for an earnest money down payment. Able recorded the document, as authorized by statute.

Able orally gave Baker permission to park his car on Blackacre without charge prior to the closing. Thereafter, Baker frequently parked his car on Blackacre.

Another property came on the market that Baker wanted more than Blackacre. Baker decided to try to escape any obligation to Able.

Baker had been told that contracts for the purchase and sale of real property require consideration and concluded that because he had made no earnest money down payment, he could refuse to close and not be liable. Baker notified Able of his intention not to close and, in fact, did refuse to close on the date set for the closing. Able brought an appropriate action to compel specific performance by Baker.

If Able wins, it will be because

(A) Baker's use of Blackacre for parking constitutes part performance.
(B) general contract rules regarding consideration apply to real estate contracts.
(C) the doctrine of equitable conversion applies.
(D) the document was recorded.

Question 36

Les leased a barn to his neighbor, Tom, for a term of three years. Tom took possession of the barn and used it for his farming purposes. The lease made Les responsible for structural repairs to the barn, unless they were made necessary by actions of Tom.

One year later, Les conveyed the barn and its associated land to Lottie "subject to the lease to Tom." Tom paid the next month's rent to Lottie. The next day a portion of an exterior wall of the barn collapsed because of rot in the interior structure of the wall. The wall had appeared to be sound, but a competent engineer, on inspection, would have discovered its condition. Neither Lottie nor Tom had the barn inspected by an engineer. Tom was injured as a result of the collapse of the wall.

Les had known that the wall was dangerously weakened by rot and needed immediate repairs, but had not told Tom or Lottie. There is no applicable statute.

Tom brought an appropriate action against Les to recover damages for the injuries he sustained. Lottie was not a party.

Which of the following is the most appropriate comment concerning the outcome of this action?

(A) Tom should lose, because Lottie assumed all of Les's obligations by reason of Tom's attornment to her.
(B) Tom should recover, because there is privity between lessor and lessee and it cannot be broken unilaterally.
(C) Tom should recover, because Les knew of the danger but did not warn Tom.
(D) Tom should lose, because he failed to inspect the barn.

Question 37

Able conveyed Blackacre to Baker by a warranty deed. Baker recorded the deed four days later. After the conveyance but prior to Baker's recording of the deed, Smollett properly filed a judgment against Able.

The two pertinent statutes in the jurisdiction provide the following: 1) any judgment properly filed shall, for ten years from filing, be a lien on the real property then owned or subsequently acquired by any person against whom the judgment is rendered, and 2) no conveyance or mortgage of real property shall be good against subsequent purchasers for value and without notice unless the same be recorded according to law.

The recording act has no provision for a grace period.

Smollett joined both Able and Baker in an appropriate action to foreclose the judgment lien against Blackacre.

If Smollett is unsuccessful, it will be because

(A) Able's warranty of title to Baker defeats Smollett's claim.
(B) Smollett is not a purchaser for value.
(C) any deed is superior to a judgment lien.
(D) four days is not an unreasonable delay in recording a deed.

Question 38

Olwen owned 80 acres of land, fronting on a town road. Two years ago, Olwen sold to Buck the back 40 acres. The 40 acres sold to Buck did not adjoin any public road. Olwen's deed to Buck expressly granted a right-of-way over a specified strip of Olwen's retained 40 acres, so Buck could reach the town road. The deed was promptly and properly recorded.

Last year, Buck conveyed the back 40 acres to Sam. They had discussed the right-of-way over Olwen's land to the road, but Buck's deed to Sam made no mention of it. Sam began to use the right-of-way as Buck had, but Olwen sued to enjoin such use by Sam.

The court should decide for

(A) Sam, because he has an easement by implication.
(B) Sam, because the easement appurtenant passed to him as a result of Buck's deed to him.
(C) Olwen, because Buck's easement in gross was not transferable.
(D) Olwen, because Buck's deed failed expressly to transfer the right-of-way to Sam.

Question 39

Sixty years ago by a properly executed and recorded deed, Albert conveyed Greenacre, a tract of land: "To Louis for life, then to Louis's widow for her life, then to Louis's child or children in equal shares." At that time, Louis, who was Albert's grandson, was six years old.

Shortly thereafter, Albert died testate. Louis was his only heir at law. Albert's will left his entire estate to First Church.

Twenty-five years ago, when he was 41, Louis married Maria who was then 20 years old; they had one child, Norman. Maria and Norman were killed in an automobile accident three years ago when Norman was 21. Norman died testate, leaving his entire estate to the American Red Cross. His father, Louis, was Norman's sole heir at law.

Two years ago, Louis married Zelda. They had no children. This year, Louis died testate, survived by his widow, Zelda, to whom he left his entire estate.

The common-law Rule Against Perpetuities is unchanged by statute in the jurisdiction.

In an appropriate action to determine the ownership of Greenacre, the court should find that title is vested in

(A) First Church, because the widow of Louis was unborn at the time of conveyance and, hence, the remainder violated the Rule Against Perpetuities.
(B) Zelda, because her life estate and her inheritance from Louis (who was Albert's sole heir at law and who was Norman's sole heir at law) merged the entire title in her.
(C) the American Red Cross, because Norman had a vested remainder interest (as the only child of Louis) that it inherited, the life estate to Louis's widow being of no force and effect.
(D) Zelda for life under the terms of Albert's deed, with the remainder to the American Red Cross as the successor in interest to Norman, Louis's only child.

Question 40

Able entered into a written contract with Baker to sell Greenacre. The contract was dated June 19 and called for a closing date on the following August 19. There was no other provision in the contract concerning the closing date. The contract contained the following clause: "subject to the purchaser, Baker, obtaining a satisfactory mortgage at the current rate." On the date provided for closing, Baker advised Able that he was unable to close because his mortgage application was still being processed by a bank. Able desired to declare the contract at an end and consulted his attorney in regard to his legal position.

Which of the following are relevant in advising Able of his legal position?

I. Is time of the essence?
II. Parol evidence rule.
III. Statute of Frauds.
IV. Specific performance.

(A) I and III only.
(B) II and IV only.
(C) II, III, and IV only.
(D) I, II, III, and IV.

Question 41

Adam owns his home, Blackacre, which was mortgaged to Bank by a duly recorded purchase money mortgage. Last year, Adam replaced all of Blackacre's old windows with new windows.

Each new window consists of a window frame with three inserts: regular windows, storm windows, and screens. The windows are designed so that each insert can be easily inserted or removed from the window frame without tools to adjust to seasonal change and to facilitate the cleaning of the inserts.

The new windows were expensive. Adam purchased them on credit, signed a financing statement, and granted a security interest in the windows to Vend, the supplier of the windows. Vend promptly and properly filed and recorded the financing statement before the windows were installed. Adam stored the old windows in the basement of Blackacre.

This year, Adam has suffered severe financial reverses and has defaulted on his mortgage obligation to Bank and on his obligation to Vend.

Bank brought an appropriate action to enjoin Vend from its proposed repossession of the window inserts.

In the action, the court should rule for

(A) Bank, because its mortgage was recorded first.
(B) Bank, because windows and screens, no matter their characteristics, are an integral part of a house.
(C) Vend, because the inserts are removable.
(D) Vend, because the availability of the old windows enables Bank to return Blackacre to its original condition.

Question 42

Owen, the owner of Greenacre, a tract of land, mortgaged Greenacre to ABC Bank to secure his preexisting obligation to ABC Bank. The mortgage was promptly and properly recorded. Owen and

Newton then entered into a valid written contract for the purchase and sale of Greenacre, which provided for the transfer of "a marketable title, free of encumbrances." The contract did not expressly refer to the mortgage.

Shortly after entering into the contract, Newton found another property that much better suited her needs and decided to try to avoid her contract with Owen. When Newton discovered the existence of the mortgage, she asserted that the title was encumbered and that she would not close. Owen responded by offering to provide for payment and discharge of the mortgage at the closing from the proceeds of the closing. Newton refused to go forward, and Owen brought an appropriate action against her for specific performance.

If the court holds for Owen in this action, it will most likely be because

(A) the mortgage is not entitled to priority because it was granted for preexisting obligations.
(B) the doctrine of equitable conversion supports the result.
(C) Owen's arrangements for the payment of the mortgage fully satisfied Owen's obligation to deliver marketable title.
(D) the existence of the mortgage was not Newton's real reason for refusing to close.

Question 43

Eight years ago, Orben, prior to moving to a distant city, conveyed Blackacre, an isolated farm, to his son, Sam, by a quitclaim deed. Sam paid no consideration. Sam, who was 19 years old, without formal education, and without experience in business, took possession of Blackacre and operated the farm but neglected to record his deed. Subsequently, Orben conveyed Blackacre to Fred by warranty deed. Fred, a substantial land and timber promoter, paid valuable consideration for the deed to him. He was unaware of Sam's possession, his quitclaim deed, or his relationship to Orben. Fred promptly and properly recorded his deed and began removing timber from the land. Immediately upon learning of Fred's actions, Sam recorded his deed and brought an appropriate action to enjoin Fred from removing the timber and to quiet title in Sam. The recording act of the jurisdiction provides:

"No conveyance or mortgage of real property shall be good against subsequent purchasers for value and without notice unless the same be recorded according to law."

In this action, Fred should

(A) prevail, because a warranty deed for valuable consideration takes priority over a quitclaim deed without consideration.
(B) prevail, because Orben's subsequent conveyance to Fred revoked the gift to Sam.
(C) lose, because Sam's possession charged Fred with notice.
(D) lose, because the equities favor Sam.

Question 44

Brown owned Blackacre, a tract of undeveloped land. Blackacre abuts Whiteacre, a tract of land owned by Agency, the state's governmental energy agency. At Whiteacre, Agency has operated a waste-to-electricity recycling facility for 12 years. Blackacre and Whiteacre are in a remote area and Whiteacre is the only developed parcel of real estate within a ten-mile radius. The boundary line between Blackacre and Whiteacre had never been surveyed or marked on the face of the earth.

During the past 12 years, some of the trucks bringing waste to the Agency facility have dumped their loads so that the piles of waste extend from Whiteacre onto a portion of Blackacre. However, prior to the four-week period during each calendar year when the Agency facility is closed for inspection and repairs, the waste piles are reduced to minimal levels so that during each of the four-week closures no waste was, in fact, piled on Blackacre. Neither Brown nor any representative of Agency knew the facts about the relation of the boundary line to the waste piles.

The time for acquiring title by adverse possession in the jurisdiction is ten years.

Last year, Brown died, and his son, Silas, succeeded him as the owner of Blackacre. Silas became aware of the facts, demanded that Agency stop using Blackacre for the piling of waste, and, when Agency refused his demand, brought an appropriate action to enjoin any such use of Blackacre in the future.

If Agency prevails in that action, it will be because

(A) the facts constitute adverse possession and title to the portion of Blackacre concerned has vested in Agency.
(B) Brown's failure to keep himself informed as to Agency's use of Blackacre and his failure to object constituted implied consent to the continuation of that use.
(C) the interest of the public in the conversion of waste to energy overrides any entitlement of Silas to equitable remedies.
(D) the power of eminent domain of the state makes the claim of Silas moot.

Question 45

Ogle owned Greenacre, a tract of land, in fee simple. Five years ago, he executed and delivered to Lilly an instrument in the proper form of a warranty deed that conveyed Greenacre to Lilly "for and during the term of her natural life." No other estate or interest or person taking an interest was mentioned. Lilly took possession of Greenacre and has remained in possession.

Fifteen months ago, Ogle died, leaving a will that has been duly admitted to probate. The will, inter alia, had the following provision:

"I devise Greenacre to Mina for her natural life and from and after Mina's death to Rex, his heirs and assigns, forever."

Administration of Ogle's estate has been completed. Mina claims the immediate right to possession of Greenacre. Rex also asserts a right to immediate possession.

In an appropriate lawsuit to which Lilly, Mina, and Rex are parties, who should be adjudged to have the right to immediate possession?

(A) Lilly, because no subsequent act of Ogle would affect her life estate.
(B) Mina, because Ogle's will was the final and definitive expression of his intent.
(C) Mina, because Lilly's estate terminated with the death of Ogle.
(D) Rex, because Lilly's estate terminated with Ogle's death and all that Ogle had was the right to transfer his reversion in fee simple.

Question 46

Able was the owner of Greenacre, a large tract of land. Able entered into a binding written contract with Baker for the sale and purchase of Greenacre for $125,000. The contract required Able to convey marketable record title.

Baker decided to protect his interest and promptly and properly recorded the contract.

Thereafter, but before the date scheduled for the closing, Charlie obtained and properly filed a final judgment against Able in the amount of $1 million in a personal injury suit. A statute in the jurisdiction provides: "Any judgment properly filed shall, for ten years from filing, be a lien on the real property then owned or subsequently acquired by any person against whom the judgment is rendered."

The recording act of the jurisdiction authorizes recording of contracts and also provides: "No conveyance or mortgage of real property shall be good against subsequent purchasers for value and without notice unless the same be recorded according to law."

There are no other relevant statutory provisions.

At the closing, Baker declined to accept the title of Able on the ground that Charlie's judgment lien encumbered the title he would receive and rendered it unmarketable. Able brought an appropriate action against Baker for specific performance of the contract and joined Charlie as a party.

In this action, the judgment should be for

(A) Able, because in equity a purchaser takes free of judgment liens.
(B) Able, because the contract had been recorded.
(C) Baker, because Able cannot benefit from Baker's action in recording the contract.
(D) Baker, because the statute creating judgment liens takes precedence over the recording act.

Question 47

Oker owned in fee simple two adjoining lots, Lots 1 and 2. He conveyed in fee simple Lot 1 to Frank. The deed was in usual form of a warranty deed with the following provision inserted in the appropriate place:

"Grantor, for himself, his heirs and assigns, does covenant and agree that any reasonable expense incurred by grantee, his heirs and assigns, as the result of having to repair the retaining wall presently situated on Lot 1 at the common boundary with Lot 2, shall be reimbursed one-half the costs of repairs; and by this provision the parties intend a covenant running with the land."

Frank conveyed Lot 1 in fee simple to Sara by warranty deed in usual and regular form. The deed omitted any reference to the retaining wall or any covenant. Fifty years after Oker's conveyance to Frank, Sara conveyed Lot 1 in fee simple to Tim by warranty deed in usual form; this deed omitted any reference to the retaining wall or the covenant.

There is no statute that applies to any aspect of the problems presented except a recording act and a statute providing for acquisition of title after ten years of adverse possession.

All conveyances by deeds were for a consideration equal to fair market value.

The deed from Oker to Frank was never recorded. All other deeds were promptly and properly recorded.

Lot 2 is now owned by Henry, who took by intestate succession from Oker, now dead.

Tim expended $3,500 on the retaining wall. Then he obtained all of the original deeds in the chain from Oker to him. Shortly thereafter, Tim discovered the covenant in Oker's deed to Frank. He demanded that Henry pay $1,750, and when Henry refused, Tim instituted an appropriate action to recover that sum from Henry. In such action, Henry asserted all defenses available to him.

If judgment is for Henry, it will be because

(A) Tim is barred by adverse possession.
(B) Frank's deed from Oker was never recorded.
(C) Tim did not know about the covenant until after he had incurred the expenses and, hence, could not have relied on it.
(D) Tim's expenditures were not proved to be reasonable and customary.

Question 48

Anna entered into a valid written contract to purchase Blackacre, a large tract of land, from Jones for its fair market value of $50,000. The contract was assignable by Anna. Anna duly notified Jones to convey title to Anna and Charles, Charles being Anna's friend whom Anna had not seen for many years.

When Anna learned that Charles would have to sign certain documents in connection with the closing, she prevailed upon her brother, Donald, to attend the closing and pretend to be Charles. Anna and Donald attended the closing, and Jones executed an instrument in the proper form of a deed, purporting to convey Blackacre to Anna and Charles, as tenants in common. Donald pretended that he was Charles, and he signed Charles's name to all the required documents. Anna provided the entire $50,000 consideration for the transaction. The deed was promptly and properly recorded.

Unknown to Anna or Donald, Charles had died several months before the closing. Charles's will, which was duly probated, devised "All my real estate to my nephew, Nelson" and the residue of his estate to Anna.

Anna and Nelson have been unable to agree as to the status or disposition of Blackacre. Nelson brought an appropriate action against Jones and Anna to quiet legal title to an undivided one-half interest in Blackacre.

The court should hold that legal title to Blackacre is vested

(A) all in Jones.
(B) all in Anna.
(C) one-half in Anna and one-half in Jones.
(D) one-half in Anna and one-half in Nelson.

Question 49

Able, who owned Blackacre, a residential lot improved with a dwelling, conveyed it for a valuable consideration to Baker. The dwelling had been constructed by a prior owner. Baker had inspected Blackacre prior to the purchase and discovered no defects. After moving in, Baker became aware that sewage seeped into the basement when the toilets were flushed. Able said that this defect had been present for years and that he had taken no steps to hide the facts from Baker. Baker paid for the necessary repairs and brought an appropriate action against Able to recover his cost of repair.

If Baker wins, it will be because

(A) Able failed to disclose a latent defect.
(B) Baker made a proper inspection.
(C) the situation constitutes a health hazard.
(D) Able breached the implied warranty of habitability and fitness for purpose.

Question 50

Pauline and Doris own adjacent parcels of land. On each of their parcels was a low-rise office building. The two office buildings were of the same height.

Last year Doris decided to demolish the low-rise office building on her parcel and to erect a new high-rise office building of substantially greater height on the parcel as permitted by the zoning and building ordinances. She secured all the governmental approvals necessary to pursue her project.

As Doris's new building was in the course of construction, Pauline realized that the shadows it would create would place her (Pauline's) building in such deep shade that the rent she could charge for space in her building would be substantially reduced.

Pauline brought an appropriate action against Doris to enjoin the construction in order to eliminate the shadow problem and for damages. Pauline presented uncontroverted evidence that her evaluation as to the impact of the shadow on the fair rental value of her building was correct. There is no statute or ordinance (other than the building and zoning ordinances) that is applicable to the issues before the court.

The court should

(A) grant to Pauline the requested injunction.
(B) award Pauline damages measured by the loss of rental value, but not an injunction.
(C) grant judgment for Doris, because she had secured all the necessary governmental approvals for the new building.
(D) grant judgment for Doris, because Pauline has no legal right to have sunshine continue to reach the windows of her building.

Question 51

Seller owned Blackacre, improved with an aging four-story warehouse. The warehouse was built to the lot lines on all four sides. On the street side, recessed loading docks permitted semi-trailers to be backed in. After the tractors were unhooked, the trailers extended into the street and occupied most of one lane of the street. Over the years, as trailers became larger, the blocking of the street became more severe. The municipality advised Seller that the loading docks could not continue to be used because the trailers blocked the street; it gave Seller 90 days to cease and desist.

During the 90 days, Seller sold and conveyed Blackacre by warranty deed for a substantial consideration to Buyer. The problem of the loading docks was not discussed in the negotiations.

Upon expiration of the 90 days, the municipality required Buyer to stop using the loading docks. This action substantially reduced the value of Blackacre.

Buyer brought an appropriate action against Seller seeking cancellation of the deed and return of all monies paid.

Such action should be based upon a claim of

(A) misrepresentation.
(B) breach of the covenant of warranty.
(C) failure of consideration.
(D) mutual mistake.

Question 52

Ody, owner of Profitacre, executed an instrument in the proper form of a deed, purporting to convey Profitacre "to Leon for life, then to Ralph in fee simple." Leon, who is Ody's brother and Ralph's father, promptly began to manage Profitacre, which is valuable income-producing real estate. Leon collected all rents and paid all expenses, including real estate taxes. Ralph did not object, and this state of affairs continued for five years until 1987. In that year, Leon executed an instrument in the proper form of a deed, purporting to convey Profitacre to Mona. Ralph, no admirer of Mona, asserted his right to ownership of Profitacre. Mona asserted her ownership and said that if Ralph had any rights he was obligated to pay real estate taxes, even though Leon had been kind enough to pay them in the past.

Income from Profitacre is ample to cover expenses, including real estate taxes.

In an appropriate action to determine the rights of the parties, the court should decide

(A) Leon's purported deed forfeited his life estate, so Ralph owns Profitacre in fee simple.
(B) Mona owns an estate for her life, is entitled to all income, and must pay real estate taxes; Ralph owns the remainder interest.
(C) Mona owns an estate for the life of Leon, is entitled to all income, and must pay real estate taxes; Ralph owns the remainder interest.
(D) Mona owns an estate for the life of Leon and is entitled to all income; Ralph owns the remainder interest, and must pay real estate taxes.

Question 53

Homer and Ethel were jointly in possession of Greenacre in fee simple as tenants in common. They joined in a mortgage of Greenacre to Fortunoff Bank. Homer erected a fence along what he considered to be the true boundary between Greenacre and the adjoining property, owned by Mitchell. Shortly thereafter, Homer had an argument with Ethel and gave up his possession to Greenacre. The debt secured by the mortgage had not been paid.

Mitchell surveyed his land and found that the fence erected a year earlier by Homer did not follow the true boundary. Part of the fence was within Greenacre. Part of the fence encroached on Mitchell's land. Mitchell and Ethel executed an agreement fixing the boundary line in accordance with the fence constructed by Homer. The agreement, which met all the formalities required in the jurisdiction, was promptly and properly recorded.

A year after the agreement was recorded, Homer temporarily reconciled his differences with Ethel and resumed joint possession of Greenacre. Thereafter, Homer repudiated the boundary line agreement and brought an appropriate action against Mitchell and Ethel to quiet title along the original true boundary.

In such action, Homer will

(A) win, because Fortunoff Bank was not a party to the agreement.

(B) win, because one tenant in common cannot bind another tenant in common to a boundary line agreement.

(C) lose, because the agreement, as a matter of law, was mutually beneficial to Ethel and Homer.

(D) lose, because Ethel was in sole possession of said premises at the time the agreement was signed.

Question 54

Ashton owned Woodsedge, a tract used for commercial purposes, in fee simple and thereafter mortgaged it to First Bank. She signed a promissory note secured by a duly executed and recorded mortgage. There was no "due on sale" clause, that is, no provision that, upon sale, the whole balance then owing would become due and owing. Ashton conveyed Woodsedge to Beam "subject to a mortgage to First Bank, which the grantee assumes and agrees to pay." Beam conveyed Woodsedge to Carter "subject to an existing mortgage to First Bank." A copy of the note and the mortgage that secured it had been exhibited to each grantee.

After Carter made three timely payments, no further payments were made by any party. In fact, the real estate had depreciated to a point where it was worth less than the debt.

There is no applicable statute or regulation.

In an appropriate foreclosure action, First Bank joined Ashton, Beam, and Carter as defendants. At the foreclosure sale, although the fair market value for Woodsedge in its depreciated state was obtained, a deficiency resulted.

First Bank is entitled to collect a deficiency judgment against

(A) Ashton only.
(B) Ashton and Beam only.
(C) Beam and Carter only.
(D) Ashton, Beam, and Carter.

Question 55

Oliver, owner of Blackacre, needed money. Blackacre was fairly worth $100,000, so Oliver tried to borrow $60,000 from Len on the security of Blackacre. Len agreed, but only if Oliver would convey Blackacre to Len outright by warranty deed, with Len agreeing orally to reconvey to Oliver once the loan was paid according to its terms. Oliver agreed, conveyed Blackacre to Len by warranty deed, and Len paid Oliver $60,000 cash. Len promptly and properly recorded Oliver's deed.

Now, Oliver has defaulted on repayment with $55,000 still due on the loan. Oliver is still in possession.

Which of the following best states the parties' rights in Blackacre?

(A) Len's oral agreement to reconvey is invalid under the Statute of Frauds, so Len owns Blackacre outright.

(B) Oliver, having defaulted, has no further rights in Blackacre, so Len may obtain summary eviction.

(C) The attempted security arrangement is a creature unknown to the law, hence a nullity; Len has only a personal right to $55,000 from Oliver.

(D) Len may bring whatever foreclosure proceeding is appropriate under the laws of the jurisdiction.

Question 56

Oscar, owner of Greenacre, conveyed Greenacre by quitclaim deed as a gift to Ann, who did not then record her deed. Later, Oscar conveyed Greenacre by warranty deed to Belle, who paid valuable consideration, knew nothing of Ann's claim, and promptly and properly recorded. Next, Ann recorded her deed. Then Belle conveyed Greenacre by quitclaim deed to her son Cal as a gift. When the possible conflict with Ann was discovered, Cal recorded his deed.

Greenacre at all relevant times has been vacant unoccupied land.

The recording act of the jurisdiction provides: "No unrecorded conveyance or mortgage of real property shall be good against subsequent purchasers for value without notice, who shall first record." No other statute is applicable.

Cal has sued Ann to establish who owns Greenacre.

The court will hold for

(A) Cal, because Ann was a donee.

(B) Cal, because Belle's purchase cut off Ann's rights.
(C) Ann, because she recorded before Cal.
(D) Ann, because Cal was a subsequent donee.

Question 57

Test owned Blackacre, a vacant one-acre tract of land in State. Five years ago, he executed a deed conveying Blackacre to "Church for the purpose of erecting a church building thereon." Three years ago, Test died leaving Sonny as his sole heir at law. His duly probated will left "all my Estate, both real and personal, to my friend Fanny."

Church never constructed a church building on Blackacre and last month Church, for a valid consideration, conveyed Blackacre to Developer.

Developer brought an appropriate action to quiet title against Sonny, Fanny, and Church, and joined the appropriate state official. Such official asserted that a charitable trust was created which has not terminated.

In such action, the court should find that title is now in

(A) Developer.
(B) Sonny.
(C) Fanny.
(D) the state official.

Question 58

Alice owned a commercial property, Eastgate, consisting of a one-story building rented to various retail stores and a very large parking lot. Two years ago, Alice died and left Eastgate to her nephew, Paul, for life, with remainder to her godson, Richard, his heirs and assigns. Paul was 30 years old and Richard was 20 years old when Alice died. The devise of Eastgate was made subject to any mortgage on Eastgate in effect at the time of Alice's death.

When Alice executed her will, the balance of the mortgage debt on Eastgate was less than $5,000. A year before her death, Alice suffered financial reverses; and in order to meet her debts, she had mortgaged Eastgate to secure a loan of $150,000. The entire principal of the mortgage remained outstanding when she died. As a result, the net annual income from Eastgate was reduced not only by real estate

taxes and regular maintenance costs, but also by the substantial mortgage interest payments that were due each month.

Paul was very dissatisfied with the limited benefit that he was receiving from the life estate. When, earlier this year, Acme, Inc., proposed to purchase Eastgate, demolish the building, pay off the mortgage, and construct a 30-story office building, Paul was willing to accept Acme's offer. However, Richard adamantly refused the offer, even though Richard, as the remainderman, paid the principal portion of each monthly mortgage amortization payment. Richard was independently wealthy and wanted to convert Eastgate into a public park when he became entitled to possession.

When Acme realized that Richard would not change his mind, Acme modified its proposal to a purchase of the life estate of Paul. Acme was ready to go ahead with its building plans, relying upon a large life insurance policy on Paul's life to protect it against the economic risk of Paul's death. Paul's life expectancy was 45 years.

When Richard learned that Paul had agreed to Acme's modified proposal, Richard brought an appropriate action against them to enjoin their carrying it out.

There is no applicable statute.

The best argument for Richard is that

(A) Acme cannot purchase Paul's life estate, because life estates are not assignable.
(B) the proposed demolition of the building constitutes waste.
(C) Richard's payment of the mortgage principal has subrogated him to Paul's rights as a life tenant and bars Paul's assignment of the life estate without Richard's consent.
(D) continued existence of the one-story building is more in harmony with the ultimate use as a park than the proposed change in use.

Question 59

Oren owned Purpleacre, a tract of land, in fee simple. By will duly admitted to probate after his death, Oren devised Purpleacre to "any wife who survives me with remainder to such of my children as are living at her death."

Oren was survived by Wen, his wife, and by three children, Cynthia, Cam, and Camelia. Thereafter, Cam died and by will duly admitted to probate devised his entire estate to David. Cynthia and Camelia were Cam's heirs at law.

Later Wen died. In an appropriate lawsuit to which Cynthia, Camelia, and David are parties, title to Purpleacre is at issue.

In such lawsuit, judgment should be that title to Purpleacre is in

(A) Cynthia, Camelia, and David, because the earliest vesting of remainders is favored and reference to Wen's death should be construed as relating to time of taking possession.
(B) Cynthia, Camelia, and David, because the provision requiring survival of children violates the Rule Against Perpetuities since the surviving wife might have been a person unborn at the time of writing of the will.
(C) Cynthia and Camelia, because Cam's remainder must descend by intestacy and is not devisable.
(D) Cynthia and Camelia, because the remainders were contingent upon surviving the life tenant.

Question 60

Beach owned a tract of land called Blackacre. An old road ran through Blackacre from the abutting public highway. The road had been used to haul wood from Blackacre. Without Beach's permission and with no initial right, Daniel, the owner of Whiteacre, which adjoined Blackacre, traveled over the old road for a period of 15 years to obtain access to Whiteacre, although Whiteacre abutted another public road. Occasionally, Daniel made repairs to the old road.

The period of time to acquire rights by prescription in the jurisdiction is ten years.

After the expiration of 15 years, Beach conveyed a portion of Blackacre to Carrol. The deed included the following clause: "together with the right to pass and repass at all times and for all purposes over the old road." Carrol built a house fronting on the old road.

The road was severely damaged by a spring flood, and Carrol made substantial repairs to the road. Carrol asked Daniel and Beach to contribute one-third each to the cost of repairing the flood damage. They both refused, and Carrol brought an appropriate action to compel contribution from Beach and Daniel.

In this action, Carrol will

(A) lose as to both defendants.
(B) win as to both defendants.
(C) win as to Beach, but lose as to Daniel.
(D) win as to Daniel, but lose as to Beach.

Question 61

Oxnard owned Goldacre, a tract of land, in fee simple. At a time when Goldacre was in the adverse possession of Amos, Eric obtained the oral permission of Oxnard to use as a road or driveway a portion of Goldacre to reach adjoining land, Twin Pines, which Eric owned in fee simple. Thereafter, during all times relevant to this problem, Eric used this road across Goldacre regularly for ingress and egress between Twin Pines and a public highway.

Amos quit possession of Goldacre before acquiring title by adverse possession. Without any further communication between Oxnard and Eric, Eric continued to use the road for a total period, from the time he first began to use it, sufficient to acquire an easement by prescription. Oxnard then blocked the road and refused to permit its continued use. Eric brought suit to determine his right to continue use of the road. Eric should

(A) win, because his user was adverse to Amos and once adverse it continued adverse until some affirmative showing of a change.
(B) win, because Eric made no attempt to renew permission after Amos quit possession of Goldacre.
(C) lose, because his user was with permission.
(D) lose, because there is no evidence that he continued adverse user for the required period after Amos quit possession.

Questions 62-63 are based on the following fact situation.

A brother and sister, Bruce and Sharon, acquired as joint tenants a twenty-acre parcel of land called Greenacre. They contributed equally to the purchase price. Several years later, Bruce proposed that they build an apartment development on Greenacre. Sharon rejected the proposal but orally agreed with Bruce that Bruce could go ahead on his own on the northerly half of Greenacre and Sharon could do what she wished with the southerly half of Greenacre. Bruce proceeded to build an apartment development on, and generally developed and improved, the northerly ten acres of Greenacre. Sharon orally permitted the southerly ten acres of Greenacre to be used by the Audubon Society as a nature preserve. Bruce died, leaving his entire estate to his son, Stanley. The will named Sharon as executrix of his will, but she refused to serve.

Question 62

In an appropriate action to determine the respective interests of Sharon and Stanley in Greenacre, if Stanley is adjudged to be the owner of the northerly ten acres of Greenacre, the most likely reason for the judgment will be that

(A) the close blood relationship between Sharon and Bruce removes the necessity to comply with the Statute of Frauds.
(B) Sharon's conduct during Bruce's lifetime estops her from asserting title to the northerly half of Greenacre.
(C) the joint tenancy was terminated by the oral agreement of Sharon and Bruce at the time it was made.
(D) Sharon had a fiduciary obligation to her nephew Stanley by reason of her being named executrix of Bruce's will.

Question 63

In an appropriate action to determine the respective interests of Sharon and Stanley in Greenacre, if Sharon is adjudged to be the owner of all of Greenacre, the most likely reason for the judgment will be that

(A) the Statute of Frauds prevents the proof   of Sharon's oral agreement.
(B) Bruce could not unilaterally sever the joint tenancy.
(C) Sharon's nomination as executrix of Bruce's estate does not prevent her from asserting her claim against Stanley.

(D) the record title of the joint tenancy in Greenacre can be changed only by a duly recorded instrument.

Question 64

Homer and Purcell entered into a valid, enforceable written contract by which Homer agreed to sell and Purcell agreed to purchase Blackacre, which was Homer's residence. One of the contract provisions was that after closing Homer had the right to remain in residence at Blackacre for up to 30 days before delivering possession to Purcell. The closing took place as scheduled. Title passed to Purcell and Homer remained in possession. Within a few days after the closing, the new house next door which was being constructed for Homer was burned to the ground, and at the end of the 30-day period Homer refused to move out of Blackacre; instead, Homer tendered to Purcell a monthly rental payment in excess of the fair rental value of Blackacre. Purcell rejected the proposal and that day brought an appropriate action to gain immediate possession of Blackacre. The contract was silent as to the consequences of Homer's failure to give up possession within the 30-day period, and the jurisdiction in which Blackacre is located has no statute dealing directly with this situation, although the landlord-tenant law of the jurisdiction requires a landlord to give a tenant 30 days notice before a tenant may be evicted. Purcell did not give Homer any such 30-day statutory notice. Purcell's best legal argument in support of his action to gain immediate possession is that Homer is a

(A) trespasser ab initio.
(B) licensee.
(C) tenant at sufferance.
(D) tenant from month to month.

Questions 65-67 are based on the following fact situation.

In 1970, Oscar, owner of a 100-acre tract, prepared and duly recorded a subdivision plan called Happy Acres. The plan showed 90 one-acre lots and a ten-acre tract in the center that was designated "Future Public School." Oscar published and distributed a brochure promoting Happy Acres which emphasized the proximity of the lots to the school property and indicated potential tax savings "because the school district will not have to expend tax money to acquire this property." There is no specific statute concerning the dedication of school sites.

Oscar sold 50 of the lots to individual purchasers. Each deed referred to the recorded plan and also contained the following clause: "No mobile home shall be erected on any lot within Happy Acres." Sarah was one of the original purchasers from Oscar.

In 1976, Oscar sold the remaining 40 lots and the ten-acre tract to Max by a deed which referred to the plan and contained the restriction relating to mobile homes. Max sold the 40 lots to individual purchasers and the ten-acre tract to Pete. None of the deeds from Max referred to the plan or contained any reference to mobile homes.

Question 65

Assume for this question only that Pete has announced his intention of erecting a fast food restaurant on the ten-acre tract and that Sarah has filed an action to enjoin Pete. If Sarah wins, it will be because

(A) Sarah has an equitable servitude concerning the use of the tract.
(B) Sarah, as a taxpayer, has legal interest in the use of the tract.
(C) Sarah is a creditor beneficiary of Oscar's promise with respect to the tract.
(D) Pete is not a bona fide purchaser.

Question 66

Assume for this question only that Joe, who purchased his lot from Max, has placed a mobile home on it and that Sarah brings an action against Joe to force him to remove it. The result of this action will be in favor of

(A) Sarah, because the restrictive covenant in her deed runs with the land.
(B) Sarah, because the presence of the mobile home may adversely affect the market value of her land.
(C) Joe, because his deed did not contain the restrictive covenant.
(D) Joe, because he is not a direct but a remote grantee of Oscar.

Question 67

Assume for this question only that in 1977 the school board of the district in which Happy Acres is situated has voted to erect a new school on the ten-acre tract. In an appropriate action between the school board and Pete to determine title, the result will be in favor of

(A) Pete, because the school board has been guilty of laches.
(B) Pete, because his deed did not refer to the subdivision plan.
(C) the school board, because Pete had constructive notice of the proposed use of the tract.
(D) the school board, because there has been a dedication and acceptance of the tract.

Questions 68-69 are based on the following fact situation.

In 1930, Owens, the owner in fee simple of Barrenacres, a large, undeveloped tract of land, granted an easement to the Water District "to install, inspect, repair, maintain, and replace pipes" within a properly delineated strip of land twenty feet wide across Barrenacres. The easement permitted the Water District to enter Barrenacres for only the stated purposes. The Water District promptly and properly recorded the deed. In 1931, the Water District installed a water main which crossed Barrenacres within the described strip; the Water District has not since entered Barrenacres.

In 1935, Owens sold Barrenacres to Peterson, but the deed, which was promptly and properly recorded, failed to refer to the Water District easement. Peterson built his home on Barrenacres in 1935, and since that time he has planted and maintained, at great expense in money, time, and effort, a formal garden area which covers, among other areas, the surface of the twenty-foot easement strip.

In 1976, the Water District proposed to excavate the entire length of its main in order to inspect, repair, and replace the main, to the extent necessary. At a public meeting, at which Peterson was present, the Water District announced its plans and declared its intent to do as little damage as possible to any property involved. Peterson objected to the Water District plans.

Question 68

Peterson asked his attorney to secure an injunction against the Water District and its proposed entry upon his property. The best advice that the attorney can give is that Peterson's attempt to secure injunctive relief will be likely to

(A) succeed, because Peterson's deed from Owens did not mention the easement.
(B) succeed, because more than forty years have passed since the Water District last entered Barrenacres.
(C) fail, because the Water District's plan is within its rights.
(D) fail, because the Water District's plan is fair and equitable.

Question 69

Assume that Peterson reserved his rights and after the Water District completed its work sued for the $5,000 in damages he suffered by reason of the Water District entry. Peterson's attempt to secure damages probably will

(A) succeed, because his deed from Owens did not mention the easement.
(B) succeed, because of an implied obligation imposed on the Water District to restore the surface to its condition prior to entry.
(C) fail, because of the public interest in maintaining a continuous water supply.
(D) fail, because the Water District acted within its rights.

Questions 70-71 are based on the following fact situation.

Devlin was the owner of a large subdivision. Parnell became interested in purchasing a lot but could not decide between Lot 40 and Lot 41. The price and fair market value of each of those two lots was $5,000. Parnell paid Devlin $5,000, which Devlin accepted, and Devlin delivered to Parnell a deed which was properly executed, complete, and ready for recording in every detail except that the space in the deed for the lot number was left blank. Devlin told Parnell to fill in either Lot 40 or Lot 41 according to his decision and then to record the deed. Parnell visited the development the next day and completely changed his mind, selecting Lot 25. He filled in Lot 25 and duly recorded the deed. The price of Lot 25 and its fair market value was $7,500.

Question 70

Immediately upon learning what Parnell had done, Devlin brought an appropriate action against Parnell to rescind the transaction. If Devlin loses, the most likely basis for the judgment is that

(A) Devlin's casual business practices created his loss.
(B) the need for certainty in land title records controls.
(C) the agency implied to complete the deed cannot be restricted by the oral understanding.
(D) the recording of the deed precludes any questioning of its provisions in its recorded form.

Question 71

Assume the following facts for this question only. Before Devlin had time to learn of Parnell's actions, Parnell sold Lot 25 to Caruso for $6,000 by a duly and properly executed, delivered, and recorded warranty deed. Caruso knew that Devlin had put a price of $7,500 on Lot 25, but he knew no other facts regarding the Devlin-Parnell transaction. Caruso's attorney accurately reported Parnell's record title to be good, marketable, and free of encumbrances. Neither Caruso nor his attorney made any further investigation outside the record. Devlin brought an appropriate action against Caruso to recover title to Lot 25. If Devlin loses, the most likely basis for the judgment is that

(A) the Statute of Frauds prevents the introduction of any evidence of Devlin's and Parnell's agreement.
(B) recording of the deed from Devlin to Parnell precludes any question of its genuineness.
(C) as between Devlin and a bona fide purchaser, Devlin is estopped.
(D) the clean hands doctrine bars Devlin from relief.

Question 72

By her validly executed will, Sallie devised a certain tract of land to her son, Ben, for his life with remainder to such of Ben's children as should be living at his death, "Provided, however, that no such child of Ben shall mortgage or sell, or attempt to mortgage or sell his or her interest in the property prior to attaining 25 years of age: and, if any such child of Ben shall violate this provision, then upon such violation his or her interest shall pass to and become the property of the remaining children of Ben then living, share and share alike."

Sallie's will included an identical provision for each of her four other children concerning four other tracts of land. The residuary clause of the will gave the residuary estate to Sallie's five children equally. Sallie died and was survived by the five children named in her will and by eleven grandchildren. Several additional grandchildren have since been born.

In an action for a declaration of rights, it was claimed that the attempted gifts to Sallie's grandchildren were entirely void and that the interests following the life estates to Sallie's children passed to the children absolutely by the residuary clause. Assuming that the action was properly brought with all necessary parties and with a guardian ad litem appointed to represent the interests of unborn and infant grandchildren, the decision should be that

(A) the attempted gifts to grandchildren are void under the Rule Against Perpetuities.
(B) the attempted gifts to grandchildren are void as unlawful restraints on alienation.
(C) the provisions concerning grandchildren are valid and will be upheld according to their terms.
(D) even if the provisions against sale or mortgage by the grandchildren are void, the remainders to grandchildren are otherwise valid and will be given effect.

Question 73

Seth was an elderly widower who lived alone on a small farm which he owned. Except for the farm, including the house and its furnishings, and the usual items of personal clothing and similar things, Seth owned substantially no property. Under proper management, the farm was capable of producing an adequate family income. Because of the usual deterioration accompanying old age, Seth was unable to do farm work or even to provide for his own personal needs. Seth entered into an oral contract with his nephew, Jim, by which Seth agreed to convey the farm to Jim and Jim agreed to move into the house with Seth, operate the farm, and take care of Seth for the rest of his life. The oral contract was silent as to when the land was to be conveyed. Jim, who lived about fifty miles away where he was operating a small business of his own, terminated his business and moved in with Seth. With the assistance of his wife, Jim gave Seth excellent care until Seth died intestate about five years after the date of the contract. In his final years Seth was confined to his bed and required much personal service of an intimate and arduous sort.

Seth was survived by his only son, Sol, who was also Seth's sole heir and next of kin. Sol resided in a distant city and gave his father no attention in his father's final years. Sol showed up for Seth's funeral and demanded that Jim vacate the farm immediately. Upon Jim's refusal to do so, Sol brought an appropriate action for possession. Jim answered by way of a counterclaim to establish Jim's right to possession and title to the farm.

If the court's decision is in favor of Jim, it will be because

(A) the land is located in a state where the Statute of Frauds will not be applied if there has been such part performance as will result in an irreparable hardship if the contract is not performed.
(B) the land is located in a state where the Statute of Frauds will not be applied if there has been such part performance that is by its very nature unequivocally referable to the contract.
(C) Sol is precluded by the "clean hands" doctrine from enforcing his claim against Jim.
(D) the blood relationship of uncle-nephew is sufficient to remove the necessity for any writing to satisfy the Statute of Frauds.

Question 74

The following events took place in a state that does not recognize the common-law marriage. The state does recognize the common-law estate of tenancy by the entirety and has no statute on the subject.

Wade Sloan and Mary Isaacs, who were never formally married, lived together over a seven-year period. During this time Mary identified herself as "Mrs. Sloan" with the knowledge and consent of Wade. Wade and Mary maintained several charge accounts at retail stores under the names "Mr. and Mrs. Wade Sloan," and they filed joint income tax returns as Mr. and Mrs. Sloan. Within this period Wade decided to buy a home. The deed was in proper form and identified the grantees as "Wade Sloan and Mary Sloan his wife, and their heirs and assigns forever as tenants by the entirety." Wade made a down payment of $10,000 and gave a note and mortgage for the unpaid balance. Both Wade and Mary signed the note and mortgage for the unpaid balance. Both Wade and Mary signed the note and mortgage as husband and wife. Wade made the monthly payments as they became due until he and Mary had a disagreement and he abandoned her and the house. Mary then made the payments for three months. She then brought an action against Wade for partition of the land in question. The prayer for partition should be

(A) denied, because a tenant by the entirety has no right to partition.
(B) denied, because Wade has absolute title to the property.
(C) granted, because the tenancy by the entirety that was created by the deed was severed when Wade abandoned Mary.
(D) granted, because the estate created by the deed was not a tenancy by the entirety.

Question 75

Blackacre is a three-acre tract of land with a small residence. Olga, the owner of Blackacre, rented it to Terrence at a monthly rental of $200. After Terrence had been in possession of Blackacre for several years, Terrence and Olga orally agreed that Terrence would purchase Blackacre from Olga for the sum of $24,000, payable at the rate of $200 a month for ten years and also would pay the real estate taxes and the expenses of insuring and maintaining Blackacre.

Olga agreed to give Terrence a deed to Blackacre after five years had passed and $12,000 had been paid on account and to accept from Terrence a note secured by a mortgage for the balance. Terrence continued in possession of Blackacre and performed his obligations as orally agreed. Terrence, without consulting Olga, made improvements for which he paid $1,000. When Terrence had paid $12,000, he tendered a proper note and mortgage to Olga and demanded the delivery of the deed as agreed. Olga did not deny the oral agreement but told Terrence that she has changed her mind, and she refused to complete the transaction. Terrence then brought an action for specific performance. Olga pleaded the Statute of Frauds as her defense. If Olga wins, it will be because

(A) nothing Terrence could have done would have overcome the original absence of a written agreement.
(B) the actions and payments of Terrence are as consistent with his being a tenant as with an oral contract.
(C) Terrence did not secure Olga's approval for the improvements that he made.
(D) Olga has not received any unconscionable benefit, and, therefore, Terrence is not entitled to equitable relief.

Question 76

Alice conveyed Twinoaks Farm "to Barbara, her heirs and assigns, so long as the premises are used for residential and farm purposes, then to Charles and his heirs and assigns." The jurisdiction in which Twinoaks Farm is located has adopted the common-law Rule Against Perpetuities unmodified by statute. As a consequence of the conveyance, Alice's interest in Twinoaks Farm is

(A) nothing.
(B) a possibility of reverter.
(C) a right of entry for condition broken.
(D) a reversion in fee simple absolute.

Question 77

Lawnacre was conveyed to Celeste and Donald by a deed which, in the jurisdiction in which Lawnacre is situated, created a cotenancy in equal shares and with the right of survivorship. The jurisdiction has no statute directly applicable to any of the problems posed.

Celeste, by deed, conveyed "my undivided one-half interest in Lawnacre" to Paul. Celeste has since died. In an appropriate action between Paul and Donald in which title to Lawnacre is at issue, Donald will

(A) prevail, because he is the sole owner of Lawnacre.
(B) prevail if, but only if, the cotenancy created in Celeste and Donald was a tenancy by the entirety.
(C) not prevail if he had knowledge of the conveyance prior to Celeste's death.
(D) not prevail, because Paul and Donald own Lawnacre as tenants in common.

Question 78

Tess occupied an apartment in a building owned by Len. She paid rent of $125 in advance each month. During the second month of occupancy, Tess organized the tenants in the building as a tenants' association and the association made demands of Len concerning certain repairs and improvements the tenants wanted. When Tess tendered rent for the third month, Len notified her that rent for the fourth and subsequent months would be $200 per month. Tess protested and pointed out that all other tenants paid rent of $125 per month. Thereupon, Len gave the required statutory notice that the tenancy was being terminated at the end of the third month. By an appropriate proceeding, Tess contests Len's right to terminate. If Tess succeeds, it will be because

(A) a periodic tenancy was created by implication.
(B) the doctrine prohibiting retaliatory eviction is part of the law of the jurisdiction.
(C) the $200 rent demanded violates the agreement implied by the rate charged to other tenants.
(D) the law implies a term of one year in the absence of any express agreement.

Questions 79-80 are based on the following fact situation.

Meadowview is a large tract of undeveloped land. Black, the owner of Meadowview, prepared a development plan creating 200 house lots in Meadowview with the necessary streets and public areas. The plan was fully approved by all necessary governmental agencies and duly recorded. However, construction of the streets, utilities, and other aspects of the development of Meadowview has not yet begun, and none of the streets can be opened as public ways until they are completed in accordance with the applicable ordinances of the municipality in which Meadowview is located.

College Avenue, one of the streets laid out as part of the Meadowview development, abuts Whiteacre, an adjacent one-acre parcel owned by White. Whiteacre has no access to any public way except an old, poorly developed road which is inconvenient and cannot be used without great expense. White sold Whiteacre to Breyer. The description used in the deed from White to Breyer was the same as that used in prior deeds except that the portion of the description which formerly said, "thence by land of Black, north-easterly a distance of 200 feet, more or less," was changed to "thence by College Avenue as laid out on the Plan of Meadowview North 46- East 201.6 feet," with full reference to the plan and its recording data.

Breyer now seeks a building permit which will show that Breyer intends to use College Avenue for access to Whiteacre. Black objects to the granting of a building permit on the grounds that he has never granted any right to White or Breyer to use College Avenue. There are no governing statutes or ordinances relating to the problem. Black brings an appropriate action in which the right of Breyer to use College Avenue without an express grant from Black is at issue.

Question 79

The best argument for Black in this action is that

(A) Breyer's right must await the action of appropriate public authorities to open College Avenue as a public street, since no private easements arose by implication.
(B) the Statute of Frauds prevents the introduction of evidence which might prove the necessity for Breyer to use College Avenue.
(C) Breyer's right to College Avenue is restricted to the assertion of a way by necessity and the facts preclude the success of such a claim.

(D) Breyer would be unjustly enriched if he were permitted to use College Avenue.

Question 80

The best argument for Breyer in this action is that

(A) there is a way by necessity over Meadowview's lands to gain access to a public road.
(B) the deed from White to Breyer referred to the recorded plan and therefore created rights to use the streets delineated on the plan.
(C) sale of lots in Meadowview by reference to its plan creates private easements in the streets shown in the plan.
(D) the recording of the plan is a dedication of the streets shown on the plan to public use.

Question 81

Realco Realtors acquired a large tract of land upon which Realco developed a mobile home subdivision. The tract was divided into 60 lots, appropriate utilities were installed, and a plat of the entire tract, including a Declaration of Restrictions, was properly drawn and recorded. The Declaration of Restriction included the following: "3. Ownership and/or occupancy are restricted to persons 21 years of age or over, one family per lot." As the separate lots were sold, the deed to each lot included the following provision: "As shown on recorded plat [properly identified by page and plat book reference] and subject to the restrictions therein contained." One of the lots was purchased by Dawson, who now resides in a mobile home on the lot together with his wife and two children, aged 11 and 13. Other lot owners in the subdivision brought action against Dawson to enjoin further occupancy by the children under 21 years of age. If judgment is for Dawson, the issue that most likely will determine the case will be whether

(A) the mobile home is treated as personalty or realty.
(B) the restriction constitutes an unlawful restraint on alienation.
(C) enforcement of the restriction is considered a violation of the equal protection clause of the Fourteenth Amendment of the United States Constitution.
(D) the terms of the restriction are expressly repeated verbatim in Dawson's deed.

Question 82

Lester, the owner in fee simple of a small farm consisting of thirty acres of land improved with house and several outbuildings, leased the same to Tanner for a ten-year period. After two years had expired, the government condemned twenty acres of the property and allocated the compensation award to Lester and Tanner according to their respective interest so taken. It so happened, however, that the twenty acres taken embraced all of the farm's tillable land, leaving only the house, outbuildings, and a small woodlot. There is no applicable statute in the jurisdiction where the property is located nor any provision in the lease relating to condemnation. Tanner quit possession, and Lester brought suit against him to recover rent. Lester will

(A) lose, because there has been a frustration of purpose which excuses Tanner from further performance of his contract to pay rent.
(B) lose, because there has been a breach of the implied covenant of quiet enjoyment by Lester's inability to provide Tanner with possession of the whole of the property for the entire term.
(C) win, because of the implied warranty on the part of the tenant to return the demised premises in the same condition at the end of the term as they were at the beginning.
(D) win, because the relationship of landlord and tenant was unaffected by the condemnation, thus leaving Tanner still obligated to pay rent.

Question 83

Maria is the owner and possessor of Goodacre, on which there is a lumber yard. Maria conveyed to Reliable Electric Company the right to construct and use an overhead electric line across Goodacre to serve other properties. The conveyance was in writing, but the writing made no provision concerning the responsibility for repair or maintenance of the line. Reliable installed the poles and erected the electric line in a proper and workmanlike manner. Neither Maria nor Reliable took any steps toward the maintenance or repair of the line after it was built. Neither party complained to the other about any failure to repair. Because of the failure to repair or properly maintain the line, it fell to the ground during a storm. In doing so, it caused a fire in the lumber yard and did considerable damage. Maria sued Reliable Electric Company to recover for damages to the lumber yard. The decision should be for

(A) Maria, because the owner of an easement has a duty to so maintain the easement as to avoid unreasonable interference with the use of the servient tenement by its lawful possessor.

(B) Maria, because the owner of an easement is absolutely liable for any damage caused to the servient tenement by the exercise of the easement.

(C) Reliable Electric Company, because the possessor of the servient tenement has a duty to give the easement holder notice of defective conditions.

(D) Reliable Electric Company, because an easement holder's right to repair is a right for his own benefit, and is therefore inconsistent with any duty to repair for the benefit of another.

Question 84

Metterly, the owner in fee simple of Brownacre, by quitclaim deed conveyed Brownacre to her daughter, Doris, who paid no consideration for the conveyance. The deed was never recorded. About a year after the delivery of the deed, Metterly decided that this gift had been ill-advised. She requested that Doris destroy the deed, which Doris dutifully and voluntarily did. Within the month following the destruction of the deed, Metterly and Doris were killed in a common disaster. Each of the successors in interest claimed title to Brownacre. In an appropriate action to determine the title to Brownacre, the probable outcome will be that

(A) Metterly was the owner of Brownacre, because Doris was a donee and therefore could not acquire title by quitclaim deed.

(B) Metterly was the owner of Brownacre, because title to Brownacre reverted to her upon the voluntary destruction of the deed by Doris.

(C) Doris was the owner of Brownacre, because her destruction of the deed to Brownacre was under the undue influence of Metterly.

(D) Doris was the owner of Brownacre, because the deed was merely evidence of her title, and its destruction was insufficient to cause title to pass back to Metterly.

Question 85

A water pipe burst in the basement of Supermart, a grocery store, flooding the basement and damaging cases of canned goods on the floor. The plumbing contractor's workmen, in repairing the leak, knocked over several stacks of canned goods in cases, denting the cans. After settling its claims against the landlord for the water leak and against the plumbing contractor for the damage done by his workmen, Supermart put the goods on special sale.

Four weeks later Dotty was shopping in Supermart. Several tables in the market were covered with assorted canned foods, all of which were dirty and dented. A sign on each of the tables read: "Damaged Cans—Half Price."

Dotty was having Guest for dinner that evening and purchased two dented cans of tuna, packed by Canco, from one of the tables displaying the damaged cans. Before Guest arrived, Dotty prepared a tuna casserole which she and Guest ate. Both became ill and the medical testimony established that the illness was caused by the tuna's being unfit for consumption. The tuna consumed by Dotty and Guest came from the case that was at the top of one of the stacks knocked over by the workmen. The tuna in undamaged cans from the same Canco shipment was fit for consumption.

If Guest asserts a claim against Dotty, Dotty most likely will

(A) be held strictly liable in tort for serving spoiled tuna.

(B) be held liable only if she were negligent.

(C) not be held liable unless her conduct was in reckless disregard of the safety of Guest.

(D) not be held liable, because Guest was a social visitor.

Question 86

Owens contracted to sell a tract of land, Overlea, to Painter by general warranty deed. However, at the closing Painter did not carefully examine the deed and accepted a quitclaim deed without covenants of title. Painter later attempted to sell Overlea to Thompson, who refused to perform because Owens had conveyed an easement for a highway across Overlea before Painter bought the property.

Painter sued Owens for damages. Which of the following arguments will most likely succeed in Owens' defense?

(A) The existence of the easement does not violate the contract.

(B) The mere existence of an easement which is not being used does not give rise to a cause of action.

(C) Painter's cause of action must be based on the deed and not on the contract.

(D) The proper remedy is rescission of the deed.

Question 87

Lord leased a warehouse building and the lot on which it stood to Taylor for a term of ten years. The lease contained a clause prohibiting Taylor from subletting his interest. Can Taylor assign his interest under the lease?

(A) Yes, because restraints on alienation of land are strictly construed.

(B) Yes, because disabling restraints on alienation of land are invalid.

(C) No, because the term "subletting" includes "assignment" when the term is employed in a lease.

(D) No, because, even in the absence of an express prohibition on assignment, a tenant may not assign without the landlord's permission.

Question 88

The following facts concern a tract of land in a state which follows general United States law. Each instrument is in proper form, recorded, marital property rights were waived when necessary, and each person named was adult and competent at the time of the named transaction.

1. In 1940 Oleg, the owner, conveyed his interest in fee simple "to my brothers Bob and Bill, their heirs and assigns as joint tenants with right of survivorship."

2. In 1950 Bob died, devising his interest to his only child, "Charles, for life, and then to Charles' son, Sam, for life, and then to Sam's children, their heirs and assigns."

3. In 1970 Bill died, devising his interest "to my friend, Frank, his heirs and assigns."

4. In 1972 Frank conveyed by quitclaim deed "to Paul, his heirs and assigns whatever right, title and interest I own."

Paul has never married. Paul has contracted to convey marketable record title in the land to Patrick. Can Paul do so?

(A) Yes, without joinder of any other person in the conveyance.

(B) Yes, if Charles, Sam, and Sam's only child (Gene, aged 25) will join in the conveyance.

(C) No, regardless of who joins in the conveyance, because Sam may have additional children whose interests cannot be defeated.

(D) No, regardless of who joins in the conveyance, because a title acquired by quitclaim deed is impliedly unmerchantable.

Questions 89-90 are based on the following fact situation.

Oscar, the owner in fee simple, laid out a subdivision of 325 lots on 150 acres of land. He obtained governmental approval (as required by applicable ordinances) and, between 1968 and 1970, he sold 140 of the lots, inserting in each of the 140 deeds the following provision:

"The Grantee, for himself and his heirs, assigns and successors, covenants and agrees that the premises conveyed herein shall have erected thereon one single-family dwelling and that no other structure (other than a detached garage, normally incident to a single-family dwelling) shall be erected or maintained; and, further, that no use shall ever be made or permitted to be made than occupancy by a single family for residential purposes only."

Because of difficulty encountered in selling the remaining lots for single family use, in January 1971, Oscar advertised the remaining lots with prominent emphasis: "These lots are not subject to any restriction and purchasers will find them adaptable to a wide range of uses."

Question 89

Payne had purchased one of the 140 lots and brought suit against Oscar to establish that the remaining 185 lots, as well as the 140 sold previously, can be used only for residential purposes by single families. Assuming that procedural requirements have been met to permit adjudication of the issue Payne has tendered, which of the following is the most appropriate comment?

(A) Oscar should win because the provision binds only the grantee.

(B) The outcome turns on whether a common development scheme had been established for the entire subdivision.

(C) The outcome turns on whether there are sufficient land areas devoted to multiple-family uses within the municipality to afford reasonable opportunity for all economic classes to move into the area so as to satisfy the standards of equal protection of the law.

(D) Payne should win under an application of the doctrine which requires construction of deeds to resolve any doubt against the grantor.

Question 90

Suppose that Oscar sold 50 lots during 1971 without inserting in the deeds any provisions relating to structures or uses. Doyle purchased one of the 50 lots and proposes to erect a service station and to conduct a retail business for the sale of gasoline, etc. Pringle purchased a lot from Boyer. Boyer had purchased from Oscar in 1968 and the deed had the provision that is quoted in the fact situation. Pringle brings suit to prevent Doyle from erecting the service station and from conducting a retail business. In the litigation between Pringle and Doyle, which of the following constitutes the best defense for Doyle?

(A) Oscar's difficulty in selling with provisions relating to use establishes a change in circumstances which renders any restrictions which may once have existed unenforceable.

(B) Enforcement of the restriction, in view of the change of circumstances, would be an unreasonable restraint on alienation.

(C) Since the proof (as stated) does not establish a danger of monetary loss to Pringle, Pringle has failed to establish one of the necessary elements in a cause of action to prevent Doyle from using his lot for business purposes.

(D) The facts do not establish a common building or development scheme for the entire subdivision.

Question 91

Odum owned Brightacre (a tract of land) in fee simple. He conveyed it "to Pike, his heirs and assigns; but if Farley shall be living thirty years from the date of this deed, then to Farley, his heirs and assigns." The limitation "to Farley, his heirs and assigns" is

(A) valid, because Farley's interest is a reversion.

(B) valid, because the interest will vest, if at all, within a life in being.

(C) valid, because Farley's interest is vested subject to divestment.

(D) invalid.

Question 92

Homer conveyed his home to his wife, Wanda, for life, remainder to his daughter, Dixie. There was a $20,000 mortgage on the home, requiring monthly payment covering interest to date plus a portion of the principal. Which of the following statements about the monthly payment is correct?

(A) Wanda must pay the full monthly payment.

(B) Wanda must pay a portion of the monthly payment based on an apportionment of the value between Wanda's life estate and Dixie's remainder.

(C) Wanda must pay the portion of the monthly payment which represents interest.

(D) Dixie must pay the full monthly payment.

Question 93

For this question only, assume that Ohner and Byer were bound by a contract for the sale of lot 101 for $5,000, that on May 3 Ohner telephoned Byer that because he had just discovered that a shopping center was going to be erected adjacent to the Grove subdivision, he would "have to have $6,000 for each of the lots including lot 101," that Byer thereupon agreed to pay him $6,000 for lot 101, and that on May 6 Byer telegraphed, "Accept your offer with respect to the rest of the lots." Assuming that two contracts were formed and that there is no controlling statute, Byer will most likely be required to pay

(A) only $5,000 for each of the fifty lots.

(B) only $5,000 for lot 101, but $6,000 for the remaining forty-nine lots.

(C) $6,000 for each of the fifty lots.

(D) $6,000 for lot 101, but only $5,000 for the remaining forty-nine lots.

Questions 94-95. Assume for the purposes of these questions that you are counsel to the state legislative committee that is responsible for real estate laws in your state.

Question 94

The committee wants you to draft a statute governing the recording of deeds that fixes priorities of title, as reflected on the public record, as definitely as possible. Which of the following, divorced from other policy considerations, would best accomplish this particular result?

(A) Eliminate the requirement of witnesses to deeds.
(B) Make time of recording the controlling factor.
(C) Make irrebuttable the declarations in the deeds that valuable consideration was paid.
(D) Make the protection of bona fide purchasers the controlling factor.

Question 95

The committee wants you to draft legislation to make all restrictions on land use imposed by deeds (now or hereafter recorded) unenforceable in the future so that public land-use planning through zoning will have exclusive control in matters of land use. Which of the following is LEAST likely to be a consideration in the drafting of such legislation?

(A) Compensation for property rights taken by public authority
(B) Impairment of contract
(C) Sovereign immunity
(D) Police power

Questions 96-97 are based on the following fact situation.

Trease owned Hilltop in fee simple. By his will, he devised as follows: "Hilltop to such of my grandchildren who shall reach the age of 21; and by this provision I intend to include all grandchildren whenever born." At the time of his death, Trease had three children and two grandchildren.

Question 96

Courts hold such a devise valid under the common-law Rule Against Perpetuities. What is the best explanation of that determination?

(A) All of Trease's children would be measuring lives.
(B) The rule of convenience closes the class of beneficiaries when any grandchild reaches the age of 21.
(C) There is a presumption that Trease intended to include only those grandchildren born prior to his death.
(D) There is a subsidiary rule of construction that dispositive instruments are to be interpreted so as to uphold interests rather than to invalidate them under the Rule Against Perpetuities.

Question 97

Which of the following additions to or changes in the facts of the preceding question would produce a violation of the common-law Rule Against Perpetuities?

(A) A posthumous child was born to Trease.
(B) Trease's will expressed the intention to include all afterborn grandchildren in the gift.
(C) The instrument was an inter vivos conveyance rather than a will.
(D) Trease had no grandchildren living at the time of his death.

Questions 98-99 are based on the following fact situation.

Seller and Buyer execute an agreement for the sale of real property on September 1, 1971. The jurisdiction in which the property is located recognized the principle of equitable conversion and has no statute pertinent to this problem.

Question 98

Assume for this question only that Seller dies before closing and his will leaves his personal property to Perry and his real property to Rose. There being no breach of the agreement by either party, which of the following is correct?

(A) Death, an eventuality for which the parties could have provided, terminates the agreement if they did not so provide.
(B) Rose is entitled to the proceeds of the sale when it closes, because the doctrine of equitable conversion does not apply to these circumstances.
(C) Perry is entitled to the proceeds of the sale when it closes.
(D) Title was rendered unmarketable by Seller's death.

Question 99

Assume for this question only that Buyer dies before closing, there being no breach of the agreement by either party. Which of the following is appropriate in most jurisdictions?

(A) Buyer's heir may specifically enforce the agreement.
(B) Seller has the right to return the down payment and cancel the contract.
(C) Death terminates the agreement.

(D) Any title acquired would be unmarketable by reason of Buyer's death.

Questions 100-101 are based on the following fact situation.

Ohner holds title in fee simple to a tract of 1,500 acres. He desires to develop the entire tract as a golf course, country club, and residential subdivision. He contemplates forming a corporation to own and to operate the golf course and country club; the stock in the corporation will be distributed to the owners of lots in the residential portions of the subdivision, but no obligation to issue the stock is to ripen until all the residential lots are sold. The price of the lots is intended to return enough money to compensate Ohner for the raw land, development costs (including the building of the golf course and the country club facilities), and developer's profit, if all of the lots are sold. Ohner's market analyses indicate that he must create a scheme of development that will offer prospective purchasers (and their lawyers) a very high order of assurance that several aspects will be clearly established:

1. Aside from the country club and golf course, there will be no land use other than for residential use and occupancy in the 1,500 acres.
2. The residents of the subdivision will have unambiguous right of access to the club and golf course facilities.
3. Each lot owner must have an unambiguous right to transfer his lot to a purchaser with all original benefits.
4. Each lot owner must be obligated to pay annual dues to a pro rata share (based on the number of lots) of the club's annual operating deficit (whether or not such owner desires to make use of club and course facilities).

Question 100

In the context of all aspects of the scheme, which of the following will offer the best chance of implementing the requirement that each lot owner pay annual dues to support the club and golf course?

(A) Covenant
(B) Easement
(C) Mortgage
(D) Personal contractual obligation by each purchaser

Question 101

Of the following, the greatest difficulty that will be encountered in establishing the scheme is that

(A) any judicial recognition will be construed as state action which, under current doctrines, raises a substantial question whether such action would be in conflict with the Fourteenth Amendment.
(B) the scheme, if effective, renders title unmarketable.
(C) one or more of the essential aspects outlined by Ohner will result in a restraint on alienation.
(D) there is a judicial reluctance to recognize an affirmative burden to pay money in installments and over an indefinite period as a burden which can be affixed to bind future owners of land.

Question 102

Rogers gave Mitchell a power of attorney containing the following provision:

"My attorney, Mitchell, is specifically authorized to sell and convey any part or all of my real property."

Mitchell conveyed part of Rogers' land to Stone by deed in the customary form containing covenants of title. Stone sues Rogers for breach of a covenant. The outcome of Stone's suit will be governed by whether

(A) deeds without covenants are effective to convey realty.
(B) the jurisdiction views the covenants as personal or running with the land.
(C) Stone is a bona fide purchaser.
(D) the power to "sell and convey" is construed to include the power to execute the usual form of deed used to convey realty.

Question 103

Testator devised his farm "to my son, Selden, for life, then to Selden's children and their heirs and assigns." Selden, a widower, had two unmarried adult children.

In appropriate action to construe the will, the court will determine that the remainder to children is

(A) indefeasibly vested.
(B) contingent.
(C) vested subject to partial defeasance.
(D) vested subject to complete defeasance.

Question 104

Allen and Barker are equal tenants in common of a strip of land 10 feet wide and 100 feet deep which lies between the lots on which their respective homes are situated. Both Allen and Barker need the use of the 10-foot strip as a driveway; and each fears that a new neighbor might seek partition and leave him with an unusable 5-foot strip. The best advice about how to solve their problem is

(A) a covenant against partition.
(B) an indenture granting cross easements in the undivided half interest of each.
(C) partition into two separate 5-foot wide strips and an indenture granting cross easements.
(D) a trust to hold the strip in perpetuity.

Question 105

In 1967 Owen held Blackacre, a tract of land, in fee simple absolute. In that year he executed and delivered to Price a quitclaim deed which purported to release and quitclaim to Price all of the right, title and interest of Owen in Blackacre. Price accepted the quitclaim and placed the deed in his safety deposit box.

Owen was indebted to Crider in the amount of $35,000. In September, 1971, Owen executed and delivered to Crider a warranty deed, purporting to convey the fee simple to Blackacre, in exchange for a full release of the debt he owed to Crider. Crider immediately recorded his deed.

In December, 1971, Price caused his quitclaim deed to Blackacre to be recorded and notified Crider that he (Price) claimed title.

Assume that there is no evidence of occupancy of Blackacre and assume, further, that the jurisdiction where Blackacre is situated has a recording statute which required good faith and value as elements of the junior claimant's priority. Which of the following is the best comment concerning the conflicting claims of Price and Crider?

(A) Price cannot succeed, because the quitclaim through which he claims prevents him from being bona fide (in good faith).
(B) The outcome will turn on the view taken as to whether Crider paid value within the meaning of the statute requiring this element.
(C) The outcome will turn on whether Price paid value (a fact not given in the statement).
(D) Price's failure to record until December, 1971, estops him from asserting title against Crider.

Question 106

Hank owned a secondhand goods store. He often placed merchandise on the sidewalk, sometimes for short intervals, sometimes from 7:00 a.m. until 6:00 p.m. Pedestrians from time to time stopped and gathered to look at the merchandise. Fred had moved into an apartment which was situated immediately above Hank's store; a street-level stairway entrance was located about twenty feet to the east. On several occasions, Fred had complained to Hank about the situation because not only were his view and peace of mind affected, but his travel on the sidewalk was made more difficult. Fred owned and managed a restaurant two blocks to the west of his apartment and made frequent trips back and forth. There was a back entrance to his apartment through a parking lot; this entrance was about two hundred feet farther in walking distance from his restaurant. Once Fred complained to the police, whereupon Hank was arrested under a local ordinance which prohibited the placing of goods or merchandise on public sidewalks and imposed, as its sole sanction, a fine for its violation.

One day, the sidewalk in front of Hank's store was unusually cluttered because he was cleaning and mopping the floor of his shop. Fred and his fifteen-year-old son, Steve, saw a bus they wished to take, and they raced down the stairs and onto the cluttered sidewalk in front of Hank's store, Fred in the lead. While dodging merchandise and people, Fred fell. Steve tripped over him and suffered a broken arm. Fred also suffered broken bones and was unable to attend to his duties for six weeks.

If, prior to the day of his personal injuries, Fred had asserted a claim based on public nuisance for injunctive relief against Hank for his obstruction of the sidewalk in violation of the ordinance, the defense on which Hank would have most likely prevailed is that

(A) Fred consented to the obstruction by continuing to rent his apartment.
(B) the violation of the ordinance was not unreasonable.
(C) remedy of abatement by self-help was adequate.
(D) there was no claim for special damage.

Questions 107-108 are based on the following fact situation.

By way of a gift, Pat executed a deed naming his daughter, Marian, as grantee. The deed contained descriptions as follows:

(1) All of my land and dwelling known as 44 Main Street, Midtown, United States, being one acre.

(2) All that part of my farm, being a square with 200-foot sides, the southeast corner of which is in the north line of my neighbor, Julia Brown.

The deed contained covenants of general warranty, quiet enjoyment, and right to convey.

Pat handed the deed to Marian who immediately returned it to her father for safekeeping. Her father kept it in his safe deposit box. The deed was not recorded.

The property at 44 Main Street covered 7/8 of an acre of land, had a dwelling and a garage situated thereon, and was subject to a right of way, described in prior deeds, in favor of Jack, a neighbor. Pat owned no other land on Main Street. Jack had not used the right of way for ten years and it was not visible on inspection of the property.

Question 107

The description of 44 Main Street was

(A) sufficient, because the discrepancy in area is not fatal.
(B) not sufficient, because it contained no metes and bounds.
(C) not sufficient, because the acreage given was not correct.
(D) not sufficient, because a deed purporting to convey more than a grantor owns is void ab initio.

Question 108

The description of part of Pat's farm

(A) is sufficient if consideration has been paid.
(B) is sufficient because no ambiguity therein appears on the face of the deed.
(C) could be enforced if the deed contained a covenant of seisin.
(D) is insufficient because of vagueness.

Questions 109-110 are based on the following fact situation.

Owner held 500 acres in fee simple absolute. In 1960 Owner platted and obtained all required governmental approvals of two subdivisions of 200 acres each.

In 1960 and 1961 commercial buildings and parking facilities were constructed on one, Royal Center, in accordance with the plans disclosed by the plat for each subdivision. Royal Center continues to be used for commercial purposes.

The plat of the other, Royal Oaks, showed 250 lots, streets, and utility and drainage easements. All of the lots in Royal Oaks were conveyed during 1960 and 1961. The deeds contained provisions, expressly stated to be binding upon the grantee, his heirs and assigns, requiring the lots to be used only for single-family, residential purposes until 1985. The deeds expressly stated that these provisions were enforceable by the owner of any lot in the Royal Oaks subdivision.

At all times since 1949, the 200 acres of Royal Center have been zoned for shopping center use, and the 200 acres in Royal Oaks have been zoned for residential use in a classification which permits both single-family and multiple-family use.

Question 109

In an appropriate attack upon the limitation to residential user by single families, if the evidence disclosed no fact in addition to those listed above, the most probable judicial resolution would be that

(A) there is no enforceable restriction because judicial recognition constitutes state action which is in conflict with the Fourteenth Amendment to the United States Constitution.
(B) there is no enforceable restriction because of Owner's conflict of interest in that he did not make the restriction applicable to the 100 acres he retains.
(C) the restriction in user set forth in the deeds will be enforced at the suit of any present owner of a lot in Royal Oaks residential subdivision.
(D) any user consistent with zoning will be permitted but that such users so permitted as are in conflict with the restrictions in the deeds will give rise to a right to damages from Owner or Owner's successor.

Question 110

For this question only, assume that Owner now desires to open his remaining 100 acres as a residential subdivision of 125 lots (with appropriate streets, etc.). He has, as an essential element of his scheme, the feature that the restrictions should be identical with those he planned for the original Royal Oaks residential subdivision and, further, that lot owners in Royal Oaks should be able to enforce (by lawsuits) restrictions on the lots in the 100 acres. The zoning for the 100 acres is identical with that for the 200 acres of Royal Oaks residential subdivision. Which of the following best states the chance of success for his scheme?

(A) He can restrict use only to the extent of that imposed by zoning (that is, to residential user by not more than four dwelling units per lot).
(B) He cannot restrict the 100 acres to residential user because of the conflicting user for retail commercial purposes in the 200 acres comprising the shopping center.
(C) He cannot impose any enforceable restriction to residential user only.
(D) Any chance of success depends upon the 100 acres being considered by the courts as a part of a common development scheme which also includes the 200 acres of Royal Oaks.

Questions 111-112 are based on the following fact situation.

Ogden was the fee simple owner of three adjoining vacant lots fronting on a common street in a primarily residential section of a city which had no zoning laws. The lots were identified as Lots 1, 2, and 3. Ogden conveyed Lot 1 to Akers and Lot 2 to Bell. Ogden retained Lot 3, which consisted of three acres of woodland. Bell, whose lot was between the other two, built a house on his lot. Bell's house included a large window on the side facing Lot 3. The window provided a beautiful view from Bell's living room, thereby adding value to Bell's house.

Akers erected a house on his lot. Ogden made no complaint to either Akers or Bell concerning the houses they built. After both Akers and Bell had completed their houses, the two of them agreed to and did build a common driveway running from the street to the rear of their respective lots. The driveway was built on the line between the two houses so that one-half of the way was located on each lot. Akers and Bell exchanged right-of-way deeds by which each of them conveyed to the other, his heirs and assigns, an easement to continue the right of way. Both deeds were properly recorded. After Akers and Bell had lived in their respective houses for thirty years, a new public street was built bordering on the rear of Lots 1, 2, and 3. Akers informed Bell that, since the new street removed the need for their common driveway, he considered the right-of-way terminated; therefore, he intended to discontinue its use and expected Bell to do the same. At about the same time, Ogden began the erection of a six-story apartment house on Lot 3. If the apartment house is completed, it will block the view from Bell's window and will substantially reduce the value of Bell's lot.

Question 111

In an action brought by Bell to enjoin Akers from interfering with Bell's continued use of the common driveway between the two lots, the decision should be for

(A) Akers, because the termination of the necessity for the easement terminated the easement.
(B) Akers, because the continuation of the easement after the change of circumstances would adversely affect the marketability of both lots without adding any commensurate value to either.
(C) Bell, because an incorporeal hereditament lies in grant and cannot be terminated without a writing.
(D) Bell, because the removal of the need for the easement created by express grant does not affect the right to the easement.

Question 112

In an action brought by Bell to enjoin Ogden from erecting the apartment building in such a way as to obstruct the view from Bell's living room window, the decision should be for

(A) Bell, because Ogden's proposed building would be an obstruction of Bell's natural right to an easement for light and air.

(B) Bell, because Bell was misled by Ogden's failure to complain when Bell was building his house.

(C) Ogden if, but only if, it can be shown that Ogden's intention to erect such a building was made known to Bell at or prior to the time of Ogden's conveyance to Bell.

(D) Ogden, because Bell has no easement for light, air, or view.

Question 113

Morgan conveyed Greenacre, her one-family residence, to "Perez for life, remainder to Rowan, her heirs and assigns, subject, however, to First Bank's mortgage thereon." There was an unpaid balance on the mortgage of $10,000, which is payable in $1,000 annual installments plus interest at 6 percent on the unpaid balance, with the next payment due on July 1. Perez is now occupying Greenacre. The reasonable rental value of the property exceeds the sum necessary to meet all current charges. There is no applicable statute.

Under the rules governing contributions between life tenants and remaindermen, how should the burden for payment be allocated?

(A) Rowan must pay the principal payment, but Perez must pay the interest to First Bank.

(B) Rowan must pay both the principal and interest payments to First Bank.

(C) Perez must pay both the principal and interest payments to First Bank.

(D) Perez must pay the principal payment, but Rowan must pay the interest to First Bank.

Question 114

Anders conveyed her only parcel of land to Burton by a duly executed and delivered warranty deed, which provided:

To have and to hold the described tract of land in fee simple, subject to the understanding that within one year from the date of the instrument said grantee shall construct and thereafter maintain and operate on said premises a public health center.

The grantee, Burton, constructed a public health center on the tract within the time specified and operated it for five years. At the end of this period, Burton converted the structure into a senior citizens' recreational facility. It is conceded by all parties in interest that a senior citizens' recreational facility is not a public health center.

In an appropriate action, Anders seeks a declaration that the change in the use of the facility has caused the land and structure to revert to her. In this action, Anders should

(A) win, because the language of the deed created a determinable fee, which leaves a possibility of reverter in the grantor.

(B) win, because the language of the deed created a fee subject to condition subsequent, which leaves a right of entry or power of termination in the grantor.

(C) lose, because the language of the deed created only a contractual obligation and did not provide for retention of property interest by the grantor.

(D) lose, because an equitable charge is enforceable only in equity.

Question 115

Talbot and Rogers, as lessees, signed a valid lease for a house. Lane, the landlord, duly executed the lease and delivered possession of the premises to the lessees.

During the term of the lease, Rogers verbally invited Andrews to share the house with the lessees. Andrews agreed to pay part of the rent to Lane, who did not object to this arrangement, despite a provision in the lease that provided that "any assignment, subletting or transfer of any rights under this lease without the express written consent of the landlord is strictly prohibited, null, and void." Talbot objected to Andrews' moving in, even if Andrews were to pay a part of the rent.

When Andrews moved in, Talbot brought an appropriate action against Lane, Rogers, and Andrews for a declaratory judgment that Rogers had no right to assign. Rogers' defense was that he and Talbot were tenants in common of a term for years, and that he, Rogers, had a right to assign a fractional interest in his undivided one-half interest. In this action, Talbot will

(A) prevail, because a cotenant has no right to assign all or any part of a leasehold without the consent of all interested parties.

(B) prevail, because the lease provision prohibits assignment.

(C) not prevail, because he is not the beneficiary of the non-assignment provision in the lease.

(D) not prevail, because his claim amounts to a void restraint on alienation.

Questions 116-117 are based on the following fact situation.

The owner of Newacre executed and delivered to a power company a right-of-way deed for the building and maintenance of an overhead power line across Newacre. The deed was properly recorded. Newacre then passed through several intermediate conveyances until it was conveyed to Sloan about ten years after the date of the right-of-way deed. All the intermediate deeds were properly recorded, but none of them mentioned the right-of-way.

Sloan entered into a written contract to sell Newacre to Jones. By the terms of the contract, Sloan promised to furnish an abstract of title to Jones. Sloan contracted directly with Abstract Company to prepare and deliver an abstract to Jones, and Abstract Company did so. The abstract omitted the right-of-way deed. Jones delivered the abstract to his attorney and asked the attorney for an opinion as to title. The attorney signed and delivered to Jones a letter stating that, from the attorney's examination of the abstract, it was his "opinion that Sloan had a free and unencumbered marketable title to Newacre."

Sloan conveyed Newacre to Jones by a deed which included covenants of general warranty and against encumbrances. Jones paid the full purchase price. After Jones had been in possession of Newacre for more than a year, he learned about the right-of-way deed. Sloan, Jones, Abstract Company, and Jones' attorney were all without actual knowledge of the existence of the right-of-way to the conveyance from Sloan to Jones.

Question 116

If Jones sues Abstract Company for damages caused to Jones by the presence of the right-of-way, the most likely result will be a decision for

(A) Jones, because Jones was a third-party creditor beneficiary of the contract between Sloan and Abstract Company.

(B) Jones, because the abstract prepared by Abstract Company constitutes a guarantee of Jones' title to Newacre.

(C) Abstract Company, because Abstract Company had no knowledge of the existence of the right-of-way.

(D) Abstract Company, because there was no showing that any fraud was practiced upon Jones.

Question 117

If Jones sues Sloan because of the presence of the right-of-way, the most likely result will be a decision for

(A) Jones, because Sloan is liable for his negligent misrepresentation.

(B) Jones, because the covenants in Sloan's deed to Jones have been breached.

(C) Sloan, because Jones relied upon Abstract Company, not Sloan, for information concerning title.

(D) Sloan, because Sloan was without knowledge of any defects in the title to Newacre.

Question 118

In 1965 Hubert Green executed his will which in pertinent part provided, "I hereby give, devise, and bequeath Greenvale to my surviving widow for life, remainder to such of my children as shall live to attain the age of 30 years, but if any child dies under the age of 30 years survived by a child or children, such child or children shall take and receive the share which his, her, or their parent would have received had such parent lived to attain the age of 30 years."

At the date of writing his will, Green was married to Susan, and they had two children, Allan and Beth. Susan died in 1970 and Hubert married Waverly in 1972. At his death in 1980, Green was survived by his wife, Waverly, and three children, Allan, Beth, and Carter. Carter, who was born in 1974, was his child by Waverly.

In a jurisdiction which recognizes the common law Rule Against Perpetuities unmodified by statute, the result of the application of the rule is that the

(A) remainder to the children and to the grandchildren is void because Green could have subsequently married a person who was unborn at the time Green executed his will.

(B) remainder to the children is valid, but the substitutionary gift to the grandchildren is void because Green could have subsequently married a person who was unborn at the time Green executed his will.

(C) gift in remainder to Allan and Beth or their children is valid, but the gift to Carter or his children is void.

(D) remainder to the children and the substitutionary gift to the grandchildren are valid.

Question 119

At a time when Ogawa held Lot 1 in the Fairoaks subdivision in fee simple, Vine executed a warranty deed that recited that Vine conveyed Lot 1, Fairoaks, to Purvis. The deed was promptly and duly recorded.

After the recording of the deed from Vine to Purvis, Ogawa conveyed Lot 1 to Vine by a warranty deed that was promptly and duly recorded. Later, Vine conveyed the property to Rand by warranty deed and the deed was promptly and duly recorded. Rand paid the fair market value of Lot 1 and had no knowledge of any claim of Purvis.

In an appropriate action, Rand and Purvis contest title to Lot 1. In this action, judgment should be for

(A) Purvis, because Purvis' deed is senior to Rand's.

(B) Rand, because Rand paid value without notice of Purvis' claim.

(C) Purvis or Rand, depending on whether a subsequent grantee is bound, at common law, by the doctrine of estoppel by deed.

(D) Purvis or Rand, depending on whether Purvis' deed is deemed recorded in Rand's chain of title.

Question 120

Arthur and Celia, brother and sister, both of legal age, inherited Goodacre, their childhood home, from their father. They thereby became tenants in common.

Goodacre had never been used as anything except a residence. Arthur had been residing on Goodacre with his father at the time his father died. Celia had been residing in a distant city. After their father's funeral, Arthur continued to live on Goodacre, but Celia returned to her own residence.

There was no discussion between Arthur and Celia concerning their common ownership, nor had there ever been any administration of their father's estate. Arthur paid all taxes, insurance, and other carrying charges on Goodacre. He paid no rent or other compensation to Celia, nor did Celia request any such payment.

Thirty years later, a series of disputes arose between Arthur and Celia for the first time concerning their respective rights to Goodacre. The jurisdiction where the land is located recognizes the usual common-law types of cotenancies, and there is no applicable legislation on the subject.

If Arthur claims the entire title to Goodacre in fee simple and brings an action against Celia to quiet title in himself, and if the state where the land is located has an ordinary 20-year adverse possession statute, the decision should be for

(A) Arthur, because during the past 30 years Arthur has exercised the type of occupancy ordinarily considered sufficient to satisfy the adverse possession requirements.

(B) Arthur, because the acts of the parties indicate Celia's intention to renounce her right to inheritance.

(C) Celia, because there is no evidence that Arthur has performed sufficient acts to constitute her ouster.

(D) Celia, because one cotenant cannot acquire title by adverse possession against another.

Question 121

Johnson and Tenniel owned Brownacre as joint tenants with the right of survivorship. Johnson executed a mortgage on Brownacre to Lowden in order to secure a loan. Subsequently, but before the indebtedness was paid to Lowden, Johnson died intestate with Stokes as her only heir at law. The jurisdiction at which Brownacre is located recognizes the title theory of mortgages.

In an appropriate action, the court should determine that title to Brownacre is vested

(A) in Tenniel, with the entire interest subject to the mortgage.
(B) in Tenniel, free and clear of the mortgage.
(C) half in Tenniel, free of the mortgage and half in Stokes, subject to the mortgage.
(D) half in Tenniel and half in Stokes, with both subject to the mortgage.

Question 122

Simmons and Boyd entered into a written contract for the sale and purchase of Wideacre. The contract provided that "Simmons agrees to convey a good and marketable title to Boyd sixty days from the date of this contract." The purchase price was stated as $60,000.

At the time set for closing Simmons tendered a deed in the form agreed to in the contract. Boyd's examination of the record prior to the date of closing had disclosed, however, that the owner of record was not Simmons, but Olson. Further investigation by Boyd revealed that, notwithstanding the state of the record, Simmons had been in what Boyd conceded as adverse possession for fifteen years. The period of time to acquire title by adverse possession in the jurisdiction is ten years. Boyd refuses to pay the purchase price or to take possession "because of the inability of Simmons to transfer a marketable title."

In an appropriate action by Simmons against Boyd for specific performance, Simmons will

(A) prevail, because he has obtained a "good and marketable title" by adverse possession.
(B) prevail, because Simmons' action for specific performance is an action in rem even though Olson is not a party.
(C) not prevail, because Boyd cannot be required to buy a lawsuit even if the probability is great that Boyd would prevail against Olson.
(D) not prevail, because Simmons' failure to disclose his lack of record title constitutes fraud.

Question 123

Martinez, a widower, owns in fee simple a ranch, Ranchacre. Martinez has one child, Enrique, who is married. Enrique has one child, Ana Maria, who is also married but has no children. In an effort to dispose of Ranchacre to his descendants and to honor a request by Ana Maria that she be skipped in any disposition, Martinez conveys Ranchacre to his son,

Enrique, for life with the remainder to Ana Maria's children in fee simple.

What interest, if any, is created in favor of Ana Maria's unborn children at the time of the conveyance?

(A) A contingent remainder
(B) A vested remainder subject to divestment
(C) A springing use
(D) None

Question 124

Opus, the owner of Stoneacre, entered into a written agreement with Miner. Under this written agreement, which was acknowledged and duly recorded, Miner, for a five-year period, was given the privilege to enter on Stoneacre to remove sand, gravel, and stone in whatever quantities Miner desired. Miner was to make monthly payments to Opus on the basis of the amount of sand, gravel, and stone removed during the previous month. Under the terms of the agreement, Miner's privilege was exclusive against all others except Opus, who reserved the right to use Stoneacre to any purpose whatsoever, including the removal of sand, gravel, and stone.

One year after the agreement was entered into, the state brought a condemnation action to take Stoneacre for a highway interchange. In the condemnation action, is Miner entitled to compensation?

(A) Yes, because he has a license, which is a property right protected by the due process clause.
(B) Yes, because he has a profit à prendre, which is a property right protected by the due process clause.
(C) No, because he has a license, and licenses are not property rights protected by the due process clause.
(D) No, because he has a profit à prendre, which is not a property right protected by the due process clause.

Question 125

For a valuable consideration, Amato, the owner of Riveracre, signed and gave to Barton a duly executed instrument that provided as follows: "The grantor may or may not sell Riveracre during her lifetime, but at her death, or if she earlier decides to sell, the property will be offered to Barton at $500 per acre. Barton shall exercise this right, if at all, within sixty days of receipt of said offer to sell." Barton recorded the instrument. The instrument was not valid as a will.

Is Barton's right under the instrument valid?

(A) Yes, because the instrument is recorded.
(B) Yes, because Barton's right to purchase will vest or fail within the period prescribed by the Rule Against Perpetuities.
(C) No, because Barton's right to purchase is a restraint on the owner's power to make a testamentary disposition.
(D) No, because Barton's right to purchase is an unreasonable restraint on alienation.

Question 126

Andres conveyed Applewood Farm "to Bogatz, her heirs and assigns, so long as the premises are used for residential and farm purposes, then to Cohen and his heirs." The common law Rule Against Perpetuities, unmodified by statute, is part of the law of the jurisdiction in which Applewood Farm is located. As a consequence of the conveyance, Cohen's interest in Applewood Farm is

(A) nothing.
(B) a valid executory interest.
(C) a possibility of reverter.
(D) a right of entry for condition broken.

Question 127

A ten-lot subdivision was approved by the proper governmental authority. The authority's action was pursuant to a map filed by Diaz, which included an undesignated parcel in addition to the ten numbered lots. The shape of the undesignated parcel is different and somewhat larger than any one of the numbered lots. Subdivision building restrictions were imposed on "all the lots shown on said map."

Diaz contracts to sell the unnumbered lot, described by metes and bounds, to Butts. Is title to the parcel marketable?

(A) Yes, because the undesignated parcel is not a lot to which the subdivision building restrictions apply.
(B) Yes, because the undesignated parcel is not part of the subdivision.

(C) No, because the undesignated parcel has never been approved by the proper governmental authority.
(D) No, because the map leaves it uncertain whether the unnumbered lot is subject to the building restrictions.

Question 128

Fernwood Realty Company developed a residential development, known as the Fernwood Development, which included single-family dwellings, town houses, and high-rise apartments for a total of 25,000 dwelling units. Included in the deed to each unit was a covenant under which the grantee and the grantee's "heirs and assigns" agreed to purchase electrical power only from a plant Fernwood promised to build and maintain within the development. Fernwood constructed the plant and the necessary power lines. The plant did not supply power outside the development. An appropriate and fair formula was used to determine price.

After constructing and selling 12,500 of the units, Fernwood sold its interest in the development to Gaint Realty Investors. Gaint operated the power plant and constructed and sold the remaining 12,500 units. Each conveyance from Gaint contained the same covenant relating to electrical power that Fernwood had included in the 12,500 conveyances it had made.

Page bought a dwelling unit from Olm, who had purchased it from Fernwood. Subsequently, Page, whose lot was along the boundary of the Fernwood development, ceased buying electrical power from Gaint and began purchasing power from General Power Company, which provided such service in the area surrounding the Fernwood development. Both General Power and Gaint have governmental authorization to provide electrical services to the area. Gaint instituted an appropriate action against Page to enjoin her from obtaining electrical power from General Power. If judgment is for Page, it most likely will be because

(A) the covenant does not touch and concern the land.
(B) the mixture of types of residential units is viewed as preventing one common development scheme.
(C) the covenant is a restraint on alienation.
(D) there is no privity of estate between Page and Gaint.

Question 129

Ortega owned Blackacre in fee simple and by his will specifically devised Blackacre as follows: "To my daughter, Eugenia, her heirs and assigns, but if Eugenia dies survived by a husband and a child or children, then to Eugenia's husband during his lifetime with remainder to Eugenia's children, their heirs and assigns. Specifically provided, however, that if Eugenia dies survived by a husband and no child, Blackacre is specifically devised to my nephew, Luis, his heirs and assigns."

While Ortega's will was in probate, Luis quitclaimed all interest in Blackacre to Eugenia's husband, José. Three years later, Eugenia died, survived by José but no children. Eugenia left a will devising her interest in Blackacre to José. The only applicable statute provides that any interest in land is freely alienable.

Luis instituted an appropriate action against José to establish title to Blackacre. Judgment should be for

(A) Luis, because his quitclaim deed did not transfer his after acquired title.
(B) Luis, because José took nothing under Ortega's will.
(C) José, because Luis had effectively conveyed his interest to Jose.
(D) José, because the doctrine of after acquired title applies to a devise by will.

Questions 130-131 are based on the following fact situation.

Orris had title to Brownacre in fee simple. Without Orris' knowledge, Hull entered Brownacre in 1950 and constructed an earthen dam across a watercourse. The earthen dam trapped water that Hull used to water a herd of cattle he owned. After twelve years of possession of Brownacre, Hull gave possession of Brownacre to Burns. At the same time, Hull also purported to transfer his cattle and all his interests in the dam and water to Burns by a document that was sufficient as a bill of sale to transfer personal property but was insufficient as a deed to transfer real property.

One year later, Burns entered into a lease with Orris to lease Brownacre for a period of five years. After the end of the five-year term of the lease, Burns remained on Brownacre for an additional three years and then left Brownacre. At that time Orris conveyed Brownacre by a quitclaim deed to Powell. The period

of time to acquire title by adverse possession in the jurisdiction is ten years.

Question 130

After Orris' conveyance to Powell, title to Brownacre was in:

(A) Hull.
(B) Orris.
(C) Burns.
(D) Powell.

Question 131

After Orris' conveyance to Powell, title to the earthen dam was in:

(A) the person who then held title to Brownacre in fee simple.
(B) Burns, as purchaser of the dam under the bill of sale.
(C) the person who then owned the water rights as an incident thereto.
(D) Hull, as the builder of the dam.

Question 132

While hospitalized, Marsh requested her attorney to draw a deed conveying her home to her son, Simon. While Marsh remained in the hospital, the deed was drawn, properly executed, and promptly and properly recorded. On being informed of the existence of the deed, Simon told his mother, "I want no part of the property; take the deed right back." Marsh recovered and left the hospital, but shortly thereafter, before any other relevant event, Simon died intestate.

Marsh brought an appropriate action against Simon's heirs to determine title.

If Marsh wins, it will be because

(A) the court will impose a constructive trust to carry out the intent of the deceased son.
(B) the presumption of delivery arising from the recording is not valid unless the grantee has knowledge at the time of the recording.
(C) Simon's declaration was a constructive reconveyance of the land.
(D) there was no effective acceptance of delivery of the deed.

Question 133

Constance owned Greenacre in fee simple. She executed two instruments in the proper form of deeds. The first instrument purported to convey an undivided one-half interest in Greenacre to Henry and his wife, Audrey, as joint tenants with right of survivorship.

The second instrument purported to convey an undivided one-half interest in Greenacre to Susan, the only child of Henry. Susan was thirteen years old at the time. The common-law joint tenancy is unmodified by statute.

No actual consideration was paid for the deeds. Constance handed the two deeds to Henry. Henry promptly and properly recorded the deed to himself and Audrey and put the deed to his daughter, Susan, in a safe-deposit box without recording it.

The same year, Henry, Audrey, and Susan were on a vacation when the plane in which they were flying went down, and all three were killed simultaneously. Henry, Audrey, and Susan died intestate. The applicable statute in the jurisdiction provides that "when title to property on its devolution depends on priority of death and there is insufficient evidence that the persons have died otherwise than simultaneously, the property of each person shall be disposed of as if he had survived." An appropriate action was instituted by the heirs of Henry, Audrey, and Susan. Constance, who is not an heir of any of the deceased, was a party to the action.

The court should determine that title to Greenacre is

(A) entirely in Constance.
(B) one-half in the heirs of Henry and one-half in the heirs of Audrey.
(C) one-half in Constance, one-quarter in the heirs of Henry, and one-quarter in the heirs of Audrey.
(D) one-half in the heirs of Susan, one-quarter in the heirs of Henry, and one-quarter in the heirs of Audrey.

Question 134

Otto conveyed Goldacre to "Andy, his heirs and assigns, but if Andy dies and is not survived by children by his present wife, Jane, then to Bob and his heirs and assigns." Shortly after taking possession, Andy discovered rich metal deposits on the land, opened a mining operation, and removed and sold a considerable quantity of valuable ore without giving Bob any notice of his action. Andy has no children. Andy, Jane, and Bob are all still

living. Bob brought an action in equity for an accounting of the value of the ore removed and for an injunction against further removal.

If the decision is for Andy, it will be because

(A) Bob has no interest in Goldacre.
(B) the right to take minerals is an incident of a defeasible fee simple.
(C) the right to take minerals is an incident of the right to possession.
(D) there was no showing that Andy acted in bad faith.

Question 135

Taylor and Scott, an unmarried couple, purchased a condominium as tenants in common and lived in the condominium for three years. Subsequently, they made a verbal agreement that, on the death of either of them, the survivor would own the entire condominium, and, as a result, they decided they did not need wills.

Two years later, Taylor and Scott were involved in the same automobile accident. Taylor was killed immediately. Scott died one week later. Both died intestate. Taylor's sole heir is his brother, Mark. Scott's sole heir is her mother, Martha. Mark claimed one-half of the condominium, and Martha claimed all of it. The jurisdiction has no applicable statute except for the Statute of Frauds; nor does it recognize common-law marriages.

In an appropriate action by Martha claiming the entire ownership of the condominium, the court will find that

(A) Martha owns the entire interest because Taylor and Scott did not make wills in reliance upon their oral agreement.
(B) Martha owns the entire interest because she is entitled to reformation of the deed to reflect the verbal agreement.
(C) Mark and Martha each own an undivided one-half interest because Taylor and Scott each died as the result of the same accident.
(D) Mark and Martha each own an undivided one-half interest because the Statute of Frauds applies.

Question 136

Oaks, the owner of Blackacre, conveyed a right-of-way to United Utility "for the underground transportation of gas by pipeline, the location of right-of-way to be mutually agreed upon by Oaks and United Utility." United Utility then installed a six-inch pipeline at a location selected by it and not objected to by Oaks. Two years later, United Utility advised Oaks of its intention to install an additional six-inch pipeline parallel to and three feet laterally from the original pipeline. In an appropriate action, Oaks sought a declaration that United Utility has no right to install the second pipeline.

If Oaks prevails, it will be because

(A) any right implied to expand the original use of the right-of-way creates an interest that violates the Rule Against Perpetuities.
(B) the original installation by United Utility defined the scope of the easement.
(C) Oaks did not expressly agree to the location of the right-of-way.
(D) the assertion of the right to install an additional pipeline constitutes inverse condemnation.

Question 137

Frank owned two adjacent parcels, Blackacre and Whiteacre. Blackacre fronts on a poor unpaved public road, while Whiteacre fronts on Route 20, a paved major highway. Fifteen years ago, Frank conveyed to his son, Sam, Blackacre "together with a right-of-way 25 feet wide over the east side of Whiteacre to Route 20." At that time, Blackacre was improved with a ten-unit motel.

Ten years ago, Frank died. His will devised Whiteacre "to my son, Sam, for life, remainder to my daughter, Doris." Five years ago, Sam executed an instrument in the proper form of a deed, purporting to convey Blackacre and Whiteacre to Joe in fee simple. Joe then enlarged the motel to 12 units. Six months ago, Sam died and Doris took possession of Whiteacre. She brought an appropriate action to enjoin Joe from using the right-of-way.

In this action, who should prevail?

(A) Doris, because merger extinguished the easement.
(B) Doris, because Joe has overburdened the easement.
(C) Joe, because he has an easement by necessity.
(D) Joe, because he has the easement granted by Frank to Sam.

Question 138

Orin owned in fee simple Blueacre, a farm of 300 acres. He died and by will duly admitted to probate devised Blueacre to his surviving widow, Wilma, for life with remainder in fee simple to his three children, Cindy, Clara, and Carter. All three children survived Orin.

At the time of Orin's death, there existed a mortgage on Blueacre that Orin had given ten years before to secure a loan for the purchase of the farm. At his death, there remained unpaid $40,000 in principal, payable in installments of $4,000 per year for the next ten years. In addition, there was due interest at the rate of 10 percent per annum, payable annually with the installment of principal. Wilma took possession and out of a gross income of $50,000 per year realized $25,000 net after paying all expenses and charges except the installment of principal and interest due on the mortgage.

Carter and Cindy wanted the three children, including Clara, to each contribute one-third of the amounts needed to pay the mortgage installments. Clara objected, contending that Wilma should pay all of these amounts out of the profits she had made in operation of the farm. When foreclosure of the mortgage seemed imminent, Clara sought legal advice.

If Clara obtained sound advice relating to her rights, she was told that

(A) her only protection lies in instituting an action for partition to compel the sale of the life estate of Wilma and to obtain the value of Clara's one-third interest in remainder.
(B) she could obtain appropriate relief to compel Wilma personally to pay the sums due because the income is more than adequate to cover these amounts.
(C) she could be compelled personally to pay her share of the amounts due because discharge of the mortgage enhances the principal.
(D) she could not be held personally liable for any amount but that her share in remainder could be lost if the mortgage installments are not paid.

Question 139

Rohan executed and delivered a promissory note and a mortgage securing the note to Acme Mortgage Company, which was named as payee in the note and as mortgagee in the mortgage. The note included a statement that the indebtedness evidenced by the note was "subject to the terms of a contract between the maker and the payee of the note executed on the same day" and that the note was "secured by a mortgage of even date." The mortgage was promptly and properly recorded. Subsequently, Acme sold the Rohan note and mortgage to XYZ Bank and delivered to XYZ Bank a written assignment of the Rohan note and mortgage. The assignment was promptly and properly recorded. Acme retained possession of both the note and the mortgage in order to act as collecting agent. Later, being short of funds, Acme sold the note and mortgage to Peterson at a substantial discount. Acme executed a written assignment of the note and mortgage to Peterson and delivered to him the note, the mortgage, and the assignment. Peterson paid value for the assignment without actual knowledge of the prior assignment to XYZ Bank and promptly and properly recorded his assignment. The principal of the note was not then due, and there had been no default in payment of either interest or principal.

If the issue of ownership of the Rohan note and mortgage is subsequently raised in an appropriate action by XYZ Bank to foreclose, the court should hold that

(A) Peterson owns both the note and the mortgage.
(B) XYZ Bank owns both the note and the mortgage.
(C) Peterson owns the note and XYZ Bank owns the mortgage.
(D) XYZ Bank owns the note and Peterson owns the mortgage.

Question 140

Owen owned Greenacre, a tract of land, in fee simple. By warranty deed he conveyed Greenacre to Lafe for life "and from and after the death of Lafe to Rem, her heirs and assigns."

Subsequently Rem died, devising all of her estate to Dan. Rem was survived by Hannah, her sole heir at law.

Shortly thereafter Lafe died, survived by Owen, Dan, and Hannah.

Title to Greenacre now is in

(A) Owen, because the contingent remainder never vested and Owen's reversion was entitled to possession immediately upon Lafe's death.

(B) Dan, because the vested remainder in Rem was transmitted by her will.
(C) Hannah, because she is Rem's heir.
(D) either Owen or Hannah, depending upon whether the destructibility of contingent remainders is recognized in the applicable jurisdiction.

Question 141

Susan owned Goldacre, a tract of land, in fee simple. By warranty deed, she conveyed Goldacre in fee simple to Ted for a recited consideration of "$10 and other valuable consideration." The deed was promptly and properly recorded. One week later, Susan and Ted executed a written document that stated that the conveyance of Goldacre was for the purpose of establishing a trust for the benefit of Benton, a child of Susan's. Ted expressly accepted the trust and signed the document with Susan. This written agreement was not authenticated to be eligible for recordation and there never was an attempt to record it.

Ted entered into possession of Goldacre and distributed the net income from Goldacre to Benton at appropriate intervals.

Five years later, Ted conveyed Goldacre in fee simple to Patricia by warranty deed. Patricia paid the fair market value of Goldacre, had no knowledge of the written agreement between Susan and Ted, and entered into possession of Goldacre.

Benton made demand upon Patricia for distribution of income at the next usual time Ted would have distributed. Patricia refused. Benton brought an appropriate action against Patricia for a decree requiring her to perform the trust Ted had theretofore recognized.

In such action, judgment should be for

(A) Benton, because a successor in title to the trustee takes title subject to the grantor's trust.
(B) Benton, because equitable interests are not subject to the recording act.
(C) Patricia, because, as a bona fide purchaser, she took free of the trust encumbering Ted's title.
(D) Patricia, because no trust was ever created since Susan had no title at the time of the purported creation.

Question 142

Anna owned Blackacre, which was improved with a dwelling. Beth owned Whiteacre, an adjoining unimproved lot suitable for constructing a dwelling. Beth executed and delivered a deed granting to Anna an easement over the westerly 15 feet of Whiteacre for convenient ingress and egress to a public street, although Anna's lot did abut another public street. Anna did not then record Beth's deed. After Anna constructed and started using a driveway within the described 15-foot strip in a clearly visible manner, Beth borrowed $10,000 cash from Bank and gave Bank a mortgage on Whiteacre. The mortgage was promptly and properly recorded. Anna then recorded Beth's deed granting the easement. Beth subsequently defaulted on her loan payments to Bank.

The recording act of the jurisdiction provides: "No conveyance or mortgage of real property shall be good against subsequent purchasers for value and without notice unless the same be recorded according to law."

In an appropriate foreclosure action as to Whiteacre, brought against Anna and Beth, Bank seeks, among other things, to have Anna's easement declared subordinate to Bank's mortgage, so that the easement will be terminated by completion of the foreclosure.

If Anna's easement is NOT terminated, it will be because

(A) the recording of the deed granting the easement prior to the foreclosure action protects Anna's rights.
(B) the easement provides access from Blackacre to a public street.
(C) Anna's easement is appurtenant to Blackacre and thus cannot be separated from Blackacre.
(D) visible use of the easement by Anna put Bank on notice of the easement.

Question 143

A little more than five years ago, Len completed construction of a single-family home located on Homeacre, a lot that Len owned. Five years ago, Len and Tina entered into a valid five-year written lease of Homeacre that included the following language: "This house is rented as is, without certain necessary or useful items. The parties agree that Tina may acquire and install such items as she wishes at her expense, and that she may remove them if she wishes at the termination of this lease."

Tina decided that the house needed, and she paid cash to have installed, standard-sized combination screen/storm windows, a freestanding refrigerator to

fit a kitchen alcove built for that purpose, a built-in electric stove and oven to fit a kitchen counter opening left for that purpose, and carpeting to cover the plywood living room floor.

Last month, by legal description of the land, Len conveyed Homeacre to Pete for $100,000. Pete knew of Tina's soon-expiring tenancy, but did not examine the written lease. As the lease expiration date approached, Pete learned that Tina planned to vacate on schedule, and learned for the first time that Tina claimed and planned to remove all of the above-listed items that she had installed.

Pete promptly brought an appropriate action to enjoin Tina from removing those items.

The court should decide that Tina may remove

(A) none of the items.
(B) only the refrigerator.
(C) all items except the carpet.
(D) all of the items.

Question 144

Olivia, owner in fee simple of Richacre, a large parcel of vacant land, executed a deed purporting to convey Richacre to her nephew, Grant. She told Grant, who was then 19, about the deed and said that she would give it to him when he reached 21 and had received his undergraduate college degree. Shortly afterward Grant searched Olivia's desk, found and removed the deed, and recorded it.

A month later, Grant executed an instrument in the proper form of a warranty deed purporting to convey Richacre to his fiance, Bonnie. He delivered the deed to Bonnie, pointing out that the deed recited that it was given in exchange for "$1 and other good and valuable consideration," and that to make it valid Bonnie must pay him $1. Bonnie, impressed and grateful, did so. Together, they went to the recording office and recorded the deed. Bonnie assumed Grant had owned Richacre, and knew nothing about Grant's dealing with Olivia. Neither Olivia's deed to Grant nor Grant's deed to Bonnie said anything about any conditions.

The recording act of the jurisdiction provides: "No conveyance or mortgage of real property shall be good against subsequent purchasers for value and without notice unless the same be recorded according to law."

Two years passed. Grant turned 21, then graduated from college. At the graduation party, Olivia was chatting with Bonnie and for the first time learned the foregoing facts.

The age of majority in the jurisdiction is 18 years.

Olivia brought an appropriate action against Bonnie to quiet title to Richacre.

The court will decide for

(A) Olivia, because Grant's deed to Bonnie before Grant satisfied Olivia's conditions was void, as Bonnie had paid only nominal consideration.
(B) Olivia, because her deed to Grant was not delivered.
(C) Bonnie, because Grant has satisfied Olivia's oral conditions.
(D) Bonnie, because the deed to her was recorded.

Question 145

Alex and Betty, who were cousins, acquired title in fee simple to Blackacre, as equal tenants in common, by inheritance from Angela, their aunt. During the last 15 years of her lifetime, Angela allowed Alex to occupy an apartment in the house on Blackacre, to rent the other apartment in the house to various tenants, and to retain the rent. Alex made no payments to Angela; and since Angela's death 7 years ago, he has made no payments to Betty. For those 22 years, Alex has paid the real estate taxes on Blackacre, kept the building on Blackacre insured, and maintained the building. At all times, Betty has lived in a distant city and has never had anything to do with Angela, Alex, or Blackacre.

Recently, Betty needed money for the operation of her business and demanded that Alex join her in selling Blackacre. Alex refused.

The period of time to acquire title by adverse possession in the jurisdiction is 10 years. There is no other applicable statute.

Betty brought an appropriate action against Alex for partition. Alex asserted all available defenses and counterclaims.

In that action, the court should

(A) deny partition and find that title has vested in Alex by adverse possession.
(B) deny partition, confirm the tenancy in common, but require an accounting to determine if either

Betty or Alex is indebted to the other on account of the rental payment, taxes, insurance premiums, and maintenance costs.
(C) grant partition and require, as an adjustment, an accounting to determine if either Betty or Alex is indebted to the other on account of the rental payments, taxes, insurance premiums, and maintenance costs.
(D) grant partition to Betty and Alex as equal owners, but without an accounting.

Question 146

Janet had a season ticket for the Scorpions' hockey games at Central Arena (Section B, Row 12, Seat 16). During the intermission between the first and second periods of a game between the Scorpions and the visiting Hornets, Janet solicited signatures for a petition urging that the coach of the Scorpions be fired.

Central Arena and the Scorpions are owned by ABC, Inc., a privately owned entity. As evidenced by many prominently displayed signs, ABC prohibits all solicitations anywhere within Central Arena at any time and in any manner. ABC notified Janet to cease her solicitation of signatures.

Janet continued to seek signatures on her petition during the Scorpions' next three home games at Central Arena. Each time, ABC notified Janet to cease such solicitation. Janet announced her intention to seek signatures on her petition again during the Scorpions' next home game at Central Arena. ABC wrote a letter informing Janet that her season ticket was canceled and tendering a refund for the unused portion. Janet refused the tender and brought an appropriate action to establish the right to attend all home games.

In this action, the court will decide for

(A) ABC, because it has a right and obligation to control activities on realty it owns and has invited the public to visit.
(B) ABC, because Janet's ticket to hockey games created only a license.
(C) Janet, because, having paid value for the ticket, her right to be present cannot be revoked.
(D) Janet, because she was not committing a nuisance by her activities.

Question 147

Several years ago, Bart purchased Goldacre, financing a large part of the purchase price by a loan from Mort that was secured by a mortgage. Bart made the installment payments on the mortgage regularly until last year. Then Bart persuaded Pam to buy Goldacre, subject to the mortgage to Mort. They expressly agreed that Pam would not assume and agree to pay Bart's debt to Mort. Bart's mortgage to Mort contained a due-on-sale clause stating, "If Mortgagor transfers his/her interest without the written consent of Mortgagee first obtained, then at Mortgagee's option the entire principal balance of the debt secured by this Mortgage shall become immediately due and payable." However, without seeking Mort's consent, Bart conveyed Goldacre to Pam, the deed stating in pertinent part " . . . , subject to a mortgage to Mort [giving details and recording data]."

Pam took possession of Goldacre and made several mortgage payments, which Mort accepted. Now, however, neither Pam nor Bart has made the last three mortgage payments. Mort has brought an appropriate action against Pam for the amount of the delinquent payments.

In this action, judgment should be for

(A) Pam, because she did not assume and agree to pay Bart's mortgage debt.
(B) Pam, because she is not in privity of estate with Mort.
(C) Mort, because Bart's deed to Pam violated the due-on-sale clause.
(D) Mort, because Pam is in privity of estate with Mort.

Question 148

Corp, a corporation, owned Blackacre in fee simple, as the real estate records showed. Corp entered into a valid written contract to convey Blackacre to Barbara, an individual. At closing, Barbara paid the price in full and received an instrument in the proper form of a deed, signed by duly authorized corporate officers on behalf of Corp, purporting to convey Blackacre to Barbara. Barbara did not then record the deed or take possession of Blackacre.

Next, George (who had no knowledge of the contract or the deed) obtained a substantial money judgment against Corp. Then, Barbara recorded the deed from Corp. Thereafter, George properly filed the judgment against Corp.

A statute of the jurisdiction provides: "Any judgment properly filed shall, for ten years from filing, be a lien on the real property then owned or subsequently

acquired by any person against whom the judgment is rendered."

Afterward, Barbara entered into a valid written contract to convey Blackacre to Polly. Polly objected to Barbara's title and refused to close.

The recording act of the jurisdiction provides: "Unless the same be recorded according to law, no conveyance or mortgage of real property shall be good against subsequent purchasers for value and without notice."

Barbara brought an appropriate action to require Polly to complete the purchase contract.

The court should decide for

(A) Polly, because George's judgment was obtained before Barbara recorded the deed from Corp.
(B) Polly, because even though Corp's deed to Barbara prevented George's judgment from being a lien on Blackacre, George's filed judgment poses a threat of litigation.
(C) Barbara, because Barbara recorded her deed before George filed his judgment.
(D) Barbara, because Barbara received the deed from Corp before George filed his judgment.

Question 149

Arthur's estate plan included a revocable trust established 35 years ago with ABC Bank as trustee. The principal asset of the trust has always been Blackacre, a very profitable, debt-free office building. The trust instrument instructs the trustee to pay the net income to Arthur for life, and, after the death of Arthur, to pay the net income to his wife, Alice, for life; and, after her death, "to distribute the net trust estate as she may appoint by will, or in default of her exercise of this power of appointment, to my son (her stepson), Charles."

Arthur died 30 years ago survived by Alice and Charles. Arthur had not revoked or amended the trust agreement. A few years after Arthur's death, Alice remarried; she then had a child, Marie; was widowed for a second time; and, last year, died. Her will contained only one dispositive provision: "I give my entire estate to my daughter, Marie, and I intentionally make no provision for my stepson, Charles." Marie is now 22 years old. The common-law Rule Against Perpetuities is unmodified by statute in the jurisdiction. There are no other applicable statutes.

Charles brought an appropriate action against Marie to determine who was entitled to the net trust estate and thus to Blackacre.

If the court rules for Marie, it will be because

(A) Alice's life estate and general power of appointment merge into complete ownership in Alice.
(B) the Rule Against Perpetuities does not apply to general powers of appointment.
(C) the jurisdiction deems "entire estate" to be a reference to Blackacre or to Alice's general power of appointment.
(D) Alice intended that Charles should not benefit by reason of her death.

Question 150

Sal owned five adjoining rectangular lots, numbered 1 through 5 inclusive, all fronting on Main Street. All of the lots are in a zone limited to one- and two-family residences under the zoning ordinance. Two years ago, Sal conveyed Lots 1, 3, and 5. None of the three deeds contained any restrictions. Each of the new owners built a one-family residence.

One year ago, Sal conveyed Lot 2 to Peter. The deed provided that each of Peter and Sal, their respective heirs and assigns, would use Lots 2 and 4 respectively only for one-family residential purposes. The deed was promptly and properly recorded. Peter built a one-family residence on Lot 2.

Last month, Sal conveyed Lot 4 to Betty. The deed contained no restrictions. The deed from Sal to Peter was in the title report examined by Betty's lawyer. Betty obtained a building permit and commenced construction of a two-family residence on Lot 4.

Peter, joined by the owners of Lots 1, 3, and 5, brought an appropriate action against Betty to enjoin the proposed use of Lot 4, or, alternatively, damages caused by Betty's breach of covenant.

Which is the most appropriate comment concerning the outcome of this action?

(A) All plaintiffs should be awarded their requested judgment for injunction because there was a common development scheme, but award of damages should be denied to all.
(B) Peter should be awarded appropriate remedy, but recovery by the other plaintiffs is doubtful.
(C) Injunction should be denied, but damages should be awarded to all plaintiffs, measured by

diminution of market value, if any, suffered as a result of the proximity of Betty's two-family residence.
(D) All plaintiffs should be denied any recovery or relief because the zoning preempts any private scheme of covenants.

Question 151

Abel owned Blackacre in fee simple. Three years ago, Abel and Betty agreed to a month-to-month tenancy with Betty paying Abel rent each month. After six months of Betty's occupancy, Abel suggested to Betty that she could buy Blackacre for a monthly payment of no more than her rent. Abel and Betty orally agreed that Betty would pay $25,000 in cash, the annual real estate taxes, the annual fire insurance premiums, and the costs of maintaining Blackacre, plus the monthly mortgage payments that Abel owed on Blackacre. They further orally agreed that within six years Betty could pay whatever mortgage balances were then due and Abel would give her a warranty deed to the property. Betty's average monthly payments did turn out to be about the same as her monthly rent.

Betty fully complied with all of the obligations she had undertaken. She made some structural modifications to Blackacre. Blackacre is now worth 50% more than it was when Abel and Betty made their oral agreement. Betty made her financing arrangements and was ready to complete the purchase of Blackacre, but Abel refused to close. Betty brought an appropriate action for specific performance against Abel to enforce the agreement.

The court should rule for

(A) Abel, because the agreements were oral and violated the statute of frauds.
(B) Abel, subject to the return of the $25,000, because the arrangement was still a tenancy.
(C) Betty, because the doctrine of part performance applies.
(D) Betty, because the statute of frauds does not apply to oral purchase and sale agreements between landlords and tenants in possession.

Question 152

Alex and Brenda owned in fee simple Greenacre as tenants in common, each owning an undivided one-half interest. Alex and Brenda joined in mortgaging Greenacre to Marge by a properly recorded mortgage that contained a general warranty clause. Alex became disenchanted with land-owning and notified

Brenda that he would no longer contribute to the payment of installments due Marge. After the mortgage was in default, and Marge made demand for payment of the entire amount of principal and interest due, Brenda tendered to Marge, and Marge deposited, a check for one-half of the amount due Marge. Brenda then demanded a release of Brenda's undivided one-half interest. Marge refused to release any interest in Greenacre. Brenda promptly brought an action against Marge to quiet title to an undivided one-half interest in Greenacre.

In such action, Brenda should

(A) lose, because Marge's title had been warranted by an express provision of the mortgage.
(B) lose, because there was no redemption from the mortgage.
(C) win, because Brenda is entitled to marshalling.
(D) win, because the cotenancy of the mortgagors was in common and not joint.

Question 153

Otis owned in fee simple Lots 1 and 2 in an urban subdivision. The lots were vacant and unproductive. They were held as a speculation that their value would increase. Otis died and, by his duly probated will, devised the residue of his estate (of which Lots 1 and 2 were part) to Lena for life with remainder in fee simple to Rose. Otis's executor distributed the estate under appropriate court order, and notified Lena that future real estate taxes on Lots 1 and 2 were Lena's responsibility to pay.

Except for the statutes relating to probate and those relating to real estate taxes, there is no applicable statute.

Lena failed to pay the real estate taxes due for Lots 1 and 2. To prevent a tax sale of the fee simple, Rose paid the taxes and demanded that Lena reimburse her for same. When Lena refused, Rose brought an appropriate action against Lena to recover the amount paid.

In such action, Rose should recover

(A) the amount paid, because a life tenant has the duty to pay current charges.
(B) the present value of the interest that the amount paid would earn during Lena's lifetime.
(C) nothing, because Lena's sole possession gave the right to decide whether or not taxes should be paid.

(D) nothing, because Lena never received any income from the lots.

Question 154

By a writing, Oner leased his home, Blackacre, to Tenn for a term of three years, ending December 31 of last year, at the rent of $1,000 per month. The lease provided that Tenn could sublet and assign.

Tenn lived in Blackacre for one year and paid the rent promptly. After one year, Tenn leased Blackacre to Agrit for one year at a rent of $1,000 per month.

Agrit took possession of Blackacre and lived there for six months but, because of her unemployment, paid no rent. After six months, on June 30 Agrit abandoned Blackacre, which remained vacant for the balance of that year. Tenn again took possession of Blackacre at the beginning of the third and final year of the term but paid Oner no rent.

At the end of the lease term, Oner brought an appropriate action against both Tenn and Agrit to recover $24,000, the unpaid rent.

In such action Oner is entitled to a judgment

(A) against Tenn individually for $24,000, and no judgment against Agrit.
(B) against Tenn individually for $18,000, and against Agrit individually for $6,000.
(C) against Tenn for $12,000, and against Tenn and Agrit jointly and severally for $12,000.
(D) against Tenn individually for $18,000, and against Tenn and Agrit jointly and severally for $6,000.

Question 155

Olive owned Blackacre, a single-family residence. Fifteen years ago, Olive conveyed a life estate in Blackacre to Lois.

Fourteen years ago, Lois, who had taken possession of Blackacre, leased Blackacre to Trent for a term of 15 years at the monthly rental of $500.

Eleven years ago, Lois died intestate leaving Ron as her sole heir.

Trent regularly paid rent to Lois and, after Lois's death, to Ron until last month.

The period in which to acquire title by adverse possession in the jurisdiction is 10 years.

In an appropriate action, Trent, Olive, and Ron each asserted ownership of Blackacre.

The court should hold that title in fee simple is in

(A) Olive, because Olive held a reversion and Lois has died.
(B) Ron, because Lois asserted a claim adverse to Olive when Lois executed a lease to Trent.
(C) Ron, because Trent's occupation was attributable to Ron, and Lois died 11 years ago.
(D) Trent, because of Trent's physical occupancy and because Trent's term ended with Lois's death.

Question 156

Olivia owned Blackacre, her home. Her daughter, Dawn, lived with her and always referred to Blackacre as "my property." Two years ago, Dawn, for a valuable consideration, executed and delivered to Bruce an instrument in the proper form of a warranty deed purporting to convey Blackacre to Bruce in fee simple, reserving to herself an estate for two years in Blackacre. Bruce promptly and properly recorded his deed.

One year ago, Olivia died and by will, duly admitted to probate, left her entire estate to Dawn.

One month ago, Dawn, for a valuable consideration, executed and delivered to Carl an instrument in the proper form of a warranty deed purporting to convey Blackacre to Carl, who promptly and properly recorded the deed. Dawn was then in possession of Blackacre and Carl had no actual knowledge of the deed to Bruce. Immediately thereafter, Dawn gave possession to Carl.

The recording act of the jurisdiction provides: "No conveyance or mortgage of real property shall be good against subsequent purchasers for value and without notice unless the same be recorded according to law."

Last week, Dawn fled the jurisdiction. Upon learning the facts, Carl brought an appropriate action against Bruce to quiet title to Blackacre.

If Carl wins, it will be because

(A) Dawn had nothing to convey to Bruce two years ago.
(B) Dawn's deed to Bruce was not to take effect until after Dawn's deed to Carl.
(C) Carl was first in possession.

(D) Dawn's deed to Bruce was not in Carl's chain of title.

Question 157

Owner owned Greenacre, a tract of land, in fee simple. Owner executed an instrument in the proper form of a deed, purporting to convey Greenacre to Purchaser in fee simple. The instrument recited that the conveyance was in consideration of "$5 cash in hand paid and for other good and valuable consideration." Owner handed the instrument to Purchaser and Purchaser promptly and properly recorded it.

Two months later, Owner brought an appropriate action against Purchaser to cancel the instrument and to quiet title. In support, Owner proved that no money in fact had been paid by Purchaser, notwithstanding the recitation, and that no other consideration of any kind had been supplied by Purchaser.

In such action, Owner should

(A) lose, because any remedy Owner might have had was lost when the instrument was recorded.
(B) lose, because the validity of conveyance of land does not depend upon consideration being paid, whether recited or not.
(C) prevail, because the recitation of consideration paid may be contradicted by parol evidence.
(D) prevail, because recordation does not make a void instrument effective.

Question 158

Ven owned Goldacre, a tract of land, in fee simple. Ven and Pur entered into a written agreement under which Pur agreed to buy Goldacre for $100,000, its fair market value. The agreement contained all the essential terms of a real estate contract to sell and buy, including a date for closing. The required $50,000 down payment was made. The contract provided that in the event of Pur's breach, Ven could retain the $50,000 deposit as liquidated damages.

Before the date set for the closing in the contract, Pur died. On the day that Addy was duly qualified as administratrix of the estate of Pur, which was after the closing date, Addy made demand for return of the $50,000 deposit. Ven responded by stating that he took such demand to be a declaration that Addy did not intend to complete the contract and that Ven considered the contract at an end. Ven further asserted that Ven was entitled to retain, as liquidated damages, the $50,000. The reasonable market value of Goldacre had increased to $110,000 at that time.

Addy brought an appropriate action against Ven to recover the $50,000. In answer, Ven made no affirmative claim but asserted that he was entitled to retain the $50,000 as liquidated damages as provided in the contract.

In such lawsuit, judgment should be for

(A) Addy, because the provision relied upon by Ven is unenforceable.
(B) Addy, because the death of Pur terminated the contract as a matter of law.
(C) Ven, because the court should enforce the express agreement of the contracting parties.
(D) Ven, because the doctrine of equitable conversion prevents termination of the contract upon the death of a party.

Question 159

Owen owned Blackacre in fee simple, as the land records showed, when he contracted to sell Blackacre to Bryer. Two weeks later, Bryer paid the agreed price and received a warranty deed. A week thereafter, when neither the contract nor the deed had been recorded and while Owen remained in possession of Blackacre, Cred properly filed her money judgment against Owen. She knew nothing of Bryer's interest.

A statute in the jurisdiction provides: "Any judgment properly filed shall, for ten years from filing, be a lien on the real property then owned or subsequently acquired by any person against whom the judgment is rendered."

The recording act of the jurisdiction provides: "No conveyance or mortgage of real property shall be good against subsequent purchasers for value and without notice unless the same be recorded according to law."

Cred brought an appropriate action to enforce her lien against Blackacre in Bryer's hands.

If the court decides for Bryer, it will most probably be because

(A) the doctrine of equitable conversion applies.
(B) the jurisdiction's recording act does not protect creditors.
(C) Owen's possession gave Cred constructive notice of Bryer's interest.

(D) Bryer was a purchaser without notice.

Question 160

Alpha and Beta owned Greenacre, a large farm, in fee simple as tenants in common, each owning an undivided one-half interest. For five years Alpha occupied Greenacre and conducted farming operations. Alpha never accounted to Beta for any income but Alpha did pay all real estate taxes when the taxes were due and kept the buildings located on Greenacre insured against loss from fire, storm, and flood. Beta lived in a distant city and was interested only in realizing a profit from the sale of the land when market conditions produced the price Beta wanted.

Alpha died intestate survived by Hera, Alpha's sole heir. Thereafter Hera occupied Greenacre but was inexperienced in farming operations. The result was a financial disaster. Hera failed to pay real estate taxes for two years. The appropriate governmental authority held a tax sale to recover the taxes due. At such sale Beta was the only bidder and obtained a conveyance from the appropriate governmental authority upon payment of an amount sufficient to discharge the amounts due for taxes, plus interest and penalties, and the costs of holding the tax sale. The amount paid was one-third of the reasonable market value of Greenacre.

Thereafter Beta instituted an appropriate action against Hera to quiet title in and to recover possession of Greenacre. Hera asserted all defenses available to Hera.

Except for the statutes related to real estate taxes and tax sales, there is no applicable statute.

In this lawsuit, Beta is entitled to a decree quieting title so that Beta is the sole owner in fee simple of Greenacre

(A) because Beta survived Alpha.
(B) because Hera defaulted in the obligations undertaken by Alpha.
(C) unless Hera pays Beta one-half of the reasonable market value of Greenacre.
(D) unless Hera pays Beta one-half of the amount Beta paid for the tax deed.

Question 161

Opal owned several vacant lots in ABC Subdivision. She obtained a $50,000 loan from a lender, Bank, and executed and delivered to Bank a promissory note and mortgage describing Lots 1, 2, 3, 4, and 5. The mortgage was promptly and properly recorded.

Upon payment of $10,000, Opal obtained a release of Lot 2 duly executed by Bank. She altered the instrument of release to include Lot 5 as well as Lot 2 and recorded it. Opal thereafter sold Lot 5 to Eva, an innocent purchaser, for value.

Bank discovered that the instrument of release had been altered and brought an appropriate action against Opal and Eva to set aside the release as it applied to Lot 5. Opal did not defend against the action, but Eva did.

The recording act of the jurisdiction provides: "No unrecorded conveyance or mortgage of real property shall be good against subsequent purchasers for value without notice, who shall first record."

The court should rule for

(A) Eva, because Bank was negligent in failing to check the recordation of the release.
(B) Eva, because she was entitled to rely on the recorded release.
(C) Bank, because Eva could have discovered the alteration by reasonable inquiry.
(D) Bank, because the alteration of the release was ineffective.

Question 162

Owner owned a hotel, subject to a mortgage securing a debt Owner owed to Lender One. Owner later acquired a nearby parking garage, financing a part of the purchase price by a loan from Lender Two, secured by a mortgage on the parking garage. Two years thereafter, Owner defaulted on the loan owed to Lender One, which caused the full amount of that loan to become immediately due and payable. Lender One decided not to foreclose the mortgage on Owner's hotel at that time, but instead brought an action, appropriate under the laws of the jurisdiction and authorized by the mortgage loan documents, for the full amount of the defaulted loan. Lender One obtained and properly filed a judgment for that amount.

A statute of the jurisdiction provides: "Any judgment properly filed shall, for ten years from filing, be a lien on the real property then owned or subsequently acquired by any person against whom the judgment is rendered."

There is no other applicable statute, except the statute providing for judicial foreclosure of mortgages, which places no restriction on deficiency judgments.

Lender One later brought an appropriate action for judicial foreclosure of its first mortgage on the hotel and of its judgment lien on the parking garage. Lender Two was joined as a party defendant, and appropriately counterclaimed for foreclosure of its mortgage on the parking garage, which was also in default. All procedures were properly followed and the confirmed foreclosure sales resulted as follows:

Lender One purchased the hotel for $100,000 less than its mortgage balance.

Lender One purchased the parking garage for an amount that is $200,000 in excess of Lender Two's mortgage balance.

The $200,000 surplus arising from the bid paid by Lender One for the parking garage should be paid

(A) $100,000 to Lender One and $100,000 to Owner.
(B) $100,000 to Lender Two and $100,000 to Owner.
(C) $100,000 to Lender One and $100,000 to Lender Two.
(D) $200,000 to Owner.

Question 163

Vendor owned Greenacre, a tract of land, in fee simple. Vendor entered into a valid written agreement with Purchaser under which Vendor agreed to sell and Purchaser agreed to buy Greenacre by installment purchase. The contract stipulated that Vendor would deliver to Purchaser, upon the payment of the last installment due, "a warranty deed sufficient to convey the fee simple." The contract contained no other provision that could be construed as referring to title.

Purchaser entered into possession of Greenacre. After making 10 of the 300 installment payments obligated under the contract, Purchaser discovered that there was outstanding a valid and enforceable mortgage on Greenacre, securing the payment of a debt in the amount of 25% of the purchase price Purchaser had agreed to pay. There was no evidence that Vendor had ever been late in payments due under the mortgage and there was no evidence of any danger of insolvency of Vendor. The value of Greenacre now is four times the amount due on the debt secured by the mortgage.

Purchaser quit possession of Greenacre and demanded that Vendor repay the amounts Purchaser had paid under the contract. After Vendor refused the demand, Purchaser brought an appropriate action against Vendor to recover damages for Vendor's alleged breach of the contract.

In such action, should damages be awarded to Purchaser?

(A) No, because the time for Vendor to deliver marketable title has not arrived.
(B) No, because Purchaser assumed the risk by taking possession.
(C) Yes, because in the absence of a contrary express agreement, an obligation to convey marketable title is implied.
(D) Yes, because the risk of loss assumed by Purchaser in taking possession relates only to physical loss.

Question 164

Thirty years ago Able, the then-record owner of Greenacre, a lot contiguous to Blueacre, in fee simple, executed and delivered to Baker an instrument in writing which was denominated "Deed of Conveyance." In pertinent part it read, "Able does grant to Baker and her heirs and assigns a right-of-way for egress and ingress to Blueacre." If the quoted provision was sufficient to create an interest in land, the instrument met all other requirements for a valid grant. Baker held record title in fee simple to Blueacre, which adjoined Greenacre.

Twelve years ago Charlie succeeded to Able's title in fee simple in Greenacre and seven years ago Dorcas succeeded to Baker's title in fee simple in Blueacre by a deed which made no mention of a right-of-way or driveway. At the time Dorcas took title, there existed a driveway across Greenacre which showed evidence that it had been used regularly to travel between Main Road, a public road, and Blueacre. Blueacre did have frontage on Side Road, another public road, but this means of access was seldom used because it was not as convenient to the dwelling situated on Blueacre as was Main Road. The driveway originally was established by Baker.

Dorcas has regularly used the driveway since acquiring title. The period of time required to acquire rights by prescription in the jurisdiction is ten years.

Six months ago Charlie notified Dorcas that Charlie planned to develop a portion of Greenacre as a residential subdivision and that Dorcas should cease any use of the driveway. After some negotiations, Charlie offered to permit Dorcas to construct another driveway to connect with the streets of the proposed subdivision. Dorcas declined this offer on the ground that travel from Blueacre to Main Road would be more circuitous.

Dorcas brought an appropriate action against Charlie to obtain a definitive adjudication of the respective rights of Dorcas and Charlie. In such lawsuit Charlie relied upon the defense that the location of the easement created by the grant from Able to Baker was governed by reasonableness and that Charlie's proposed solution was reasonable.

Charlie's defense should

(A) fail, because the location had been established by the acts of Baker and Able.
(B) fail, because the location of the easement had been fixed by prescription.
(C) prevail, because the reasonableness of Charlie's proposal was established by Dorcas's refusal to suggest any alternative location.
(D) prevail, because the servient owner is entitled to select the location of a right-of-way if the grant fails to identify its location.

Question 165

Art, who owned Blackacre in fee simple, conveyed Blackacre to Bea by warranty deed. Celia, an adjoining owner, asserted title to Blackacre and brought an appropriate action against Bea to quiet title to Blackacre. Bea demanded that Art defend Bea's title under the deed's covenant of warranty, but Art refused. Bea then successfully defended at her own expense.

Bea brought an appropriate action against Art to recover Bea's expenses incurred in defending against Celia's action to quiet title to Blackacre.

In this action, the court should decide for

(A) Bea, because in effect it was Art's title that was challenged.
(B) Bea, because Art's deed to her included the covenant of warranty.
(C) Art, because the title Art conveyed was not defective.
(D) Art, because Celia may elect which of Art or Bea to sue.

Question 166

Ollie owned a large tract of land known as Peterhill. During Ollie's lifetime, Ollie conveyed the easterly half (East Peterhill), situated in the municipality of Hawthorn, to Abel, and the westerly half (West Peterhill), situated in the municipality of Sycamore, to Betty. Each of the conveyances, which were promptly and properly recorded, contained the following language:

The parties agree for themselves and their heirs and assigns that the premises herein conveyed shall be used only for residential purposes; that each lot created within the premises herein conveyed shall contain not less than five acres; and that each lot shall have not more than one single-family dwelling. This agreement shall bind all successor owners of all or any portion of Peterhill and any owner of any part of Peterhill may enforce this covenant.

After Ollie's death, Abel desired to build houses on one-half acre lots in the East Peterhill tract as authorized by current applicable zoning and building codes in Hawthorn. The area surrounding East Peterhill in Hawthorn was developed as a residential community with homes built on one-half acre lots. West Peterhill was in a residential area covered by the Sycamore zoning code, which allowed residential development only on five-acre tracts of land.

In an appropriate action brought by Betty to enjoin Abel's proposed construction on one-half acre lots, the court will find the quoted restriction to be

(A) invalid, because of the change of circumstance in the neighborhood.
(B) invalid, because it conflicts with the applicable zoning code.
(C) valid, but only so long as the original grantees from Ollie own their respective tracts of Peterhill.
(D) valid, because the provision imposed an equitable servitude.

Question 167

Three years ago Adam conveyed Blackacre to Betty for $50,000 by a deed that provided: "By accepting this deed, Betty covenants for herself, her heirs and assigns, that the premises herein conveyed shall be used solely for residential purposes and, if the premises are used for nonresidential purposes, Adam, his heirs and assigns, shall have the right to repurchase the premises for the sum of one thousand dollars ($1,000)." In order to pay the $50,000 purchase price for Blackacre, Betty obtained a

$35,000 mortgage loan from the bank. Adam had full knowledge of the mortgage transaction. The deed and mortgage were promptly and properly recorded in proper sequence. The mortgage, however, made no reference to the quoted language in the deed.

Two years ago Betty converted her use of Blackacre from residential to commercial without the knowledge or consent of Adam or of the bank. Betty's commercial venture failed, and Betty defaulted on her mortgage payments to the bank. Blackacre now has a fair market value of $25,000.

The bank began appropriate foreclosure proceedings against Betty. Adam properly intervened, tendered $1,000, and sought judgment that Betty and the bank be ordered to convey Blackacre to Adam, free and clear of the mortgage.

The common-law Rule Against Perpetuities is unmodified by statute.

If the court rules against Adam, it will be because

(A) the provision quoted from the deed violates the Rule Against Perpetuities.
(B) the Bank had no actual knowledge of, and did not consent to, the violation of the covenant.
(C) the rights reserved by Adam were subordinated, by necessary implication, to the rights of the bank as the lender of the purchase money.
(D) the consideration of $1,000 was inadequate.

Question 168

Theresa owned Blueacre, a tract of land, in fee simple. Theresa wrote and executed, with the required formalities, a will that devised Blueacre to "my daughter, Della, for life with remainder to my descendants per stirpes." At the time of writing the will, Theresa had a husband and no descendants living other than her two children, Della and Seth.

Theresa died and the will was duly admitted to probate. Theresa's husband predeceased her. Theresa was survived by Della, Seth, four grandchildren, and one great-grandchild. Della and Seth were Theresa's sole heirs at law.

Della and Seth brought an appropriate action for declaratory judgment as to title of Blueacre. Guardians ad litem were appointed and all other steps were taken so that the judgment would bind all persons interested whether born or unborn.

In that action, if the court rules that Della has a life estate in the whole of Blueacre and that the remainder is contingent, it will be because the court chose one of several possible constructions and that the chosen construction

(A) related all vesting to the time of writing of the will.
(B) related all vesting to the death of Theresa.
(C) implied a condition that remaindermen survive Della.
(D) implied a gift of a life estate to Seth.

The correct answer is (C). This question tests the law of life estates and future interests.. A grantor who wishes to make a conveyance effective upon his or her decease must use a testamentary instrument, rather than a deed, to fulfill that purpose. A life estate is a possessory interest in a parcel of real property that lasts for the life of some person. A life estate creates a future interest that becomes effective upon the end of a measuring lifetime. That future interest may either be a reversion or a remainder.

Question 169

Six years ago, Oscar, owner of Blackacre in fee simple, executed and delivered to Albert an instrument in the proper form of a warranty deed, purporting to convey Blackacre to "Albert and his heirs." At that time, Albert was a widower who had one child, Donna.

Three years ago, Albert executed and delivered to Bea an instrument in the proper form of a warranty deed, purporting to convey Blackacre to "Bea." Donna did not join in the deed. Bea was and still is unmarried and childless.

The only possibly applicable statute in the jurisdiction states that any deed will be construed to convey the grantor's entire estate, unless expressly limited.

Last month, Albert died, never having remarried. Donna is his only heir.

Blackacre is now owned by

(A) Donna, because Albert's death ended Bea's life estate pur autre vie.
(B) Bea in fee simple pursuant to Albert's deed.
(C) Donna and Bea as tenants in common of equal shares.
(D) Donna and Bea as joint tenants, because both survived Albert.

Question 170

Martin, the owner in fee simple of Orchardacres, mortgaged Orchardacres to Marie to secure the payment of the loan she made to him. The loan was due at the end of the growing season of the year in which it was made. Martin maintained and operated an orchard on the land, which was his sole source of income. Halfway through the growing season, Martin experienced severe health and personal problems and, as a result, left the state; his whereabouts were unknown. Marie learned that no one was responsible for the cultivation and care of the orchard on Orchardacres. She undertook to provide, through employees, the care of the orchard and the harvest for the remainder of the growing season. The net profits were applied to the debt secured by the mortgage on Orchardacres.

During the course of the harvest, Paul, a business invitee, was injured by reason of a fault in the equipment used. Under applicable tort case law, the owner of the premises would be liable for Paul's injuries. Paul brought an appropriate action against Marie to recover damages for the injuries suffered, relying on this aspect of tort law.

In such lawsuit, judgment should be for

(A) Paul, if, but only if, the state is a title theory state, because in other jurisdictions a mortgagee has no title interest but only a lien.
(B) Paul, because Marie was a mortgagee in possession.
(C) Marie, because she acted as agent of the owner only to preserve her security interest.
(D) Marie, if, but only if, the mortgage expressly provided for her taking possession in the event of danger to her security interest.

Question 171

Adam owned Blackacre. Adam entered into a written three-year lease of Blackacre with Bertha. Among other provisions, the lease prohibited Bertha from "assigning this lease, in whole or in part, and from subletting Blackacre, in whole or in part." In addition to a house, a barn, and a one-car garage, Blackacre's 30 acres included several fields where first Adam, and now Bertha, grazed sheep.

During the following months, Bertha:

I. By a written agreement allowed her neighbor Charles exclusive use of the garage for storage, under lock and key, of his antique Packard automobile for two years, charging him $240.

II. Told her neighbor Doris that Doris could use the fields to practice her golf as long as she did not disturb Bertha's sheep.

Which, if any, of Bertha's actions constituted a violation of the lease?

(A) I only.
(B) II only.
(C) Both I and II.
(D) Neither I nor II.

Question 172

Bill owned in fee simple Lot 1 in a properly approved subdivision, designed and zoned for industrial use. Gail owned the adjoining Lot 2 in the same subdivision. The plat of the subdivision was recorded as authorized by statute.

Twelve years ago, Bill erected an industrial building wholly situated on Lot 1 but with one wall along the boundary common with Lot 2. The construction was done as authorized by a building permit, validly obtained under applicable statutes, ordinances, and regulations. Further, the construction was regularly inspected and passed as being in compliance with all building code requirements.

Lot 2 remained vacant until six months ago, when Gail began excavation pursuant to a building permit authorizing the erection of an industrial building situated on Lot 2 but with one wall along the boundary common with Lot 1. The excavation caused subsidence of a portion of Lot 1 that resulted in injury to Bill's building. The excavation was not done negligently or with any malicious intent to injure. In the jurisdiction, the time to acquire title by adverse possession or rights by prescription is 10 years.

Bill brought an appropriate action against Gail to recover damages resulting from the injuries to the building on Lot 1.

In such lawsuit, judgment should be for

(A) Bill, if, but only if, the subsidence would have occurred without the weight of the building on Lot 1.
(B) Bill, because a right for support, appurtenant to Lot 1, had been acquired by adverse possession or prescription.

(C) Gail, because Lots 1 and 2 are urban land, as distinguished from rural land and, therefore, under the circumstances Bill had the duty to protect any improvements on Lot 1.
(D) Gail, because the construction and the use to be made of the building were both authorized by the applicable law.

MBE MASTER

AMERIBAR BAR REVIEW

Multistate Bar Examination Released Questions – Section 8

TORTS

Question 1

Walter, a 16-year-old, purchased an educational chemistry set manufactured by Chemco.

Walter invited his friend and classmate, Peter, to assist him in a chemistry project. Referring to a library chemistry book on explosives and finding that the chemistry set contained all of the necessary chemicals, Walter and Peter agreed to make a bomb. During the course of the project, Walter carelessly knocked a lighted Bunsen burner into a bowl of chemicals from the chemistry set. The chemicals burst into flames, injuring Peter.

In a suit by Peter against Chemco, based on strict liability, Peter will

(A) prevail, if the chemistry set did not contain a warning that its contents could be combined to form dangerous explosives.
(B) prevail, because manufacturers of chemistry sets are engaged in an abnormally dangerous activity.
(C) not prevail, because Walter's negligence was the cause in fact of Peter's injury.
(D) not prevail, if the chemistry set was as safe as possible, consistent with its educational purposes, and its benefits exceeded its risks.

Question 2

As Paul, a bartender, was removing the restraining wire from a bottle of champagne produced and bottled by Winery, Inc., the plastic stopper suddenly shot out of the bottle. The stopper struck and injured Paul's eye. Paul had opened other bottles of champagne, and occasionally the stoppers had shot out with great force, but Paul had not been injured.

Paul has brought an action against Winery, Inc., alleging that the bottle that caused his injury was defective and unreasonably dangerous because its label did not warn that the stopper might suddenly shoot out during opening. The state has merged contributory negligence and unreasonable assumption of risk into a pure comparative fault system that is applied in strict products liability actions.

If the jury finds that the bottle was defective and unreasonably dangerous because it lacked a warning, will Paul recover a judgment in his favor?

(A) No, if the jury finds that a legally sufficient warning would not have prevented Paul's injury.
(B) No, if a reasonable bartender would have realized that a stopper could eject from the bottle and hit his eye.
(C) Yes, with damages reduced by the percentage of any contributory fault on Paul's part.
(D) Yes, with no reduction in damages, because foreseeable lack of caution is the reason for requiring a warning.

Question 3

Able and Baker are students in an advanced high school Russian class. During an argument one day in the high school cafeteria, in the presence of other students, Able, in Russian, accused Baker of taking money from Able's locker.

In a suit by Baker against Able based on defamation, Baker will

(A) prevail, because Able's accusation constituted slander per se.
(B) prevail, because the defamatory statement was made in the presence of third persons.
(C) not prevail, unless Able made the accusation with knowledge of falsity or reckless disregard of the truth.
(D) not prevail, unless one or more of the other students understood Russian.

Questions 4-5 are based on the following fact situation.

Doe, the governor of State, signed a death warrant for Rend, a convicted murderer. Able and Baker are active opponents of the death penalty. At a demonstration protesting the execution of Rend, Able and Baker carried large signs that stated, "Governor Doe - Murderer." Television station XYZ broadcast news coverage of the demonstration, including pictures of the signs carried by Able and Baker.

Question 4

If Governor Doe asserts a defamation claim against XYZ, will Doe prevail?

(A) Yes, because the signs would cause persons to hold Doe in lower esteem.
(B) Yes, if Doe proves that XYZ showed the signs with knowledge of falsity or reckless disregard of the truth that Doe had not committed homicide.
(C) No, unless Doe proves he suffered pecuniary loss resulting from harm to his reputation proximately caused by the defendants' signs.
(D) No, if the only reasonable interpretation of the signs was that the term "murderer" was intended as a characterization of one who would sign a death warrant.

Question 5

If Doe asserts against XYZ a claim for damages for intentional infliction of emotional distress, will Doe prevail?

(A) Yes, if the broadcast showing the signs caused Doe to suffer severe emotional distress.
(B) Yes, because the assertion on the signs was extreme and outrageous.
(C) No, unless Doe suffered physical harm as a consequence of the emotional distress caused by the signs.
(D) No, because XYZ did not publish a false statement of fact with "actual malice."

Question 6

At a country auction, Powell acquired an antique cabinet that he recognized as a "Morenci," an extremely rare and valuable collector's item. Unfortunately, Powell's cabinet had several coats of varnish and paint over the original finish. Its potential value could only be realized if these layers could be removed without damaging the original finish. Much of the value of Morenci furniture depends on the condition of a unique oil finish, the secret of which died with Morenci, its inventor.

A professional restorer of antique furniture recommended that Powell use Restorall to remove the paint and varnish from the cabinet. Powell obtained and read a sales brochure published by Restorall, Inc., which contained the following statement: "This product will renew all antique furniture. Will not damage original oil finishes."

Powell purchased some Restorall and used it on his cabinet, being very careful to follow the accompanying instructions exactly. Despite Powell's care, the original Morenci finish was irreparably damaged. When finally

refinished, the cabinet was worth less than 20% of what it would have been worth if the Morenci finish had been preserved.

If Powell sues Restorall, Inc., to recover the loss he has suffered as a result of the destruction of the Morenci finish, will Powell prevail?

(A) Yes, unless no other known removal technique would have preserved the Morenci finish.
(B) Yes, if the loss would not have occurred had the statement in the brochure been true.
(C) No, unless the product was defective when sold by Restorall, Inc.
(D) No, if the product was not dangerous to persons.

Question 7

Palko is being treated by a physician for asbestosis, an abnormal chest condition that was caused by his on-the-job handling of materials containing asbestos. His physician has told him that the asbestosis is not presently cancerous, but that it considerably increases the risk that he will ultimately develop lung cancer.

Palko brought an action for damages, based on strict product liability, against the supplier of the materials that contained asbestos. The court in this jurisdiction has ruled against recovery of damages for negligently inflicted emotional distress in the absence of physical harm.

If the supplier is subject to liability to Palko for damages, should the award include damage for emotional distress he has suffered arising from his knowledge of the increased risk that he will develop lung cancer?

(A) No, because Palko's emotional distress did not cause his physical condition.
(B) No, unless the court in this jurisdiction recognizes a cause of action for an increased risk of cancer.
(C) Yes, because the supplier of a dangerous product is strictly liable for the harm it causes.
(D) Yes, because Palko's emotional distress arises from bodily harm caused by his exposure to asbestos.

Question 8

In an action brought against Driver by Walker's legal representative, the only proofs that the legal representative offered on liability were that: (1) Walker, a pedestrian, was killed instantly while walking on the shoulder of the highway; (2) Driver was driving the car that struck Walker; and (3) there were no living witnesses to the accident other than Driver, who denied negligence.

Assume the jurisdiction has adopted a rule of pure comparative negligence.

If, at the end of the plaintiff's case, Driver moves for a directed verdict, the trial judge should

(A) grant the motion, because the legal representative has offered no specific evidence from which reasonable jurors may conclude that Driver was negligent.
(B) grant the motion, because it is just as likely that Walker was negligent as that Driver was negligent.
(C) deny the motion, unless Walker was walking with his back to traffic, in violation of the state highway code.
(D) deny the motion, because, in the circumstances, negligence on the part of Driver may be inferred.

Question 9

Dent operates a residential rehabilitation center for emotionally disturbed and ungovernable children who have been committed to his custody by their parents or by juvenile authorities. The center's purpose is to modify the behavior of the children through a teaching program carried out in a family-like environment. Though the children are not permitted to leave the center without his permission, there are no bars or guards to prevent them from doing so. It has been held in the state where the center is located that persons having custody of children have the same duties and responsibilities that they would have if they were the parents of the children.

Camden, aged 12, who had been in Dent's custody for six months, left the center without permission. Dent became aware of Camden's absence almost immediately, but made no attempt to locate him or secure his return, though reports reached him that Camden had been seen in the vicinity. Thirty-six hours after Camden left the center, Camden committed a brutal assault upon Pell, a five-year-old child, causing Pell to suffer extensive permanent injury.

If an action is brought against Dent on behalf of Pell to recover damages for Pell's injuries, will Pell prevail?

(A) No, because parents are not personally liable for their child's intentional torts.
(B) Yes, if Camden was old enough to be liable for battery.
(C) Yes, because Camden was in Dent's custody.
(D) No, unless Dent knew or had reason to know that Camden had a propensity to attack younger children.

Question 10

Landco owns and operates a 12-story apartment building containing 72 apartments, 70 of which are rented. Walker has brought an action against Landco alleging that while he was walking along a public sidewalk adjacent to Landco's apartment building a flower pot fell from above and struck him on the shoulder, causing extensive injuries. The action was to recover damages for those injuries.

If Walker proves the foregoing facts and offers no other evidence explaining the accident, will his claim survive a motion for directed verdict offered by the defense?

(A) Yes, because Walker was injured by an artificial condition of the premises while using an adjacent public way.
(B) Yes, because such an accident does not ordinarily happen in the absence of negligence.
(C) No, if Landco is in no better position than Walker to explain the accident.
(D) No, because there is no basis for a reasonable inference that Landco was negligent.

Question 11

Peter and Donald were in the habit of playing practical jokes on each other on their respective birthdays. On Peter's birthday, Donald sent Peter a cake containing an ingredient that he knew had, in the past, made Peter very ill. After Peter had eaten a piece of the cake, he suffered severe stomach pains and had to be taken to the hospital by ambulance. On the way to the hospital, the ambulance driver suffered a heart attack, which caused the ambulance to swerve from the road and hit a tree. As a result of the collision, Peter suffered a broken leg.

In a suit by Peter against Donald to recover damages for Peter's broken leg, Peter will

(A) prevail, because Donald knew that the cake would be harmful or offensive to Peter.

(B) prevail, only if the ambulance driver was negligent.

(C) not prevail, because Donald could not reasonably be expected to foresee injury to Peter's leg.

(D) not prevail, because the ambulance driver's heart attack was a superseding cause of Peter's broken leg.

Questions 12-14 are based on the following fact situation.

Dora, who was eight years old, went to the grocery store with her mother. Dora pushed the grocery cart while her mother put items into it. Dora's mother remained near Dora at all times. Peterson, another customer in the store, noticed Dora pushing the cart in a manner that caused Peterson no concern. A short time later, the cart Dora was pushing struck Peterson in the knee, inflicting serious injury.

Question 12

If Peterson brings an action, based on negligence, against the grocery store, the store's best defense will be that

(A) a store owes no duty to its customers to control the use of its shopping carts.

(B) a store owes no duty to its customers to control the conduct of other customers.

(C) any negligence of the store was not the proximate cause of Peterson's injury.

(D) a supervised child pushing a cart does not pose an unreasonable risk to other customers.

Question 13

If Peterson brings an action, based on negligence, against Dora's mother, will Peterson prevail?

(A) Yes, if Dora was negligent.

(B) Yes, because Dora's mother is responsible for any harm caused by Dora.

(C) Yes, because Dora's mother assumed the risk of her child's actions.

(D) Yes, if Dora's mother did not adequately supervise Dora's actions.

Question 14

If Peterson brings an action, based on negligence, against Dora, Dora's best argument in defense would be that

(A) Dora exercised care commensurate with her age, intelligence, and experience.

(B) Dora is not subject to tort liability.

(C) Dora was subject to parental supervision.

(D) Peterson assumed the risk that Dora might hit Peterson with the cart.

Question 15

Dayton operates a collection agency. He was trying to collect a $400 bill for medical services rendered to Pratt by Doctor.

Dayton went to Pratt's house and when Martina, Pratt's mother, answered the door, Dayton told Martina he was there to collect a bill owed by Pratt. Martina told Dayton that because of her illness, Pratt had been unemployed for six months, that she was still ill and unable to work, and that she would pay the bill as soon as she could.

Dayton, in a loud voice, demanded to see Pratt and said that if he did not receive payment immediately, he would file a criminal complaint charging her with fraud. Pratt, hearing the conversation, came to the door. Dayton, in a loud voice, repeated his demand for immediate payment and his threat to use criminal process.

If Pratt asserts a claim against Dayton, based on infliction of emotional distress, will Pratt prevail?

(A) Yes, if Pratt suffered severe emotional distress as a result of Dayton's conduct.

(B) Yes, unless the bill for medical services was valid and past due.

(C) No, unless Pratt suffered physical harm as a result of Dayton's conduct.

(D) No, if Dayton's conduct created no risk of physical harm to Pratt.

Question 16

A car driven by Dan entered land owned by and in the possession of Peter, without Peter's permission.

Which, if any, of the following allegations, without additional facts, would provide a sufficient basis for a claim by Peter against Dan?

I.   Dan intentionally drove his car onto Peter's land.

II. Dan negligently drove his car onto Peter's land.

III. Dan's car damaged Peter's land.

(A) I only.
(B) III only.
(C) I, II, or III.
(D) Neither I, nor II, nor III

Question 17

Palmco owns and operates a beachfront hotel. Under a contract with City to restore a public beach, Dredgeco placed a large and unavoidably dangerous stone-crushing machine on City land near Palmco's hotel. The machine creates a continuous and intense noise that is so disturbing to the hotel guests that they have canceled their hotel reservations in large numbers, resulting in a substantial loss to Palmco.

Palmco's best chance to recover damages for its financial losses from Dredgeco is under the theory that the operation of the stone-crushing machine constitutes

(A) an abnormally dangerous activity.
(B) a private nuisance.
(C) negligence.
(D) a trespass.

Question 18

While Patty was riding her horse on what she thought was a public path, the owner of a house next to the path approached her, shaking a stick and shouting, "Get off my property." Unknown to Patty, the path on which she was riding crossed the private property of the shouting owner. When Patty explained that she thought the path was a public trail, the man cursed her, approached Patty's horse, and struck the horse with the stick. As a result of the blow, the horse reared, causing Patty to fear that she would fall. However, Patty managed to stay on the horse, and then departed. Neither Patty nor the horse suffered bodily harm.

If Patty brings an action for damages against the property owner, the result should be for

(A) Patty, for trespass to her chattel property.
(B) Patty, for battery and assault.
(C) the defendant, because Patty suffered no physical harm.
(D) the defendant, because he was privileged to exclude trespassers from his property.

Question 19

While driving his car, Plaintiff sustained injuries in a three-car collision. Plaintiff sued the drivers of the other two cars, D-1 and D-2, and each defendant crossclaimed against the other for contribution. The jurisdiction has adopted a rule of pure comparative negligence and allows contribution based upon proportionate fault. The rule of joint and several liability has been retained.

The jury has found that Plaintiff sustained damages in the amount of $100,000, and apportioned the causal negligence of the parties as follows: Plaintiff 40%, D-1 30%, and D-2 30%.

How much, if anything, can Plaintiff collect from D-1, and how much, if anything, can D-1 then collect from D-2 in contribution?

(A) Nothing, and then D-1 can collect nothing from D-2.
(B) $30,000, and then D-1 can collect nothing from D-2,
(C) $40,000, and then D-1 can collect $10,000 from D-2.
(D) $60,000, and then D-1 can collect $30,000 from D-2.

Question 20

Desmond fell while attempting to climb a mountain, and lay unconscious and critically injured on a ledge that was difficult to reach. Pearson, an experienced mountain climber, was himself seriously injured while trying to rescue Desmond. Pearson's rescue attempt failed, and Desmond died of his injuries before he could be reached.

Pearson brought an action against Desmond's estate for compensation for his injuries. In this jurisdiction, the traditional common-law rules relating to contributory negligence and assumption of risk remain in effect.

Will Pearson prevail in his action against Desmond's estate?

(A) Yes, if his rescue attempt was reasonable.
(B) Yes, because the law should not discourage attempts to assist persons in helpless peril.
(C) No, unless Desmond's peril arose from his own failure to exercise reasonable care.
(D) No, because Pearson's rescue attempt failed and therefore did not benefit Desmond.

Question 21

As a result of an accident at the NPP nuclear power plant, a quantity of radioactive vapor escaped from the facility and two members of the public were exposed to excessive doses of radiation. According to qualified medical opinion, that exposure will double the chance that these two persons will ultimately develop cancer. However, any cancer that might be caused by this exposure will not be detectable for at least ten years. If the two exposed persons do develop cancer, it will not be possible to determine whether it was caused by this exposure or would have developed in any event.

If the exposed persons assert a claim for damages against NPP shortly after the escape of the radiation, which of the following questions will NOT present a substantial issue?

(A) Will the court recognize that the plaintiffs have suffered a present legal injury?

(B) Can the plaintiffs prove the amount of their damages?

(C) Can the plaintiffs prove that any harm they may suffer was caused by this exposure?

(D) Can the plaintiffs prevail without presenting evidence of specific negligence on the part of NPP?

Question 22

In preparation for a mountain-climbing expedition, Alper purchased the necessary climbing equipment from Outfitters, Inc., a retail dealer in sporting goods. A week later, Alper fell from a rock face when a safety device he had purchased from Outfitters malfunctioned because of a defect in its manufacture. Thereafter, Rollins was severely injured when he tried to reach and give assistance to Alper on the ledge to which Alper had fallen. Rollins's injury was not caused by any fault on his own part.

If Rollins brings an action against Outfitters, Inc., to recover damages for his injuries, will Rollins prevail?

(A) No, unless Outfitters could have discovered the defect by a reasonable inspection of the safety device.

(B) No, because Rollins did not rely on the representation of safety implied from the sale of the safety device by Outfitters.

(C) Yes, unless Alper was negligent in failing to test the safety device.

(D) Yes, because injury to a person in Rollins's position was foreseeable if the safety device failed.

Question 23

Plaintiff was a passenger in a car that was struck in the rear by a car driven by First. The collision resulted from First's negligence in failing to keep a proper lookout. Plaintiff's physician found that the collision had aggravated a mild osteoarthritic condition in her lower back and had brought on similar, but new, symptoms in her neck and upper back.

Six months after the first accident, Plaintiff was a passenger in a car that was struck in the rear by a car driven by Second. The collision resulted from Second's negligence in failing to keep a proper lookout. Plaintiff's physician found that the second collision had caused a general worsening of Plaintiff's condition, marked by a significant restriction of movement and muscle spasms in her back and neck. The physician believes Plaintiff's worsened condition is permanent, and he can find no basis for apportioning responsibility for her present worsened condition between the two automobile collisions.

Plaintiff brought an action for damages against First and Second. At the close of Plaintiff's evidence, as outlined above, each of the defendants moved for a directed verdict in his favor on the ground that Plaintiff had failed to produce evidence on which the jury could determine how much damage each defendant had caused. The jurisdiction adheres to the common-law rules regarding joint and several liability.

Plaintiff's best argument in opposition to the defendants' motions would be that the defendants are jointly and severally liable for Plaintiff's entire harm, because

(A) the wrongdoers, rather than their victim, should bear the burden of the impossibility of apportionment.

(B) the defendants breached a common duty that each of them owed to Plaintiff.

(C) each of the defendants was the proximate cause in fact of all of Plaintiff's damages.

(D) the defendants are joint tortfeasors who aggravated Plaintiff's preexisting condition.

Question 24

Airco operates an aircraft maintenance and repair business serving the needs of owners of private airplanes. Flyer contracted with Airco to replace the engine in his plane with a more powerful engine of foreign manufacture. Airco purchased the replacement engine through a representative of the manufacturer and installed it in Flyer's plane. A short time after it was put into use, the new engine failed, and the plane crashed into a warehouse owned by Landers, destroying the warehouse and its contents. Airco was guilty of no negligence in the procurement, inspection, or installation of the engine. The failure of the engine was caused by a defect that would not be disclosed by inspection and testing procedures available to an installer. There was no negligence on the part of Flyer, who escaped the disabled plane by parachute.

Landers recovered a judgment for damages from Flyer for the destruction of his warehouse and its contents, and Flyer has asserted a claim against Airco to recover compensation on account of that liability.

In that action, Flyer will recover

(A) full compensation, because the engine was defective.
(B) no compensation, because Airco was not negligent.
(C) contribution only, because Airco and Flyer were equally innocent.
(D) no compensation, because Landers's judgment established Flyer's responsibility to Landers.

Question 25

While driving at a speed in excess of the statutory limit, Dant negligently collided with another car, and the disabled vehicles blocked two of the highway's three northbound lanes. When Page approached the scene two minutes later, he slowed his car to see if he could help those involved in the collision. As he slowed, he was rear-ended by a vehicle driven by Thomas. Page, who sustained damage to his car and was seriously injured, brought an action against Dant to recover damages. The jurisdiction adheres to the traditional common-law rules pertaining to contributory negligence.

If Dant moves to dismiss the action for failure to state a claim upon which relief may be granted, should the motion be granted?

(A) Yes, because it was Thomas, not Dant, who collided with Page's car and caused Page's injuries.
(B) Yes, if Page could have safely passed the disabled vehicles in the traffic lane that remained open.
(C) No, because a jury could find that Page's injury arose from a risk that was a continuing consequence of Dant's negligence.
(D) No, because Dant was driving in excess of the statutory limit when he negligently caused the first accident.

Question 26

Pocket, a bank vice president, took substantial kickbacks to approve certain loans that later proved worthless. Upon learning of the kickbacks, Dudd, the bank's president, fired Pocket, telling him, "If you are not out of this bank in ten minutes, I will have the guards throw you out bodily." Pocket left at once.

If Pocket asserts a claim against Dudd based on assault, will Pocket prevail?

(A) No, because the guards never touched Pocket.
(B) No, because Dudd gave Pocket ten minutes to leave.
(C) Yes, if Dudd intended to cause Pocket severe emotional distress.
(D) Yes, because Dudd threatened Pocket with a harmful or offensive bodily contact.

Questions 27-28 are based on the following fact situation.

Dooley was a pitcher for the City Robins, a professional baseball team. While Dooley was throwing warm-up pitches on the sidelines during a game, he was continuously heckled by some spectators seated in the stands above the dugout behind a wire mesh fence. On several occasions, Dooley turned and looked directly at the hecklers with a scowl on his face, but the heckling continued. Dooley wound up as though he was preparing to pitch in the direction of his catcher; however the ball traveled from his hand at high speed, at a 90-degree angle from the line to the catcher and directly toward the hecklers in the stands. The ball passed through the wire mesh fence and struck Patricia, one of the hecklers.

Patricia brought an action for damages against Dooley and the City Robins, based upon negligence and battery. The trial court directed a verdict for the defendants on the battery count. The jury found for the defendants on the negligence count because the jury determined that Dooley could not foresee that the ball would pass through the wire mesh fence.

Patricia has appealed the judgments on the battery counts, contending that the trial court erred in directing verdicts for Dooley and the City Robins.

Question 27

On appeal, the judgment entered on the directed verdict in Dooley's favor on the battery claim should be

(A) affirmed, because the jury found on the evidence that Dooley could not foresee that the ball would pass through the fence.
(B) affirmed, if there was evidence that Dooley was mentally ill and that his act was the product of his mental illness.
(C) reversed and the case remanded, if a jury could find on the evidence that Dooley intended to cause the hecklers to fear being hit.
(D) reversed and the case remanded, because a jury could find that Dooley's conduct was extreme and outrageous, and the cause of physical harm to Patricia.

Question 28

For this question only, assume that, On appeal, the court holds that the question of whether Dooley committed a battery is a jury issue.

The judgment entered on the directed verdict in favor of the City Robins should then be

(A) reversed and the case remanded, because a jury could find the City Robins vicariously liable for a battery committed by Dooley in the course of his employment.
(B) reversed and the case remanded, only if a jury could find negligence on the part of the Robins' management.
(C) affirmed, because an employer is not vicariously liable for a servant's battery.
(D) affirmed, if Dooley's act was a knowing violation of team rules.

Question 29

Dieter parked her car in violation of a city ordinance that prohibits parking within ten feet of a fire hydrant. Because Grove was driving negligently, his car sideswiped Dieter's parked car. Plaintiff, a passenger in Grove's car, was injured in the collision.

If Plaintiff asserts a claim against Dieter to recover damages for his injuries, basing his claim on Dieter's violation of the parking ordinance, will Plaintiff prevail?

(A) Yes, because Dieter was guilty of negligence per se.
(B) Yes, if Plaintiff would not have been injured had Dieter's car not been parked where it was.
(C) No, because Dieter's parked car was not an active or efficient cause of Plaintiff's injury.
(D) No, if prevention of traffic accidents was not a purpose of the ordinance.

Question 30

Dorfman's dog ran into the street in front of Dorfman's home and began chasing cars. Peterson, who was driving a car on the street, swerved to avoid hitting the dog, struck a telephone pole, and was injured.

If Peterson asserts a claim against Dorfman, will Peterson prevail?

(A) Yes, because Dorfman's dog was a cause in fact of Peterson's injury.
(B) Yes, if Dorfman knew his dog had a propensity to chase cars and did not restrain it.
(C) No, because a dog is a domestic animal.
(D) No, unless a statute or ordinance made it unlawful for the owner to allow a dog to be unleashed on a public street.

Question 31

Dower, an inexperienced driver, borrowed a car from Puder, a casual acquaintance, for the express purpose of driving it several blocks to the local drug store. Instead, Dower drove the car, which then was worth $12,000, 100 miles to Other City. While Dower was driving in Other City the next day, the car was hit by a negligently driven truck and sustained damage that will cost $3,000 to repair. If repaired, the car will be fully restored to its former condition.

If Puder asserts a claim against Dower based on conversion, Puder should recover a judgment for

(A) $12,000.
(B) $3,000.

(C) $3,000 plus damages for the loss of the use of the car during its repair.

(D) nothing, unless Dower was negligent and his negligence was a substantial cause of the collision.

Question 32

Deland operates a bank courier service that uses armored trucks to transport money and securities. One of Deland's armored trucks was parked illegally, too close to a street intersection. Pilcher, driving his car at an excessive speed, skidded into the armored truck while trying to make a turn. The truck was not damaged, but Pilcher was injured.

Pilcher has brought an action against Deland to recover damages for his loss resulting from the accident. The jurisdiction follows a pure comparative negligence rule.

In this action, Pilcher should recover

(A) nothing, because Deland was not an active or efficient cause of Pilcher's loss.

(B) nothing, if Deland was less negligent than Pilcher.

(C) his entire loss, reduced by a percentage that reflects the negligence attributed to Pilcher.

(D) his entire loss, because Deland's truck suffered no damage.

Question 33

While walking on a public sidewalk, Anson was struck by a piece of lumber that fell from the roof of Bruce's house. Bruce had hired Chase to make repairs to his roof, and the lumber fell through negligence on Chase's part.

If Anson brings an action against Bruce to recover damages for the injury caused to him by Chase's negligence, will Anson prevail?

(A) Yes, under the res ipsa loquitur doctrine.

(B) Yes, if Chase's act was a breach of a nondelegable duty owed by Bruce to Anson.

(C) No, if Chase was an independent contractor rather than Bruce's servant.

(D) No, if Bruce exercised reasonable care in hiring Chase to do the repair work.

Question 34

Star, who played the lead role in a television soap opera, was seriously injured in an automobile accident caused by Danton's negligent driving. As a consequence of Star's injury, the television series was canceled, and Penn, a supporting actor, was laid off.

In an action against Danton, can Penn recover for his loss of income attributable to the accident?

(A) Yes, because Danton's negligence was the cause in fact of Penn's loss.

(B) Yes, unless Penn failed to take reasonable measures to mitigate his loss.

(C) No, unless Danton should have foreseen that by injuring Star he would cause harm to Penn.

(D) No, because Danton's liability does not extend to economic loss to Penn that arises solely from physical harm to Star.

Question 35

Ann's three-year-old daughter, Janet, was killed in an automobile accident. At Ann's direction, Janet's body was taken to a mausoleum for interment. Normally, the mausoleum's vaults are permanently sealed with marble plates secured by "tamper-proof" screws. After Janet's body was placed in the mausoleum, however, only a fiberglass panel secured by caulking compound covered her vault. About a month later, Janet's body was discovered in a cemetery located near the mausoleum. It had apparently been left there by vandals who had taken it from the mausoleum.

As a result of this experience, Ann suffered great emotional distress.

If Ann sues the mausoleum for the damages arising from her emotional distress, will she prevail?

(A) No, because Ann experienced no threat to her own safety.

(B) No, unless the mausoleum's behavior was extreme and outrageous.

(C) Yes, if the mausoleum failed to use reasonable care to safeguard the body.

(D) Yes, unless Ann suffered no physical harm as a consequence of her emotional distress.

Question 36

Prad entered Drug Store to make some purchases. As he was searching the aisles for various items, he noticed a display card containing automatic pencils. The display card was on a high shelf behind a cashier's counter. Prad saw a sign on the counter that read, "No Admittance, Employees Only." Seeing no clerks in the vicinity to help him, Prad went behind the counter to get a pencil. A clerk then appeared behind the counter and asked whether she could help him. He said he just wanted a pencil and that he could reach the display card himself. The clerk said nothing further. While reaching for the display card, Prad stepped sideways into an open shaft and fell to the basement, ten feet below. The clerk knew of the presence of the open shaft, but assumed incorrectly that Prad had noticed it.

Prad sued Drug Store to recover damages for the injuries he sustained in the fall. The jurisdiction has adopted a rule of pure comparative negligence, and it follows traditional common-law rules governing the duties of a land possessor.

Will Prad recover a judgment against Drug Store?

(A) No, because Prad was a trespasser.
(B) No, unless Prad's injuries resulted from the defendant's willful or wanton misconduct.
(C) Yes, because the premises were defective with respect to a public invitee.
(D) Yes, if the clerk had reason to believe that Prad was unaware of the open shaft.

Question 37

In the course of a bank holdup, Robber fired a gun at Guard. Guard drew his revolver and returned the fire. One of the bullets fired by Guard ricocheted, striking Plaintiff.

If Plaintiff asserts a claim against Guard based upon battery, will Plaintiff prevail?

(A) Yes, unless Plaintiff was Robber's accomplice.
(B) Yes, under the doctrine of transferred intent.
(C) No, if Guard fired reasonably in his own defense.
(D) No, if Guard did not intend to shoot Plaintiff.

Question 38

Jones and Smith, who were professional rivals, were attending a computer industry dinner where each was to receive an award for achievement in the field of data processing. Smith engaged Jones in conversation and expressed the opinion that if they joined forces, they could do even better. Jones replied that she would not consider Smith as a business partner and when Smith demanded to know why, told him that he, Smith, was incompetent.

The exchange was overheard by Brown, who attended the dinner. Smith suffered emotional distress but no pecuniary loss.

If Smith asserts a claim against Jones based on defamation, will Smith prevail?

(A) No, because Smith suffered no pecuniary loss.
(B) No, because Jones's statement was made to Smith and not to Brown.
(C) No, unless Jones should have foreseen that her statement would be overheard by another person.
(D) No, unless Jones intended to cause Smith emotional distress.

Question 39

The Pinners, a retired couple, had lived in their home in a residential neighborhood for 20 years when the Darleys moved into the house next door and built a swimming pool in the back yard. The four young Darley children frequently played in the pool after school. They often were joined by other neighborhood children. The Pinners were in the habit of reading and listening to classical music in the afternoons. Sometimes they took naps. The boisterous sounds of the children playing in the pool disturbed the Pinners' customary enjoyment of quiet afternoons.

In the Pinners' nuisance action for damages against the Darleys, the Pinners should

(A) prevail, if the children's noise constituted a substantial interference with the Pinners' use and enjoyment of their home.
(B) prevail, because the Pinners' interest in the quiet enjoyment of their home takes precedence in time over the Darleys' interests.
(C) not prevail, unless the noise constituted a substantial and unreasonable disturbance to persons of normal sensibilities.
(D) not prevail, because the children's interest in healthy play has priority over the Pinners' interest in peace and quiet.

Question 40

Jones, who was driving his car at night, stopped the car and went into a nearby tavern for a drink. He left the car standing at the side of the road, projecting three feet into the traffic lane. The lights were on and his friend, Peters, was asleep in the back seat. Peters awoke, discovered the situation, and went back to sleep. Before Jones returned, his car was hit by an automobile approaching from the rear and driven by Davis. Peters was injured.

Peters sued Davis and Jones jointly to recover the damages he suffered resulting from the accident. The jurisdiction has a pure comparative negligence rule and has abolished the defense of assumption of risk. In respect to other issues, the rules of the common law remain in effect.

Peters should recover

(A) nothing, if Peters was more negligent than either Davis or Jones.
(B) nothing, unless the total of Davis's and Jones's negligence was greater than Peters's.
(C) from Davis and Jones, jointly and severally, the amount of damages Peters suffered reduced by the percentage of the total negligence that is attributed to Peters.
(D) from Davis and Jones, severally, a percentage of Peters's damages equal to the percentage of fault attributed to each of the defendants.

Question 41

Peavey was walking peacefully along a public street when he encountered Dorwin, whom he had never seen before. Without provocation or warning, Dorwin picked up a rock and struck Peavey with it. It was later established that Dorwin was mentally ill and suffered recurrent hallucinations.

If Peavey asserts a claim against Dorwin based on battery, which of the following, if supported by evidence, will be Dorwin's best defense?

(A) Dorwin did not understand that his act was wrongful.
(B) Dorwin did not desire to cause harm to Peavey.
(C) Dorwin did not know that he was striking a person.
(D) Dorwin thought Peavey was about to attack him.

Question 42

Penstock owned a large tract of land on the shore of a lake. Drury lived on a stream that ran along one boundary of Penstock's land and into the lake. At some time in the past, a channel had been cut across Penstock's land from the stream to the lake at a point some distance from the mouth of the stream. From where Drury lived, the channel served as a convenient shortcut to the lake. Erroneously believing that the channel was a public waterway,

Drury made frequent trips through the channel in his motorboat. His use of the channel caused no harm to the land through which it passed.

If Penstock asserts a claim for damages against Drury based on trespass, which of the following would be a correct disposition of the case?

(A) Judgment for Penstock for nominal damages, because Drury intentionally used the channel.
(B) Judgment for Drury, if he did not use the channel after learning of Penstock's ownership claim.
(C) Judgment for Drury, because he caused no harm to Penstock's land.
(D) Judgment for Drury, because when he used the channel he believed it was a public waterway.

Question 43

David built in his backyard a garage that encroached two feet across the property line onto property owned by his neighbor, Prudence. Thereafter, David sold his property to Drake. Prudence was unaware, prior to David's sale to Drake, of the encroachment of the garage onto her property. When she thereafter learned of the encroachment, she sued David for damages for trespass.

In this action, will Prudence prevail?

(A) No, unless David was aware of the encroachment when the garage was built.
(B) No, because David no longer owns or possesses the garage.
(C) Yes, because David knew where the garage was located, whether or not he knew where the property line was.
(D) Yes, unless Drake was aware of the encroachment when he purchased the property.

Question 44

Daniel and a group of his friends are fanatical basketball fans who regularly meet at each others' homes to watch basketball games on television. Some of the group are fans of team A, and others are fans of team B. When the group has watched televised games between these two teams, fights sometimes have broken out among the group. Despite this fact, Daniel invited the group to his home to watch a championship game between teams A and B.

During the game, Daniel's guests became rowdy and antagonistic. Fearing that they would begin to fight, and that a fight would damage his possessions, Daniel asked his guests to leave. They refused to go and soon began to fight. Daniel called the police, and Officer was sent to Daniel's home. Officer sustained a broken nose in his efforts to stop the fighting.

Officer brought an action against Daniel alleging that Daniel was negligent in inviting the group to his house to watch this championship game. Daniel has moved to dismiss the complaint.

The best argument in support of this motion would be that

(A) a rescuer injured while attempting to avert a danger cannot recover damages from the endangered person.
(B) a police officer is not entitled to a recovery based upon the negligent conduct that created the need for the officer's professional intervention.
(C) as a matter of law, Daniel's conduct was not the proximate cause of Officer's injury.
(D) Daniel did not owe Officer a duty to use reasonable care, because Officer was a mere licensee on Daniel's property.

Question 45

Supermarket is in a section of town where there are sometimes street fights and where pedestrians are occasionally the victims of pickpockets and muggers. In recognition of the unusual number of robberies in the area, the supermarket posted signs in the store and in its parking lot that read:

Warning: There are pickpockets and muggers at work in this part of the city. Supermarket is not responsible for the acts of criminals.

One evening, Lorner drove to Supermarket to see about a special on turkeys that Supermarket was advertising. She decided that the turkeys were too large and left the store without purchasing anything. In the parking lot, she was attacked by an unknown man who raped her and then ran away.

If Lorner sues Supermarket, the result should be for the

(A) plaintiff, if Supermarket failed to take reasonable steps to protect customers against criminal attack in its parking lot.
(B) plaintiff, because Supermarket is liable for harm to business invitees on its premises.
(C) defendant, if the warning signs were plainly visible to Lorner.
(D) defendant, because the rapist was the proximate cause of Lorner's injuries.

Question 46

Peter, who was 20 years old, purchased a new, high-powered sports car that was marketed with an intended and recognized appeal to youthful drivers. The car was designed with the capability to attain speeds in excess of 100 miles per hour. It was equipped with tires designed and tested only for a maximum safe speed of 85 miles per hour. The owner's manual that came with the car stated that "continuous driving over 90 miles per hour requires high-speed-capability tires," but the manual did not describe the speed capability of the tires sold with the car.

Peter took his new car out for a spin on a straight, smooth country road where the posted speed limit was 55 miles per hour. Intending to test the car's power, he drove for a considerable distance at over 100 miles per hour. While he was doing so, the tread separated from the left rear tire, causing the car to leave the road and hit a tree. Peter sustained severe injuries.

Peter has brought a strict product liability action in tort against the manufacturer of the car. You should assume that pure comparative fault principles apply to this case.

Will Peter prevail?

(A) No, because Peter's driving at an excessive speed constituted a misuse of the car.
(B) No, because the car was not defective.
(C) Yes, if the statement in the manual concerning the tires did not adequately warn of the danger of high-speed driving on the tires mounted on the car.
(D) Yes, unless Peter's driving at a speed in excess of the posted speed limit was negligence per se that, by the law of the jurisdiction, was not excusable.

Question 47

Electco operates a factory that requires the use of very high voltage electricity. Paul owns property adjacent to the Electco plant where he has attempted to carry on a business that requires the use of sensitive electronic equipment. The effectiveness of Paul's electronic equipment is impaired by electrical interference arising from the high voltage currents used in Electco's plant. Paul has complained to Electco several times, with no result. There is no way that Electco, by taking reasonable precautions, can avoid the interference with Paul's operation that arises from the high voltage currents necessary to Electco's operation.

In Paul's action against Electco to recover damages for the economic loss caused to him by the electrical interference, will Paul prevail?

(A) Yes, because Electco's activity is abnormally dangerous.
(B) Yes, for loss suffered by Paul after Electco was made aware of the harm its activity was causing to Paul.
(C) No, unless Electco caused a substantial and unreasonable interference with Paul's business.
(D) No, because Paul's harm was purely economic and did not arise from physical harm to his person or property.

Question 48

Doe negligently caused a fire in his house, and the house burned to the ground. As a result, the sun streamed into Peter's yard next door, which previously had been shaded by Doe's house. The sunshine destroyed some delicate and valuable trees in Peter's yard that could grow only in the shade. Peter has brought a negligence action against Doe for the loss of Peter's trees. Doe has moved to dismiss the complaint.

The best argument in support of this motion would be that

(A) Doe's negligence was not the active cause of the loss of Peter's trees.
(B) Doe's duty to avoid the risks created by a fire did not encompass the risk that sunshine would damage Peter's trees.
(C) the loss of the trees was not a natural and probable consequence of Doe's negligence.
(D) Peter suffered a purely economic loss, which is not compensable in a negligence action.

Question 49

Dan, an eight-year-old, rode his bicycle down his driveway into a busy highway and Driver had to stop her car suddenly to avoid colliding with the bike. Because of the sudden stop, Driver's two-year-old son, Peter, who was sitting on the seat without any restraint, was thrown into the dashboard and injured. Had Peter been properly restrained in a baby car seat, as required by a state safety statute of which his mother was aware, he would not have been injured.

In an action brought on Peter's behalf against Dan's parents to recover for Peter's injuries, Peter will

(A) not prevail, because parents are not vicariously liable for the negligent acts of their children.
(B) not prevail, because Peter's injury was attributable to his mother's knowing violation of a safety statute.
(C) prevail, if Dan's parents knew that he sometimes drove into the highway, and they took no steps to prevent it.
(D) prevail, if Dan's riding into the highway was negligent and the proximate cause of Peter's injuries.

Question 50

While Hill was in her kitchen, she heard the screech of automobile tires. She ran to the window and saw a tricycle flying through the air. The tricycle had been hit by a car driven by Weber, who had been speeding. She also saw a child's body in the grass adjacent to the street. As a result of her shock from this experience, Hill suffered a heart attack.

In a claim by Hill against Weber, the issue on which Hill's right to recover will depend is whether

(A) a person can recover damages based on the defendant's breach of a duty owed to another.
(B) it is foreseeable that a person may suffer physical harm caused solely by an injury inflicted on another.
(C) a person can recover damages caused by shock unaccompanied by bodily impact.
(D) a person can recover damages for harm resulting from shock caused solely by another's peril or injury.

Question 51

Defendant left her car parked on the side of a hill. Two minutes later, the car rolled down the hill and struck and injured Plaintiff.

In Plaintiff's negligence action against Defendant, Plaintiff introduced into evidence the facts stated above, which are undisputed. Defendant testified that, when she parked her car, she turned the front wheels into the curb and put on her emergency brakes, which were in good working order. She also introduced evidence that, in the weeks before this incident, juveniles had been seen tampering with cars in the neighborhood. The jury returned a verdict in favor of Defendant, and Plaintiff moved for a judgment notwithstanding the verdict.

Plaintiff's motion should be

(A) granted, because it is more likely than not that Defendant's negligent conduct was the legal cause of Plaintiff's injuries.
(B) granted, because the evidence does not support the verdict.
(C) denied, because, given Defendant's evidence, the jury was not required to draw an inference of negligence from the circumstances of the accident.
(D) denied, if Defendant was in no better position than Plaintiff to explain the accident.

Question 52

David owned a shotgun that he used for hunting. David knew that his old friend, Mark, had become involved with a violent gang that recently had a shoot-out with a rival gang. David, who was going to a farm to hunt quail, placed his loaded shotgun on the back seat of his car. On his way to the farm, David picked up Mark to give him a ride to a friend's house. After dropping off Mark at the friend's house, David proceeded to the farm, where he discovered that his shotgun was missing from his car. Mark had taken the shotgun and, later in the day, Mark used it to shoot Paul, a member of the rival gang. Paul was severely injured.

Paul recovered a judgment for his damages against David, as well as Mark, on the ground that David was negligent in allowing Mark to obtain possession of the gun, and was therefore liable jointly and severally with Mark for Paul's damages. The jurisdiction has a statute that allows contribution based upon proportionate fault and adheres to the traditional common-law rules on indemnity.

If David fully satisfies the judgment, David then will have a right to recover from Mark

(A) indemnity for the full amount of the judgment, because Mark was an intentional tortfeasor.
(B) contribution only, based on comparative fault, because David himself was negligent.
(C) one-half of the amount of the judgment.
(D) nothing, because David's negligence was a substantial proximate cause of the shooting.

Question 53

Chemco manufactured a liquid chemical product known as XRX. Some XRX leaked from a storage tank on Chemco's property, seeped into the groundwater, flowed to Farmer's adjacent property, and polluted Farmer's well. Several of Farmer's cows drank the polluted well water and died.

If Farmer brings an action against Chemco to recover the value of the cows that died, Farmer will

(A) prevail, because a manufacturer is strictly liable for harm caused by its products.
(B) prevail, because the XRX escaped from Chemco's premises.
(C) not prevail, unless Farmer can establish that the storage tank was defective.
(D) not prevail, unless Chemco failed to exercise reasonable care in storing the XRX.

Question 54

Plaintiff, a jockey, was seriously injured in a race when another jockey, Daring, cut too sharply in front of her without adequate clearance. The two horses collided, causing Plaintiff to fall to the ground, sustaining injury. The State Racetrack Commission ruled that, by cutting in too sharply, Daring committed a foul in violation of racetrack rules requiring adequate clearance for crossing lanes. Plaintiff has brought an action against Daring for damages in which one count is based on battery.

Will Plaintiff prevail on the battery claim?

(A) Yes, if Daring was reckless in cutting across in front of Plaintiff's horse.
(B) Yes, because the State Racetrack Commission determined that Daring committed a foul in violation of rules applicable to racing.
(C) No, unless Daring intended to cause impermissible contact between the two horses or apprehension of such contact by Plaintiff.
(D) No, because Plaintiff assumed the risk of accidental injury inherent in riding as a jockey in a horse race.

Question 55

The Daily Sun, a newspaper, printed an article that stated:

Kitchen, the popular restaurant on the town square, has closed its doors. Kitchen employees have told the Daily Sun that the closing resulted from the owner's belief that Kitchen's general manager has embezzled thousands of dollars from the restaurant over the last several years. A decision on reopening the restaurant will be made after the completion of an audit of Kitchen's books.

Plaintiff, who is Kitchen's general manager, brought a libel action against the Daily Sun based on the publication of this article. The parties stipulated that Plaintiff never embezzled any funds from Kitchen. They also stipulated that Plaintiff is well known among many people in the community because of his job with Kitchen.

The case went to trial before a jury.

The defendant's motion for a directed verdict in its favor, made at the close of the evidence, should be granted if the

(A) record contains no evidence that Plaintiff suffered special harm as a result of the publication.
(B) record contains no evidence that the defendant was negligent as to the truth or falsity of the charge of embezzlement.
(C) evidence is not clear and convincing that the defendant published the article with "actual malice."
(D) record contains uncontradicted evidence that the article accurately reported what the employees told the Daily Sun.

Question 56

Surgeon performed a sterilization operation on Patient. After the surgery, Surgeon performed a test that showed that Patient's fallopian tubes were not severed, as was necessary for sterilization. Surgeon did not reveal the failure of the operation to Patient, who three years later became pregnant and delivered a baby afflicted with a severe birth defect that will require substantial medical care throughout its life. The birth defect resulted from a genetic defect unknown to, and undiscoverable by, Surgeon. Patient brought an action on her own behalf against Surgeon, seeking to recover the cost of her medical care for the delivery of the baby, and the baby's extraordinary future medical expenses for which Patient will be responsible.

Which of the following questions is relevant to the lawsuit and currently most difficult to answer?

(A) Did Surgeon owe a duty of care to the baby in respect to medical services rendered to Patient three years before the baby was conceived?
(B) Can a person recover damages for a life burdened by a severe birth defect based on a physician's wrongful failure to prevent that person's birth from occurring?

(C) Did Surgeon owe a duty to Patient to inform her that the sterilization operation had failed?
(D) Is Patient entitled to recover damages for the baby's extraordinary future medical expenses?

Question 57

Drew, the owner of a truck leasing company, asked Pat, one of Drew's employees, to deliver $1,000 to the dealership's main office. The following week, as a result of a dispute over whether the money had been delivered, Drew instructed Pat to come to the office to submit to a lie detector test.

When Pat reported to Drew's office for the test, it was not administered. Instead, without hearing Pat's story, Drew shouted at him, "You're a thief!" and fired him. Drew's shout was overheard by several other employees who were in another office, which was separated from Drew's office by a thin partition. The next day, Pat accepted another job at a higher salary. Several weeks later, upon discovering that the money had not been stolen, Drew offered to rehire Pat.

In a suit for slander by Pat against Drew, Pat will

(A) prevail, because Pat was fraudulently induced to go to the office for a lie detector test, which was not, in fact, given.
(B) prevail, if Drew should have foreseen that the statement would be overheard by other employees.
(C) not prevail, if Drew made the charge in good faith, believing it to be true.
(D) not prevail, because the statement was made to Pat alone and intended for his ears only.

Question 58

For five years, Rancher had kept his horse in a ten-acre field enclosed by a six-foot woven wire fence with six inches of barbed wire on top. The gate to the field was latched and could not be opened by an animal. Rancher had never had any trouble with people coming onto his property and bothering the horse, and the horse had never escaped from the field. One day, however, when Rancher went to the field, he found that the gate was open and the horse was gone. Shortly before Rancher's discovery, Driver was driving with due care on a nearby highway when suddenly Rancher's horse darted in front of his car. When Driver attempted to avoid hitting the horse, he lost control of the car, which then crashed into a tree. Driver was injured.

Driver sued Rancher to recover damages for his injuries and Rancher moved for summary judgment.

If the facts stated above are undisputed, the judge should

(A) deny the motion, because, pursuant to the doctrine of res ipsa loquitur, a jury could infer that Rancher was negligent.
(B) deny the motion, because an animal dangerous to highway users escaped from Rancher's property and caused the collision.
(C) grant the motion, because there is no evidence that Rancher was negligent.
(D) grant the motion, because Rancher did not knowingly permit the horse to run at large.

Question 59

Penkov suffered a severe loss when his manufacturing plant, located in a shallow ravine, was flooded during a sustained rainfall. The flooding occurred because City had failed to maintain its storm drain, which was located on City land above Penkov's premises, and because Railroad had failed to maintain its storm drain, which was located on Railroad land below Penkov's premises. The flooding would not have occurred if either one of the two storm drains had been maintained properly.

Penkov sued Railroad to recover compensation for his loss. The evidence in the case established that the failures of the two drains were caused by the respective negligence of City and Railroad. There is no special rule insulating City from liability.

In his action against Railroad, Penkov should recover

(A) nothing, because he should have joined City, without whose negligence he would have suffered no loss.
(B) nothing, unless he introduces evidence that enables the court reasonably to apportion responsibility between City and Railroad.
(C) one-half his loss, in the absence of evidence that enables the court to allocate responsibility fairly between City and Railroad.
(D) all of his loss, because but for Railroad's negligence none of the flooding would have occurred.

Question 60

The manager of a department store noticed that Paula was carrying a scarf with her as she examined various items in the blouse department. The manager recognized the scarf as an expensive one carried by the store. Paula was trying to find a blouse that matched a color in the scarf, and, after a while, found one. The manager then saw Paula put the scarf into her purse, pay for the blouse, and head for the door. The manager, who was eight inches taller than Paula, blocked Paula's way to the door and asked to see the scarf in Paula's purse. Paula produced the scarf, as well as a receipt for it, showing that it had been purchased from the store on the previous day. The manager then told Paula there was no problem, and stepped out of her way.

If Paula brings a claim against the store based on false imprisonment, the store's best defense would be that

(A) by carrying the scarf in public view and then putting it into her purse, Paula assumed the risk of being detained.
(B) the manager had a reasonable belief that Paula was shoplifting and detained her only briefly for a reasonable investigation of the facts.
(C) Paula should have realized that her conduct would create a reasonable belief that facts existed warranting a privilege to detain.
(D) Paula was not detained, but was merely questioned about the scarf.

Question 61

John's father, Jeremiah, died in Hospital. Hospital maintains a morgue with refrigerated drawers a bit larger than a human body. Jeremiah's body was placed in such a drawer awaiting pickup by a mortician. Before the mortician called for the body, a Hospital orderly placed two opaque plastic bags in the drawer with Jeremiah's body. One bag contained Jeremiah's personal effects, and the other contained an amputated leg from some other Hospital patient. It is stipulated that Hospital was negligent to allow the amputated leg to get into Jeremiah's drawer. The mortician delivered the two opaque plastic bags to John, assuming both contained personal effects. John was shocked when he opened the bag containing the amputated leg. John sued Hospital to recover for his emotional distress. At the trial, John testified that the experience had been extremely upsetting, that he had had recurring nightmares about it, and that his family and business relationships had been adversely affected for a period of several months. He did not seek medical or psychiatric treatment for his emotional distress.

Who should prevail?

(A) John, because of the sensitivity people have regarding the care of the bodies of deceased relatives.

(B) John, because hospitals are strictly liable for mishandling dead bodies.

(C) Hospital, because John did not require medical or psychiatric treatment.

(D) Hospital, because John suffered no bodily harm.

Question 62

While Prudence was leaving an elevator, it suddenly dropped several inches, causing her to fall. An investigation of the accident revealed that the elevator dropped because it had been negligently maintained by the Acme Elevator Company. Acme had a contract with the owner of the building to inspect and maintain the elevator. Prudence's fall severely aggravated a preexisting physical disability.

If Prudence sues Acme Elevator Company for damages for her injuries, she should recover

(A) nothing, if Acme could not reasonably have been expected to foresee the extent of the harm that Prudence suffered as a result of the accident.

(B) nothing, if the accident would not have caused significant harm to an ordinarily prudent elevator passenger.

(C) damages for the full amount of her disability, because a tortfeasor must take its victim as it finds her.

(D) damages for the injury caused by the falling elevator, including the aggravation of her preexisting disability.

Question 63

Gardner's backyard, which is landscaped with expensive flowers and shrubs, is adjacent to a golf course. While Driver was playing golf on the course, a thunderstorm suddenly came up. As Driver was returning to the clubhouse in his golf cart, lightning struck a tree on the course, and the tree began to fall in Driver's direction. In order to avoid being hit by the tree, Driver deliberately steered his cart onto Gardner's property, causing substantial damage to Gardner's expensive plantings.

In an action by Gardner against Driver to recover damages for the harm to his plantings, Gardner will

(A) prevail, because, although occasioned by necessity, Driver's entry onto Gardner's property was for Driver's benefit.

(B) prevail, for nominal damages only, because Driver was privileged to enter Gardner's property.

(C) not prevail, because the lightning was an act of God.

(D) not prevail, because Driver's entry onto Gardner's property was occasioned by necessity and therefore privileged.

Questions 64-65 are based on the following fact situation.

Dumont, a real estate developer, was trying to purchase land on which he intended to build a large commercial development. Perkins, an elderly widow, had rejected all of Dumont's offers to buy her ancestral home, where she had lived all her life and which was located in the middle of Dumont's planned development. Finally, Dumont offered her $250,000. He told her that it was his last offer and that if she rejected it, state law authorized him to have her property condemned.

Perkins then consulted her nephew, a law student, who researched the question and advised her that Dumont had no power of condemnation under state law. Perkins had been badly frightened by Dumont's threat, and was outraged when she learned that Dumont had lied to her.

Question 64

If Perkins sues Dumont for damages for emotional distress, will she prevail?

(A) Yes, if Dumont's action was extreme and outrageous.

(B) Yes, because Perkins was frightened and outraged.

(C) No, if Perkins did not suffer emotional distress that was severe.

(D) No, if it was not Dumont's purpose to cause emotional distress.

Question 65

If Perkins asserts a claim based on misrepresentation against Dumont, will she prevail?

(A) Yes, if Dumont knew he had no legal power of condemnation.

(B) Yes, if Dumont tried to take unfair advantage of a gross difference between himself and Perkins in commercial knowledge and experience.

(C) No, if Dumont's offer of $250,000 equaled or exceeded the market value of Perkins's property.

(D) No, because Perkins suffered no pecuniary loss.

Questions 66-67 are based on the following fact situation.

Perkins and Morton were passengers sitting in adjoining seats on a flight on Delval Airline. There were many empty seats on the aircraft.

During the flight, a flight attendant served Morton nine drinks. As Morton became more and more obviously intoxicated and attempted to engage Perkins in a conversation, Perkins chose to ignore Morton. This angered Morton, who suddenly struck Perkins in the face, giving her a black eye.

Question 66

If Perkins asserts a claim for damages against Delval Airline based on negligence, Perkins will

(A) not recover, because a person is not required by law to come to the assistance of another who is imperiled by a third party.
(B) not recover, if Perkins could easily have moved to another seat.
(C) recover, because a common carrier is strictly liable for injuries suffered by a passenger while aboard the carrier.
(D) recover, if the flight attendants should have perceived Morton's condition and acted to protect Perkins before the blow was struck.

Question 67

If Perkins asserts a claim for damages against Delval Airline based on battery, she will

(A) prevail, because she suffered an intentionally inflicted harmful or offensive contact.
(B) prevail, if the flight attendant acted recklessly in continuing to serve liquor to Morton.
(C) not prevail, because Morton was not acting as an agent or employee of Delval Airline.
(D) not prevail, unless she can establish some permanent injury from the contact.

Question 68

At the trial of an action against Grandmother on behalf of Patrick, the following evidence has been introduced. Grandson and his friend, Patrick, both aged eight, were visiting at Grandmother's house when, while exploring the premises, they discovered a hunting rifle in an unlocked gun cabinet. They removed it from the cabinet and were examining it when the rifle, while in Grandson's hands, somehow discharged. The bullet struck and injured Patrick. The gun cabinet was normally locked. Grandmother had opened it for dusting several days before the boys' visit, and had then forgotten to relock it. She was not aware that it was unlocked when the boys arrived.

If the defendant moves for a directed verdict in her favor at the end of the plaintiff's case, that motion should be

(A) granted, because Grandmother is not legally responsible for the acts of Grandson.
(B) granted, because Grandmother did not recall that the gun cabinet was unlocked.
(C) denied, because a firearm is an inherently dangerous instrumentality.
(D) denied, because a jury could find that Grandmother breached a duty of care she owed to Patrick.

Question 69

Landco purchased a large tract of land intending to construct residential housing on it. Landco hired Poolco to build a large in-ground swimming pool on the tract. The contract provided that Poolco would carry out blasting operations that were necessary to create an excavation large enough for the pool. The blasting caused cracks to form in the walls of Plaintiff's home in a nearby residential neighborhood.

In Plaintiff's action for damages against Landco, Plaintiff should

(A) prevail, only if Landco retained the right to direct and control Poolco's construction of the pool.
(B) prevail, because the blasting that Poolco was hired to perform damaged Plaintiff's home.
(C) not prevail, if Poolco used reasonable care in conducting the blasting operations.
(D) not prevail, if Landco used reasonable care to hire a competent contractor.

Question 70

Davis has a small trampoline in his backyard which, as he knows, is commonly used by neighbor children as well as his own. The trampoline is in good condition, is not defective in any way, and normally is surrounded by mats to prevent injury if a user should fall off. Prior to leaving with his family for the day, Davis leaned the trampoline up against the side of the house and placed the mats in the garage.

While the Davis family was away, Philip, aged 11, a new boy in the neighborhood, wandered into Davis's yard and saw the trampoline. Philip had not previously been aware of its presence, but, having frequently used a trampoline before, he decided to set it up, and started to jump. He lost his balance on one jump and took a hard fall on the bare ground, suffering a serious injury that would have been prevented by the mats.

An action has been brought against Davis on Philip's behalf to recover damages for the injuries Philip sustained from his fall. In this jurisdiction, the traditional common-law rules pertaining to contributory negligence have been replaced by a pure comparative negligence rule.

In his action against Davis, will Philip prevail?

(A) No, if children likely to be attracted by the trampoline would normally realize the risk of using it without mats.

(B) No, if Philip failed to exercise reasonable care commensurate with his age, intelligence, and experience.

(C) No, because Philip entered Davis's yard and used the trampoline without Davis's permission.

(D) No, because Philip did not know about the trampoline before entering Davis's yard and thus was not "lured" onto the premises.

Question 71

In his employment, Grinder operates a grinding wheel. To protect his eyes, he wears glasses, sold under the trade name "Safety Glasses," manufactured by Glassco. The glasses were sold with a warning label stating that they would protect only against small, flying objects. One day, the grinding wheel Grinder was using disintegrated and fragments of the stone wheel were thrown off with great force. One large fragment hit Grinder, knocking his safety glasses up onto his forehead. Another fragment then hit and injured his eye.

Grinder brought an action against Glassco for the injury to his eye. The jurisdiction adheres to the traditional common-law rule pertaining to contributory negligence.

In this action, will Grinder prevail?

(A) Yes, because the safety glasses were defective in that they did not protect him from the disintegrating wheel.

(B) Yes, because the glasses were sold under the trade name "Safety Glasses."

(C) No, because the glasses were not designed or sold for protection against the kind of hazard Grinder encountered.

(D) No, if Grinder will be compensated under the workers' compensation law.

Questions 72-74 are based on the following fact situation.

Oscar purchased a large bottle of No-Flake dandruff shampoo, manufactured by Shampoo Company. The box containing the bottle stated in part: "CAUTION-- Use only 1 capful at most once a day. Greater use may cause severe damage to the scalp." Oscar read the writing on the box, removed the bottle, and threw the box away. Oscar's roommate, Paul, asked to use the No-Flake, and Oscar said, "Be careful not to use too much." Paul thereafter used No-Flake twice a day, applying two or three capfuls each time, notwithstanding the label statement that read: "Use no more than one capful per day. See box instructions." The more he used No-Flake, the more inflamed his scalp became, the more it itched, and the more he used. After three weeks of such use, Paul finally consulted a doctor who diagnosed his problem as a serious and irreversible case of dermatitis caused by excessive exposure to the active ingredients in No-Flake. These ingredients are uniquely effective at controlling dandruff, but there is no way to remove a remote risk to a small percentage of persons who may contract dermatitis as the result of applying for prolonged periods of time amounts of No-Flake substantially in excess of the directions. This jurisdiction adheres to the traditional common-law rules pertaining to contributory negligence and assumption of risk.

Question 72

Based upon the foregoing facts, if Paul sues Shampoo Company to recover damages for his dermatitis, his most promising theory of liability will be that the No-Flake shampoo

(A) had an unreasonably dangerous manufacturing defect.

(B) had an unreasonably dangerous design defect.

(C) was inherently dangerous.

(D) was inadequately labeled to warn of its dangers.

Question 73

If Paul asserts a claim for his injuries against Shampoo Company based on strict liability in tort, which of the following would constitute a defense?

I.   Paul misused the No-Flake shampoo.
II. Paul was contributorily negligent in continuing to use No-Flake shampoo when his scalp began to hurt and itch.
III. Paul was a remote user and not in privity with Shampoo Company.

(A) I only.
(B) I and II only.
(C) II and III only.
(D) Neither I, nor II, nor III.

Question 74

If Paul asserts a claim against Oscar for his dermatitis injuries, Oscar's best defense will be that

(A)   Paul was contributorily negligent.
(B)   Paul assumed the risk.
(C)   Oscar had no duty toward Paul, who was a gratuitous donee.
(D)   Oscar had no duty toward Paul, because Shampoo Company created the risk and had a nondelegable duty to foreseeable users.

Question 75

While Driver was taking a leisurely spring drive, he momentarily took his eyes off the road to look at some colorful trees in bloom. As a result, his car swerved a few feet off the roadway, directly toward Walker, who was standing on the shoulder of the road waiting for a chance to cross. When Walker saw the car bearing down on him, he jumped backwards, fell, and injured his knee.

Walker sued Driver for damages, and Driver moved for summary judgment. The foregoing facts are undisputed.

Driver's motion should be

(A) denied, because the record shows that Walker apprehended an imminent, harmful contact with Driver's car.
(B) denied, because a jury could find that Driver negligently caused Walker to suffer a legally compensable injury.
(C) granted, because the proximate cause of Walker's injury was his own voluntary act.
(D) granted, because it is not unreasonable for a person to be distracted momentarily.

Question 76

Diggers Construction Company was engaged in blasting operations to clear the way for a new road. Diggers had erected adequate barriers and posted adequate warning signs in the vicinity of the blasting. Although Paul read and understood the signs, he entered the area to walk his dog. As a result of the blasting, Paul was hit by a piece of rock and sustained head injuries. The jurisdiction follows the traditional common-law rules governing the defenses of contributory negligence, assumption of risk, and last clear chance.

In an action by Paul against Diggers to recover damages for his injuries, Paul will

(A) not prevail, if Diggers exercised reasonable care to protect the public from harm.
(B) not prevail, because Paul understood the signs and disregarded the warnings.
(C) prevail, because Paul was harmed by Diggers's abnormally dangerous activity.
(D) prevail, unless Paul failed to use reasonable care to protect himself from harm.

Question 77

Allen and Bradley were law school classmates who had competed for the position of editor of the law review. Allen had the higher grade point average, but Bradley was elected editor, largely in recognition of a long and important note that had appeared in the review over her name.

During the following placement interview season, Allen was interviewed by a representative of a nationally prominent law firm. In response to the interviewer's request for information about the authorship of the law review note, Allen said that he had heard that the note attributed to Bradley was largely the work of another student.

The firm told Bradley that it would not interview her because of doubts about the authorship of the note. This greatly distressed Bradley. In fact the note had been prepared by Bradley without assistance from anyone else.

If Bradley asserts a claim against Allen based on defamation, Bradley will

(A) recover, because Allen's statement was false.

(B) recover, if Allen had substantial doubts about the accuracy of the information he gave the interviewer.

(C) not recover, unless Bradley proves pecuniary loss.

(D) not recover, because the statement was made by Allen only after the interviewer inquired about the authorship of the note.

Questions 78-79 are based on the following fact situation.

Pat sustained personal injuries in a three-car collision caused by the concurrent negligence of the three drivers, Pat, Donald, and Drew. In Pat's action for damages against Donald and Drew, the jury apportioned the negligence 30% to Pat, 30% to Donald, and 40% to Drew. Pat's total damages were $100,000.

Question 78

Assume for this question only that a state statute provides for a system of pure comparative negligence, joint and several liability of concurrent tortfeasors, and contribution based upon proportionate fault.

If Pat chooses to execute against Donald alone, she will be entitled to collect at most

(A) $70,000 from Donald, and then Donald will be entitled to collect $40,000 from Drew.

(B) $30,000 from Donald, and then Donald will be entitled to collect $10,000 from Drew.

(C) $30,000 from Donald, and then Donald will be entitled to collect nothing from Drew.

(D) nothing from Donald, because Donald's percentage of fault is not greater than that of Pat.

Question 79

Assume for this question only that the state has retained the common-law rule pertaining to contribution and that the state's comparative negligence statute provides for a system of pure comparative negligence but abolishes joint and several liability.

If Pat chooses to execute against Donald alone, she will be entitled to collect at most

(A) $70,000 from Donald, and then Donald will be entitled to collect $40,000 from Drew.

(B) $30,000 from Donald, and then Donald will be entitled to collect $10,000 from Drew.

(C) $30,000 from Donald, and then Donald will be entitled to collect nothing from Drew.

(D) nothing from Donald, because Donald's percentage of fault is not greater than that of Pat.

Question 80

Patten suffered from a serious, though not immediately life-threatening, impairment of his circulatory system. Patten's cardiologist recommended a cardiac bypass operation and referred Patten to Dr. Cutter. Cutter did not inform Patten of the 2% risk of death associated with this operation. Cutter defended his decision not to mention the risk statistics to Patten because "Patten was a worrier and it would significantly lessen his chances of survival to be worried about the nonsurvival rate."

Cutter successfully performed the bypass operation and Patten made a good recovery. However, when Patten learned of the 2% risk of death associated with the operation, he was furious that Cutter had failed to disclose this information to him.

If Patten asserts a claim against Cutter based on negligence, will Patten prevail?

(A) No, if Cutter used his best personal judgment in shielding Patten from the risk statistic.

(B) No, because the operation was successful and Patten suffered no harm.

(C) Yes, if Patten would have refused the operation had he been informed of the risk.

(D) Yes, because a patient must be told the risk factor associated with a surgical procedure in order to give an informed consent.

Question 81

Lender met Borrower on the street, demanded that Borrower pay a debt owed to Lender, and threatened to punch Borrower in the nose. A fight ensued between them. Mann came upon the scene just as Lender was about to kick Borrower in the head. Noting that Lender was getting the better of the fight, Mann pointed a gun at Lender and said, "Stop, or I'll shoot." If Lender asserts a claim against Mann based on assault, will Lender prevail?

(A) Yes, because Mann threatened to use deadly force.

(B) Yes, unless Mann was related to Borrower.

(C) No, if it was apparent that Lender was about to inflict serious bodily harm upon Borrower.

(D) No, because Lender was the original aggressor by threatening Borrower with a battery.

Questions 82-83 are based on the following fact situation.

Professor Merrill, in a lecture in her psychology course at a private university, described an experiment in which a group of college students in a neighboring city rushed out and washed cars stopped at traffic lights during the rush hour. She described how people reacted differently—with shock, joy, and surprise. At the conclusion of her report, she said, "You understand, of course, that you are not to undertake this or any other experiment unless you first clear it with me." Four of Merrill's students decided to try the same experiment but did not clear it with Merrill.

One subject of their experiment, Carr, said, "I was shocked. There were two people on each side of the car. At first I thought negatively. I thought they were going to attack me and thought of driving away. Then I quieted down and decided there were too many dirty cars in the city anyway."

Charitable immunity has been abolished in the jurisdiction.

Question 82

If Carr asserts a claim against the students who washed his car, his best theory is

(A) assault.
(B) negligence.
(C) invasion of privacy.
(D) false imprisonment.

Question 83

If Carr has a valid claim against the students, will he also prevail against the university?

(A) Yes, if the students would not have performed the experiment but for Merrill's lecture.
(B) Yes, if Carr's claim against the students is based on negligence.
(C) No, because the students were not Merrill's employees.
(D) No, because Merrill did not authorize the car wash as a class project.

Questions 84-85 are based on the following fact situation.

Passer was driving his pickup truck along a lonely road on a very cold night. Passer saw Tom, who was a stranger, lying in a field by the side of the road and apparently injured. Passer stopped his truck, alighted, and, upon examining Tom, discovered that Tom was intoxicated and in danger of suffering from exposure to the cold. However, Passer returned to his truck and drove away without making any effort to help Tom. Tom remained lying at the same place and was later injured when struck by a car driven by Traveler, who was drowsy and inattentive, had veered off the road into the field and hit Tom. Traveler did not see Tom prior to hitting him.

Question 84

If Tom asserts a claim against Passer for damages for his injuries, will Tom prevail?

(A) Yes, because by stopping and examining Tom, Passer assumed a duty to aid him.
(B) Yes, if a reasonably prudent person under the circumstances would have aided Tom.
(C) No, if Passer did not, in any way, make Tom's situation worse.
(D) No, because Tom himself created the risk of harm by becoming intoxicated.

Question 85

If Tom asserts a claim against Traveler, will Tom prevail?

(A) Yes, because Traveler was negligent in going off the road.
(B) Yes, because Tom was in a helpless condition.
(C) No, because Traveler did not see Tom before Tom was struck.
(D) No, because Tom's intoxication was the cause in fact of his harm.

Question 86

Roofer entered into a written contract with Orissa to repair the roof of Orissa's home, the repairs to be done "in a workmanlike manner." Roofer completed the repairs and took all of his equipment away, with the exception of a 20-foot extension ladder, which was left against the side of the house. He intended to come back and get the ladder the next morning. At that time, Orissa and her family were away on a trip. During the night, a thief, using the ladder to gain access to an upstairs window, entered the house and stole some valuable jewels. Orissa has asserted a claim against Roofer for damages for the loss of the jewels.

In her claim against Roofer, Orissa will

(A) prevail, because by leaving the ladder, Roofer became a trespasser on Orissa's property.
(B) prevail, because by leaving the ladder, Roofer created the risk that a person might unlawfully enter the house.
(C) not prevail, because the act of the thief was a superseding cause.
(D) not prevail, because Orissa's claim is limited to damages for breach of contract.

Question 87

As a result of an accident at the NPP nuclear power plant, a quantity of radioactive vapor escaped from the facility and two members of the public were exposed to excessive doses of radiation. According to qualified medical opinion, that exposure will double the chance that these two persons will ultimately develop cancer. However, any cancer that might be caused by this exposure will not be detectable for at least ten years. If the two exposed persons do develop cancer, it will not be possible to determine whether it was caused by this exposure or would have developed in any event.

If the exposed persons assert a claim for damages against NPP shortly after the escape of the radiation, which of the following questions will NOT present a substantial issue?

(A) Will the court recognize that the plaintiffs have suffered a present legal injury?
(B) Can the plaintiffs prove the amount of their damages?
(C) Can the plaintiffs prove that any harm they may suffer was caused by this exposure?
(D) Can the plaintiffs prevail without presenting evidence of specific negligence on the part of NPP?

Questions 88-90 are based on the following fact situation.

House owns his home in City. On the lawn in front of his home and within five feet of the public sidewalk there was a large tree. The roots of the tree caused the sidewalk to buckle severely and become dangerous. An ordinance of City requires adjacent landowners to keep sidewalks in safe condition. House engaged Contractor to repair the sidewalk, leaving it to Contractor to decide how the repair should be made.

Contractor dug up the sidewalk, cut back the roots of the tree, and laid a new sidewalk. Two days after House had paid Contractor the agreed price of the repair, the tree fell over onto the street and damaged a parked car belonging to Driver.

Driver has asserted claims against House and Contractor, and both defendants admit that cutting the roots caused the tree to fall.

Question 88

The theory on which Driver is most likely to prevail against House is that House is

(A) strictly liable, because the tree was on his property.
(B) liable for Contractor's negligence if, to House's knowledge, Contractor was engaged in hazardous activity.
(C) liable, because he assumed responsibility when he paid Contractor for the repair.
(D) liable on the basis of respondeat superior.

Question 89

In the claim of Driver against Contractor, the best defense of Contractor is that

(A) the tree was on the property of House.
(B) he repaired the sidewalk at the direction of House.
(C) he could not reasonably foresee that the tree would fall.
(D) he was relieved of liability when House paid for the repair.

Question 90

If Driver recovers a judgment against House, does House have any recourse against Contractor?

(A) No, if payment by House was an acceptance of the work.

(B) No, because House selected Contractor to do the work.

(C) Yes, if the judgment against House was based on vicarious liability.

(D) Yes, because House's conduct was not a factual cause of the harm.

Question 91

In 1960 Omar, the owner in fee simple absolute, conveyed Stoneacre, a five-acre tract of land. The relevant, operative words of the deed conveyed to "Church [a duly organized religious body having power to hold property] for the life of my son, Carl, and from and after the death of my said son, Carl, to all of my grandchildren and their heirs and assigns in equal shares; provided, Church shall use the premises for church purposes only."

In an existing building on Stoneacre, Church immediately began to conduct religious services and other activities normally associated with a church.

In 1975, Church granted to Darin a right to remove sand and gravel from a one-half acre portion of Stoneacre upon the payment of royalty. Darin has regularly removed sand and gravel since 1975 and paid royalty to Church. Church has continued to conduct religious services and other church activities on Stoneacre.

All four of the living grandchildren of Omar, joined by a guardian ad litem to represent unborn grandchildren, instituted suit against Church and Darin seeking damages for the removal of sand and gravel and an injunction preventing further acts of removal. There is no applicable statute. Which of the following best describes the likely disposition of this lawsuit?

(A) The plaintiffs should succeed, because the interest of Church terminated with the first removal of sand and gravel.

(B) Church and Darin should be enjoined, and damages should be recovered but impounded for future distribution.

(C) The injunction should be granted, but damages should be denied, because Omar and Carl are not parties to the action.

(D) Damages should be awarded, but the injunction should be denied.

Question 92

Ohner owns the Acme Hotel. When the International Order of Badgers came to town for its convention, its members rented 400 of the 500 rooms, and the hotel opened its convention facilities to them. Badgers are a rowdy group, and during their convention they littered both the inside and the outside of the hotel with debris and bottles. The hotel manager knew that objects were being thrown out of the hotel windows. At his direction, hotel employees patrolled the hallways telling the guests to refrain from such conduct. Ohner was out of town and was not aware of the problems which were occurring. During the convention, as Smith walked past the Acme Hotel on the sidewalk, he was hit and injured by an ashtray thrown out of a window in the hotel. Smith sued Ohner for damages for his injuries.

Will Smith prevail in his claim against Ohner?

(A) Yes, because a property owner is strictly liable for acts on his premises if such acts cause harm to persons using the adjacent public sidewalks.

(B) Yes, if the person who threw the ashtray cannot be identified.

(C) No, because Ohner had no personal knowledge of the conduct of the hotel guests.

(D) No, if the trier of fact determines that the hotel employees had taken reasonable precautions to prevent such an injury.

Question 93

Leader is a labor leader in Metropolis. Ten years ago he was divorced. Both he and his first wife have since married other persons. Recently, News, a newspaper in another city, ran a feature article on improper influences it asserted had been used by labor officials to secure favorable rulings from government officials. The story said that in 1960 Leader's first wife, with Leader's knowledge and concurrence, gave sexual favors to the mayor of Metropolis and then persuaded him to grant concessions to Leader's union, with which Metropolis was then negotiating a labor contract. The story named Leader and identified his first wife by her former and current surnames. The reporter for News believed the story to be true, since it had been related to him by two very reliable sources.

Leader's first wife suffered emotional distress and became very depressed. If she asserts a claim based on defamation against News, she will

(A) prevail, because the story concerned her personal, private life.

(B) prevail if the story was false.

(C) not prevail, because News did not print the story with knowledge of its falsity or with reckless disregard for its truth or falsity.

(D) not prevail if News exercised ordinary care in determining if the story was true or false.

Questions 94-95 are based on the following fact situation.

In 1976, Utility constructed a new plant for the generation of electricity. The plant burns lignite, a low grade fuel which is available in large quantities.

Although the plant was constructed in accordance with the best practicable technology, the plant emits a substantial quantity of invisible fumes. The only way Utility can reduce the fumes is by the use of scrubbing equipment that would cost $50,000,000 to install and would increase the retail price of generated electricity by 50 percent while reducing the volume of fumes by only 20 percent. Because of the expense of such equipment and its relative ineffectiveness, no other generating plants burning lignite use such equipment.

The plant was located in a sparsely settled rural area, remote from the large city served by Utility.

Farmer owned a farm adjacent to the plant. He had farmed the land for forty years and lived on the premises. The prevailing winds carried fumes from the new plant over Farmer's land. His 1975 crop was less than half the average size of this crop over the five years immediately preceding the construction of the plant. It can be established that the fumes caused the crop reduction.

Farmer's hay fever, from which he had long suffered, became worse in 1976. Physicians advised him that the lignite fumes were affecting it and that serious lung disease would soon result unless he moved away from the plant. He did so, selling his farm at its reasonable market value, which was then $10,000 less than before the construction of the plant.

Question 94

If Farmer asserts a claim based on nuisance against Utility for damages for personal injuries, will Farmer prevail?

(A) No, because there is no practicable way for Utility to reduce the fumes.

(B) No, because Utility's acts constituted a public nuisance.

(C) Yes, because Farmer's personal injuries were within the scope of the liability imposed on Utility.

(D) Yes, because the generation of electricity is an ultra-hazardous activity.

Question 95

If Farmer asserts a claim based on negligence against Utility for crop damages, will Farmer prevail?

(A) No, because Utility was not negligent.

(B) No as to 1976 crop damage, because Farmer did not mitigate damages by selling his farm in 1975.

(C) Yes as to 20 percent of his crop damage, because use of available equipment would have reduced the fumes by 20 percent.

(D) Yes, because operation of the plant constitutes a nuisance.

Questions 96-98 are based on the following fact situation.

Sand Company operated an installation for distributing sand and gravel. The installation was adjacent to a residential area. On Sand's grounds there was a chute with polished metal sides for loading sand and gravel into trucks. The trucks being loaded stopped on the public street below the chute.

After closing hours, a plywood screen was placed in the chute and the ladder used for inspection was removed to another section of the installation. For several months, however, a number of children, 8 to 10 years of age, had been playing on Sand's property and the adjoining street after closing hours. The children found the ladder and also discovered that they could remove the plywood screen from the chute and slide down to the street below. Sand knew of this activity.

One evening, the children were using the chute as a play device. As an automobile driven by Commuter approached the chute, Ladd, an 8-year-old boy, slid down just in front of the automobile. Commuter applied her brakes, but they suddenly failed, and she hit and injured Ladd. Commuter saw the child in time to have avoided hitting him if her brakes had worked properly. Two days previously, Commuter had taken her car to Garage to have her brakes inspected. Garage inspected the brakes and told her that the brakes were in perfect working order. Claims were asserted on behalf of Ladd by his proper legal representative against Sand, Commuter, and Garage.

Question 96

On Ladd's claim against Sand, will Ladd prevail?

(A) Yes, if Sand could have effectively secured the chute at moderate cost.
(B) Yes, because Sand is strictly liable for harm resulting from an artificial condition on its property.
(C) No, if Commuter had the last clear chance to avoid the injury.
(D) No, because Ladd was a trespasser.

Question 97

On Ladd's claim against Commuter, Commuter's best defense is that

(A) her conduct was not the cause in fact of the harm.
(B) she used reasonable care in the maintenance of her brakes.
(C) she could not reasonably foresee Ladd's presence in the street.
(D) she did not act willfully and wantonly.

Question 98

On Ladd's claim against Garage, will Ladd prevail?

(A)   Yes, because Garage is strictly liable in tort.
(B)   Yes, if Garage was negligent in inspecting Commuter's brakes.
(C)   No, if Ladd was in the legal category of a bystander.
(D)   No, because Sand's conduct was an independent and superseding cause.

Questions 99-100 are based on the following fact situation.

Section 1 of the Vehicle Code of State makes it illegal to cross a street in a central business district other than at a designated crosswalk. Section 2 of the Code prohibits parking any motor vehicle so that it blocks any part of a designated crosswalk. Ped wanted to cross Main Street in the central business district of City, located in State, but a truck parked by Trucker was blocking the designated crosswalk. Ped stepped out into Main Street and carefully walked around the back of the truck. Ped was struck by a motor vehicle negligently operated by Driver.

Question 99

If Ped asserts a claim against Driver, Ped's failure to be in the crosswalk will have which of the following effects?

(A) It is not relevant in determining the right of Ped.
(B) It may be considered by the trier of the facts on the issue of Driver's liability.
(C) It will bar Ped's recovery unless Driver saw Ped in time to avoid the impact.
(D) It will bar Ped's recovery as a matter of law.

Question 100

If Ped asserts a claim against Trucker, the most likely result is that Ped will

(A) prevail, because Trucker's violation of a state statute makes him strictly liable for all injuries caused thereby.
(B) prevail, because the probable purpose of Section 2 of the Vehicle Code of State was to safeguard pedestrians in using crosswalk.
(C) not prevail, because Ped assumed the risk of injury when he crossed the street outside the crosswalk.
(D) not prevail, because Driver's conduct was the actual cause of Ped's harm.

Questions 101-103 are based on the following fact situation.

Husband and Wife, walking on a country road, were frightened by a bull running loose on the road. They climbed over a fence to get onto the adjacent property, owned by Grower. After climbing over the fence, Husband and Wife damaged some of Grower's plants which were near the fence. The fence was posted with a large sign, "No Trespassing."

Grower saw Husband and Wife and came toward them with his large watchdog on a long leash. The dog rushed at Wife. Grower had intended only to frighten Husband and Wife, but the leash broke, and before Grower could restrain the dog, the dog bit Wife.

Question 101

If Wife asserts a claim based on battery against Grower, will Wife prevail?

(A) Yes, because Grower intended that the dog frighten Wife.
(B) Yes, because the breaking of the leash establishes liability under res ipsa loquitur.

(C) No, because Wife made an unauthorized entry on Grower's land.

(D) No, because Grower did not intend to cause any harmful contact with Wife.

Question 102

If Husband asserts a claim based on assault against Grower, will Husband prevail?

(A) Yes, because the landowner did not have a privilege to use excessive force.

(B) Yes, if Husband reasonably believed that the dog might bite him.

(C) No, if the dog did not come in contact with him.

(D) No, if Grower was trying to protect his property.

Question 103

If Grower asserts a claim against Wife and Husband for damage to his plants, will Grower prevail?

(A) Yes, because Wife and Husband entered on his land without permission.

(B) Yes, because Grower had posted his property with a "No Trespassing" sign.

(C) No, because Wife and Husband were confronted by an emergency situation.

(D) No, because Grower used excessive force toward Wife and Husband.

Questions 104-108 are based on the following fact situation.

Storekeeper, the owner of a large hardware store, sells power saws for both personal and commercial use. He often takes old power saws as trade-ins on new ones. The old power saws are then completely disassembled and rebuilt with new bearings by Storekeeper's employees and sold by Storekeeper as "reconditioned saws."

Purchaser, the owner and operator of a cabinetmaking shop, informed Storekeeper that he wanted to buy a reconditioned circular saw for use in his cabinet-making business. However, the blade that was on the saw he picked out had very coarse teeth for cutting rough lumber. Purchaser told Storekeeper that he wanted a saw blade that would cut plywood. Storekeeper exchanged the coarse blade for a new one with finer teeth that would cut plywood smoothly. The new blade was manufactured by Saw-Blade Company, which uses all available techniques to inspect its products for defects. The reconditioned saw had been manufactured by Power Saw Company.

The week after the saw was purchased, Employee, who works for Purchaser in Purchaser's cabinetmaking shop, was injured while using the saw. Employee's arm was severely cut. As a result, the cabinetmaking shop was shut down for a week until a replacement for Employee could be found.

Question 104

If Employee was injured while cutting plywood when the shaft holding the saw blade came loose when a bearing gave way and the shaft and blade flew off the saw, and if Employee asserts a claim based on strict liability in tort against Power Saw Company, Employee will probably

(A) recover if the shaft that came loose was a part of the saw when it was new.

(B) recover, because Power Saw Company was in the business of manufacturing dangerous machines.

(C) not recover, because Employee was not the buyer of the power saw.

(D) not recover, because the saw had been rebuilt by Storekeeper.

Question 105

If Employee was injured while cutting plywood when the shaft holding the saw blade came loose when a bearing gave way and the shaft and blade flew off the saw, and if Purchaser asserts a claim based on strict liability in tort against Storekeeper for loss of business because of the injury to Employee, Purchaser probably will

(A) not recover, because economic loss from injury to an employee is not within the scope of Storekeeper's duty.

(B) not recover, because Storekeeper was not the manufacturer of the power saw.

(C) recover, because Storekeeper knew the power saw was to be used in Purchaser's cabinetmaking business.

(D) recover, because the reconditioned power saw was the direct cause of Purchaser's loss of business.

Question 106

If Employee was injured while cutting plywood when the shaft holding the saw blade came loose when a bearing gave way and the shaft and blade flew off the saw, and if Employee asserts a claim based on strict liability in tort against Storekeeper, Employee probably will

(A) not recover unless Purchaser told Storekeeper that Employee would use the power saw.
(B) not recover if Employee failed to notice that the shaft was coming loose.
(C) recover unless Employee knew that the shaft was coming loose.
(D) recover unless Storekeeper used all possible care in reconditioning the power saw.

Question 107

If Employee was cutting a sheet of plywood, and while he was doing so, the saw blade flew to pieces and severely cut Employee's arm, and if Employee asserts a claim against Storekeeper, the theory on which Employee is most likely to prevail is

(A) strict liability in tort.
(B) express warranty.
(C) negligence, relying on res ipsa loquitur.
(D) negligence, relying on the sale of an inherently dangerous product.

Question 108

If Employee was cutting a sheet of hard plastic, and while he was doing so, the saw blade flew to pieces and severely cut Employee's arm, and if Employee asserts a claim based on strict liability in tort against Saw-Blade Company, the defense most likely to prevail is

(A) Employee did not purchase the saw blade.
(B) the blade was being put to an improper use.
(C) Employee was contributorily negligent in using the blade to cut hard plastic.
(D) Saw-Blade Company used every available means to inspect the blade for defects.

Questions 109-110 are based on the following fact situation.

Photo, a free-lance photographer, took a picture of Player in front of Shoe Store. Player was a nationally known amateur basketball star who had received much publicity in the press. At the time, the window display in Shoe Store featured "Jumpers," a well-known make of basketball shoes. Photo sold the picture, greatly enlarged, to Shoe Store and told Shoe Store that Photo had Player's approval to do so and that Player had consented to Shoe Store's showing the enlarged picture in the window. Shoe Store made no effort to ascertain whether Player had given his consent to Photo. In fact, Player did not even know that Photo had taken the picture. Shoe Store put the enlarged picture in the window with the display of "Jumpers" shoes. The college that Player attended believed that Player had intentionally endorsed Shoe Store and "Jumpers" shoes, and the college cancelled his athletic scholarship.

Question 109

If Player asserts a claim based on defamation against Shoe Store, will Player prevail?

(A) Yes, if Shoe Store was reckless in accepting Photo's statement that Photo had Player's approval.
(B) Yes, because the defamatory material was in printed form.
(C) No, if Shoe Store believed Photo's statement that Photo had Player's approval.
(D) No, because the picture of Player was not defamatory per se.

Question 110

If Player asserts a claim based on invasion of privacy against Shoe Store, will Player prevail?

(A) Yes, because Photo had no right to take Player's picture.
(B) Yes, because Shoe Store, without Player's permission, used Player's picture for profit.
(C) No, because Player was already a basketball star who had received much publicity in the press.
(D) No, because Shoe Store believed it had permission to put the picture in the window.

Questions 111-112 are based on the following fact situation.

Johnson wanted to purchase a used motor vehicle. The used car lot of Car Company, in a remote section away from town, was enclosed by a ten-foot chain link fence. While Johnson and Sales Representative, an employee of Car Company, were in the used car lot looking at cars, a security guard locked the gate at 1:30 p.m., because it was Saturday and the lot was supposed to be closed after 1:00 p.m. Saturday until Monday morning. At 1:45 p.m., Johnson and Sales Representative discovered they were locked in.

There was no traffic in the vicinity and no way in which help could be summoned. After two hours, Johnson began to panic at the prospect of remaining undiscovered and without food and water until Monday morning. Sales Representative decided to wait in a car until help should come. Johnson tried to climb over the fence and, in doing so, fell and was injured. Johnson asserts a claim against Car Company for damages for his injuries.

Question 111

If Johnson's claim is based on negligence, is the defense of assumption of the risk applicable?

(A) Yes, if a reasonable person would have recognized that there was some risk of falling while climbing the fence.
(B) Yes, because Sales Representative, as Car Company's agent, waited for help.
(C) No, if it appeared that there was no other practicable way of getting out of the lot before Monday.
(D) No, because Johnson was confined as the result of a volitional act.

Question 112

If Johnson's claim is based on false imprisonment, will Johnson prevail?

(A) Yes, because he was confined against his will.
(B) Yes, because he was harmed as a result of his confinement.
(C) No, unless the security guard was negligent in locking the gate.
(D) No, unless the security guard knew that someone was in the lot at the time the guard locked the gate.

Questions 113-114 are based on the following fact situation.

In 1940, Cattle Company paid $30,000 for a 150-acre tract of agricultural land well suited for a cattle feed lot. The tract was ten miles from the city of Metropolis, then a community of 50,000 people, and five miles from the nearest home. By 1976, the city limits extended to Cattle Company's feed lot, and the city had a population of 350,000. About 10,000 people lived within three miles of the cattle-feeding operation.

The Cattle Company land is outside the city limits and no zoning ordinance applies. The Cattle Company land is now worth $300,000, and $25,000 has been invested in buildings and pens. Cattle Company, conscious of its obligations to its neighbors, uses the best and most sanitary feed lot procedures, including chemical sprays, to keep down flies and odors and frequently removes manure. Despite these measures, residents of Metropolis complain of flies and odors. An action has been filed by five individual homeowners who live within half a mile of the Cattle Company feed lot. The plaintiffs' homes are valued currently at $25,000 to $40,000 each. Flies in the area are five to ten times more numerous than in other parts of Metropolis, and extremely obnoxious odors are frequently carried by the wind to the plaintiffs' homes. The flies and odors are a substantial health hazard.

Question 113

If plaintiffs assert a claim based on public nuisance, plaintiffs will

(A) prevail if plaintiffs sustained harm different from that suffered by the public at large.
(B) prevail if Cattle Company's acts interfered with any person's enjoyment of his property.
(C) not prevail, because only the state may bring an action based on public nuisance.
(D) not prevail, because plaintiffs came to the nuisance.

Question 114

If plaintiffs assert a claim based on private nuisance, plaintiffs will

(A) prevail, because Cattle Company's activity unreasonably interfered with plaintiffs' use and enjoyment of their property.
(B) prevail, because Cattle Company's activity constitutes an inverse condemnation of their property.
(C) not prevail, because Cattle Company had operated the feed lot for more than 25 years.

(D) not prevail, because Cattle Company uses the most reasonable procedures to keep down flies and odors.

Questions 115-117 are based on the following fact situation.

Motorist arranged to borrow his friend Owner's car to drive for one day while Motorist's car was being repaired. Owner knew that the brakes on his car were faulty and might fail in an emergency. Owner forgot to tell Motorist about the brakes when Motorist picked up the car, but Owner did telephone Spouse, Motorist's wife, and told her about them. Spouse, however, forgot to tell Motorist.

Motorist was driving Owner's car at a reasonable rate of speed and within the posted speed limit, with Spouse as a passenger. Another car, driven by Cross, crossed in front of Motorist at an intersection and in violation of the traffic signal. Motorist tried to stop, but the brakes failed, and the two cars collided. If the brakes had been in proper working order, Motorist could have stopped in time to avoid the collision. Motorist and Spouse were injured.

Question 115

If Motorist asserts a claim against Cross, Motorist will

(A) recover the full amount of his damages, because Motorist himself was not at fault.
(B) recover only a proportion of his damages, because Spouse was also at fault.
(C) not recover, because Spouse was negligent and a wife's negligence is imputed to her husband.
(D) not recover, because the failure of the brakes was the immediate cause of the collision.

Question 116

If the jurisdiction has adopted "pure" comparative negligence and Spouse asserts a claim against Cross, Spouse will

(A) recover in full for her injuries, because Motorist, who was driving the car in which she was riding, was not himself at fault.
(B) recover a proportion of her damages based on the respective degrees of her negligence and that of Cross.
(C) not recover, because but for the failure of the brakes the collision would not have occurred.

(D) not recover, because she was negligent and her negligence continued until the moment of impact.

Question 117

If Motorist asserts a claim against Owner, will Motorist prevail?

(A) Yes, in negligence, because Owner knew the brakes were faulty and failed to tell Motorist.
(B) Yes, in strict liability in tort, because the car was defective and Owner lent it to Motorist.
(C) No, because Owner was a gratuitous lender, and thus his duty of care was slight.
(D) No, because the failure of Spouse to tell Motorist about the brakes was the cause in fact of Motorist's harm.

Questions 118-120 are based on the following fact situation.

A water pipe burst in the basement of Supermart, a grocery store, flooding the basement and damaging cases of canned goods on the floor. The plumbing contractor's workmen, in repairing the leak, knocked over several stacks of canned goods in cases, denting the cans. After settling its claims against the landlord for the water leak and against the plumbing contractor for the damage done by his workmen, Supermart put the goods on special sale.

Four weeks later Dotty was shopping in Supermart. Several tables in the market were covered with assorted canned foods, all of which were dirty and dented. A sign on each of the tables read: "Damaged Cans—Half Price."

Dotty was having Guest for dinner that evening and purchased two dented cans of tuna, packed by Canco, from one of the tables displaying the damaged cans. Before Guest arrived, Dotty prepared a tuna casserole which she and Guest ate. Both became ill and the medical testimony established that the illness was caused by the tuna's being unfit for consumption. The tuna consumed by Dotty and Guest came from the case that was at the top of one of the stacks knocked over by the workmen. The tuna in undamaged cans from the same Canco shipment was fit for consumption.

Question 118

If Dotty asserts a claim against Canco based on negligence, the doctrine of res ipsa loquitur is

(A) applicable, because the tuna was packed in a sealed can.
(B) applicable, because Canco as the packer is strictly liable.
(C) not applicable, because the case of tuna had been knocked over by the workmen.
(D) not applicable, because of the sign on the table from which Dotty purchased the tuna.

Question 119

If Guest asserts a claim against Dotty, Dotty most likely will

(A) be held strictly liable in tort for serving spoiled tuna.
(B) be held liable only if she were negligent.
(C) not be held liable unless her conduct was in reckless disregard of the safety of Guest.
(D) not be held liable, because Guest was a social visitor.

Question 120

If Guest asserts a claim against Supermart, the most likely result is that Guest will

(A) recover on the theory of res ipsa loquitur.
(B) recover on the theory of strict liability in tort.
(C) not recover, because Supermart gave proper warning.
(D) not recover, because Guest was not the purchaser of the cans.

Question 121

Diner, a drive-in hamburger and ice cream stand, recently opened for business in the suburban town of Little City. Diner's business hours are from 9:00 a.m. to midnight. It is in an area that for fifteen years has been zoned for small retail businesses, apartment buildings, and one- and two-family residences. The zoning code specifies that "small retail business" includes "businesses where food and drink are dispensed for consumption on the premises." Diner was the first drive-in in Little City. For seven years Mr. and Mrs. Householder have owned and lived in their single-family residence, which is across the street from Diner.

On opening day a brass band played in the parking lot of Diner until midnight, and the noise of cars and the unusual activity as a result of the new business prevented the Householders from getting to sleep until well after midnight, long after their usual time. Diner is heavily patronized during the day and night by high school students. The noise of cars, the lights of the cars, the lights illuminating the parking lot at Diner, and the noise from the loudspeaker of the ordering system prevented the Householders from sleeping before midnight. Paper cups, napkins, and other items from the drive-in are regularly blown into the Householders' front yard by the prevailing wind. The traffic to and from Diner is so heavy on the street in front of their house that the Householders are afraid to allow their small children to play in the front yard.

The Householders have asserted a claim against Diner based on private nuisance. The most likely effect of the fact that Householders were in the area before Diner is that it

(A) requires that the Householders' interest be given priority.
(B) is irrelevant because of the zoning ordinance.
(C) is irrelevant because conforming economic uses are given priority.
(D) is some, but not controlling, evidence.

Questions 122-123 are based on the following fact situation.

Peter was rowing a boat on a mountain lake when a storm suddenly arose. Fearful that the boat might sink, Peter rowed to a boat dock on shore and tied the boat to the dock. The shore property and dock were the private property of Owner.

While the boat was tied at the dock, Owner came down and ordered Peter to remove the boat, because the action of the waves was causing the boat to rub against a bumper on the dock. When Peter refused, Owner untied the boat and cast it adrift. The boat sank.

Peter was wearing a pair of swimming trunks, nothing else. He had a pair of shoes and a parka in the boat, but they were lost when Owner set it adrift. Peter was staying at a cabin one mile from Owner's property. The only land routes back were a short rocky trail that was dangerous during the storm, and a 15-mile road around the lake. The storm continued with heavy rain and hail, and Peter having informed Owner of the location of his cabin, asked Owner to take him back there in Owner's car. Owner said, "You got here by yourself and you'll have to get back home yourself." After one hour the storm stopped, and Peter walked home over the trail.

Question 122

A necessary element in determining if Peter is liable for a trespass is whether

(A) Owner had clearly posted his property with a sign indicating that it was private property.
(B) Peter knew that the property belonged to a private person.
(C) Peter had reasonable grounds to believe the property belonged to a private person.
(D) Peter had reasonable grounds to believe his boat might be swamped and sink.

Question 123

If Peter asserts a claim against Owner for loss of the boat, the most likely result is that Owner will

(A) have no defense under the circumstances.
(B) prevail, because Peter was a trespasser ab initio.
(C) prevail, because the boat might have damaged the dock.
(D) prevail, because Peter became a trespasser when he refused to remove the boat.

Question 124

Pauline, an unmarried female, was prominent in the women's liberation movement. She recently gave birth to a baby and publicly announced that she had no intention of marrying the father or disclosing his identity. The local newspaper, Journal, decided to do a series of articles on Pauline entitled "The Perils of Pauline."

The first article about Pauline discussed her parents. The article correctly stated that Mary, her mother, had died recently and Frank, her father, is still living. The article referred to the fact that at the time of Pauline's birth there were rumors that she had been born six months after the marriage of Mary and Frank, that Frank was not in fact her father, and that a person identified as Albert, who had played minor roles in two motion pictures, was her real father. Albert has lived in retirement for the last ten years.

If Pauline asserts a claim based on invasion of privacy against Journal for the statements in the first article about her birth and it is established that the statements are true the most likely result is that Pauline will

(A) not prevail, because truth is a complete defense.
(B) not prevail, because of her announcement concerning the birth of her own child.
(C) prevail, because the statements hold her up to ridicule and contempt.
(D) prevail, because her statements are embarrassing to her.

Questions 125-127 are based on the following fact situation.

An ordinance of City makes it unlawful to park a motor vehicle on a City street within ten feet of a fire hydrant. At 1:55 p.m. Parker, realizing he must be in Bank before it closed at 2:00 p.m., and finding no other space available, parked his automobile in front of a fire hydrant on a City street. Parker then hurried into the bank, leaving his aged neighbor, Ned, as a passenger in the rear seat of the car. About 5 minutes later, and while Parker was still in Bank, Driver was driving down the street. Driver swerved to avoid what he mistakenly thought was a hole in the street and side-swiped Parker's car. Parker's car was turned over on top of the hydrant, breaking the hydrant and causing a small flood of water. Parker's car was severely damaged and Ned was badly injured. There is no applicable guest statute.

Question 125

If Ned asserts a claim against Parker, the most likely result is that Ned will

(A) recover, because Parker's action was negligence per se.
(B) recover, because Parker's action was a continuing wrong which contributed to Ned's injuries.

(C) not recover, because a reasonably prudent person could not foresee injury to Ned as a result of Parker's action.

(D) not recover, because a violation of a city ordinance does not give rise to a civil cause of action.

Question 126

If Parker asserts a claim against Driver for damage to Parker's automobile, the most likely result is that Parker will

(A) recover, because the purpose of the ordinance is to provide access to the fire hydrant.

(B) recover, because Driver's negligence was later in time than Parker's act of parking.

(C) not recover, because Parker was contributorily negligent as a matter of law.

(D) not recover, because Parker's action in parking unlawfully was a continuing wrong.

Question 127

If City asserts a claim against Driver for the damage to the fire hydrant and Driver was negligent in swerving his car, his negligence is

(A) a cause in fact and a legal cause of City's harm.

(B) a cause in fact, but not a legal cause, of City's harm because Parker parked illegally.

(C) a legal cause, but not a cause in fact, of City's harm because Parker's car struck the hydrant.

(D) neither a legal cause nor a cause in fact of City's harm.

Question 128

Philip was a 10-year-old boy. Macco was a company that sold new and used machinery. Macco stored discarded machinery, pending sale for scrap, on a large vacant area it owned. This area was unfenced and was one-quarter mile from the housing development where Philip lived. Macco knew that children frequently played in the area and on the machinery. Philip's parents had directed him not to play on the machinery because it was dangerous.

One day Philip was playing on a press in Macco's storage area. The press had several wheels, each geared to the other. Philip climbed on the largest wheel, which was about five feet in diameter. Philip's weight caused the wheel to rotate, his foot was caught between two wheels that were set in motion, and he was severely injured.

A claim for relief was asserted by Philip through a duly appointed guardian. Macco denied liability and pleaded Philip's contributory fault as a defense.

In determining whether Maaco breached a duty to Philip, which of the following is the most significant?

(A) Whether the press on which Philip was injured was visible from a public way.

(B) Whether the maintenance of the area for the storage of discarded machinery was a private nuisance.

(C) Whether the maintenance of the area for the storage of discarded machinery was a public nuisance.

(D) Whether Maaco could have eliminated the risk of harm without unduly interfering with Macco's normal operations.

Questions 129-130 are based on the following fact situation.

Si was in the act of siphoning gasoline from Neighbor's car in Neighbor's garage and without his consent when the gasoline exploded and a fire followed. Rescuer, seeing the fire, grabbed a fire extinguisher from his car and put out the fire, saving Si's life and Neighbor's car and garage. In doing so, Rescuer was badly burned.

Question 129

If Rescuer asserts a claim against Si for personal injuries, Rescuer will

(A) prevail, because he saved Si's life.

(B) prevail, because Si was at fault in causing the fire.

(C) not prevail, because Rescuer knowingly assumed the risk.

(D) not prevail, because Rescuer's action was not a foreseeable consequence of Si's conduct.

Question 130

If Rescuer asserts a claim against Neighbor for personal injuries, Rescuer will

(A) prevail, because he saved Neighbor's property.
(B) prevail, because he acted reasonably in an emergency.
(C) not prevail, because Neighbor was not at fault.
(D) not prevail, because Rescuer knowingly assumed the risk.

Questions 131-132 are based on the following fact situation.

In City of State Y, Maple Street is a local public thoroughfare, designated as a one-way street for northbound traffic. Pine Street is a public thoroughfare, designated as a one-way street for east-bound traffic. Maple and Pine Streets intersect at right angles. The intersection is controlled by traffic lights. There are two sets of lights, one at the northeast corner and one at the northwest corner, for traffic on Maple Street. There are two sets of lights, one at the northeast corner and one at the southeast corner, for traffic on Pine Street.

Trucker was making a delivery to a market on the east side of Maple Street, just north of its intersection with Pine Street. There being insufficient space for his truck and enclosed trailer, he parked it with the rear of the trailer extending entirely across the crosswalk on the north side of the intersection. The height of the trailer was such that it entirely obscured the traffic light on the northeast corner from the view of traffic moving east on Pine Street. Unknown to Trucker, the traffic light at the southeast corner was not functioning, because a collision seventy-two hours earlier had knocked down the pole from which the light was suspended.

Visitor, on his first trip to City, was driving east on Pine Street. Not seeing any traffic light or pole, he entered the intersection at a time when the light was red for eastbound traffic and green for northbound traffic. Driver, proceeding north on Maple Street and seeing the green light, entered the intersection without looking for any cross traffic and struck Visitor's car. Driver received personal injuries, and Visitor's car was damaged severely as a result of the impact.

Statutes of State Y make it a misdemeanor (1) to park a motor vehicle so that any part projects into a crosswalk and (2) to enter an intersection contrary to a traffic signal.

Question 131

If Driver asserts a claim against Trucker and establishes that Trucker was negligent, the likely result is that Trucker's negligence is

(A) a legal but not an actual cause of Driver's injuries.
(B) an actual but not a legal cause of Driver's injuries.
(C) both an actual and a legal cause of Driver's injuries.
(D) neither an actual nor a legal cause of Driver's injuries.

Question 132

If Driver asserts a claim against City, the theory on which he has the best chance of prevailing is that City

(A) is strictly liable for harm caused by a defective traffic signal.
(B) was negligent in not replacing the broken pole within seventy-two hours.
(C) had an absolute duty to maintain installed traffic signals in good operating order.
(D) created a dangerous trap by not promptly replacing the broken pole.

Question 133

Henry hated Wanda, his former wife, for divorcing him and marrying John a short time thereafter. About a month after Wanda married John, Henry secretly entered Wanda and John's rented apartment during their absence by using a master key. Henry placed a microphone behind the book stand in the bedroom of the apartment, drilled a hole in the nearby wall and poked the wires from the microphone through the hole into the space in the wall, with the result that the microphone appeared to be connected with wires going into the adjoining apartment. Actually the microphone was not connected to anything. Henry anticipated that Wanda would discover the microphone in a few days and would be upset by the thought that someone had been listening to her conversations with John in their bedroom.

Shortly thereafter, as he was putting a book on the stand, John noticed the wires behind the book stand and discovered the hidden microphone. He then called Wanda and showed her the microphone and wires. Wanda fainted and, in falling, struck her head on the book stand and suffered a mild concussion. The next day John telephoned Henry and accused him of planting the microphone. Henry laughingly admitted it. Because of his concern about Wanda and his anger at Henry, John is emotionally upset and unable to go to work.

If Wanda asserts a claim against Henry based on infliction of mental distress, the fact that John was the person who showed her the microphone will

(A) relieve Henry of liability, because John was careless in so doing.
(B) relieve Henry of liability, because John's conduct was the immediate cause of Wanda's harm.
(C) not relieve Henry of liability, because Henry's goal was achieved.
(D) not relieve Henry of liability, because the conduct of a third person is irrelevant in emotional distress cases.

Questions 134-135 are based on the following fact situation.

Dave is a six-year-old boy who has a well-deserved reputation for bullying younger and smaller children. His parents have encouraged him to be aggressive and tough. Dave, for no reason, knocked down, kicked and severely injured Pete, a four-year-old. A claim for relief has been asserted by Pete's parents for their medical and hospital costs and for Pete's injuries.

Question 134

If the claim is asserted against Dave's parents, the most likely result is they will be

(A) liable, because parents are strictly liable for the torts of their children.
(B) liable, because Dave's parents encouraged him to be aggressive and tough.
(C) not liable, because a six-year-old cannot commit a tort.
(D) not liable, because parents cannot be held liable for the tort of a child.

Question 135

If the claim is asserted against Dave, the most likely result is Dave will be

(A) liable, because he intentionally harmed Pete.
(B) liable, because, as a six-year-old, he should have known his conduct was wrongful.
(C) not liable, because a child under seven is not liable in tort.
(D) not liable, because he is presumed to be under his parents' control and they have the sole responsibility.

Question 136

Customer, aged twenty, went into Store at approximately 6:45 p.m to look at some suits that were on sale. The clerks were busy, and one of them told him that he should wait on himself. Customer selected three suits from a rack and went into the dressing room to try them on. Signs posted on the walls of Store state that closing time is 9:00 p.m.; however, because of a special awards banquet for employees, Store was closed at 7:00 p.m. on this day. The employees, in a hurry to get to the banquet, did not check the dressing rooms or turn off the lights before leaving. When Customer emerged from the dressing room a few minutes after 7:00 p.m., he was alone and locked in. Customer tried the front door but it was secured on the outside by a bar and padlock, so he went to the rear door. Customer grabbed the door knob and vigorously shook the door. It did not open, but the activity set off a mechanism that had been installed because of several recent thefts committed by persons who had hidden in the store until after closing time. The mechanism sprayed a chemical mist in Customer's face, causing him to become temporarily blind. The mechanism also activated an alarm carried by Store's employee, Watchman, who was just coming to work. Watchman unlocked the front door, ran into the store, and grabbed Customer. Customer, who was still unable to see, struck out at this person and hit a metal rack, injuring his hand. Watchman then identified himself, and Customer did the same. After assuring himself that Customer was telling the truth, Watchman allowed him to leave.

If Customer is to prevail on a claim against Store based on battery from the use of the chemical spray, Customer must establish that

(A) he suffered severe bodily harm.
(B) the spray mist was an offensive or harmful contact.
(C) he suffered severe emotional distress.
(D) his conduct was not a factual cause of the chemical's spraying him.

Question 137

Dock had been the unsuccessful suitor of Mary, who had recently announced her engagement to Paul. Angered by her engagement, Dock sent Mary the following letter: "I hope you know what you are doing. The man you think you love wears women's clothes when at home. A Friend."

The receipt of this letter caused Mary great emotional distress. She hysterically telephoned Paul, read him the letter, and told him that she was breaking their engagement. The contents of the letter were not revealed to others. Paul, who was a young attorney in the state attorney's office, suffered serious humiliation and emotional distress as a result of the broken engagement.

If Paul asserts a claim against Dock based on defamation and it is proved that Dock's statement was true, such proof will be

(A) a defense by itself.
(B) a defense only if Dock was not actuated by malice.
(C) a defense only if Dock reasonably believed it to be true.
(D) no defense by itself.

Question 138

Construction Company contracted to build a laundry for Wash Company on the latter's vacant lot in a residential area. As a part of its work, Construction Company dug a trench from the partially completed laundry to the edge of a public sidewalk; waterlines were to be installed in the trench. Because of the contour of the land, the trench was dug to a depth ranging from 7 to 9 feet. Construction Company did not place any barriers around the trench and permitted it to lie open for almost a week while waiting for the delivery of water pipes. This was known to Wash Company, but it raised no objection.

During the time the trench was open, a series of heavy rains fell, causing 5 feet of surface water to gather in the bottom of the trench. While this condition existed, 5-year-old Tommy, who was playing on the vacant lot with friends, stumbled and fell into the trench. Robert, an adult passerby, saw this and immediately lowered himself into the trench to rescue Tommy. However, his doing so caused the rain-soaked walls of the trench to collapse, killing both him and Tommy.

In a claim for wrongful death by Tommy's administrator against Construction Company, the most likely result is that plaintiff will

(A) recover, because the defendant left the open trench unprotected.
(B) recover, because construction companies are strictly liable for inherently dangerous conditions.
(C) not recover, because Tommy was a trespasser.

(D) not recover, because Tommy's death was a result of the collapse of the trench, an independent intervening cause.

Question 139

Doctor, a licensed physician, resided in her own home. The street in front of the home had a gradual slope. Doctor's garage was on the street level, with a driveway entrance from the street.

At two in the morning Doctor received an emergency call. She dressed and went to the garage to get her car and found a car parked in front of her driveway. That car was occupied by Parker, who, while intoxicated, had driven to that place and now was in a drunken stupor in the front seat. Unable to rouse Parker, Doctor pushed him into the passenger's side of the front seat and got in on the driver's side.
Doctor released the brake and coasted the car down the street, planning to pull into a parking space that was open. When Doctor attempted to stop the car, the brakes failed to work, and the car crashed into the wall of Owner's home, damaging Owner's home and Parker's car and injuring Doctor and Parker. Subsequent examination of the car disclosed that the brake linings were badly worn. A state statute prohibits the operation of a motor vehicle unless the brakes are capable of stopping the vehicle within specified distances at specified speeds. The brakes on Parker's car were incapable of stopping the vehicle within the limits required by the statute. Another state statute makes it a criminal offense to be intoxicated while driving a motor vehicle.

If Parker asserts a claim against Doctor for his injuries, Parker will probably

(A) recover, because Doctor was negligent as a matter of law.
(B) recover, because Doctor had no right to move the car.
(C) not recover, because his brakes were defective.
(D) not recover, because he was in a drunken stupor when injured.

Question 140

Auto Company, a corporation, was a small dealer in big new cars and operated a service department. Peter wanted to ask Mike, the service manager, whether Auto Company would check the muffler on his small foreign car. Peter parked on the street near the service department with the intention of entering that part of the building by walking through one of the three large entrances designed for use by automobiles.

There was no street entrance to the service department for individuals, and customers as well as company employees often used one of the automobile entrances.

As Peter reached the building, he glanced behind him to be sure no vehicle was approaching that entrance. Seeing none, he walked through the entrance, but immediately he was struck on the back of the head and neck by the large overhead door which was descending. The blow knocked Peter unconscious and caused permanent damage.

Peter did not know how the door was raised and lowered; however, the overhead door was operated by the use of either of two switches in the building. One switch was located in the office of the service manager and the other was located near the door in the service work area for the convenience of the mechanics. On this occasion, no one was in the service work area except three Auto Company mechanics. Mike, who had been in his office, and the three mechanics denied having touched a switch that would have lowered the door. Subsequent investigation showed, however, that the switches were working properly and that all of the mechanisms for moving the door were in good working order.

If Peter asserts a claim based on negligence against Auto Company, Peter probably will

(A) recover, because Auto Company is strictly liable under the circumstance.
(B) recover, because an employee of Auto Company was negligent.
(C) not recover, because Peter was a licensee.
(D) not recover, because Peter assumed the risk.

Question 141

Householder hired Contractor to remodel her, Householder's, kitchen. She had learned of him through a classified advertisement he placed in the local newspaper. During the telephone conversation in which she hired him, he stated he was experienced and qualified to do all necessary work. Because of his low charge for his work, they agreed in writing that on acceptance of his job by Householder, he would have no further liability to her or to anyone else for any defects in materials or workmanship, and that she would bear all such costs.

Householder purchased a dishwasher manufactured by Elex Company from Dealer, who was in the retail electrical appliance business. The washer was sold by Dealer with only the manufacturer's warranty and with no warranty by Dealer; Elex Company restricted its warranty to ninety days on parts and labor. Contractor installed the dishwasher.

Two months after Householder accepted the entire job, she was conversing in her home with Accountant, an acquaintance who had agreed to prepare her income tax return gratuitously. As they talked, they noticed that the dishwasher was operating strangely, repeatedly stopping and starting. At Householder's request, Accountant gave it a cursory examination and, while inspecting it, received a violent electrical shock which did him extensive harm. The dishwasher had an internal wiring defect which allowed electrical current to be carried into the framework and caused the machine to malfunction. The machine had not been adequately grounded by Contractor during installation; if it had been, the current would have been led harmlessly away. The machine carried instructions for correct grounding, which Contractor had not followed.

If Accountant asserts a claim based on strict liability against Elex Company for damages, the probable result is that Accountant will

(A) recover, because the dishwasher was defectively made.
(B) recover, because Elex Company is vicariously liable for the improper installation.
(C) not recover, because he assumed the risk by inspecting the machine.
(D) not recover, because he was not the purchaser.

Questions 142-143 are based on the following fact situation.

Mrs. Ritter, a widow, recently purchased a new uncrated electric range for her kitchen from Local Retailer. The range has a wide oven with a large oven door. The crate in which Stove Company, the manufacturer, shipped the range carried a warning label that the stove would tip over with a weight of 25 pounds or more on the oven door. Mrs. Ritter has one child—Brenda, aged 3. Recently, at about 5:30 p.m., Brenda was playing on the floor of the kitchen while Mrs. Ritter was heating water in a pan on the stove. The telephone rang and Mrs. Ritter went into the living room to answer it. While she was gone Brenda decided to find out what was cooking. She opened the oven door and climbed on it to see what was in the pan. Brenda's weight (25 pounds) on the door caused the stove to tip over forward. Brenda fell to the floor and the hot water spilled over her, burning her severely. Brenda screamed. Mrs. Ritter ran to the kitchen and immediately gave her first aid treatment for burns. Brenda thereafter received medical treatment.

Brenda's burns were painful. They have now healed and do not bother her, but she has ugly scars on her legs and back. Brenda's claim is asserted on her behalf by the proper party.

Question 142

If Brenda asserts a claim based on strict liability against Stove Company, she must establish that

(A) the defendant negligently designed the stove.
(B) stoves made by other manufacturers do not turn over with a 25-pound weight on the oven door.
(C) the defendant failed to warn the Ritters that the stove would turn over easily.
(D) the stove was defective and unreasonably dangerous to her.

Question 143

If Brenda asserts a claim based on strict liability against Local Retailer, she must establish that

(A) Local Retailer did not inform Mrs. Ritter of the warning on the crate.
(B) the stove was substantially in the same condition at the time it tipped over as when it was purchased from Local Retailer.
(C) Local Retailer made some change in the stove design or had improperly assembled it so that it tipped over more easily.
(D) Local Retailer knew or should have known that the stove was dangerous because of the ease with which it tipped over.

Question 144

Mrs. Dennis' 12-year-old daughter, Gala, had some difficulty getting along with other children in the neighborhood, especially with the younger ones. Thinking the experience would be good for her, Mrs. Dennis recommended Gala to Mr. Parrent as a baby sitter for his five-year-old boy, Robby, but did not mention Gala's difficulties or her lack of prior experience as a baby sitter. The Dennises and the Parrents were longstanding social acquaintances. On the evening Gala was to sit, the Parrents told Gala that she should treat Robby firmly, but that it would be preferable not to spank him since he did not take kindly to it. They did not tell Gala they had experienced trouble retaining baby sitters because of Robby's temper tantrums.

Later in the evening when Robby became angry upon being told to go to his room for being naughty, Gala spanked him, but only moderately hard. Robby then threw a hard-backed book at Gala, hitting her in the eye. As Gala tried to catch Robby to take him to his room, Robby fled around the house and out the back door, knocking over and breaking an expensive lamp.

The back yard was completely dark. Gala heard Robby screaming and banging at the back door, which had closed and locked automatically, but she did nothing. After twenty minutes had passed, she heard a banging and crying at the front door, but still she did nothing. Then the noise stopped. In a few minutes Gala went outside and found Robby lying on the steps unconscious and injured.

If a claim is asserted on behalf of Robby against Mrs. Dennis for damages based on Gala's conduct, Mrs. Dennis will probably be liable, because

(A) parents are vicariously liable for the intentional torts of their children.
(B) she has a nondelegable duty to control the actions of her child.
(C) respondeat superior applies.
(D) she was negligent.

Question 145

The most generally accepted basis on which a court will hold that X has a legal duty to aid another is the recognition by X that there is immediate danger of serious harm to

(A) another human being from a stranger's wrongful conduct.

(B) his neighbor from a stranger's wrongful conduct.
(C) his cousin from a stranger's wrongful conduct.
(D) another human being from X's own non-negligent conduct.

Questions 146-149 are based on the following fact situation.

Walker, a pedestrian, started north across the street in a clearly marked north-south crosswalk with the green traffic light in her favor. Walker was in a hurry, and so before reaching the north curb on the street, she cut to her left diagonally across the street to the east-west crosswalk and started across it. Just after reaching the east-west crosswalk, the traffic light turned green in her favor. She proceeded about five steps further across the street to the west in the crosswalk when she was struck by a car approaching from her right that she thought would stop, but did not. The car was driven by Driver, 81 years of age, who failed to stop his car after seeing that the traffic light was red against him. Walker had a bone disease, resulting in very brittle bones, that is prevalent in only 0.02 percent of the population. As a result of the impact Walker suffered a broken leg and the destruction of her family heirloom, a Picasso original painting that she was taking to her bank for safekeeping. The painting had been purchased by Walker's grandmother for $750 but was valued at $500,000 at the time of the accident.

Walker has filed suit against Driver. Driver's attorney has alleged that Walker violated a state statute requiring that pedestrians stay in crosswalks, and that if Walker had not violated the statute she would have had to walk 25 feet more to reach the impact point and therefore would not have been at a place where she could have been hit by Driver. Walker's attorney ascertains that there is a statute as alleged by Driver, that his measurements are correct, that there is a state statute requiring observance of traffic lights, and that Driver's license expired two years prior to the collision.

Question 146

The violation of the crosswalk statute by Walker should not defeat her cause of action against Driver because

(A) Driver violated the traffic light statute at a later point in time than Walker's violation.
(B) pedestrians are entitled to assume that automobile drivers will obey the law.
(C) Walker was hit while in the crosswalk.

(D) the risks that the statute was designed to protect against probably did not include an earlier arrival at another point.

Question 147

The failure of Driver to have a valid driver's license has which of the following effects?

(A) It makes Driver liable to Walker because Driver is a trespasser on the highway.
(B) It would not furnish a basis for liability.
(C) It proves that Driver is an unfit driver in this instance.
(D) It makes Driver absolutely liable for Walker's injury.

Question 148

If Walker establishes liability on the part of Driver for her physical injuries, should Walker's recovery include damages for a broken leg?

(A) No, since only 0.02 percent of the population have bones as brittle as Walker's.
(B) No, unless a person of ordinary health would probably have suffered a broken leg from the impact.
(C) Yes, because Driver could foresee that there would be unforeseeable consequences of the impact.
(D) Yes, even though the extent of the injury was not a foreseeable consequence of the impact.

Question 149

Walker's violation of the crosswalk statute should not be considered by the jury because

(A) there is no dispute in the evidence about factual cause.
(B) as a matter of law the violation of the statute results in liability for all resulting harm.
(C) as a matter of law Driver's conduct was an independent intervening cause.
(D) as a matter of law the injury to Walker was not the result of a risk the statute was designed to protect against.

Question 150

Paulsen was eating in a restaurant when he began to choke on a piece of food that had lodged in his throat. Dow, a physician who was sitting at a nearby table, did not wish to become involved and did not render any assistance, although prompt medical attention would have been effective in removing the obstruction from Paulsen's throat. Because of the failure to obtain prompt medical attention, Paulsen suffered severe brain injury from lack of oxygen.

If Paulsen asserts a claim against Dow for his injuries, will Paulsen prevail?

(A) Yes, if the jurisdiction relieves physicians of malpractice liability for emergency first aid.
(B) Yes, if a reasonably prudent person with Dow's experience, training, and knowledge would have assisted Paulsen.
(C) No, because Dow was not responsible for Paulsen's condition.
(D) No, because Dow knew that Paulsen was substantially certain to sustain serious injury.

Questions 151-152 are based on the following fact situation.

Parents purchased a new mobile home from Seller. The mobile home was manufactured by Mobilco and had a ventilating system designed by Mobilco with both a heating unit and an air conditioner. Mobilco installed a furnace manufactured by Heatco and an air conditioning unit manufactured by Coolco.

Each was controlled by an independent thermostat installed by Mobilco. Because of the manner in which Mobilco designed the ventilating system, the first time the ventilating system was operated by Parents, cold air was vented into Parents' bedroom to keep the temperature at 68°F (20°C). The cold air then activated the heater thermostat, and hot air was pumped into the bedroom of Child, the six-month-old child of Parents. The temperature in Child's room reached more than 170°F (77°C) before Child's mother became aware of the condition and shut the system off manually. As a result, Child suffered permanent physical injury.

Claims have been asserted by Child, through a duly appointed guardian, against Mobilco, Seller, Heatco, and Coolco.

Question 151

If Child's claim against Seller is based on negligence, the minimum proof necessary to establish Seller's liability is that the ventilating system

(A) was defective.
(B) was defective and had not been inspected by Seller.
(C) was defective and had been inspected by Seller, and the defect was not discovered.
(D) was defective, and the defect would have been discovered if Seller had exercised reasonable care in inspecting the system.

Question 152

If Child's claims against Mobilco, Heatco, and Coolco are based on strict liability in tort, Child will probably recover against

(A) Mobilco only, because the ventilating system was defectively designed by Mobilco.
(B) Heatco only, because it was the excessive heat from the furnace that caused Child's injuries.
(C) Mobilco and Heatco only, because the combination of Mobilco's design and Heatco's furnace caused Child's injuries.
(D) Mobilco, Heatco, and Coolco, because the combination of Mobilco's design, Heatco's furnace, and Coolco's air conditioning unit caused Child's injuries.

Question 153

Light Company is the sole distributor of electrical power in City. The Company owns and maintains all of the electric poles and equipment in City. Light Company has complied with the National Electrical Safety Code, which establishes minimum requirements for the installation and maintenance of power poles. The Code has been approved by the federal and state governments.

Light Company has had to replace insulators on its poles repeatedly because unknown persons repeatedly shoot at and destroy them. This causes the power lines to fall to the ground. On one of these occasions, Paul, Faber's 5-year-old son, wandered out of Faber's yard, intentionally touched a downed wire, and was seriously burned.

If a claim on Paul's behalf is asserted against Light Company, the probable result is that Paul will

(A) recover if Light Company could have taken reasonable steps to prevent the lines from falling when the insulators were destroyed.
(B) recover, because a supplier of electricity is strictly liable in tort.

(C) not recover unless Light Company failed to exercise reasonable care to stop the destruction of the insulators.

(D) not recover, because the destruction of the insulators was intentional.

Question 154

The city of Metropolis has an ordinance that makes it an offense, punishable by fine, for the owner of a dog to permit the dog to run unleashed on a public way.

Smythe, a police officer, observed a small dog running loose in the street. As he picked the dog up, Nelson, who was seated in her car lawfully parked at the curb, called out, "Oh, thank you, Officer for returning Fido." Smythe asked Nelson whether the dog was hers, and when she acknowledged ownership, he asked her to see her driver's license. Nelson gave her name and address, but she refused to produce a driver's license. Smythe then told her to produce her driver's license if she did not want to go to jail. Nelson responded by saying, "Isn't this ridiculous?" Smythe took her by the arm and said, "Let's go. You are under arrest."

Nelson cried out that Smythe was hurting her but he refused to release her arm, and she struck him with her free hand. Smythe then dragged Nelson from her car, forced her into his squad car, and took her to the police station.

The incident took place on the street in front of the apartment where Nelson and her aged father, Joplin, lived. Smythe did not know that Joplin had observed what took place from a window in the apartment.

If Nelson's father, Joplin, asserts a claim against Smythe for the intentional infliction of emotional distress, will Joplin prevail?

(A) Yes, if Smythe's acts caused Joplin severe emotional distress.

(B) Yes, if it is found that Smythe's behavior was extreme and outrageous with respect to Nelson.

(C) No, because Smythe did not know that Joplin was watching.

(D) No, because Joplin was not within the zone of physical danger.

Question 155

A group of children, ranging in age from 8 to 15, regularly played football on the common area of an apartment complex owned by O'Neill. Most of the children lived in the apartment complex, but some lived elsewhere. O'Neill knew that the children played on the common area and had not objected.

Peter, a 13-year-old who did not live in the apartment complex, fell over a sprinkler head while running for a pass and broke his leg. Although Peter had played football on the common area before, he had never noticed the sprinkler heads, which protruded one inch above the ground and were part of a permanently installed underground sprinkler system.

If a claim is asserted on Peter's behalf, Peter will

(A) prevail if the sprinkler head was a hazard that Peter probably would not discover.

(B) prevail, because O'Neill had not objected to children playing on the common area.

(C) not prevail, because Peter did not live in the apartment complex.

(D) not prevail unless the sprinkler heads were abnormally dangerous to users of the common area.

Questions 156-157 are based on the following fact situation.

Innes worked as a secretary in an office in a building occupied partly by her employer and partly by Glass, a retail store. The two areas were separated by walls and were in no way connected, except that the air conditioning unit served both areas and there was a common return-air duct.

Glass began remodeling, and its employees did the work, which included affixing a plastic surfacing material to counters. To fasten the plastic to the counters, the employees purchased glue, with the brand name Stick, that was manufactured by Steel, packaged in a sealed container by Steel, and retailed by Paint Company.

In the course of the remodeling job, one of Glass' employees turned on the air conditioning and caused fumes from the glue to travel from Glass through the air conditioning unit and into Innes' office. The employees did not know that there was common duct work for the air conditioners. Innes was permanently blinded by the fumes from the glue.

The label on the container of glue read, "DANGER. Do not smoke near this product. Extremely flammable. Contains Butanone, Tuluol and Hexane. Use with adequate ventilation. Keep out of the reach of children."

The three chemicals listed on the label are very toxic and harmful to human eyes. Steel had received no reports of eye injuries during the ten years that the product had been manufactured and sold.

Question 156

If Innes asserts a claim against Paint Company, the most likely result is that she will

(A) recover if she can recover against Steel.
(B) recover, because Innes was an invitee of a tenant in the building.
(C) not recover unless Paint Company was negligent.
(D) not recover, because the glue came in a sealed package.

Question 157

If Innes asserts a claim against Glass, the most likely result is that she will

(A) recover, because a user of a product is held to the same standard as the manufacturer.
(B) recover, because the employees of Glass caused the fumes to enter her area of the building.
(C) not recover, because Glass used the glue for its intended purposes.
(D) not recover, because the employees of Glass had no reason to know that the fumes could injure Innes.

Question 158

Siddon worked as a private duty nurse and on occasion worked in Doctors' Hospital. The hospital called Registry, the private duty referral agency through which Siddon usually obtained employment, and asked that in the future she not be assigned to patients in Doctors' Hospital. Registry asked the hospital why it had made the request. Doctors' Hospital sent a letter to Registry giving as the reason for its request that significant amounts of narcotics had disappeared during Siddon's shift from the nursing stations at which she had worked.

If Siddon asserts a claim based on defamation against Doctors' Hospital, Siddon will

(A) recover, because the hospital accused Siddon of improper professional conduct.
(B) recover if Siddon did not take the narcotics.
(C) not recover if narcotics disappeared during Siddon's shifts.
(D) not recover if the hospital reasonably believed that Siddon took the narcotics.

Question 159

Ellis, an electrical engineer, designed an electronic game known as Zappo. Ellis entered into a licensing agreement with Toyco under which Toyco agreed to manufacture Zappo according to Ellis' specifications and to market it and pay a royalty to Ellis.

Carla, whose parents had purchased a Zappo game for her, was injured while playing the game. Carla recovered a judgment against Toyco on the basis of a finding that the Zappo game was defective because of Ellis' improper design.

In a claim for indemnity against Ellis, will Toyco prevail?

(A) Yes, because as between Ellis and Toyco, Ellis was responsible for the design of Zappo.
(B) Yes, because Toyco and Ellis were joint tortfeasors.
(C) No, because Toyco, as the manufacturer, was strictly liable to Carla.
(D) No, if Toyco, by a reasonable inspection, could have discovered the defect in the design of Zappo.

Questions 160-161 are based on the following fact situation.

Gasco owns a storage facility where flammable gases are stored in liquified form under high pressure in large spherical tanks. The facility was constructed for Gasco by Acme Company, a firm that specializes in the construction of such facilities. After the facility had been in use for five years, an explosion in the facility started a large fire that blanketed the surrounding countryside with a high concentration of oily smoke and soot. Farber owns a large truck farm near the facility. His entire lettuce crop was destroyed by oil deposits left by the smoke. Johnson, who lives near the facility, inhaled a large amount of the smoke and thereafter became obsessed by a fear that the inhalation would destroy his health and ultimately cause his death.

Question 160

If Farber asserts a claim against Gasco for the loss of his lettuce crop and is unable to show any negligence on the part of Gasco, will Farber prevail?

(A) Yes, because the operation of the storage facility was an abnormally dangerous activity.
(B) Yes, because the intrusion of the smoke onto Farber's farm amounted to a trespass.
(C) No, if the explosion was caused by internal corrosion that reasonable inspection procedures would not have disclosed.
(D) No, if the explosion was caused by negligent construction on Acme's part.

Question 161

If Farber asserts a claim against Acme Company for the loss of his lettuce crop will Farber prevail?

(A) No, if Acme did not design the storage facility.
(B) No, because Acme was an independent contractor.
(C) Yes, because the operation of the storage facility was an abnormally dangerous activity.
(D) Yes, if the explosion resulted from a defect of which Acme was aware.

Question 162

When Mary Weld visited Dugan's Alleys to participate in the weekly bowling league competition held there, she brought her 2-year-old son, Bobby, along and left him in a nursery provided by Dugan for the convenience of his customers. The children in the nursery were normally supervised by three attendants, but at this particular time, as Mary Weld knew, there was only one attendant present to care for about twenty children of assorted ages.

About thirty minutes later, while the attendant was looking the other way, Bobby suddenly started to cry. The attendant found him lying on his back, picked him up, and called his mother. It was later discovered that Bobby had suffered a skull fracture.

If a claim is asserted against Dugan on Bobby's behalf, will Bobby prevail?

(A) Yes, because Dugan owed the child the highest degree of care.
(B) Yes, because a 2-year-old is incapable of contributory negligence.
(C) No, unless Dugan or his employees failed to exercise reasonable care to assure Bobby's safety.

(D) No, if Mary Weld assumed the risk by leaving Bobby in the nursery.

Question 163

Astin left her car at Garrison's Garage to have repair work done. After completing the repairs, Garrison took the car out for a test drive and was involved in an accident that caused damages to Placek.

A statute imposes liability on the owner of an automobile for injuries to a third party that are caused by the negligence of any person driving the automobile with the owner's consent. The statute applies to situations of this kind, even if the owner did not specifically authorize the mechanic to test-drive the car.

Placek sued Astin and Garrison jointly for damages arising from the accident. In that action, Astin cross-claims to recover from Garrison the amount of any payment Astin may be required to make to Placek. The trier of fact has determined that the accident was caused solely by negligent driving on Garrison's part, and that Placek's damages were $100,000.

In this action, the proper outcome will be that

(A) Placek should have judgment for $50,000 each against Astin and Garrison; Astin should recover nothing from Garrison.
(B) Placek should have judgment for $100,000 against Garrison only.
(C) Placek should have judgment for $100,000 against Astin and Garrison jointly, and Astin should have judgment against Garrison for 50 percent of any amount collected from Astin by Placek.
(D) Placek should have judgment for $100,000 against Astin and Garrison jointly, and Astin should have judgment against Garrison for any amount collected from Astin by Placek.

Question 164

Dever drove his car into an intersection and collided with a fire engine that had entered the intersection from Dever's right. The accident was caused by negligence on Dever's part. As a result of the accident, the fire engine was delayed in reaching Peters' house, which was entirely consumed by fire. Peters' house was located about ten blocks from the scene of the accident.

If Peters asserts a claim against Dever, Peters will recover

(A) the part of his loss that would have been prevented if the collision had not occurred.
(B) the value of his house before the fire.
(C) nothing if Dever had nothing to do with causing the fire.
(D) nothing, because Dever's conduct did not create an apparent danger to Peters.

Question 165

Miller applied to the state liquor board for transfer of the license of Miller's Bar and Grill to a new site. The board held a hearing on the application.

At that hearing, Hammond appeared without being subpoenaed and stated that Miller had underworld connections. Although Hammond did not know this information to be true, he had heard rumors about Miller's character and had noticed several underworld figures going in and out of Miller's Bar and Grill. In fact, Miller had no underworld connections.

In a claim against Hammond based on defamation, Miller will

(A) not recover if Hammond reasonably believed his statement to be true.
(B) not recover if the board granted Miller's application.
(C) recover, because Hammond's statement was false.
(D) recover, because Hammond appeared before the board voluntarily.

Question 166

Purvis purchased a used car from Daley, a used car dealer. Knowing them to be false, Daley made the following statements to Purvis prior to the sale:

Statement 1. This car has never been involved in an accident.

Statement 2. This car gets 25 miles to the gallon on the open highway.

Statement 3. This is as smooth-riding a car as you can get.

If Purvis asserts a claim against Daley based on deceit, which of the false statements made by Daley would support Purvis' claim?

(A) Statement 1 only

(B) Statement 2 only
(C) Statements 1 and 2 only
(D) Statements 2 and 3 only

Question 167

Acorp and Beeco are companies that each manufacture pesticide X. Their plants are located along the same river. During a specific 24-hour period, each plant discharged pesticide into the river. Both plants were operated negligently and such negligence caused the discharge of the pesticide into the river.

Landesmann operated a cattle ranch downstream from the plants of Acorp and Beeco. Landesmann's cattle drank from the river and were poisoned by the pesticide. The amount of the discharge from either plant alone would not have been sufficient to cause any harm to Landesmann's cattle.

If Landesmann asserts a claim against Acorp. and Beeco, what, if anything, will Landesmann recover?

(A) Nothing, because neither company discharged enough pesticide to cause harm to Landesmann's cattle.
(B) Nothing, unless Landesmann can establish how much pesticide each plant discharged.
(C) One-half of Landesmann's damages from each company.
(D) The entire amount of Landesmann's damages, jointly and severally, from the two companies.

Questions 168-169 are based on the following fact situation.

Cycle Company manufactured a bicycle that it sold to Bike Shop, a retail bicycle dealer, which in turn sold it to Roth. Shortly thereafter, while Roth was riding the bicycle along a city street, he saw a traffic light facing him turn from green to amber. He sped up, hoping to cross the intersection before the light turned red. However, Roth quickly realized that he could not do so and applied the brake, which failed. To avoid the traffic that was then crossing in front of him, Roth turned sharply to his right and onto the sidewalk, where he struck Perez, a pedestrian. Both Perez and Roth sustained injuries.

Question 168

If Roth asserts a claim against Bike Shop based on strict liability in tort, will Roth prevail?

(A) Yes, if the brake failed because of a defect present when the bicycle left the factory of Cycle Company.

(B) Yes, because the brake failed while Roth was riding the bicycle.

(C) No, if Roth contributed to his own injury by speeding up.

(D) No, if Bike Shop carefully inspected the bicycle before selling it.

Question 169

If Perez asserts a claim based on negligence against Cycle Company and if it is found that the brake failure resulted from a manufacturing defect in the bicycle, will Perez prevail?

(A) Yes, because Cycle Company placed a defective bicycle into the stream of commerce.

(B) Yes, if the defect could have been discovered through the exercise of reasonable care by Cycle Company.

(C) No, because Perez was not a purchaser of the bicycle.

(D) No, if Roth was negligent in turning into the sidewalk.

Questions 170-171 are based on the following fact situation.

Morris was driving north on an interstate highway at about 50 miles per hour when a tractor-trailer rig, owned and driven by Dixon, passed her. The tractor was pulling a refrigerated meat trailer fully loaded with beef carcasses hanging freely from the trailer ceiling. When Dixon cut back in front of Morris, the shifting weight of the beef caused the trailer to overturn. Morris was unable to avoid a collision with the overturned trailer and was injured.

The trailer had been manufactured by Trailco. A number of truckers had complained to Trailco that the design of the trailer, which allowed the load to swing freely, was dangerous. Dixon knew of the dangerous propensity of the trailer. A restraining device that could be installed in the trailer would prevent the load from shifting and was available at nominal cost. Dixon knew of the restraining device but had not installed it.

Question 170

If Morris asserts a claim based on strict liability tort against Trailco, she will

(A) recover unless Morris was negligently driving when the truck overturned.

(B) recover, because Dixon's knowledge of the dangerous propensity of the trailer does not relieve Trailco of liability.

(C) not recover, because there was no privity of contract between Morris and Trailco.

(D) not recover if Dixon was negligent in failing to install the restraining device in the trailer.

Question 171

If Morris asserts a claim for her injuries against Dixon, she will

(A) prevail if the use of a restraining device would have prevented the trailer from overturning.

(B) prevail, because Dixon is strictly liable to Morris for injuries resulting from defects in the trailer.

(C) not prevail unless Dixon was driving in a negligent manner at the time Morris was injured.

(D) not prevail, because Dixon was not the manufacturer or seller of the trailer.

Questions 172-174 are based on the following fact situation.

Poe ordered some merchandise from Store. When the merchandise was delivered, Poe decided that it was not what he had ordered, and he returned it for credit. Store refused to credit Poe's account, continued to bill him, and, after 90 days, turned the account over to Kane, a bill collector, for collection.

Kane called at Poe's house at 7 p.m. on a summer evening while many of Poe's neighbors were seated on their porches. When Poe opened the door, Kane, who was standing just outside the door, raised an electrically amplified bullhorn to his mouth. In a voice that could be heard a block away, Kane called Poe a "deadbeat" and asked him when he intended to pay his bill to Store.

Poe, greatly angered, slammed the door shut. The door struck the bullhorn and jammed it forcibly against Kane's face. As a consequence, Kane lost some of his front teeth.

Question 172

If Poe asserts a claim based on defamation against Kane, will Poe prevail?

(A) Yes, if Kane's remarks were heard by any of Poe's neighbors.

(B) Yes, because Kane's conduct was extreme and outrageous.
(C) No, unless Kane knew that Poe owed no money to Store.
(D) No, unless Poe suffered some special damage.

Question 173

If Poe asserts a claim based on intentional infliction of emotional distress against Kane, will Poe prevail?

(A) Yes, because Kane's conduct was extreme and outrageous.
(B) Yes, because Kane was intruding on Poe's property.
(C) No, unless Poe suffered physical harm.
(D) No, if Poe still owed Store for the merchandise.

Question 174

If Kane asserts a claim of battery against Poe will Kane prevail?

(A) Yes, because Poe had not first asked Kane to leave the property.
(B) Yes, if Poe knew that the door was substantially certain to strike the bullhorn.
(C) No, if Kane's conduct triggered Poe's response.
(D) No, because Kane was an intruder on Poe's property.

Question 175

Plummer, a well-known politician, was scheduled to address a large crowd at a political dinner. Just as he was about to sit down at the head table, Devon pushed Plummer's chair to one side. As a result, Plummer fell to the floor. Plummer was embarrassed at being made to look foolish before a large audience but suffered no physical harm.

If Plummer asserts a claim against Devon for damages because of his embarrassment, will Plummer prevail?

(A) Yes, if Devon knew that Plummer was about to sit on the chair.
(B) Yes, if Devon negligently failed to notice that Plummer was about to sit on the chair.
(C) No, because Plummer suffered no physical harm along with his embarrassment.
(D) No, if in moving the chair Devon intended only a good-natured practical joke on Plummer.

Questions 176-177 are based on the following fact situation.

When Denton heard that his neighbor, Prout, intended to sell his home to a minority purchaser, Denton told Prout that Prout and his wife and children would meet with "accidents" if he did so. Prout then called the prospective purchaser and told him that he was taking the house off the market.

Question 176

If Prout asserts a claim against Denton for assault, Prout will

(A) recover if Denton intended to place Prout in fear of physical harm.
(B) recover, because Denton's conduct was extreme and outrageous.
(C) not recover if Denton took no action that threatened immediate physical harm to Prout.
(D) not recover, because Prout's action removed any threat of harmful force.

Question 177

If Prout asserts a claim against Denton for intentional infliction of emotional distress Prout will

(A) recover if Prout suffered severe emotional distress as a consequence of Denton's conduct.
(B) recover, because Denton intended to frighten Prout.
(C) not recover, because Denton made no threat of immediate physical harm to Prout or his family.
(D) not recover if Prout suffered no physical harm as a consequence of Denton's conduct.

Question 178

While on a hiking trip during the late fall, Page arrived, toward the end of the day, at a clearing where several similar cabins were located, none of which was occupied. One of the cabins belonged to Levin, Page's friend, who had given Page permission to use it. Page entered one of the cabins, which she thought was Levin's, and prepared to spend the night. In fact the cabin was owned, not by Levin, but by Dwyer.

When the night turned cold, Page started a fire in the stove. Unknown to Page, there was a defect in the stove that allowed carbon monoxide fumes to escape into the cabin. During the night the fumes caused serious injury to Page.

If Page asserts a claim against Dwyer for her injury, will Page recover?

(A) Yes, if Dwyer knew that the stove was defective.
(B) Yes, if Dwyer could have discovered the defect in the stove by a reasonable inspection.
(C) No, because Dwyer had no reason to anticipate Page's presence in the cabin.
(D) No, unless Page needed to use the cabin for her own protection.

Question 179

Telco, a local telephone company, negligently allowed one of its telephone poles, located between a street and a sidewalk, to become termite-ridden. Rhodes, who was intoxicated and driving at an excessive rate of speed, lost control of her car and hit the weakened telephone pole. One week later, the pole fell and struck Walker, a pedestrian who was walking on the sidewalk. The pole fell because of the combination of the force of the impact and the pole's termite-ridden condition.

If Walker asserts a claim against Telco and Rhodes, will Walker prevail?

(A) Yes, against Telco but not Rhodes.
(B) Yes, against Rhodes but not Telco.
(C) Yes, against Telco and Rhodes, each for one-half of his damages.
(D) Yes, against both Telco and Rhodes for the full amount of his damages.

Question 180

In 1956, Silo Cement Company constructed a plant for manufacturing ready-mix concrete in Lakeville. At that time Silo was using bagged cement, which caused little or no dust. In 1970, Petrone bought a home approximately 1,800 feet from the Silo plant.

One year ago, Silo stopped using bagged cement and began to receive cement in bulk shipments. Since then at least five truck-loads of cement have passed Petrone's house daily. Cement blows off the trucks and into Petrone's house. When the cement arrives at the Silo plant, it is blown by forced air from the trucks into the storage bin. As a consequence cement dust fills the air surrounding the plant to a distance of 2,000 feet. Petrone's house is the only residence within 2,000 feet of the plant.

If Petrone asserts a claim against Silo based on nuisance, will Petrone prevail?

(A) Yes, unless using bagged cement would substantially increase Silo's costs.

(B) Yes, if the cement dust interfered unreasonably with the use and enjoyment of Petrone's property.
(C) No, because Silo is not required to change its industrial methods to accommodate the needs of one individual.
(D) No, if Silo's methods are in conformity with those in general use in the industry.

Question 181

Abco developed a new drug, ZB, for treatment of Wegener's disease. Abco extensively tested ZB for several years on animals and human volunteers and had observed no undesirable side effects. The Federal Drug Administration (FDA) then approved ZB for sale as a prescription drug.

Five other drug companies, each acting independently, developed drugs identical to ZB. Each of these drugs was also approved by the FDA for sale as a prescription drug. True Blue Drug, a wholesaler, bought identically-shaped pills from all six of the manufacturers and sold the pills to drugstores as Wegener's X.

This drug had a long-delayed side effect. Sons of male users of Wegener's X are sterile. One such son, Crane, brought an action against Abco for his damages. Abco, through True Blue Drug, supplied about 10 percent of the Wegener's X sold in the state where Crane lived. It is not possible to establish which of the six companies supplied the particular pills that Crane's father took.

If Crane asserts a claim against Abco based on strict liability in tort, which of the following will be a decisive question in determining whether Crane will prevail?

(A) Does the res ipsa loquitur doctrine apply?
(B) Can liability be imposed on Abco without proof that Abco knew that the drug had an undesirable side effect?
(C) Is Abco relieved of liability by the FDA approval of the drug?
(D) Can liability be imposed on Abco without showing that its pills were used by Crane's father?

Question 182

After being notified by Dr. Josephs that Nurse Norris' employment with his office was terminated, Norris applied for a position with Hospital. In her application, Norris listed her former employment with Josephs. Josephs, in response to a telephone inquiry from Hospital, stated that "Norris lacked professional competence." Although Josephs believed that to be a fair assessment of Norris, his adverse rating was based on one episode of malpractice for which he blamed Norris but which in fact was chargeable to another doctor. Because of Josephs' adverse comment on her qualifications, Norris was not employed by Hospital.

If Norris asserts a claim based on defamation against Josephs, will Norris prevail?

(A) Yes, because Josephs was mistaken in the facts on which he based his opinion of Norris' competence.
(B) Yes, because Josephs' statement reflected adversely on Norris' professional competence.
(C) No, if Norris authorized Hospital to make inquiry of her former employer.
(D) No, if Josephs had reasonable grounds for his belief that Norris was not competent.

Question 183

Chemco designed and built a large tank on its premises for the purpose of storing highly toxic gas. The tank developed a sudden leak and escaping toxic gas drifted into the adjacent premises, where Nyman lived. Nyman inhaled the gas and died as a result.

In a suit brought by Nyman's personal representative against Chemco, which of the following must be established if the claim is to prevail?

I.   The toxic gas that escaped from Chemco's premises was the cause of Nyman's death.
II. The tank was built in a defective manner.
III. Chemco was negligent in designing the tank.

(A) I only
(B) I and II only
(C) I and III only
(D) I, II, and III

Question 184

As a result of an accident at the NPP nuclear power plant, a quantity of radioactive vapor escaped from the facility and two members of the public were exposed to excessive doses of radiation. According to qualified medical opinion, that exposure will double the chance that these two persons will ultimately develop cancer. However, any cancer that might be caused by this exposure will not be detectable for at least ten years. If the two exposed persons do develop

cancer, it will not be possible to determine whether it was caused by this exposure or would have developed in any event.

If the exposed persons assert a claim for damages against NPP shortly after the escape of the radiation, which of the following questions will NOT present a substantial issue?

(A) Will the court recognize that the plaintiffs have suffered a present legal injury?
(B) Can the plaintiffs prove the amount of their damages?
(C) Can the plaintiffs prove that any harm they may suffer was caused by this exposure?
(D) Can the plaintiffs prevail without presenting evidence of specific negligence on the part of NPP?

Question 185

Dieter parked her car in violation of a city ordinance that prohibits parking within ten feet of a fire hydrant. Because Grove was driving negligently, his car sideswiped Dieter's parked car. Plaintiff, a passenger in Grove's car, was injured in the collision.

If Plaintiff asserts a claim against Dieter to recover damages for his injuries, basing his claim on Dieter's violation of the parking ordinance, will Plaintiff prevail?

(A) Yes, because Dieter was guilty of negligence per se.
(B) Yes, if Plaintiff would not have been injured had Dieter's car not been parked where it was.
(C) No, because Dieter's parked car was not an active or efficient cause of Plaintiff's injury.
(D) No, if prevention of traffic accidents was not a purpose of the ordinance.

Question 186

Neighbor, who lived next door to Homeowner, went into Homeowner's garage without permission and borrowed Homeowner's chain saw. Neighbor used the saw to clear broken branches from the trees on Neighbor's own property. After he had finished, Neighbor noticed several broken branches on Homeowner's trees that were in danger of falling on Homeowner's roof. While Neighbor was cutting Homeowner's branches, the saw broke.

In a suit for conversion by Homeowner against Neighbor, will Homeowner recover?

(A) Yes, for the actual damage to the saw.
(B) Yes, for the value of the saw before Neighbor borrowed it.
(C) No, because when the saw broke Neighbor was using it to benefit Homeowner.
(D) No, because Neighbor did not intend to keep the saw.

Question 187

Homeowner hired Arsonist to set fire to Homeowner's house so that Homeowner could collect the insurance proceeds from the fire. After pouring gasoline around the house, Arsonist lit the fire with his cigarette lighter and then put the lighter in his pocket. As Arsonist was standing back admiring his work, the lighter exploded in his pocket. Arsonist suffered severe burns to his leg.

Arsonist brought an action against the manufacturer of the lighter based on strict product liability. Under applicable law, the rules of pure comparative fault apply in such actions.

Will Arsonist prevail?

(A) Yes, if the lighter exploded because of a defect caused by a manufacturing error.
(B) Yes, if Arsonist can establish that the lighter was the proximate cause of his injury.
(C) No, because the lighter was not being used for an intended or reasonably foreseeable purpose.
(D) No, because Arsonist was injured in the course of committing a felony by the device used to perpetrate the felony.

Question 188

Karen was crossing Main Street at a crosswalk. John, who was on the sidewalk nearby, saw a speeding automobile heading in Karen's direction. John ran into the street and pushed Karen out of the path of the car. Karen fell to the ground and broke her leg.

In an action for battery brought by Karen against John, will Karen prevail?

(A) Yes, because John could have shouted a warning instead of pushing Karen out of the way.
(B) Yes, if Karen was not actually in danger and John should have realized it.
(C) No, because the driver of the car was responsible for Karen's injury.
(D) No, if John's intent was to save Karen, not to harm her.

Question 189

Perry suffered a serious injury while participating in an impromptu basketball game at a public park. The injury occurred when Perry and Dever, on opposing teams, each tried to obtain possession of the ball when it rebounded from the backboard after a missed shot at the basket. During that encounter, Perry was struck and injured by Dever's elbow. Perry now seeks compensation from Dever.

At the trial, evidence was introduced tending to prove that the game had been rough from the beginning, that elbows and knees had frequently been used to discourage interference by opposing players, and that Perry had been one of those making liberal use of such tactics.

In this action, will Perry prevail?

(A) Yes, if Dever intended to strike Perry with his elbow.
(B) Yes, if Dever intended to cause a harmful or offensive contact with Perry.
(C) No, because Perry impliedly consented to rough play.
(D) No, unless Dever intentionally used force that exceeded the players' consent.

Question 190

The police in City notified local gas station attendants that a woman, known as Robber, recently had committed armed robberies at five City gas stations. The police said that Robber was approximately 75 years old, had white hair, and drove a vintage, cream-colored Ford Thunderbird. Attendants were advised to call police if they saw her, but not to attempt to apprehend her. Armed robbery is a felony under state law.

Traveler was passing through City on a cross-country journey. Traveler was a 75-year-old woman who had white hair and drove a vintage, cream-colored Ford Thunderbird. When Traveler drove into Owner's gas station, Owner thought Traveler must be the robber wanted by the police. After checking the oil at Traveler's request, Owner falsely informed Traveler that she had a broken fan belt, that her car could not be driven without a new belt, that it would take him about an hour to replace it, and that she should stay in his office for consultation about the repair. Traveler was greatly annoyed that her journey was delayed, but she stayed in Owner's office while she waited for her car.

Owner telephoned the police and, within the hour, the police came and questioned Traveler. The police immediately determined that Traveler was not Robber, and Traveler resumed her journey without further delay.

In Traveler's action for false imprisonment against Owner, Traveler will

(A) not prevail, if Owner reasonably believed that Traveler was Robber.
(B) not prevail, because Traveler suffered no physical or mental harm.
(C) prevail, if Traveler reasonably believed she could not leave Owner's premises.
(D) prevail, because Owner lied to Traveler about the condition of her car.

Question 191

Powell, who was an asbestos insulation installer from 1955 to 1965, contracted asbestosis, a serious lung disorder, as a result of inhaling airborne asbestos particles on the job. The asbestos was manufactured and sold to Powell's employer by the Acme Asbestos Company. Because neither Acme nor anyone else discovered the risk to asbestos installers until 1966, Acme did not provide any warnings of the risks to installers until after that date.

Powell brought an action against Acme based on strict liability in tort for failure to warn. The case is to be tried before a jury. The jurisdiction has not adopted a comparative fault rule in strict liability cases.

In this action, an issue that is relevant to the case and is a question for the court to decide as a matter of law, rather than for the jury to decide as a question of fact, is whether

(A) a satisfactory, safer, alternative insulation material exists under today's technology.
(B) the defendant should be held to the standard of a prudent manufacturer who knew of the risks, regardless of whether the risks were reasonably discoverable before 1966.
(C) the defendant should reasonably have known of the risks of asbestos insulation materials before 1966, even though no one else had discovered the risks.
(D) the asbestos insulation materials to which the plaintiff was exposed were inherently dangerous.

Question 192

Company designed and built a processing plant for the manufacture of an explosive chemical. Engineer was retained by Company to design a filter system for the processing plant. She prepared an application for a permit to build the plant's filter system and submitted it to the state's Department of Environmental Protection (DEP). As required by DEP regulations, Engineer submitted a blueprint to the DEP with the application for permit. The blueprint showed the entire facility and was signed and sealed by her as a licensed professional engineer.

After the project was completed, a portion of the processing plant exploded, injuring Plaintiff. During discovery in an action by Plaintiff against Engineer, it was established that the explosion was caused by a design defect in the processing plant that was unrelated to the filter system designed by Engineer.

In that action, will Plaintiff prevail?

(A) Yes, if Engineer signed, sealed, and submitted a blueprint that showed the design defect.
(B) Yes, because all of the plant's designers are jointly and severally liable for the defect.
(C) No, because Engineer owed no duty to Plaintiff to prevent the particular risk of harm.
(D) No, if Engineer was an independent contractor.

Question 193

Mom rushed her eight-year-old daughter, Child, to the emergency room at Hospital after Child fell off her bicycle and hit her head on a sharp rock. The wound caused by the fall was extensive and bloody.

Mom was permitted to remain in the treatment room, and held Child's hand while the emergency room physician cleaned and sutured the wound. During the procedure, Mom said that she was feeling faint and stood up to leave the room. While leaving the room, Mom fainted and, in falling, struck her head on a metal fixture that protruded from the emergency room wall. She sustained a serious injury as a consequence.

If Mom sues Hospital to recover damages for her injury, will she prevail?

(A) Yes, because Mom was a public invitee of Hospital's.
(B) Yes, unless the fixture was an obvious, commonly used, and essential part of Hospital's equipment.

(C) No, unless Hospital's personnel failed to take reasonable steps to anticipate and prevent Mom's injury.

(D) No, because Hospital's personnel owed Mom no affirmative duty of care.

Question 194

For ten years, Vacationer and Neighbor have owned summer vacation homes on adjoining lots. A stream flows through both lots. As a result of a childhood swimming accident, Vacationer is afraid of water and has never gone close to the stream.

Neighbor built a dam on her property that has completely stopped the flow of the stream to Vacationer's property.

In a suit by Vacationer against Neighbor, will Vacationer prevail?

(A) Yes, if the damming unreasonably interferes with the use and enjoyment of Vacationer's property.

(B) Yes, if Neighbor intended to affect Vacationer's property.

(C) No, because Vacationer made no use of the stream.

(D) No, if the dam was built in conformity with all applicable laws.

Question 195

Fran, who was driving at an excessive speed, applied her brakes to stop at a traffic light. Due to damp, fallen leaves, her car skidded and came to a halt perpendicular to the roadway. Sid, who was also driving at an excessive speed and was immediately behind Fran, saw Fran's car perpendicular to the roadway. Although Sid had sufficient distance to come to a slow, controlled stop, he decided not to slow down but, rather, to swerve to the left in an effort to go around Fran's car. Due to oncoming traffic, the space was insufficient and Sid's car collided with Fran's car, severely injuring Fran.

Fran filed a personal injury action against Sid in a jurisdiction in which contributory negligence is a bar to recovery.

Will Fran prevail?

(A) Yes, if the jury finds that Sid was more than 50% at fault.

(B) Yes, if the jury finds that Sid had the last clear chance.

(C) No, if the jury finds that Fran's conduct was in any way a legal cause of the accident.

(D) No, if the jury finds that, in speeding, Fran assumed the risk.

Question 196

Employer retained Doctor to evaluate medical records of prospective employees. Doctor informed Employer that Applicant, a prospective employee, suffered from AIDS. Employer informed Applicant of this and declined to hire her.

Applicant was shocked by this news and suffered a heart attack as a result. Subsequent tests revealed that Applicant in fact did not have AIDS. Doctor had negligently confused Applicant's file with that of another prospective employee.

If Applicant sued Doctor for damages, on which of the following causes of action would Applicant recover?

    I.   Invasion of privacy.
    II. Negligent misrepresentation.
    III. Negligent infliction of emotional distress.

(A) III only.
(B) I and II only.
(C) II and III only.
(D) I, II, and III.

Question 197

While approaching an intersection with the red light against him, Motorist suffered a heart attack that rendered him unconscious. Motorist's car struck Child, who was crossing the street with the green light in her favor. Under the state motor vehicle code, it is an offense to drive through a red traffic light.

Child sued Motorist to recover for her injuries. At trial it was stipulated that (1) immediately prior to suffering the heart attack, Motorist had been driving within the speed limit, had seen the red light, and had begun to slow his car; (2) Motorist had no history of heart disease and no warning of this attack; (3) while Motorist was unconscious, his car ran the red light.

On cross motions for directed verdicts on the issue of liability at the conclusion of the proofs, the court should

(A) grant Child's motion, because Motorist ran a red light in violation of the motor vehicle code.

(B) grant Child's motion, because, in the circumstances, reasonable persons would infer that Motorist was negligent.

(C) grant Motorist's motion, because he had no history of heart disease or warning of the heart attack.

(D) deny both motions and submit the case to the jury, to determine whether, in the circumstances, Motorist's conduct was that of a reasonably prudent person.

Question 198

In a trial to a jury, Owner proved that Power Company's negligent maintenance of a transformer caused a fire that destroyed his restaurant. The jury returned a verdict for Owner in the amount of $450,000 for property loss and $500,000 for emotional distress. The trial judge entered judgment in those amounts. Power Company appealed that part of the judgment awarding $500,000 for emotional distress.

On appeal, the judgment should be

(A) affirmed, because Power Company negligently caused Owner's emotional distress.

(B) affirmed, because harm arising from emotional distress is as real as harm caused by physical impact.

(C) reversed, because the law does not recognize a claim for emotional distress incident to negligently caused property loss.

(D) reversed, unless the jury found that Owner suffered physical harm as a consequence of the emotional distress caused by his property loss.

Question 199

Patron ate a spicy dinner at Restaurant on Sunday night. He enjoyed the food and noticed nothing unusual about the dinner.

Later that evening, Patron had an upset stomach. He slept well through the night, went to work the next day, and ate three meals. His stomach discomfort persisted, and by Tuesday morning he was too ill to go to work.

Eventually, Patron consulted his doctor, who found that Patron was infected with a bacterium that can be contracted from contaminated food. Food can be contaminated when those who prepare it do not adequately wash their hands.

Patron sued Restaurant for damages. He introduced testimony from a health department official that various health code violations had been found at Restaurant both before and after Patron's dinner, but that none of Restaurant's employees had signs of bacterial infection when they were tested one month after the incident.

Restaurant's best argument in response to Patron's suit would be that

(A) no one else who ate at Restaurant on Sunday complained about stomach discomfort.

(B) Restaurant instructs its employees to wash their hands carefully and is not responsible if any employee fails to follow these instructions.

(C) Patron has failed to establish that Restaurant's food caused his illness.

(D) Patron assumed the risk of an upset stomach by choosing to eat spicy food.

Question 200

When Parents were told that their child, Son, should repeat second grade, they sought to have him evaluated by a psychologist. The psychologist, who charged $300, determined that Son had a learning disability. Based upon the report, the school board placed Son in special classes. At an open meeting of the school board, Parents asked that the $300 they had paid to the psychologist be reimbursed by the school district. A reporter attending the meeting wrote a newspaper article about this request, mentioning Son by name.

In a privacy action brought by Son's legal representative against the newspaper, the plaintiff will

(A) recover, because the story is not newsworthy.

(B) recover, because Son is under the age of consent.

(C) not recover, if the story is a fair and accurate report of what transpired at the meeting.

(D) not recover, if Parents knew that the reporter was present.

Questions 201-202 are based on the following fact situation.

Adam's car sustained moderate damage in a collision with a car driven by Basher. The accident was caused solely by Basher's negligence. Adam's car was still drivable after the accident. Examining the car the next morning, Adam could see that a rear fender had to be replaced. He also noticed that gasoline had dripped onto the garage floor. The collision had caused a small leak in the gasoline tank.

Adam then took the car to Mechanic, who owns and operates a body shop, and arranged with Mechanic to repair the damage. During their discussion Adam neglected to mention the gasoline leakage. Thereafter, while Mechanic was loosening some of the damaged material with a hammer, he caused a spark, igniting vapor and gasoline that had leaked from the fuel tank. Mechanic was severely burned.

Mechanic has brought an action to recover damages against Adam and Basher. The jurisdiction has adopted a pure comparative negligence rule in place of the traditional common-law rule of contributory negligence.

Question 201

In this action, will Mechanic obtain a judgment against Basher?

(A) No, unless there is evidence that Basher was aware of the gasoline leak.
(B) No, if Mechanic would not have been harmed had Adam warned him about the gasoline leak.
(C) Yes, unless Mechanic was negligent in not discovering the gasoline leak himself.
(D) Yes, if Mechanic's injury was a proximate consequence of Basher's negligent driving.

Question 202

In this action, will Mechanic obtain a judgment against Adam?

(A) No, because it was Mechanic's job to inspect the vehicle and repair whatever needed repair.
(B) No, unless Adam was aware of the risk that the gasoline leak represented.
(C) Yes, if a reasonable person in Adam's position would have warned Mechanic about the gasoline leak.
(D) Yes, because the car was unreasonably dangerous when Adam delivered it to Mechanic.

Question 203

The warden of State Prison prohibits the photographing of the face of any prisoner without the prisoner's consent. Photographer, a news photographer, wanted to photograph Mobster, a notorious organized crime figure incarcerated at State Prison. To circumvent the warden's prohibition, Photographer flew over the prison exercise yard and photographed Mobster. Prisoner, who was imprisoned for a technical violation of a regulatory statute, happened to be standing next to Mobster when the photograph was taken.

When the picture appeared in the press, Prisoner suffered severe emotional distress because he believed that his business associates and friends would think he was consorting with gangsters. Prisoner suffered no physical harm as the result of his emotional distress. Prisoner brought an action against Photographer for intentional or reckless infliction of emotional distress.

What is the best argument that Photographer can make in support of a motion for summary judgment?

(A) No reasonable person could conclude that Photographer intended to photograph Prisoner.
(B) Prisoner did not suffer any physical injury arising from the emotional distress.
(C) As a news photographer, Photographer was privileged to take photographs that others could not.
(D) No reasonable person could conclude that Photographer's conduct was extreme and outrageous as to Prisoner.

Question 204

Vintner is the owner of a large vineyard and offers balloon rides to visitors who wish to tour the grounds from the air. During one of the rides, Vintner was forced to make a crash landing on his own property. Without Vintner's knowledge or consent, Trespasser had entered the vineyard to camp for a couple of days. Trespasser was injured when he was hit by the basket of the descending balloon.

If Trespasser sues Vintner to recover damages for his injuries, will Trespasser prevail?

(A) No, unless the crash landing was made necessary by negligence on Vintner's part.
(B) No, unless Vintner could have prevented the injury to Trespasser after becoming aware of Trespasser's presence.
(C) Yes, because even a trespasser may recover for injuries caused by an abnormally dangerous activity.
(D) Yes, if the accident occurred at a place which Vintner knew was frequented by intruders.

Question 205

Farmer owns a small farm with several head of cattle, which are kept in a fenced grazing area. One day the cattle were frightened by a thunderstorm, an occasional occurrence in the area. The cattle broke through the fence, entered onto Neighbor's property, and severely damaged Neighbor's crops. Under the law of the state, landowners are not required to erect fences to prevent the intrusion of livestock.

If Neighbor sues Farmer to recover for the damage done to his crops, will Neighbor prevail?

(A) Yes, because Farmer's cattle caused the damage to Neighbor's crops.
(B) Yes, if Farmer's cattle had panicked during previous thunderstorms.
(C) No, unless the fence was negligently maintained by Farmer.
(D) No, because the thunderstorm was a force of nature.

Question 206

Pat had been under the care of a cardiologist for three years prior to submitting to an elective operation that was performed by Surgeon. Two days thereafter, Pat suffered a stroke, resulting in a coma, caused by a blood clot that lodged in her brain. When it appeared that she had entered a permanent vegetative state, with no hope of recovery, the artificial life-support system that had been provided was withdrawn, and she died a few hours later. The withdrawal of artificial life support had been requested by her family, and duly approved by a court. Surgeon was not involved in that decision, or in its execution.

The administrator of Pat's estate thereafter filed a wrongful death action against Surgeon, claiming that Surgeon was negligent in having failed to consult a cardiologist prior to the operation. At the trial the plaintiff offered evidence that accepted medical practice would require examination of the patient by a cardiologist prior to the type of operation that Surgeon performed.

In this action, the plaintiff should

(A) prevail, if Surgeon was negligent in failing to have Pat examined by a cardiologist prior to the operation.
(B) prevail, if the blood clot that caused Pat's death was caused by the operation which Surgeon performed.
(C) not prevail, absent evidence that a cardiologist, had one examined Pat before the operation,

would probably have provided advice that would have changed the outcome.
(D) not prevail, because Surgeon had nothing to do with the withdrawal of artificial life support, which was the cause of Pat's death.

Question 207

The day after Seller completed the sale of his house and moved out, one of the slates flew off the roof during a windstorm. The slate struck Pedestrian, who was on the public sidewalk. Pedestrian was seriously injured.

The roof is old and has lost several slates in ordinary windstorms on other occasions.

If Pedestrian sues Seller to recover damages for his injuries, will Pedestrian prevail?

(A) Yes, because the roof was defective when Seller sold the house.
(B) Yes, if Seller should have been aware of the condition of the roof and should have realized that it was dangerous to persons outside the premises.
(C) No, because Seller was neither the owner nor the occupier of the house when Pedestrian was injured.
(D) No, if Pedestrian knew that in the past slates had blown off the roof during windstorms.

Question 208

Orderly, a male attendant who worked at Hospital, had sexual relations with Patient, a severely retarded person, in her room at Hospital.

In a tort action brought on Patient's behalf against Hospital, Patient will

(A) not prevail, if Orderly's actions were outside the scope of his employment.
(B) not prevail, if Patient initiated the relationship with Orderly and encouraged his actions.
(C) prevail, if Orderly was an employee of Hospital.
(D) prevail, if Hospital failed to use reasonable care to protect Patient from such conduct.

Question 209

Passenger departed on an ocean liner knowing that it would be a rough voyage due to predicted storms. The ocean liner was not equipped with the type of lifeboats required by the applicable statute.

Passenger was swept overboard and drowned in a storm so heavy that even a lifeboat that conformed to the statute could not have been launched.

In an action against the operator of the ocean liner brought by Passenger's representative, will Passenger's representative prevail?

(A) Yes, because the ocean liner was not equipped with the statutorily required lifeboats.
(B) Yes, because in these circumstances common carriers are strictly liable.
(C) No, because the storm was so severe that it would have been impossible to launch a statutorily required lifeboat.
(D) No, because Passenger assumed the risk by boarding the ocean liner knowing that it would be a rough voyage.

Question 210

The Rapido is a sports car manufactured by the Rapido Motor Co. The Rapido has an excellent reputation for mechanical reliability with one exception, that the motor may stall if the engine has not had an extended warm-up. Driver had just begun to drive her Rapido in city traffic without a warm-up when the engine suddenly stalled. A car driven by Troody rear-ended Driver's car. Driver suffered no external physical injuries as a result of the collision. However, the shock of the crash caused her to suffer a severe heart attack.

Driver brought an action against the Rapido Motor Co. based on strict liability in tort. During the trial, the plaintiff presented evidence of an alternative engine design of equal cost that would eliminate the stalling problem without impairing the functions of the engine in any way. The defendant moves for a directed verdict at the close of the evidence.

This motion should be

(A) denied, because the jury could find that an unreasonably dangerous defect in the engine was a proximate cause of the collision.
(B) denied, if the jury could find that the Rapido was not crashworthy.
(C) granted, because Troody's failure to stop within an assured clear distance was a superseding cause of the collision.
(D) granted, if a person of normal sensitivity would not have suffered a heart attack under these circumstances.

Question 211

Driver was driving his car near Owner's house when Owner's child darted into the street in front of Driver's car. As Driver swerved and braked his car to avoid hitting the child, the car skidded up into Owner's driveway and stopped just short of Owner, who was standing in the driveway and had witnessed the entire incident. Owner suffered serious emotional distress from witnessing the danger to his child and to himself. Neither Owner nor his property was physically harmed.

If Owner asserts a claim for damages against Driver, will Owner prevail?

(A) Yes, because Driver's entry onto Owner's land was unauthorized.
(B) Yes, because Owner suffered serious emotional distress by witnessing the danger to his child and to himself.
(C) No, unless Driver was negligent.
(D) No, unless Owner's child was exercising reasonable care.

Question 212

Traveler was a passenger on a commercial aircraft owned and operated by Airline. The aircraft crashed into a mountain, killing everyone on board. The flying weather was good.

Traveler's legal representative brought a wrongful death action against Airline. At trial, the legal representative offered no expert or other testimony as to the cause of the crash.

On Airline's motion to dismiss at the conclusion of the legal representative's case, the court should

(A) grant the motion, because the legal representative has offered no evidence as to the cause of the crash.
(B) grant the motion, because the legal representative has failed to offer evidence negating the possibility that the crash may have been caused by mechanical failure that Airline could not have prevented.
(C) deny the motion, because the jury may infer that the aircraft crashed due to Airline's negligence.
(D) deny the motion, because in the circumstances common carriers are strictly liable.

Question 213

Because of Farmer's default on his loan, the bank foreclosed on the farm and equipment that secured the loan. Among the items sold at the resulting auction was a new tractor recently delivered to Farmer by the retailer. Shortly after purchasing the tractor at the auction, Pratt was negligently operating the tractor on a hill when it rolled over due to a defect in the tractor's design. He was injured as a result. Pratt sued the auctioneer, alleging strict liability in tort. The jurisdiction has not adopted a comparative fault rule in strict liability cases.

In this suit, the result should be for the

(A) plaintiff, because the defendant sold a defective product that injured the plaintiff.
(B) plaintiff, if the defendant failed to inspect the tractor for defects prior to sale.
(C) defendant, because he should not be considered a "seller" for purposes of strict liability in tort.
(D) defendant, because the accident was caused in part by Pratt's negligence.

Question 214

Adam owns Townacres in fee simple, and Bess owns the adjoining Greenacres in fee simple. Adam has kept the lawns and trees on Townacres trimmed and neat. Bess "lets nature take its course" at Greenacres. The result on Greenacres is a tangle of underbrush, fallen trees, and standing trees that are in danger of losing limbs. Many of the trees on Greenacres are near Townacres. In the past, debris and large limbs have been blown from Greenacres onto Townacres. By local standards Greenacres is an eyesore that depresses market values of real property in the vicinity, but the condition of Greenacres violates no applicable laws or ordinances.

Adam demanded that Bess keep the trees near Townacres trimmed. Bess refused.

Adam brought an appropriate action against Bess to require Bess to abate what Adam alleges to be a nuisance. In the lawsuit, the only issue is whether the condition of Greenacres constitutes a nuisance.

The strongest argument that Adam can present is that the condition of Greenacres

(A) has an adverse impact on real estate values.
(B) poses a danger to the occupants of Townacres.
(C) violates community aesthetic standards.
(D) cannot otherwise be challenged under any law or ordinance.

Question 215

Homeowner owns a house on a lake. Neighbor owns a house across a driveway from Homeowner's property. Neighbor's house sits on a hill and Neighbor can see the lake from his living room window.

Homeowner and Neighbor got into an argument and Homeowner erected a large spotlight on his property that automatically comes on at dusk and goes off at sunrise. The only reason Homeowner installed the light was to annoy Neighbor. The glare from the light severely detracts from Neighbor's view of the lake.

In a suit by Neighbor against Homeowner, will Neighbor prevail?

(A) Yes, because Homeowner installed the light solely to annoy Neighbor.
(B) Yes, if, and only if, Neighbor's property value is adversely affected.
(C) No, because Neighbor's view of the lake is not always obstructed.
(D) No, if the spotlight provides added security to Homeowner's property.

Question 216

Driver negligently drove his car into Pedestrian, breaking her leg. Pedestrian's leg was put in a cast, and she used crutches to get about. While shopping at Market, her local supermarket, Pedestrian nonnegligently placed one of her crutches on a banana peel that had been negligently left on the floor by the manager of Market's produce department. Pedestrian's crutch slipped on the peel, and she fell to the floor, breaking her arm. Had Pedestrian stepped on the banana peel at a time when she did not have to use crutches, she would have regained her balance.

Pedestrian sued Driver and Market for her injuries. Pedestrian will be able to recover from

(A) Driver, for her broken leg only.
(B) Driver, for both of her injuries.
(C) Market, for both of her injuries.
(D) Driver, for her broken leg only, and Market, for her broken arm only.

Question 217

Athlete, a professional football player, signed a written consent for his team's physician, Doctor, to perform a knee operation. After Athlete was under a general anesthetic, Doctor asked Surgeon, a world famous orthopedic surgeon, to perform the operation.

Surgeon's skills were superior to Doctor's, and the operation was successful.

In an action for battery by Athlete against Surgeon, Athlete will

(A) prevail, because Athlete did not agree to allow Surgeon to perform the operation.
(B) prevail, because the consent form was in writing.
(C) not prevail, because Surgeon's skills were superior to Doctor's.
(D) not prevail, because the operation was successful.

Question 218

Actor, a well-known movie star, was drinking Vineyard wine at a nightclub. A bottle of the Vineyard wine, with its label plainly showing, was on the table in front of Actor. An amateur photographer asked Actor if he could take his picture and Actor said, "Yes." Subsequently, the photographer sold the photo to Vineyard. Vineyard, without Actor's consent, used the photo in a wine advertisement in a nationally circulated magazine. The caption below the photo stated, "Actor enjoys his Vineyard wine."

If Actor sues Vineyard to recover damages as a result of Vineyard's use of the photograph, will Actor prevail?

(A) No, because Actor consented to being photographed.
(B) No, because Actor is a public figure.
(C) Yes, because Vineyard made commercial use of the photograph.
(D) Yes, unless Actor did, in fact, enjoy his Vineyard wine.

Question 219

As Seller, an encyclopedia salesman, approached the grounds on which Hermit's house was situated, he saw a sign that said, "No salesmen. Trespassers will be prosecuted. Proceed at your own risk." Although Seller had not been invited to enter, he ignored the sign and drove up the driveway toward the house. As he rounded a curve, a powerful explosive charge buried in the driveway exploded, and Seller was injured.

Can Seller recover damages from Hermit for his injuries?

(A) Yes, if Hermit was responsible for the explosive charge under the driveway.
(B) Yes, unless Hermit, when he planted the charge, intended only to deter, not to harm, a possible intruder.
(C) No, because Seller ignored the sign, which warned him against proceeding further.
(D) No, if Hermit reasonably feared that intruders would come and harm him or his family.

Question 220

Del's sporting goods shop was burglarized by an escaped inmate from a nearby prison. The inmate stole a rifle and bullets from a locked cabinet. The burglar alarm at Del's shop did not go off because Del had negligently forgotten to activate the alarm's motion detector.

Shortly thereafter, the inmate used the rifle and ammunition stolen from Del in a shooting spree that caused injury to several people, including Paula.

If Paula sues Del for the injury she suffered, will Paula prevail?

(A) Yes, if Paula's injury would have been prevented had the motion detector been activated.
(B) Yes, because Del was negligent in failing to activate the motion detector.
(C) No, because the storage and sale of firearms and ammunition is not an abnormally dangerous activity.
(D) No, unless there is evidence of circumstances suggesting a high risk of theft and criminal use of firearms stocked by Del.

Made in the USA
Charleston, SC
05 June 2011